엠브이피 보카

편입 VOCA 대표 수험서

# MVP

## Vol 2 워크북

김영편입 컨텐츠평가연구소 편저

KB124657

김영편입

# PREFACE

## MVP Workbook is
### a smart and wise way to Memorize your Vocabulary Powerfully!

편입영어시험을 준비하는 학생들은 실전 대비를 위해 수많은 어휘를 암기해야 합니다. 그러나 단순히 많은 양의 단어를 외우는 것만으로는 문제 해결력이 생기지 않으니, 다양한 방식으로 단어를 학습하고 이를 실제 문제에 적용하는 훈련이 필요합니다.

"MVP 워크북"은 이러한 학생들의 고민을 덜어주기 위해 기획된 책으로, "MVP"의 DAY별 표제어를 바탕으로하여 DAILY CHECKUP을 제공합니다. "MVP"에서 외운 표제어의 뜻을 써보고, 20지 선택형 논리완성 문제를 통해 문장의 빈칸을 유추하고 단어의 쓰임을 확인할 수 있도록 했습니다. 그리고 각 표제어에 대한 동의어 암기를 빠르게 확인할 수 있도록 뜻이 다른 어휘 찾기 문제를 수록했습니다. 또한, 편입영어시험의 가장 대표적 유형인 동의어 문제를 수록하여 암기한 어휘를 실전문제에 적용하는 연습을 했으며, APPENDIX에는 한국외대 문맥상 동의어 문제와 이화여대 반의어 기출문제를 수록했습니다.

단순한 동의어 문제에서 벗어나 다양한 문제 유형을 통해 단어를 암기하는 학습법은 어휘 공부를 하는 학생들에게 큰 도움이 될 것입니다. 이제 "MVP 워크북"을 통해 자신의 어휘력을 한 단계 업그레이드 해보세요!

김영편입 단행본팀

# CONTENTS

**교재의 내용에 오류가 있나요?**

www.kimnbook.co.kr ➡ 자료실 ➡ 도서 정오표

도서 정오표에 반영되지 않은 새로운 오류가 있을 때에는
교재 오류 신고 게시판에 글을 남겨주세요. 정성껏 답변해 드리겠습니다.

# HOW TO STUDY

STEP 01

## MVP 표제어와 관련된 동의어, 반의어, 파생어의 통합적 어휘 암기

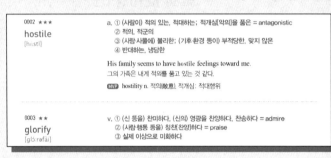

각 DAY별 표제어 50개와 동의어, 반의어, 파생어를 암기합니다.

각 DAY의 어휘 수준은 초급부터 고급까지 다양하므로, 빠른 학습을 위해 이미 알고 있는 단어는 건너뛰고 모르는 단어들을 중점적으로 외웁니다.

STEP 02

## MVP 표제어 뜻 쓰기

문제 풀이에 앞서 표제어 50개를 가볍게 확인할 수 있도록 구성했습니다.

표제어의 뜻을 빈칸에 써봄으로써 학습한 어휘의 암기 여부를 확인할 수 있습니다.

# 20지 선택형 논리완성

[2] Select **the most** appropriate word from the box below. Each word should be used only once.

| | | | |
|---|---|---|---|
| ① commerce | ② exert | ⑪ outspoken | ⑯ virtuoso |
| ③ circuitous | ⑦ dotage | ⑫ hostile | ⑰ artificial |
| ④ satire | ⑧ signify | ⑬ cohort | ⑱ usurpation |
| ⑤ subdue | ⑨ parallel | ⑭ laudable | ⑲ prescribe |
| ⑥ verdant | ⑩ innocence | ⑮ glorify | ⑳ buttress |

1 Despite the accusations against him, the evidence presented in court ultimately proved his _____.

2 Voltaire's *Candide* is a brilliant example of literary _____, using humor and wit to criticize society and its institutions.

3 In international relations, countries may become _____ towards each other when diplomatic tensions rise.

4 Proteins not only constitute much of the physical fabric of the body; they also _____ sensitive control over all the chemical processes inside the cell.

5 The campaigns of Alexander the Great did not result in the establishment of a new empire, but rather in _____ of an existing empire — that of the Persians.

6 Some athletes are known for being _____, never hesitating to express their opinions on various issues beyond the game.

7 Mr. Eliot's manners leave nothing to be desired. His behavior is usually _____.

8 Not anxious to return to work, he took the most _____ route he could think of, and a fifteen-minute trip took him three-quarters of an hour.

9 The martial arts instructor demonstrated various techniques to safely _____ an aggressive opponent without causing harm.

10 The attorney worked to gather substantial evidence to _____ the defendant's claim of innocence.

다시 한번 표제어를 학습하는 효과를 얻을 수 있도록 각 DAY별 표제어로 구성했습니다.

기출문제와의 연계성을 높이기 위해 이화여대 20지 선택형 논리완성과 같은 문제로 구성했습니다.

각 문제는 문맥상 빈칸에 들어갈 단어를 추론할 수 있는 문장들로 출제되었습니다.

# 뜻이 다른 어휘 찾기 문제

[3] Choose the one which is different from the others.

| | | | |
|---|---|---|---|
| 11 ① antithesis | ② concession | ③ antipode | ④ inverse |
| 12 ① grudge | ② whim | ③ caprice | ④ vagary |
| 13 ① revere | ② respect | ③ recant | ④ esteem |
| 14 ① sordid | ② squalid | ③ filthy | ④ stolid |
| 15 ① inflexible | ② quixotic | ③ rigid | ④ rigorous |
| 16 ① crafty | ② cunning | ③ sly | ④ naive |
| 17 ① eccentricity | ② quirk | ③ banality | ④ peculiarity |
| 18 ① timid | ② irksome | ③ irritating | ④ tedious |
| 19 ① mimicry | ② infringement | ③ mimesis | ④ imitation |
| 20 ① tension | ② anxiety | ③ strain | ④ inertia |

각 DAY별 10개의 문제가 있으며, MVP 표제어와 함께 제시된 동의어의 암기 여부를 빠르게 확인할 수 있는 문제들로 구성했습니다.

* STEP 01-04가 끝난 후 체크박스에 표시한 단어 및 틀린 문제의 단어를 개인 단어장에 정리하면서 다시 한 번 어휘를 암기합니다.

# HOW TO STUDY

STEP 05

## ACTUAL TEST & 정답

ACTUAL TEST는 5일 간의 표제어를 바탕으로 출제된 기출문제와 예상 문제로 구성됐습니다.

100문항에 제한시간 60분을 두어 빠른 속도로 문제를 풀 수 있도록 했습니다.

선택지의 단어 또한 주요 기출어휘로 구성되어 있으므로, 정답을 확인하며 암기가 미진한 단어의 경우 어휘 옆에 있는 체크박스에 표시를 해두고 다시 한번 단어장에 정리를 합니다.

STEP 06

## APPENDIX 01 문제 & 정답

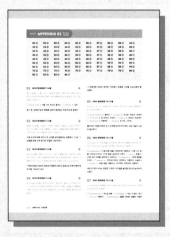

2014~2023학년도 한국외대에서 출제됐던 문맥상 동의어 유형 총 84문제를 수록했습니다.

문제 속에 밑줄 친 단어는 여러 가지 뜻을 갖고 있는 다의어로, 제시어의 뜻이 모두 선택지에 제시되어 있는 것이 특징입니다.

따라서 문맥을 파악하고 문장에서 쓰인 제시어의 문맥상의 동의어를 고르는 연습을 해야 합니다.

## STEP 07   APPENDIX 02 문제 & 정답

2014~2023학년도 이화여대에서
출제됐던 반의어 유형 총 59문제를
수록했습니다.

편입 시험에서 반의어 문제의 출제
비율은 높지 않지만, 한 단어의 반대
되는 뜻을 익히면 해당 단어의 의미를
더욱 명확하게 기억할 수 있고 두 단어를
동시에 기억하기 쉬워집니다.

정답에는 어휘를 상세하게 수록하여
사전의 도움 없이도 어휘 학습이 가능
하도록 했으며, 해당 문제의 출제 연도를
함께 표기했습니다.

## STEP 08   학습플랜 체크 및 복습

학습 계획을 세우고 관리할 수 있는 기능을 제공합니다.

학습 진도를 체크하면서 빠진 부분이 없는지 꼼꼼히 확인하고,
틀렸던 단어나 어려웠던 단어를 주기적으로 반복 학습하여
영단어를 효율적으로 외울 수 있도록 합니다.

학습이 완료되면 좌측 체크박스(□)에 표기를 하여 진도를 확인
합니다.

# 📋 학습플랜 다양한 문제를 통한 집중 반복 학습으로 영단어 암기 효과 극대화

| | 1일 | 2일 | 3일 | 4일 | 5일 | 주간 Review |
|---|---|---|---|---|---|---|
| 1주 | ☐ MVP DAY 01 <br> ☐ MVP 01 DAILY CHECKUP | ☐ MVP DAY 02 <br> ☐ MVP 02 DAILY CHECKUP | ☐ MVP DAY 03 <br> ☐ MVP 03 DAILY CHECKUP | ☐ MVP DAY 04 <br> ☐ MVP 04 DAILY CHECKUP | ☐ MVP DAY 05 <br> ☐ MVP 05 DAILY CHECKUP | ☐ MVP DAY 01-05 <br> ☐ MVP 01-05 ACTUAL TEST |
| 2주 | ☐ MVP DAY 06 <br> ☐ MVP 06 DAILY CHECKUP | ☐ MVP DAY 07 <br> ☐ MVP 07 DAILY CHECKUP | ☐ MVP DAY 08 <br> ☐ MVP 08 DAILY CHECKUP | ☐ MVP DAY 09 <br> ☐ MVP 09 DAILY CHECKUP | ☐ MVP DAY 10 <br> ☐ MVP 10 DAILY CHECKUP | ☐ MVP DAY 06-10 <br> ☐ MVP 06-10 ACTUAL TEST |
| 3주 | ☐ MVP DAY 11 <br> ☐ MVP 11 DAILY CHECKUP | ☐ MVP DAY 12 <br> ☐ MVP 12 DAILY CHECKUP | ☐ MVP DAY 13 <br> ☐ MVP 13 DAILY CHECKUP | ☐ MVP DAY 14 <br> ☐ MVP 14 DAILY CHECKUP | ☐ MVP DAY 15 <br> ☐ MVP 15 DAILY CHECKUP | ☐ MVP DAY 11-15 <br> ☐ MVP 11-15 ACTUAL TEST |
| 4주 | ☐ MVP DAY 16 <br> ☐ MVP 16 DAILY CHECKUP | ☐ MVP DAY 17 <br> ☐ MVP 17 DAILY CHECKUP | ☐ MVP DAY 18 <br> ☐ MVP 18 DAILY CHECKUP | ☐ MVP DAY 19 <br> ☐ MVP 19 DAILY CHECKUP | ☐ MVP DAY 20 <br> ☐ MVP 20 DAILY CHECKUP | ☐ MVP DAY 16-20 <br> ☐ MVP 16-20 ACTUAL TEST |
| 5주 | ☐ MVP DAY 21 <br> ☐ MVP 21 DAILY CHECKUP | ☐ MVP DAY 22 <br> ☐ MVP 22 DAILY CHECKUP | ☐ MVP DAY 23 <br> ☐ MVP 23 DAILY CHECKUP | ☐ MVP DAY 24 <br> ☐ MVP 24 DAILY CHECKUP | ☐ MVP DAY 25 <br> ☐ MVP 25 DAILY CHECKUP | ☐ MVP DAY 21-25 <br> ☐ MVP 21-25 ACTUAL TEST |
| 6주 | ☐ MVP DAY 26 <br> ☐ MVP 26 DAILY CHECKUP | ☐ MVP DAY 27 <br> ☐ MVP 27 DAILY CHECKUP | ☐ MVP DAY 28 <br> ☐ MVP 28 DAILY CHECKUP | ☐ MVP DAY 29 <br> ☐ MVP 29 DAILY CHECKUP | ☐ MVP DAY 30 <br> ☐ MVP 30 DAILY CHECKUP | ☐ MVP DAY 26-30 <br> ☐ MVP 26-30 ACTUAL TEST |

어휘 암기와 문제 풀이를 통해 기본 어휘 실력을 높이는 **MVP 60일 완성 Study Planner**

| | 1일 | 2일 | 3일 | 4일 | 5일 | 주간 Review |
|---|---|---|---|---|---|---|
| **7주** | ☐ MVP DAY **31**<br>☐ MVP **31**<br>DAILY<br>CHECKUP | ☐ MVP DAY **32**<br>☐ MVP **32**<br>DAILY<br>CHECKUP | ☐ MVP DAY **33**<br>☐ MVP **33**<br>DAILY<br>CHECKUP | ☐ MVP DAY **34**<br>☐ MVP **34**<br>DAILY<br>CHECKUP | ☐ MVP DAY **35**<br>☐ MVP **35**<br>DAILY<br>CHECKUP | ☐ MVP DAY **31-35**<br>☐ MVP **31-35**<br>ACTUAL<br>TEST |
| **8주** | ☐ MVP DAY **36**<br>☐ MVP **36**<br>DAILY<br>CHECKUP | ☐ MVP DAY **37**<br>☐ MVP **37**<br>DAILY<br>CHECKUP | ☐ MVP DAY **38**<br>☐ MVP **38**<br>DAILY<br>CHECKUP | ☐ MVP DAY **39**<br>☐ MVP **39**<br>DAILY<br>CHECKUP | ☐ MVP DAY **40**<br>☐ MVP **40**<br>DAILY<br>CHECKUP | ☐ MVP DAY **36-40**<br>☐ MVP **36-40**<br>ACTUAL<br>TEST |
| **9주** | ☐ MVP DAY **41**<br>☐ MVP **41**<br>DAILY<br>CHECKUP | ☐ MVP DAY **42**<br>☐ MVP **42**<br>DAILY<br>CHECKUP | ☐ MVP DAY **43**<br>☐ MVP **43**<br>DAILY<br>CHECKUP | ☐ MVP DAY **44**<br>☐ MVP **44**<br>DAILY<br>CHECKUP | ☐ MVP DAY **45**<br>☐ MVP **45**<br>DAILY<br>CHECKUP | ☐ MVP DAY **41-45**<br>☐ MVP **41-45**<br>ACTUAL<br>TEST |
| **10주** | ☐ MVP DAY **46**<br>☐ MVP **46**<br>DAILY<br>CHECKUP | ☐ MVP DAY **47**<br>☐ MVP **47**<br>DAILY<br>CHECKUP | ☐ MVP DAY **48**<br>☐ MVP **48**<br>DAILY<br>CHECKUP | ☐ MVP DAY **49**<br>☐ MVP **49**<br>DAILY<br>CHECKUP | ☐ MVP DAY **50**<br>☐ MVP **50**<br>DAILY<br>CHECKUP | ☐ MVP DAY **46-50**<br>☐ MVP **46-50**<br>ACTUAL<br>TEST |
| **11주** | ☐ MVP DAY **51**<br>☐ MVP **51**<br>DAILY<br>CHECKUP | ☐ MVP DAY **52**<br>☐ MVP **52**<br>DAILY<br>CHECKUP | ☐ MVP DAY **53**<br>☐ MVP **53**<br>DAILY<br>CHECKUP | ☐ MVP DAY **54**<br>☐ MVP **54**<br>DAILY<br>CHECKUP | ☐ MVP DAY **55**<br>☐ MVP **55**<br>DAILY<br>CHECKUP | ☐ MVP DAY **51-55**<br>☐ MVP **51-55**<br>ACTUAL<br>TEST |
| **12주** | ☐ MVP DAY **56**<br>☐ MVP **56**<br>DAILY<br>CHECKUP | ☐ MVP DAY **57**<br>☐ MVP **57**<br>DAILY<br>CHECKUP | ☐ MVP DAY **58**<br>☐ MVP **58**<br>DAILY<br>CHECKUP | ☐ MVP DAY **59**<br>☐ MVP **59**<br>DAILY<br>CHECKUP | ☐ MVP DAY **60**<br>☐ MVP **60**<br>DAILY<br>CHECKUP | ☐ MVP DAY **56-60**<br>☐ MVP **56-60**<br>ACTUAL<br>TEST |

# MVP

## Vol.2 워크북

# 01 ~60

## DAILY CHECKUP
## &
## ACTUAL TEST

[1] Write the meaning of the following words.

| | |
|---|---|
| ☐ innocent | ☐ virtuoso |
| ☐ hostile | ☐ laud |
| ☐ glorify | ☐ tension |
| ☐ deceased | ☐ squalid |
| ☐ antithesis | ☐ rigid |
| ☐ multiple | ☐ entrepreneur |
| ☐ refund | ☐ approximately |
| ☐ dotage | ☐ signify |
| ☐ satire | ☐ cohort |
| ☐ proficient | ☐ illustrate |
| ☐ exert | ☐ verdant |
| ☐ artificial | ☐ check |
| ☐ whim | ☐ prescribe |
| ☐ formidable | ☐ mimesis |
| ☐ commerce | ☐ fix |
| ☐ drastic | ☐ circuitous |
| ☐ usurp | ☐ guffaw |
| ☐ primitive | ☐ subdue |
| ☐ ramp | ☐ crafty |
| ☐ esteem | ☐ buttress |
| ☐ beneficial | ☐ quirk |
| ☐ transit | ☐ parallel |
| ☐ acknowledge | ☐ irksome |
| ☐ peninsula | ☐ skull |
| ☐ outspoken | ☐ disprove |

[2] Select <u>the most</u> appropriate word from the box below. Each word should be used only once.

| | | | |
|---|---|---|---|
| ① commerce | ② exert | ③ outspoken | ④ virtuoso |
| ⑤ circuitous | ⑥ dotage | ⑦ hostile | ⑧ artificial |
| ⑨ satire | ⑩ signify | ⑪ cohort | ⑫ usurpation |
| ⑬ subdue | ⑭ parallel | ⑮ laudable | ⑯ prescribe |
| ⑰ verdant | ⑱ innocence | ⑲ glorify | ⑳ buttress |

1     Despite the accusations against him, the evidence presented in court ultimately proved his _____.

2     Voltaire's *Candide* is a brilliant example of literary _____, using humor and wit to criticize society and its institutions.

3     In international relations, countries may become _____ towards each other when diplomatic tensions rise.

4     Proteins not only constitute much of the physical fabric of the body; they also _____ sensitive control over all the chemical processes inside the cell.

5     The campaigns of Alexander the Great did not result in the establishment of a new empire, but rather in _____ of an existing empire — that of the Persians.

6     Some athletes are known for being _____, never hesitating to express their opinions on various issues beyond the game.

7     Mr. Eliot's manners leave nothing to be desired. His behavior is usually _____.

8     Not anxious to return to work, he took the most _____ route he could think of, and a fifteen-minute trip took him three-quarters of an hour.

9     The martial arts instructor demonstrated various techniques to safely _____ an aggressive opponent without causing harm.

10     The attorney worked to gather substantial evidence to _____ the defendant's claim of innocence.

**[3] Choose the one which is different from the others.**

11    ① antithesis          ② concession        ③ antipode          ④ inverse

12    ① grudge              ② whim              ③ caprice           ④ vagary

13    ① revere              ② respect           ③ recant            ④ esteem

14    ① sordid              ② squalid           ③ filthy            ④ stolid

15    ① inflexible          ② quixotic          ③ rigid             ④ rigorous

16    ① crafty              ② cunning           ③ sly               ④ naive

17    ① eccentricity        ② quirk             ③ banality          ④ peculiarity

18    ① timid               ② irksome           ③ irritating        ④ tedious

19    ① mimicry             ② infringement      ③ mimesis           ④ imitation

20    ① tension             ② anxiety           ③ strain            ④ inertia

## ✓ Answers

1    ⑱    | 그에 대한 혐의에도 불구하고 법정에 제시된 증거는 결국 그의 무죄를 입증했다.

2    ⑨    | 볼테르(Voltaire)의 『캉디드』는 유머와 재치를 이용하여 사회와 제도를 비판한 문학 풍자의 훌륭한 예이다.

3    ⑦    | 국제관계에서 외교적 긴장이 고조되면 국가들은 서로 적대적으로 될 수도 있다.

4    ②    | 단백질은 신체의 물리 조직의 많은 부분을 구성할 뿐만 아니라 세포 안에서 일어나는 모든 화학 과정을 민감하게 통제한다.

5    ⑫    | 알렉산더 대왕(Alexander the Great)의 출정은 새로운 제국을 수립하는 결과가 아니라, 오히려 기존 제국, 즉 페르시아 제국을 찬탈하는 결과를 가져왔다.

6    ③    | 일부 선수들은 경기 외의 다양한 문제에 대해 의견을 표현하는 것을 주저하지 않고 거침없이 말하는 것으로 유명하다.

7    ⑮    | 엘리엇(Eliot)씨의 태도는 전혀 흠잡을 데가 없다. 그의 행동은 항상 칭찬할 만하다.

8    ⑤    | 그는 직장으로 되돌아가고 싶지 않아서, 생각할 수 있는 가장 빙 돌아가는 길을 선택해 15분 걸릴 거리를 45분에 걸려 갔다.

9    ⑬    | 무술 강사는 공격적인 상대를 해를 끼치지 않고 안전하게 제압할 수 있는 다양한 기술을 시연했다.

10   ⑳    | 그 변호사는 피고인의 무죄 주장을 지지해 줄 실질적인 증거를 수집하려고 노력했다.

- - - - - - - - - - - - - - - - - - - - - - - - - - - - - - - - - - - - - - - - - - - - - - - - - -

11 ②    12 ①    13 ③    14 ④    15 ②    16 ④    17 ③    18 ①    19 ②    20 ④

## ☑ DAILY CHECKUP

[1] Write the meaning of the following words.

| | |
|---|---|
| ☐ elementary | ☐ nexus |
| ☐ dogma | ☐ dichotomy |
| ☐ modify | ☐ withdraw |
| ☐ stationary | ☐ ostensible |
| ☐ altruistic | ☐ photosynthesis |
| ☐ rapture | ☐ surplus |
| ☐ deprive | ☐ calculate |
| ☐ impasse | ☐ introvert |
| ☐ liberal | ☐ maze |
| ☐ volition | ☐ pragmatic |
| ☐ evaporate | ☐ grief |
| ☐ flaccid | ☐ anomalous |
| ☐ bankrupt | ☐ seize |
| ☐ epitome | ☐ yoke |
| ☐ pester | ☐ involve |
| ☐ conventional | ☐ congenial |
| ☐ risible | ☐ trigger |
| ☐ summit | ☐ scope |
| ☐ dispel | ☐ resign |
| ☐ prodigal | ☐ byproduct |
| ☐ agriculture | ☐ jubilant |
| ☐ hibernate | ☐ adduce |
| ☐ client | ☐ fraud |
| ☐ thoughtful | ☐ plunder |
| ☐ flout | ☐ civilization |

[2] Select <u>the most</u> appropriate word from the box below. Each word should be used only once.

| | | | |
|---|---|---|---|
| ① elementary | ② impasse | ③ plundered | ④ adduce |
| ⑤ prodigality | ⑥ grief | ⑦ introvert | ⑧ altruistic |
| ⑨ yoke | ⑩ flaccid | ⑪ ostensible | ⑫ dichotomy |
| ⑬ hibernated | ⑭ liberal | ⑮ epitome | ⑯ modified |
| ⑰ dispelled | ⑱ fraud | ⑲ dogma | ⑳ trigger |

**1** Because experience had convinced her that he was both self-seeking and avaricious, she rejected the likelihood that his donation had been _____.

**2** The negotiations reached a(n) _____ with both sides refusing to compromise.

**3** When a plant doesn't receive enough water, its leaves and stems may appear wilted and _____ due to dehydration.

**4** The grand palace, with its opulent design and luxurious furnishings, stands as the _____ of elegance and extravagance in architecture.

**5** When I listened to his cogent arguments, all my doubts were _____ and I was forced to agree with his point of view.

**6** She is most frugal in matters of business, but in her private life she reveals a streak of _____.

**7** Their _____ goal was to clean up government corruption, but their real aim was to unseat the government.

**8** The cybersecurity team worked diligently to uncover and prevent online _____ activities aimed at stealing sensitive user information.

**9** The tomb of the pharaoh was discovered, but it had already been _____ by grave robbers long before the archaeologists arrived.

**10** Learning the _____ principles of mathematics is crucial for building a strong foundation in more advanced mathematical concepts.

[3] Choose the one which is different from the others.

11  ① stationary      ② motionless      ③ static          ④ restless

12  ① harass          ② pester          ③ pacify          ④ torment

13  ① alien           ② conventional    ③ traditional     ④ customary

14  ① risible         ② voluminous      ③ ludicrous       ④ facetious

15  ① amorphous       ② anomalous       ③ aberrant        ④ atypical

16  ① jubilant        ② exultant        ③ conceivable     ④ joyful

17  ① compatible      ② congenial       ③ sympathetic     ④ tangible

18  ① withdraw        ② redeem          ③ recede          ④ retreat

19  ① tout            ② flout           ③ mock            ④ scorn

20  ① deliberate      ② thoughtful      ③ forthright      ④ prudent

## ✔Answers

1  ⑧   ┃ 그녀는 경험적으로 그가 이기적이고 탐욕스럽다고 확신했기 때문에, 그의 기부가 이타적이었을 가능성을 부인했다.

2  ②   ┃ 그 협상은 양측 모두 타협을 거부하는 가운데 난국에 부딪혔다.

3  ⑩   ┃ 식물이 물을 충분히 공급받지 못하면, 식물의 잎과 줄기는 탈수로 인해 시들고 축 늘어진 것처럼 보일지도 모른다.

4  ⑮   ┃ 그 대궁전은 화려한 디자인과 호화로운 가구로 인해 건축 양식에서 우아함과 화려함의 전형이 되어 있다.

5  ⑰   ┃ 그의 설득력 있는 주장을 들었을 때, 나의 모든 의구심은 제거되었고 그의 관점에 동의할 수밖에 없었다.

6  ⑤   ┃ 그녀는 사업적인 면에서는 가장 검소하지만, 사생활에서는 낭비하는 구석이 있다.

7  ⑪   ┃ 그들의 표면상의 목표는 정부의 부패를 척결하는 것이었지만, 진짜 목표는 현 정부를 몰아내는 것이었다.

8  ⑱   ┃ 사이버 보안팀은 민감한 사용자 정보를 훔치는 것을 목표로 한 온라인 사기 행위를 적발하고 방지하기 위해 열심히 노력했다.

9  ③   ┃ 파라오의 무덤이 발견되었지만, 고고학자들이 도착하기 훨씬 전에 이미 무덤 도굴꾼들에 의해 약탈당했다.

10 ①   ┃ 수학의 기본 원리를 익히는 것은 고급 수학 개념의 기초를 단단히 다지는 데 중요하다.

------------------------------------------------------------------------------

11 ④    12 ③    13 ①    14 ②    15 ①    16 ③    17 ④    18 ②    19 ①    20 ③

[1] Write the meaning of the following words.

| | |
|---|---|
| ☐ upheaval | ☐ apparent |
| ☐ provisional | ☐ muggy |
| ☐ abide | ☐ infer |
| ☐ species | ☐ disparate |
| ☐ belligerent | ☐ emergency |
| ☐ consume | ☐ vanquish |
| ☐ stagnant | ☐ gingerly |
| ☐ rue | ☐ domicile |
| ☐ propaganda | ☐ humane |
| ☐ demean | ☐ lineage |
| ☐ aftermath | ☐ whisper |
| ☐ modulate | ☐ outcry |
| ☐ showy | ☐ factual |
| ☐ partake | ☐ avocation |
| ☐ culprit | ☐ enlarge |
| ☐ invigorate | ☐ botany |
| ☐ talkative | ☐ resume |
| ☐ scorn | ☐ pseudonym |
| ☐ founder | ☐ nonchalant |
| ☐ custom | ☐ zodiac |
| ☐ expect | ☐ cardinal |
| ☐ chimerical | ☐ interminable |
| ☐ drown | ☐ blame |
| ☐ replica | ☐ threat |
| ☐ pierce | ☐ susceptible |

[2] Select <u>the most</u> appropriate word from the box below. Each word should be used only once.

| | | | |
|---|---|---|---|
| ① demean | ② cardinal | ③ talkative | ④ provisional |
| ⑤ nonchalant | ⑥ replica | ⑦ whisper | ⑧ propaganda |
| ⑨ invigorate | ⑩ belligerent | ⑪ modulate | ⑫ vanquish |
| ⑬ humane | ⑭ domicile | ⑮ stagnant | ⑯ drown |
| ⑰ chimerical | ⑱ factual | ⑲ enlarge | ⑳ partake |

1   These marks are only _____ and can be revised at any time until finalized at the Board of Examiners meeting.

2   His constant provocation and aggressive behavior during the negotiations only served to make the situation more _____.

3   _____ water around a home should always be removed, as it becomes a breeding place for mosquitoes.

4   Resorting to insults and derogatory comments is a common way to _____ others, but it's not conducive to healthy communication.

5   After a long and exhausting workout, many people turn to a refreshing drink to help _____ their bodies and replenish lost nutrients.

6   At the company's annual workshop, Mark, who is usually quite introverted, surprised everyone by becoming extremely _____ and engaging in conversations with almost everyone.

7   Bourgeois sociologists have long regarded Utopias as _____ schemes for transforming society, and they included Marxism among such daydreams.

8   The athlete needed to summon all his strength and determination to _____ his rival and secure the gold medal.

9   Despite the unexpected turn of events, she remained remarkably _____, as if nothing had disrupted her composure.

10   It takes training to be able to distinguish a(n) _____ from an original work of art.

[3] Choose the one which is different from the others.

11  ① notoriety        ② upheaval        ③ turbulence       ④ convulsion

12  ① rue              ② relieve         ③ regret           ④ repent

13  ① flashy           ② gaudy           ③ crude            ④ showy

14  ① scorn            ② contempt        ③ disdain          ④ fallacy

15  ① rashly           ② gingerly        ③ carefully        ④ cautiously

16  ① pedigree         ② lineage         ③ dotage           ④ descent

17  ① incessant        ② infinite        ③ interminable     ④ intermittent

18  ① susceptible      ② versatile       ③ prone            ④ vulnerable

19  ① sultry           ② sweltering      ③ muggy            ④ murky

20  ① dismissive       ② disparate       ③ different        ④ dissimilar

## ✓Answers

1 ④ | 이 점수들은 단지 잠정적인 것이어서 심사 위원회 회의에서 최종적으로 승인될 때까지 언제라도 수정될 수 있다.

2 ⑩ | 협상 과정에서 그의 끊임없는 반대 의견 표명과 공격적인 행동은 상황을 더욱 적대적으로 만들 뿐이었다.

3 ⑮ | 집 주위의 고여 있는 물은 모기가 번식하는 장소가 되기 때문에 항상 없애야 한다.

4 ① | 모욕과 경멸적인 말을 하는 것은 다른 사람을 비하하는 일반적인 방법이지만 건강한 의사소통에 도움이 되지 않는다.

5 ⑨ | 길고 고단한 운동 후, 많은 사람들은 몸에 활력을 주고 잃어버린 영양분을 보충하는 데 도움을 줄 청량음료를 찾는다.

6 ③ | 회사의 연례 워크숍에서 평소 매우 내성적인 마크(Mark)는 매우 수다스러워지고 거의 모든 사람과 대화함으로써 모두를 놀라게 했다.

7 ⑰ | 부르주아 사회학자들은 오랫동안 유토피아를 사회를 변화시키기 위한 비현실적인 계획으로 간주해 왔으며, 그들은 마르크스주의를 그러한 공상에 포함시켰다.

8 ⑫ | 그 운동선수는 경쟁자를 이겨 금메달을 획득하기 위해 모든 힘과 결단력을 모아야 했다.

9 ⑤ | 예기치 못한 상황의 전환에도 불구하고, 그녀는 아무것도 그녀의 평정심을 방해하지 않았다는 듯이 매우 태연했다.

10 ⑥ | 복제품과 원본 예술작품을 구별하려면 훈련이 필요하다.

11 ①   12 ②   13 ③   14 ④   15 ①   16 ③   17 ④   18 ②   19 ④   20 ①

**[1]** Write the meaning of the following words.

| | |
|---|---|
| ☐ adroit | ☐ vindicate |
| ☐ chronicle | ☐ treatise |
| ☐ prototype | ☐ magnify |
| ☐ successive | ☐ roseate |
| ☐ notify | ☐ promote |
| ☐ counter | ☐ diplomat |
| ☐ distort | ☐ conform |
| ☐ eulogy | ☐ banquet |
| ☐ differentiate | ☐ enrich |
| ☐ brazen | ☐ quixotic |
| ☐ patriotism | ☐ hazard |
| ☐ improvise | ☐ abstain |
| ☐ momentous | ☐ furtive |
| ☐ feat | ☐ innate |
| ☐ contemporary | ☐ stimulate |
| ☐ synopsis | ☐ receptacle |
| ☐ recognize | ☐ exhaust |
| ☐ devoid | ☐ junction |
| ☐ archaeology | ☐ overwhelm |
| ☐ pious | ☐ archaic |
| ☐ criticize | ☐ gamut |
| ☐ inmate | ☐ technical |
| ☐ slap | ☐ stun |
| ☐ loquacious | ☐ biopsy |
| ☐ writ | ☐ prevail |

[2] Select <u>the most</u> appropriate word from the box below. Each word should be used only once.

| | | | |
|---|---|---|---|
| ① differentiated | ② chronicled | ③ notify | ④ counter |
| ⑤ contemporary | ⑥ magnify | ⑦ roseate | ⑧ innate |
| ⑨ improvise | ⑩ momentous | ⑪ archaic | ⑫ distort |
| ⑬ quixotic | ⑭ pious | ⑮ exhaustible | ⑯ slap |
| ⑰ stunned | ⑱ enrich | ⑲ furtive | ⑳ vindicated |

**1**    The historian diligently _____ the events of the past, providing us with a detailed record of our history.

**2**    Some media outlets have been known to _____ the truth in pursuit of sensational headlines, leading to misinformation.

**3**    When the musician forgot the sheet music during the concert, he had to rely on his ability to _____ in order to continue playing.

**4**    The monk's _____ lifestyle, characterized by prayer and self-denial, inspired many to seek a more spiritual path.

**5**    Despite the initial doubts and criticism, her groundbreaking research was eventually recognized and _____ by the scientific community.

**6**    I'm afraid you will have to alter your _____ views in the light of the tragic news that has just been reported in the website today.

**7**    In the middle of a recession and high unemployment, it would be _____ to imagine that you could quit your job and find another easily.

**8**    The teacher suspected cheating as soon as he noticed the pupil's _____ glances at his classmate's paper.

**9**    As the population grows, we are witnessing a water shortage. Rivers are _____ and droughts have always afflicted many areas where agriculture is reliant on rainfall.

**10**    Interest rates were hiked modestly to _____ the effects of inflation.

[3] Choose the one which is different from the others.

| 11 | ① adroit | ② deft | ③ adept | ④ languid |
|----|----------|--------|---------|-----------|
| 12 | ① consecutive | ② preliminary | ③ successive | ④ ensuing |
| 13 | ① brazen | ② impudent | ③ unparalleled | ④ unabashed |
| 14 | ① evanescent | ② loquacious | ③ verbose | ④ garrulous |
| 15 | ① abstain | ② indulge | ③ forbear | ④ refrain |
| 16 | ① stimulate | ② provoke | ③ exploit | ④ prompt |
| 17 | ① insinuate | ② criticize | ③ censure | ④ fulminate |
| 18 | ① promote | ② attribute | ③ further | ④ develop |
| 19 | ① overwhelm | ② dominate | ③ surrender | ④ overcome |
| 20 | ① gamut | ② range | ③ sphere | ④ gaffe |

✓ **Answers**

1 ② | 역사가는 과거의 사건을 열심히 기록하여 우리에게 역사에 대한 상세한 기록을 제공한다.

2 ⑫ | 일부 언론 매체는 선정적인 기사를 얻기 위해 진실을 왜곡하며 잘못된 정보를 낳는 것으로 알려져 왔다.

3 ⑨ | 그 음악가는 콘서트 중에 악보를 잊어버렸을 때, 연주를 계속하기 위해 즉흥 연주 능력에 의존해야 했다.

4 ⑭ | 기도와 금욕을 특징으로 하는 스님의 경건한 삶의 방식은 많은 사람들이 좀 더 영적인 길을 찾도록 영감을 주었다.

5 ⑳ | 초기의 의심과 비판에도 불구하고, 그녀의 획기적인 연구는 결국 과학계에서 인정받고 입증되었다.

6 ⑦ | 오늘 웹사이트에 보도된 비극적 뉴스에 비추어 볼 때 당신의 낙관적 견해를 바꿔야 할 것 같다.

7 ⑬ | 경기 침체와 높은 실업률 속에서 직장을 그만두고 또 다른 직장을 쉽게 구할 수 있다고 생각하는 것은 비현실적이다.

8 ⑲ | 선생님은 그 학생이 반 친구의 시험지를 몰래 힐끗 보는 것을 알아채자마자 부정행위를 한 것으로 의심했다.

9 ⑮ | 인구가 증가함에 따라 우리는 물 부족을 목격하고 있다. 강은 고갈될 수 있으며 가뭄은 강우에 의존해 농사를 짓는 많은 지역에 항상 피해를 입혀왔다.

10 ④ | 인플레이션 효과를 반감시키기 위해 금리를 소폭 인상했다.

11 ④   12 ②   13 ③   14 ①   15 ②   16 ③   17 ①   18 ②   19 ③   20 ④

[1] Write the meaning of the following words.

| | |
|---|---|
| ☐ humiliate | ☐ precarious |
| ☐ affluent | ☐ reduce |
| ☐ peddler | ☐ stopgap |
| ☐ steady | ☐ comprehensive |
| ☐ descry | ☐ tribulation |
| ☐ ethnic | ☐ revile |
| ☐ plod | ☐ admission |
| ☐ subtle | ☐ laborious |
| ☐ boon | ☐ wrath |
| ☐ insinuate | ☐ distinctive |
| ☐ monetary | ☐ mesmerize |
| ☐ discrepancy | ☐ cautious |
| ☐ contradict | ☐ nirvana |
| ☐ zest | ☐ vertical |
| ☐ animate | ☐ exhibit |
| ☐ imperious | ☐ mishap |
| ☐ preclude | ☐ breathtaking |
| ☐ spendthrift | ☐ clue |
| ☐ drought | ☐ gleam |
| ☐ oblong | ☐ abject |
| ☐ stem | ☐ foresee |
| ☐ insurrection | ☐ ruddy |
| ☐ gratify | ☐ punishment |
| ☐ frantic | ☐ uplift |
| ☐ cavity | ☐ epoch |

[2] Select <u>the most</u> appropriate word from the box below. Each word should be used only once.

| | | | |
|---|---|---|---|
| ① boon | ② tribulation | ③ nirvana | ④ descry |
| ⑤ steady | ⑥ monetary | ⑦ insinuate | ⑧ oblong |
| ⑨ precluded | ⑩ stem | ⑪ cavity | ⑫ mesmerize |
| ⑬ comprehensive | ⑭ spendthrift | ⑮ mishap | ⑯ contradict |
| ⑰ insurrection | ⑱ foresaw | ⑲ animated | ⑳ clue |

1     His reputation as a(n) _____ was well-known, often squandering his money on lavish purchases and extravagant vacations.

2     Not a day passed by that was not the better because this man, humble as he was, had lived. He never stepped aside from his own path, yet would always give a(n) _____ to his neighbors.

3     She didn't directly accuse him of wrongdoing but chose to _____ that he may have been involved in the mysterious disappearance of the documents.

4     The participants allowed the debate to degenerate into an acrimonious dispute; the urgency of the topic _____ cordiality expected at such events.

5     The government was faced with a challenging situation when a group of individuals organized a(n) _____ in an attempt to overthrow the established regime.

6     The actor's portrayal of the character was so captivating that it could _____ anyone who watched the performance, drawing them into the story.

7     The theater performance was so _____ that it felt like the characters on stage had come to life.

8     The scientist's findings seemed to directly _____ the prevailing theory in the field, challenging the established understanding of the phenomenon.

9     Every small detail could potentially be a valuable _____ that leads to the solution.

10    The meteorologist accurately _____ the approaching storm and warned residents to take necessary precautions.

[3] Choose the one which is different from the others.

**11**　① laconic　　② affluent　　③ opulent　　④ prosperous

**12**　① arrogant　　② haughty　　③ squalid　　④ imperious

**13**　① unstable　　② insecure　　③ precarious　　④ meticulous

**14**　① revile　　② confiscate　　③ abuse　　④ vituperate

**15**　① delude　　② embarrass　　③ shame　　④ humiliate

**16**　① zest　　② flavor　　③ connoisseur　　④ savor

**17**　① gratify　　② content　　③ fulfill　　④ harass

**18**　① frantic　　② ghastly　　③ frenzied　　④ insane

**19**　① empirical　　② extemporaneous　　③ stopgap　　④ makeshift

**20**　① laborious　　② arduous　　③ lackadaisical　　④ onerous

## ✓ Answers

**1** ⑭　┃ 그는 낭비벽이 심한 사람으로 잘 알려져 있었고, 종종 사치스러운 물건과 호화로운 휴가에 돈을 낭비했다.

**2** ① 　┃ 변변치 않은 사람이었지만 이 남자는 살아있음으로써 지나가는 하루하루가 모두 더 나은 날들이었다. 그는 결코 자신의 길에서 벗어난 적이 없었고 항상 이웃에게 이로움을 주곤 했다.

**3** ⑦ 　┃ 그녀는 그의 잘못을 직접 비난하지는 않았지만, 문서들이 의문스럽게 사라진 것에 그가 연관되었을지도 모른다는 것을 넌지시 말하기로 했다.

**4** ⑨ 　┃ 참가자들은 토론이 폭언이 오가는 논쟁으로 악화되게 내버려 두었다. 주제의 긴급함이 이와 같은 행사에서 기대되는 정중한 행동을 불가능하게 했다.

**5** ⑰ 　┃ 현 정권을 전복하기 위해 한 무리의 개인들이 반란을 일으키자, 정부는 어려운 상황에 직면했다.

**6** ⑫ 　┃ 등장인물을 묘사한 그 배우의 연기가 너무나 매력적이어서 공연을 보는 모든 사람을 매료시켰고 관객을 이야기 속으로 끌어들였다.

**7** ⑲ 　┃ 연극 공연은 너무 생동감이 넘쳐 마치 무대 위의 인물들이 살아난 듯한 느낌이 들었다.

**8** ⑯ 　┃ 그 과학자의 연구 결과는 그 분야의 일반적인 이론과 직접적으로 모순되는 것처럼 보였고, 현상에 대한 확립된 이해에 도전했다.

**9** ⑳ 　┃ 모든 작은 세부사항은 잠재적으로 해결책을 이끌어내는 귀중한 단서가 될 수 있다.

**10** ⑱ 　┃ 기상학자는 다가오는 폭풍을 정확하게 예측했고 주민들에게 필요한 예방 조치를 취할 것을 경고했다.

- - - - - - - - - - - - - - - - - - - - - - - - - - - - - - - - - - - - - - - - - - - - -

**11** ①　　**12** ③　　**13** ④　　**14** ②　　**15** ①　　**16** ③　　**17** ④　　**18** ②　　**19** ①　　**20** ③

[01-100] Choose the one that is closest in meaning to the underlined part.

**01** He is the guy everyone goes to when they have any IT related issues. Even though he is an accountant, he is very <u>proficient</u> at troubleshooting software and hardware issues.
① muggy　　　　② skillful
③ gibberish　　　④ ephemeral

**02** Imagine a restaurant where your every <u>whim</u> is catered to, your every want satisfied, your every request granted without hesitation.
① sloth　　　　　② rubbish
③ caprice　　　　④ gratitude

**03** The wrestler was not very big, but his skill and speed made him a <u>formidable</u> opponent.
① malevolent　　② insolent
③ lecherous　　　④ daunting

**04** When I was ten years old, my life changed <u>drastically</u>. I found myself adopted forcefully and against my parents' will.
① violently　　　② gradually
③ elastically　　　④ incessantly

**05** The examples of the Hitler and Stalin regimes show us with terrible clarity what can happen when men <u>usurp</u> the role of gods.
① divide　　　　　② provoke
③ deteriorate　　④ seize

**06** George W. Carver was <u>esteemed</u> for his contributions in the fields of botany and chemistry.
① respected　　　② overlooked
③ criticized　　　④ compensated

**07** Because animals such as hedgehogs, shrews and moles live on insects, they are very <u>beneficial</u> to humans.
① distressing　　② helpful
③ forgiving　　　④ careful

**08** He is very <u>outspoken</u>; he's a man who does not mince words.
① exemplary　　② forthright
③ arbitrary　　　④ agitative

**09** Kristin's dedication to her job is <u>laudable</u>, but she doesn't have the necessary skills to be a good executive officer.
① laughable　　② commendable
③ regrettable　　④ dependable

**10** Americans have separated Clinton's <u>squalid</u> personal behavior from his official stewardship.
① filthy　　　　　② unsullied
③ despotic　　　④ lofty

11 We usually depict the Renaissance as a clear, bubbling river of novelty that broke the medieval dam of <u>rigidified</u> scholasticism.
① overwhelmed    ② religious
③ formalistic    ④ peripheral

12 The travel brochure recommends a rather <u>circuitous</u> route to the hotel in order to help travelers avoid congested roads.
① roundabout    ② makeshift
③ steadfast    ④ easygoing

13 In every culture it seems that one or two animals are considered <u>crafty</u> while others are looked upon as lacking in intelligence.
① artistic    ② humanistic
③ capable    ④ cunning

14 The two treaties that <u>buttress</u> the world's post-Cold War security architecture — setting strict limits and enforcing transparency on both the U.S. and Russian arsenals — will soon be terminated.
① support    ② envision
③ design    ④ build

15 The disappointment and inadequacy of reproduction proved ever more <u>irksome</u>.
① deadening    ② irreparable
③ integral    ④ irresistible

16 It will be difficult to <u>modify</u> the agreement after it has been signed because it will be subject to Congressional approval.
① improve    ② discard
③ change    ④ renew

17 The principle of cinematography is that an action is recorded in a series of <u>stationary</u> images projected in rapid succession.
① printed    ② related
③ motionless    ④ introduced

18 When an enemy appears, ground squirrels show <u>altruistic</u> behaviour. They risk their own lives to give alarm calls to nearby relatives.
① egoistic    ② unselfish
③ eccentric    ④ mysterious

19 The government has seen the power transition in the United States as an occasion to tackle the <u>impasse</u> on the Korean Peninsula issue.
① defiance    ② praise
③ retard    ④ deadlock

20 Genuine love is <u>volitional</u> rather than emotional.
① violent    ② willing
③ disheartening    ④ unconscious

21 Today much of this enthusiasm has not only <u>evaporated</u> but turned into antipathy.
① increased    ② disappeared
③ transformed    ④ sharpened

22 From his dark expertly cut hair to his hand-made shoes he was the <u>epitome</u> of the new young man.
① summary    ② intelligence
③ fortitude    ④ indigence

23 We can't attract people's attention with conventional catchphrases.
 ① feasible    ② superficial
 ③ banal       ④ original

24 The economist sought to dispel all fears of a depression.
 ① disperse    ② entangle
 ③ coincide    ④ hurl

25 The prodigal expenditure on military budget during a time of peace created a stir in the Cabinet.
 ① lavish      ② various
 ③ tangible    ④ sporadic

26 Besides the ostensible conflict between religions in the Crusades, internal pressures within the medieval Roman Catholic Church itself could be cited as helping to propel the call to holy war.
 ① offensive   ② seeming
 ③ feasible    ④ genuine

27 There is enough food to feed all the people on Earth — but not everyone gets enough to eat. This is mainly due to the way food is distributed and the challenges involved in moving food from areas of surplus to areas of great need.
 ① efficiency  ② cultivation
 ③ nourishment ④ excess

28 The introverted student became outspoken after a life-changing experience.
 ① talkative   ② candid
 ③ shy         ④ vocal

29 In the weeks leading up to the emergence of Amy's agoraphobia, she experiences something unexpected and anomalous.
 ① anorexic    ② atypical
 ③ aspiring    ④ anxious

30 The raid on the cabin led to the seizure of 25 kilograms of pure heroine.
 ① detection   ② consumption
 ③ disruption  ④ capture

31 When such young people go to a university they probably discover congenial souls and enjoy a few years of great happiness.
 ① kindred     ② virtuous
 ③ romantic    ④ immortal

32 He adduced several facts to support his theory.
 ① misused     ② abolished
 ③ memorized   ④ presented

33 Bank frauds are on the rise due to the loss of employment and drop in personal finances.
 ① credits     ② deceits
 ③ charges     ④ deposits

34 This syllabus is provisional and subject to amendment without notice.
 ① concise     ② reliable
 ③ inflexible  ④ temporary

35 China regards Taiwan as a part of China and pressures its allies to abide by that position.
 ① govern      ② disturb
 ③ restrict    ④ follow

36 World and earth are always intrinsically and essentially in conflict, belligerent by nature.
① combative
② harmonious
③ common
④ neutral

37 In the Chinese tradition, humidity and stagnant water are considered as the source of endemic and epidemic illness.
① mobile
② warm
③ static
④ tepid

38 As a result, they have been left with the demeaning legal status of "noncitizens," which deprives them of a number of rights, including the right to vote and run for public office.
① detaining
② sustaining
③ degrading
④ emerging

39 Poverty and sickness are often the aftermaths of war.
① symptoms
② reasons
③ consequences
④ influences

40 Consciously or subconsciously, we're meant to understand that the new Asian girlfriend is a downgraded version of our beloved white protagonist: Culprits include season two of *Friends* (Ross has a new girlfriend who is Chinese American).
① offenders
② plaintiffs
③ suspects
④ witnesses

41 The Blue Line was expected to resume service on a nearly normal schedule.
① recollect
② resolve
③ restrict
④ recommence

42 Reading the manuscript carefully, researchers tried to replicate the original experiment.
① create
② analyze
③ duplicate
④ modify

43 Every day at meal-times you go out, apparently to a restaurant, and loaf an hour in the Luxembourg Gardens, watching the pigeons.
① ostensibly
② irreversibly
③ utterly
④ impassably

44 Scientists are trying to pull together disparate ideas in astronomy.
① complementary
② different
③ compatible
④ original

45 Since I was afraid of banging my bare feet against the furniture, I walked through the darkened room gingerly.
① boldly
② quietly
③ awkwardly
④ carefully

46 All people have their own particular lineage, which has varying degrees of importance in their everyday lives.
① ancestry
② dimensions
③ qualifications
④ genetic traits

47 After he was promoted to vice president of the company, he became scornful of his former friends.
① disdainful
② respectful
③ protective
④ negligent

**48** In the nineteenth century, many women writers used <u>pseudonyms</u> because they were afraid of being labeled "unladylike."

① synonyms

② feminine names

③ eponyms

④ pen names

**49** The actress waited her turn to audition for the leading role, trying her best to look <u>nonchalant</u>.

① indecorous  ② nonessential

③ indifferent  ④ undignified

**50** As a salesman, your <u>cardinal</u> rule is to do everything you can to satisfy the customer.

① religious  ② gigantic

③ principal  ④ potential

**51** We used to stay late into the night engaged in <u>interminable</u> arguments upon arts and literature.

① useful  ② unceasing

③ intolerable  ④ pointless

**52** Patients suffering from liver disease may be <u>susceptible</u> to bacterial infections.

① available  ② digressive

③ prone  ④ invincible

**53** Her <u>adroit</u> handling of the boat saved us from going onto the rocks.

① erudite  ② dexterous

③ tangible  ④ inherent

**54** The paintings meticulously <u>chronicle</u> the fall of the Roman empire.

① ephemeralize  ② recount

③ diarize  ④ ingerminate

**55** The witness's version of the accident turned out to be a complete <u>distortion</u>.

① agenda

② routine

③ misrepresentation

④ mishap

**56** Mr. Kim's <u>eulogy</u> of Mr. Lee at his funeral was both eloquent and emotional.

① prayer  ② hatred

③ speech  ④ praise

**57** A <u>brazen-faced</u> person typically is too engaged with himself or herself to appreciate the beauty in others and the world.

① distracted  ② stubborn

③ insolent  ④ punctual

**58** When the pandemic slashed audience capacity by two-thirds or shuttered theatre venues completely, companies had to learn to <u>improvise</u>. Theatre Calgary showed the way with its summer online production of *Romeo and Juliet*.

① postpone  ② obliterate

③ nullify  ④ extemporize

**59** The Industrial Revolution marked a <u>momentous</u> change in human history.

① sudden  ② tectonic

③ momentary  ④ ominous

60 About half the children managed the feat of waiting for 15 minutes, mainly by keeping their attention away from the tempting reward.
① accomplishment
② tedium
③ engrossment
④ practice

61 She found it easier to study contemporary writers than those of the nineteenth century.
① critical     ② modern
③ unknown     ④ productive

62 Although the two men work together very well, they couldn't be more different: Henry is relaxed and loquacious, whereas James is tense and silent most of the time.
① lenient     ② verbose
③ amicable     ④ conceited

63 Arafat's go-it-alone strategy was vindicated by the crushing defeat of Arab governments in the 1967 war.
① blamed     ② blackened
③ acquitted     ④ proved

64 They had no other choice but to magnify the budget.
① obliterate     ② enlarge
③ assess     ④ distribute

65 James Whistler promoted the idea of art for art's sake.
① fought     ② got through
③ disproved     ④ put forward

66 Although attitudes towards conformity have not been fixed historically and have changed over time, in general, Americans seem to dread the idea of being, acting and looking just like their neighbors.
① pursuit of individuality
② agreement with customs or rules
③ state of being poised
④ flexibility in judgement

67 Not infrequently this may present certain hazards for the individual.
① fortunes     ② dangers
③ hopes     ④ prejudices

68 They agreed to abstain from any actions that might endanger the peace process.
① support     ② refrain
③ resist     ④ interfere

69 My movements feel unwittingly furtive. I turn into something of a ghost.
① elusive     ② inhumane
③ languid     ④ harrowing

70 Political convictions lead us to lazy thinking. But there's an even more fundamental impulse at play: our innate desire for an easy answer.
① conflicting     ② deliberate
③ natural     ④ ultimate

71 Stronger measures will have to be taken to stimulate domestic consumption and foreign investment.
① endorse     ② impose
③ affect     ④ promote

72 Joyce has attempted in *Ulysses* to render as exhaustively, as precisely and as directly as it is possible in words to do, what our participation in life is like — or rather, what it seems to us like as from moment to moment we live.

① tiredly
② enthusiastically
③ descriptively
④ thoroughly

73 We had difficulty in reading the archaic language.

① confusing
② old
③ foreign
④ learned

74 English prevails in transportation and the media.

① exists
② preserves
③ continues
④ predominates

75 Studies have shown that the more affluent workers become, the less sympathetic they tend to be towards a progressive political party.

① radical
② insensible
③ selfish
④ wealthy

76 I could only just descry the vessel in full sail, at such a distance that I soon lost sight of it.

① understand
② discern
③ purify
④ ride

77 During the debate, the senator tried to insinuate his opponent was not qualified for office.

① elucidate
② intimidate
③ denounce
④ suggest

78 There is a huge discrepancy in the reviews about the cleanliness of the hotel.

① difference
② protest
③ falsity
④ indignation

79 This morning's editorial contradicted what the Prime Minister said yesterday about the economy.

① rejected
② supported
③ denied
④ praised

80 Though the king had been a kind leader, his daughter was imperious and demanding during her rule.

① chary
② imperturbable
③ implacable
④ authoritarian

81 The temporary cease-fire agreement does not preclude possible retaliatory attacks later.

① presume
② prescribe
③ precede
④ prevent

82 The savings of the wealthy and middle class, increasing far beyond the possibilities of sound investment, had been drawn into frantic speculation in stocks or real estate.

① unauthorized
② frenzied
③ concealed
④ prohibited

83 Because of the recent flow of Burmese refugees over the Thai border, the situation of the children has become increasingly precarious.

① hampered
② rugged
③ ambiguous
④ perilous

84 Neither country has <u>comprehensive</u> AIDS awareness programs or adequate health care.
① useful
② understandable
③ magic
④ extensive

85 Descartes is most remembered and <u>reviled</u> for his insistence upon the strict separation of mind and body.
① memorized
② criticized
③ obfuscated
④ misunderstood

86 Keeping a second house and garden tidy all year round can be a <u>laborious</u> task.
① unnatural
② industrious
③ enjoyable
④ onerous

87 In the ancient civilizations of Greece and Rome, thunder was believed to be a manifestation of the <u>wrath</u> of the gods.
① spirit
② voice
③ power
④ anger

88 The Italian master's 1921 oil painting on canvas is celebrated for its <u>distinctive</u> brush strokes, the graceful yet rigid lines of the silhouette, and the choice of its restrained yet exquisite colors.
① painstaking
② mediocre
③ ornamented
④ distinguishing

89 There was that word again: deal. Limbaugh repeated it over and over, <u>mesmerized</u> by his sudden discovery of the heart of the matter.
① hypnotized
② reconciled
③ persuaded
④ influenced

90 Even though his <u>cautious</u> approach has potential advantages, it looks a bit awkward in this urgent situation.
① aggressive
② discreet
③ optimistic
④ sensitive

91 Though many scientific breakthroughs have resulted from <u>mishaps</u>, it has taken brilliant thinkers to recognize their potential.
① misunderstandings
② accidents
③ misfortunes
④ incidentals

92 I do not condemn the good intentions of those who gave birth to these <u>abject</u> social policy failures.
① exquisite
② sophisticated
③ sublime
④ miserable

93 The prophet <u>foresaw</u> a severe famine in the land.
① predicted
② worried
③ outspoke
④ overestimated

94 The uncompromising modernity of the new writing is also <u>uplifting</u>.
① unconventional
② unmistakable
③ inspiring
④ exaggerating

95 The <u>epoch</u> of mountain building only served to speed up the processes of evolution.
① long period of time
② termination
③ brief moment
④ cessation

**96** <u>Hostile</u> feelings and violent responses often seem to be sublimated into sporting activities.

① delicate        ② hospitable

③ antagonistic      ④ undefined

**97** It is much harder to <u>exert</u> self-control when you're feeling fatigued and your body is run down.

① preserve        ② exercise

③ maintain        ④ ameliorate

**98** The medicines that <u>vanquish</u> the cancer cells could unfortunately leave some unpleasant side effects.

① replicate        ② mutate

③ defeat          ④ precipitate

**99** In the middle of a recession and high unemployment, it would be <u>quixotic</u> to imagine that you could quit your job and find another easily.

① hackneyed      ② affirmative

③ plausible        ④ impractical

**100** The new government has promised an end to the food shortages and <u>interminable</u> queues for basic household items.

① endless        ② sumptuous

③ inconceivable    ④ cohesive

[1] Write the meaning of the following words.

| | |
|---|---|
| ☐ outweigh | ☐ insular |
| ☐ flippant | ☐ mangle |
| ☐ panel | ☐ ecology |
| ☐ sporadic | ☐ prolong |
| ☐ declare | ☐ reminiscent |
| ☐ anthology | ☐ vow |
| ☐ infringe | ☐ spokesman |
| ☐ chronic | ☐ collaborate |
| ☐ expend | ☐ witticism |
| ☐ burden | ☐ accuse |
| ☐ snooze | ☐ peerless |
| ☐ defunct | ☐ outlook |
| ☐ hearsay | ☐ stall |
| ☐ mutable | ☐ transient |
| ☐ allay | ☐ finance |
| ☐ crucial | ☐ plea |
| ☐ paraphrase | ☐ equitable |
| ☐ terrain | ☐ aptitude |
| ☐ lucrative | ☐ nonplus |
| ☐ inception | ☐ germ |
| ☐ disregard | ☐ foreboding |
| ☐ kin | ☐ sociable |
| ☐ revoke | ☐ cavil |
| ☐ binary | ☐ dividend |
| ☐ consensus | ☐ medieval |

[2] Select <u>the most</u> appropriate word from the box below. Each word should be used only once.

| | | | |
|---|---|---|---|
| ① consensus | ② defunct | ③ allay | ④ dividend |
| ⑤ mutable | ⑥ stall | ⑦ infringe | ⑧ mangle |
| ⑨ prolong | ⑩ reminiscent | ⑪ paraphrase | ⑫ peerless |
| ⑬ revoke | ⑭ nonplus | ⑮ lucrative | ⑯ cavil |
| ⑰ snooze | ⑱ collaborate | ⑲ outweigh | ⑳ declare |

1    It's essential to understand the boundaries of copyright law and not knowingly _____ on the intellectual property rights of others.

2    The company, once a thriving industry leader, is now _____ and no longer operational.

3    In the realm of fashion, trends are notoriously _____, making it essential for designers to stay updated with ever-changing styles.

4    The failure of the company to win the _____ contract signaled the beginning of its collapse.

5    The authorities decided to _____ the driver's license of the individual who repeatedly violated traffic laws.

6    Although a full-fledged negotiation appeared out of the question, there was a growing _____ in favor of addressing the other party's objections.

7    The old photographs in the album were _____ of cherished memories from family vacations long ago.

8    Her dedication and talent in the field of mathematics earned her a reputation as a(n) _____ scholar with no equal in her generation.

9    His tendency to _____ at every decision made the project challenging, as he often found fault even in the smallest of choices.

10    Innovation often thrives when individuals from diverse backgrounds come together to _____ on new ideas and solutions.

[3] Choose the one which is different from the others.

**11**  ① frivolous      ② flippant      ③ spurious      ④ impertinent

**12**  ① incessant      ② sporadic      ③ intermittent      ④ periodic

**13**  ① hearsay      ② gossip      ③ rumor      ④ mantra

**14**  ① insular      ② indecisive      ③ parochial      ④ provincial

**15**  ① foreboding      ② premonition      ③ providence      ④ presentiment

**16**  ① engrossed      ② sociable      ③ affable      ④ amiable

**17**  ① impartial      ② fair      ③ equitable      ④ esoteric

**18**  ① witticism      ② parlance      ③ jest      ④ joke

**19**  ① discern      ② ignore      ③ overlook      ④ disregard

**20**  ① strain      ② onus      ③ opus      ④ burden

## ✓ Answers

**1** ⑦  | 저작권법의 범위를 이해하고 타인의 지식재산권을 고의로 침해하지 않는 것이 중요하다.

**2** ②  | 한때 번성했던 업계의 선두였던 이 회사는 이제 없어졌으며 더 이상 사업을 하지 않는다.

**3** ⑤  | 패션 영역에서, 유행은 잘 변하는 것으로 악명이 높으며 디자이너들은 끊임없이 변화하는 스타일을 계속해서 최신으로 유지하는 것이 중요하다.

**4** ⑮  | 그 회사가 채산성이 높은 계약을 따내지 못한 것이 몰락하기 시작한 신호가 되었다.

**5** ⑬  | 당국은 반복적으로 교통법규를 위반한 사람의 운전면허를 취소하기로 결정했다.

**6** ①  | 비록 완전한 협상은 불가능해 보였지만, 다른 당의 반대 의견도 고심하여 다루는 쪽으로 점점 합의가 이뤄지고 있었다.

**7** ⑩  | 앨범에 담긴 오래된 사진들은 오래전 가족 휴가 때의 소중한 추억을 회상하게 했다.

**8** ⑫  | 수학 분야에서 그녀의 헌신과 재능은 그녀의 세대에서 필적할 사람이 없는 뛰어난 학자로서의 명성을 얻게 해주었다.

**9** ⑯  | 모든 결정에서 트집을 잡는 그의 성향은 그 프로젝트를 어렵게 만들었는데, 그는 종종 아주 사소한 선택을 할 때조차 트집을 잡았다.

**10** ⑱  | 혁신은 다양한 배경을 가진 사람들이 모여 새로운 아이디어와 해결책을 위해 협력할 때 종종 잘 되어간다.

........................................................................................

**11** ③      **12** ①      **13** ④      **14** ②      **15** ③      **16** ①      **17** ④      **18** ②      **19** ①      **20** ③

[1] Write the meaning of the following words.

| | |
|---|---|
| ☐ subtract | ☐ dissertation |
| ☐ blunder | ☐ nullify |
| ☐ conspiracy | ☐ homologous |
| ☐ inscribe | ☐ pasture |
| ☐ peculiar | ☐ instant |
| ☐ scrawl | ☐ equator |
| ☐ amicable | ☐ remove |
| ☐ epic | ☐ orator |
| ☐ destitute | ☐ lower |
| ☐ swell | ☐ travail |
| ☐ raconteur | ☐ characteristic |
| ☐ cultivate | ☐ abjure |
| ☐ fanatic | ☐ preface |
| ☐ monotonous | ☐ reprehensible |
| ☐ disaster | ☐ minstrel |
| ☐ tighten | ☐ defer |
| ☐ symptom | ☐ competent |
| ☐ virago | ☐ erode |
| ☐ postulate | ☐ unilateral |
| ☐ aid | ☐ occurrence |
| ☐ fractious | ☐ grueling |
| ☐ status | ☐ prosper |
| ☐ interrupt | ☐ womb |
| ☐ mainstay | ☐ bondage |
| ☐ compel | ☐ apprehend |

[2] Select <u>the most</u> appropriate word from the box below. Each word should be used only once.

| | | | |
|---|---|---|---|
| ① conspiracy | ② travail | ③ competent | ④ nullify |
| ⑤ apprehend | ⑥ destitute | ⑦ homologous | ⑧ prosper |
| ⑨ reprehensible | ⑩ instant | ⑪ postulate | ⑫ amicable |
| ⑬ remove | ⑭ cultivate | ⑮ abjure | ⑯ scrawl |
| ⑰ monotonous | ⑱ subtract | ⑲ swell | ⑳ unilateral |

**1**  Many consider the moon landing to be one of the greatest achievements in history, but there are some who believe it was a staged _____.

**2**  The divorce proceedings were surprisingly _____ with the couple cooperating and finding mutually acceptable solutions to their issues.

**3**  Even had he possessed the poetic faculty, of which, as far as we can judge, he was utterly _____, the want of a language would have prevented him from being a great poet.

**4**  Many people find a repetitive and unchanging daily routine to be quite _____, as it lacks excitement and variety.

**5**  The president has used his veto power to _____ laws passed by the congress that were deemed not to be in the interests of the state.

**6**  The novel's protagonist endured many hardships and trials, symbolizing the human capacity to persevere through life's _____.

**7**  When faced with the consequences of his actions, the suspect had the choice to either stand by his claims or to _____ his statements in front of the court.

**8**  When such _____ remarks are circulated, we can only blame and despise those who produce them.

**9**  In spite of many attempts at being polite, he began to shun the _____ woman who never let him get a word in edgewise.

**10**  The goal of the police is to swiftly _____ the suspects before they evade capture.

[3] Choose the one which is different from the others.

| 11 | ① gaffe | ② blunder | ③ slip | ④ gambit |
|---|---|---|---|---|
| 12 | ① fractious | ② obedient | ③ grouchy | ④ unruly |
| 13 | ① indulge | ② intervene | ③ disturb | ④ interrupt |
| 14 | ① defer | ② postpone | ③ fall back | ④ put off |
| 15 | ① erode | ② abrogate | ③ abrade | ④ corrode |
| 16 | ① grid | ② mainstay | ③ pillar | ④ prop |
| 17 | ① compel | ② coerce | ③ repel | ④ impel |
| 18 | ① thrall | ② succor | ③ bondage | ④ slavery |
| 19 | ① saturnine | ② exhausting | ③ arduous | ④ grueling |
| 20 | ① inscribe | ② carve | ③ engrave | ④ detach |

## ✔Answers

1 ① | 많은 사람들은 달 착륙을 역사상 가장 위대한 업적 중 하나로 생각하지만, 그것이 꾸며진 음모였다고 믿는 사람들도 있다.

2 ⑫ | 이혼 절차는 부부가 서로 협력하여 그들의 문제에 대해 상호 수용할 수 있는 해결책을 찾음으로써 놀랍게도 우호적이었다.

3 ⑥ | 우리가 판단할 수 있는 한, 그가 전적으로 부족했던 시적 재능을 갖고 있었다고 하더라도, 언어의 부족 때문에 그는 위대한 시인이 되지 못했을 것이다.

4 ⑰ | 많은 사람들은 반복적이고 변하지 않는 일상이 흥미로움과 다양성이 부족하기 때문에 매우 단조롭다고 생각한다.

5 ④ | 대통령은 자신의 거부권을 이용하여 의회를 통과한 법률들을 무효화했는데, 그 법률들은 국익을 위한 것이 아니라고 여겨진 것들이었다.

6 ② | 소설의 주인공은 많은 고난과 시련을 견뎌냈으며, 이는 인생의 고난을 견디어 내는 인간의 능력을 상징했다.

7 ⑮ | 자신의 행동이 초래한 결과에 직면했을 때, 용의자는 법정에서 자신의 주장을 고수하거나 진술을 철회하는 선택권을 가지게 되었다.

8 ⑨ | 그런 괘씸한 소문이 유포되었을 때, 우리는 단지 그런 소문을 지어낸 사람들을 비난하고 혐오할 수 있을 뿐이다.

9 ⑳ | 예의 바르게 행동하려고 많은 노력을 했음에도 불구하고 그는 그에게 말할 기회를 주지 않은 일방석인 그 여자를 피하기 시작했다.

10 ⑤ | 경찰의 목표는 용의자가 검거를 피하기 전에 신속하게 체포하는 것이다.

----

11 ④   12 ②   13 ①   14 ③   15 ②   16 ①   17 ③   18 ②   19 ①   20 ④

[1] Write the meaning of the following words.

| | |
|---|---|
| ☐ contagious | ☐ astronomical |
| ☐ pension | ☐ cite |
| ☐ justify | ☐ rift |
| ☐ sumptuous | ☐ gloomy |
| ☐ insomnia | ☐ enigma |
| ☐ profound | ☐ transpire |
| ☐ shelter | ☐ mores |
| ☐ exacting | ☐ prey |
| ☐ superstition | ☐ curtail |
| ☐ quagmire | ☐ fluent |
| ☐ announce | ☐ nomad |
| ☐ magniloquent | ☐ overnight |
| ☐ disappoint | ☐ antibody |
| ☐ stalwart | ☐ disinterested |
| ☐ camaraderie | ☐ forestall |
| ☐ bar | ☐ capacity |
| ☐ fracas | ☐ visceral |
| ☐ intend | ☐ purchase |
| ☐ synergy | ☐ witch |
| ☐ apprise | ☐ beatific |
| ☐ ludicrous | ☐ recline |
| ☐ reincarnation | ☐ post-mortem |
| ☐ impromptu | ☐ sage |
| ☐ hinge | ☐ express |
| ☐ demeanor | ☐ tendentious |

[2] Select the most appropriate word from the box below. Each word should be used only once.

| | | | |
|---|---|---|---|
| ① stalwart | ② camaraderie | ③ contagious | ④ tendentious |
| ⑤ superstition | ⑥ forestall | ⑦ sage | ⑧ shelter |
| ⑨ pension | ⑩ justify | ⑪ visceral | ⑫ nomad |
| ⑬ exacting | ⑭ prey | ⑮ impromptu | ⑯ quagmire |
| ⑰ transpire | ⑱ ludicrous | ⑲ apprise | ⑳ disappoint |

**1**      Some researchers argue that pain can be _____; The pain sensations of others can be felt by some people, just by witnessing their agony.

**2**      The lawyer endeavored to _____ her argument with compelling evidence and sound reasoning during the trial.

**3**      Reconstructing the skeletons of extinct species like dinosaurs is a(n) _____ process that requires much patience and effort by paleontologists.

**4**      When you've been climbing alone for hours, there's a tremendous sense of _____ when you meet another climber.

**5**      As the political situation continued to deteriorate, the country found itself sinking deeper into a complex and challenging _____ with no clear solution in sight.

**6**      The proposal to build a skyscraper in the small, rural town seemed utterly _____, as it contradicted the town's quaint charm and lacked any practical justification.

**7**      With no script or preparation, the actors delivered a(n) _____ performance that captivated the audience and showcased their spontaneity.

**8**      Despite advancements in science, some people still hold on to _____, believing in charms and rituals for luck and protection.

**9**      In search of adventure and a life less tethered, he embraced the lifestyle of a modern-day _____, traveling from place to place with no permanent home.

**10**      Strict sanitary procedures help to _____ outbreaks of disease.

**[3] Choose the one which is different from the others.**

**11**  ① lavish      ② sumptuous      ③ supercilious      ④ extravagant

**12**  ① bombastic      ② magniloquent      ③ pompous      ④ sedulous

**13**  ① illusion      ② fracas      ③ brawl      ④ quarrel

**14**  ① demeanor      ② defiance      ③ conduct      ④ behavior

**15**  ① puzzle      ② conundrum      ③ homage      ④ enigma

**16**  ① disinterested      ② fair      ③ impartial      ④ subjective

**17**  ① blissful      ② truculent      ③ beatific      ④ rapturous

**18**  ① fluent      ② eloquent      ③ fragile      ④ voluble

**19**  ① immature      ② gloomy      ③ dismal      ④ melancholy

**20**  ① obstruct      ② hinder      ③ bar      ④ stumble

## ✔ Answers

**1** ③  ｜ 몇몇 연구원들은 고통이 전염될 수 있다고 주장하는데, 일부 사람들은 타인들의 고통을 보는 것만으로도 그들의 고통을 느낄 수 있다는 것이다.

**2** ⑩  ｜ 그 변호사는 재판 과정에서 설득력 있는 증거와 올바른 논거로 그녀의 주장을 정당화하려고 노력했다.

**3** ⑬  ｜ 공룡처럼 멸종한 종(種)의 뼈대를 다시 맞추는 일은 고생물학자의 많은 인내와 노력을 필요로 하는 힘든 과정이다.

**4** ②  ｜ 몇 시간을 혼자서 등산하고 있을 때 또 다른 등산가를 만나면 엄청난 동료 의식이 생긴다.

**5** ⑯  ｜ 정치 상황이 계속 악화되면서, 그 나라는 뚜렷한 해결책이 보이지 않는 복잡하고 어려운 수렁에 더욱 깊이 빠져들게 되었다.

**6** ⑱  ｜ 작은 시골 마을에 초고층 건물을 짓겠다는 제안은 그 마을의 고풍스러운 매력과 모순되고 실질적인 명분도 전혀 없었기 때문에 정말 터무니없어 보였다.

**7** ⑮  ｜ 대본이나 준비 없이 배우들은 관객을 사로잡으며 그들의 자발성을 보여주는 즉흥적인 연기를 선보였다.

**8** ⑤  ｜ 과학의 발전에도 불구하고 일부 사람들은 여전히 미신을 고수하며 행운과 보호를 위한 부적과 의식을 믿는다.

**9** ⑫  ｜ 모험과 덜 얽매인 삶을 찾아, 그는 일정한 주거지 없이 이곳저곳을 여행하며 현대 유목민의 삶의 방식을 받아들였다.

**10** ⑥  ｜ 엄격한 위생 절차가 질병의 발생을 예방하는 데 도움이 된다.

- - - - - - - - - - - - - - - - - - - - - - - - - - - - - - - - - - - - - - - - - - - - - - - - -

**11** ③    **12** ④    **13** ①    **14** ②    **15** ③    **16** ④    **17** ②    **18** ③    **19** ①    **20** ④

[1] Write the meaning of the following words.

| | |
|---|---|
| ☐ permanent | ☐ precursor |
| ☐ snore | ☐ domestic |
| ☐ exorbitant | ☐ epigram |
| ☐ corroborate | ☐ migrate |
| ☐ arson | ☐ orifice |
| ☐ striking | ☐ brittle |
| ☐ procrastinate | ☐ council |
| ☐ immigrant | ☐ leisurely |
| ☐ discrete | ☐ astonish |
| ☐ source | ☐ corporal |
| ☐ hoard | ☐ detest |
| ☐ munificent | ☐ sanctum |
| ☐ alleviate | ☐ wage |
| ☐ caustic | ☐ kingdom |
| ☐ dedicate | ☐ superfluous |
| ☐ subsequent | ☐ objurgate |
| ☐ bedrock | ☐ protest |
| ☐ inquisitive | ☐ metabolism |
| ☐ evict | ☐ nocturnal |
| ☐ roughly | ☐ alumnus |
| ☐ vapor | ☐ trip |
| ☐ fulfill | ☐ coma |
| ☐ aristocracy | ☐ inimical |
| ☐ soar | ☐ pundit |
| ☐ tortuous | ☐ reproduce |

[2] Select <u>the most</u> appropriate word from the box below. Each word should be used only once.

| | | | |
|---|---|---|---|
| ① alleviate | ② bedrock | ③ subsequent | ④ epigram |
| ⑤ objurgate | ⑥ corroborate | ⑦ domestic | ⑧ corporal |
| ⑨ evict | ⑩ migrate | ⑪ arson | ⑫ nocturnal |
| ⑬ hoard | ⑭ procrastinate | ⑮ sanctum | ⑯ tortuous |
| ⑰ detest | ⑱ inquisitive | ⑲ reproduce | ⑳ permanent |

**1**  Genetic evidence has been used to _____ Darwin's theory of evolution, proving its veracity beyond a reasonable doubt.

**2**  The investigation revealed that the fire had been intentionally set, leading authorities to suspect an act of _____ as the cause.

**3**  When depression is the underlying mood disorder, antidepressants can _____ feelings of sadness, hopelessness, or difficulty with sleep and concentration.

**4**  Despite the looming deadline, he had a tendency to _____, often delaying important tasks until the last possible moment.

**5**  Known for her _____ nature, she was always curious and never afraid to explore new ideas.

**6**  In cases of persistent non-payment, landlords may decide to take legal action to forcibly _____ tenants from the property.

**7**  The legal process was long, complex, and filled with intricate details, making it a(n) _____ ordeal for everyone involved.

**8**  In the interview, the musicians expressed how much they _____ autotune, preferring the raw authenticity of a live performance.

**9**  In the performance review, the supervisor did not hesitate to _____ employees who consistently failed to meet the company's standards.

**10**  Animals that are active during the daytime are called diurnal, and those that come out at night are known as _____.

[3] Choose the one which is different from the others.

**11** ① exorbitant ② excessive ③ ebullient ④ immoderate

**12** ① remarkable ② authentic ③ striking ④ salient

**13** ① obtrusive ② munificent ③ generous ④ lavish

**14** ① vitriolic ② acerbic ③ caustic ④ tentative

**15** ① carry out ② fulfill ③ put off ④ execute

**16** ① brittle ② resilient ③ fragile ④ breakable

**17** ① downplay ② astonish ③ startle ④ astound

**18** ① superfluous ② redundant ③ prerequisite ④ excess

**19** ① pundit ② guru ③ expert ④ hermit

**20** ① harmful ② innocuous ③ inimical ④ adverse

## ✔ Answers

**1** ⑥ | 유전적 증거는 다윈의 진화론을 확증하는 데 사용되었으며, 합리적인 의심을 넘어 그것의 정확성을 입증했다.

**2** ⑪ | 조사 결과 화재가 고의로 발생한 것으로 드러나 당국은 방화를 화재의 원인으로 의심하고 있다.

**3** ① | 우울증이 근원적인 기분 장애일 때, 항우울제는 슬픔, 절망감, 또는 수면과 집중 곤란을 완화해 줄 수 있다.

**4** ⑭ | 마감일이 임박했음에도 불구하고, 그는 미루는 경향이 있었고, 종종 중요한 일들을 가능한 마지막 순간까지 미루었다.

**5** ⑱ | 호기심 많은 성격으로 알려진 그녀는 항상 호기심이 많았으며 새로운 아이디어를 탐구하는 것을 두려워하지 않았다.

**6** ⑨ | 지속해서 (월세를) 지불하지 않는 경우 집주인은 임차인을 건물에서 강제로 퇴거시키는 법적 조치를 취할 수 있다.

**7** ⑯ | 그 법적 절차는 길고 복잡하며 난해한 세부사항들로 가득 차 있어서 모든 당사자들에게 우여곡절의 험난한 시련이 되었다.

**8** ⑰ | 인터뷰에서 음악가들은 라이브 공연의 수정되지 않는 진정성을 선호하면서 음정 보정을 얼마나 싫어하는지 말했다.

**9** ⑤ | 인사평가에서 그 관리자는 회사의 기준을 계속해서 충족하지 못하는 직원들을 책망하는 것을 서슴지 않았다.

**10** ⑫ | 낮에 활발하게 활동하는 동물들은 주행성이라고 불리고, 밤에 나와서 활동하는 동물들은 야행성으로 불린다.

**11** ③  **12** ②  **13** ①  **14** ④  **15** ③  **16** ②  **17** ①  **18** ③  **19** ④  **20** ②

**[1] Write the meaning of the following words.**

| | |
|---|---|
| ☐ lukewarm | ☐ formal |
| ☐ condone | ☐ effigy |
| ☐ skyscraper | ☐ precise |
| ☐ progressive | ☐ rhapsodize |
| ☐ acclivity | ☐ agreeable |
| ☐ inhibit | ☐ henchman |
| ☐ demanding | ☐ unprecedented |
| ☐ expert | ☐ discomfit |
| ☐ beseech | ☐ performance |
| ☐ residue | ☐ slip |
| ☐ motif | ☐ immaculate |
| ☐ supplant | ☐ litter |
| ☐ commonplace | ☐ generalize |
| ☐ spur | ☐ turmoil |
| ☐ predicament | ☐ range |
| ☐ flaunt | ☐ covetous |
| ☐ triumph | ☐ zeitgeist |
| ☐ oracle | ☐ worship |
| ☐ curb | ☐ denizen |
| ☐ streak | ☐ panic |
| ☐ mural | ☐ ancillary |
| ☐ anxiety | ☐ entertain |
| ☐ congruous | ☐ mirth |
| ☐ instrument | ☐ document |
| ☐ vex | ☐ brusque |

[2] Select the most appropriate word from the box below. Each word should be used only once.

| | | | |
|---|---|---|---|
| ① progressive | ② lukewarm | ③ document | ④ predicament |
| ⑤ range | ⑥ congruous | ⑦ generalize | ⑧ condone |
| ⑨ acclivity | ⑩ supplant | ⑪ rhapsodize | ⑫ formal |
| ⑬ covetous | ⑭ discomfit | ⑮ curb | ⑯ mirth |
| ⑰ demanding | ⑱ slip | ⑲ entertain | ⑳ panic |

1    The management has promised to guarantee job security, but remained _____ about other demands.

2    As a teacher, it's important to create a classroom culture that does not _____ cheating, fostering an environment of academic honesty.

3    Top athletes often train in exceptionally _____ conditions to push their limits and achieve peak performance.

4    In the ever-evolving world of technology, newer innovations often emerge to _____ older methods and technologies, rendering them obsolete.

5    In the intricate web of international relations, diplomatic negotiations often arise to resolve disputes and prevent nations from falling into a political _____.

6    If we don't do something to _____ spending, we are going to run out of money.

7    In the highly competitive art auction, collectors and enthusiasts alike cast _____ glances at the rare masterpiece, each hoping to claim it as their own.

8    As the comedic performance unfolded on stage, the audience erupted in waves of _____, filling the theater with joyous laughter.

9    In critical thinking, it's crucial to scrutinize individual cases carefully and not hastily _____, as doing so may oversimplify complex situations and lead to inaccurate assessments.

10   The false rumor of an impending disaster spread quickly, causing unnecessary _____ among the population.

[3] Choose the one which is different from the others.

**11**  ① inhibit     ② impede     ③ hurtle     ④ restrain

**12**  ① beseech     ② implore     ③ plead     ④ subordinate

**13**  ① soak up     ② flaunt     ③ boast     ④ show off

**14**  ① vex     ② appease     ③ annoy     ④ bother

**15**  ① maneuver     ② turmoil     ③ fuss     ④ tumult

**16**  ① brusque     ② curt     ③ surly     ④ tactful

**17**  ① worship     ② succumb     ③ adore     ④ revere

**18**  ① flawless     ② immaculate     ③ irrevocable     ④ impeccable

**19**  ① commonplace     ② hackneyed     ③ banal     ④ irregular

**20**  ① smother     ② spur     ③ incite     ④ stimulate

## ✔Answers

**1** ② ｜ 경영진은 고용 안정 보장을 약속했지만, 기타 요구에 대해서는 미온적인 자세를 견지했다.

**2** ⑧ ｜ 교사로서 부정행위를 용납하지 않는 학급 문화를 조성하고 정직한 학업 환경을 조성하는 것이 중요하다.

**3** ⑰ ｜ 최고의 운동선수들은 자신들의 한계를 끌어올리고 최고의 성과를 이루기 위해 매우 힘든 환경에서 훈련하는 경우가 많다.

**4** ⑩ ｜ 계속 진화하는 기술 세계에서, 더 새로운 혁신은 종종 오래된 방법과 기술을 대체하기 위해 등장하여 오래된 기술을 쓸모가 없게 만든다.

**5** ④ ｜ 복잡하게 얽혀 있는 국제관계에서, 외교적 협상은 분쟁을 해결하고 국가가 정치적 곤경에 빠지는 것을 방지하기 위해 종종 이루어진다.

**6** ⑮ ｜ 지출을 제한하는 조치를 취하지 않으면, 우리는 돈이 다 떨어질 것이다.

**7** ⑬ ｜ 경쟁이 치열한 미술품 경매에서, 수집가들과 애호가들 모두는 희귀한 걸작을 탐내는 눈길로 바라보며 그 작품이 자신의 것이 되길 바라고 있다.

**8** ⑯ ｜ 코미디 공연이 무대 위에 열리자 관객들이 환희의 물결을 일으키며 극장을 즐거운 웃음으로 가득 채웠다.

**9** ⑦ ｜ 비판적 사고를 할 때 개별 사례를 신중하게 분석하고 섣불리 일반화하지 않는 것이 중요한데, 섣부른 일반화는 복잡한 상황을 지나치게 단순화하고 잘못된 평가를 할 수 있기 때문이다.

**10** ⑳ ｜ 재난이 임박했다는 거짓된 소문이 빠르게 퍼져 주민들 사이에 불필요한 공포를 불러일으켰다.

- - - - - - - - - - - - - - - - - - - - - - - - - - - - - - - - - - - - - - - - - - - - -

**11** ③    **12** ④    **13** ①    **14** ②    **15** ①    **16** ④    **17** ②    **18** ③    **19** ④    **20** ①

# ACTUAL TEST

[01-100] Choose the one that is closest in meaning to the underlined part.

**01** We must pay attention to the side effects of some drug, which often <u>outweigh</u> the possible benefits.
① maximize          ② minimize
③ promote           ④ exceed

**02** His <u>flippant</u> actions and words earned a few laughs from his peers, but they also got him several days of detention.
① restrained        ② enraged
③ frivolous         ④ immoral

**03** More than 100 people have been killed this year in <u>sporadic</u> outbursts of ethnic violence.
① intermittent      ② continuous
③ frequent          ④ distant

**04** Finding serious <u>infringement</u> of copyright, the court ruled in favor of the plaintiff.
① pretense          ② violation
③ infliction        ④ nuisance

**05** The employee manual clearly explains that management has little tolerance for <u>chronic</u> tardiness.
① habitual          ② conventional
③ reckless          ④ incompetent

**06** In the situation of language learning, exposure to language and motivation are <u>crucial</u> factors.
① final             ② drastic
③ meager            ④ vital

**07** The artist is also a rising business woman, having inked <u>lucrative</u> deals with Pepsi, Reebok, and other famous brands within the past year.
① smooth            ② perceptive
③ decremental       ④ remunerative

**08** Professor Clark continued his research work and <u>disregarded</u> his colleague's advice.
① ignored           ② deplored
③ explored          ④ implored

**09** Race is a social construct, not a biological trait. That's the scientific <u>consensus</u> — so why do many people still dispute it?
① inquiry           ② accord
③ objectivity       ④ candor

**10** Senior party officials took the podium, arguing the government's tax audit was aimed at <u>prolonging</u> its rule at next year's presidential election.
① enforcing         ② elongating
③ consolidating     ④ guaranteeing

11 Susan Miller <u>collaborated on</u> a novel with her brother.
① worked together on
② purchased
③ gathered together with
④ completed

12 A new study shows that robots are more persuasive when they're presented as a <u>peer</u>, as opposed to an authority figure.
① collage      ② conductor
③ college      ④ colleague

13 Noise pollution differs from other forms of pollution in a number of ways. Noise is <u>transient</u>; once the pollution stops, the environment is free of it.
① flagrant      ② temporary
③ arduous      ④ causal

14 Diversity is a mantra in this society, especially in the enlightened academic and liberal circles that feel empowered to make our society less racist and more <u>equitable</u>.
① divergent      ② allowable
③ agreeable      ④ impartial

15 Poe uses the concept of death and characters' deteriorating mental conditions in order to give a sense of <u>foreboding</u> and mystery to the story.
① hypocrisy      ② nonchalance
③ barrenness      ④ presentiment

16 Though twins, they are not identical. One is <u>sociable</u>, empathetic, cautious. The other a loner, moody, reckless.
① withdrawn      ② gregarious
③ timorous      ④ bashful

17 When one is unfamiliar with the customs, it is easy to make a <u>blunder</u>.
① commitment      ② enemy
③ injury      ④ mistake

18 I think there was a <u>conspiracy</u> to keep me out of the committee.
① fealty      ② loyalty
③ plot      ④ treachery

19 They <u>inscribed</u> the words on the wall.
① wrote      ② read
③ translated      ④ removed

20 The kiwi is <u>a peculiar</u> flightless creature with furry feathers and a long, curved beak.
① a particular      ② a solemn
③ an awkward      ④ an odd

21 The dissolution of the business partnership was quite <u>amicable</u>, so the former partners remained on good terms.
① historic      ② friendly
③ leisurely      ④ efficient

22 Millions of <u>destitute</u> immigrants have been absorbed and Hong Kong has created one of the most successful societies on earth.
① anguished      ② indigent
③ desperate      ④ exhausted

23 After gold was discovered in California in 1848, the population there swelled.

① retracted    ② acquiesced

③ curtailed    ④ burgeoned

24 A political fanatic, he has fought with revolutionaries all over the world.

① incumbent    ② candidate

③ zealot    ④ jealousy

25 Her monotonous tone of voice made the students think twice about taking her courses.

① critical    ② intriguing

③ questioning    ④ tedious

26 Stimulation is a great distraction for sensitive babies who become fractious when being changed.

① amenable    ② frivolous

③ ambivalent    ④ irritable

27 There is nothing the international community can do to compel Iran to suspend uranium enrichment.

① reserve    ② enumerate

③ meddle    ④ obligate

28 The Student Council voted to nullify some regulations passed by former councils.

① invalidate

② join legally

③ examine carefully

④ enforce

29 The obligation to close was satisfied without physical contact or as much emotional travail.

① drudgery    ② upside

③ perusal    ④ vanity

30 It is our reprehensible nature to welcome flattery.

① amiable    ② ignoble

③ blameworthy    ④ commonplace

31 They showed no deference to their lord, ignoring all his commands.

① interest    ② fright

③ respect    ④ doubt

32 I don't think Jason will succeed in his new job, for he is not competent to do that type of work.

① gullible    ② valuable

③ conspicuous    ④ able

33 Her release after only three days erodes confidence in the judicial system.

① restores    ② enhances

③ destroys    ④ adjusts

34 The global nature of climate change arises from the fact that irrespective of where on earth greenhouse gases are emitted they are rapidly absorbed into the atmosphere and spread around the earth. The consequences of the resulting global climate change, however, are projected to be far from uniform, with some countries expected to suffer far greater adverse impacts than others. In addition, unilateral action by any

one country cannot alter this situation significantly. It therefore requires concerted remedial cooperative action at the international level to address the problem.

① unauthorized

② zero-sum

③ conventional

④ one-sided

35 It is the penultimate day of a grueling three-week tour of Europe, during which she has cast herself in the role of educator in front of the UK and EU Parliaments.

① exhausting ② enjoyable

③ extravagant ④ empowering

36 According to a news report, a woman, who has no previous police record, was apprehended picking flowers from an office park for her grandmother's grave.

① witnessed ② seized

③ discovered ④ blamed

37 The new potentially more contagious omicron variant of the coronavirus popped up in more European countries just days after being identified in South Africa.

① transmittable ② valid

③ strong ④ spoiled

38 In the movies the death of a child justifies both serious acts of violent revenge and violent displays of serious acting.

① criticizes ② encourages

③ validates ④ determines

39 They love his sumptuous croon and his songs about eggshell hearts breaking on the stones of romance.

① luxurious ② chippy

③ inexpensive ④ infectious

40 The changes in society brought about by the coronavirus, and the associated governmental measures and restrictions, have been nothing short of profound.

① explosive ② catastrophic

③ seismic ④ divisive

41 In their stories of the trial, the reporters ridiculed the magniloquent speeches of the defense attorney.

① berserk ② sedulous

③ prosaic ④ grandiloquent

42 Even among the FTA's most stalwart opponents, there is a tacit awareness that globalization and other factors are unavoidably changing the country's economy.

① steadfast ② adroit

③ ascetic ④ coherent

43 He will apprise them of Indian intransigence with reference to suspension in talks between Pakistan and India.

① deprive ② accuse

③ relieve ④ inform

44 I am serious; this is not a ludicrous issue.

① laughable ② lubricating

③ negligible ④ luminant

45 The professor wasn't prepared to talk to the class, but she gave a very good <u>impromptu</u> lecture without any notes.
① extemporaneous
② thoughtful
③ unthoughtful
④ well-designed

46 Parts of his case <u>hinged</u> on the viability of the idea that memory can be manifested without awareness of remembering.
① depended
② departed
③ looked
④ let

47 As a result, they have been left with the <u>demeaning</u> legal status of "noncitizens," which deprives them of a number of rights, including the right to vote and run for public office.
① detaining
② sustaining
③ degrading
④ emerging

48 His famous book on the origin of the universe has been <u>cited</u> by scientists and scholars the world over.
① read
② quoted
③ brought
④ discussed

49 The company's sales picture is <u>gloomy</u> this year.
① promising
② precise
③ delicate
④ dark

50 The professor's lecture was full of <u>enigmatic</u> references to Greek poetry.
① enlightening
② disturbing
③ entertaining
④ puzzling

51 Taboos can reduce anxiety in a number of situations through what a person does not do. Taboos often originate from beliefs that if a certain action is performed, some tragedy or misfortune will <u>transpire</u>.
① forgo
② occur
③ vanish
④ resort

52 Many states have <u>curtailed</u> smoking in public areas by banning smoking in restaurants and bars.
① abolished
② discouraged
③ reduced
④ targeted

53 Chinese states experienced tense relations with the <u>nomadic</u> people in the past.
① wandering
② fierce
③ nocturnal
④ pristine

54 Surrealism rests in the belief in the superior reality of certain forms of association neglected heretofore, in the omnipotence of the dream, and in the <u>disinterested</u> play of thought.
① flustered
② tedious
③ mundane
④ detached

55 In order to <u>forestall</u> outbreaks of retaliatory violence, we arranged a week-long series of mass rallies and demonstrations throughout the country.
① scold
② investigate
③ endure
④ prevent

56 The terminal has the <u>capacity</u> to ship approximately 16 million tones of coal a year.
① volume      ② equipment
③ possibility      ④ employee

57 The response was less analytical than <u>visceral</u>.
① efficacious      ② instinctive
③ sycophantic      ④ responsive

58 The newspaper is notorious for the <u>tendentious</u> account of the affair, so people don't believe it wholeheartedly.
① biased      ② trendy
③ sensational      ④ exaggerated

59 In some countries, the <u>exorbitant</u> cost of staging a 'proper' funeral can lead families to financial ruin.
① cheap      ② negotiable
③ sparse      ④ expensive

60 There are many physical as well as moral facts which <u>corroborate</u> this opinion, and some few that would seem to weigh against it.
① report      ② confirm
③ collect      ④ refute

61 The windchill factor, the combination of low temperature and wind speed, <u>strikingly</u> increases the degree of cold felt by a person who is outdoors.
① effectively      ② remarkably
③ certainly      ④ unquestionably

62 One of the hallmark symptoms of ADHD is <u>procrastination</u>.
① action      ② change
③ stalling      ④ excess

63 Atoms are composed of <u>discrete</u> units called protons, neutrons and electrons.
① transferable      ② distinct
③ derived      ④ absolute

64 Unfortunately, the antibiotics that were first used as treatment failed to <u>alleviate</u> what was presumed to be community-associated pneumonia.
① provoke      ② soothe
③ eliminate      ④ aggravate

65 Mr. Davis is a very <u>dedicated</u> and talented member of the team.
① stout      ② capable
③ tranquil      ④ devoted

66 If the two ingredients are mixed together during the bread-baking process, a spongy and elastic mass consisting of tiny gas bubbles is formed. When this mixture is <u>subsequently</u> heated, the gluten becomes firm instead of elastic.
① bulkily      ② exceedingly
③ oppressively      ④ later

67 The <u>bedrock</u> on which psychoanalysis rests is a belief in the unconscious.
① foundation      ② impasse
③ viewpoint      ④ bias

**68** The main function of the stage curtain is to conceal the audience from inquisitive eyes.

① apathetic      ② curious

③ sorrowful      ④ attractive

**69** Landlords enclosed farmlands and evicted the peasants in favor of sheep cultivation.

① fostered      ② enrolled

③ excluded      ④ tempted

**70** Gray and Burns were precursors of the Romantic Movement in English Literature.

① forerunners      ② navigators

③ recipients      ④ morticians

**71** When birds migrate, they sometimes fly in formation.

① grow new feathers

② move from one place to another

③ feel death is near

④ search for food and water

**72** This may help to undermine the brittle truce that exists between the two countries.

① indissoluble      ② fragile

③ long-term      ④ mutual

**73** What constitutes corporal punishment is also wide-ranging: everything from a light slap on the hand to an all-out whipping with a belt or a paddle.

① intangible      ② excessive

③ physical      ④ rude

**74** Blackmail and kidnapping are the things we all detest.

① abhor      ② adore

③ desire      ④ disguise

**75** Israel's Prime Minister Naftali Bennett wages war on COVID-19 at home while building ties with the UAE and guarding against Iran.

① conducts      ② campaigns

③ ceases      ④ cements

**76** In those days, color was primarily used either to highlight text or to add superfluous screen decoration.

① redundant      ② superior

③ inferior      ④ superlative

**77** Langdon was having trouble concentrating as a scattering of a park's nocturnal residents were already emerging from the shadows.

① busy      ② gathered

③ night      ④ wild

**78** This target is inimical to Jane because she is in France now.

① hostile      ② infrared

③ pervasive      ④ beneficial

**79** AlphaGo's triumph was a pivotal moment for most Go pundits as well as for me.

① judges      ② fans

③ experts      ④ players

80 Frostbitten fingers and toes should be treated with lukewarm water.
① tepid　　　② boiling
③ frigid　　　④ steamy

81 Legalization of addictive drugs would not condone use of any addictive substance.
① prevent　　② concur
③ detain　　　④ overlook

82 Blue seems to inhibit hunger. So, if you're planing to lose weight, try adding a blue light to your refrigerator.
① reduce　　② satisfy
③ sustain　　④ deprive

83 Chan only gave him that anxious and beseeching look I had seen so many times before.
① begging　　② fearful
③ aggressive　④ depressed

84 The three Democratic veterans elected to Congress in 2006 were supplanted by seven Republican veterans in subsequent elections.
① followed　　② supported
③ flanked　　　④ superseded

85 This spurred the hospital to ramp up services that offer free car seats and car-safety education to families in those areas.
① annihilated　② inaugurated
③ provoked　　④ released

86 The unprecedented global predicament in the post-war era requires a new discourse of liberation.
① quandary　　② proliferation
③ fluctuation　④ apex

87 A leading human rights organization is urging Greece's new government to take urgent action to curb an alarming increase in attacks against the people from Asia and Africa.
① ransom　　② restrain
③ promote　　④ exterminate

88 Parts of the mural had been destroyed, apparently by the Maya themselves, as if they had wanted to erase the history it revealed.
① coral　　　② annals
③ painting　　④ pyramid

89 Gold, a psychologist, believes that there are several reasons siblings don't turn to each other more for instrumental help.
① mechanical　② susceptible
③ obsolete　　④ useful

90 During Eisenhower's first term, the conduct of Senator Joseph R. McCarthy was one of the most vexing problems facing the administration.
① serious　　② notorious
③ annoying　　④ unsolvable

**91** Snowfall this winter created an <u>unprecedented</u> demand for road salt.

① abundant     ② temporary

③ exceptional     ④ excessive

**92** On the site, you can read <u>immaculate</u> digital reproductions of Schoenberg's correspondence.

① impeccable     ② constructive

③ streaming     ④ monumental

**93** The <u>turmoil</u> in the city following the earthquake brought out all the fire-fighters and police.

① terror     ② liberation

③ commotion     ④ emergency

**94** On their safari, the hunters stalked lions, tigers, and other ferocious <u>denizens</u> of the jungle.

① dwellers     ② scavengers

③ hosts     ④ conservators

**95** She was offended by his <u>brusque</u> reply.

① abrupt     ② candid

③ concise     ④ gentle

**96** The angels in the painting have <u>beatific</u> smiles.

① sardonic     ② perfunctory

③ blissful     ④ convincing

**97** Nevertheless, no special measures aimed at pulling our economy from the <u>quagmire</u> are on the horizon.

① predicament     ② plateau

③ perspective     ④ frugality

**98** The authorities have <u>revoked</u> their original decision to allow development of this rural area.

① executed     ② postponed

③ demanded     ④ repealed

**99** The lawyers sought to examine the books of the <u>defunct</u> corporation.

① fraudulent     ② nonexistent

③ indigent     ④ autonomous

**100** His opinions were <u>mutable</u> and easily influenced by anyone who had any powers of persuasion.

① impudent     ② meticulous

③ capricious     ④ tentative

## ☑ DAILY CHECKUP

[1] Write the meaning of the following words.

| | |
|---|---|
| ☐ virtual | ☐ docile |
| ☐ astrology | ☐ plaintiff |
| ☐ distend | ☐ inhabit |
| ☐ staunch | ☐ marsh |
| ☐ poverty | ☐ frank |
| ☐ infinitesimal | ☐ junk |
| ☐ expire | ☐ lease |
| ☐ suffrage | ☐ state-of-the-art |
| ☐ gorge | ☐ turnpike |
| ☐ cannibal | ☐ scramble |
| ☐ proceed | ☐ cordial |
| ☐ disciple | ☐ wont |
| ☐ brilliant | ☐ barometer |
| ☐ ovation | ☐ phonetic |
| ☐ ameliorate | ☐ frighten |
| ☐ erroneous | ☐ catalyst |
| ☐ cherish | ☐ sway |
| ☐ antinomy | ☐ restive |
| ☐ reinforce | ☐ enchant |
| ☐ influx | ☐ acrimonious |
| ☐ priceless | ☐ decay |
| ☐ muffle | ☐ valetudinarian |
| ☐ analogy | ☐ override |
| ☐ trustworthy | ☐ granary |
| ☐ hoax | ☐ coincide |

[2] Select <u>the most</u> appropriate word from the box below. Each word should be used only once.

| | | | |
|---|---|---|---|
| ① antinomy | ② ovation | ③ priceless | ④ analogy |
| ⑤ docile | ⑥ decay | ⑦ influx | ⑧ wont |
| ⑨ coincide | ⑩ ameliorate | ⑪ gorge | ⑫ catalyst |
| ⑬ expire | ⑭ reinforce | ⑮ override | ⑯ suffrage |
| ⑰ valetudinarian | ⑱ astrology | ⑲ acrimonious | ⑳ infinitesimal |

**1** The term used to denote the right to vote, especially as a fundamental aspect of civic participation and representation, is known as _____.

**2** No sooner had the Nobel peace laureate finished his speech before congress than they gave him a standing _____.

**3** Social reform movements historically sought to enact changes that would _____ the hardships experienced by marginalized communities.

**4** In philosophical discourse, a contradiction between two seemingly valid principles is referred to as _____.

**5** Her inherently _____ disposition made her a natural leader, as she was easily adaptable and cooperative in challenging situations.

**6** The dispute became so _____ that we were afraid the adversaries would come to blows.

**7** Her tendency to overreact to minor symptoms and frequent health-related concerns led others to label her as a(n) _____.

**8** The president's ability to _____ decisions made by lower-ranking officials showcased the extent of executive authority.

**9** It takes so long for plastic to _____ that scientists say it could take thousands of years for a plastic bag to break down.

**10** The invention of the telephone was a great _____ in improving communications.

**[3] Choose the one which is different from the others.**

**11**  ① firm          ② staunch       ③ wistful        ④ steadfast

**12**  ① unassuming     ② erroneous      ③ incorrect      ④ spurious

**13**  ① marsh          ② swamp          ③ bog            ④ dune

**14**  ① state-of-the-art ② senile       ③ up-to-date     ④ modern

**15**  ① apathetic      ② sincere        ③ affectionate   ④ cordial

**16**  ① intimidate     ② frighten       ③ embolden       ④ scare

**17**  ① forthright     ② furtive        ③ frank          ④ outspoken

**18**  ① adherent       ② disciple       ③ guru           ④ pupil

**19**  ① condense       ② distend        ③ expand         ④ dilate

**20**  ① restive        ② obedient       ③ impatient      ④ restless

## ✔Answers

1 ⑯ ┃ 특히 시민 참여와 대표의 기본적인 측면으로서의 투표할 권리를 나타내기 위해 사용되는 용어는 참정권으로 알려져 있다.

2 ② ┃ 노벨 평화상 수상자가 의회에서 연설을 마치자마자 의원들이 수상자에게 기립박수를 보냈다.

3 ⑩ ┃ 사회 개혁 운동은 역사적으로 소외된 공동체가 겪는 어려움을 개선할 변화를 수행하고자 노력했다.

4 ① ┃ 철학적 담론에서는 겉으로 보기에 타당해 보이는 두 원칙 사이의 모순을 이율배반이라고 한다.

5 ⑤ ┃ 타고난 유순한 성격 덕분에 그녀는 어려운 상황에서도 쉽게 적응하고 협력할 수 있었기 때문에 타고난 지도자가 되었다.

6 ⑲ ┃ 논쟁이 너무나 신랄해져서 우리는 상대가 주먹다짐할까 봐 두려웠다.

7 ⑰ ┃ 가벼운 증상과 잦은 건강 관련 문제에 과민 반응하는 그녀의 성향으로 인해 다른 사람들은 그녀를 건강에 지나치게 신경 쓰는 사람이라고 한다.

8 ⑮ ┃ 하급 관리들의 결정을 뒤엎어버릴 수 있는 대통령의 능력이 행정권의 정도를 보여주었다.

9 ⑥ ┃ 플라스틱이 썩는 데 너무나 오랜 시간이 걸려서 과학자들은 비닐봉지가 분해되는 데 수천 년이 걸릴 수 있다고 말한다.

10 ⑫ ┃ 전화의 발명은 통신기술의 발달에 있어서 중요한 촉매 역할을 했다.

- - - - - - - - - - - - - - - - - - - - - - - - - - - - - - - - - - - - - - - - - - - - - - - - -

**11** ③  **12** ①  **13** ④  **14** ②  **15** ①  **16** ③  **17** ②  **18** ③  **19** ①  **20** ②

**[1] Write the meaning of the following words.**

| | |
|---|---|
| ☐ revere | ☐ tepid |
| ☐ clandestine | ☐ rascal |
| ☐ signature | ☐ pro-life |
| ☐ provoke | ☐ incidence |
| ☐ arena | ☐ mobilize |
| ☐ industrious | ☐ extraordinary |
| ☐ dissident | ☐ detect |
| ☐ preside | ☐ gastronomy |
| ☐ hospitable | ☐ burgeon |
| ☐ trumpet | ☐ implication |
| ☐ cubicle | ☐ opinionated |
| ☐ appliance | ☐ dreg |
| ☐ paternal | ☐ conceal |
| ☐ delineate | ☐ nostalgia |
| ☐ sufficient | ☐ unveil |
| ☐ whistle-blower | ☐ antagonistic |
| ☐ flexible | ☐ fratricide |
| ☐ escalate | ☐ stingy |
| ☐ intricate | ☐ brainstorm |
| ☐ leeway | ☐ absolve |
| ☐ vie | ☐ pedestrian |
| ☐ staggering | ☐ squash |
| ☐ prejudice | ☐ eunuch |
| ☐ conciliatory | ☐ maunder |
| ☐ fallout | ☐ quintessence |

[2] Select <u>the most</u> appropriate word from the box below. Each word should be used only once.

| | | | |
|---|---|---|---|
| ① clandestine | ② conciliatory | ③ eunuch | ④ revered |
| ⑤ paternal | ⑥ provoked | ⑦ delineate | ⑧ presided |
| ⑨ tepid | ⑩ nostalgia | ⑪ mobilize | ⑫ intricate |
| ⑬ detect | ⑭ dissident | ⑮ prejudice | ⑯ vie |
| ⑰ stingy | ⑱ escalate | ⑲ pedestrian | ⑳ leeway |

**1**    Though Socrates was _____ by his students who found truth in his teachings, his philosophy became a threat to the existent government.

**2**    Rather than following the dictates of Socialist Realism, the style officially endorsed by the Soviet government, Komar and Melamid chose a(n) _____ role. After much difficulty, they immigrated to the United States in 1978.

**3**    Authors often use vivid language to _____ the setting, allowing readers to visualize the details of the story.

**4**    The CIA's decision to conduct a(n) _____ operation for infiltrating terrorist organizations underscores the necessity for covert tactics in national security measures.

**5**    The flexible schedule provided by the online course allowed students the _____ to complete assignments at their own pace.

**6**    Harry Reid has recently assumed a(n) _____ attitude that is not commended by his coworkers who continue to disparage compromises.

**7**    Despite the chef's reputation for exquisite cuisine, the restaurant received only _____ reviews from the food critics.

**8**    Her visit to the childhood neighborhood filled her with a sense of _____, reminiscing about the days gone by.

**9**    The jury's decision seemed to be based more on _____ than on a fair evaluation of the facts presented during the trial.

**10**    He didn't want them to think he was _____, but he really did hate spending money.

[3] Choose the one which is different from the others.

11  ① industrious      ② diligent        ③ hardworking      ④ militant

12  ① friendly         ② palatial        ③ hospitable       ④ welcoming

13  ① astonishing      ② staggering      ③ convincing       ④ stunning

14  ① prodigy          ② rascal          ③ knave            ④ rogue

15  ① opinionated      ② sagacious       ③ adamant          ④ stubborn

16  ① exonerate        ② absolve         ③ censure          ④ acquit

17  ① mumble           ② mutter          ③ maunder          ④ mourn

18  ① shrivel          ② burgeon         ③ bud              ④ sprout

19  ① unveil           ② disclose        ③ secrete          ④ divulge

20  ① quintessence     ② epitome         ③ core             ④ bigotry

## ✔ Answers

**1** ④ ┃ 소크라테스(Socrates)는 그의 가르침 속에서 진리를 발견했던 그의 제자들로부터는 존경을 받았지만, 그의 철학은 당시의 정부에게는 위협이 되었다.

**2** ⑭ ┃ 소련 정부가 공식적으로 승인한 양식인 사회주의 리얼리즘의 요구를 따르기보다 코마(Komar)와 멜라미드(Melamid)는 체제에 반대하는 역할을 선택했다. 많은 어려움을 겪은 후에, 그들은 1978년 미국으로 이주했다.

**3** ⑦ ┃ 작가들은 종종 생생한 언어를 사용하여 배경을 묘사함으로써 독자들이 이야기의 세부 사항을 마음속에 그려볼 수 있게 한다.

**4** ① ┃ CIA가 테러조직에 침투하기 위해 비밀 작전을 수행하기로 한 결정은 국가안보 조치에 있어 비밀 전술의 필요성을 강조한다.

**5** ⑳ ┃ 온라인 강의가 제공하는 유연한 일정 덕분에 학생들은 자신의 페이스대로 과제를 마칠 수 있는 여유를 얻을 수 있게 되었다.

**6** ② ┃ 해리 레이드(Harry Reid)는 최근 타협적인 태도를 취해왔는데 그의 그런 태도는 협상을 계속해서 비난하는 동료들로부터 칭찬받지 못한다.

**7** ⑨ ┃ 셰프의 훌륭한 요리에 대한 명성에도 불구하고, 그 레스토랑은 음식 평론가들로부터 미온적인 평가만을 받았다.

**8** ⑩ ┃ 어린 시절 살던 동네를 방문한 그녀는 지나간 날들을 추억하며 향수를 느꼈다.

**9** ⑮ ┃ 배심원단의 결정은 재판 중에 제시된 사실에 대한 공정한 평가보다는 편견에 더 근거한 것처럼 보였다.

**10** ⑰ ┃ 그는 그들이 그를 인색하다고 생각하는 것은 원하지 않았지만, 정말 돈을 쓰기 싫어했다.

........................................................................................

**11** ④    **12** ②    **13** ③    **14** ①    **15** ②    **16** ③    **17** ④    **18** ①    **19** ③    **20** ④

## ☑ DAILY CHECKUP

[1] Write the meaning of the following words.

| | |
|---|---|
| ☐ detrimental | ☐ curiosity |
| ☐ loiter | ☐ stoic |
| ☐ intractable | ☐ publication |
| ☐ propagate | ☐ creep |
| ☐ amphitheater | ☐ mess |
| ☐ contribute | ☐ orchestrate |
| ☐ sundry | ☐ renegade |
| ☐ apathy | ☐ capricious |
| ☐ composite | ☐ shriek |
| ☐ sylvan | ☐ hybrid |
| ☐ perspiration | ☐ nutty |
| ☐ requite | ☐ wither |
| ☐ skinny | ☐ grievance |
| ☐ anticipate | ☐ foster |
| ☐ esoteric | ☐ barrage |
| ☐ spin-off | ☐ presumptuous |
| ☐ irritate | ☐ deserve |
| ☐ digit | ☐ otiose |
| ☐ blink | ☐ archipelago |
| ☐ knack | ☐ execute |
| ☐ motivate | ☐ mulish |
| ☐ translucent | ☐ therapy |
| ☐ recycle | ☐ deploy |
| ☐ verbatim | ☐ parcel |
| ☐ assent | ☐ felicitous |

[2] Select <u>the most</u> appropriate word from the box below. Each word should be used only once.

| | | | |
|---|---|---|---|
| ① sylvan | ② intractable | ③ translucent | ④ verbatim |
| ⑤ renegade | ⑥ execute | ⑦ orchestrate | ⑧ propagate |
| ⑨ esoteric | ⑩ felicitous | ⑪ capricious | ⑫ anticipate |
| ⑬ creep | ⑭ presumptuous | ⑮ spin-off | ⑯ wither |
| ⑰ hybrid | ⑱ curiosity | ⑲ irritate | ⑳ deserve |

**1** The disease posed a(n) _____ challenge for the medical team as it proved highly resistant to treatment.

**2** We have many magnificent monologues spoken by Jesus in this Gospel. These monologues are so deep, so powerful, and so _____ that they cannot be comprehended by conventional thinking.

**3** Many coaches and players complained that the officiating was so _____ that it was impossible to tell what was a foul and what wasn't.

**4** Offering unsolicited advice without being asked can sometimes be perceived as _____ as it assumes authority without invitation.

**5** Her _____ choice of words during the presentation captivated the audience, making the message clear and engaging.

**6** To successfully bring a plan to fruition, it's crucial to efficiently plan and _____ every step with precision.

**7** The lack of rainfall caused the once lush garden to _____, showing signs of losing its vitality.

**8** The internet has enabled information to _____ rapidly, allowing ideas and news to spread across the globe within seconds.

**9** The Beijing views Taiwan as a(n) "_____ province," since Chinese nationalists fled there and established a government after losing the civil war in 1949.

**10** The continuous noise from construction nearby can _____ many residents.

[3] Choose the one which is different from the others.

**11**  ① exclusive      ② sundry      ③ assorted      ④ miscellaneous

**12**  ① knack      ② elation      ③ ability      ④ flair

**13**  ① gripe      ② grievance      ③ humility      ④ complaint

**14**  ① otiose      ② futile      ③ fruitless      ④ remediable

**15**  ① mature      ② obstinate      ③ stubborn      ④ mulish

**16**  ① abstinent      ② hedonistic      ③ stoic      ④ ascetic

**17**  ① damaging      ② pernicious      ③ detrimental      ④ derelict

**18**  ① aloofness      ② nonchalance      ③ anomaly      ④ apathy

**19**  ① assent      ② abase      ③ concur      ④ consent

**20**  ① evaluate      ② foster      ③ encourage      ④ promote

## ✓ Answers

**1** ② ┃ 이 질병은 치료에 대한 내성이 매우 높은 것으로 증명되었기 때문에 의료진에게 다루기 힘든 도전이 되었다.

**2** ⑨ ┃ 이 복음서에는 예수가 말한 많은 장엄한 독백이 들어있다. 이 독백들은 너무나 깊이 있고 너무나 영향력이 크고 너무나 난해해서 통상적인 사고로는 이해할 수 없다.

**3** ⑪ ┃ 많은 코치들과 선수들은 심판이 너무 변덕스러워서 어떤 것이 반칙이고 어떤 것이 아닌지 구분하기 불가능했다고 불평했다.

**4** ⑭ ┃ 부탁하지도 않았는데 청하지도 않은 충고를 하는 것은 권하지도 않은 권위를 취하는 것이므로 주제넘은 것으로 인식될 수 있다.

**5** ⑩ ┃ 발표 중 그녀의 적절한 단어 선택은 청중을 사로잡았고 메시지를 명확하고 매력적으로 만들었다.

**6** ⑥ ┃ 계획을 성공적으로 결실을 맺기 위해서는 능률적으로 계획하고 모든 단계를 정확하게 실행하는 것이 중요하다.

**7** ⑯ ┃ 강우량이 부족해 한때 무성했던 정원이 시들게 되었고 생명력을 잃을 조짐을 보였다.

**8** ⑧ ┃ 인터넷을 통해 정보가 빠르게 전파될 수 있게 되었고, 아이디어와 뉴스가 단 몇 초 만에 전 세계로 퍼지게 되었다.

**9** ⑤ ┃ 중국 민족주의자들이 1949년 내전에서 패한 뒤 대만으로 도망쳐 정부를 수립했기 때문에, 중국 정부는 대만을 '변절한 지방'으로 간주한다.

**10** ⑲ ┃ 인근의 건설공사에서 계속되는 소음은 많은 주민들을 짜증 나게 할 수 있다.

- - - - - - - - - - - - - - - - - - - - - - - - - - - - - - - - - - - - - - - - - - - - - - - - - - - - - - - - -

**11** ①    **12** ②    **13** ③    **14** ④    **15** ①    **16** ②    **17** ④    **18** ③    **19** ②    **20** ①

☑ **DAILY CHECKUP**

[1] Write the meaning of the following words.

| | |
|---|---|
| ☐ glance | ☐ etymology |
| ☐ abrogate | ☐ trial |
| ☐ ineluctable | ☐ honorarium |
| ☐ streamline | ☐ premature |
| ☐ degree | ☐ vilify |
| ☐ chant | ☐ remote |
| ☐ splendid | ☐ oxymoron |
| ☐ primate | ☐ massive |
| ☐ frugal | ☐ tout |
| ☐ property | ☐ notable |
| ☐ egocentric | ☐ diabetes |
| ☐ scrape | ☐ confer |
| ☐ accomplice | ☐ memorandum |
| ☐ mortify | ☐ intense |
| ☐ burglar | ☐ unnerve |
| ☐ disseminate | ☐ origin |
| ☐ stigma | ☐ cater |
| ☐ recoil | ☐ pupil |
| ☐ aesthetic | ☐ figurative |
| ☐ constitution | ☐ retain |
| ☐ lunatic | ☐ cosmopolitan |
| ☐ probe | ☐ bellwether |
| ☐ impetus | ☐ supervise |
| ☐ whiz | ☐ dour |
| ☐ arrange | ☐ exclaim |

[2] Select <u>the most</u> appropriate word from the box below. Each word should be used only once.

| | | | |
|---|---|---|---|
| ① abrogated | ② egocentric | ③ recoil | ④ burglar |
| ⑤ pupil | ⑥ streamline | ⑦ exclaim | ⑧ oxymoron |
| ⑨ unnerved | ⑩ supervised | ⑪ frugal | ⑫ etymology |
| ⑬ premature | ⑭ lunatic | ⑮ stigma | ⑯ accomplice |
| ⑰ disseminate | ⑱ remote | ⑲ touted | ⑳ honorarium |

**1**   The peace treaty between the two sovereign states has been _____, formally ending the mutual agreement to stop hostilities.

**2**   Developing drugs can be hit or miss, but now a tiny, DNA-based sensor may help _____ the task.

**3**   Business travel has rebounded from the Great Recession, but lots of travelers remain _____ when spending company money on the road.

**4**   Abbas is extremely unpopular among Palestinians, many of whom view the Palestinian Authority as a(n) _____ to the Israeli occupation because it coordinates with Israel on security matters.

**5**   The purpose of the campaign was to _____ crucial information to communities, ensuring it reached as many people as possible.

**6**   The distinguished speaker was offered a generous _____ for delivering the keynote address at the conference.

**7**   The spectre of defaults and the speed and scale of the price plunge have _____ financial markets.

**8**   The manager _____ the project closely and ensured that all tasks were completed on schedule.

**9**   Clean fuel is actually a(n) _____ because no one can burn fuel cleanly enough.

**10**   Someone who acts in a way that's totally erratic could be seen as a bit of a(n) _____.

[3] Choose the one which is different from the others.

**11**　① ineluctable　② inevitable　③ inescapable　④ inextirpable

**12**　① magnificent　② splendid　③ shoddy　④ gorgeous

**13**　① surrender　② mortify　③ embarrass　④ humiliate

**14**　① stimulus　② hindrance　③ impetus　④ momentum

**15**　① vilify　② vacillate　③ defame　④ revile

**16**　① vulnerable　② noteworthy　③ conspicuous　④ notable

**17**　① bleak　② dour　③ succulent　④ morose

**18**　① figurative　② straightforward　③ allegorical　④ metaphorical

**19**　① leader　② vanguard　③ bellwether　④ vagabond

**20**　① intense　② acute　③ astute　④ fierce

## ✓Answers

**1** ①　┃ 두 주권 국가 간의 평화 조약이 파기되어, 적대 행위를 중단하기로 한 상호 협정이 공식적으로 종료되었다.

**2** ⑥　┃ 약물 개발은 주먹구구식으로 이루어질 수 있지만, 이제 작은 DNA기반 센서가 작업을 간소화시키는 데 도움이 될 수 있을지도 모른다.

**3** ⑪　┃ 출장 여행이 대침체에서 회복되었지만, 많은 여행자들은 회사의 경비를 여행에 쓸 때 여전히 절약한다.

**4** ⑯　┃ 압바스(Abbas) 수반은 팔레스타인 주민들 사이에서 굉장히 인기가 없으며, 그들 중 다수는 팔레스타인 당국이 안보 문제에 관해 이스라엘과 협력하기 때문에 당국을 이스라엘 점령의 공범자로 생각한다.

**5** ⑰　┃ 그 캠페인의 목적은 중요한 정보를 지역사회에 전파하여 가능한 한 많은 사람들에게 전달되도록 하는 것이었다.

**6** ⑳　┃ 그 저명한 연사는 학회에서 기조연설을 한 것에 대해 넉넉한 사례금을 받았다.

**7** ⑨　┃ 채무 불이행의 불안과 가격 폭락의 속도와 규모가 금융시장을 무기력하게 하였다.

**8** ⑩　┃ 그 관리자는 모든 작업이 예정대로 완료되도록 프로젝트를 면밀히 감독했다.

**9** ⑧　┃ 사실 연료를 완전히 깨끗하게 태울 수는 없으므로 청정연료라는 것은 모순적인 말이다.

**10** ⑭　┃ 완전히 엉뚱한 방식으로 행동하는 사람은 약간 미친 사람으로 보일 수 있다.

- - - - - - - - - - - - - - - - - - - - - - - - - - - - - - - - - - - - - - - - - - - - - - - - - - - - - - - - - -

**11** ④　**12** ③　**13** ①　**14** ②　**15** ②　**16** ①　**17** ③　**18** ②　**19** ④　**20** ③

[1] Write the meaning of the following words.

| | |
|---|---|
| ☐ specific | ☐ fledgling |
| ☐ deduct | ☐ ventriloquism |
| ☐ gullible | ☐ admonish |
| ☐ indemnify | ☐ subsistence |
| ☐ pregnant | ☐ bootless |
| ☐ fraction | ☐ clout |
| ☐ enormous | ☐ extravagant |
| ☐ asperity | ☐ goblin |
| ☐ personalize | ☐ reveal |
| ☐ despicable | ☐ euthanasia |
| ☐ prodigy | ☐ superior |
| ☐ trample | ☐ tatter |
| ☐ antique | ☐ augury |
| ☐ morbid | ☐ wholesome |
| ☐ collate | ☐ idiosyncrasy |
| ☐ insatiable | ☐ noxious |
| ☐ duplicate | ☐ consult |
| ☐ rip-off | ☐ partition |
| ☐ harsh | ☐ onomatopoeia |
| ☐ abeyance | ☐ balk |
| ☐ ostracize | ☐ rote |
| ☐ discourse | ☐ casualty |
| ☐ sip | ☐ picturesque |
| ☐ melancholy | ☐ strategy |
| ☐ jurisdiction | ☐ lacerate |

[2] Select <u>the most</u> appropriate word from the box below. Each word should be used only once.

| | | | |
|---|---|---|---|
| ① indemnify | ② deducted | ③ collate | ④ melancholy |
| ⑤ lacerate | ⑥ gullible | ⑦ ventriloquism | ⑧ euthanasia |
| ⑨ morbid | ⑩ onomatopoeia | ⑪ prodigy | ⑫ rote |
| ⑬ reveal | ⑭ extravagant | ⑮ tatter | ⑯ ostracized |
| ⑰ fledgling | ⑱ duplicate | ⑲ balk | ⑳ noxious |

1    His tendency to believe even the most implausible stories made him appear rather _____ among his peers.

2    The insurance company is not required to _____ for an accident caused by the negligence of the insured.

3    His remarkable ability to master complex concepts at such a young age hinted at his potential to become a true _____ in the field of music.

4    Her fascination with dark and macabre subjects led others to perceive her interests as somewhat _____.

5    His constant tendency to contradict others and challenge established ideas caused him to be _____ by his classmates, leading to a sense of alienation.

6    The country wants to boost its own _____ auto industry, feeble though it is, so it is trying harder to make car exports.

7    The release of _____ fumes into the air has caused serious air pollution.

8    The sharp thorns on the rose bush were poised to _____ anyone who dared to reach for the flowers without caution.

9    A majority of Canadians would support a law legalizing physician-assisted _____ for persons suffering from terminally ill.

10   The billionaire's penchant for hosting elaborate parties with rare delicacies and excessive decorations reflected his _____ taste for luxury.

[3] Choose the one which is different from the others.

11  ① affinity        ② asperity        ③ acerbity        ④ acrimony

12  ① petulant       ② insatiable       ③ unquenchable    ④ voracious

13  ① cessation      ② suspension      ③ aberration      ④ abeyance

14  ① vain           ② futile          ③ bootless        ④ interminable

15  ① clout          ② tension         ③ influence       ④ leverage

16  ① healthy        ② salubrious      ③ wholesome       ④ licentious

17  ① augury         ② attrition       ③ harbinger       ④ omen

18  ① unanimity      ② idiosyncrasy    ③ peculiarity     ④ quirk

19  ① trample        ② crush           ③ squash          ④ observe

20  ① abominable     ② mean            ③ virtuous        ④ despicable

## ✓Answers

1  ⑥  | 가장 믿기 어려운 이야기조차 믿는 그의 경향은 동료들 사이에서 그를 다소 속이기 쉬운 것처럼 보이게 했다.

2  ①  | 보험사는 피보험자의 부주의로 발생한 사고에 대해 보상할 의무가 없다.

3  ⑪  | 어린 나이에 복잡한 개념을 완전히 익힐 수 있는 그의 놀라운 능력은 음악 분야에서 진정한 천재가 될 그의 잠재력을 암시했다.

4  ⑨  | 어둡고 무시무시한 주제에 대한 그녀의 강한 흥미는 다른 사람들이 그녀의 관심사를 다소 병적인 것으로 인식하게 했다.

5  ⑯  | 다른 사람들의 말에 반박하고 기성관념에 도전하는 그의 한결같은 경향은 그를 학우들로부터 배척당하게 하여 소외감을 느끼게 했다.

6  ⑰  | 자동차 산업이 미약하지만 그 나라는 초기 단계에 있는 자국의 자동차 산업을 신장시키길 원한다. 그래서 이 나라는 자동차 수출을 위해 더 열심히 노력하고 있다.

7  ⑳  | 유해한 연기가 공기 중으로 방출되면서 심각한 대기 오염이 발생했다.

8  ⑤  | 장미 덤불에 있는 날카로운 가시는 조심하지 않고 꽃을 향해 손을 뻗는 사람은 누구나 찔리게 할 수 있었다.

9  ⑧  | 대부분의 캐나다 사람들은 불치병을 앓고 있는 사람에 대해 의사의 도움을 받는 안락사를 합법화하는 법을 지지한다.

10 ⑭  | 산해진미와 화려한 장식으로 정성을 들인 파티를 주최하기를 좋아하는 억만장자의 성향은 사치에 대한 그의 호화로운 취향을 반영했다.

11 ①    12 ①    13 ③    14 ④    15 ②    16 ④    17 ②    18 ①    19 ④    20 ③

# ACTUAL TEST

[01-100] Choose the one that is closest in meaning to the underlined part.

**01** In his rage, he flung <u>virtually</u> everything within reach at the wall.
① practically　② prosaically
③ sporadically　④ specifically

**02** Even a decade ago, "mainstream" Republicans, even if they <u>staunchly</u> opposed abortion, avoided claiming that women and doctors conspired to commit infanticide.
① tactfully　② arbitrarily
③ steadfastly　④ cogently

**03** Cobalt in <u>infinitesimal</u> amounts is one of the metals essential to life.
① minute　② prescribed
③ limited　④ restricted

**04** The trade agreement between the two countries will <u>expire</u> in three years.
① cease　② negotiate
③ amend　④ adopt

**05** The movement for women's <u>suffrage</u> was a social, economic and political reform movement, aimed at extending the suffrage to women.
① voting right
② freedom
③ monogamy
④ divorce right

**06** Bears are not choosy. They <u>gorge on</u> insects, berries, nuts, small mammals, ham sandwiches, and garbage with equal relish.
① chase to catch
② fill themselves with
③ get along well with
④ hate to eat

**07** <u>Brilliantly</u> colored flowers attract insects.
① Delicately　② Harmoniously
③ Sensibly　④ Brightly

**08** The local government is trying to <u>ameliorate</u> the difficult conditions caused by the ongoing drought.
① improve　② provoke
③ remove　④ spread

**09** The neural connections that are most heavily used are <u>reinforced</u>, while those that are rarely, if ever, used atrophy and disappear over time.
① encompassed　② contemplated
③ absolved　④ buttressed

**10** The newly constructed terminal 3 at Kennedy International Airport is very helpful in accommodating the <u>influx</u> of visitors.
① rush　② drop
③ income　④ inflation

11 Although <u>docile</u> around humans, German shepherds are fierce defenders of their territory.

① aggressive      ② intelligent

③ obedient      ④ stubborn

12 Anthropologists believe that in the sixteenth century a few thousand Inuits <u>inhabited</u> northern Canada.

① threatened      ② fought over

③ dominated      ④ lived in

13 I take it that you have been quite <u>frank</u> with me.

① false      ② patient

③ loyal      ④ honest

14 Jane's father, instead of getting angry, greeted Mark <u>cordially</u> and made him feel relieved.

① in a friendly manner

② in a hostile manner

③ in an indifferent manner

④ in a loyal manner

15 We should have made more efficient plans to capture such <u>restive</u> animals.

① remorseful      ② restless

③ reminiscent      ④ regressive

16 What <u>enchanted</u> him in this case was the nicety of procedure, which began by deceiving and by murdering.

① embarrassed      ② attracted

③ imprisoned      ④ imputed

17 There was an <u>acrimonious</u> dispute about the new labor law between the two parties.

① a bitter      ② a discouraging

③ an amicable      ④ an enlightening

18 Every time I make a suggestion at work, my boss <u>overrides</u> me.

① rejects      ② lauds

③ scolds      ④ praises

19 His birthday party was arranged to <u>coincide</u> with our trip.

① adjourn      ② synchronize

③ succeed      ④ interrupt

20 There are not many people in this society who one can <u>revere</u>.

① implicate      ② respect

③ condescend      ④ agitate

21 Today, the form of combat called "battle royal" is a staple of professional wrestling, but in the 1950s, it was relegated to back rooms and more <u>clandestine</u> functions.

① exasperating      ② surreptitious

③ hyperbolic      ④ licentious

22 Farce, a dramatic form whose principal purpose is to <u>provoke</u> laughter, does not attempt to portray life realistically.

① cause      ② appreciate

③ reward      ④ ridicule

23 Until recently there was much difficulty in finding other investments not requiring <u>industrious</u> personal attention, and not liable to be affected by political vicissitudes.

① diligent    ② occasional

③ various    ④ endless

24 Foreign leaders are expected to flock to the Czech Republic for Friday's state ceremony for the <u>dissident</u> playwright who led the nation through the bloodless 1989 Velvet Revolution that toppled Soviet-backed communism.

① opposing    ② loyal

③ fashionable    ④ notorious

25 In the absence of the chairman, the vice-chairman was called upon to <u>preside</u>.

① direct    ② goof up

③ mess up    ④ confuse

26 To achieve a just society we have to reason together about the meaning of the good life, and to create a public culture <u>hospitable</u> to the disagreements that will inevitably arise.

① amenable    ② clinical

③ antagonistic    ④ parsimonious

27 Assuming that all humankind constitutes one "race," what words could we use to <u>delineate</u> physical differences, such as lighter or darker skin tones and wider or narrower noses?

① differentiate    ② portray

③ disregard    ④ embellish

28 The prime minister and the opposition party leader let their dispute over the new bill <u>escalate</u> to ugly and destructive proportions.

① stagnate    ② resume

③ intensify    ④ dwindle

29 The <u>intricate</u> directions were difficult to understand.

① vague    ② unusual

③ routine    ④ complicated

30 In the 1880s, five railroads operating between New York and Chicago <u>vied</u> for passengers and freight traffic, and two more were under construction.

① rallied    ② waited

③ competed    ④ searched

31 From flamboyance to sublimity, from <u>staggering</u> athleticism to icy artistry, figure skating truly has it all.

① astonishing    ② masculine

③ dazzling    ④ intense

32 Stereotypes about race exist in all cultures and can sometimes lead to <u>prejudice</u>.

① unanimity    ② friction

③ bias    ④ hierarchy

33 Even his patience and <u>conciliatory</u> nature could not hold the Left-Wing Group together.

① confronting    ② indistinct

③ definite    ④ peacemaking

34 The other way of using music is as background accompaniment — like a tepid bath in which you induce a drowsy reverie.
① hot
② luxurious
③ stylish
④ lukewarm

35 Korean people are now enjoying better dental health, as shown by the declining incidence of tooth decay.
① treatment
② result
③ occurrence
④ expansion

36 It is helpful to know the major locations where the pulse can be detected because monitoring the pulse is important clinically.
① perceived
② mended
③ eluded
④ suspended

37 With burgeoning market freedom come growing educational and commercial pressures.
① developing
② confining
③ weakening
④ declining

38 From what she said, the implication was that they were splitting up.
① suggestion
② supply
③ indictment
④ tone

39 The success of these films, and a few others, even prompted the New York Times to write a feature hailing the dawn of a new era of originality in big budget movies. Hollywood bigwigs opined that "originality" and "quality" were the next big thing.
① jeered
② praised
③ brooded
④ observed

40 Government concealed the fact that public medical insurances program had been a total disaster.
① grumbled
② despised
③ dissembled
④ applauded

41 She is rather antagonistic to the church members.
① opposed
② ignorant
③ charitable
④ curious

42 My father was a stingy old man who resented every penny he spent on us.
① an upright
② a discreet
③ a strict
④ a frugal

43 As part of the king's historic decision, he decided to absolve all those villains who languished in the tower.
① torture
② encourage
③ maintain
④ forgive

44 The movie received some glowing reviews from film critics, but I found it pedestrian.
① exaggerated
② officious
③ embellished
④ uninteresting

45 His biography, which was written by his close friend, was detrimental to his fame.
① harmful
② influential
③ ineffective
④ advantageous

46 Clinton could face a legal nightmare as intractable as Nixon's.
① unruly
② tragic
③ terrible
④ scandalous

47 The smell of freshly shed <u>perspiration</u> filled the small room.

① whisper      ② sweat

③ inspiration      ④ respiration

48 The infamous Hatfield-McCoy feud began in earnest when, in 1882, the Hatfield <u>requited</u> the slaying of Ellison Hatfield by executing three McCoy brothers.

① avenged      ② compensated

③ reimbursed      ④ accentuated

49 *New Yorker* short stories often include <u>esoteric</u> allusions to obscure people and events.

① querulous      ② acerbic

③ recondite      ④ inverse

50 They have failed to make themselves comfortable in the talk of people in the street; no one taught them the <u>knack</u>, of course, and they were not keen to learn.

① conversation      ② skill

③ communication      ④ reputation

51 It is hard for us to realize that the great men who led the American Revolution were considered <u>renegades</u> by supporters of the British king.

① descendants      ② apostates

③ sycophants      ④ patrons

52 That he should ask her to marry him was rather <u>presumptuous</u> on his part.

① creditable      ② foolish

③ impertinent      ④ aggressive

53 Farmers use pesticides to protect their crops, but some pesticides can kill so many living things that nature itself may <u>wither</u> and die.

① grow      ② dry up

③ condense      ④ float

54. At a time when they wanted to focus on the economy, Chinese leaders face a surprise political challenge: A possible Google pullout that could anger China's public and embolden other companies to vent <u>grievance</u>.

① remorse      ② complaint

③ misfortune      ④ condolence

55 A certain amount of parental abrasiveness may <u>foster</u> self-direction and independence in young girls, perhaps because it forces the child to assert herself in the environment.

① avert      ② incriminate

③ nurture      ④ dispatch

56 Adolescents cannot escape the constant <u>barrage</u> of ads on television and radio and in magazines and newspapers.

① exaggeration      ② blast

③ gust      ④ infiltration

57 In 1972, the United States abolished the death sentence with the U. S. Supreme Court ruling that the punishment was arbitrary and <u>capricious</u>.

① incompatible      ② invariable

③ changeable      ④ dependable

58 The president's duty is to <u>execute</u> the laws to the best of his ability.
① carry out  ② carry on
③ put on  ④ put out

59 The two senators appeared equally <u>mulish</u> in their debate; neither would yield even the smallest concession.
① malicious  ② impeccable
③ solicitous  ④ obstinate

60 Twenty years ago, many of these service members were toddlers. Some were not born. But the attacks led them to a country that few could have found on a map before they received their <u>deployment</u> orders.
① institution  ② trench
③ arrangement  ④ proposition

61 The movie can be taken as a <u>felicitous</u> satire on what today's mainstream cinema offers.
① comedic  ② clumsy
③ fallacious  ④ apt

62 The President's job is to <u>abrogate</u> any law that fosters inequality among citizens.
① resolve  ② pass
③ observe  ④ repeal

63 Some philosophers regard the traditional claim as so incontestable, and the externalist conclusion as so <u>ineluctable</u>, that they are driven to reject externalism.
① flamboyant  ② reductionistic
③ indulgent  ④ inescapable

64 In 1914, John R. Bray <u>streamlined</u> the animation process, using assembly-line techniques to turn out cartoons.
① revolutionized  ② bypassed
③ invented  ④ simplified

65 Quilts were traditionally a <u>frugal</u> way of making use of worn-out clothing.
① ingenuous  ② creative
③ predictable  ④ thrifty

66 He also dropped more dark hints about "having fun and games," which Bowen took to mean recruiting him as an <u>accomplice</u> for hunting children.
① collaborator  ② decoy
③ interrogator  ④ bait

67 It would be <u>mortifying</u> to find myself ten francs short and be obliged to borrow from my guest.
① surprising  ② humiliating
③ disturbing  ④ complacent

68 He launched a series of course books and handbooks that <u>disseminated</u> the Birmingham approach to a much wider audience.
① recanted  ② diffused
③ deteriorated  ④ intercepted

69 There is no <u>stigma</u> attached to what you are doing.
① purpose  ② disgrace
③ illness  ④ honor

**70** Much of the impetus for Environmentalism came from the German Wihelm Heinrich Riehl, who laid the foundations for European conservatism in the middle of the nineteenth century.

① esteem      ② favorite

③ stimulus      ④ destination

**71** Shall we arrange next month's meeting?

① set forth      ② set out

③ set up      ④ set to

**72** He was vilified, hounded, and forced into exile by the government agency.

① accused      ② arrested

③ chased      ④ interrogated

**73** He lives in a remote village.

① small      ② beautiful

③ strange      ④ distant

**74** In the 1920s, America's consumer culture touted youthfulness as a commercial product that one could actually purchase.

① defined      ② criticized

③ mystified      ④ trumpeted

**75** Disposal of the dead brings closure to the living and confers respect on the departed.

① taxes      ② consults

③ revokes      ④ accords

**76** 'Star Wars: The Last Jedi' director Rian Johnson has said that solely catering to fans is "a mistake."

① blaming      ② challenging

③ indulging      ④ preaching

**77** Television encourages passive, rather than active, listening. When you watch television, you are listening in a way that does not require you to retain anything.

① maintain      ② sacrifice

③ dispense with      ④ be distracted

**78** It is important for a manager to supervise the work of his staff.

① oversee      ② estimate

③ undertake      ④ aid

**79** A powerful orator, Jim is, in fact, less dour than he's made out to be.

① strong      ② faithful

③ sullen      ④ calm

**80** They capture gullible young people into debt distress very early and the companies shame them using unconventional techniques if they fail to pay.

① starving      ② stabilizing

③ naive      ④ entire

**81** It is difficult to realize the enormously important role of language in our social behavior.

① conveniently      ② immensely

③ politely      ④ slightly

**82** US Secretary of State Hillary Clinton has called Russia and China despicable for opposing UN action aimed at stopping the bloodshed in Syria.

① disparate      ② complacent

③ ingenious      ④ abominable

83 A university is a place to be stripped of your naïveté, to have heated debates, to hear your core beliefs trampled on.
① weighed          ② vindicated
③ advocated        ④ crushed

84 The modern Goth culture movement is often criticized because its followers focus on morbid subjects.
① abstruse         ② dismal
③ invariable        ④ indecent

85 This was a woman with an insatiable appetite for the visual world and the talent to capture it on film.
① suitable          ② bottomless
③ abrupt            ④ absurd

86 Since last October, 323 people have died trying to cross into the United States, often in the harsh and remote deserts of Arizona.
① cruel             ② humid
③ spacious          ④ poisonous

87 When the newspaper columnist began writing about the Bavarian town's Nazi past, many of its citizens ostracized her.
① banished          ② nurtured
③ decapitated       ④ appraised

88 While it is necessary to provide these fledgling poets with an opportunity to present their work, it is not essential that we admire everything they write.
① prestigious       ② unknown
③ experimental      ④ inexperienced

89 "Seek ye first the good things of the mind," Bacon admonishes us.
① appeals           ② transforms
③ advises           ④ rebukes

90 Mary has enormous clout in the company because her father is its president.
① investment        ② influence
③ burden            ④ ambition

91 He indulges himself in extravagant tastes and habits.
① peculiar          ② probable
③ provident         ④ profuse

92 Several years ago while sheltering from a typhoon in a sleazy motel in Cincinnati I came across a tattered beer-stained notice above a public telephone. It reads simply: "This isn't a rehearsal. This is Life. Don't miss it."
① ragged            ② dirty
③ desolate          ④ savaged

93 To stress the individuality and even uniqueness of every work of art is wholesome as a reaction against facile generalizations.
① worthy            ② pernicious
③ imposing          ④ impressive

94 Even though some genetic mutations may be useful under some circumstances, most are unconditionally noxious in all existing environment.
① deleterious       ② decrepit
③ onerous           ④ odious

**95** The doctor's interest was aroused by an idiosyncrasy in John's skull: there seemed to be a coin slot in the back of his head.

① discovery     ② phenomenon

③ image     ④ peculiarity

**96** One of the chief aims of American foreign policy in the period following World War Ⅱ was to balk Soviet attempts to export communism to the Third World.

① block     ② reverse

③ monitor     ④ emulate

**97** His remarkable recovery defied all medical augury.

① attention     ② supervision

③ assistance     ④ portent

**98** Trading on the stock market has temporarily been put in abeyance while the trade commission investigates stock-in-trade manipulation.

① charge     ② cessation

③ dissent     ④ practice

**99** The potential new method in which Japan could attack other countries is unnerving its neighboring countries.

① indulging     ② sanctioning

③ enervating     ④ discriminating

**100** There is widespread public apathy towards car accidents in this country.

① indifference     ② resentment

③ delusion     ④ consent

**[1]** Write the meaning of the following words.

| | |
|---|---|
| ☐ orthodox | ☐ regulate |
| ☐ debase | ☐ prognosis |
| ☐ paleontology | ☐ blue |
| ☐ swindle | ☐ ceremony |
| ☐ inapt | ☐ edify |
| ☐ milieu | ☐ vigilant |
| ☐ equivocal | ☐ horde |
| ☐ clog | ☐ graduate |
| ☐ artery | ☐ truism |
| ☐ seeming | ☐ flat |
| ☐ lag | ☐ bravado |
| ☐ riot | ☐ exquisite |
| ☐ conversant | ☐ culminate |
| ☐ associate | ☐ nugatory |
| ☐ fiat | ☐ precede |
| ☐ dynamic | ☐ quota |
| ☐ intercede | ☐ upbraid |
| ☐ scheme | ☐ reasonable |
| ☐ desultory | ☐ posture |
| ☐ contretemps | ☐ succumb |
| ☐ span | ☐ meretricious |
| ☐ woe | ☐ task |
| ☐ abstruse | ☐ aloof |
| ☐ dub | ☐ phase |
| ☐ monk | ☐ imbue |

[2] Select <u>the most</u> appropriate word from the box below. Each word should be used only once.

| | | | |
|---|---|---|---|
| ① prognosis | ② riot | ③ imbue | ④ culminate |
| ⑤ debase | ⑥ horde | ⑦ upbraid | ⑧ fiat |
| ⑨ milieu | ⑩ equivocal | ⑪ intercede | ⑫ desultory |
| ⑬ abstruse | ⑭ quota | ⑮ bravado | ⑯ clog |
| ⑰ succumb | ⑱ vigilant | ⑲ conversant | ⑳ swindle |

1   The scandalous revelations about the politician's misconduct threatened to _____ his once sterling reputation.

2   The famed faith healer turned out to be a fraud because he had pretended to have a disease-curing power in order to _____ people.

3   His words to the press were deliberately _____ — he didn't deny the reports but neither did he confirm them.

4   The controversial decision incited public uproar and heightened the possibility of a citywide _____.

5   Her approach to the project seemed aimless and unfocused, which resulted in a rather _____ outcome in the end.

6   The writings of the great philosopher René Descartes are _____; many readers have difficulty in following his complex, intricately woven arguments.

7   When I am travelling alone, I tell myself I should remain _____ at all times when I walk by myself in an unfamiliar street.

8   His tendency to flaunt his accomplishments and assertiveness often hinted at his reliance on a veneer of _____.

9   Rather than offering constructive feedback, the manager tended to _____ his team members for their shortcomings.

10   Despite her resilience, she eventually began to _____ to the pressures of the demanding workload.

[3] Choose the one which is different from the others.

**11** ① orthodox     ② honorary     ③ conventional     ④ established

**12** ① ostensible     ② apparent     ③ substantial     ④ seeming

**13** ① disguise     ② contretemps     ③ argument     ④ quarrel

**14** ① gloomy     ② depressed     ③ blue     ④ flamboyant

**15** ① truism     ② austerity     ③ bromide     ④ cliché

**16** ① futile     ② nugatory     ③ mundane     ④ vain

**17** ① gaudy     ② garish     ③ meretricious     ④ vainglorious

**18** ① aloof     ② auxiliary     ③ apathetic     ④ indifferent

**19** ① enlighten     ② edify     ③ evince     ④ instruct

**20** ① boon     ② woe     ③ affliction     ④ grief

## ✔ Answers

**1** ⑤ | 그 정치인의 위법 행위에 대한 불명예스러운 폭로는 한때 훌륭했던 그의 평판을 떨어뜨릴 위험이 있었다.

**2** ⑳ | 그 유명한 신앙 치료사는 사기꾼으로 밝혀졌는데, 왜냐하면 그는 사람들을 속이기 위해 병을 치료하는 능력이 있는 것처럼 행동했기 때문이다.

**3** ⑩ | 그는 언론에 계획적으로 모호하게 답변했다. 그는 보도를 부인하지도 않았지만 사실로 확증하지도 않았다.

**4** ② | 논란을 일으킨 결정은 비난 여론을 들끓게 했고 시 전역에서 폭동이 일어날 가능성을 높였다.

**5** ⑫ | 그 프로젝트에 대한 그녀의 접근법은 방향을 잃고 불분명해 보여 결국 다소 일관성이 없는 결과물을 낳았다.

**6** ⑬ | 위대한 철학자 르네 데카르트(René Descartes)의 글들은 난해하다. 그래서 많은 독자들은 그의 복잡하고 난해하게 얽힌 주장을 이해하는 데 어려움을 겪는다.

**7** ⑱ | 홀로 여행할 때, 낯선 거리를 혼자서 걷고 있으면 나는 항상 경계해야 한다고 나 자신에게 말한다.

**8** ⑮ | 자신의 공적과 자기주장을 과시하는 그의 성향은 종종 그가 허세를 부리는 겉모습에 의존하고 있음을 암시했다.

**9** ⑦ | 그 관리자는 건설적인 피드백을 주기보다는 팀원들의 단점을 비난하는 경향이 있었다.

**10** ⑰ | 그녀의 회복력에도 불구하고, 그녀는 결국 과중한 업무량의 압박에 굴복하기 시작했다.

- - - - - - - - - - - - - - - - - - - - - - - - - - - - - - - - - - - - - - - - - - - - - - - - - - - - -

**11** ②    **12** ③    **13** ①    **14** ④    **15** ②    **16** ③    **17** ④    **18** ②    **19** ③    **20** ①

[1] Write the meaning of the following words.

| | |
|---|---|
| ☐ benign | ☐ celestial |
| ☐ mollify | ☐ insult |
| ☐ pauper | ☐ sophomoric |
| ☐ criminal | ☐ fetch |
| ☐ puberty | ☐ trivial |
| ☐ sustain | ☐ bust |
| ☐ regent | ☐ applause |
| ☐ shackle | ☐ lubricate |
| ☐ intrepid | ☐ dauntless |
| ☐ demur | ☐ epistle |
| ☐ acid | ☐ offensive |
| ☐ enumerate | ☐ moan |
| ☐ prize | ☐ counteract |
| ☐ stupendous | ☐ foolhardy |
| ☐ demotic | ☐ alter |
| ☐ heir | ☐ knave |
| ☐ normative | ☐ reproach |
| ☐ conservation | ☐ vain |
| ☐ inflame | ☐ aplomb |
| ☐ puritanical | ☐ copy |
| ☐ scrutiny | ☐ torrid |
| ☐ glut | ☐ proverb |
| ☐ energetic | ☐ dilate |
| ☐ retrograde | ☐ orbit |
| ☐ mechanic | ☐ writhe |

[2] Select <u>the most</u> appropriate word from the box below. Each word should be used only once.

| | | | |
|---|---|---|---|
| ① benign | ② enumerate | ③ celestial | ④ knave |
| ⑤ writhe | ⑥ acid | ⑦ applause | ⑧ lubricate |
| ⑨ inflame | ⑩ fetch | ⑪ retrograde | ⑫ glut |
| ⑬ normative | ⑭ aplomb | ⑮ demotic | ⑯ dilate |
| ⑰ trivial | ⑱ shackle | ⑲ sustain | ⑳ mollify |

**1** Her sincere apology was meant to _____ the anger of her friend, hoping to ease the tension in their relationship.

**2** His words, sharp and biting, had an unmistakable _____ quality that left a lasting impact on those who heard them.

**3** Rather than calming the situation, his words only served to further _____ the already tense atmosphere.

**4** The new policy, instead of advancing progress, seemed to have a(n) _____ effect on the company's growth.

**5** Although initially significant, the issue eventually revealed itself to be rather _____ in the broader context of the situation.

**6** The purpose of oiling the machinery was to _____ the gears and ensure their smooth functioning.

**7** His ability to deliver the speech with such _____ spoke volumes about his confidence.

**8** Tired-looking eyes can be a red flag for chronic allergies, which _____ blood vessels and cause them leak. This creates puffiness and a dark purple-blue hue in the sensitive skin under the eyes.

**9** The athlete's injury caused him to _____ in pain, unable to conceal the intense discomfort during the match.

**10** To Sandra's relief, the biopsy revealed that the tumor on her skin was _____.

[3] Choose the one which is different from the others.

**11**  ① pernicious    ② intrepid    ③ brave    ④ dauntless

**12**  ① demur    ② dissent    ③ gainsay    ④ endorse

**13**  ① enormous    ② congenial    ③ stupendous    ④ colossal

**14**  ① puritanical    ② abstinent    ③ prodigal    ④ austere

**15**  ① abusive    ② tantalizing    ③ offensive    ④ insulting

**16**  ① rash    ② reckless    ③ foolhardy    ④ prudent

**17**  ① relinquish    ② reproach    ③ reprimand    ④ rebuke

**18**  ① proverb    ② adage    ③ lexicon    ④ aphorism

**19**  ① arid    ② broiling    ③ torrid    ④ pristine

**20**  ① futile    ② modest    ③ vain    ④ useless

## ✓ Answers

**1** ⑳  | 그녀의 진심 어린 사과는 친구의 화를 누그러뜨리고 그들의 관계의 긴장을 완화하기 위한 것이었다.

**2** ⑥  | 날카롭고 신랄한 그의 말은 그 말을 듣는 사람들에게 오래 지속되는 영향을 미치는 틀림없이 신랄한 특징을 가지고 있었다.

**3** ⑨  | 그의 말은 상황을 진정시키기는커녕 이미 긴장된 분위기를 더욱 악화시킬 뿐이었다.

**4** ⑪  | 새로운 정책은 발전을 이루는 대신 회사의 성장을 후퇴시키는 영향을 미치는 것처럼 보였다.

**5** ⑰  | 그 문제는 처음에는 중요했지만, 그 상황의 더 넓은 맥락에서 볼 때 결국 다소 사소한 것으로 드러났다.

**6** ⑧  | 기계에 기름을 바르는 목적은 기어에 윤활유를 발라 마찰을 줄이고 기어가 원활하게 작동하도록 하는 것이었다.

**7** ⑭  | 그처럼 침착하게 연설하는 그의 능력은 그의 자신감에 대해 많은 것을 말해줬다.

**8** ⑯  | 피곤해 보이는 눈은 만성 알레르기에 대한 위험신호일 수 있는데, 만성 알레르기는 혈관을 팽창시켜 혈관이 새게 만들며, 이것이 눈 밑의 민감한 피부를 부어오르게 하고 짙은 자주색을 띠게 한다.

**9** ⑤  | 부상으로 경기 중 극심한 불편함을 감출 수 없던 그 선수는 고통에 몸부림쳤다.

**10** ①  | 산드라(Sandra)에게는 안심이 되게도, 생체 조직 검사를 통해 피부에 난 종양이 양성이라고 밝혀졌다.

- - - - - - - - - - - - - - - - - - - - - - - - - - - - - - - - - - - - - - - - - - - - - - - - - -

**11** ①    **12** ④    **13** ②    **14** ③    **15** ②    **16** ④    **17** ①    **18** ③    **19** ④    **20** ②

[1] Write the meaning of the following words.

| | |
|---|---|
| ☐ flourish | ☐ quisling |
| ☐ hoarse | ☐ extant |
| ☐ priority | ☐ bait |
| ☐ subliminal | ☐ respiration |
| ☐ contemplate | ☐ displace |
| ☐ inviolable | ☐ voluptuous |
| ☐ slaughter | ☐ tuition |
| ☐ attire | ☐ eviscerate |
| ☐ explode | ☐ promising |
| ☐ affectation | ☐ cloister |
| ☐ catholic | ☐ up-to-date |
| ☐ bygone | ☐ stroke |
| ☐ dike | ☐ footage |
| ☐ propitious | ☐ mortal |
| ☐ interim | ☐ gasp |
| ☐ revolve | ☐ fabulous |
| ☐ stronghold | ☐ windfall |
| ☐ culpable | ☐ implant |
| ☐ minion | ☐ alluvial |
| ☐ policy | ☐ cliché |
| ☐ deify | ☐ transgress |
| ☐ lax | ☐ session |
| ☐ gourmet | ☐ drab |
| ☐ accompany | ☐ pagan |
| ☐ checkered | ☐ outline |

[2] Select <u>the most</u> appropriate word from the box below. Each word should be used only once.

| | | | |
|---|---|---|---|
| ① eviscerate | ② hoarse | ③ cloister | ④ voluptuous |
| ⑤ gasp | ⑥ transgress | ⑦ catholic | ⑧ promising |
| ⑨ propitious | ⑩ stroke | ⑪ quisling | ⑫ mortal |
| ⑬ stronghold | ⑭ culpable | ⑮ windfall | ⑯ bygone |
| ⑰ deify | ⑱ priority | ⑲ contemplate | ⑳ pagan |

1    Her taste in literature was rather _____ as she enjoyed a wide range of genres and authors.


2    After cheering at the concert all night, her voice was so _____ that she could barely speak the next day.


3    Some people believe that the appearance of a black cat is a(n) _____ sign; others believe that black cats are ominous.


4    Despite his efforts to deflect blame, the evidence made him appear _____ in the company's financial discrepancies.


5    Throughout various periods in history, rulers were so esteemed that people would _____ them and treat them with an almost divine reverence and honor.


6    His analysis of the scientific theory aimed to _____ any inconsistencies, leaving no room for doubt.


7    In Greek mythology, even the mightiest warriors were subject to the _____ vulnerabilities of human life.


8    The unexpected inheritance from a distant relative was a sudden _____ that significantly improved the family's financial situation.


9    The teacher's firmness made it clear that any attempt to _____ the classroom rules would not be tolerated.


10   The ancient civilization practiced _____ rituals as part of their religious traditions, worshipping nature and various deities.

[3] Choose the one which is different from the others.

11  ① apparel        ② vanity         ③ attire          ④ costume
12  ① pretense       ② affectation    ③ alacrity        ④ simulation
13  ① tentative      ② provisional    ③ interim         ④ permanent
14  ① attentive      ② lax            ③ lenient         ④ slack
15  ① bait           ② fodder         ③ decoy           ④ lure
16  ① platitude      ② banality       ③ cliché          ④ crux
17  ① sacrosanct     ② inveterate     ③ inviolable      ④ divine
18  ① concealed      ② subconscious   ③ sublime         ④ subliminal
19  ① conservative   ② up-to-date     ③ modern          ④ contemporary
20  ① embed          ② insert         ③ implant         ④ incense

## ✓ Answers

1  ⑦   | 그녀는 다양한 장르와 작가를 좋아했기 때문에 문학에 대한 그녀의 취향은 다소 폭넓었다.

2  ②   | 밤새도록 콘서트에서 환호성을 지른 후, 그녀의 목소리는 너무 쉬어서 다음날 거의 말을 할 수 없었다.

3  ⑨   | 일부 사람들은 검은 고양이의 출현이 길조라고 생각하지만, 다른 사람들은 검은 고양이를 불길하다고 생각한다.

4  ⑭   | 비난을 피하려는 노력에도 불구하고, 그 증거는 그가 회사의 재무상의 불일치(오류)에 책임이 있는 것처럼 보이게 만들었다.

5  ⑰   | 역사적으로 여러 시대에 걸쳐 통치자들은 매우 존경받았기 때문에 사람들은 그들을 신격화하고 거의 신성한 존경심과 명예를 가지고 그들을 대했다.

6  ①   | 그 과학 이론에 대한 그의 분석은 모순되는 것을 제거하고 의심의 여지를 남기지 않는 것을 목표로 했다.

7  ⑫   | 그리스 신화에서는 가장 강력한 전사들조차 인간의 생명에 치명적인 취약성에 노출되어 있었다.

8  ⑮   | 먼 친척으로부터의 예상치 못한 상속은 가족의 재정 상황을 크게 개선한 뜻밖의 횡재였다.

9  ⑥   | 선생님의 단호한 의지는 교실 규칙을 위반하려는 어떤 시도도 용납되지 않을 것임을 분명히 했다.

10 ⑳   | 고대 문명은 자연과 다양한 신을 숭배하는 종교적 전통의 일부로서 이교도의 의식을 행했다.

········································································································

11 ②    12 ③    13 ④    14 ①    15 ②    16 ④    17 ②    18 ③    19 ①    20 ④

[1] Write the meaning of the following words.

| | |
|---|---|
| ☐ lucid | ☐ fortuitous |
| ☐ recollect | ☐ sprout |
| ☐ equivalent | ☐ miscarriage |
| ☐ ruse | ☐ nourish |
| ☐ suspect | ☐ wretched |
| ☐ diminutive | ☐ amount |
| ☐ particle | ☐ trepidation |
| ☐ bloodshed | ☐ mammoth |
| ☐ chary | ☐ arithmetic |
| ☐ struggle | ☐ besiege |
| ☐ cascade | ☐ jurisprudence |
| ☐ innovation | ☐ excrete |
| ☐ strenuous | ☐ fashionable |
| ☐ raucous | ☐ overturn |
| ☐ departure | ☐ cuisine |
| ☐ muster | ☐ divulge |
| ☐ starvation | ☐ irascible |
| ☐ proxy | ☐ pilfer |
| ☐ controversial | ☐ odor |
| ☐ thesaurus | ☐ grandiloquent |
| ☐ profitable | ☐ equipment |
| ☐ vegetate | ☐ spurn |
| ☐ acute | ☐ arid |
| ☐ cower | ☐ depose |
| ☐ holdout | ☐ consternation |

[2] Select <u>the most</u> appropriate word from the box below. Each word should be used only once.

| | | | |
|---|---|---|---|
| ① cascade | ② trepidation | ③ lucid | ④ mammoth |
| ⑤ arid | ⑥ excrete | ⑦ divulge | ⑧ odor |
| ⑨ jurisprudence | ⑩ equivalent | ⑪ nourish | ⑫ bloodshed |
| ⑬ strenuous | ⑭ raucous | ⑮ cower | ⑯ sprout |
| ⑰ diminutive | ⑱ profitable | ⑲ grandiloquent | ⑳ depose |

1    Even though it was only a small glass of juice, the nutrition drink claimed to include an amount of vitamins and minerals _____ to that found in a full day's worth of fruits and vegetables.

2    The ongoing conflict in the region threatened to spiral into a situation of severe _____ if immediate intervention wasn't initiated.

3    His explanation was so clear and _____ that even complex concepts became easily understandable to everyone in the audience.

4    People in smoke-affected areas are advised not to do _____ exercise outdoors and to wear masks outdoors where air pollution levels are particularly bad.

5    The lively concert turned the once serene park into a(n) _____ gathering with cheering crowds and energetic performances.

6    Entering the haunted house, she felt a sense of unease and _____ as unknown sounds echoed in the dark.

7    The officials all spoke on condition of anonymity because they were not permitted to _____ details of the investigation.

8    His tendency to use _____ language made his communication style seem more ostentatious than informative.

9    The lecturer's presentation was so dull and _____ that it made it hard for the audience to stay engaged.

10    The rebels planned to stage a coup to _____ the dictator.

[3] Choose the one which is different from the others.

**11**  ① maneuver  ② subterfuge  ③ ruse  ④ distortion

**12**  ① recollect  ② recall  ③ surmise  ④ reminisce

**13**  ① rash  ② chary  ③ circumspect  ④ discreet

**14**  ① muster  ② scatter  ③ assemble  ④ convene

**15**  ① miserable  ② dismal  ③ wretched  ④ fiery

**16**  ① accidental  ② willful  ③ fortuitous  ④ serendipitous

**17**  ① grouchy  ② irascible  ③ aristocratic  ④ irritable

**18**  ① tranquility  ② consternation  ③ bewilderment  ④ dismay

**19**  ① rebuff  ② disdain  ③ spurn  ④ embrace

**20**  ① besiege  ② precipitate  ③ beleaguer  ④ beset

## ✔Answers

1 ⑩ | 비록 작은 한 잔의 주스에 불과했지만, 그 영양음료에는 하루치의 과일과 채소에서 발견되는 것과 같은 양의 비타민과 미네랄이 포함되어 있다고 주장했다.

2 ⑫ | 이 지역에서 계속되는 분쟁은 즉각적인 개입이 개시되지 않으면 심각한 유혈사태로 치달을 위험이 있었다.

3 ③ | 그의 설명은 매우 알아듣기 쉽고 명쾌해서 복잡한 개념도 청중 모두가 쉽게 이해할 수 있었다.

4 ⑬ | 연기가 퍼진 지역의 사람들은 실외에서 격심한 운동을 하지 말고 대기 오염 수준이 특히 나쁠 경우에는 실외에서 마스크를 착용하라는 충고를 들었다.

5 ⑭ | 활기 넘치는 콘서트는 한때 조용했던 공원을 환호하는 군중과 에너지 넘치는 공연이 가득한 소란스러운 집회로 바꾸어 놓았다.

6 ② | 흉가에 들어서자 그녀는 어둠 속에서 알 수 없는 소리가 울려 퍼지면서 불안감과 두려움을 느꼈다.

7 ⑦ | 공무원들 모두 익명을 조건으로 말했는데, 그들은 그 조사에 대한 세부사항을 밝히는 것이 허용되지 않았기 때문이었다.

8 ⑲ | 과장된 언어를 사용하는 그의 성향은 그의 의사소통 방식을 유익하기보다 과시적으로 보이게 만들었다.

9 ⑤ | 강연자의 발표가 너무 지루하고 무미건조해서 청중들이 몰두하기 어렵게 했다.

10 ⑳ | 반군은 독재자를 물러나게 하기 위해 쿠데타를 일으킬 계획이었다.

11 ④    12 ③    13 ①    14 ②    15 ④    16 ②    17 ③    18 ①    19 ④    20 ②

[1] Write the meaning of the following words.

| | |
|---|---|
| ☐ unwilling | ☐ parasite |
| ☐ abyss | ☐ extraterrestrial |
| ☐ inculpate | ☐ doldrums |
| ☐ prominent | ☐ stray |
| ☐ complexion | ☐ layer |
| ☐ evaluate | ☐ bearing |
| ☐ hunch | ☐ arouse |
| ☐ devastate | ☐ vitriolic |
| ☐ protagonist | ☐ clap |
| ☐ solution | ☐ fulcrum |
| ☐ carcinogenic | ☐ intrinsic |
| ☐ mull | ☐ robe |
| ☐ ridicule | ☐ observe |
| ☐ aghast | ☐ misanthrope |
| ☐ conjecture | ☐ poisonous |
| ☐ predatory | ☐ quotient |
| ☐ sequence | ☐ drench |
| ☐ glaze | ☐ frigid |
| ☐ biennial | ☐ lull |
| ☐ sprain | ☐ acrophobia |
| ☐ folklore | ☐ chide |
| ☐ tenable | ☐ tribute |
| ☐ craze | ☐ ephemeral |
| ☐ sanitary | ☐ wrist |
| ☐ renew | ☐ digest |

[2] Select <u>the most</u> appropriate word from the box below. Each word should be used only once.

| | | | |
|---|---|---|---|
| ① complexion | ② mull | ③ quotient | ④ abyss |
| ⑤ conjecture | ⑥ evaluate | ⑦ predatory | ⑧ ephemeral |
| ⑨ sprain | ⑩ misanthrope | ⑪ craze | ⑫ sanitary |
| ⑬ parasite | ⑭ bearing | ⑮ acrophobia | ⑯ carcinogenic |
| ⑰ intrinsic | ⑱ tenable | ⑲ lull | ⑳ chide |

1  After the economic downturn, the company found itself on the edge of a(n) _____ with declining profits and uncertain prospects.

2  Before making a decision, she liked to take her time and _____ over the various options available to her.

3  Despite initial doubts, his argument proved to be _____ after considering all the evidence presented.

4  Gender-neutral clothing is back in vogue, but the _____ has mirrored broader social changes throughout the 20th century.

5  The scientist discovered a tiny organism acting as a hidden _____ that takes nutrients from its host.

6  His disdain for humanity and preference for solitude earned him the reputation of a(n) _____.

7  When legendary director Alfred Hitchcock created a film about a detective with an intense fear of heights, he named the film *Vertigo*, not _____; perhaps he thought Vertigo was catchier.

8  The beauty of the cherry blossoms is _____; it lasts only for a brief period before fading away.

9  The teacher didn't hesitate to _____ the students for their lack of preparation ahead of the exam.

10  A substance that is _____ is likely to cause cancer.

[3] Choose the one which is different from the others.

**11**　① prominent　② conspicuous　③ invisible　④ outstanding

**12**　① intuition　② hunch　③ premonition　④ mistreatment

**13**　① flatter　② ridicule　③ deride　④ scoff

**14**　① stagnation　② ennui　③ doldrums　④ recession

**15**　① vitriolic　② acerbic　③ caustic　④ placid

**16**　① unwilling　② reluctant　③ voluntary　④ hesitant

**17**　① exonerate　② inculpate　③ accuse　④ incriminate

**18**　① aghast　② docile　③ astonished　④ stunned

**19**　① swerve　② deviate　③ forestall　④ stray

**20**　① fulcrum　② prop　③ strut　④ succor

[01-100] Choose the one that is closest in meaning to the underlined part.

01 When people see that their disease cannot be cured by orthodox methods, they turn to alternative therapies.
① meticulous      ② innovative
③ conventional    ④ ingenious

02 He made many mistakes that debased the value of the member.
① altered      ② discarded
③ exalted      ④ lowered

03 The wealthy and cruel dictator was ultimately convicted of swindling his own people and made his own country bankrupt.
① defrauding    ② abolishing
③ ruining       ④ rendering

04 Our cultural milieu, including news and social media, is increasingly visually oriented.
① custom        ② property
③ environment   ④ perspective

05 Teachers who speak equivocally may cause their students to become confused.
① quickly        ② ambiguously
③ aggressively   ④ loudly

06 Weeds clog waterways, destroy wildlife habitats, and impede farming.
① drain         ② grow along
③ float on      ④ obstruct

07 He is conversant with all aspects of sculpture from modelling to casting techniques.
① well-mannered   ② argumentative
③ talkative       ④ familiar

08 A neutral nation volunteered to intercede in the interest of achieving peace.
① mediate      ② intercept
③ organize     ④ participate

09 So wrote Rowland Hill, the greatest postal performer in history, who in 1837 devised a scheme to reduce and standardize postal rates and to shift the burden of payment from the addressee to the sender.
① necessity    ② contrivance
③ document     ④ forfeit

10 Today these subjects are still discussed in a half-hearted and desultory way.
① unmethodical   ② misguided
③ disguised      ④ systematic

11 Valenti almost found himself retired because of this contretemps.
① curmudgeon    ② conundrum
③ hame          ④ argy-bargy

12 The parallel between the abstruseness of contemporary art and that of modern science is too obvious to be missed.
① purity ② vulgarity
③ abdication ④ reconditeness

13 The first massive electronic computers were soon dubbed "electronic brains."
① replaced ② named
③ preceded by ④ created as

14 When patients have access to diagnosis and treatment, the prognosis for tuberculosis sufferers is quite good, with most expected to make a full recovery.
① prospect ② symptoms
③ deterioration ④ operation

15 He unceremoniously dropped out of the presidential race, as he knew he did not stand a chance of success.
① conscientiously ② abruptly
③ deliberately ④ meticulously

16 His purpose was not to entertain but to edify.
① simulate ② divert
③ scold ④ instruct

17 Supervisors must be vigilant when it comes to safety. They must continually educate workers.
① watchful ② indolent
③ drowsy ④ imprudent

18 Some organism will succumb to the lack of oxygen and its death may easily pass unnoticed.

① stick ② yield
③ impose ④ transfer

19 Under this conductor's poised and animated direction arose a distinctive performance of the *Requiem*, with flowing tempi, exquisite dynamic shading, and absolute perfection in the orchestra.
① lackadaisical ② profuse
③ querulous ④ sublime

20 Most emergency evacuation plans state that precedence must be given to the injured.
① approval ② procession
③ relocation ④ priority

21 Military advisors were upbraided for presenting global reductions in nuclear stockpiles as progress.
① alienated ② reprimanded
③ overawed ④ scavenged

22 The Philippines' trade has been flat this year, due to low international commodities prices and local investors' reluctance to diversify into new areas of business.
① exuberant ② inactive
③ insatiable ④ extravagant

23 His father remains aloof from the day-to-day activities of his family.
① separated from
② upward of
③ bored with
④ exhausted from

24 In the United States educational system, intermediate school is the transitional phase between the primary grades and high school.
① stage
② notion
③ pattern
④ alternative

25 Sylvia has a benign personality. She is not at all unpleasant to be with.
① intense
② ordered
③ weak
④ gentle

26 The troop withdrawal will not end tensions between Russia and Georgia or entirely mollify the West.
① appease
② coerce
③ persuade
④ encourage

27 Their leader remained intrepid even in the face of great danger.
① fearless
② reckless
③ calm
④ stable

28 Solving problems effectively requires a sustained effort. You cannot give up too soon.
① fastidious
② aggressive
③ continuous
④ decent

29 After the doctor from the public health department had enumerated all the dreadful sounding diseases that were rampant in the water park, I decided I didn't want to visit it after all.
① allotted
② incarnated
③ validated
④ listed

30 To climb Mount Everest on a bicycle would be a stupendous accomplishment.
① unintelligent
② strenuous
③ monumental
④ energetic

31 She is not at all puritanical, and she aims to make sure the team has fun.
① profligate
② penurious
③ salacious
④ moralistic

32 Any pronouncement about educational technology needs to be scrutinized with great care to ascertain what part of the process is involved — the machinery, the software, or the methodology.
① utilized
② selected
③ systemized
④ examined

33 There is a glut of lawyers on the market, and many law school graduates cannot get good jobs.
① pool
② excess
③ demand
④ trade

34 Despite having lived what he considered to be a trivial life, George had actually had a tremendous impact on everyone he knew.
① frivolous
② prodigious
③ remorseful
④ insolvent

35 In spite of the scale of the famine, the relief workers struggled on with dauntless optimism.
① haughty
② ill-advised
③ intrepid
④ feeble

36 We cannot condone such <u>knavery</u> in public officials.
　① conjecture　　② frailty
　③ iniquity　　　④ complaint

37 Joe looked at me for a single instant with something faintly like <u>reproach</u>. Utterly ridiculous as his cravat was, and as his collars were, I was conscious of a sort of dignity in the look.
　① approbation　　② prohibition
　③ tolerance　　　④ reprimand

38 By contemporary accounts, the orchestra played them with increasing <u>aplomb</u>.
　① malaise　　　　② collectedness
　③ cacophony　　　④ idiosyncrasy

39 Once one had crossed the <u>torrid</u> regions, where human survival had long been assumed to be impossible, one would find lands that were as fertile and habitable as the northern hemisphere.
　① scorching　　　② benign
　③ equatorial　　　④ connecting

40 Although it's <u>proverbial</u> that you can't miss what you never had, or what never truly was, romantic notions of black people's unity and struggle in the past magnify the despair of present realities.
　① provable　　　② illuminating
　③ well-known　　④ controversial

41 The pupils of our eyes <u>dilate</u> when the level of light is low.
　① paralyze　　　② recoil
　③ focus　　　　④ expand

42 The jute, a relative of the basswood trees, <u>flourishes</u> in warm, humid climates.
　① amplifies　　　② swells
　③ thrives　　　　④ prolongs

43 An understudy performs when the lead singer's voice becomes <u>hoarse</u>.
　① fatigued　　　② rough
　③ thin　　　　　④ famous

44 The country's three <u>slaughterhouses</u> reported processing just under 100,000 donkeys in two years.
　① abattoirs　　　② gallows
　③ penitentiaries　④ arboretums

45 This is not just a local idea; it's <u>catholic</u>.
　① bounded　　　② official
　③ religious　　　④ universal

46 Other owners find the sale price they are likely to receive discouraging, and they prefer to wait for a more <u>propitious</u> time to sell.
　① voluntary　　　② auspicious
　③ conducive　　　④ perspicacious

47 The government is taking <u>interim</u> measures to help those in immediate need.
　① solid　　　　② temporary
　③ desirable　　④ unreflected

**48** The police officer was dismissed for <u>culpable</u> neglect of duty.

① chronic　　　② blameworthy

③ felicitous　　④ trustworthy

**49** The collectors were <u>lax</u> in delivering revenues to the Royal Treasury with virtually no system of accountable book-keeping.

① firm　　　　② loose

③ resilient　　④ careful

**50** The 33 year-old woman arriving in Rome from Sao Paulo in Brazil was wearing tight-fitting clothes to enhance her <u>voluptuousness</u>, hoping that her looks might distract the attention of border police.

① awkwardness

② seductiveness

③ carelessness

④ pleasance

**51** Those who <u>transgress</u> the laws of society can be punished.

① disagree with

② disperse

③ violate

④ interfere with

**52** Many songbirds in temperate zones reveal a <u>drab</u> plumage during the winter.

① variegated　　② enticing

③ colorless　　　④ distinct

**53** The address he delivered was <u>lucid</u> with many balanced statements.

① short　　　　② compact

③ clear　　　　④ enlightening

**54** He tried, but he couldn't <u>recollect</u> the story.

① repeat　　　　② understand

③ remember　　 ④ change

**55** Theorists have been <u>chary</u> of analyzing the spiritual role of music.

① apprehensive　② quiescent

③ facetious　　　④ obdurate

**56** Aging Korea will burden young workers. The government needs to make <u>strenuous</u> efforts to help individuals prolong the period of economic activity by creating jobs for senior citizens.

① arduous　　　② efficient

③ continuing　　④ controversial

**57** The work Christmas party gradually grew more <u>raucous</u>.

① erroneous　　② mellifluous

③ sanctimonious　④ boisterous

**58** The Revolutionary forces had to <u>muster up</u> enough men to oppose the British army.

① finance　　　　② convince

③ disguise　　　④ gather

**59** Unlike the unequivocal accounts provided by eyewitnesses, the evidence provided by the flight recorder was more <u>controvertible</u>, leading to the development of several different theories to explain the crash.

① lucid　　　　② ambiguous

③ infallible　　④ theoretical

**60** Gift cards are America's most popular present. They are <u>profitable</u> because retailers receive money for them up front, and around 10% of them are never redeemed.

① convenient  ② lucrative
③ productive  ④ responsible

**61** I am <u>acutely</u> aware that my beliefs have never been tested by personal experience.

① abstractly  ② reasonably
③ commonly  ④ strongly

**62** The timing of the man's investment in the mining company turned out to be <u>fortuitous</u>, resulting in an unexpectedly quick profit.

① lucky  ② rational
③ careful  ④ sensible

**63** The conditions of the refugee camps are <u>wretched</u> despite great efforts by humanitarian organizations.

① convincing  ② trivial
③ decent  ④ miserable

**64** I thought Carol would be nervous when she made her speech, but she delivered it without <u>trepidation</u>.

① dexterity  ② fortitude
③ fright  ④ avarice

**65** The fortress was <u>besieged</u> by the enemy until the inhabitants were starving.

① deserted  ② constructed
③ blockaded  ④ occupied

**66** The most medically interesting amphibians found to date are the dart-poison frogs of Central and South America, whose skins <u>excrete</u> a variety of valuable compounds.

① make up  ② set out
③ let out  ④ give in

**67** A new look at the human Y chromosome has <u>overturned</u> longstanding ideas about its evolutionary history.

① reaffirmed  ② reclaimed
③ redeemed  ④ revoked

**68** The accused would not <u>divulge</u> his connection with the crime.

① disclose  ② conceal
③ contradict  ④ recognize

**69** There is nothing clear but the allegation of an <u>irascible</u> doctor at the other end of the telephone, ringing up somebody late at night.

① inclement  ② choleric
③ desperate  ④ genial

**70** This variety of hybrid tea rose is more <u>odorous</u> than the one you have in your garden.

① mundane  ② stingy
③ oblique  ④ fragrant

**71** The senator speaks in the <u>grandiloquent</u> style of the old-fashioned orator.

① magnanimous  ② bombastic
③ prosaic  ④ discursive

72 His compatriot Swift, who shared his distaste for universal benignity, has the crazed Gulliver go step further, spurning his kinsfolk and falling in love with a breed of alien quadrupeds.

① hating      ② rejecting

③ saving      ④ leaving

73 Global warming will exacerbate the problem, especially in poor, arid areas.

① hot      ② dry

③ insipid      ④ torrent

74 It was evident that to establish order they had to depose the king.

① dethrone      ② thaw

③ melt      ④ cope

75 No need for consternation. Everything is under control.

① impatience      ② dismay

③ contest      ④ anomaly

76 The Internet probably deserves its abysmal reputation among business executives. They're barraged daily with hype about the World Wide Web and the Net's flashy multimedia strip with its glitzy movie clips and virtual shopping malls.

① awful      ② terrific

③ comforting      ④ agreeable

77 A number of prominent figures from different political parties and elements who had supported other presidential candidates who lost in the first round of the presidential election are expected to declare their support for the man.

① silent      ② indulgent

③ imminent      ④ eminent

78 The computer presents three-dimensional images that enable doctors to see around the injured muscle, so that the effects of the injury on the surrounding tissue can be evaluated.

① removed      ② prescribed

③ determined      ④ treated

79 Prices on steakhouse menus are higher than they were three years ago, and the drought that has devastated corn crops in the Midwest will only push them higher.

① triggered      ② enhanced

③ destroyed      ④ manipulated

80 She is the protagonist of change in our department.

① bondman      ② antagonist

③ principal      ④ subordination

81 Meanwhile, Egypt and Jordan, the only Arab nations to recognize Israel, openly mulled over breaking off relations, a move that could take years to repair.

① suggested

② criticized

③ pondered over

④ were wary of

82 Many people can afford to buy motorcars at anything from two hundred pounds who would be aghast at the idea of spending half a guinea occasionally on a book.
① alarmed ② wise
③ lavishing ④ discouraged

83 There has been some conjecture about possible merger.
① assiduity ② ignorance
③ surmise ④ indigestion

84 Many of his colleagues eventually agreed that Dr. Brown's theory was tenable.
① redundant ② tolerable
③ logical ④ efficient

85 Whether this rug is red or green is nugatory to someone who is colorblind.
① tentative ② subtle
③ worthless ④ vulnerable

86 He launched a vitriolic attack on the prime minister, accusing him of shielding corrupt friends.
① cowardly ② tactful
③ discreet ④ acerbic

87 The factory is the fulcrum of our town because most of our citizens work there.
① pride ② attraction
③ caliber ④ pivot

88 Studying the past has the intrinsic value of satisfying our curiosity about ourselves.
① inherent ② obsolete
③ exquisite ④ uncertain

89 Simply excuse yourself during any lull, saying you need a drink or want to say hello to someone else.
① pause ② clamor
③ agitation ④ commotion

90 He chided the younger boys that the teacher began training along with him.
① soothed ② complimented
③ threatened ④ scolded

91 A postage stamp has been issued to pay tribute to Helen Keller and her teacher, Anne Sullivan.
① redeem ② spawn
③ honor ④ reimburse

92 A little less than 7% of New Mexico's rivers are perennial, with the remaining 93% being ephemeral, according to state officials.
① chronic ② inveterate
③ temporary ④ contaminated

93 That is why one of the biggest antitrust investigations of an American company in years ended with a slap on the wrist Thursday, when the Federal Trade Commission closed its investigation of Google's search practices without bringing a complaint.
① a slap on the back
② a slap in the face
③ a severe punishment
④ a soft punishment

**94** The bond market normally revives after the summer <u>doldrums</u>.

① serenity      ② depression

③ humidity      ④ venture

**95** <u>Predatory</u> lenders prey on those who have a low-level of education.

① plundering      ② fastidious

③ beleaguered      ④ whimsical

**96** Winston Churchill warned the English people that if they gave in to the Nazis, they would "sink into the <u>abyss</u> of a new Dark Age."

① dawn      ② cult

③ gulf      ④ usher

**97** The government has implemented a number of measures to <u>counteract</u> the effects of the rise in the value in the won.

① strengthen      ② offset

③ pursue      ④ commence

**98** Every human life is sacred and <u>inviolable</u> from its conception to its natural end.

① sacrosanct      ② blithe

③ phlegmatic      ④ mercurial

**99** The shop used free gifts as a <u>bait</u> to attract new customers.

① substitute      ② precedent

③ decoy      ④ resort

**100** The illegal policy brought <u>windfall</u> profits overnight to voucher issuers.

① makeshift      ② bonanza

③ stopgap      ④ setback

[1] Write the meaning of the following words.

| | |
|---|---|
| ☐ robust | ☐ vandalize |
| ☐ paralysis | ☐ prolific |
| ☐ stately | ☐ crouch |
| ☐ confiscate | ☐ gifted |
| ☐ duress | ☐ bystander |
| ☐ intimidate | ☐ rescue |
| ☐ stratum | ☐ mendicant |
| ☐ arduous | ☐ domain |
| ☐ exhort | ☐ formulate |
| ☐ practically | ☐ awe |
| ☐ submerge | ☐ trunk |
| ☐ cortege | ☐ sluggard |
| ☐ synonym | ☐ orient |
| ☐ prune | ☐ backlash |
| ☐ luxurious | ☐ attend |
| ☐ traverse | ☐ oral |
| ☐ imply | ☐ monarch |
| ☐ wordplay | ☐ homing |
| ☐ cutting-edge | ☐ jury |
| ☐ brace | ☐ voracious |
| ☐ finite | ☐ spike |
| ☐ carriage | ☐ intransigent |
| ☐ itinerant | ☐ epigraph |
| ☐ delve | ☐ dissuade |
| ☐ chemistry | ☐ gusto |

[2] Select <u>the most</u> appropriate word from the box below. Each word should be used only once.

| | | | |
|---|---|---|---|
| ① stately | ② confiscate | ③ gusto | ④ gifted |
| ⑤ dissuaded | ⑥ duress | ⑦ voracious | ⑧ imply |
| ⑨ backlash | ⑩ formulated | ⑪ cutting-edge | ⑫ intimidate |
| ⑬ exhort | ⑭ traverse | ⑮ itinerant | ⑯ submerge |
| ⑰ vandalized | ⑱ prolific | ⑲ awe | ⑳ intransigent |

1    The customs officer has the authority to _____ any goods that violate import regulations.

2    Her confrontational tone was used to _____ her colleagues into submission, but it only led to strained relationships.

3    The witness's testimony seemed unreliable as it was given under _____ and appeared to be influenced by external pressures.

4    The motivational speaker's aim was to _____ students to take action and pursue their goals relentlessly.

5    For years, he was known as the "homeless billionaire" for his _____ life in which he lived in fine hotels around the world but did not own a home.

6    Volunteers were working to clean the Washington Monument on Wednesday after it was _____ with a vulgar, anti-government statement in red paint.

7    Her exceptional intellect and remarkable talents made her stand out as a(n) _____ student among her peers.

8    The Asian carp, a(n) _____ eater that has no predators, now dominates the Mississippi and Illinois rivers and their tributaries.

9    The controversial decision by the government sparked a significant _____ among the citizens and led to protests and unrest.

10    Despite multiple attempts at negotiation, the leader remained _____ and unwilling to compromise on any terms.

[3] Choose the one which is different from the others.

11  ① strenuous        ② arduous        ③ demanding        ④ frivolous

12  ① entourage        ② cortege        ③ cadre            ④ retinue

13  ① naysayer         ② sluggard       ③ dawdler          ④ drone

14  ① sturdy           ② robust         ③ lethargic        ④ vigorous

15  ① onlooker         ② partaker       ③ bystander        ④ spectator

16  ① capsize          ② orient         ③ adjust           ④ align

17  ① prop             ② strengthen     ③ protrude         ④ brace

18  ① delve            ② deride         ③ examine          ④ investigate

19  ① excuse           ② rescue         ③ salvage          ④ save

20  ① limited          ② bounded        ③ finite           ④ interminable

## ✓Answers

1 ②    | 세관원은 수입 규정을 위반한 모든 물품을 압수할 권한이 있다.

2 ⑫    | 그녀의 대립적인 말투는 동료들을 위협하여 굴복시키려고 사용되었지만, 그것은 단지 관계를 긴장되게 했다.

3 ⑥    | 증인의 증언은 강압에 의해 행해졌고 외압의 영향을 받은 것 같았으므로 신빙성이 없어 보였다.

4 ⑬    | 동기부여 강연가의 목표는 학생들에게 행동으로 옮기고 끊임없이 목표를 추구하도록 권고하는 것이었다.

5 ⑮    | 수년간 그는 전 세계의 고급 호텔에서 살았지만 집을 소유하지 않는 그의 이동 생활로 인해 '집 없는 억만장자'로 알려져 있었다.

6 ⑰    | 저속한 반정부적인 문장을 빨간 페인트로 칠하여 워싱턴 기념비가 훼손된 후 수요일 자원봉사자들이 기념비를 청소하고 있었다.

7 ④    | 그녀의 특출난 지적 능력과 놀라운 재능은 그녀를 또래 학생들 사이에서 영재 학생으로 두드러지게 했다.

8 ⑦    | 천적이 없는 게걸스러운 포식자인 아시아 잉어는 지금 미시시피주와 일리노이주의 강들과 지류들을 지배하고 있다.

9 ⑨    | 논란이 되는 정부의 결정은 시민들 사이에 상당한 반발을 불러일으켰고, 시위와 소요로 이어졌다.

10 ⑳   | 여러 번의 협상 시도에도 불구하고, 그 지도자는 여전히 비타협적이었고 어떤 조건에서도 타협할 의지가 없었다.

- - - - - - - - - - - - - - - - - - - - - - - - - - - - - - - - - - - - - - - - - - - - - -

11 ④    12 ③    13 ①    14 ③    15 ②    16 ①    17 ③    18 ②    19 ①    20 ④

# ☑ DAILY CHECKUP

[1] Write the meaning of the following words.

| | |
|---|---|
| ☐ abdicate | ☐ anthropology |
| ☐ volatile | ☐ substantial |
| ☐ diagram | ☐ convene |
| ☐ beget | ☐ basement |
| ☐ integrate | ☐ turbid |
| ☐ shrub | ☐ decelerate |
| ☐ down-to-earth | ☐ prohibitive |
| ☐ promulgate | ☐ caucus |
| ☐ mortgage | ☐ surmount |
| ☐ auspicious | ☐ utopian |
| ☐ demagogue | ☐ opprobrium |
| ☐ flummox | ☐ resort |
| ☐ ally | ☐ convex |
| ☐ insidious | ☐ emphasis |
| ☐ treaty | ☐ forthcoming |
| ☐ stipulate | ☐ nurture |
| ☐ pendent | ☐ convoy |
| ☐ limp | ☐ weigh |
| ☐ extreme | ☐ excerpt |
| ☐ holocaust | ☐ gibberish |
| ☐ monumental | ☐ chastise |
| ☐ escapade | ☐ radiant |
| ☐ compact | ☐ predilection |
| ☐ groan | ☐ mire |
| ☐ irrespective | ☐ amulet |

[2] Select <u>the most</u> appropriate word from the box below. Each word should be used only once.

| | | | |
|---|---|---|---|
| ① abdicate | ② beget | ③ monumental | ④ opprobrium |
| ⑤ convex | ⑥ nurture | ⑦ demagogue | ⑧ amulet |
| ⑨ emphasis | ⑩ turbid | ⑪ convoy | ⑫ volatile |
| ⑬ auspicious | ⑭ gibberish | ⑮ down-to-earth | ⑯ prohibitive |
| ⑰ pendent | ⑱ insidious | ⑲ groan | ⑳ utopian |

1    Everybody welcomed the decline of unemployment rates, which was a(n) _____ sign for our economy.

2    The charismatic politician displayed traits of a(n) _____ by manipulating emotions rather than relying on rational arguments.

3    We were all impressed by how _____ the movie star turned out to be; she was frank in talking and did not have any feeling of superiority, self-assertiveness, or showiness.

4    The heavy rainfall turned the once clear stream into a(n) _____ river, making it difficult to see the bottom.

5    The author's vision of a society without conflict seemed _____ in its perfect ideals but unrealistic in its execution.

6    Despite the mixture's _____ nature, we found that by lowering the temperature in the laboratory we could dramatically reduce its tendency to vaporize.

7    The controversial policy announcement drew immediate _____ from various advocacy groups and the public alike.

8    The professor's lecture was so filled with disjointed thoughts that the students struggled to extract any semblance of logic from the stream of _____ he presented.

9    The _____ was believed to ward off evil and bring good fortune.

10   The CEO's sudden decision to _____ responsibility caused chaos within the company, leaving a leadership vacuum.

[3] Choose the one which is different from the others.

**11**  ① integrate  ② merge  ③ impart  ④ incorporate

**12**  ① browbeat  ② flummox  ③ bewilder  ④ perplex

**13**  ① proclaim  ② proliferate  ③ declare  ④ promulgate

**14**  ① vagary  ② escapade  ③ prank  ④ impetus

**15**  ① convene  ② adjourn  ③ assemble  ④ gather

**16**  ① chastise  ② chide  ③ ordain  ④ rebuke

**17**  ① predilection  ② preference  ③ liking  ④ qualm

**18**  ① predicament  ② plight  ③ indulgence  ④ mire

**19**  ① sullen  ② radiant  ③ bright  ④ resplendent

**20**  ① overcome  ② surmount  ③ crusade  ④ conquer

## ✓ Answers

**1** ⑬  | 실업률 하락을 모두가 환영했는데, 이것은 우리 경제에 좋은 징조였다.

**2** ⑦  | 카리스마 넘치는 정치가는 이성적인 주장에 의지하기보다는 감정을 조종함으로써 선동가의 특성을 보였다.

**3** ⑮  | 우리는 모두 그 유명 영화배우가 알고 보니 매우 진솔하다는 것에 감명을 받았다. 그녀는 말하는 데 있어서 솔직했고, 우월감이나 주제넘음이나 허영심을 갖고 있지 않았다.

**4** ⑩  | 폭우로 인해 한때 맑았던 시내가 탁한 색의 강으로 바뀌어 바닥을 볼 수 없게 되었다.

**5** ⑳  | 그 작가의 갈등 없는 사회에 대한 비전은 그 완벽한 이상적인 면에서는 이상향적인 것 같았지만 실행 면에서는 비현실적인 것 같았다.

**6** ⑫  | 그 혼합물의 휘발성에도 불구하고, 우리는 연구실에서 그것의 온도를 낮춤으로써 증발하려는 성질을 급격히 줄일 수 있다는 사실을 알게 되었다.

**7** ④  | 논란이 된 정책 발표는 다양한 압력 단체와 대중 모두로부터 즉각적인 비난을 불러일으켰다.

**8** ⑭  | 그 교수의 강의는 너무 일관성이 없는 생각들로 가득 차서 학생들은 그가 설명하는 횡설수설한 말들로부터 그 어떤 논리 비슷한 것이라도 도출해 내려고 노력했다.

**9** ⑧  | 그 부적은 악을 물리치고 행운을 가져다준다고 여겨졌다.

**10** ①  | 책임을 포기하기로 한 대표이사의 갑작스러운 결정은 사내에 혼란을 일으켜 리더십 공백을 초래했다.

**11** ③  **12** ①  **13** ②  **14** ④  **15** ②  **16** ③  **17** ④  **18** ③  **19** ①  **20** ③

[1] Write the meaning of the following words.

| | |
|---|---|
| ☐ notorious | ☐ surmise |
| ☐ adulate | ☐ diffident |
| ☐ parvenu | ☐ object |
| ☐ convey | ☐ wizardry |
| ☐ penitence | ☐ artful |
| ☐ instigate | ☐ carcass |
| ☐ reticent | ☐ kindle |
| ☐ deplete | ☐ visionary |
| ☐ heap | ☐ equilibrium |
| ☐ prosaic | ☐ irresistible |
| ☐ bask | ☐ sow |
| ☐ superficial | ☐ allegiance |
| ☐ turnkey | ☐ regale |
| ☐ fragile | ☐ pretext |
| ☐ mumble | ☐ compelling |
| ☐ spot | ☐ beverage |
| ☐ crutch | ☐ flint |
| ☐ eavesdrop | ☐ exotic |
| ☐ acquaintance | ☐ dowager |
| ☐ lachrymose | ☐ guarantee |
| ☐ storage | ☐ sturdy |
| ☐ consolidate | ☐ reward |
| ☐ manuscript | ☐ mollycoddle |
| ☐ glimpse | ☐ trajectory |
| ☐ invective | ☐ portion |

[2] Select <u>the most</u> appropriate word from the box below. Each word should be used only once.

| | | | |
|---|---|---|---|
| ① penitence | ② bask | ③ mumbled | ④ eavesdrop |
| ⑤ equilibrium | ⑥ lachrymose | ⑦ trajectory | ⑧ reward |
| ⑨ pretext | ⑩ reticent | ⑪ heap | ⑫ prosaic |
| ⑬ fragile | ⑭ parvenu | ⑮ kindle | ⑯ regaled |
| ⑰ wizardry | ⑱ compelling | ⑲ convey | ⑳ visionary |

**1** Upon realizing the consequences of his actions, the offender displayed genuine _____ for his wrongdoing.

**2** Luther was _____ on the subject of his accomplishments: he didn't like to talk about himself.

**3** His narrative felt mundane and _____ as it lacked the creative spark that captures readers' imagination.

**4** Ecuador heavily regulates tourism in the Galapagos as part of its environmental conservation policies, but the travel guidebook publisher Fodor's says the islands' _____ ecosystems remain vulnerable.

**5** The walls in our old house were so thin that you could easily _____ on the discussions in the next room.

**6** The novel's tragic ending had a(n) _____ effect on the readers, leaving them deeply moved and sorrowful.

**7** Uncle Jim _____ everyone with his hilarious anecdotes and witty jokes.

**8** The meditation practice aimed to restore inner _____ and bring a sense of peace to the individual's mind.

**9** The apology seemed more like a(n) _____ for avoiding taking responsibility for the mistake.

**10** He _____ his answers, despite repeated requests to speak up, and was impatient with many of the questions.

[3] Choose the one which is different from the others.

| 11 | ① superficial | ② cursory | ③ ostensible | ④ palpable |
| 12 | ① reinforce | ② consolidate | ③ streamline | ④ strengthen |
| 13 | ① infamous | ② notorious | ③ curious | ④ flagitious |
| 14 | ① denunciation | ② exculpation | ③ invective | ④ tirade |
| 15 | ① adulate | ② blandish | ③ flatter | ④ emulate |
| 16 | ① cunning | ② crafty | ③ whimsical | ④ artful |
| 17 | ① provoke | ② instigate | ③ incite | ④ libel |
| 18 | ① impotent | ② irresistible | ③ overwhelming | ④ compelling |
| 19 | ① allegiance | ② fidelity | ③ enmity | ④ loyalty |
| 20 | ① robust | ② puny | ③ sturdy | ④ stalwart |

✔**Answers**

1 ① ┃ 범죄자는 자신의 행동의 결과를 깨닫자, 그의 잘못에 대해 진정한 회개를 했다.

2 ⑩ ┃ 루터(Luther)는 자신의 성과라는 주제에 대해서는 말을 삼갔다. 그는 자신에 관해 이야기하는 것을 좋아하지 않았다.

3 ⑫ ┃ 그의 이야기는 독자들의 상상력을 사로잡는 창의적인 번득임이 부족했기 때문에 재미없고 단조롭게 느껴졌다.

4 ⑬ ┃ 에콰도르는 환경보존 정책의 일환으로 갈라파고스 제도의 관광을 엄격하게 규제하지만, 여행 가이드북 출판사인 포도스는 갈라파고스 제도의 망가지기 쉬운 생태계는 여전히 (환경오염에) 취약하다고 말한다.

5 ④ ┃ 오래된 집의 벽은 너무 얇아서 옆방의 대화를 쉽게 엿들을 수 있었다.

6 ⑥ ┃ 그 소설의 비극적 결말은 독자들에게 눈물을 자아냈으며 깊은 감동과 슬픔을 안겨주었다.

7 ⑯ ┃ 짐(Jim) 삼촌은 재미있는 일화와 재치 있는 농담으로 모두를 즐겁게 했다.

8 ⑤ ┃ 명상 수행은 내면의 균형을 회복하고 개인의 마음에 평화를 가져오는 것을 목표로 했다.

9 ⑨ ┃ 그 사과는 실수에 대한 책임을 회피하기 위한 구실처럼 보였다.

10 ③ ┃ 큰 소리로 똑똑히 답변해 달라는 거듭된 요청에도 불구하고, 그는 대답을 중얼거렸고 많은 질문에 조급해졌다.

11 ④    12 ③    13 ③    14 ②    15 ④    16 ③    17 ④    18 ①    19 ③    20 ②

☑ **DAILY CHECKUP**

[1] Write the meaning of the following words.

| | |
|---|---|
| ☐ titular | ☐ index |
| ☐ discretion | ☐ entreat |
| ☐ pretentious | ☐ article |
| ☐ assort | ☐ canvass |
| ☐ epiphany | ☐ masculine |
| ☐ suppress | ☐ landslide |
| ☐ indiscriminate | ☐ crack |
| ☐ recruit | ☐ stalemate |
| ☐ sham | ☐ insuperable |
| ☐ corporeal | ☐ upset |
| ☐ fray | ☐ photogenic |
| ☐ disproportionate | ☐ sally |
| ☐ pare | ☐ grotesque |
| ☐ amphibian | ☐ chronology |
| ☐ speculate | ☐ fauna |
| ☐ mogul | ☐ watershed |
| ☐ browse | ☐ outrageous |
| ☐ venture | ☐ tutelage |
| ☐ affordable | ☐ stentorian |
| ☐ repast | ☐ decode |
| ☐ conjugal | ☐ precept |
| ☐ extract | ☐ numerical |
| ☐ hollow | ☐ cure-all |
| ☐ guru | ☐ mischief |
| ☐ run-of-the-mill | ☐ binocular |

[2] Select <u>the most</u> appropriate word from the box below. Each word should be used only once.

| | | | |
|---|---|---|---|
| ① titular | ② discretion | ③ tutelage | ④ pretentious |
| ⑤ guru | ⑥ precept | ⑦ stalemate | ⑧ fray |
| ⑨ stentorian | ⑩ disproportionate | ⑪ indiscriminate | ⑫ conjugal |
| ⑬ affordable | ⑭ speculate | ⑮ upset | ⑯ entreat |
| ⑰ outrageous | ⑱ canvass | ⑲ watershed | ⑳ cure-all |

**1** Moscow denies aiming at civilian targets, but its _____ shelling has wrought wide destruction in urban centers.

**2** The diplomat handled the delicate negotiations with _____ to avoid disrupting the fragile peace talks.

**3** The company's commitment to providing _____ options allowed a wider range of customers to access its products.

**4** Her affected mannerisms and exaggerated gestures made her come across as _____ to the public.

**5** The political candidate planned to _____ the entire district in order to gather support for the upcoming election.

**6** The entrepreneur sought advice from a marketing _____ to enhance their business strategies.

**7** The negotiations reached a(n) _____ as neither party was willing to compromise on their demands.

**8** Recognizing the gravity of the situation, she decided to _____ the council for their assistance in resolving the community's pressing issues.

**9** The debate quickly descended into a heated _____ as opposing viewpoints clashed fiercely.

**10** The comedian's suggestive jokes were considered _____ by some as she often pushed the boundaries of acceptable humor.

[3] Choose the one which is different from the others.

11  ① repeal  ② suppress  ③ quell  ④ subdue

12  ① fraud  ② sham  ③ affinity  ④ hoax

13  ① void  ② empty  ③ hollow  ④ prodigal

14  ① grotesque  ② florid  ③ absurd  ④ ludicrous

15  ① ordinary  ② run-of-the-mill  ③ top-notch  ④ mediocre

16  ① prank  ② frolic  ③ mischief  ④ permeation

17  ① morose  ② corporeal  ③ palpable  ④ tangible

18  ① insuperable  ② imperative  ③ insurmountable  ④ impassable

19  ① decipher  ② decode  ③ tangle  ④ crack

20  ① classify  ② assort  ③ categorize  ④ scatter

## ✓ Answers

1  ⑪  | 러시아는 민간인을 겨냥한 공격을 부인했지만, 무차별적인 포격으로 도심이 광범위하게 파괴되었다.

2  ②  | 그 외교관은 결렬되기 쉬운 평화 회담이 중단되는 것을 피하기 위해 까다로운 협상을 신중하게 다루었다.

3  ⑬  | 합리적인 가격에 선택할 수 있는 제품을 제공하는 것에 대한 회사의 헌신 덕분에 더 폭넓은 고객이 그 회사의 제품에 접근할 수 있게 되었다.

4  ④  | 그녀의 가식적인 태도와 과장된 몸짓으로 인해 그녀는 대중에게 허세 부리는 사람이라는 인상을 주었다.

5  ⑱  | 그 후보자는 다가오는 선거에서 지지를 모으기 위해 지역구 전체를 유세할 계획이었다.

6  ⑤  | 그 사업가는 그들의 사업 전략을 강화하기 위해 마케팅 전문가에게 조언을 구했다.

7  ⑦  | 어느 쪽도 자신들의 요구 사항을 타협할 의사가 없어 협상이 교착상태에 빠졌다.

8  ⑯  | 상황의 심각성을 인식한 그녀는 지역사회의 긴급한 문제를 해결하는 데 의회의 도움을 요청하기로 결정했다.

9  ⑧  | 서로 다른 의견들이 격렬하게 대립하면서 토론은 순식간에 격렬한 싸움으로 빠져들었다.

10  ⑰  | 그 코미디언의 외설적인 농담은 종종 용인되는 유머의 한계를 넘었기 때문에 일부 사람들은 그 농담들을 터무니없는 것으로 간주했다.

11 ①    12 ③    13 ④    14 ②    15 ③    16 ④    17 ①    18 ②    19 ③    20 ④

[1] Write the meaning of the following words.

| | |
|---|---|
| ☐ mundane | ☐ impudent |
| ☐ exasperate | ☐ coalesce |
| ☐ depot | ☐ pugnacious |
| ☐ gaze | ☐ voyage |
| ☐ apogee | ☐ zoom |
| ☐ resonant | ☐ trilogy |
| ☐ psychology | ☐ dutiful |
| ☐ disfigure | ☐ sleight |
| ☐ sheen | ☐ crawl |
| ☐ account | ☐ malaise |
| ☐ preposterous | ☐ nominate |
| ☐ stain | ☐ askance |
| ☐ bulletin | ☐ cumulative |
| ☐ initiate | ☐ begrudge |
| ☐ heterodox | ☐ gnome |
| ☐ surveillance | ☐ flip |
| ☐ wallow | ☐ pigment |
| ☐ vassal | ☐ juggernaut |
| ☐ tailor | ☐ swear |
| ☐ steadfast | ☐ quorum |
| ☐ chauvinist | ☐ evidence |
| ☐ epidemic | ☐ occult |
| ☐ cataclysm | ☐ peril |
| ☐ ragamuffin | ☐ retrieve |
| ☐ propel | ☐ level-headed |

[2] Select the most appropriate word from the box below. Each word should be used only once.

| ① chauvinist | ② vassal | ③ swear | ④ resonant |
|---|---|---|---|
| ⑤ retrieve | ⑥ exasperate | ⑦ preposterous | ⑧ begrudge |
| ⑨ sheen | ⑩ initiate | ⑪ surveillance | ⑫ tailor |
| ⑬ steadfast | ⑭ cumulative | ⑮ epidemic | ⑯ occult |
| ⑰ sleight | ⑱ zoom | ⑲ cataclysm | ⑳ gnome |

1 His unwavering determination showcased his _____ resolve to succeed against all odds.

2 Merriam Webster Dictionary defines "male _____ pig" in a straightforward way, noting that the term means "a man who thinks women are not equal to men."

3 The government's expansion of digital _____ raised questions about citizens' right to privacy.

4 He says that settling humans on other worlds, such as Mars, could preserve civilization if Earth were to experience a(n) _____, such as a large asteroid impact.

5 He was known to _____ vehemently when frustrated, using colorful language to express his displeasure.

6 The inability to reach a consensus among the team members began to _____ the mediator who struggled to maintain patience during the prolonged discussion.

7 Although most people do not believe in _____ practices, the attraction to the supernatural, such as psychic powers or astrology, remains strong.

8 Using the right software, he was able to quickly _____ the lost files from his computer.

9 She couldn't help but _____ her colleagues' success, feeling envious of their achievements.

10 The two candidates denounced each other by saying that the pledges of the other person are absolutely _____.

[3] Choose the one which is different from the others.

**11** ① arrogant      ② presumptuous      ③ bashful      ④ impudent

**12** ① suspiciously      ② askance      ③ skeptically      ④ gingerly

**13** ① apogee      ② aeon      ③ apex      ④ acme

**14** ① sober      ② mundane      ③ banal      ④ humdrum

**15** ① level-headed      ② discreet      ③ arbitrary      ④ reasonable

**16** ① dissident      ② heretical      ③ heterodox      ④ nonchalant

**17** ① nominate      ② acquaint      ③ appoint      ④ designate

**18** ① unite      ② detach      ③ coalesce      ④ merge

**19** ① impel      ② drive      ③ deluge      ④ propel

**20** ① preliminary      ② dutiful      ③ obedient      ④ faithful

## ✓Answers

**1** ⑬ | 그의 흔들리지 않는 결단력은 모든 역경을 이겨내고 성공하겠다는 확고한 의지를 보여주었다.

**2** ① | 메리엄 웹스터 사전은 '남성 우월주의자'를 직설적으로 정의하며, 이 용어는 '여성이 남성과 동등하지 않다고 생각하는 남성'을 뜻한다고 명시한다.

**3** ⑪ | 정부의 디지털 감시 확대로 인해 시민의 개인 정보 보호 권리에 대한 의문이 제기되었다.

**4** ⑲ | 그는 지구가 거대한 소행성 충돌과 같은 대재앙을 겪을 경우 화성과 같은 다른 세계에 인류를 정착시키는 것이 문명을 보존할 수 있다고 말한다.

**5** ③ | 그는 좌절감을 느끼면 격렬하게 욕설을 퍼붓고, 불만을 표현하기 위해 다채로운 언어를 사용하는 것으로 유명했다.

**6** ⑥ | 팀원들 간에 합의점을 찾지 못한 것은 장시간의 토론 과정에서 인내심을 유지하기 위해 애쓰던 중재자를 화나게 하기 시작했다.

**7** ⑯ | 대부분의 사람들은 주술적인 의식을 믿지 않지만, 초능력과 점성술과 같은 초자연적인 행위에 끌리는 매력은 여전히 강하다.

**8** ⑤ | 올바른 소프트웨어를 사용하여 그는 컴퓨터에서 잃어버린 파일을 빠르게 복구할 수 있었다.

**9** ⑧ | 그녀는 동료들의 성과를 부러워하며 그들의 성공을 시기하지 않을 수 없었다.

**10** ⑦ | 두 후보는 상대방의 공약이 완전히 터무니없는 것이라고 말하며 서로를 비난했다.

---

**11** ③    **12** ④    **13** ②    **14** ①    **15** ③    **16** ④    **17** ②    **18** ②    **19** ③    **20** ①

# ACTUAL TEST

문항수 / 시간 100문항 ⏱60분

▶▶▶ ANSWERS P.344

[01-100] Choose the one that is closest in meaning to the underlined part.

**01** When an opinion poll is taken, its <u>robustness</u> increases with the size and randomness of the sample.
① interpretation ② irrelevance
③ testimony ④ power

**02** Taxi drivers <u>paralyzed</u> public services.
① despised ② disabled
③ displaced ④ degraded

**03** Voters were impressed by his <u>stately</u> speech made just two days before the election.
① national ② dignified
③ spontaneous ④ well-planned

**04** Korea Deposit Insurance Corporation will sell artwork <u>confiscated</u> from the suspended savings banks in South Korea this year at foreign auctions.
① drafted ② donated
③ impounded ④ dispatched

**05** We will do our best to defend our country's sovereignty and will never give in under <u>duress</u>.
① coercion ② quarantine
③ exuberance ④ surveillance

**06** Attempts to <u>intimidate</u> people into voting for the governing party did not work.
① encourage ② discourage
③ frighten ④ cox

**07** It was about this time I conceived the bold and <u>arduous</u> project of arriving at moral perfection.
① averse ② fastidious
③ austere ④ strenuous

**08** The evangelist will <u>exhort</u> all sinners in his audiences to reform.
① exasperate ② obliterate
③ cast away ④ advise

**09** By the time Ibn Battuta returned to Tangier, he had <u>traversed</u> — by foot, by donkey, by camel and by boat — nearly the entire length of the Muslim world and beyond on a quest for knowledge and experience.
① crossed ② conquered
③ surveyed ④ witnessed

**10** Today the study of biology is entering an exciting new age, where we can achieve an unprecedented level of accuracy through the use of <u>cutting-edge</u> technology.
① scientific ② extensive
③ in-depth ④ innovative

**11** The revelation came as traders <u>braced themselves</u> for another turbulent week, with mounting expectations that central banks may soon cut rates to prevent market mayhem leading to an economic downturn.

① anticipated     ② headed

③ prepared     ④ stood

**12** In my view, Luke was an <u>itinerant</u> physician who plied his trade in places like Troas and Philippi.

① sickly     ② temporary

③ traveling     ④ proficient

**13** We all practice two basic ways of thinking, whether we have names for them or not; We can <u>delve into</u> something and try to separate its parts, or we can look at two or more things that seem separated and try to fit them together.

① examine     ② recruit

③ divide     ④ dissolve

**14** Agatha Christie was a <u>prolific</u> writer, publishing 66 detective novels and 14 short story collections in her career.

① original     ② productive

③ tolerant     ④ celebrated

**15** My aging immune system is without doubt more <u>sluggish</u> than it used to be.

① slow     ② weak

③ quick     ④ swift

**16** It has not yet risen to an organized consumer movement, but there are unmistakable signs of a <u>backlash</u> against the 75 million handheld communications devices now on the American scene.

① negative reaction

② physical violence

③ political controversy

④ religious discrimination

**17** A <u>voracious</u> reader, my aunt frequented wonderfully cozy bookstores that dotted the college towns she lived in.

① considerable     ② enthusiastic

③ imaginative     ④ speedy

**18** I wonder why the manager maintained such an <u>intransigent</u> position.

① noncommittal     ② flatfooted

③ squalid     ④ amicable

**19** Stigma and discrimination associated with HIV/AIDS, and sometimes community or even governmental denial of the disease, too often <u>dissuade</u> individuals from getting tested or receiving medical care.

① deter     ② convince

③ bar     ④ prescribe

**20** There's no handbook for how to <u>abdicate</u>, but Oprah Winfrey offered up a pretty good model for monarchs who don't want to go quietly.

① renounce     ② reverberate

③ restitute     ④ resonate

21 Ingredients for hand sanitizers are not cheap these days, because of volatile commodity prices for ethyl alcohol and glycerin.

① elastic　　　　② unreliable
③ immobile　　　④ unstable

22 Sabella nevertheless remained a beloved figure in football, admired for his humility and down-to-earth way of life.

① alternative　　② conciliatory
③ practical　　　④ holistic

23 The principal promulgated orderly rules for pupil conduct.

① instigated　　　② procured
③ announced　　　④ retracted

24 With a hundred people promising donations of $100 each, the fund-raising drive got off to a most auspicious start.

① irreparable　　② false
③ preliminary　　④ favorable

25 The demagogue employed every means of appealing to the passions and prejudices of the crowd.

① tyrant　　　　② agitator
③ critic　　　　　④ pedagogue

26 Investors have been flummoxed by the unusual array of circumstances weighing down the economy.

① marginalized　② baffled
③ braced　　　　④ summoned

27 He died of an insidious disease before the doctors realized he was sick.

① a furtive　　　② an obvious
③ an unilateral　④ a meaningless

28 German sociologist Ulrich Beck, who observed the shock of the Chernobyl nuclear accident, published "Risk Society." It is a theory on risk that stipulates that industrialization and modernization brings technological development and material prosperity, but also greater risk.

① insinuates　　② specifies
③ negates　　　④ reverses

29 When a late spring frost touches a wooded area, it can leave a fearful mark. Tender leaves, just budding, turn black and become limp.

① lanky　　　　② stiff and firm
③ burnt　　　　④ lifeless and drooping

30 In 1974 Hank Aaron broke Babe Ruth's monumental lifetime record of 714 home-runs.

① archaic　　　② degrading
③ outstanding　④ entire

31 There are still concerns about the safety of nuclear power, as seen most recently at the Fukushima nuclear power plant in Japan. The country had to close its nuclear reactor when the plant was hit by a tsunami and, as a consequence, began releasing substantial amounts of radioactive materials.

① ignorable　　② considerable
③ dangerous　　④ essential

**32** Legislatures won't <u>convene</u> until January at the earliest, so it's unclear how many bills are being drafted and on which subjects.

① intervene      ② gather

③ adjourn      ④ dissemble

**33** The poem depicts the <u>turbid</u> state of the soldier's mind the night before the decisive battle was set to begin.

① fearless      ② adamant

③ morose      ④ confused

**34** During the Colonial Period, it was <u>prohibitively</u> expensive to ship anything across the Appalachian Mountains.

① momentarily      ② extraordinarily

③ strangely      ④ tolerably

**35** At the end of the third quarter, the visitors were ahead by 18 points, a lead that our team was unable to <u>surmount</u>.

① devour      ② overcome

③ decline      ④ denude

**36** Unhappy people often <u>resort to</u> violence as a means of expressing their suffering.

① put up with

② suffer from

③ find fault with

④ make use of

**37** Korea has <u>nurtured</u> small business by giving them money and special advantages to help them grow and become successful.

① hold back      ② promoted

③ disregarded      ④ disciplined

**38** Faults seen through anger are like objects seen through a mist: they appear larger. If a man is hungry, then let him eat food: but he should never hunger and thirst for anger if he intends to <u>chastise</u>.

① vindicate      ② upbraid

③ commend      ④ succor

**39** Politicians often manifest a <u>predilection</u> for making statements for short term political gain that are either nonsensical or contradictory to past positions they have held.

① provision for      ② probability of

③ liking for      ④ prospect of

**40** Instead of the familiar Asia that remained <u>mired</u> in a distant and static past, Japan suddenly came to represent modernity or even postmodernity.

① exotic      ② pure

③ essentialized      ④ stagnant

**41** <u>Amulets</u> are typically part of folk religion or paganism.

① trinkets      ② totems

③ talismans      ④ tartans

**42** Professional hockey teams are <u>notorious</u> for the fights among players during games.

① exciting      ② unbearable

③ expecting      ④ infamous

43 Here had been her sin; here, her sorrow; and here was yet to be her penitence. She had returned, therefore, and resumed, of her own free will, the symbol of which we have related so dark a tale.

① penalty      ② salvage

③ grudge       ④ contrition

44 The captain instigated an unexpected reaction as a response to the behavior of the angry woman.

① projected    ② provoked

③ instructed   ④ investigated

45 He was reticent about the reasons for the quarrel.

① reserved     ② querulous

③ hilarious    ④ dogmatic

46 Once the water was depleted, the explorers had to give up hope.

① disproved    ② exhausted

③ malingered   ④ appeased

47 After a while it occurs to them that they ought to return to the drawing-room and the prosaic routine of everyday life.

① exuberant    ② consonant

③ mundane      ④ pastoral

48 Because her research gave only a superficial analysis of the issue, the professor could not give her more than a passing grade.

① redundant    ② superfluous

③ wide-spread  ④ shallow

49 We see a solid vault of apartment houses around the fragile-seeming home.

① grotesque    ② refined

③ frail        ④ formidable

50 The child mumbled so badly that I could not understand a word he said.

① ranted       ② rambled

③ muttered     ④ baffled

51 Wild animals are known to listen to each other for clues about lurking predators, effectively eavesdropping on other species' chatter.

① overhearing  ② gazing

③ camouflaging ④ mimicking

52 In writing a book of this kind, my main aim has been to acquaint the reader with what is the generally accepted view of the authors and periods under discussion.

① familiarize  ② explain

③ question     ④ acquire

53 Finally they decided to consolidate the two companies into one.

① lavish       ② prevent

③ merge        ④ impress

54 The idea is this data will provide a unique glimpse into what really goes on in families that hasn't been available through traditional methods of self-report.

① opportunity  ② extension

③ meaning      ④ looking

**55** We <u>surmised</u> that the traffic delay was caused by some accident on the highway.
① assessed ② supposed
③ decided ④ confessed

**56** Sara was <u>diffident</u> when offering a comment on the professor's lecture.
① wanton ② modest
③ hidebound ④ propathetic

**57** Her teacher's praise <u>kindled</u> a spark of hope inside her.
① inspired ② dampened
③ discouraged ④ confused

**58** Any shift by China concerning North Korea has the potential to significantly alter the political <u>equilibrium</u> in Asia.
① balance ② agitation
③ desertion ④ frustration

**59** The dynamic contradiction between national <u>allegiance</u> and international sympathies defined Einstein's search for a Jewish identity.
① dedication ② deterioration
③ fertility ④ delinquency

**60** If this is their <u>pretext</u>, it is an insult to me.
① pretension ② excuse
③ engagement ④ prestige

**61** To everyone's displeasure, John was <u>pretentious</u> when bragging about his big salary and tremendous benefits.
① prominent ② explicable
③ showy ④ exponential

**62** In her speech, she offered several <u>compelling</u> examples to support her ideas.
① controversial ② illusionary
③ doubtful ④ unavoidable

**63** Kim likes to collect <u>exotic</u> plants.
① unusual ② expensive
③ common ④ beautiful

**64** These <u>sturdy</u> looking girls are afraid of getting involved in this issue.
① attractive ② unfriendly
③ friendly ④ stalwart

**65** The decision concerning how to supply these from the various monastic properties and incomes at his disposal was left entirely to the abbot's <u>discretion</u>.
① piety ② sagacity
③ inclination ④ avarice

**66** First as a <u>dutiful</u> daughter, then as a wife, mother and teacher, Nancy has repressed her own desires her entire life.
① virtuous ② surrogate
③ obedient ④ freewheeling

**67** Luke's teachers introduced the children to a set of dinosaur models, which he promptly scrutinized. On the drive home from school, he <u>regaled</u> his mother with tales of triceratops and tyrannosaurus and velociraptors.
① bored ② related
③ inspired ④ entertained

**68** In the novel *Silent Spring*, Rachel Carson forcefully decried the indiscriminate use of pesticides.

① haphazard      ② innovative

③ unpleasant      ④ indispensable

**69** *Venus* is the rare film that suggests that the aged are neither magical saints nor tragic cases, but corporeal creatures like the rest of us.

① bilious      ② palpable

③ impervious      ④ intuitable

**70** The movie showed a man who was deprived of his conjugal rights.

① legal      ② spousal

③ conjuring      ④ performative

**71** The other day a waiter at an Italian restaurant in Moscow tried to explain to a customer why a run-of-the-mill Tuscan wine on the menu was so expensive. "If we list it cheap," he said, "New Russians won't buy it."

① tasty      ② native

③ average      ④ envious

**72** Over 15 Igbo groups of diverse fields had met to work out a position that could be canvassed by the Southeast geopolitical zone.

① botched      ② prattled

③ emaciated      ④ scrutinized

**73** That politician's speech was one of the most grotesque I've ever heard.

① emotional      ② beautiful

③ original      ④ dreadful

**74** Being fired by Apple and finding himself unemployed was a watershed moment for Steve Jobs.

① destructive      ② significant

③ upsetting      ④ humiliating

**75** She was a pleasant-looking woman of about forty, with a deep voice, almost manly in its stentorian tones, and had a large sensible square body, with feet to match — these last encased in good thick boots.

① tranquil      ② delightful

③ deafening      ④ twisted

**76** He was concerned only with mundane matters, especially the daily stock market quotations.

① global      ② futile

③ spiritual      ④ worldly

**77** Feeling exasperated may be a side effect of too much medication.

① irritable      ② drowsy

③ forlorn      ④ dizzy

**78** The apogee of the Viennese style of music, Mozart's music continues to mesmerize audiences well into the 21st century.

① zenith      ② nadir

③ perigee      ④ longitude

**79** Then suddenly something different happened and he had to account for the accident.

① maintain      ② recollect

③ explain      ④ deny

80 Her preposterous speech embarrassed her co-workers.

① rude      ② prospective

③ ambiguous      ④ ridiculous

81 Since the man still wasn't responding to medical treatment, the claims adjuster decided to place him under surveillance.

① observation      ② manipulation

③ protection      ④ recovery

82 They often tried to obscure, downplay, or tailor their racial self-understanding to conform to the needs of the larger culture.

① adjust      ② abandon

③ improve      ④ curtail

83 Freedom fighters are defined positively as idealistic people who steadfastly refuse to accept foreign invaders, while insurgents are seen as rebels against a government which claims legitimacy, but in fact the words refer to the same people from opposing perspectives.

① stealthily      ② capriciously

③ petulantly      ④ tenaciously

84 Mary Harris's expectations as a wife and mother were shattered when she lost her entire family, her husband and their four children, in a yellow-fever epidemic in 1867.

① pestilence      ② epoch

③ incidence      ④ villainy

85 The Civil War was really a social cataclysm in which the capitalists, laborers, and farmers of the North and West drove from power in the national government the planting aristocracy of the South.

① upheaval      ② culmination

③ barometer      ④ milepost

86 Garrison's verbal attacks on Douglas after their split were just as pugnacious as his attacks on others he had broken with in the movement.

① ebullient      ② truculent

③ effervescent      ④ unruffled

87 The understanding was based on more than just impressions of their malaise.

① supremacy      ② misbehavior

③ unease      ④ temperament

88 In the United States, a party can nominate a single candidate for office.

① refuse      ② keep

③ change      ④ name

89 China is an unbeatable industrial juggernaut that will steamroll its competitors in its relentless quest for wealth and power.

① maverick      ② machination

③ largess      ④ leviathan

90 The occult rites of the organization were revealed only to members.

① mystical      ② facile

③ devious      ④ peculiar

91 A team of navy divers was dispatched to retrieve the sunken ship.

① hurl      ② revive

③ forfeit      ④ salvage

92 Political, cultural and economic sages are still looking <u>askance</u> at President Biden's expensive plan to forgive some student debt.
① spontaneously  ② stringently
③ relentlessly  ④ skeptically

93 Magicians take advantage of the ability to redirect gaze and attention to enhance their <u>sleight</u> of hand.
① competitiveness  ② dexterity
③ splendor  ④ agility

94 It is extremely <u>impudent</u> for Japan's high-ranking diplomat to talk about trust between the two countries.
① impertinent  ② attentive
③ nebulous  ④ bureaucratic

95 They tried to live according to his <u>precept</u> that the unexamined life was not worthy of a man.
① preference  ② pride
③ teaching  ④ dignity

96 While the President seems uniquely immune to disgrace, the rest of our politicians remain vulnerable to <u>opprobrium</u>.
① vilification  ② artifice
③ tenacity  ④ impetus

97 The book sold well because of the <u>outrageous</u> bits, but it's hard to believe many people read it from cover to cover.
① far-sighted  ② effusive
③ eclectic  ④ preposterous

98 With no solution in sight, it is the vendors who are bearing the brunt of the political <u>stalemate</u>.
① dispute  ② breach
③ impasse  ④ libel

99 The honorary professor also mentioned that <u>speculative</u> foreign capitalists would take advantage of the new bill with South Korean companies having no means for protecting themselves.
① reflective  ② ablaze
③ sentient  ④ risky

100 The mutual <u>invective</u> between the ruling and opposition parties shows no sign of ceasing.
① tolerance  ② denunciation
③ consent  ④ interference

[1] Write the meaning of the following words.

| | |
|---|---|
| ☐ voluntary | ☐ punctuate |
| ☐ enunciate | ☐ cursory |
| ☐ simian | ☐ agnostic |
| ☐ contempt | ☐ indoctrinate |
| ☐ defraud | ☐ amiss |
| ☐ inordinate | ☐ truce |
| ☐ moniker | ☐ glitter |
| ☐ release | ☐ hubris |
| ☐ denouement | ☐ rig |
| ☐ splenetic | ☐ prerogative |
| ☐ adore | ☐ exemplify |
| ☐ sewage | ☐ unkempt |
| ☐ blight | ☐ compile |
| ☐ enterprise | ☐ succinct |
| ☐ nosedive | ☐ feudalism |
| ☐ penniless | ☐ wield |
| ☐ strand | ☐ leash |
| ☐ confluence | ☐ pill |
| ☐ annual | ☐ bail |
| ☐ inkling | ☐ delectable |
| ☐ fugitive | ☐ giddy |
| ☐ touchstone | ☐ overtake |
| ☐ chubby | ☐ captious |
| ☐ discourage | ☐ mechanism |
| ☐ municipal | ☐ replete |

[2] Select <u>the most</u> appropriate word from the box below. Each word should be used only once.

| | | | |
|---|---|---|---|
| ① nosedived | ② confluence | ③ hubris | ④ cursory |
| ⑤ touchstone | ⑥ contempt | ⑦ glitter | ⑧ leash |
| ⑨ enunciate | ⑩ compiled | ⑪ exemplify | ⑫ stranded |
| ⑬ wield | ⑭ penniless | ⑮ fugitive | ⑯ overtake |
| ⑰ inordinate | ⑱ succinct | ⑲ denouement | ⑳ discouraged |

1    It is not less absurd than wicked to treat manual labor with _____ since to it we owe all the visible results of civilization.

2    Credit card debt, which _____ during the pandemic as Americans used government stimulus to pay down balances, has rebounded to all-time highs.

3    The authorities launched a widespread search to apprehend the _____ who had escaped custody.

4    Due to time constraints, she gave the document only a(n) _____ glance and missed important details.

5    His excessive _____ made him believe he was invincible, but it ultimately led to his downfall.

6    Instead of expressing himself in a(n) _____ way, he always writes more words than needed, and uses a dictionary to check his spelling, which is time-consuming.

7    In all press conferences, the speakers _____ their words carefully to avoid being misquoted.

8    The travelers were left _____ at the airport due to the sudden cancellation of flights.

9    Leaders should understand how to _____ power without abusing it, ensuring fair and just decisions.

10   As the race progressed, the athlete managed to steadily _____ the competitors and claimed victory in the end.

[3] Choose the one which is different from the others.

| 11 | ① fleece | ② defraud | ③ flatter | ④ swindle |
| 12 | ① unwilling | ② voluntary | ③ discretionary | ④ spontaneous |
| 13 | ① suggestion | ② hint | ③ inkling | ④ invocation |
| 14 | ① indoctrinate | ② indulge | ③ brainwash | ④ inculcate |
| 15 | ① perspective | ② prerogative | ③ perquisite | ④ privilege |
| 16 | ① slovenly | ② unkempt | ③ undefined | ④ untidy |
| 17 | ① ill-tempered | ② conciliatory | ③ splenetic | ④ peevish |
| 18 | ① devious | ② delectable | ③ enjoyable | ④ pleasant |
| 19 | ① captious | ② censorious | ③ fault-finding | ④ commendatory |
| 20 | ① dizzy | ② giddy | ③ audacious | ④ vertiginous |

## ✓ Answers

1  ⑥  Ⅰ 육체노동을 경멸한다는 것은 불합리할 뿐 아니라 나쁜 일이다. 왜냐하면 우리가 육체노동을 통해 현존하는 모든 문명의 결실을 얻었기 때문이다.

2  ①  Ⅰ 미국인들이 팬데믹 동안 정부 부양책을 이용해 대출금 잔액을 상환하면서 급감했던 신용카드 부채가 사상 최고치로 다시 증가했다.

3  ⑮  Ⅰ 당국은 구금 중 탈출한 도망자를 체포하기 위해 대대적인 수색에 착수했다.

4  ④  Ⅰ 시간적 제약 때문에 그녀는 서류를 대충 훑어보기만 해서 중요한 세부 사항을 놓쳤다.

5  ③  Ⅰ 그의 지나친 오만함으로 인해 그는 자신이 무적이라고 믿었으나 그것으로 결국 몰락하게 되었다.

6  ⑱  Ⅰ 자신의 생각을 간결한 방식으로 표현하는 대신에 그는 언제나 필요 이상으로 많은 단어를 쓰고 사전을 이용해 철자를 확인하다 보니 시간이 많이 소모된다.

7  ⑨  Ⅰ 모든 기자 회견에서, 연설자들은 자신들의 말이 잘못 인용되는 것을 막기 위해 조심스럽게 똑똑히 발음한다.

8  ⑫  Ⅰ 갑작스러운 항공편 결항으로 여행객들이 공항에 발이 묶였다.

9  ⑬  Ⅰ 지도자는 권력을 남용하지 않고 행사할 수 있는 방법을 이해하고 공정하고 정의로운 결정을 내릴 수 있도록 해야 한다.

10  ⑯  Ⅰ 경주가 진행되면서 그 선수는 꾸준히 경쟁자들을 추월하여 결국 승리를 거두었다.

- - - - - - - - - - - - - - - - - - - - - - - - - - - - - - - - - - - - - - - - - - - - - - - - -

11 ③    12 ①    13 ④    14 ②    15 ①    16 ③    17 ②    18 ①    19 ④    20 ③

☑ **DAILY CHECKUP**

[1] Write the meaning of the following words.

| | |
|---|---|
| ☐ nuisance | ☐ juxtapose |
| ☐ stupefy | ☐ obloquy |
| ☐ boisterous | ☐ estranged |
| ☐ autopsy | ☐ forgo |
| ☐ sightly | ☐ blizzard |
| ☐ destination | ☐ potential |
| ☐ challenging | ☐ dodder |
| ☐ expostulate | ☐ shelf |
| ☐ catastrophe | ☐ insane |
| ☐ grudge | ☐ swarm |
| ☐ overweening | ☐ luxuriant |
| ☐ inoculation | ☐ paean |
| ☐ testify | ☐ amplify |
| ☐ ethnocentrism | ☐ menopause |
| ☐ refractory | ☐ trim |
| ☐ predisposition | ☐ vicarious |
| ☐ invade | ☐ sleuth |
| ☐ didactic | ☐ command |
| ☐ surfeit | ☐ holdup |
| ☐ pander | ☐ proclaim |
| ☐ misdemeanor | ☐ multifarious |
| ☐ wishy-washy | ☐ allegory |
| ☐ currency | ☐ reprimand |
| ☐ abet | ☐ facet |
| ☐ revenue | ☐ conscript |

[2] Select <u>the most</u> appropriate word from the box below. Each word should be used only once.

| | | | |
|---|---|---|---|
| ① boisterous | ② testify | ③ reprimanded | ④ nuisance |
| ⑤ amplified | ⑥ ethnocentrism | ⑦ command | ⑧ refractory |
| ⑨ pander | ⑩ vicarious | ⑪ sightly | ⑫ expostulate |
| ⑬ didactic | ⑭ invade | ⑮ misdemeanor | ⑯ challenging |
| ⑰ juxtapose | ⑱ forgo | ⑲ inoculation | ⑳ potential |

1  Home fans at the stadium became _____ as their team scored the winning goal in the final minutes.

2  Anyone who judges people or traditions based on his own cultural standards is guilty of _____.

3  Since they had always been well-behaved, I was completely surprised by their _____ behavior.

4  The book's tone was highly _____ as it aimed to impart moral lessons throughout the narrative.

5  The court classified the offense as a(n) _____ due to its nonviolent nature and lesser impact on society.

6  Parents scold their children before others, but kids should not be severely _____ in front of others, for it could have a bad effect on them.

7  Watching the team win brought him _____ satisfaction as if he had personally achieved victory.

8  Someone charged with a crime might decide to _____ the right to remain silent and instead confess.

9  James Joyce's *Ulysses* is a serious undertaking for any novice reader; likewise, Proust's work can be _____.

10  The recurring software glitch in the system became a significant _____ for the IT department.

**[3] Choose the one which is different from the others.**

11  ① grudge ② concord ③ malice ④ rancor

12  ① arrogant ② overweening ③ antediluvian ④ conceited

13  ① cohesion ② surfeit ③ excess ④ plethora

14  ① slander ② calumny ③ obloquy ④ pretext

15  ① irresolute ② quick-witted ③ indecisive ④ wishy-washy

16  ① proclaim ② declare ③ vacillate ④ pronounce

17  ① lush ② exuberant ③ luxuriant ④ barren

18  ① stupefy ② squander ③ numb ④ paralyze

19  ① anthem ② hymn ③ vista ④ paean

20  ① impede ② abet ③ incite ④ instigate

## ✓ Answers

1  ①  ┃ 경기장의 홈 팬들은 자신들의 팀이 마지막 몇 분을 남겨두고 결승골을 넣자 떠들썩해졌다.

2  ⑥  ┃ 자신의 문화적 기준에 따라 사람이나 전통을 판단하는 사람은 자민족 중심주의라는 잘못을 범한다.

3  ⑧  ┃ 그들은 언제나 품행이 단정했었기 때문에, 나는 그들의 고집 센 행동에 굉장히 놀랐다.

4  ⑬  ┃ 이 책의 어조는 이야기 전반에 걸쳐 도덕적 교훈을 전달하는 것을 목표로 했기 때문에 매우 교훈적이었다.

5  ⑮  ┃ 법원은 폭력적이지 않은 특성과 사회에 미치는 영향이 적다는 이유로 그 범죄를 경범죄로 분류했다.

6  ③  ┃ 부모는 다른 사람들 앞에서 자신의 아이들을 꾸짖지만, 다른 사람들 앞에서 아이들을 심하게 질책해서는 안 된다. 왜냐하면 아이들에게 좋지 않은 영향을 미칠 수 있기 때문이다.

7  ⑩  ┃ 팀의 승리를 지켜본 그는 마치 자신이 승리를 거둔 듯한 대리만족을 느꼈다.

8  ⑱  ┃ 범죄 혐의로 기소된 사람은 묵비권을 포기하고 대신 자백하기로 결정할 수도 있다.

9  ⑯  ┃ 제임스 조이스(James Joyce)의 『율리시스』는 초보자가 읽기에 쉽지 않으며, 프루스트(Proust)의 작품도 마찬가지로 힘겨울 수 있다.

10 ④  ┃ 시스템에서 반복적으로 발생하는 소프트웨어 결함은 IT 부서에 심각한 골칫거리가 되었다.

11 ②  12 ③  13 ①  14 ④  15 ②  16 ③  17 ④  18 ②  19 ③  20 ①

☑ **DAILY CHECKUP**

[1] Write the meaning of the following words.

| | |
|---|---|
| ☐ indulge | ☐ clement |
| ☐ demise | ☐ transfuse |
| ☐ frivolous | ☐ unwittingly |
| ☐ epitaph | ☐ conflict |
| ☐ secure | ☐ shrug |
| ☐ predecessor | ☐ nostrum |
| ☐ revive | ☐ exonerate |
| ☐ pedantic | ☐ gradual |
| ☐ staple | ☐ coagulate |
| ☐ brainwash | ☐ restitution |
| ☐ void | ☐ prudent |
| ☐ amnesia | ☐ flinch |
| ☐ mince | ☐ scavenger |
| ☐ parody | ☐ insipid |
| ☐ linguist | ☐ byword |
| ☐ hustle | ☐ assimilate |
| ☐ banter | ☐ editorial |
| ☐ stimulus | ☐ causality |
| ☐ prevailing | ☐ scam |
| ☐ overlook | ☐ dictate |
| ☐ commemoration | ☐ subversive |
| ☐ abstemious | ☐ turnover |
| ☐ rhetoric | ☐ acrid |
| ☐ dire | ☐ weather |
| ☐ gait | ☐ millennium |

[2] Select the most appropriate word from the box below. Each word should be used only once.

| | | | |
|---|---|---|---|
| ① abstemious | ② nostrum | ③ subversive | ④ assimilated |
| ⑤ turnover | ⑥ exonerate | ⑦ indulge | ⑧ overlook |
| ⑨ restitution | ⑩ parody | ⑪ prudent | ⑫ rhetoric |
| ⑬ transfused | ⑭ demise | ⑮ causality | ⑯ weather |
| ⑰ insipid | ⑱ flinch | ⑲ shrug | ⑳ stimulus |

1    The economic downturn led to the _____ of several small businesses in the region.

2    Despite being surrounded by indulgent treats, she remained _____ and chose only the healthiest options.

3    The teacher's focus on big ideas sometimes caused her to _____ small mistakes in students' assignments.

4    The compelling testimonies of multiple witnesses provided the crucial support needed to ultimately _____ the defendant.

5    Since so many car accidents have happened at that intersection, it would be _____ for the city to put a stop sign in the area.

6    The novel's storyline was so _____ that even the most ardent readers struggled to maintain interest in its lackluster plot.

7    After the conflict was resolved, the court ordered the defendant to provide _____ for the damages caused to the plaintiff's property.

8    The new immigrants brought different languages and different cultures to the United States, but gradually most of them _____ to the dominant American culture they found here.

9    Truly to transgress, you must believe that the conventions you are bucking have some force. So once transgression itself has become the norm, it ceases to be _____.

10    They had to _____ the storm before continuing their journey across the open sea.

**[3] Choose the one which is different from the others.**

**11** ① flattery  ② banter  ③ chaff  ④ raillery

**12** ① appalling  ② dire  ③ trivial  ④ dreadful

**13** ① unintentionally  ② accidentally  ③ unwittingly  ④ knowingly

**14** ① clement  ② lenient  ③ gentle  ④ fervid

**15** ① bitter  ② savory  ③ acrid  ④ pungent

**16** ① congeal  ② clot  ③ coagulate  ④ dilute

**17** ① steady  ② gradual  ③ abrupt  ④ progressive

**18** ① scam  ② hoard  ③ swindle  ④ mulct

**19** ① decree  ② command  ③ dictate  ④ allege

**20** ① hack  ② hustle  ③ hurry  ④ rush

## ✓ Answers

**1** ⑭  | 경기 침체로 이 지역의 몇몇 소규모 기업들이 폐업했다.

**2** ①  | 그녀는 마음껏 먹을 수 있는 음식에 둘러싸여 있음에도 불구하고 절제를 유지하고 가장 건강한 음식만을 골랐다.

**3** ⑧  | 그 선생님은 큰 아이디어에 집중하는 바람에 학생들의 과제에서 작은 실수를 때때로 간과했다.

**4** ⑥  | 여러 증인의 설득력 있는 증언은 궁극적으로 피고인의 무죄를 입증하는 데 필요한 결정적인 도움이 되었다.

**5** ⑪  | 그 교차로에서 너무나 많은 교통사고가 발생했기 때문에, 시 당국이 그 구역에 정지 표지판을 세우는 게 현명할 것이다.

**6** ⑰  | 소설의 줄거리가 너무 무미건조해서 가장 열심인 독자들조차 그 밋밋한 줄거리에 관심을 유지하려고 애썼다.

**7** ⑨  | 분쟁이 해결된 후, 법원은 피고에게 원고의 재산에 발생한 손해를 배상하라고 명령했다.

**8** ④  | 새 이민자들이 다른 언어와 문화를 미국에 들여왔지만 점차로 그것들 대부분은 그들이 이곳에서 발견한 주요 미국 문화에 동화되었다.

**9** ③  | 진정으로 (기존 체제를) 위반하려면, 당신이 맞서고 있는 그 관습들에 어떤 힘이 있다고 믿어야 한다. 그러므로 일단 위반 그 자체가 규범이 되고 나면, 그것은 더 이상 체제 전복적이지 않다.

**10** ⑯  | 그들은 망망대해를 계속 여행하기 전에 폭풍을 뚫고 나아가야 했다.

........................................................................................

**11** ①  **12** ③  **13** ④  **14** ④  **15** ②  **16** ④  **17** ③  **18** ②  **19** ④  **20** ①

[1] Write the meaning of the following words.

| | |
|---|---|
| ☐ punctual | ☐ heterogeneous |
| ☐ importune | ☐ supplement |
| ☐ adage | ☐ anatomy |
| ☐ withstand | ☐ synthetic |
| ☐ traumatic | ☐ luster |
| ☐ schism | ☐ convivial |
| ☐ collude | ☐ bailout |
| ☐ drudgery | ☐ voluble |
| ☐ consonant | ☐ ore |
| ☐ excavate | ☐ astute |
| ☐ pristine | ☐ prowess |
| ☐ figment | ☐ numb |
| ☐ spiteful | ☐ inventory |
| ☐ acquiesce | ☐ knell |
| ☐ respective | ☐ expedition |
| ☐ paramour | ☐ arrest |
| ☐ bifurcate | ☐ tenant |
| ☐ standoff | ☐ blankly |
| ☐ intermittent | ☐ rogue |
| ☐ epilogue | ☐ grim |
| ☐ momentary | ☐ corps |
| ☐ pervert | ☐ sparkle |
| ☐ cavalcade | ☐ dorsal |
| ☐ deport | ☐ malediction |
| ☐ outset | ☐ forsake |

[2] Select the most appropriate word from the box below. Each word should be used only once.

| | | | |
|---|---|---|---|
| ① punctual | ② bifurcate | ③ dorsal | ④ prowess |
| ⑤ acquiesce | ⑥ withstand | ⑦ malediction | ⑧ grim |
| ⑨ convivial | ⑩ forsake | ⑪ collude | ⑫ schism |
| ⑬ synthetic | ⑭ voluble | ⑮ heterogeneous | ⑯ pristine |
| ⑰ numb | ⑱ knell | ⑲ standoff | ⑳ figment |

1   Transforming yourself from chronically late to perfectly _____ is a big task.

2   Many ancient civilizations collapsed when their environment could not _____ the strain of supporting their growing populations.

3   Despite their apparent rivalry, the two companies were discovered to secretly _____ in an attempt to control the market.

4   Before Columbus conquered South America, groups of nomadic people clustered around the Amazon River, leaving the surrounding rainforest _____ and untouched.

5   It was difficult to imagine Matthew, a(n) _____ man, as a psychiatrist; listening while others talked was not his style.

6   The knight's legendary _____ on the battlefield made him a revered figure among his comrades and feared by his enemies.

7   The bitter cold of the winter morning left my fingers and toes feeling completely _____.

8   In a fit of anger, he uttered a vehement _____ towards those who had wronged him.

9   The unwavering soldier swore to never _____ his duty regardless of the personal sacrifices it demanded.

10  The disagreement caused a deep _____ within the group and led to factions forming with differing ideologies.

[3] Choose the one which is different from the others.

**11** ① adage ② anecdote ③ axiom ④ precept

**12** ① badger ② importune ③ jostle ④ implore

**13** ① zeal ② drudgery ③ travail ④ chore

**14** ① dig ② burrow ③ excavate ④ deposit

**15** ① spiteful ② transcendent ③ malevolent ④ malicious

**16** ① perpetual ② intermittent ③ periodic ④ sporadic

**17** ① canny ② shrewd ③ obtuse ④ astute

**18** ① scoundrel ② knave ③ rogue ④ hardliner

**19** ① demur ② deport ③ banish ④ expatriate

**20** ① misuse ② pontificate ③ pervert ④ distort

## ✓ Answers

**1** ① ｜ 상습적으로 늦는 사람에서 완벽히 시간을 엄수하는 사람으로 스스로 변화하는 것은 쉽지 않은 일이다.

**2** ⑥ ｜ 많은 고대 문명들은 그들의 환경이 증가하는 인구를 부양하는 일의 중압감을 견디어 낼 수 없었을 때 붕괴했다.

**3** ⑪ ｜ 명백한 경쟁 관계임에도 불구하고 두 회사는 시장을 장악하기 위해 비밀리에 담합을 한 것으로 밝혀졌다.

**4** ⑯ ｜ 콜럼버스(Columbus)가 남아메리카를 정복하기 이전에, 유목민 무리들이 아마존 강 주변에서 무리를 이루어 살았는데, 이들은 주변의 열대우림을 자연 그대로 두었다.

**5** ⑭ ｜ 입심 좋은 매튜(Matthew)를 정신과 의사라고 상상하기란 어려웠다. 다른 사람이 말을 하는 동안 듣기만 하는 것은 그의 스타일이 아니었다.

**6** ④ ｜ 전장에서 그 기사의 전설적인 용맹함은 그를 동료들 사이에서 존경받는 인물로 만들었고 적들에게 두려움의 대상이 되게 했다.

**7** ⑰ ｜ 겨울 아침의 매서운 추위로 인해 손가락과 발가락이 완전히 감각을 잃었다.

**8** ⑦ ｜ 홧김에 그는 자신을 부당하게 취급한 사람들을 향해 거센 저주를 퍼부었다.

**9** ⑩ ｜ 확고한 의지를 가지고 있던 군인은 개인적으로 어떤 희생을 치르더라도 결코 자신의 의무를 저버리지 않을 것임을 맹세했다.

**10** ⑫ ｜ 그 의견 차이는 집단 내에 깊은 분열을 야기했고, 서로 다른 이념을 가진 파벌이 형성되었다.

- - - - - - - - - - - - - - - - - - - - - - - - - - - - - - - - - - - - - - - - - - - - - - - - - - - - - - - - - - - -

**11** ② **12** ③ **13** ① **14** ④ **15** ② **16** ① **17** ③ **18** ④ **19** ① **20** ②

**[1] Write the meaning of the following words.**

| | |
|---|---|
| ☐ overall | ☐ descant |
| ☐ interlocutor | ☐ picky |
| ☐ daze | ☐ appetite |
| ☐ sobriquet | ☐ quarantine |
| ☐ bewail | ☐ skeleton |
| ☐ pedigree | ☐ mnemonic |
| ☐ stymie | ☐ infuriate |
| ☐ discursive | ☐ exile |
| ☐ hypnosis | ☐ repudiate |
| ☐ wince | ☐ cherubic |
| ☐ ripe | ☐ genre |
| ☐ equity | ☐ vivacious |
| ☐ flounder | ☐ liquor |
| ☐ ingrate | ☐ thaw |
| ☐ mythology | ☐ coy |
| ☐ suspend | ☐ proliferate |
| ☐ tremor | ☐ brisk |
| ☐ calculus | ☐ scruple |
| ☐ abusive | ☐ deterrent |
| ☐ stereotype | ☐ envision |
| ☐ crash | ☐ punitive |
| ☐ entrust | ☐ fault |
| ☐ luscious | ☐ rave |
| ☐ yardstick | ☐ composure |
| ☐ converge | ☐ amalgamate |

[2] Select <u>the most</u> appropriate word from the box below. Each word should be used only once.

| | | | |
|---|---|---|---|
| ① quarantine | ② deterrent | ③ abusive | ④ infuriate |
| ⑤ tremor | ⑥ ingrate | ⑦ exile | ⑧ flounder |
| ⑨ discursive | ⑩ wince | ⑪ picky | ⑫ proliferate |
| ⑬ descant | ⑭ stymied | ⑮ coy | ⑯ scruple |
| ⑰ entrust | ⑱ thawed | ⑲ bewail | ⑳ rave |

**1** Unable to contain her grief, she began to _____ the loss of her cherished pet.

**2** The two boxers battled toe-to-toe until the final round when the longtime champion of the ring was finally _____ by his young opponent's stamina.

**3** His speech was so _____ that it jumped from one topic to another, making it challenging for the audience to follow his main points.

**4** He was considered a(n) _____ who always took but never acknowledged the kindness or support he received from others.

**5** The anonymity of the Internet frees some people to send _____ messages that are offensive to others.

**6** Due to the outbreak, the health officials ordered a mandatory _____ for those who had been in close contact with the infected individuals.

**7** The blatant disregard for their concerns only served to _____ the already frustrated protesters.

**8** Street food vendors continue to _____ in America as more customers are turning to food trucks for their affordability and convenience.

**9** Installing high-quality security cameras throughout the neighborhood served as a powerful _____ against potential burglaries and vandalism.

**10** After the failed rebellion, the defeated leaders faced the prospect of either imprisonment or _____ from their homeland, choosing the latter to avoid captivity.

[3] Choose the one which is different from the others.

**11**  ① decorum      ② sobriquet      ③ moniker      ④ nickname

**12**  ① fairness      ② impartiality      ③ equity      ④ bigotry

**13**  ① delicious      ② luscious      ③ bland      ④ savory

**14**  ① repudiate      ② impede      ③ disclaim      ④ deny

**15**  ① angelic      ② cherubic      ③ vitriolic      ④ seraphic

**16**  ① blend      ② amalgamate      ③ sneer      ④ compound

**17**  ① composure      ② gratitude      ③ aplomb      ④ equanimity

**18**  ① vivacious      ② lively      ③ stolid      ④ spirited

**19**  ① punishing      ② disciplinary      ③ punitive      ④ retaliatory

**20**  ① explicate      ② daze      ③ stupefy      ④ stun

## ✓Answers

**1** ⑲ | 슬픔을 참을 수 없었던 그녀는 소중히 여겨온 그녀의 애완동물을 잃고 통곡하기 시작했다.

**2** ⑭ | 두 명의 복서는 마지막 라운드까지 정면으로 맞서서 싸웠으며 마지막 라운드에서 복싱계의 오랜 챔피언은 그의 어린 상대의 체력에 결국 좌절되었다.

**3** ⑨ | 그의 연설은 너무 두서가 없다 보니 한 주제에서 또 다른 주제로 갑자기 바뀌어서 청중이 그의 주요 요점을 따라가는 것을 어렵게 했다.

**4** ⑥ | 그는 다른 사람들로부터 받은 친절이나 지원을 항상 받아들이기는 하지만 결코 인정하지 않는 은혜를 모르는 사람으로 여겨졌다.

**5** ③ | 인터넷이 지닌 익명성 때문에 어떤 사람들은 다른 사람들에게 불쾌한 모욕적인 메시지를 보낼 수 있게 되었다.

**6** ① | 전염병 발병으로 인해 보건 당국은 감염된 개인과 밀접하게 접촉한 사람들에 대해 의무 격리를 명령했다.

**7** ④ | 그들의 우려를 노골적으로 무시한 것은 이미 좌절한 시위자들을 분노하게 만들었을 뿐이었다.

**8** ⑫ | 더 많은 고객들이 적당한 가격과 편리함으로 인해 푸드 트럭을 이용하고 있기 때문에 거리의 음식 노점상은 미국에서 계속 급증하고 있다.

**9** ② | 동네 곳곳에 고급 보안 카메라를 설치한 것은 일어날 수 있는 도난 및 공공 기물 파손에 대한 강력한 억제책으로 작용했다.

**10** ⑦ | 반란이 실패한 후, 패배한 지도자들은 투옥되거나 고국에서 추방될 예정이었고, 투옥되는 것을 피하고자 후자(망명)를 선택했다.

**11** ①      **12** ④      **13** ③      **14** ②      **15** ③      **16** ③      **17** ②      **18** ③      **19** ④      **20** ①

# ACTUAL TEST

[01-100] Choose the one that is closest in meaning to the underlined part.

**01** Our English class wrote essay on this Schopenhauer quote: "Hatred comes from the heart; <u>contempt</u> from the head; and neither feeling is quite within our control."
① scorn
② humility
③ dignity
④ reverence

**02** To show his professor how hard-working he was, he spent an <u>inordinate</u> amount of time on his assignments.
① onerous
② excessive
③ designated
④ exhaustive

**03** As French president, Jacques Chirac was called all sorts of names, not the least for his vociferous opposition to the U.S.-led war in Iraq. Now he has a <u>moniker</u> that will stick: Convicted criminal.
① certificate
② medal
③ nickname
④ honor

**04** It is very difficult to succeed in the music business; nine out of ten bands that <u>release</u> a first record fail to produce a second.
① pay for
② distribute
③ overturn
④ itemize

**05** Dr. Samuel Johnson <u>adored</u> the female nurse and was surprised at her curative power.
① found
② esteemed
③ obtained
④ rejected

**06** His <u>splenetic</u> tweets about foreigners were quoted in court opinions blocking his immigration initiatives.
① eccentric
② vibrant
③ peevish
④ effusive

**07** The farmers fear that the previous night's frost had <u>blighted</u> the potato crops entirely.
① damaged
② fertilized
③ sanitized
④ cultivated

**08** The show <u>took a nosedive</u> this season, a victim of too much hype and a repetitive format.
① flourished
② finished
③ remained
④ plummeted

**09** In the musician's mind a <u>fugitive</u> set of notes began slowly to form into a tune.
① melodious
② temporary
③ awe-inspiring
④ of real value

**10** It is the worship of money that I wish to consider: the belief that all values may be measured in terms of money, and that money is the ultimate <u>touchstone</u> of success in life.
① test
② source
③ challenge
④ objective

11 All such communicative events are <u>punctuated</u> routinely by various units of traditional material that are memorable and repeatable.
① described      ② articulated
③ emphasized      ④ addressed

12 What do a rabbit, a bee, an apple, a pine cone, and a buttercup have in common? A <u>cursory</u> glance doesn't reveal much in common.
① staring      ② probing
③ casual      ④ precise

13 Saussure's 1916 book, *Cours de linguistique générale*, inspired Guillaume, as it did Jakobson, not to be an <u>indoctrinated</u> follower but to go beyond Saussure's seminal ideas.
① inculcated      ② incarnated
③ inflected      ④ inseminated

14 What went wrong was a combination of the storm's bad timing and the <u>hubris</u> of the residents who thought they were immune to the realities of bad weather.
① indecency      ② hauteur
③ blandishment      ④ larceny

15 Liberty is the Englishman's <u>prerogative</u>; we must preserve that at the expense of our life.
① prejudice      ② prediction
③ project      ④ privilege

16 Jeremy hated his neighbor's <u>unkempt</u> lawn: he thought its neglected appearance had a detrimental effect on neighborhood property values.
① truncated      ② redolent
③ disheveled      ④ unwitting

17 Our website <u>compiles</u> news headlines and summaries from other sources, and it allows you to scan them all in one place.
① copies      ② remits
③ delivers      ④ edits

18 The message from the union was <u>succinct</u>: no workers would report for work the next day.
① tedious      ② tardy
③ brief      ④ final

19 Well aware of the threat from unpredictable dictatorships <u>wielding</u> missiles and weapons of mass destruction, he had not expected to be fighting a war within a year of taking office.
① using      ② hiding
③ covering      ④ wanting

20 John used to be laid back and easygoing, but since his parents' divorce he is <u>captious</u> about everything.
① arduous      ② complacent
③ quibbling      ④ supercilious

21 Homo sapiens is a storytelling animal that thinks in stories rather than in numbers and graphs. We believe that the universe itself works like a story, replete with heroes and villains, conflicts and resolutions, climaxes and happy endings.

① related       ② drawn

③ constructed    ④ filled

22 He stopped, stupefied and utterly at a loss when he saw that his wife was beginning to cry.

① stunned       ② elated

③ enjoyed       ④ beamed

23 The crowd gathered at the city center were boisterous to say the least; they were in no mood for observing holiday commemoration.

① somber       ② bizarre

③ flamboyant    ④ rowdy

24 Doctors inject thin needles filled with a chemical solution into unsightly veins, causing them to shrink and become normalized again.

① faint        ② clogged

③ invisible      ④ repulsive

25 The freeze on population funds was a catastrophe for poor women and their children.

① disaster      ② blessing

③ surprise      ④ disappointment

26 I hope you do not bear me any grudge.

① unfriendly feelings

② bad conscience

③ material loss

④ secret suspicion

27 Overweening personal ambition is no virtue; but while I had it, I could have danced on a bed of nails.

① Persuasive     ② Elegant

③ Categorical     ④ Immoderate

28 This was accomplished by inoculating material from the brains of individuals who had died of a disease named kuru into the brains of three female chimpanzees.

① transforming    ② extricating

③ vaccinating     ④ impinging

29 Precision oncology will benefit around 1.5% of patients with relapsed and refractory solid tumours.

① mutable       ② manipulative

③ inevitable     ④ intractable

30 The didactic goal of the documentary *The Idea of North* is one of the main distinctions between *North* and a musical composition.

① dialectic      ② preachy

③ nebulous      ④ discerning

31 The child's misdemeanor was never taken seriously by his parents.

① sickness

② wrong doings

③ mistakes

④ rude words

32 The two students responsible for the racist incidents of last spring have already suffered public obloquy.
① disgrace          ② eulogy
③ soliloquy         ④ oblivion

33 In most cases of family conflict, repair is possible and preferable to estrangement.
① errand           ② establishment
③ reconciliation    ④ distancing

34 As an act of solidarity with his fellow employees, the president of the company volunteered to forgo his salary.
① renege           ② bestow
③ dole             ④ waive

35 All behaviors have an inherited basis, but strictly speaking it is only a potentiality that is inherited.
① learnability      ② possibility
③ likeness          ④ quantity

36 He enjoys watching sports games on TV for vicarious pleasure, for he wanted to be a football star in his youth.
① precious          ② vigorous
③ substitute        ④ indispensable

37 All the countries have proclaimed their loyalty to the alliance.
① forsaken          ② declared
③ declaimed         ④ provoked

38 Employees who consistently arrive to work late may be formally reprimanded by their supervisor.
① undermined       ② ridiculed
③ admonished       ④ discharged

39 Just as her work has given voice to this little-remarked facet of African-American culture, it has affirmed the unique vantage point of the black woman.
① restoration       ② embellishment
③ decadence         ④ aspect

40 A life of indulgence, a "gay life," as it is falsely called, is a miserable mockery of happiness.
① frugality          ② discipline
③ luxury            ④ complaint

41 Pop culture knows that people love nothing more than imagining their own demise.
① death             ② fame
③ heritage          ④ vanity

42 The first germ-line gene manipulations are unlikely to be attempted for frivolous reasons.
① personal          ② experimental
③ fallacious         ④ imprudent

43 Britain's trading company, the Hudson Bay Company, wanted to secure a foothold in Alaska's fur-trade market.
① lock              ② obtain
③ tighten           ④ keep

44 Schlosser doesn't <u>mince</u> words when it comes to E. coli contamination. He says it like it is: Manure gets mixed with meat.
① coin
② experiment
③ emphasize
④ mitigate

45 This murky history helps explain why the book describes what the Venetian could not possibly have seen, and <u>overlooks</u> sights that any traveler to China must have witnessed — like the Great Wall, foot-binding and chopsticks.
① scrutinizes
② glances at
③ recollects
④ passes over

46 In order to live longer, you should have <u>abstemious</u> habits.
① typical
② inconsistent
③ abstinent
④ indulgent

47 Increasing fuel prices will have <u>dire</u> consequences for the poor.
① terrible
② beneficial
③ desirable
④ tangible

48 The open-air garden is accessible to the public and will most likely establish itself as a convenient gathering place in midtown in <u>clement</u> weather.
① abrupt
② circuitous
③ moderate
④ prodigious

49 The confession of one prisoner <u>exonerated</u> the other suspects.
① infuriated
② denounced
③ condemned
④ acquitted

50 The crowd in the stadium is <u>gradually</u> getting bigger.
① in general
② at once
③ by degrees
④ for good

51 A substance was generously applied to the open wound to <u>coagulate</u> the blood.
① consecrate
② contaminate
③ constrain
④ congeal

52 If she undertakes to make full <u>restitution</u> and you can verify that she is doing so, your problem is solved.
① reparation
② restraint
③ repentance
④ replacement

53 Marine ecologists claim that the number of the great white sharks will inevitably dwindle unless <u>prudent</u> controls are enacted.
① legal
② sensible
③ massive
④ timely

54 Be sure to maintain a positive image of your company. Mindless, <u>insipid</u> advertising can make clients turn away.
① incipient
② boring
③ impudent
④ rash

55 A large percentage of these adolescents have <u>assimilated</u> into American society with little or no knowledge of their countries of origin.
① infused
② imbued
③ absorbed
④ arrived

56 The president is the only person authorized to <u>dictate</u> policy.

① underscore     ② deposit

③ dispatch     ④ decree

57 Beijing describes the group as an "evil cult" with <u>subversive</u> intentions.

① lukewarm     ② rebellious

③ sinister     ④ vicious

58 He made <u>an acrid</u> attack on American imperialism.

① a complete     ② an undeniable

③ a pungent     ④ a vigorous

59 When you're feeling <u>under the weather</u>, there's nothing better than climbing into bed with a mug of something hot.

① unwell     ② anxious

③ isolated     ④ uplifting

60 The successful salesman is always <u>punctual</u> for his appointments.

① on time     ② prepared

③ anxious     ④ anticipating

61 Early on, Mrs Guigou sought to distract attention from her looks with seriousness, rigour and — toward <u>importunate</u> men — icy disdain.

① troublesome

② brutal

③ condescending

④ disrespectful

62 This new building is not firm enough to <u>withstand</u> the total weight of the key structure and other subsidiary supportive equipment.

① project     ② array

③ endure     ④ ignite

63 Virtual reality holds exciting potential for 'exposure therapy,' in which patients are encouraged to relive <u>traumatic</u> memories.

① painful     ② puerile

③ hallucinatory     ④ drastic

64 The <u>schism</u> is sharply felt in Jerusalem, known for its conservative and religious populations.

① deviation     ② split

③ encroachment     ④ mediation

65 How many women still <u>collude</u> in the myth of male superiority, believing it's "nicer" when boys and men finish first?

① collide     ② confer

③ connive     ④ convert

66 Ice shelves, yet unpolluted <u>pristine</u> compositions, tend to be the most commonly studied glacial formation.

① immaculate     ② barren

③ mellow     ④ stale

67 After she <u>acquiesced</u> on her employer's suggestions, things went much more smoothly.

① consented     ② disagreed

③ complimented     ④ revised

68 Japan promised Wednesday to hand over two anti-whale activists who were seized after they leapt aboard a harpoon ship in icy Antarctic waters, but a standoff quickly emerged as the sides traded accusations of piracy on the high seas.

① deadlock      ② equilibrium

③ decisiveness      ④ tranquility

69 In the northeastern United States, it rains intermittently throughout the spring.

① abundantly      ② steadily

③ periodically      ④ daily

70 The former government minister was sentenced to 18 months imprisonment for perjury and attempting to pervert the course of justice.

① delay      ② resolve

③ distort      ④ modify

71 Discourse analysis is uniquely heterogeneous among the many subdisciplines of linguistics.

① ubiquitous      ② genealogical

③ diverse      ④ logical

72 A convivial host, Drew interacted with all his friends and acquaintances who came to his party.

① jolly      ② complicated

③ moody      ④ enigmatic

73 She can deploy the conventional cultural referent of the voluble woman in a comic frame.

① glib      ② sumptuous

③ taciturn      ④ wily

74 The 21st century has already been proclaimed the "Chinese century," and shock waves from China's frenzied entrepreneurialism, manufacturing prowess and low-cost labor are rocking industries throughout the world.

① affordability      ② diversity

③ skill      ④ individuality

75 He looked at me very blankly and tiredly, then said, having to share his worry with someone.

① easily      ② vacantly

③ shortly      ④ perfidiously

76 "We'll try it," the professor said to me grimly, "with every adjustment of the microscope known to man."

① wisely      ② kindly

③ sternly      ④ drily

77 Some survey questions are designed to elicit the malediction from the followers.

① contumacy      ② acclamation

③ acclimation      ④ slander

78 Conservatives often forsake the principle of states' rights when it does not fit their ideological goals.

① abandon      ② embrace

③ interpret      ④ impose

79 When Warren Buffett makes investments in struggling companies that eventually turnaround, he is lauded as an astute investor and reaps billions in profits.

① amicable      ② inert

③ shrewd      ④ speculative

80 AI can take the drudgery out of mundane jobs such as office administration.
① contemplation ② toil
③ agility ④ strife

81 Diderot paid tribute to role of women as interlocutors in shaping the intellectual conventions of the age.
① spectators ② speculators
③ efficient clerks ④ conversationalists

82 The firm he heads, which he joined straight out of high school, has the requisite pedigree: it is the oldest bicycle manufacturer in the Bicycle Kingdom.
① asset ② condition
③ honour ④ breed

83 The cause of the common cold has continuously stymied scientists.
① worried ② amazed
③ thwarted ④ motivated

84 Placing blame on the news media, he delivered a discursive, defensive analysis of why he was not responsible for dividing Americans.
① ebullient ② incoherent
③ somnolent ④ obdurate

85 You can never be an ingrate to your parents.
① a libertine
② an ungrateful person
③ an enemy
④ a betrayer

86 As diverse as it is vast, China encompasses myriad terrains and cultures. While the nation's ultra-modern, hyper-connected major cities are advancing to the future, time feels suspended in the open countryside that remains rooted in tradition.
① dismissed ② postponed
③ prevented ④ stopped

87 Stronger commitment was promised for digital technologies, particularly services and devices to speed the convergence between broadcasting and telecommunications.
① congregation ② optimum
③ union ④ renovation

88 Those patients who carried contagious diseases were clustered, so they were quarantined from other patients.
① coalesced ② curtailed
③ protracted ④ segregated

89 Abercrombie & Fitch's skin-filled ads and nightclub vibration delighted American teenagers and infuriated parents.
① amused ② enraged
③ summoned ④ motivated

90 Chaucer not only came to doubt the worth of his extraordinary body of work but repudiated it.
① reinterpreted ② revised
③ rejuvenated ④ renounced

91 The couples had a great time dancing to such vivacious music.
① tired      ② gloomy
③ lively      ④ easily

92 Affirmative action programs to improve women's and minority groups' access to education have proliferated since the early 1970s. At the primary and secondary levels of public education, affirmative action first led to a redesigning of teaching programs and textbooks.
① declined      ② improved
③ deteriorated      ④ multiplied

93 Convicted thieves and counterfeiters often received the death penalty, which was thought to be a deterrent to other criminals.
① beacon      ② amphibian
③ eminence      ④ hindrance

94 The scrupulous care he put into his work helped him advance at the company.
① unrelenting      ② obsessive
③ escalating      ④ meticulous

95 There was a state of tremulous excitement for him when he found the map in the cave.
① fleeting      ② trembling
③ traumatic      ④ facetious

96 The soul is placed in the body like a rough diamond, and must be polished, or the luster of it will never appear.
① sheen      ② immortality
③ vanity      ④ rapture

97 Property owners sometimes unwittingly find themselves facing civil and criminal penalties because they didn't secure a permit for engaging in even normal activities like farming or homebuilding.
① thoroughly      ② sternly
③ punctiliously      ④ involuntarily

98 Many people who were somewhat "wishy-washy" about politics are now more committed towards the goal of genuine democracy.
① liberal      ② indecisive
③ apathetic      ④ conclusive

99 To Americans able to pay their debt to government agencies, such penalties, which can range from a few dollars to hundreds, are a minor nuisance.
① impasse      ② barrier
③ annoyance      ④ grievance

100 She was charged with aiding and abetting the burglar because she drove the getaway car.
① inciting      ② imitating
③ chasing      ④ defrauding

[1] Write the meaning of the following words.

| | |
|---|---|
| ☐ harvest | ☐ ambidextrous |
| ☐ inscrutable | ☐ mudslinging |
| ☐ crescendo | ☐ libido |
| ☐ preeminent | ☐ groove |
| ☐ encourage | ☐ correlation |
| ☐ axiom | ☐ reject |
| ☐ prick | ☐ foolproof |
| ☐ string | ☐ discount |
| ☐ depraved | ☐ blasphemy |
| ☐ treasury | ☐ outlet |
| ☐ vociferous | ☐ minimal |
| ☐ ablation | ☐ dungeon |
| ☐ prod | ☐ wrangle |
| ☐ concerned | ☐ tumor |
| ☐ rubbish | ☐ fraternal |
| ☐ diagonal | ☐ elocution |
| ☐ simulate | ☐ vice versa |
| ☐ bureaucracy | ☐ juice |
| ☐ finicky | ☐ opt |
| ☐ coddle | ☐ contraption |
| ☐ intimacy | ☐ allude |
| ☐ sweltering | ☐ sequela |
| ☐ exculpate | ☐ glamorous |
| ☐ static | ☐ barnstorm |
| ☐ patch | ☐ retroactive |

[2] Select <u>the most</u> appropriate word from the box below. Each word should be used only once.

| | | | |
|---|---|---|---|
| ① encourage | ② vociferous | ③ exculpate | ④ intimacy |
| ⑤ static | ⑥ groove | ⑦ elocution | ⑧ blasphemy |
| ⑨ inscrutable | ⑩ concerned | ⑪ allude | ⑫ preeminent |
| ⑬ ambidexterity | ⑭ axiom | ⑮ diagonal | ⑯ reject |
| ⑰ fraternal | ⑱ coddle | ⑲ foolproof | ⑳ prod |

1   The candidate's _____ speeches captivated the audience as his forceful and vehement delivery resonated with unwavering conviction.

2   Some individuals believe that constant attention and overprotection can inadvertently _____ the ones they care about.

3   The artist's intentions behind the abstract painting were _____, leaving viewers puzzled by the meaning hidden within its intricate layers.

4   In a long-term relationship, building trust and fostering emotional _____ are essential for maintaining a strong and meaningful connection between partners.

5   The lawyer presented compelling evidence to _____ her client, demonstrating the innocence of the accused beyond any reasonable doubt.

6   Hawkins is _____ in his field; no other contemporary scientist commands the same respect.

7   Most Americans are accustomed to thinking of lie detectors as _____ — as machines that can, without error, separate the guilty from the innocent.

8   The playwright's depiction of sacred themes in a comedic light was considered by many devote Christians as a form of outright _____.

9   The pianist's effortless transition between left and right hands while playing the complex piece showcased a remarkable level of _____.

10  The teacher's thought-provoking questions aimed to _____ into the students' critical thinking.

[3] Choose the one which is different from the others.

**11** ① depraved     ② genteel     ③ wicked     ④ immoral

**12** ① squeamish     ② fastidious     ③ finicky     ④ fictitious

**13** ① swath     ② sweltering     ③ sultry     ④ scorching

**14** ① slander     ② mudslinging     ③ moniker     ④ vilification

**15** ① dispute     ② quarrel     ③ wrangle     ④ concur

**16** ① glamorous     ② clamorous     ③ alluring     ④ charming

**17** ① yield     ② simulate     ③ pretend     ④ feign

**18** ① essence     ② core     ③ juice     ④ sedative

**19** ① gadget     ② contraption     ③ provision     ④ gizmo

**20** ① opt     ② dismiss     ③ choose     ④ select

## ✓ Answers

**1** ② ┃ 후보자의 큰 소리로 외치는 연설은 그의 힘차고 열정적인 연설이 흔들리지 않는 신념으로 가득했기 때문에 청중을 사로잡았다.

**2** ⑱ ┃ 어떤 사람들은 지속적인 관심과 과잉보호가 그들이 아끼는 사람을 자기도 모르게 응석받이로 기를 수 있다고 생각한다.

**3** ⑨ ┃ 추상화에 숨겨진 화가의 의도는 알 수 없었고, 복잡하게 층을 이루어 그려진 그림의 숨겨진 의미에 대해 관객들은 어리둥절해졌다.

**4** ④ ┃ 장기적인 관계에서 신뢰를 구축하고 정서적 친밀감을 조성하는 것은 파트너 간의 강력하고 의미 있는 관계를 유지하기 위해 필수적이다.

**5** ③ ┃ 그 변호사는 자신의 의뢰인의 무죄를 증명할 확실한 증거를 제시했고, 피고인의 무죄를 조금도 의심의 여지없이 증명했다.

**6** ⑫ ┃ 호킨스(Hawkins)는 그의 분야에서 탁월하다. 다른 어떤 현대 과학자도 그와 같은 존경을 받지 못한다.

**7** ⑲ ┃ 대부분의 미국인은 거짓말 탐지기를 확실한 것으로, 즉 오류 없이 유죄와 무죄를 구분할 수 있는 기계로 생각하는 데 익숙해져 있다.

**8** ⑧ ┃ 이 극작가가 신성한 주제를 희극적인 관점에서 묘사한 것을 많은 독실한 기독교인들은 노골적인 신성모독의 한 형태로 간주했다.

**9** ⑬ ┃ 복잡한 곡을 연주하는 동안 피아니스트가 왼손과 오른손 사이를 힘들이지 않고 전환하는 것은 놀라운 수준의 양손잡이 능력을 보여주었다.

**10** ⑳ ┃ 선생님의 생각을 자극하는 질문은 학생들의 비판적 사고를 불러일으키는 것을 목표로 했다.

**11** ②    **12** ④    **13** ①    **14** ③    **15** ④    **16** ②    **17** ①    **18** ④    **19** ③    **20** ②

☑ **DAILY CHECKUP**

[1] Write the meaning of the following words.

| | |
|---|---|
| ☐ intact | ☐ carnal |
| ☐ squander | ☐ surrender |
| ☐ detour | ☐ fluid |
| ☐ plaudit | ☐ angular |
| ☐ counsel | ☐ reclaim |
| ☐ trenchant | ☐ lash |
| ☐ subpoena | ☐ resilient |
| ☐ repel | ☐ dampen |
| ☐ viewpoint | ☐ gist |
| ☐ inviting | ☐ provincial |
| ☐ shove | ☐ cringe |
| ☐ affront | ☐ extrovert |
| ☐ cerebral | ☐ addle |
| ☐ betroth | ☐ wan |
| ☐ fraudulent | ☐ moiety |
| ☐ eradicate | ☐ almighty |
| ☐ cemetery | ☐ unify |
| ☐ dispassionate | ☐ tariff |
| ☐ pulse | ☐ devour |
| ☐ substantive | ☐ syndrome |
| ☐ goad | ☐ nimble |
| ☐ conviction | ☐ pork |
| ☐ hoary | ☐ burrow |
| ☐ ellipsis | ☐ fade |
| ☐ inundate | ☐ ordinance |

[2] Select <u>the most</u> appropriate word from the box below. Each word should be used only once.

| | | | |
|---|---|---|---|
| ① detour | ② substantive | ③ carnal | ④ squandered |
| ⑤ reclaimed | ⑥ trenchant | ⑦ almighty | ⑧ fade |
| ⑨ cringe | ⑩ devour | ⑪ provincial | ⑫ inundated |
| ⑬ subpoena | ⑭ inviting | ⑮ eradicate | ⑯ extrovert |
| ⑰ intact | ⑱ nimble | ⑲ addled | ⑳ resilient |

1  The critic's _____ review dissected the film's flaws with precise and cutting commentary.

2  He collected at least $500,000 from the score but had a gambling problem and _____ it away at the racetrack.

3  The public health initiative aimed to _____ infectious diseases by implementing widespread vaccination programs and stringent hygiene practices.

4  The small town was completely _____ by the unexpected influx of tourists during the festival, causing a strain on available accommodations.

5  This rubber ball is very _____ and immediately springs back into shape after you've squashed it.

6  Over time, memories of certain experiences tend to _____ and become less vivid in one's recollection.

7  The dinosaur's fossilized skeleton is one of the most complete and best preserved dinosaurs ever found with skull and three-meter tail _____.

8  The massive wildfire seemed to _____ everything in its path, leaving a trail of destruction across the forest.

9  Messi's _____ footwork on the soccer field allowed him to swiftly maneuver around opponents.

10  The road was closed for repairs, so the driver had to take a(n) _____ to reach his destination.

[3] Choose the one which is different from the others.

| 11 | ① flattery | ② affront | ③ indignity | ④ slight |
| 12 | ① plaudit | ② acclaim | ③ praise | ④ innuendo |
| 13 | ① deceitful | ② fraudulent | ③ versatile | ④ dishonest |
| 14 | ① detached | ② impartial | ③ dispassionate | ④ dainty |
| 15 | ① soothe | ② goad | ③ provoke | ④ urge |
| 16 | ① succumb | ② retrieve | ③ surrender | ④ capitulate |
| 17 | ① pallid | ② pale | ③ unctuous | ④ wan |
| 18 | ① ordinance | ② decree | ③ enactment | ④ veto |
| 19 | ① chastise | ② dig | ③ excavate | ④ burrow |
| 20 | ① depress | ② covet | ③ dampen | ④ discourage |

## ✔ Answers

1 ⑥ | 비평가의 날카로운 평론은 정확하고 신랄한 논평으로 영화의 결점을 상세히 분석했다.

2 ④ | 그는 그 작품으로 적어도 5십만 달러를 모았지만 도박 문제가 있어서 그 돈을 경마장에서 탕진했다.

3 ⑮ | 공중보건 계획은 광범위한 예방접종 프로그램과 엄격한 위생을 실천함으로써 전염병을 박멸하는 것을 목표로 했다.

4 ⑫ | 그 작은 마을은 축제 기간 동안 예상치 못하게 유입된 관광객들로 완전히 넘쳤고, 이로 인해 이용할 수 있는 숙박 시설에 부담이 되었다.

5 ⑳ | 이 고무공은 매우 탄력성이 좋아서 짓누른 후에 곧바로 제 모양으로 되돌아온다.

6 ⑧ | 시간이 지남에 따라 특정 경험에 대한 기억은 희미해지는 경향이 있으며 기억이 덜 생생해진다.

7 ⑰ | 그 공룡의 화석화된 뼈대는 지금껏 발견된 가장 완전하고 가장 잘 보존된 공룡들 중 하나인데, 두개골과 3미터에 달하는 꼬리는 훼손되지 않고 본래대로 있다.

8 ⑩ | 거대한 산불은 그 길에 있는 모든 것을 집어삼키는 것처럼 보였으며, 숲 전체에 파괴의 흔적을 남겼다.

9 ⑱ | 메시(Messi)는 축구장에서 민첩한 발기술로 재빠르게 상대 선수들을 따돌리고 빠져나갈 수 있었다.

10 ① | 도로가 수리를 위해 통행이 중단되었기 때문에 운전자는 목적지에 도착하기 위해 우회해야 했다.

11 ①    12 ④    13 ③    14 ④    15 ①    16 ②    17 ③    18 ④    19 ①    20 ②

[1] Write the meaning of the following words.

| | |
|---|---|
| ☐ gratuitous | ☐ apposite |
| ☐ expatiate | ☐ jumble |
| ☐ archive | ☐ miscegenation |
| ☐ concrete | ☐ term |
| ☐ reprisal | ☐ dogged |
| ☐ passe | ☐ advance |
| ☐ instantaneous | ☐ scurry |
| ☐ deteriorate | ☐ covenant |
| ☐ methodical | ☐ nuptial |
| ☐ circumvent | ☐ register |
| ☐ bauble | ☐ gumption |
| ☐ intramural | ☐ fleeting |
| ☐ directory | ☐ outbreak |
| ☐ thrust | ☐ bruise |
| ☐ extraneous | ☐ sermon |
| ☐ feces | ☐ catchy |
| ☐ supercilious | ☐ premise |
| ☐ legislature | ☐ interchange |
| ☐ butcher | ☐ cooperation |
| ☐ pole | ☐ helluva |
| ☐ snort | ☐ espionage |
| ☐ wistful | ☐ roam |
| ☐ examine | ☐ alloy |
| ☐ stolid | ☐ cul-de-sac |
| ☐ proviso | ☐ vapid |

[2] Select <u>the most</u> appropriate word from the box below. Each word should be used only once.

| | | | |
|---|---|---|---|
| ① gratuitous | ② nuptial | ③ extraneous | ④ sermon |
| ⑤ bruise | ⑥ espionage | ⑦ outbreak | ⑧ supercilious |
| ⑨ proviso | ⑩ bauble | ⑪ gumption | ⑫ interchange |
| ⑬ alloy | ⑭ dogged | ⑮ circumvent | ⑯ register |
| ⑰ helluva | ⑱ catchy | ⑲ examine | ⑳ snort |

1    The resourceful hacker sought ways to _____ the security measures, gaining unauthorized access to the system.

2    The basic law of the universe is economy. The universe does not waste a single quark; all serves a purpose and fits into a balance — there are no _____ events.

3    The aristocrats' _____ attitude made others feel belittled as they often displayed an air of superiority in their interactions.

4    The contract included a crucial _____ that outlined specific conditions under which the agreement could be terminated or modified.

5    Despite facing numerous obstacles, her _____ determination enabled her to persistently pursue her goals until she achieved success.

6    Manning was found guilty of _____ and theft in 2013 and was sentenced to 35 years in prison after she leaked classified documents to a hostile country.

7    The health department swiftly responded to the sudden _____ of a contagious virus, implementing preventive measures to contain its spread within the community.

8    The entrepreneur's success was not solely due to her intelligence but also to her unwavering determination and sheer _____ to overcome obstacles.

9    Jewelry usually contains 14 or 18 karats of gold _____ and rarely is fashioned of pure gold.

10   The advertising jingle had a(n) _____ tune that lingered in people's minds long after they heard it.

**[3] Choose the one which is different from the others.**

| 11 | ① prompt | ② instantaneous | ③ immediate | ④ instinctive |
| 12 | ① reprisal | ② reprieve | ③ retaliation | ④ revenge |
| 13 | ① excoriate | ② elaborate | ③ expatiate | ④ expound |
| 14 | ① obtuse | ② dull | ③ stolid | ④ stupendous |
| 15 | ① transitory | ② fleeting | ③ perpetual | ④ ephemeral |
| 16 | ① cul-de-sac | ② waiver | ③ dead end | ④ impasse |
| 17 | ① ransack | ② roam | ③ ramble | ④ saunter |
| 18 | ① scuttle | ② disembark | ③ hasten | ④ scurry |
| 19 | ① obsolete | ② passe | ③ predictable | ④ outdated |
| 20 | ① disorder | ② confuse | ③ jumble | ④ untangle |

[1] Write the meaning of the following words.

| | |
|---|---|
| ☐ fortify | ☐ shear |
| ☐ imbecile | ☐ infraction |
| ☐ aphasia | ☐ outgoing |
| ☐ supersede | ☐ extol |
| ☐ distinct | ☐ battalion |
| ☐ relic | ☐ wheedle |
| ☐ prevent | ☐ homage |
| ☐ craven | ☐ lurk |
| ☐ strife | ☐ enclave |
| ☐ accede | ☐ cede |
| ☐ emission | ☐ vivid |
| ☐ disparage | ☐ prophet |
| ☐ chore | ☐ truncate |
| ☐ noisome | ☐ stellar |
| ☐ concept | ☐ initiative |
| ☐ buff | ☐ utensil |
| ☐ develop | ☐ picaresque |
| ☐ prolix | ☐ confuse |
| ☐ mortician | ☐ remunerative |
| ☐ rescind | ☐ dystopia |
| ☐ tribe | ☐ blaze |
| ☐ covert | ☐ fracture |
| ☐ gesticulate | ☐ ape |
| ☐ avaricious | ☐ contrive |
| ☐ mite | ☐ gigantic |

[2] Select <u>the most</u> appropriate word from the box below. Each word should be used only once.

| | | | |
|---|---|---|---|
| ① disparage | ② truncated | ③ outgoing | ④ covert |
| ⑤ ceded | ⑥ craven | ⑦ imbecile | ⑧ superseded |
| ⑨ prolix | ⑩ prevent | ⑪ picaresque | ⑫ distinct |
| ⑬ acceded | ⑭ wheedle | ⑮ noisome | ⑯ gigantic |
| ⑰ remunerative | ⑱ rescinded | ⑲ vivid | ⑳ lurk |

1    As technology advances, older models of computers are gradually _____ by more efficient and powerful versions.

2    He is an American hero who saved American lives by killing the enemy. Now, after his death, some people _____ him by calling him a killer when what they should be doing is thanking him.

3    In the face of adversity, rather than showing courage, he displayed a(n) _____ reluctance to confront the challenges ahead.

4    The garbage left unattended for weeks emitted a(n) _____ stench that permeated the entire neighborhood.

5    Her writing style, while informative, tended to be excessively _____, often making it challenging for readers to follow her ideas concisely.

6    The approval for the project was suddenly _____ when new information surfaced about its potential risks.

7    The salesman tried to _____ the hesitant customer into purchasing the product by highlighting its numerous benefits and discounts.

8    In the online world, potential risks and threats may _____ in seemingly harmless corners of the internet.

9    In the competitive job market, individuals often seek positions that offer _____ compensation packages to ensure financial stability and growth.

10   Soldiers might take part in a(n) _____ mission to infiltrate an enemy camp.

**[3] Choose the one which is different from the others.**

**11** ① fortify      ② reinforce      ③ plunge      ④ strengthen

**12** ① conflict      ② discord      ③ strife      ④ truce

**13** ① buff      ② detractor      ③ aficionado      ④ enthusiast

**14** ① inspired      ② avaricious      ③ acquisitive      ④ greedy

**15** ① infringement      ② breach      ③ incursion      ④ infraction

**16** ① exalt      ② admire      ③ extol      ④ castigate

**17** ① homage      ② intrusion      ③ respect      ④ deference

**18** ① raze      ② contrive      ③ concoct      ④ fabricate

**19** ① leading      ② stellar      ③ scenic      ④ outstanding

**20** ① relic      ② artifact      ③ remnant      ④ asset

## ✔ Answers

**1** ⑧ | 기술이 발전함에 따라 오래된 컴퓨터 모델은 더 효율적이고 강력한 버전으로 점점 대체된다.

**2** ① | 그는 적을 죽여서 미국인들의 생명을 구한 미국의 영웅이다. 그가 죽고 난 지금, 일부 사람들은 그에게 감사해야 하는데도 그를 살인자라고 부름으로써 그의 명예를 해치고 있다.

**3** ⑥ | 그는 역경에 직면하여 용기를 보여주기보다는 앞으로 있을 도전을 맞서는 데 비겁하게 주저하는 모습을 보였다.

**4** ⑮ | 몇 주 동안 방치된 쓰레기는 동네 전체에 고약한 악취를 풍겼다.

**5** ⑨ | 그녀의 문체는 유익하지만 지나치게 장황한 경향이 있어 종종 독자들이 그녀의 생각을 간결하게 따라가는 것을 어렵게 만든다.

**6** ⑱ | 잠재적 위험에 대한 새로운 정보가 공개되자 프로젝트 승인이 갑자기 취소되었다.

**7** ⑭ | 판매원은 제품의 다양한 혜택과 할인 혜택을 강조함으로써 망설이는 고객을 설득하여 제품을 구매하도록 노력했다.

**8** ⑳ | 온라인 세계에서는 무해해 보이는 인터넷 구석구석에 잠재적인 위험과 위협이 숨어 있을 수 있다.

**9** ⑰ | 경쟁이 치열한 취업 시장에서 개인은 재정적 안정과 성장을 확보하기 위해 유리한 (급여와 복리후생을 포함한) 보상 패키지를 제공하는 자리를 찾는 경우가 많다.

**10** ④ | 병사들은 적진에 잠입하기 위한 비밀 임무에 참여할 수 있다.

- - - - - - - - - - - - - - - - - - - - - - - - - - - - - - - - - - - - - - - - - - - - - - - - -

**11** ③    **12** ④    **13** ②    **14** ①    **15** ③    **16** ④    **17** ②    **18** ①    **19** ③    **20** ④

[1] Write the meaning of the following words.

| | |
|---|---|
| ☐ vindictive | ☐ refurbish |
| ☐ burlesque | ☐ sterile |
| ☐ egotism | ☐ dusk |
| ☐ ad hoc | ☐ futile |
| ☐ crackdown | ☐ conundrum |
| ☐ instill | ☐ throttle |
| ☐ locomotion | ☐ bloated |
| ☐ matter | ☐ mortuary |
| ☐ palsy | ☐ gregarious |
| ☐ cunning | ☐ swirl |
| ☐ protocol | ☐ idiom |
| ☐ quote | ☐ cloak |
| ☐ squirt | ☐ fortnight |
| ☐ inconceivable | ☐ ascend |
| ☐ exult | ☐ entire |
| ☐ arbor | ☐ precocious |
| ☐ defile | ☐ rowdy |
| ☐ repugnant | ☐ broach |
| ☐ purify | ☐ sublime |
| ☐ wig | ☐ reference |
| ☐ milk | ☐ overrun |
| ☐ coordination | ☐ vessel |
| ☐ high-handed | ☐ distill |
| ☐ suffer | ☐ evade |
| ☐ kudos | ☐ tribunal |

[2] Select the most appropriate word from the box below. Each word should be used only once.

| | | | |
|---|---|---|---|
| ① locomotion | ② egotism | ③ purify | ④ precocious |
| ⑤ broach | ⑥ sublime | ⑦ exult | ⑧ evade |
| ⑨ sterile | ⑩ rowdy | ⑪ distill | ⑫ defile |
| ⑬ overrun | ⑭ futile | ⑮ conundrum | ⑯ ascend |
| ⑰ refurbish | ⑱ crackdown | ⑲ quote | ⑳ gregarious |

1    Her constant bragging and self-centered behavior were clear indications of her excessive _____.

2    As the final buzzer sounded, the team members began to _____, celebrating their hard-fought victory on the field.

3    The intention to _____ the sacred ground with disrespectful actions deeply offended those who revered the site for its sanctity and purity.

4    Some people came to dominate other people, and the domination was inevitable. Therefore, it would be _____ to try to change the domination today.

5    A solution that kills bacteria can be sprayed to create a(n) _____ surface for safe food preparation.

6    The ancient text's intricate _____ remained an unsolved mystery that challenged scholars and historians for centuries.

7    Unlike the _____ Capote, who was never happier than when he was in the center of a crowd of celebrities, Faulkner, in later years, grew somewhat reclusive and shunned company.

8    The classroom became quite _____ when the substitute teacher struggled to maintain order amidst the students' playful banter and excitement.

9    The fugitive attempted to _____ capture by changing identities and moving stealthily from one city to another.

10    The company invested in a significant effort to _____ its aging infrastructure.

[3] Choose the one which is different from the others.

**11** ① instill    ② imbue    ③ uproot    ④ inculcate

**12** ① provisional    ② makeshift    ③ ad hoc    ④ painstaking

**13** ① gullible    ② cunning    ③ crafty    ④ wily

**14** ① repugnant    ② reverent    ③ abhorrent    ④ obnoxious

**15** ① autocratic    ② high-handed    ③ circumspect    ④ overbearing

**16** ① credit    ② applause    ③ kudos    ④ inertia

**17** ① haughty    ② shrunken    ③ bloated    ④ arrogant

**18** ① encourage    ② throttle    ③ stifle    ④ strangle

**19** ① retaliatory    ② vindictive    ③ sympathetic    ④ revengeful

**20** ① lampoon    ② farce    ③ burlesque    ④ recitation

## ✓ Answers

**1** ②    | 그녀의 끊임없는 자랑과 자기중심적인 행동은 그녀의 지나친 이기주의를 분명히 보여주는 것이었다.

**2** ⑦    | 경기를 종료하는 버저가 울리자 팀원들은 경기장에서 힘든 경기의 승리를 축하하며 기뻐하기 시작했다.

**3** ⑫    | 성지를 무례한 행동으로 모독하려는 의도는 그곳의 신성함과 순수함을 경외하는 사람들의 기분을 몹시 상하게 했다.

**4** ⑭    | 일부 사람들이 다른 사람들을 지배하게 되었으며, 그 지배는 불가피했다. 따라서 오늘날 그 지배를 바꾸려고 애를 써봐야 소용없을 것이다.

**5** ⑨    | 박테리아를 죽이는 용액을 뿌려 안전한 음식 준비를 위해 살균한 표면을 만들 수 있다.

**6** ⑮    | 고대 문헌의 복잡한 수수께끼는 수세기 동안 학자와 역사가들에게 도전을 안겨준 풀리지 않은 미스터리로 남아 있었다.

**7** ⑳    | 명사(名士)들의 무리 한 가운데 있을 때 가장 행복해했던, 사교적인 카포티(Capote)와는 달리, 포크너(Faulkner)는 만년에 다소 은둔적이고 사람과 어울리는 것을 피했다.

**8** ⑩    | 학생들의 장난스러운 농담과 흥분 속에서 대리 교사가 질서를 유지하려고 애쓰고 있을 때 교실은 매우 소란스러워졌다.

**9** ⑧    | 도망자는 신분을 바꾸고 몰래 도시를 오가며 붙잡히는 것을 피하려 했다.

**10** ⑰    | 그 회사는 노후화된 인프라를 쇄신하기 위해 상당한 노력을 기울였다.

. . . . . . . . . . . . . . . . . . . . . . . . . . . . . . . . . . . . . . . . . . . . . . . . . . . . . . . .

**11** ③    **12** ④    **13** ①    **14** ②    **15** ③    **16** ④    **17** ②    **18** ①    **19** ③    **20** ④

# ACTUAL TEST

[01-100] Choose the one that is closest in meaning to the underlined part.

**01** Daisy stated that it was a rather <u>inscrutable</u> work of art, but he liked it.
① bizarre
② shoddy
③ insipid
④ enigmatic

**02** Germany controlled much of eastern Europe and transferred its troops to the Western Front, where most of the battles were fought. Alas, their <u>preeminence</u> did not last as American troops arrived by the thousands each day to support the Allied powers.
① supremacy
② setback
③ inception
④ failure

**03** A pilot in Chicago could shed light on the potential effects of giving cash to low-income families <u>with no strings attached</u>.
① charitably
② unconditionally
③ impartially
④ bountifully

**04** Some criminal experts contend that teenagers growing up in <u>depraved</u> areas are far more likely to turn to crime and drug abuse.
① corrupt
② secluded
③ dejected
④ unpopulated

**05** At home, in a consistent pattern, the most <u>vociferous</u> advocates of preemptory war usually claimed prescient brilliance, as when the American military rapidly dislodged the Taliban and Saddam Hussein.
① twisted
② loud
③ conscientious
④ positive

**06** She found a long stick and <u>prodded</u> the pile of logs.
① pushed
② leaped
③ built
④ hit

**07** The <u>simulation</u> (and therefore destruction) of authentic discourse, first in the United States, and then spreading to the rest of the world, is what Guy Debord would call the first quantum leap into the "society of the spectacle" and what Jean Baudrillard would recognize as a milestone in the world's slide into hyper-reality. Mass media's colonization of civil society turned into a quasi-political campaign promoting technology itself when the image-making technology of television came along.
① imitation
② affinity
③ originality
④ difference

08 <u>Intimacy</u> is valuable currency when an artist's identity and image hinge on hired-gun hitmakers and airbrushed photo shoots and social-media posts.
① friendliness ② popularity
③ resemblance ④ similarity

09 One <u>sweltering</u> late afternoon in March, I walked out to collect wood.
① very hot ② tiring
③ pretty ④ smoothing

10 The fact that the bombardiers are Saudi hardly <u>exculpates</u> the United States.
① praises ② familiarizes
③ exaggerates ④ acquits

11 As the election approaches, more and more candidates resort to <u>mudslinging</u>.
① veracity ② gimmick
③ precursor ④ slander

12 Although the Carbon 14 method of dating old objects is not <u>foolproof</u>, it is the best method available at present.
① wholly operational
② entirely serviceable
③ fully reliable
④ completely safe

13 Several of Jacob Epstein's symbolic sculptures resulted in accusations of indecency and <u>blasphemy</u>.
① impiety ② brutality
③ assault ④ derision

14 The first skateboard-like <u>contraptions</u> are thought to have appeared sometime in the 1950's in Southern California beach communities.
① conceptions ② devices
③ playthings ④ replicas

15 She <u>alluded to</u> her work experience when she said, "I've been very busy the past few years."
① avoided speaking about
② concentrated on
③ was proud of
④ spoke indirectly about

16 The Korean War of 1950-1953 destroyed most of the cities and upset the traditional society largely <u>intact</u> throughout the Japanese colonization.
① inactive ② obsolete
③ struggling ④ untouched

17 Poor planning led him to <u>squander</u> his entire fortune.
① evade ② compile
③ manipulate ④ waste

18 The argument by her lawyer was marked by <u>trenchant</u> observation.
① incisive ② negative
③ fulsome ④ cagey

19 As the kidnapper's actions were so <u>repellent</u>, it was hard to have any sympathy for her.
① reserved ② insincere
③ aggressive ④ unpleasant

**20** It was <u>an affront</u> to his vanity that you should disagree with him.

① an insult      ② a damage

③ a contempt      ④ an ignorance

**21** The announcement that they had become <u>betrothed</u> surprised their friends who had not suspected any romance.

① segregated      ② engaged

③ hospitalized      ④ fabled

**22** The report concluded that he acted neither <u>fraudulently</u> nor improperly.

① deceitfully      ② aggressively

③ violently      ④ actively

**23** Doctors are battling to <u>eradicate</u> illness such as malaria and tetanus.

① proliferate      ② decline

③ degenerate      ④ exterminate

**24** Tom was almost <u>dispassionate</u> when he heard the news of her whereabouts.

① shocked      ② competent

③ unemotional      ④ gallant

**25** The lack of <u>substantive</u> discussion of serious issues is slowing down the project.

① excursive      ② important

③ instinctive      ④ obstructive

**26** The real estate broker <u>goaded</u> the couple to put down a deposit.

① guided      ② asked

③ forced      ④ urged

**27** The jury will undoubtedly <u>convict</u> the culprit of grand larceny.

① condemn      ② extend

③ scorch      ④ supplant

**28** More than 20 towns across a huge swathe of Queensland have been cut off or flooded, and more than 200,000 people affected. In the southern town of St. George, residents are on heightened alert after the weather bureau predicted a flood peak that would <u>inundate</u> 80% of the town.

① parch      ② destroy

③ conserve      ④ engulf

**29** Some are naturally more <u>resilient</u> than others, probably because they have a tendency to be optimistic thinkers.

① attentive      ② buoyant

③ chimerical      ④ erratic

**30** All this belt-tightening further <u>dampens</u> demand. As it is, consumers are struggling.

① incite      ② saddle with

③ distend      ④ attenuate

**31** Even if language learners cannot fully grasp what is being said, they can often understand the <u>gist</u> of it.

① axis      ② jest

③ essence      ④ mettle

32 Many Pennsylvanians are very provincial, refusing to even acknowledge that there is another world.
① narrow-minded
② patriotic
③ prosaic
④ middle-of-the-road

33 Perhaps it was the flaring sunlight that addled his mind.
① demesmerized ② muddled
③ dulcified ④ meddled

34 Each day a mole devours nearly its own weight in worms and insect larvae.
① disturbs ② consumes
③ carries ④ discovers

35 The boy who had caught a gray rabbit had a very bright and nimble dog about the size of a fox.
① quick-moving ② hasty
③ delicious ④ ridiculous

36 There is too much crime and gratuitous violence on TV, which gives bad influence on the adolescents and the young.
① potent ② unnecessary
③ uncivilized ④ disastrous

37 Few of the workers signed the open letter criticizing the company, fearing reprisal from management.
① defect ② digression
③ revenge ④ recess

38 Death was not instantaneous because none of bullets hit the heart.
① serious ② immediate
③ expected ④ desired

39 Under communism, incentives are weak and work habits deteriorate.
① isolate ② degenerate
③ transfer ④ change

40 All three face being struck off if they are found guilty of running the practice in order to circumvent conditions imposed by the Law Society.
① repeal ② evade
③ castigate ④ circumscribe

41 There was so much extraneous material in the essay that it was difficult to get the author's message.
① banal ② exemplary
③ irrelevant ④ complicated

42 He showed a supercilious manner when meeting with people, which made him unpopular among his colleagues.
① submissive ② talkative
③ superfluous ④ haughty

43 Stuck in the classroom, he gazes wistfully through the window at the boys playing soccer outside.
① wantonly ② yearningly
③ dreadfully ④ pleasantly

44 Examine the contract carefully before you sign anything.
① Look in
② Look on
③ Look out
④ Look over

45 This prophecy was strengthened by apposite quotations showing the existing drift of opinion.
① diametric
② conjectured
③ extant
④ pertinent

46 J. S. Mill devoted much of his youthful energies to the advancement of the principle of utility.
① establishment
② abolishment
③ promotion
④ clarification

47 The only way to improve is through hard work and dogged perseverance.
① poignant
② tenacious
③ drowsy
④ zealous

48 Sensory memory is an image or memory that enters your mind fleetingly.
① easily
② haphazardly
③ temporarily
④ fundamentally

49 As economies bounce back from the pandemic the recovery will be patchy, as local outbreaks and clampdowns come and go.
① quarantines
② breakouts
③ visitors
④ subsidences

50 We had lots of bumps and bruises in our relationship though there was never a doubt in my mind that we loved each other.
① damages
② remedies
③ comforts
④ compassions

51 She played a catchy song on the piano.
① melancholic
② pleasant
③ melodious
④ gloomy

52 His premises were simple: twentieth century modernism originated in or resulted in obscurity; nineteenth century romanticism exalted the impalpable and irrational.
① promises
② assumptions
③ assignments
④ prompts

53 The relationship between humans and wolves has always been a troubled one. Just a century ago, more than 100,000 of the fearsome predators roamed the West, helping themselves to the abundant prey and vast territory they found there.
① pursued
② wandered around
③ stalked
④ haunted

54 Our prime minister delivered a vapid address.
① unkempt
② inane
③ urbane
④ inbred

55 We are trying to get the country out of a hole after the last government drove us into a cul-de-sac.
① derision
② pillar
③ impasse
④ delirium

56  The effect of this was to fortify them in their resolve to try to save the party.
① ease          ② lower
③ decrease       ④ strengthen

57  Lending someone your passport is an imbecile thing to do.
① a superimposed
② a transportable
③ a checked
④ an absurd

58  Every few minutes, someone introduces a new antiaging cream that allegedly supersedes all the existing ones on the market.
① predicates     ② replaces
③ antedates      ④ accumulates

59  The Italian master's 1921 oil painting on canvas is celebrated for its distinctive brush strokes, the graceful yet rigid lines of the silhouette, and the choice of its restrained yet exquisite colors.
① painstaking    ② mediocre
③ ornamented     ④ distinguishing

60  Politicians are making craven activities not to lose votes ahead of an election.
① versatile      ② tentative
③ hard-bitten    ④ cowardly

61  At the King's death the prince acceded to the throne.
① abdicated      ② proceeded
③ succeeded      ④ preceded

62  Astronomers have difficulty detecting black holes since they emit no electronic radiation. Therefore, their presence is inferred by the absence of such radiation or by the drawing of material from a nearby cloud of interstellar matter toward the black hole.
① expand         ② condense
③ release        ④ exhaust

63  In spite of their disparaging remarks, he was proud of his son's painting.
① belittling     ② equitable
③ incisive       ④ unfair

64  He is much too prolix in his writings; he writes a page when a sentence should suffice.
① pithy          ② verbose
③ sententious    ④ sacrilegious

65  After the celebrity was involved in a scandal, the cosmetic company rescinded its offer of an endorsement contract.
① renewed        ② revoked
③ rectified      ④ redrafted

66  The organization's covert program to overthrow a dictatorship has failed.
① clandestine    ② crafty
③ ruthless       ④ impetuous

67  He sacrificed his own career so that his avaricious brother could succeed.
① blatant        ② fable
③ honest         ④ greedy

68 Sometimes a habitual <u>infraction</u> of a social convention is punished merely by expressions of social disapproval or gossip.
① divergence　　② breach
③ discrimination　④ depreciation

69 Mary suggests that you should first assess your <u>outgoings</u> and make financial plans accordingly.
① dividends　　② dependents
③ drafts　　　　④ expenditures

70 He was an individualist who <u>extolled</u> mass production, and an environmentalist who wanted to dome over the Arctic.
① opposed　　② supported
③ praised　　　④ downplayed

71 Benjamin Franklin received <u>homage</u> on both sides of the Atlantic as the man who personified the peculiar genius of America.
① fame　　　　② reward
③ respect　　　④ contribution

72 In Vietnam, the guerrillas often <u>ceded</u> control of the territory during the day and returned at night to prevent political stabilization.
① ceased　　　② yielded
③ terminated　④ procrastinated

73 The venture proved to be <u>remunerative</u> to its investors.
① untenable　　② detrimental
③ chancy　　　④ lucrative

74 It may not be necessary to put a cast on a very small <u>fracture</u>.
① hypocrisy　　② affectation
③ blotch　　　④ crack

75 What we see from Russia is an illegal and illegitimate effort to destabilize a sovereign state and create a <u>contrived</u> crisis with paid operatives across an international boundary.
① potential　　② concocted
③ random　　　④ unexpected

76 This legislation can be used by malicious and <u>vindictive</u> people to get at their neighbors who might have a puppy or a dog next door.
① hysterical　　② vengeful
③ compelling　④ shameless

77 The office manager called security, and with an <u>ad hoc</u> posse, pursued me through the labyrinthine halls, nearly to my editor's door.
① rapid　　　　② adhesive
③ non-violent　④ provisional

78 Parental example is the best means of <u>instilling</u> social responsibility in children.
① ignoring　　② practicing
③ moderating　④ implanting

79 Disgusting video films filled with violence and sex will <u>defile</u> the minds of the young.
① purify　　　② contaminate
③ ridicule　　④ discipline

80 The meal was prepared perfectly, but the diners found it repugnant.
① mediocre      ② disgusting
③ tasteless      ④ sumptuous

81 A lot of people are said to have tried to milk the insurance companies.
① draw milk from a cow for
② take advantage of
③ extract money by guile from
④ render measures to develop

82 The cerebellum is a section of the brain that coordinates the movements of voluntary muscles.
① executes      ② integrates
③ differentiates   ④ activates

83 A mule is the sterile animal of a horse and donkey.
① obnoxious     ② shabby
③ barren        ④ forsaken

84 After several futile attempts to save the ship, the captain ordered it abandoned.
① vain          ② tragic
③ excessive      ④ depressed

85 Experts had long discussed the geographical conundrum of finding the middle of the ocean, but it took modern technology to provide a full solution.
① riddle        ② terrain
③ distribution    ④ barrier

86 Emily hid shyly behind her mother when she met new people, yet her brother Keith was gregarious.
① noisy         ② sociable
③ distracting     ④ unashamed

87 Basically, unless instructed by the want ad, it is best that you not broach the subject about the salary.
① look after     ② bring up
③ find out       ④ diverge from

88 The Food and Drug Administration approved puberty blockers 30 years ago to treat children with precocious puberty.
① studious      ② aggressive
③ presumptive    ④ advanced

89 Most students are confused by her lectures, but Tom can always distill her main idea.
① implicate      ② extract
③ endorse       ④ paraphrase

90 Mozart had the ability to transform the popular musical styles of his day into something sublime.
① esoteric       ② epoch-making
③ lofty         ④ unconventional

91 Having an important title seems to make people suddenly high-handed.
① overbearing    ② prescient
③ solicitous      ④ fastidious

**92** The musical *Cats* is a famous <u>burlesque</u> that indirectly expresses human nature.
① dystopia          ② parody
③ soliloquy         ④ intrigue

**93** As soon as he finished his remarks, a <u>truncated</u> version of Russia's national anthem played.
① shortened         ② patriotic
③ metrical          ④ solemn

**94** Some people often <u>wheedle</u> their way into their boss.
① plunge            ② convert
③ galvanize         ④ coax

**95** She is now the <u>stolid</u> defender of an embattled European Union and of Western liberal values.
① indefatigable     ② outspoken
③ orthodox          ④ stubborn

**96** He had no choice but to <u>surrender</u> when he was driven to the edge of the cliff.
① pursue            ② confess
③ intervene         ④ succumb

**97** Guatemala won <u>plaudits</u> during the past decade for efforts to curb impunity and graft.
① acclaim           ② serenity
③ concord           ④ haven

**98** They are tired of a legislature that is forever <u>wrangling</u> rather than lawmaking.
① quarreling        ② trudging
③ ingratiating      ④ mocking

**99** Prices on the stock market, which have been <u>static</u>, are now rising again.
① fluctuating       ② resilient
③ stationary        ④ impending

**100** The <u>finicky</u> nature of the technology has brought some unexpected problems.
① revolutionary     ② fast-moving
③ volatile          ④ fastidious

[1] Write the meaning of the following words.

| | |
|---|---|
| ☐ worldly | ☐ corpse |
| ☐ disconcert | ☐ deny |
| ☐ constellation | ☐ piebald |
| ☐ stifle | ☐ horrid |
| ☐ decorum | ☐ circuit |
| ☐ quarrelsome | ☐ nitpick |
| ☐ proscribe | ☐ effect |
| ☐ spurious | ☐ vagrant |
| ☐ ebb | ☐ resource |
| ☐ institute | ☐ butt |
| ☐ censorious | ☐ arcane |
| ☐ preliminary | ☐ phenom |
| ☐ adjudicate | ☐ uphold |
| ☐ beset | ☐ munition |
| ☐ omen | ☐ gorgeous |
| ☐ transmute | ☐ bay |
| ☐ matrix | ☐ downright |
| ☐ revamp | ☐ shroud |
| ☐ interstice | ☐ tutor |
| ☐ fascinating | ☐ frenzy |
| ☐ garrison | ☐ lullaby |
| ☐ collogue | ☐ exhume |
| ☐ infirm | ☐ suite |
| ☐ saga | ☐ rambunctious |
| ☐ noticeable | ☐ agent |

[2] Select <u>the most</u> appropriate word from the box below. Each word should be used only once.

| | | | |
|---|---|---|---|
| ① ebb | ② decorum | ③ preliminary | ④ piebald |
| ⑤ quarrelsome | ⑥ beset | ⑦ frenzy | ⑧ uphold |
| ⑨ nitpick | ⑩ deny | ⑪ adjudicate | ⑫ spurious |
| ⑬ arcane | ⑭ revamp | ⑮ vagrant | ⑯ noticeable |
| ⑰ transmute | ⑱ gorgeous | ⑲ downright | ⑳ exhume |

1    The ceremony required a display of utmost _____ with attendees expected to uphold dignified behavior and proper etiquette throughout the event.

2    The contentious atmosphere within the meeting was primarily due to the presence of _____ individuals who were prone to disputes over trivial matters.

3    His promises seemed enticing at first glance but were ultimately dismissed as _____ upon thorough investigation.

4    The board of directors decided it was imperative to overhaul and _____ the company's old-fashioned image to attract a younger demographic.

5    Through extensive research, scientists contributing to sustainable development aim to discover ways to _____ common elements into renewable sources of energy.

6    In the abandoned district, one might encounter a solitary _____, an individual moving from place to place without a permanent abode.

7    Experts in academic fields often show off the depth of their knowledge by mentioning some _____ fact as if it was common for everyone to know.

8    It is essential for citizens to actively participate in the democratic process to _____ the values of their society.

9    The authorities planned to _____ the buried artifacts in hopes of uncovering historical treasures lost to time.

10   The news of the sale sparked a shopping _____ as eager customers hurried to take advantage of the discounted prices.

[3] Choose the one which is different from the others.

**11**   ① secular        ② worldly        ③ definite       ④ mundane

**12**   ① assign         ② disconcert     ③ baffle         ④ disturb

**13**   ① suppress       ② curb           ③ stifle         ④ impart

**14**   ① proscribe      ② sanction       ③ ban            ④ prohibit

**15**   ① harbinger      ② augury         ③ omen           ④ skirmish

**16**   ① fatiguing      ② fascinating    ③ alluring       ④ enchanting

**17**   ① frail          ② feeble         ③ infirm         ④ robust

**18**   ① phenom         ② sage           ③ prodigy        ④ genius

**19**   ① evident        ② horrid         ③ horrible       ④ frightful

**20**   ① collogue       ② conspire       ③ debunk         ④ intrigue

## ✓ Answers

**1** ②  ㅣ 행사에는 최대한의 예의가 요구되었으며, 참석자들은 행사 내내 품위 있는 행동과 적절한 예절을 지켜야 했다.

**2** ⑤  ㅣ 회의에서의 논쟁적인 분위기는 주로 사소한 일에 대해 논쟁을 일으키는 경향이 있는 다투기 좋아하는 사람들의 존재 때문이었다.

**3** ⑫  ㅣ 그의 약속은 언뜻 보기에는 그럴듯해 보였지만, 철저한 조사를 통해 결국 거짓된 것으로 묵살되었다.

**4** ⑭  ㅣ 이사회는 젊은 층의 관심을 끌기 위해 회사의 오래된 이미지를 조사해서 개선하는 것이 매우 중요하다고 결정했다.

**5** ⑰  ㅣ 지속 가능한 개발에 기여하는 과학자들은 광범위한 연구를 통해 흔한 재료를 재생할 수 있는 에너지원으로 변환하는 방법을 찾는 것을 목표로 한다.

**6** ⑮  ㅣ 버려진 지역에서 우리는 영구적인 거처 없이 이리저리 옮겨 다니는 사람인 외톨이 부랑자를 만날지도 모른다.

**7** ⑬  ㅣ 학문 분야의 전문가들은 어떤 난해한 사실을 마치 누구나 알고 있는 것처럼 언급하여 지식의 깊이를 과시하곤 한다.

**8** ⑧  ㅣ 시민들이 사회의 가치를 지키기 위해서는 민주적 과정에 적극적으로 참여하는 것이 필수적이다.

**9** ⑳  ㅣ 당국은 세월에 묻혀버린 역사적 보물을 찾아내기를 기대하며 매장된 유물을 발굴할 계획이었다.

**10** ⑦  ㅣ 세일 소식에 열성적인 고객들이 할인된 가격을 이용하기 위해 서둘렀기 때문에 쇼핑 열풍이 불었다.

- - - - - - - - - - - - - - - - - - - - - - - - - - - - - - - - - - - - - - - - - - - - - - - - -

**11** ③   **12** ①   **13** ④   **14** ②   **15** ④   **16** ①   **17** ④   **18** ②   **19** ①   **20** ③

**[1] Write the meaning of the following words.**

| | |
|---|---|
| ☐ novice | ☐ glean |
| ☐ concerted | ☐ affection |
| ☐ expunge | ☐ oval |
| ☐ profligate | ☐ mote |
| ☐ assail | ☐ wail |
| ☐ livelihood | ☐ tumult |
| ☐ requisite | ☐ hue |
| ☐ sidestep | ☐ retribution |
| ☐ despondent | ☐ leery |
| ☐ induct | ☐ crux |
| ☐ privilege | ☐ diverge |
| ☐ strident | ☐ pendulum |
| ☐ denomination | ☐ voluminous |
| ☐ fester | ☐ caption |
| ☐ acupuncture | ☐ ornament |
| ☐ injurious | ☐ emend |
| ☐ bonanza | ☐ bedridden |
| ☐ dispose | ☐ interference |
| ☐ suggestion | ☐ amorphous |
| ☐ timorous | ☐ rout |
| ☐ euphoria | ☐ knead |
| ☐ compress | ☐ comrade |
| ☐ exigency | ☐ foray |
| ☐ subterranean | ☐ barrister |
| ☐ mercury | ☐ prowl |

[2] Select <u>the most</u> appropriate word from the box below. Each word should be used only once.

| | | | |
|---|---|---|---|
| ① festered | ② pendulum | ③ gleaned | ④ rout |
| ⑤ novice | ⑥ amorphous | ⑦ profligate | ⑧ concerted |
| ⑨ foray | ⑩ strident | ⑪ prowled | ⑫ diverged |
| ⑬ assail | ⑭ subterranean | ⑮ disposed | ⑯ retribution |
| ⑰ bedridden | ⑱ bonanza | ⑲ privilege | ⑳ requisite |

1     Despite numerous warnings about the consequences of _____ spending, the government continued its reckless use of resources.

2     The constant barrage of challenges and obstacles seemed to _____ her determination, yet she persisted despite the adversities.

3     His bold and progressive opinions often positioned him as a(n) _____ critic of the existing conservative political system.

4     One of the warriors was bitten by a snake, and the wound _____ and caused an unbearable stench.

5     Whether you're an experienced home buyer or a(n) _____, buying property overseas involves research and planning to avoid making a costly mistake.

6     An unexpected increase in tourism to a small town was a(n) _____ for the locals.

7     We all make mistakes at work, and hopefully many of us resolve these mistakes by acknowledging the oversight, learning whatever lessons can be _____, and moving on.

8     The concept of "an eye for an eye" often symbolizes the idea of seeking _____ as a form of justice.

9     The finance minister's opinion _____ from that of the prime minister, causing conflict within the party.

10     The artist's experimental _____ into abstract painting showcased a remarkable departure from traditional techniques.

[3] Choose the one which is different from the others.

**11** ① affiliate ② sidestep ③ avoid ④ evade

**12** ① expunge ② excel ③ erase ④ efface

**13** ① cowardly ② timorous ③ supercilious ④ timid

**14** ① abstract ② abridge ③ compress ④ expatiate

**15** ① tumult ② helm ③ commotion ④ uproar

**16** ① heedless ② leery ③ suspicious ④ cautious

**17** ① kernel ② gist ③ crux ④ trivia

**18** ① ample ② voluminous ③ meager ④ copious

**19** ① rectify ② soothe ③ emend ④ correct

**20** ① disproportionate ② despondent ③ dejected ④ discouraged

---

## ✔Answers

**1** ⑦ | 과도한 지출의 결과에 대한 수많은 경고에도 불구하고 정부는 계속해서 재원을 무분별하게 사용했다.

**2** ⑬ | 끊임없이 빗발치는 도전과 난관이 그녀의 결심에 맞서는 것 같았지만, 그녀는 그 어려움에도 불구하고 끈질기게 정진했다.

**3** ⑩ | 그의 대담하고 진보적인 의견은 종종 그를 기존의 보수적인 정치 체제에 대한 신랄한 비판자로 자리매김했다.

**4** ① | 전사들 중 한 명이 뱀에게 물렸고, 상처가 곪아서 견디기 힘든 악취를 풍겼다.

**5** ⑤ | 당신이 경험이 많은 주택구입자이든 초보자이든 간에, 해외 부동산을 구입하는 것은 값비싼 실수를 피하기 위한 조사와 계획이 수반된다.

**6** ⑱ | 작은 마을에 예상치 못한 관광 증가는 지역 주민들에게는 큰 행운이 되었다.

**7** ③ | 우리는 모두 직장에서 실수를 하는데, 아마도 우리 중 상당수는 잘못을 인정하고, 얻을 수 있는 모든 교훈을 배우고, 계속 정진함으로써 이런 실수들을 해결할 것이다.

**8** ⑯ | "눈에는 눈"이라는 개념은 종종 정의의 한 형태로서 보복을 추구한다는 생각을 상징한다.

**9** ⑫ | 재무부 장관의 의견이 총리의 의견과 달라서 당내 갈등이 빚어졌다.

**10** ⑨ | 그 화가의 추상화 분야로의 실험적인 진출은 전통적인 기법에서 눈에 띄게 벗어남을 보여주었다.

.........................................................................................

**11** ① **12** ② **13** ③ **14** ④ **15** ② **16** ① **17** ④ **18** ③ **19** ② **20** ①

[1] Write the meaning of the following words.

| | |
|---|---|
| ☐ immortal | ☐ lascivious |
| ☐ constrict | ☐ exploit |
| ☐ persiflage | ☐ contingent |
| ☐ subordinate | ☐ frontispiece |
| ☐ accrue | ☐ wreak |
| ☐ offspring | ☐ defendant |
| ☐ retaliate | ☐ comport |
| ☐ primary | ☐ runaway |
| ☐ somniloquy | ☐ antecedent |
| ☐ ghastly | ☐ vegetarian |
| ☐ trammel | ☐ inhale |
| ☐ dispatch | ☐ brick-and-mortar |
| ☐ cant | ☐ smother |
| ☐ blemish | ☐ climax |
| ☐ ritual | ☐ gravitate |
| ☐ incise | ☐ archery |
| ☐ edifice | ☐ complex |
| ☐ bamboozle | ☐ purport |
| ☐ monolithic | ☐ overrate |
| ☐ famine | ☐ husbandry |
| ☐ display | ☐ forfeit |
| ☐ nosy | ☐ derelict |
| ☐ efflorescence | ☐ symbiosis |
| ☐ unleash | ☐ precipitate |
| ☐ trend | ☐ migraine |

[2] Select <u>the most</u> appropriate word from the box below. Each word should be used only once.

| | | | |
|---|---|---|---|
| ① subordinate | ② cant | ③ incise | ④ lascivious |
| ⑤ derelict | ⑥ forfeited | ⑦ symbiosis | ⑧ husbandry |
| ⑨ ghastly | ⑩ bamboozle | ⑪ immortal | ⑫ dispatch |
| ⑬ overrated | ⑭ gravitate | ⑮ antecedent | ⑯ display |
| ⑰ unleash | ⑱ precipitated | ⑲ smother | ⑳ efflorescence |

1     The war veteran recounted the _____ horrors of battle, illustrating the harsh realities of combat.

2     North Korea is willing to _____ its troops to take part in the war, he claimed, saying further that the troops are being prepared to assist the Russian military.

3     Despite his honest intentions, the salesman's overly elaborate pitch seemed to _____ the potential buyers rather than persuade them to make a purchase.

4     The coach's motivational speech was intended to inspire the team to _____ their full potential during the upcoming match.

5     The legacy of that remarkable leader rendered him almost _____, as his teachings continued to inspire generations long after his time.

6     The novelist's vivid descriptions of the characters' _____ desires added depth to the storyline but also sparked controversy over obscenity.

7     The overprotective parents' tendency to _____ their children with constant attention and restrictions hindered the children's independence.

8     Practicing _____ involves meticulous budgeting and wise spending to ensure a secure and prosperous future.

9     The _____ ship, left stranded on the shore, served as a haunting reminder of maritime history and the passage of time.

10    The controversial decision by the government to implement new taxes _____ widespread protests and demands for reconsideration across the nation.

**[3] Choose the one which is different from the others.**

| 11 | ① persiflage | ② secrecy | ③ banter | ④ raillery |
|----|--------------|-----------|----------|------------|
| 12 | ① fetter | ② trammel | ③ retrieve | ④ shackle |
| 13 | ① embroidery | ② blemish | ③ blot | ④ flaw |
| 14 | ① meddlesome | ② intrusive | ③ nosy | ④ callous |
| 15 | ① runaway | ② prowler | ③ escapee | ④ fugitive |
| 16 | ① climax | ② acme | ③ nadir | ④ culmination |
| 17 | ① comport | ② behave | ③ conduct | ④ commence |
| 18 | ① collate | ② wreak | ③ unleash | ④ vent |
| 19 | ① abuse | ② conceive | ③ exploit | ④ misuse |
| 20 | ① contract | ② compress | ③ consent | ④ constrict |

## ✓Answers

1  ⑨ ┃ 참전 용사는 전쟁의 지독한 공포를 이야기하면서 전투의 가혹한 현실을 잘 보여주었다.

2  ⑫ ┃ 북한은 참전하기 위해 군대를 급파할 용의가 있다고 그는 주장했으며, 이어서 그 군대는 러시아 군을 돕기 위해 준비하고 있다고 말했다.

3  ⑩ ┃ 그의 정직한 의도에도 불구하고 판매원의 지나치게 정성을 들인 홍보는 잠재 고객이 구매하도록 설득하기는커녕 그들을 속이는 것처럼 보였다.

4  ⑰ ┃ 감독의 격려 인사는 팀이 곧 있을 경기에서 최대한의 잠재력을 발휘할 수 있도록 영감을 주기 위한 것이었다.

5  ⑪ ┃ 그 뛰어난 지도자의 유산은 그를 거의 불멸의 존재로 만들었는데, 이는 그의 가르침이 그가 살았던 이후로도 오랫동안 여러 세대에 계속해서 영감을 주었기 때문이었다.

6  ④ ┃ 작중인물들의 음탕한 욕망에 대한 소설가의 생생한 묘사는 줄거리에 깊이를 더해주었지만, 외설 시비를 불러일으키기도 했다.

7  ⑲ ┃ 끊임없는 관심과 제약으로 자녀들을 숨 막히게 하는 과보호하는 부모의 성향은 아이의 자립을 방해했다.

8  ⑧ ┃ 절약을 실천하는 것에는 안전하고 번영하는 미래를 보장하기 위해 꼼꼼한 예산 편성과 현명한 지출이 수반된다.

9  ⑤ ┃ 해안에 좌초된 채 방치된 그 배는 연해의 역사와 시간의 경과를 늘 상기시켜 주는 역할을 했다.

10 ⑱ ┃ 새로운 세금 정책을 시행하기로 한 정부의 논란을 불러일으킨 결정은 전국적으로 광범위한 시위와 재검토 요구를 촉발시켰다.

- - - - - - - - - - - - - - - - - - - - - - - - - - - - - - - - - - - - - - - - - - - - - - - - - - - - - - - - - - - - - - - - - - - - - - - - - - - - -

**11** ②  **12** ③  **13** ①  **14** ④  **15** ②  **16** ③  **17** ④  **18** ①  **19** ②  **20** ③

☑ **DAILY CHECKUP**

[1] Write the meaning of the following words.

| | |
|---|---|
| ☐ erudite | ☐ confabulate |
| ☐ dissolve | ☐ vestige |
| ☐ ratio | ☐ noncommittal |
| ☐ succulent | ☐ dissent |
| ☐ appeal | ☐ excruciate |
| ☐ connivance | ☐ indebted |
| ☐ phlegmatic | ☐ clamp |
| ☐ herald | ☐ sidereal |
| ☐ balmy | ☐ folly |
| ☐ revolt | ☐ roundabout |
| ☐ inure | ☐ conclave |
| ☐ copyright | ☐ whirl |
| ☐ presentiment | ☐ bluff |
| ☐ fluorescent | ☐ oculist |
| ☐ abrasive | ☐ multitude |
| ☐ lionize | ☐ authoritarian |
| ☐ testament | ☐ enliven |
| ☐ off-the-cuff | ☐ linear |
| ☐ moor | ☐ turnout |
| ☐ fiendish | ☐ inseparable |
| ☐ describe | ☐ derivative |
| ☐ garbage | ☐ protract |
| ☐ scorch | ☐ buxom |
| ☐ emolument | ☐ stake |
| ☐ jocular | ☐ cumbersome |

[2] Select <u>the most</u> appropriate word from the box below. Each word should be used only once.

| | | | |
|---|---|---|---|
| ① presentiment | ② indebted | ③ fiendish | ④ excruciate |
| ⑤ herald | ⑥ sidereal | ⑦ enliven | ⑧ inseparable |
| ⑨ protract | ⑩ revolt | ⑪ describe | ⑫ inure |
| ⑬ lionize | ⑭ confabulate | ⑮ turnout | ⑯ erudite |
| ⑰ cumbersome | ⑱ connivance | ⑲ jocular | ⑳ derivative |

**1**  The sudden increase in job opportunities in the technology sector seemed to _____ a new era of economic growth in the region.

**2**  The unfair treatment of the employees by the management sparked a collective _____ within the company.

**3**  The eerie silence in the town gave him a chilling _____ of an impending disaster though he couldn't quite pinpoint its source.

**4**  Throughout history, societies tend to _____ figures who demonstrate exceptional bravery and leadership during challenging times.

**5**  The serial killers' _____ schemes were so elaborate and malicious that they left a lasting impact on the real world.

**6**  Amid the serious discussions, his _____ remark added a lighthearted touch to the conversation, momentarily easing the tension in the room.

**7**  The toothache seemed to _____ him, causing sharp and relentless pain that made it difficult for him to focus on anything else.

**8**  The teacher's decision to _____ the class discussion not only allowed for a more in-depth exploration of the topic, but it also extended the lesson beyond the scheduled time.

**9**  The renowned scholar's published works are a testament to his _____ understanding and profound insights into various academic disciplines.

**10**  _____ bureaucratic procedures must be simplified.

[3] Choose the one which is different from the others.

**11**  ① phlegmatic  ② nefarious  ③ apathetic  ④ unemotional

**12**  ① redolent  ② fragrant  ③ balmy  ④ stifling

**13**  ① far-flung  ② fluorescent  ③ luminous  ④ glowing

**14**  ① off-the-cuff  ② prepared  ③ extemporaneous  ④ impromptu

**15**  ① scorch  ② parch  ③ wade  ④ wither

**16**  ① vestige  ② radiance  ③ sign  ④ trace

**17**  ① stupidity  ② absurdity  ③ cessation  ④ folly

**18**  ① roundabout  ② circuitous  ③ indirect  ④ straightforward

**19**  ① decisive  ② noncommittal  ③ ambiguous  ④ equivocal

**20**  ① bluff  ② breach  ③ bravado  ④ bluster

---

## ✔ Answers

**1** ⑤  ｜기술 부문의 취업 기회가 갑자기 증가하면서 이 지역 경제 성장의 새로운 시대가 도래하는 것처럼 보였다.

**2** ⑩  ｜직원에 대한 경영진의 부당한 대우는 회사 내의 집단 반발을 불러일으켰다.

**3** ①  ｜마을의 기괴한 정적은 그에게 곧 닥칠 재앙에 대한 섬뜩한 예감을 주었지만, 그 원인을 정확히 파악할 수는 없었다.

**4** ⑬  ｜역사를 통틀어 사회는 어려운 시기에 비범한 용기와 리더십을 보여주는 인물들을 치켜세우는 경향이 있다.

**5** ③  ｜연쇄 살인범들의 사악한 계략은 너무나 정교하고 악의적이어서 그들은 현실 세계에 지속적인 영향을 미쳤다.

**6** ⑲  ｜진지한 토론 중에 그가 한 우스운 말이 대화에 유쾌함을 더해주며 잠시 방 안의 긴장감을 완화했다.

**7** ④  ｜치통은 그를 극심한 고통으로 몰아넣고 날카롭고 지독한 통증을 유발하여 다른 일에 집중하기 어렵게 만드는 것 같았다.

**8** ⑨  ｜수업 토론을 연장하기로 한 선생님의 결정으로 인해 그 주제에 대한 보다 심층적인 탐구가 가능해졌을 뿐만 아니라 수업 시간이 예정된 시간보다 길어졌다.

**9** ⑯  ｜저명한 학자의 출판된 저작물은 다양한 학문 분야에 대한 그의 박식한 이해와 심오한 통찰력을 보여주는 증거이다.

**10** ⑰  ｜번거로운 행정절차는 간소화되어야 한다.

............................................................

**11** ②  **12** ④  **13** ①  **14** ②  **15** ③  **16** ②  **17** ③  **18** ④  **19** ①  **20** ②

[1] Write the meaning of the following words.

| | |
|---|---|
| ☐ assiduous | ☐ corsair |
| ☐ presume | ☐ liaison |
| ☐ behalf | ☐ hoodwink |
| ☐ imbroglio | ☐ quicksilver |
| ☐ credulous | ☐ deface |
| ☐ eschew | ☐ moratorium |
| ☐ spouse | ☐ postprandial |
| ☐ dissonant | ☐ commute |
| ☐ augment | ☐ excursion |
| ☐ curriculum | ☐ internecine |
| ☐ virulent | ☐ conduit |
| ☐ skid | ☐ blunt |
| ☐ benediction | ☐ overthrow |
| ☐ maroon | ☐ fusillade |
| ☐ proximity | ☐ urbane |
| ☐ cleave | ☐ trespass |
| ☐ acronym | ☐ dangle |
| ☐ stark | ☐ extrinsic |
| ☐ relative | ☐ insulate |
| ☐ desuetude | ☐ perquisite |
| ☐ flee | ☐ antibiotic |
| ☐ toilsome | ☐ raid |
| ☐ gentile | ☐ amputate |
| ☐ provocative | ☐ fishy |
| ☐ ruminate | ☐ supplicate |

[2] Select the most appropriate word from the box below. Each word should be used only once.

| | | | |
|---|---|---|---|
| ① eschew | ② imbroglio | ③ fusillade | ④ toilsome |
| ⑤ moratorium | ⑥ presumed | ⑦ stark | ⑧ commuted |
| ⑨ assiduous | ⑩ defaced | ⑪ excursion | ⑫ dissonant |
| ⑬ internecine | ⑭ extrinsic | ⑮ trespass | ⑯ overthrow |
| ⑰ flee | ⑱ acronym | ⑲ provocative | ⑳ insulate |

1   Amid the diplomatic _____, the ambassador struggled to find a peaceful resolution to the escalating tensions between the two countries.

2   Because he was _____ in the performance of his duties, his employers could not complain about his work.

3   In order to maintain a minimalist lifestyle, she chose to _____ lavish spending on unnecessary possessions.

4   Two children were no longer allowed to sing because their _____ voices damaged the sound of the chorus.

5   The mischievous student _____ the library book by scribbling in it with a permanent marker, causing damage to its cover and pages.

6   The hikers knew it was forbidden to enter the restricted area, yet curiosity led them to _____ onto the prohibited land.

7   The marathon runner faced a(n) _____ task as she tackled the steep hills in the final stretch of the race.

8   The Asian governments at first decided to _____ themselves from encounters with the imperialistic Western powers, but ended up opening their door.

9   The government announced a temporary _____ on all non-essential travel to the region due to escalating political tensions.

10   Cream, which means money, comes from the _____ which stands for "Cash rules everything around me."

[3] Choose the one which is different from the others.

**11** ① credulous  ② primitive  ③ naive  ④ gullible

**12** ① opportune  ② virulent  ③ lethal  ④ pernicious

**13** ① maroon  ② strand  ③ maraud  ④ isolate

**14** ① obsoletism  ② disuse  ③ desuetude  ④ debate

**15** ① ruminate  ② articulate  ③ contemplate  ④ meditate

**16** ① resumption  ② communication  ③ liaison  ④ contact

**17** ① foray  ② raid  ③ decree  ④ incursion

**18** ① avoidable  ② fishy  ③ dubious  ④ suspicious

**19** ① beseech  ② allege  ③ supplicate  ④ beg

**20** ① blunt  ② subtle  ③ dull  ④ obtuse

# ACTUAL TEST

[01-100] Choose the one that is closest in meaning to the underlined part.

**01** Mary was much <u>disconcerted</u> by the claim that to write well demanded arduous study.
① prevailed
② exulted
③ vigorous
④ embarrassed

**02** The country's raucous fans are straining the rules of <u>decorum</u> in sports that value silence, like table tennis.
① vigor
② pinnacle
③ propriety
④ commotion

**03** Some conductors <u>proscribe</u> sound amplification at their concerts.
① permit
② process
③ demand
④ ban

**04** Although the accusations against the politician were <u>spurious</u>, they were believed by enough voters to seriously damage his bid for office.
① complaisant
② superordinate
③ spruce
④ counterfeit

**05** Since the mid-1990s, cultural depictions of the AIDS crisis for gay men began to <u>ebb</u>.
① even
② bounce
③ stop
④ recede

**06** Daylight saving time was <u>instituted</u> to increase productivity.
① organized
② started
③ encouraged
④ taught

**07** After the <u>preliminary</u> exercise of prayer and song, the speaker of the day gave an address.
① preparatory
② religious
③ sympathetic
④ thorough

**08** Many universities are now planning to <u>revamp</u> their existing curriculum by integrating international examples into their courses.
① globalize
② publicize
③ downplay
④ overhaul

**09** She would give her <u>horrid</u> friends one more chance.
① horrified
② arrogant
③ cynical
④ nasty

**10** The travel brochure recommends a rather <u>circuitous</u> route to the hotel in order to help travelers avoid congested roads.
① roundabout
② makeshift
③ steadfast
④ easygoing

**11** Most people believe that the most <u>effective</u> treatment begins early in the recovery process.
① effluent
② efficacious
③ feasible
④ available

12 To converse with others effectively, we need more tools than just an extensive vocabulary and an <u>arcane</u> knowledge of the rules of grammar.

① esoteric ② inclusive

③ systematic ④ comprehensive

13 My dream house is one that would be in mountains. It would be surrounded by trees and it would have a view of a <u>gorgeous</u> lake.

① beautiful ② disturbed

③ gloomy ④ perplexed

14 The band <u>exhumed</u> some old English music hall songs and delighted modern audiences with them.

① disrupted ② rendered

③ excavated ④ composed

15 A governmental attempt to clamp down on the <u>rambunctious</u> British press turned into a new royal scandal.

① prescient ② unruly

③ obsequious ④ pedantic

16 Many companies exaggerate or <u>downright</u> lie about the effects of their food and herbal products.

① thoroughly ② plausibly

③ promptly ④ tepidly

17 As a police officer you are expected to <u>uphold</u> the law whether you agree with it or not.

① amend ② ratify

③ defend ④ transcend

18 State-run residential facilities for those who become <u>infirm</u> to remain independent are few.

① feeble ② insolvent

③ disabled ④ restless

19 I didn't talk to anyone about the dream as I wasn't sure it was a good <u>omen</u> or a bad one.

① confession ② vigor

③ artifice ④ portent

20 John Thompson is still <u>a novice</u> as far as film acting is concerned.

① a learner ② an expert

③ a genius ④ a preacher

21 He never <u>expunged</u> from his mind the shame of having to flee from the enemy.

① entrenched ② inserted

③ removed ④ prevailed

22 Not so long ago, big companies from poor nations were generally dismissed as second-rate, run by fat family dynasties or <u>profligate</u> autocrats.

① progressive ② stingy

③ frugal ④ wasteful

23 Where did the <u>assailant</u> come from?

① assistant ② attacker

③ smoke ④ ship

24 There's no <u>prerequisite</u> for Professor Smith's Italian Renaissance course, is there?

① requirement ② disadvantage

③ permission ④ disappointment

25 Shrewd Internet users can <u>sidestep</u> the real-name regulations by using other people's personal information or by capitalizing on sites run by overseas servers.
① enforce　　　② avoid
③ adhere to　　④ stipulate

26 Many Afghans feel deeply <u>despondent</u> about the direction the country is being taken in by the Taliban.
① nostalgic　　② responsible
③ elated　　　④ dejected

27 Their shared <u>strident</u> criticism of social media has come from divergent political views.
① consoling　　② severe
③ stereotyped　④ aristocratic

28 Abraham Lincoln's election to the presidency in 1860 brought to a climax the long <u>festering</u> debate about the relative powers of the federal and the state governments.
① dreary　　　② festive
③ fetching　　④ suppurating

29 The circulatory system helps <u>dispose of</u> wastes that would harm the body if they accumulated.
① intake　　　② bear up under
③ get rid of　　④ run over

30 The shy child's natural <u>timidity</u> had made her afraid to try out for the team.
① fearfulness　② reverence
③ inclination　　④ impulse

31 Addictions are really about the failure to inhibit a once-rewarded behavior, not about the degree of <u>euphoria</u> that is created.
① disruption　　② realization
③ frustration　　④ exhilaration

32 The tourist tried to <u>compress</u> all his sport clothes into one suitcase.
① expand　　　② commemorate
③ condense　　④ spend

33 Popular search keywords, which greatly influence the setting of social agendas and forming public opinions, are positioned to stand out, and the list changes in real time, adding a sense of <u>exigency</u>, though many of the keywords are inaccurate and lead to bad information or provocative subjects.
① accuracy　　② factuality
③ ingenuity　　④ urgency

34 <u>Subterranean</u> reservoirs in the United States contain far more usable water than all surface reservoirs and lakes combined.
① Naval　　　② Rainwater
③ Unpolluted　④ Underground

35 <u>Mercurial</u> individuals are similar to dramatic and especially adventurous people in their reluctance to think things out and to plan for the future.
① dogmatic　　② parsimonious
③ unscrupulous　④ capricious

36 Lincoln argued for the end of slavery with values gleaned from the Declaration of Independence.
① removed      ② amended
③ quoted      ④ garnered

37 Despite their stoical appearance, their every gesture is still troubled by their memories of their tumultuous past.
① emotional      ② pertinent
③ sarcastic      ④ violent

38 Nature always metes out a retribution for any transgression of her law.
① reticence      ② lawsuit
③ vengeance      ④ discord

39 The crux of the problem is the unique means of identification used by the author of the cuneiform passage.
① heart      ② appropriateness
③ solution      ④ fascination

40 Parents and children often have divergent beliefs about life.
① realistic      ② dissimilar
③ untruthful      ④ profound

41 Certain pine trees are deliberately dwarfed for ornamental purposes.
① medicinal      ② diverse
③ decorative      ④ constructive

42 The photographer liked amorphous subjects: clouds, spilled milk shakes, women in tent-like dresses.
① formless      ② eccentric
③ mobile      ④ transient

43 A five-cup-a-day coffee drinker himself, the 51-year-old is a picture of intensity as he prowls his office and recalls how it all began.
① opens early
② cleans up
③ feels proud of
④ moves around

44 He is, in truth, one of the immortal characters in fiction.
① imperishable      ② counterfeit
③ disreputable      ④ ostensible

45 As a young and inexperienced employee, you cannot expect to hold more than a subordinate job in that big company.
① superior      ② tedious
③ temporary      ④ subsidiary

46 When I'm boarding a plane, I always have to touch the exterior on the right side of the door. It's a personal travel ritual that somehow makes me feel safe.
① game      ② hazard
③ scheme      ④ ceremony

47 Undeniably this is another fragile edifice of the rules governing international market.
① facade      ② menace
③ structure      ④ plethora

48 Shifty Sally found it easy to bamboozle the drunk card players in the saloon and win the game.
① confuse ② benumb
③ intimidate ④ cheat

49 Politicians sought to exploit census procedures to their advantage.
① seek ② explain
③ explore ④ utilize

50 The outcome was contingent upon the effort made to succeed.
① clear ② advisable
③ dependent ④ proper

51 The movement toward equality of rights had some antecedents that helped the cause of aspiring women.
① elements ② procedures
③ precedents ④ justification

52 Watson wished to know the purport of Holmes's thesis.
① meaning ② contradistinction
③ flaw ④ rectitude

53 The security guard was fired because of his derelict attitude at his workplace.
① deserted ② careless
③ unprecedented ④ deteriorating

54 "Fundamental" is the most over-used word in the debate. There is nothing more fundamental than the markets, which had sound reasons to precipitate the crisis.

① prevent ② pacify
③ foretell ④ accelerate

55 Erudite discussion was made in the session about the origin of the English novel and its tradition.
① Boring ② Heated
③ Scholarly ④ Epoch-making

56 With the Internet, it is exceedingly easy for each of us to find like-minded types. Views that would ordinarily dissolve, simply because of an absence of social support, can be found in large numbers on the Internet.
① emerge ② increase
③ dissipate ④ oscillate

57 Instantly the rumor spread that the secretary had connived in the spy's liquidation.
① prolonged ② conspired
③ embezzled ④ annihilated

58 The election of the divisive mayor heralded a difficult period of political polarization for the city.
① divulged ② foreshadowed
③ solicited ④ decompressed

59 Work in environmental journalism for very long, and you can eventually become inured to catastrophe.
① vulnerable ② hardened
③ resurgent ④ irrevocable

60 There are in excess of fifty species of
fluorescent fungi.
① microscopic   ② poisonous
③ luminous   ④ aquatic

61 It's a testament to antibullying curriculums
in elementary schools that none of the girls
would use words like *fat* in front of an adult,
which wasn't true even three or four years
ago.
① a Bible
② an evidence
③ a question
④ a will

62 His off-the-cuff comments have ruffled
feathers at home and abroad.
① provocative   ② tactful
③ impromptu   ④ humble

63 Jones, usually laid-back and jocular, was
snappy at a media conference.
① oracular   ② obstinate
③ affectionate   ④ humorous

64 These upright stones are the vestiges of
some ancient religion.
① patterns   ② traces
③ versions   ④ proofs

65 The Sudanese government has dissented the
idea.
① bolstered   ② contrived
③ initiated   ④ opposed

66 Wendy's negotiations with an unfamiliar and
often threatening world should be excruciating
to watch.
① pestersome   ② abstruse
③ denunciatory   ④ dilatory

67 They don't realize the folly of his idea.
① stupidity   ② danger
③ difficulty   ④ advantage

68 It was a roundabout way of telling us to leave.
① rudimentary   ② circuitous
③ sporadical   ④ audible

69 Reckless distribution of complicated
derivative products throughout the global
market, detached from the real economy,
put the global financial market into crisis.
① unoriginal   ② disingenuous
③ foreign   ④ speculative

70 The jury's deliberation was protracted
because of their confusion over a point of
view.
① lengthened   ② befuddled
③ illuminated   ④ distended

71 Analog, although more cumbersome than
its digital equivalents, provides a richness
of experience unparalleled with anything
delivered from a screen.
① sluggish   ② compulsory
③ burdensome   ④ coarse

72 Through <u>assiduous</u> research work in major museums in Japan, some very rare drawings have been recovered for the spring exhibition, 2004.

① diligent        ② sufficient
③ flattered       ④ insufficient

73 Some people are <u>credulous</u> enough to believe anything they read in a newspaper.

① gullible        ② delusive
③ credible        ④ skeptical

74 He has made it easy for the Palestinians to <u>eschew</u> negotiations and stick with their U.N. strategy.

① elude           ② eradicate
③ execute         ④ elucidate

75 If the agreement is to live up to its promise, countries will have to make full use of the mechanisms for <u>augmenting</u> emissions cuts and accelerating adaptation for decades to come.

① mitigating
② griping at
③ ratcheting up
④ abominating

76 Jack and Jill were married without their parents' <u>benediction</u>.

① blessing        ② being informed
③ donation        ④ attendance

77 You can be lonely anywhere, but there is a particular flavor to the loneliness that comes from living in a city, surrounded by millions of people. Mere physical <u>proximity</u> is not enough to dispel a sense of internal isolation.

① adjacency       ② aloofness
③ complacency     ④ visibility

78 The testing of political and economic assertions against empirical evidence fell into <u>desuetude</u>; open discussion on the scientific model ceased.

① abolition       ② activation
③ beatitude       ④ vitality

79 It is useless to attempt to <u>flee</u> from every danger, some risks must be taken.

① hide oneself
② run away
③ protect oneself
④ stay away

80 In a situation of two roommates, a neatnik's passion for cleanliness may lead her to see the other's messiness not as a simple issue of lifestyle differences, but as intentional and even <u>provocative</u>.

① irritating      ② seductive
③ soothing        ④ voluntary

81 Darwin studied and <u>ruminated</u> over his unusual collection for 25 years before he synthesized his thoughts on evolution.

① modified        ② brooded
③ reminisced      ④ vaulted

82 The one-year <u>moratorium</u> on fuel tax rises was announced the day after the Prime Minister said the January 1 fuel tax rise would be put off for six months.
① refusal      ② liability
③ increment      ④ postponement

83 The problem with market research is that often it is simply too <u>blunt</u> an instrument to pick up the distinction between the bad and the merely different.
① dull      ② efficient
③ keen      ④ outdated

84 "Though they are interesting to note," the meeting manager claimed, "those facts are <u>extrinsic</u> to the matter under discussion."
① extraneous      ② agitated
③ fictive      ④ frenetic

85 When the security guard saw a light in the store after closing hours, it seemed to him that there was something <u>fishy</u> going on.
① suspicious      ② obvious
③ placid      ④ helpless

86 He promoted violence at nearly every one of his rallies until his advisors all <u>supplicated</u> him to stop.
① mandated      ② convinced
③ implored      ④ expedited

87 The government denied that there had been any collateral damage during the bombing <u>raid</u>.
① attack      ② decree
③ sight      ④ disposal

88 Spain must do more to prepare for increasingly <u>virulent</u> wildfires stoked by climate change.
① nagging      ② unextinguished
③ destructive      ④ exorbitant

89 The official spoke on the condition of anonymity to offer a candid response to the House leadership <u>imbroglio</u>.
① reluctance      ② recitation
③ quandary      ④ truancy

90 Priests are those who try to be happy by refraining from <u>worldly</u> passions.
① furious      ② secular
③ unbridled      ④ unsullied

91 Conservatives have accused social media companies of seeking to <u>stifle</u> conservative voices.
① clarify      ② glean
③ atone      ④ suppress

92 Military dictators in the 1960s to 1980s ordered roundups of <u>vagrants</u> to beautify the streets, sending thousands of homeless and disabled people and children to facilities where they were detained and forced to work.
① vagabonds      ② dissidents
③ perverts      ④ lunatics

93 The skyrocketing global wheat prices meant a <u>bonanza</u> for traders.
① solace      ② allocation
③ windfall      ④ collusion

94 Even authoritarian states like China and Russia are <u>leery</u> of dealing with a brutal and mercurial leader like North Korea's Kim Jong Un.

① wary　　　② trifling

③ reprehensive　④ indifferent

95 The soldier said he was <u>retaliating</u> for bullying by senior colleagues.

① tempering　　② revenging

③ agonizing　　④ hesitating

96 Air raid sirens now sound several times a day and the local military hospital is filled with troops coming in from the front lines with <u>ghastly</u> injuries.

① slight　　　② corporal

③ horrible　　④ strenuous

97 Under Oklahoma law, sexual battery is the intentional touching of someone's body in a "<u>lascivious</u> manner" without the person's consent.

① unctuous　　② propitiatory

③ disruptive　　④ lewd

98 Celebrity figures inevitably invite scrutiny and thereby <u>forfeit</u> the right to privacy.

① infringe　　② lose

③ trespass　　④ uphold

99 Computer scientists and engineers are rather more <u>phlegmatic</u> about the notion of quantum supremacy than commentators.

① fortuitous　　② unemotional

③ nefarious　　④ affirmative

100 He has a <u>presentiment</u> that his life will be taken by poison.

① foreboding　　② stupor

③ attachment　　④ antipathy

[1] Write the meaning of the following words.

| | |
|---|---|
| ☐ oppose | ☐ jeremiad |
| ☐ avid | ☐ curse |
| ☐ plum | ☐ orotund |
| ☐ stampede | ☐ lagoon |
| ☐ hilarious | ☐ outstrip |
| ☐ epithet | ☐ isotope |
| ☐ babble | ☐ dwarf |
| ☐ community | ☐ transitory |
| ☐ slough | ☐ spine |
| ☐ indubitable | ☐ expropriate |
| ☐ divest | ☐ aliment |
| ☐ carping | ☐ grouch |
| ☐ seam | ☐ foretell |
| ☐ portentous | ☐ brethren |
| ☐ revenge | ☐ disable |
| ☐ extinction | ☐ wry |
| ☐ fringe | ☐ chafe |
| ☐ bespoke | ☐ rape |
| ☐ misnomer | ☐ matriarch |
| ☐ graze | ☐ surreptitious |
| ☐ tithe | ☐ adulterate |
| ☐ intertwine | ☐ varnish |
| ☐ compunction | ☐ connubial |
| ☐ delirious | ☐ prognosticate |
| ☐ vicissitude | ☐ ethereal |

[2] Select <u>the most</u> appropriate word from the box below. Each word should be used only once.

| | | | |
|---|---|---|---|
| ① indubitable | ② expropriate | ③ bespoke | ④ compunction |
| ⑤ carping | ⑥ portentous | ⑦ transitory | ⑧ outstrip |
| ⑨ avid | ⑩ adulterate | ⑪ jeremiad | ⑫ intertwine |
| ⑬ varnish | ⑭ grouch | ⑮ surreptitious | ⑯ stampede |
| ⑰ orotund | ⑱ wry | ⑲ aliment | ⑳ misnomer |

**1** As the doors of the store opened on Black Friday, eager shoppers created a frantic _____ in their rush to snag the best deals on electronics and gadgets.

**2** The bookworm was known for being _____ in his pursuit of devouring literature.

**3** The evidence presented in the case was so convincing that the jury reached a(n) _____ conclusion about the defendant's guilt.

**4** The sudden appearance of the comet in the night sky was seen as a(n) _____ sign by the ancient civilizations, often interpreted as a harbinger of significant changes or events to come.

**5** Democratic leaders need to rethink their relationship with a barbaric regime that has no _____ about killing its own citizens.

**6** The singer's performance was marked by a(n) _____ voice that filled the auditorium with its powerful resonance.

**7** The state of euphoria after winning the championship was _____ but etched in memory forever.

**8** The dictator's decision to _____ the citizens' assets for personal gain exemplified the abuse of power and sparked international condemnation.

**9** The thieves' _____ actions allowed them to bypass the elaborate security measures and steal the valuable artifact from the museum unnoticed.

**10** The intention to _____ the essential oils with synthetic fragrances was a deceptive attempt to cut costs.

## [3] Choose the one which is different from the others.

**11**  ① revenge  ② reprisal  ③ retaliation  ④ siege

**12**  ① hilarious  ② queer  ③ amusing  ④ funny

**13**  ① cognizant  ② rapt  ③ ecstatic  ④ delirious

**14**  ① curse  ② anathema  ③ fuss  ④ imprecation

**15**  ① ethereal  ② heavenly  ③ celestial  ④ provident

**16**  ① prognosticate  ② procrastinate  ③ forecast  ④ predict

**17**  ① verge  ② fringe  ③ sanctuary  ④ edge

**18**  ① change  ② mutation  ③ vicissitude  ④ resiliency

**19**  ① slough  ② apathy  ③ quagmire  ④ sludge

**20**  ① prestige  ② epithet  ③ nickname  ④ sobriquet

### ✓Answers

**1** ⑯ ┃ 블랙 프라이데이에 매장 문이 열리자 열성적인 쇼핑객들은 전자 제품과 기기를 아주 좋은 가격에 낚아채기 위해 서두르면서 열광적으로 몰려들었다.

**2** ⑨ ┃ 그 책벌레는 문학 작품을 탐독하는 데 열성적인 것으로 알려져 있었다.

**3** ① ┃ 그 사건에 제시된 증거가 너무 확실해서 배심원은 피고인의 유죄에 대해 의심할 여지가 없는 결론에 도달했다.

**4** ⑥ ┃ 밤하늘에 혜성이 갑자기 나타나는 것은 고대 문명에서 불길한 징조로 여겨졌으며, 종종 앞으로 일어날 중대한 변화나 사건의 전조로 해석되었다.

**5** ④ ┃ 민주적인 지도자들은 자국민을 죽인 것에 대해 전혀 뉘우침을 보이지 않는 야만적인 정권과의 관계를 재고할 필요가 있다.

**6** ⑰ ┃ 그 가수의 공연은 객석을 강렬한 울림으로 가득 채운 낭랑한 목소리가 특징을 이루었다.

**7** ⑦ ┃ 우승 후의 행복감은 일시적이었지만 기억 속에 영원히 새겨졌다.

**8** ② ┃ 독재자가 개인적 이득을 위해 시민들의 재산을 몰수한 결정은 권력 남용의 전형적인 예가 되었고 국제적인 비난을 불러일으켰다.

**9** ⑮ ┃ 도둑들은 은밀한 행동으로 정교한 보안 조치를 피해 박물관에서 귀중한 유물을 눈에 띄지 않게 훔칠 수 있었다.

**10** ⑩ ┃ 에센셜 오일에 합성 향료를 섞는 것의 의도는 비용을 절감하려는 기만적인 시도였다.

- - - - - - - - - - - - - - - - - - - - - - - - - - - - - - - - - - - - - - - - - - - - - - - - - - - - - - - - -

**11** ④   **12** ②   **13** ①   **14** ③   **15** ④   **16** ②   **17** ③   **18** ④   **19** ②   **20** ①

[1] Write the meaning of the following words.

| | |
|---|---|
| ☐ considerate | ☐ census |
| ☐ hone | ☐ wily |
| ☐ interregnum | ☐ accolade |
| ☐ substantiate | ☐ depress |
| ☐ binding | ☐ xenophobia |
| ☐ duly | ☐ virile |
| ☐ communism | ☐ proceeds |
| ☐ inveterate | ☐ chasten |
| ☐ platitudinous | ☐ stricture |
| ☐ revision | ☐ coalition |
| ☐ extricate | ☐ routine |
| ☐ mettle | ☐ mold |
| ☐ firm | ☐ dissection |
| ☐ tract | ☐ evangelical |
| ☐ browbeat | ☐ lyric |
| ☐ ensign | ☐ outlaw |
| ☐ swallow | ☐ brook |
| ☐ grimace | ☐ noted |
| ☐ array | ☐ coterie |
| ☐ unremitting | ☐ solvent |
| ☐ puncture | ☐ thirst |
| ☐ attainment | ☐ ordain |
| ☐ rabid | ☐ flagship |
| ☐ probity | ☐ gut |
| ☐ itch | ☐ desecrate |

[2] Select <u>the most</u> appropriate word from the box below. Each word should be used only once.

| | | | |
|---|---|---|---|
| ① depress | ② probity | ③ rabid | ④ binding |
| ⑤ mettle | ⑥ platitudinous | ⑦ desecrate | ⑧ interregnum |
| ⑨ browbeat | ⑩ ordain | ⑪ solvent | ⑫ coterie |
| ⑬ outlaw | ⑭ xenophobia | ⑮ routine | ⑯ evangelical |
| ⑰ dissection | ⑱ flagship | ⑲ stricture | ⑳ extricate |

**1**    His promise was not just a mere verbal agreement; it was a(n) _____ commitment that held him accountable for his actions.

**2**    Following the monarch's unexpected death, the realm experienced a(n) _____, a time of transition and uncertainty in governance.

**3**    Despite the speaker's attempt to sound profound, his speech was filled with _____ expressions that lacked originality or depth.

**4**    The bank official desperately tried to _____ himself from the financial crisis he had helped to create, but all his influence couldn't get him out of trouble this time.

**5**    The coach used his aggressive demeanor to _____ the team into pushing harder during practice.

**6**    The company's reputation for uncompromising _____ was upheld by its CEO who set a standard of honesty and transparency in all business dealings.

**7**    The recent surge in anti-immigrant sentiment showcased a deep-rooted undercurrent of _____.

**8**    Her meticulous budgeting and prudent investments made her not just financially stable but also remarkably _____.

**9**    Do not _____ the sacred temple by writing graffiti on a wall.

**10**    The students awaited their lesson on the _____ of a frog to understand its internal anatomy better.

[3] Choose the one which is different from the others.

**11** ① ransack      ② substantiate      ③ affirm      ④ corroborate

**12** ① ingrained      ② deep-rooted      ③ inveterate      ④ broad-minded

**13** ① considerate      ② attentive      ③ mean      ④ sympathetic

**14** ① frown      ② grin      ③ grimace      ④ scowl

**15** ① unremitting      ② ceaseless      ③ transient      ④ incessant

**16** ① accolade      ② rebuttal      ③ applause      ④ compliment

**17** ① masculine      ② manly      ③ effeminate      ④ virile

**18** ① noted      ② eminent      ③ famous      ④ humdrum

**19** ① division      ② coalition      ③ alliance      ④ union

**20** ① income      ② disbursement      ③ proceeds      ④ profit

## ✓ Answers

**1** ④  | 그의 약속은 단순한 구두 합의에 불과한 것이 아니라, 그의 행동에 대한 책임을 묻는 구속력 있는 약속이었다.

**2** ⑧  | 군주의 갑작스러운 죽음 이후, 왕국은 과도기이자 불확실한 통치 시기인 정치 공백기를 경험했다.

**3** ⑥  | 의미심장하게 들리려는 화자의 시도에도 불구하고, 그의 연설은 독창성이나 깊이가 부족한 진부한 표현으로 가득 차 있었다.

**4** ⑳  | 그 은행원은 자신이 조장하여 초래된 금융위기에서 벗어나려고 필사적으로 노력했지만, 그의 모든 영향력이 이번에는 그를 위기에서 벗어나게 할 수 없었다.

**5** ⑨  | 감독은 그의 적극적인 태도를 이용해 팀을 을러대어 연습 중에 더 강하게 밀어붙이게 했다.

**6** ②  | 완고할 정도로 정직한 그 회사의 명성은 모든 사업 거래에서 공정함과 투명성을 기준으로 세운 최고경영자에 의해 유지되었다.

**7** ⑭  | 최근 반이민자 정서의 급증은 외국인 혐오증의 뿌리 깊은 저의(底意)를 보여주었다.

**8** ⑪  | 그녀의 신중한 예산 관리와 분별 있는 투자는 그녀를 재정적으로 안정적일 뿐만 아니라 놀라울 정도로 지불능력이 있게 만들었다.

**9** ⑦  | 벽에 낙서를 해서 신성한 사원을 모독하는 일이 없도록 하십시오.

**10** ⑰  | 학생들은 개구리의 해부학적 체내 구조를 더 잘 이해하기 위해 개구리 해부에 대한 수업을 기다렸다.

**11** ①      **12** ④      **13** ③      **14** ②      **15** ③      **16** ②      **17** ③      **18** ④      **19** ①      **20** ②

[1] Write the meaning of the following words.

| | |
|---|---|
| ☐ outburst | ☐ enormity |
| ☐ devious | ☐ cadaver |
| ☐ adjoin | ☐ kleptomania |
| ☐ profuse | ☐ factious |
| ☐ infiltrate | ☐ trite |
| ☐ celerity | ☐ bypass |
| ☐ forge | ☐ over-the-counter |
| ☐ pretense | ☐ anoint |
| ☐ extramural | ☐ connection |
| ☐ swerve | ☐ evacuate |
| ☐ dolmen | ☐ irreversible |
| ☐ contravene | ☐ saliva |
| ☐ agitation | ☐ nitty-gritty |
| ☐ lofty | ☐ hedge |
| ☐ metallurgy | ☐ winnow |
| ☐ replenish | ☐ serene |
| ☐ conflagration | ☐ revulsion |
| ☐ sullen | ☐ reliant |
| ☐ bandit | ☐ thermometer |
| ☐ flimsy | ☐ divert |
| ☐ grip | ☐ modish |
| ☐ parenthesis | ☐ purge |
| ☐ anticlimax | ☐ villain |
| ☐ intestine | ☐ cognate |
| ☐ befuddle | ☐ gimmick |

[2] Select <u>the most</u> appropriate word from the box below. Each word should be used only once.

| | | | |
|---|---|---|---|
| ① infiltrate | ② sullen | ③ factious | ④ winnow |
| ⑤ modish | ⑥ enormity | ⑦ forgery | ⑧ swerved |
| ⑨ trite | ⑩ gimmick | ⑪ extramural | ⑫ contravene |
| ⑬ outburst | ⑭ intestine | ⑮ cognate | ⑯ celerity |
| ⑰ evacuate | ⑱ reliant | ⑲ lofty | ⑳ befuddled |

**1**      Authorities say they found counterfeit money in his car and soon learned he was wanted on _____ charges.

**2**      The undercover agent needed to _____ the anti-government organization to gain access to crucial information without raising suspicion.

**3**      The company's decision to bypass regulations seemed to _____ the ethical standards they had previously upheld.

**4**      The famed philosopher's _____ ideals about human potential propelled generations to aspire to greatness.

**5**      Despite his friends' efforts to cheer him up, Jack remained _____ throughout the rainy evening.

**6**      The convoluted plot of the mystery novel _____ even the most seasoned readers as they struggled to untangle the web of clues and red herrings.

**7**      Bromide is a chemical compound that was commonly used in sedatives in the 1900s. It took on a figurative sense to mean a(n) _____ saying, or a person who is boring.

**8**      As soon as the mountain fire started, everyone was ordered to _____ the town.

**9**      The detective needed to _____ out the truth from the myriad of contradictory statements given by the witnesses to solve the case.

**10**      The advertisement boasted a groundbreaking feature but savvy consumers saw it as nothing more than a clever _____ designed to mask the product's shortcomings.

[3] Choose the one which is different from the others.

**11**  ① agitation      ② commotion      ③ disturbance      ④ humiliation

**12**  ① devious      ② boisterous      ③ indirect      ④ roundabout

**13**  ① weak      ② fragile      ③ flimsy      ④ sturdy

**14**  ① circumvent      ② avoid      ③ breach      ④ bypass

**15**  ① nitty-gritty      ② exteriority      ③ kernel      ④ gist

**16**  ① affecting      ② serene      ③ quiet      ④ tranquil

**17**  ① exuberance      ② revulsion      ③ abhorrence      ④ aversion

**18**  ① grip      ② clutch      ③ omission      ④ grasp

**19**  ① purge      ② expel      ③ oust      ④ fabricate

**20**  ① scoundrel      ② savant      ③ knave      ④ villain

## ✓ Answers

**1** ⑦ | 당국은 그의 차에서 위조지폐를 찾았으며 그가 위조 혐의로 지명 수배를 받고 있다는 사실을 이내 알게 됐다고 말한다.

**2** ① | 비밀 요원은 의혹을 일으키지 않고 중요한 정보에 접근하기 위해 반국가 단체에 잠입해야 했다.

**3** ⑫ | 회사가 규정을 무시하기로 한 결정은 그들이 이전에 지켜온 윤리적 기준에 위배되는 것처럼 보였다.

**4** ⑲ | 인간의 잠재력에 대한 그 유명한 철학자의 고결한 이상은 여러 세대에게 위대함에 대한 큰 뜻을 품게 했다.

**5** ② | 그를 격려하려는 친구들의 노력에도 불구하고, 잭(Jack)은 비오는 저녁 내내 시무룩했다.

**6** ⑳ | 추리소설의 대단히 난해한 줄거리는 가장 노련한 독자들도 당황하게 했는데, 이들은 단서들과 헷갈리게 하는 사실들이 뒤얽혀있는 것을 풀기 위해 애썼다.

**7** ⑨ | 브롬화물은 1900년대에 진정제로 흔히 사용된 화합물이다. 그것은 진부한 말 또는 따분한 사람이라는 비유적인 의미를 갖게 되었다.

**8** ⑰ | 산불이 나자마자, 모든 사람들은 그 마을에서 대피하라는 명령을 받았다.

**9** ④ | 형사는 사건을 해결하기 위해 증인들이 제시한 수많은 모순된 진술들로부터 진실을 가려내야 했다.

**10** ⑩ | 그 광고는 혁신적인 기능을 자랑했지만, 현명한 소비자들은 그것을 제품의 단점을 감추기 위한 영리한 속임수에 지나지 않는다고 생각했다.

- - - - - - - - - - - - - - - - - - - - - - - - - - - - - - - - - - - - - - - - - - - - - - - - - - - - -

**11** ④    **12** ②    **13** ④    **14** ③    **15** ②    **16** ①    **17** ①    **18** ③    **19** ④    **20** ②

**[1] Write the meaning of the following words.**

| | | | |
|---|---|---|---|
| ☐ exterminate | | ☐ incense | |
| ☐ verge | | ☐ obligation | |
| ☐ resplendent | | ☐ unruly | |
| ☐ spellbind | | ☐ burnish | |
| ☐ content | | ☐ expulsion | |
| ☐ amity | | ☐ logical | |
| ☐ peculate | | ☐ clot | |
| ☐ insignia | | ☐ nutrition | |
| ☐ spoil | | ☐ abscond | |
| ☐ credential | | ☐ pollen | |
| ☐ dog-in-the-manger | | ☐ defect | |
| ☐ forbear | | ☐ talisman | |
| ☐ progenitor | | ☐ musty | |
| ☐ bootleg | | ☐ egress | |
| ☐ citadel | | ☐ amortize | |
| ☐ typical | | ☐ brevity | |
| ☐ rectitude | | ☐ compound | |
| ☐ elope | | ☐ frost | |
| ☐ prone | | ☐ asunder | |
| ☐ huddle | | ☐ genuflect | |
| ☐ motion | | ☐ retrospect | |
| ☐ grandiose | | ☐ jaded | |
| ☐ stratagem | | ☐ lust | |
| ☐ deprecate | | ☐ stultify | |
| ☐ flotsam | | ☐ invulnerable | |

[2] Select <u>the most</u> appropriate word from the box below. Each word should be used only once.

| | | | |
|---|---|---|---|
| ① verge | ② nutrition | ③ amortize | ④ peculate |
| ⑤ expulsion | ⑥ forbore | ⑦ huddled | ⑧ exterminate |
| ⑨ rectitude | ⑩ stultified | ⑪ jaded | ⑫ content |
| ⑬ grandiose | ⑭ bootleg | ⑮ invulnerable | ⑯ deprecate |
| ⑰ clot | ⑱ unruly | ⑲ retrospect | ⑳ brevity |

**1** The auditor discovered that the unscrupulous employee had attempted to _____ funds from the company's accounts for personal gain.

**2** Known for his unyielding commitment to moral principles, he exemplified a rare and admirable sense of _____ in every action he took.

**3** Those who profess to favor freedom and yet _____ agitation are men who want crops without plowing up the ground.

**4** The principal found it challenging to manage the _____ group of students who consistently disrupted the quiet atmosphere of the school library.

**5** He was on the _____ of moving on from the project when a single late-night experiment proved successful.

**6** Despite the urge to retaliate, he _____ from seeking revenge, choosing instead to forgive and move forward.

**7** The gravity of his misconduct left the school with no choice but to proceed with his prompt _____.

**8** In an effort to maintain hygiene, the cleaning crew diligently works to _____ any traces of mold in the damp areas of the building.

**9** Because we are short on time, _____ would be appreciated; we need to leave in ten minutes to catch the last bus of the night.

**10** The ancient myth spoke of a magical amulet that rendered its wearer completely _____ to the dark sorcerer's spells.

**[3]** Choose the one which is different from the others.

| | | | |
|---|---|---|---|
| **11** | ① bulwark | ② citadel | ③ bastion | ④ bonanza |
| **12** | ① stratagem | ② stagnation | ③ maneuver | ④ ruse |
| **13** | ① placate | ② incense | ③ enrage | ④ infuriate |
| **14** | ① dazzling | ② brilliant | ③ resplendent | ④ withering |
| **15** | ① spellbind | ② repel | ③ charm | ④ entrance |
| **16** | ① friendliness | ② amity | ③ alacrity | ④ amicability |
| **17** | ① sage | ② forebear | ③ ancestor | ④ progenitor |
| **18** | ① abscond | ② elope | ③ trudge | ④ flee |
| **19** | ① periapt | ② amulet | ③ talisman | ④ cliche |
| **20** | ① exacerbate | ② clarify | ③ compound | ④ aggravate |

## ✓ Answers

**1** ④ ┃ 회계 감사관은 부도덕한 직원이 개인적 이익을 위해 회사 계좌에서 자금을 유용하려고 한 사실을 발견했다.

**2** ⑨ ┃ 도의에 대한 확고한 신념으로 유명한 그는 자신이 취하는 모든 행동에서 보기 드물고 존경할 만한 정직함을 보여주었다.

**3** ⑯ ┃ 자유를 지지한다고 주장하지만 (자유) 운동을 비난하는 사람들은 토지를 경작하지 않으면서 수확만 원하는 사람들이다.

**4** ⑱ ┃ 교장 선생님은 조용한 학교 도서관의 분위기를 지속적으로 방해하는 제멋대로인 학생들을 관리하기가 어렵다는 것을 알았다.

**5** ① ┃ 늦은 밤에 진행된 한 실험이 성공한 것으로 판명되었을 때, 그는 그 과제에서 다른 과제로 막 넘어가려는 참이었다.

**6** ⑥ ┃ 복수하고 싶은 충동에도 불구하고, 그는 복수하는 것을 삼가고 대신 용서하고 앞으로 나아가는 것을 택했다.

**7** ⑤ ┃ 그의 위법 행위의 심각성으로 인해 학교에서는 즉각적인 퇴학 조치를 취할 수밖에 없었다.

**8** ⑧ ┃ 좋은 위생 상태를 유지하기 위해 청소부는 건물의 습한 곳에 있는 곰팡이 자국을 제거하기 위해 부지런히 노력하고 있다.

**9** ⑳ ┃ 시간이 부족하기 때문에 간결한 것이 좋을 듯하다. 우리가 그날 밤의 막차를 타기 위해서는 10분 안에 떠나야 할 것이다.

**10** ⑮ ┃ 그 고대 신화는 부적을 착용한 사람을 사악한 마법사의 주문에도 완전히 끄떡없게 해주는 마법의 부적에 관해 이야기했다.

. . . . . . . . . . . . . . . . . . . . . . . . . . . . . . . . . . . . . . . . . . . . . . . . . . . . . . . . . . . . . . . . . . . . . . . . . . . . . . . . . . . . . . . . . . .

**11** ④    **12** ②    **13** ①    **14** ④    **15** ②    **16** ③    **17** ①    **18** ③    **19** ④    **20** ②

[1] Write the meaning of the following words.

| | |
|---|---|
| ☐ juvenile | ☐ duplicity |
| ☐ expertise | ☐ stump |
| ☐ surly | ☐ evince |
| ☐ pry | ☐ orgy |
| ☐ acquisitive | ☐ gaunt |
| ☐ detach | ☐ slime |
| ☐ cane | ☐ queue |
| ☐ insouciant | ☐ rudiment |
| ☐ scoop | ☐ clapped-out |
| ☐ apprentice | ☐ affix |
| ☐ revert | ☐ panoply |
| ☐ brash | ☐ dissipate |
| ☐ genealogy | ☐ bipolar |
| ☐ pressing | ☐ lampoon |
| ☐ forage | ☐ hostage |
| ☐ slit | ☐ filch |
| ☐ rove | ☐ mine |
| ☐ whopping | ☐ ejaculate |
| ☐ congratulation | ☐ installment |
| ☐ viscous | ☐ nominal |
| ☐ axis | ☐ belch |
| ☐ infuse | ☐ terminology |
| ☐ choleric | ☐ converse |
| ☐ troop | ☐ subject |
| ☐ feral | ☐ ornithology |

[2] Select <u>the most</u> appropriate word from the box below. Each word should be used only once.

| | | | |
|---|---|---|---|
| ① insouciant | ② pressing | ③ ejaculate | ④ hostage |
| ⑤ dissipated | ⑥ expertise | ⑦ slit | ⑧ detached |
| ⑨ apprentice | ⑩ revert | ⑪ viscous | ⑫ gaunt |
| ⑬ duplicity | ⑭ choleric | ⑮ affix | ⑯ belch |
| ⑰ infused | ⑱ converse | ⑲ lampoon | ⑳ forage |

1   Despite the imminent deadline, Sarah remained remarkably _____ about completing her project.

2   The nomadic tribes often embarked on journeys to _____ for sustenance in unfamiliar territories.

3   The artist's paintings were _____ with vibrant colors that brought life and energy to each canvas.

4   People may think of biodiversity or endangered species as something _____ from their daily lives. But those people don't understand that Earth functions as a "living planet" with many parts dependent on each other.

5   In spite of his efforts to remain composed, his _____ temperament often led to outbursts of anger and frustration.

6   The prolonged illness made him appear increasingly _____ with a sunken face and a frail physique.

7   The criminals took the innocent civilians as _____ to demand their ransom.

8   Skilled labor involves people who either have _____ in a particular skill, like tool making or printing, or who have received professional training in fields such as medicine, education and law.

9   The skilled craftsman took on a young _____ to pass on his knowledge and expertise.

10   Software users might _____ to an older version of a program with fewer bugs.

[3] Choose the one which is different from the others.

**11** ① abstruse  ② avaricious  ③ greedy  ④ acquisitive

**12** ① surly  ② dour  ③ sullen  ④ sedulous

**13** ① foolhardy  ② brash  ③ discreet  ④ reckless

**14** ① evince  ② withhold  ③ demonstrate  ④ manifest

**15** ① orgy  ② spree  ③ temperance  ④ indulgence

**16** ① nominal  ② impotent  ③ titular  ④ token

**17** ① lingo  ② jargon  ③ terminology  ④ profanity

**18** ① whopping  ② lackluster  ③ enormous  ④ massive

**19** ① orbit  ② axis  ③ axle  ④ pivot

**20** ① thieve  ② filch  ③ beguile  ④ steal

## ✔ Answers

**1** ①  | 마감일이 임박했음에도 불구하고, 사라(Sarah)는 자신의 프로젝트를 마치는 데 매우 태평했다.

**2** ⑳  | 유목민들은 낯선 지역에서 생명을 유지하는 데 필요한 것을 찾기 위해 종종 여행을 떠났다.

**3** ⑰  | 그 화가의 그림들은 각 캔버스에 활기와 에너지를 불어넣은 강렬한 색들로 가득 차 있었다.

**4** ⑧  | 사람들은 생물의 다양성 혹은 멸종 위기에 처한 종(種)을 자신들의 일상과 동떨어진 것으로 생각할지도 모른다. 그러나 이런 사람들은 지구가 서로에게 의존하는 많은 부분을 가진 '살아있는 행성'으로서 기능한다는 것을 이해하지 못한다.

**5** ⑭  | 침착함을 유지하려는 노력에도 불구하고, 그의 성마른 기질은 종종 분노와 좌절감의 폭발로 이어졌다.

**6** ⑫  | 장기간의 투병으로 인해 그는 홀쭉한 얼굴과 허약한 체격으로 점점 수척해 보였다.

**7** ④  | 범인들은 무고한 민간인들을 인질로 삼아 그들의 몸값을 요구했다.

**8** ⑥  | 숙련 노동에는 연장 제작이나 인쇄 등의 특별한 기술에 있어서 전문지식을 가지고 있는 사람 혹은 의학이나 교육, 법률과 같은 분야에서 전문적인 훈련을 받은 사람이 관련된다.

**9** ⑨  | 숙련된 장인은 어린 견습생을 맡아 지식과 전문지식을 전수했다.

**10** ⑩  | 소프트웨어 사용자는 버그가 적은 이전 버전의 프로그램으로 되돌아갈 수도 있다.

**11** ①  **12** ④  **13** ③  **14** ②  **15** ③  **16** ②  **17** ④  **18** ②  **19** ①  **20** ③

# ACTUAL TEST

[01-100] Choose the one that is closest in meaning to the underlined part.

**01** As an avid football fan, I try to see every game the Jets play.
① watchful
② skillful
③ eager
④ elementary

**02** The tavern owners stampeded us into overeating.
① misled
② lulled
③ embarrassed
④ forced

**03** She gave us a hilarious account of her first days as a teacher.
① an absurd
② an amusing
③ a dubious
④ an obvious

**04** In ancient times, eclipses were seen as portentous omens, events that ushered in fated beginnings or endings of historical import.
① oblivious
② threatening
③ obese
④ tantalizing

**05** It's a rare thing to witness the extinction of an entire class of animal.
① subsidence
② augmentation
③ extermination
④ propagation

**06** The story of *The Wizard of Oz* is based on the delirious dream Dorothy has after she bumps her head during a tornado.
① vivid
② demented
③ excruciating
④ hollow

**07** What is undeniable is that Bill had no compunction about drastic measures.
① extirpation
② quip
③ scruple
④ proclivity

**06** Since the technology for such bespoke genetic drugs debuted in 2018, about two dozen patients have received the infusions to treat a range of neurological syndromes.
① tailor-made
② state-of-the-art
③ over-the-top
④ down-to-earth

**09** He was ultimately destroyed by the vicissitudes of fortune, even though he had tried to adjust.
① wheel
② exchange
③ unexpected change
④ prophecy

**10** Mankind's greatest curse is poverty.
① bane
② symbol
③ vanguard
④ advantage

**11** Mr. Sanders is still prone to impromptu jeremiads about the health care industry, and nothing makes him happier than discussing signature policy proposals like "Medicare for All."
① initiative
② amendment
③ extremity
④ lamentation

**12** Cellular technology has <u>outstripped</u> power lines and the Internet in connecting rural areas.

① exceeded      ② deactivated

③ intensified      ④ unveiled

**13** China's Singles' Day has become the world's biggest shopping event, reaching a mind-blowing $25 billion in sales this year and <u>dwarfing</u> Black Friday and Cyber Monday combined.

① aggravating      ② perpetuating

③ reinstating      ④ overshadowing

**14** The winters in Scotland are longer and darker, so hard, warm liquor provides light and respite, no matter how <u>transitory</u>.

① transcendental      ② deceptive

③ fleeting      ④ translucent

**15** If the teams were not so evenly matched, it would be easier to <u>foretell</u> the outcome of the league.

① endorse      ② hinder

③ negate      ④ predict

**16** The researcher <u>surreptitiously</u> removed one egg a day from the bird's nest.

① quickly      ② secretly

③ occasionally      ④ forcefully

**17** The milk in these containers is <u>adulterated</u>.

① spoiled      ② expensive

③ warm      ④ leaking

**18** After viewing some of the financial indexes, a few pessimistic economists began to <u>prognosticate</u> an economic recession.

① forecast      ② truncate

③ quash      ④ polarize

**19** Many people think that Jackson is the most <u>considerate</u> one of them all.

① considerable      ② thoughtful

③ peevish      ④ dominant

**20** A number of new research studies <u>substantiate</u> the assumption that television interferes with family activities and the formation of family relationships.

① affirm      ② overturn

③ propose      ④ reject

**21** These <u>inveterate</u> travelers often visit other groups, not only seeking wage labor, but also simply out of curiosity about other peoples and places.

① habitual      ② successful

③ impoverished      ④ superstitious

**22** We are left with <u>platitudes</u> about being empirical, nuanced, and avoiding dogmatism, without a serious discussion of the important questions that are so carelessly glossed over.

① plethora      ② glitches

③ banalities      ④ trappings

**23** Inflation caused the government to <u>revise</u> its estimate of its annual expenditures.

① amend      ② transact

③ dispose of      ④ bleach

24  The farmer extricated the dog from the barbed-wire fence.
① vaunted          ② rankled
③ scrutinized      ④ removed

25  The mettle of a man is tested in adversities and he who remains in his beliefs comes out shining.
① cleverness       ② courage
③ insight          ④ promise

26  They patiently browbeat the landlord into fixing the heat and the plumbing.
① advised          ② acknowledged
③ begged           ④ threatened

27  The patients with lead poisoning could have the unremitting abdominal pain and nausea.
① incessant        ② unexplained
③ obtuse           ④ indelible

28  Everywhere citizens seem to want better government, probity in public office, and a state that cares for its people.
① misconduct       ② integrity
③ privilege        ④ surveillance

29  Non-violence, in contrast, seeks to appreciate and value the humanity and work of every person, and to build coalitions with all who seek a better life.
① obsessions       ② alliances
③ nominations      ④ nullifications

30  The interview is a routine part of the selection process.
① a temporary      ② a regular
③ a special        ④ an important

31  Instead of dissecting social or political woes, U.S. News reporters offer thoughts about solutions they have run across in recent months to a range of problems, great or small.
① dissolving       ② exacting
③ diluting         ④ analyzing

32  No one had the guts to raise a riot, but if a European woman went through the bazaars alone somebody would probably spit betel juice over her dress.
① the apprehension
② the intervention
③ the intransigence
④ the determination

33  When preparing for a foreign occupation, the military instructs troops not to desecrate sacred sites and risk offending the local population.
① beleaguer        ② adulterate
③ sanctify         ④ defile

34  In court, the judge will probably chasten the repeat offender with a lecture and a harsh sentence.
① sully            ② discipline
③ empower          ④ coax

**35** They went by <u>a devious</u> route.

① a scenic      ② an indirect

③ a straight      ④ a short

**36** Mallows are a type of flowering plant in the taxonomic family Malvaceae which grow <u>profusely</u> in woods and marshes.

① wildly      ② preciously

③ abundantly      ④ profoundly

**37** Television entered our lives robed as the bearer of communal bonds, providing a new set of common experiences, block parties, and festive gatherings shared by children and adults alike. The fantasies of television slowly <u>infiltrate</u> our own.

① simulate      ② adulterate

③ permeate      ④ evacuate

**38** Tom accepted the task with <u>celerity</u>. Before the request was completed, he was clearing the table.

① determination

② an independent spirit

③ being very quick and swift in action

④ reluctance

**39** We should <u>forge</u> partnerships with those around us and begin to dismantle the myth of solitary perfection.

① construct      ② disassemble

③ condemn      ④ discard

**40** It was pointed out that the construction of a highrise would <u>contravene</u> building code.

① submit      ② violate

③ assure      ④ obey

**41** I saw Peter glancing at his watch in some <u>agitation</u>.

① swelling      ② infection

③ nervousness      ④ clumsiness

**42** It's a landscape like no other on the planet — the colossal glaciers of the Himalaya, which for millennia have been <u>replenished</u> by monsoons that smother the mountains in new snow each summer.

① recycled      ② removed

③ restored      ④ revolved

**43** It is not so easy to abandon the whiny toddler or the <u>sullen</u> teenager.

① wary      ② unfriendly

③ morose      ④ remote

**44** Whether in Africa, India or even Cyprus, the British never hesitated to imprison nationalist leaders, often on <u>flimsy</u> charges.

① heavy      ② civil

③ feeble      ④ false

**45** Circus clowns may seem clumsy and <u>befuddled</u>, but good clowning requires a flexible body and quick mind.

① beguiled      ② confused

③ weird      ④ hilarious

**46** By the time the receiving line had ended, the bride and groom's thanks sounded <u>trite</u> and tired.

① hackneyed      ② exhausted

③ vacant      ④ tepid

**47** He was ordered to <u>evacuate</u> his building in Battery Park.

① construct  ② desert

③ rent  ④ decorate

**48** It was a <u>serene</u> summer night as the girl walked by the ocean.

① romantic  ② hot

③ calm  ④ exciting

**49** Many people in this country who admired dictatorship underwent a <u>revulsion</u> when they realized what their president was trying to do.

① repulsion  ② revelry

③ reprisal  ④ rescission

**50** Finding these programs has been a <u>diverting</u> puzzle for programmers.

① entertaining  ② platitudinous

③ prosaic  ④ tiresome

**51** Montgomery County leaders announced a costly effort to <u>purge</u> panhandlers from busy streets.

① extirpate  ② succor

③ contort  ④ abet

**52** We truly believe chocolate is beneficial to the skin, not just another <u>gimmick</u>.

① trick  ② delight

③ tidbit  ④ confectionery

**53** Time ran out before we could get down to the real <u>nitty-gritty</u>.

① liability  ② kernel

③ waiver  ④ disclaimer

**54** Bribes may be demanded in order for an official to do something he or she is already paid to do or to <u>bypass</u> laws and regulations.

① grasp  ② modify

③ manipulate  ④ avoid

**55** They should be severely punished for the <u>enormity</u> of their crimes.

① insincerity  ② villainy

③ evidence  ④ demise

**56** We must find a way to prevent the <u>extermination</u> of these animals.

① annihilation  ② extraction

③ dejection  ④ ferocity

**57** Princess Diana lived what seemed a <u>resplendent</u> life, but her beauty and wealth offer little protection against loneliness.

① haughty  ② prodigal

③ dazzling  ④ spurious

**58** National rivalries, hatreds, and intrigues will cease, and racial animosity and prejudice will be replaced by racial <u>amity</u>, understanding and cooperation.

① friendship  ② enmity

③ amenity  ④ dignity

**59** This hotel advertises that it <u>spoils</u> its guests.

① supplies beverage free to

② takes a decisive step for

③ offers free parking to

④ treats too well

**60** You must use <u>forbearance</u> in dealing with him because he is still weak from his illness.
① affinity         ② negligence
③ patience       ④ transparency

**61** Carla was something of an amateur genealogist, and her entire family was in that book, at least, as far back as 1638, when its earliest traceable <u>progenitor</u> had risen out of the nameless crowd of Londoners.
① root             ② forebear
③ successor      ④ descendant

**62** Our commitment to moral <u>rectitude</u> is to constantly act responsibly and lovingly during one's college days and throughout life.
① imperative     ② uplift
③ fortitude       ④ integrity

**63** Man is <u>prone</u> to error, even though he'd like to think he's infallible.
① pronounced    ② disposed
③ lying down     ④ averse

**64** In a sense, the <u>grandiose</u> waves of the Internet completely transformed traditional media industries and their short-term revenue projections.
① compatible     ② magnificent
③ eccentric       ④ rudimentary

**65** EU states should detain migrants who may <u>abscond</u> before they are deported.
① infringe        ② trudge
③ flee             ④ settle

**66** Kurt was so <u>incensed</u> upon discovering my mistake that he shouted at me for a full five minutes.
① irate            ② timid
③ doleful         ④ euphoric

**67** An <u>unruly</u> crowd of demonstrators suddenly turned riotous as the police appeared.
① phlegmatic     ② restive
③ obsequious    ④ onerous

**68** The way he has gone about his business undoubtedly will <u>burnish</u> his overall image.
① tarnish         ② restore
③ enhance        ④ distort

**69** The punishment of <u>expulsion</u> from the club was thought too harsh.
① nomination    ② injection
③ emancipation  ④ ejection

**70** The whole history of social reform demonstrates how much easier it is to <u>deprecate</u> evils than to take effective action against them.
① disabuse       ② adulate
③ condemn       ④ redress

**71** Whatever his <u>defects</u> as human being, and they were clearly apparent to all those who tried to befriend him, Rousseau was a genius.
① defaults        ② blemishes
③ merits          ④ mediocrity

72 The essays were written with admirable brevity.
① humor
② description
③ briefness
④ magnificence

73 These politic difficulties are compounded by the state governments' murky finances.
① decreased
② aggravated
③ caused
④ camouflaged

74 In retrospect, I think I made a good decision to study engineering.
① Speaking honestly
② Recently
③ Surprisingly
④ Looking back

75 Although the group of veteran tourists seemed a bit jaded at the beginning of the trip, the awe-inspiring wildlife and the pristine natural settings seemed to change everyone.
① bored
② versatile
③ impressed
④ confident

76 Sheila has a habit of making definitive, opinionated statements that tend to stultify conversation.
① firmly reinforce
② provide entertainment for
③ effectively facilitate
④ have an inhibiting effect on

77 People don't like prying persons who try to find out too much about the affairs of others.
① inquisitive
② candid
③ naive
④ verbose

78 We live in an acquisitive society which views success primarily in terms of material possessions.
① avaricious
② intrusive
③ attentive
④ disobedient

79 The trailer became detached from the truck that was pulling it.
① damaged
② fixed
③ fastened
④ separated

80 Your insouciant attitude at such a critical moment indicates that you do not understand the seriousness of the situation.
① indifferent
② sarcastic
③ impeccable
④ impassioned

81 The money will revert to the bank in six months.
① deposit in
② be due at
③ return to
④ be available to

82 The brash young technology start-ups of the past have become the established major corporations of today.
① laudable
② reckless
③ latent
④ baleful

83 I enclose a list of my most pressing problems.
① important
② confidential
③ sensitive
④ urgent

84 His family foraged food from the field, looking for anything they could eat.
① planted
② searched for
③ cooked
④ fostered

85 The senior steward <u>infused</u> courage into the new stewardesses.
① showed ② inspired
③ tempted ④ regarded

86 The nests of the dodo bird were, by necessity, built on the ground as the bird was flightless. The dodo's young were afforded little protection on the ground against predators, such as the <u>feral</u> dogs and wild pigs left behind by sailors.
① mutant ② untamed
③ aboriginal ④ wicked

87 Having discovered that he had invented the details of his past, Frank's friends were appalled by his <u>duplicity</u>.
① creativity ② congruence
③ deceit ④ ingenuity

88 He didn't intend to <u>evince</u> anger, but it showed most clearly in his behavior.
① repress ② draw out
③ conform ④ override

89 Five or six thousand years ago, civilization extended to the Nile Valley: at various times stock-farming and <u>rudimentary</u> agriculture penetrated further into Africa.
① repetitive ② productive
③ primitive ④ derivative

90 Most of the time, the cloudy simply dump their load of rain and <u>dissipate</u>.
① waste ② disappear
③ come along ④ use up foolishly

91 The cost was <u>nominal</u> in comparison with the enormous value of what you received.
① reasonable ② insignificant
③ manageable ④ substantial

92 The candidate's speech was <u>converse</u> to her usual pattern, and this became the turning point in her political career.
① convergent ② parallel
③ opposite ④ optimized

93 The creators of animation movie South Park have promised not to <u>lampoon</u> the president's twin teenage daughters in their new movie.
① satirize ② romanticize
③ obfuscate ④ reprimand

94 His leadership style may be <u>choleric</u>, but that is not what caused him to fulfill his horrific fate.
① outrageous ② absurd
③ irascible ④ abstruse

95 China's government has moved rapidly over the past year to impose new <u>strictures</u> on giant internet companies.
① proceeds ② covenants
③ restrictions ④ countermeasures

96 Apple, for decades, was supported by a small but <u>rabid</u> fan base, until the iPod and later the iPhone broke through to the mainstream.
① sizable ② innovative
③ fanatical ④ dexterous

**97** This little parasite that causes malaria, it's probably one of the most complex and <u>wily</u> pathogens known to humankind.
① sly  ② exotic
③ atypical  ④ susceptible

**98** The resolution backs a World Court ruling, but is not legally <u>binding</u>.
① amorphous  ② obligatory
③ factual  ④ statutory

**99** His <u>wry</u> smile is implying that he already knew something.
① wan  ② perfunctory
③ frowning  ④ reluctant

**100** Berliners will vote in a non-binding referendum on a call for the local government to <u>expropriate</u> the properties of large corporate landlords.
① confiscate  ② bequeath
③ contribute  ④ transfer

[1] Write the meaning of the following words.

| | |
|---|---|
| ☐ hereditary | ☐ deviate |
| ☐ clemency | ☐ alma mater |
| ☐ impinge | ☐ friction |
| ☐ example | ☐ sultry |
| ☐ dim | ☐ tome |
| ☐ buffoonery | ☐ expatriate |
| ☐ corrode | ☐ promiscuous |
| ☐ ado | ☐ virtue |
| ☐ stringent | ☐ gloss |
| ☐ glacier | ☐ cipher |
| ☐ prevaricate | ☐ doggerel |
| ☐ revolution | ☐ clique |
| ☐ exalt | ☐ twilight |
| ☐ libretto | ☐ barter |
| ☐ murky | ☐ anesthetic |
| ☐ wilt | ☐ yeoman |
| ☐ edict | ☐ florid |
| ☐ overlap | ☐ schizophrenia |
| ☐ contentious | ☐ pep |
| ☐ boulevard | ☐ articulate |
| ☐ roil | ☐ malpractice |
| ☐ impostor | ☐ reprove |
| ☐ slink | ☐ upholstery |
| ☐ niggardly | ☐ symmetry |
| ☐ chimney | ☐ quiescent |

[2] Select <u>the most</u> appropriate word from the box below. Each word should be used only once.

| | | | |
|---|---|---|---|
| ① clemency | ② corrode | ③ impostor | ④ impinge |
| ⑤ niggardly | ⑥ cipher | ⑦ expatriate | ⑧ bartered |
| ⑨ deviated | ⑩ quiescent | ⑪ symmetry | ⑫ malpractice |
| ⑬ virtue | ⑭ contentious | ⑮ ado | ⑯ promiscuous |
| ⑰ stringent | ⑱ wilted | ⑲ articulate | ⑳ doggerel |

1    The laboratory had _____ safety protocols in place to ensure the protection of its researchers from any potential hazards.

2    Although the candidate was warned repeatedly by his campaign staff that he had a congenial public image to uphold, he continued to release _____ campaign ads.

3    His reputation for being excessively cautious with expenditures earned him the label of a(n) _____ spender.

4    The proposed construction project raised concerns among environmentalists as it was feared to _____ on the habitats of several endangered species.

5    The author's portrayal of the protagonist as a(n) _____ living in a foreign land underscored the themes of displacement and cultural adaptation in the novel.

6    His _____ behavior, characterized by frequent changes in partners, raised eyebrows among his peers.

7    Despite the severity of his crime, the convicted felon hoped the judge would show _____ in sentencing.

8    In ancient civilizations, goods and services were often _____ as a means of trade and exchange.

9    The experts were able to clearly _____ and justify their understanding of the problem.

10    The accountant's deliberate misrepresentation of financial records was identified as a clear case of _____ within the industry.

**[3] Choose the one which is different from the others.**

**11**    ① detraction    ② buffoonery    ③ jest    ④ raillery

**12**    ① laud    ② extol    ③ exalt    ④ pledge

**13**    ① decree    ② commencement    ③ edict    ④ ordinance

**14**    ① equivocate    ② dodge    ③ procrastinate    ④ prevaricate

**15**    ① dim    ② luminous    ③ dull    ④ murky

**16**    ① ruddy    ② rubicund    ③ florid    ④ pallid

**17**    ① reprove    ② exonerate    ③ chide    ④ condemn

**18**    ① chicanery    ② clique    ③ coterie    ④ faction

**19**    ① muggy    ② sultry    ③ sparse    ④ sweltering

**20**    ① conflict    ② concord    ③ friction    ④ hostility

## ✔ Answers

**1** ⑰   | 그 연구소는 연구원들을 잠재적인 위험으로부터 보호하기 위해 엄격한 안전 규약을 마련해 두었다.

**2** ⑭   | 그 후보자는 선거 운동 참모로부터 그가 지켜야 할 친근한 대중적 이미지를 가지라는 권고를 반복적으로 받았음에도 불구하고, 그는 계속해서 논쟁이 되는 선거 광고를 내보냈다.

**3** ⑤   | 지출에 지나치게 조심스럽다는 그의 평판은 그에게 인색하게 돈을 소비하는 사람이라는 꼬리표를 붙여주었다.

**4** ④   | 제안된 건설 프로젝트가 여러 멸종 위기 종의 서식지를 침해할 것으로 우려되자 환경론자들 사이에 걱정을 불러일으켰다.

**5** ⑦   | 작가가 주인공을 외국에서 사는 국외 거주자로 묘사한 것은 소설에서 이주와 문화 적응이라는 주제를 강조한 것이었다.

**6** ⑯   | 파트너가 자주 바뀌는 것이 특징인 그의 문란한 행동은 동료들 사이에서 눈살을 찌푸리게 했다.

**7** ①   | 범죄의 엄중함에도 불구하고, 유죄를 선고받은 중범죄자는 판사가 형의 선고에 있어 관용을 베풀기를 바랐다.

**8** ⑧   | 고대 문명에서는 상품과 서비스가 교역과 교환의 수단으로 물물교환되는 경우가 많았다.

**9** ⑲   | 전문가들은 그 문제에 대한 이해를 분명히 설명하고 정당화할 수 있었다.

**10** ⑫   | 회계사가 고의로 재무 기록을 잘못 기재한 것은 업계 내에서 명백한 위법행위 사례로 확인되었다.

- - - - - - -

**11** ①   **12** ④   **13** ②   **14** ③   **15** ②   **16** ④   **17** ②   **18** ①   **19** ③   **20** ②

**[1]** Write the meaning of the following words.

| | |
|---|---|
| ☐ invalidate | ☐ cantrip |
| ☐ maleficent | ☐ swoop |
| ☐ palpitate | ☐ requiem |
| ☐ delirium | ☐ bastion |
| ☐ squeal | ☐ convoke |
| ☐ profane | ☐ erect |
| ☐ adultery | ☐ forensic |
| ☐ suck | ☐ preferment |
| ☐ cutthroat | ☐ outsource |
| ☐ nonsense | ☐ kindred |
| ☐ benighted | ☐ galore |
| ☐ extrapolate | ☐ hover |
| ☐ complicity | ☐ antediluvian |
| ☐ repose | ☐ occasion |
| ☐ indent | ☐ infernal |
| ☐ divine | ☐ cataract |
| ☐ grapple | ☐ retrogress |
| ☐ vernal | ☐ brackish |
| ☐ fuss | ☐ whitewash |
| ☐ sedate | ☐ transaction |
| ☐ despoil | ☐ congeal |
| ☐ injunction | ☐ extramarital |
| ☐ tumble | ☐ legion |
| ☐ mode | ☐ punctilious |
| ☐ attenuate | ☐ misapprehension |

[2] Select the most appropriate word from the box below. Each word should be used only once.

| | | | |
|---|---|---|---|
| ① indent | ② complicity | ③ forensic | ④ swooped |
| ⑤ punctilious | ⑥ delirium | ⑦ congeal | ⑧ transaction |
| ⑨ infernal | ⑩ retrogressed | ⑪ grapple | ⑫ extrapolated |
| ⑬ despoiled | ⑭ convoke | ⑮ repose | ⑯ squeal |
| ⑰ tumble | ⑱ attenuate | ⑲ vernal | ⑳ invalidate |

1    Despite his attempts to deny _____ in the crime, the evidence pointed directly to his involvement.

2    After days of high fever and intense hallucinations, the patient slipped into a state of uncontrollable _____.

3    The clear and convincing new evidence has the potential to completely _____ the previously established theories in the scientific community.

4    The explorers encountered unforeseen obstacles but were resolved to _____ with the difficulties to reach their destination.

5    The Roman raid that had _____ his home and enslaved him at twenty likewise brought disaster to his neighbors.

6    Previous research has shown that high-stress individuals and their spouses are at risk for a variety of negative outcomes, and that social support may _____ these effects.

7    With incredible speed, the hawk suddenly _____ down to catch its prey.

8    Recognizing the need for immediate action, the CEO resolved to _____ a meeting with stakeholders to address the company's financial challenges.

9    Before the use of _____ evidence, criminal cases relied on witness testimony rather than science.

10   The accountant's _____ attention to detail was evident as he meticulously reviewed every entry in the ledger.

[3] Choose the one which is different from the others.

11 ① maleficent     ② sublime     ③ baleful     ④ detrimental

12 ① sacrilegious     ② profane     ③ irreverent     ④ perfunctory

13 ① timorous     ② benighted     ③ savage     ④ uncivilized

14 ① sacred     ② divine     ③ earthly     ④ hallowed

15 ① frivolous     ② sedate     ③ serene     ④ tranquil

16 ① bountiful     ② abundant     ③ galore     ④ obvious

17 ① antediluvian     ② ancient     ③ ardent     ④ archaic

18 ① pulsate     ② sneer     ③ palpitate     ④ throb

19 ① adultery     ② adulation     ③ infidelity     ④ affair

20 ① ferocious     ② ruthless     ③ cutthroat     ④ perfunctory

## ✓ Answers

1 ② ┃ 범죄 공모를 부인하려는 그의 시도에도 불구하고, 그 증거는 그가 연루되었다는 것을 직접적으로 지적했다.

2 ⑥ ┃ 며칠 동안 고열과 강렬한 환각 증세를 경험한 후, 환자는 걷잡을 수 없는 정신착란 상태에 빠졌다.

3 ⑳ ┃ 분명하고 설득력 있는 새로운 증거는 과학계에서 이미 확립된 이론을 완전히 무효화할 가능성이 있다.

4 ⑪ ┃ 탐험가들은 예상하지 못한 장애에 부딪혔지만, 목적지에 도달하기 위해 어려움과 씨름하기로 결심했다.

5 ⑬ ┃ 20살에 그의 집을 약탈하고 그를 노예로 만들었던 로마인들의 침략은 그의 이웃들에게도 마찬가지의 재앙을 초래했다.

6 ⑱ ┃ 이전의 연구는 스트레스를 많이 받는 사람들과 그들의 배우자들은 다양한 부정적인 결과를 맞이할 위험이 있다는 것을 보여주었으며, 사회적 지원이 이러한 결과를 약화시킬지도 모른다는 것을 보여주었다.

7 ④ ┃ 매는 믿을 수 없는 엄청난 속도로 먹이를 잡기 위해 갑자기 내리덮쳤다.

8 ⑭ ┃ CEO는 즉각적인 조치의 필요성을 인식하고 회사의 재정적 어려움을 해결하기 위해 주주 회의를 소집하기로 결정했다.

9 ③ ┃ 법의학적 증거가 사용되기 이전에, 형사 사건은 과학보다는 증인의 증언에 의존했다.

10 ⑤ ┃ 장부의 모든 항목을 신경 써서 검토했으므로 그 회계사는 세세한 부분까지 꼼꼼하게 주의를 기울인 것이 분명했다.

11 ②    12 ④    13 ①    14 ③    15 ①    16 ④    17 ③    18 ②    19 ②    20 ④

[1] Write the meaning of the following words.

| | |
|---|---|
| ☐ draconian | ☐ bumpy |
| ☐ glimmer | ☐ vehicle |
| ☐ stratify | ☐ adjunct |
| ☐ curfew | ☐ courier |
| ☐ molest | ☐ lurid |
| ☐ insurgent | ☐ extradite |
| ☐ bedlam | ☐ gruff |
| ☐ antiseptic | ☐ nondescript |
| ☐ condemn | ☐ outskirts |
| ☐ ruthless | ☐ forlorn |
| ☐ equanimity | ☐ inebriate |
| ☐ surrogate | ☐ prime |
| ☐ overhear | ☐ approbation |
| ☐ wreck | ☐ flunk |
| ☐ homily | ☐ scurvy |
| ☐ dizzy | ☐ milestone |
| ☐ condiment | ☐ expurgate |
| ☐ fiddle | ☐ crass |
| ☐ precipitous | ☐ idolatry |
| ☐ endurance | ☐ uxorious |
| ☐ regiment | ☐ bungle |
| ☐ peregrination | ☐ refection |
| ☐ commiserate | ☐ denigrate |
| ☐ manslaughter | ☐ sympathy |
| ☐ trump | ☐ telltale |

[2] Select <u>the most</u> appropriate word from the box below. Each word should be used only once.

| | | | |
|---|---|---|---|
| ① draconian | ② denigrate | ③ idolatry | ④ extradited |
| ⑤ scurvy | ⑥ insurgent | ⑦ refection | ⑧ nondescript |
| ⑨ inebriated | ⑩ forlorn | ⑪ courier | ⑫ wreck |
| ⑬ expurgate | ⑭ overhear | ⑮ curfew | ⑯ molest |
| ⑰ surrogate | ⑱ bungled | ⑲ stratify | ⑳ condemned |

**1** The _____ group, fueled by dissatisfaction with the status quo, sought to overturn the existing power structures through unconventional means.

**2** The sudden imposition of a midnight _____ disrupted the plans of many night workers who relied on late hours to earn their livelihood.

**3** Byron's influence on European poetry, music, novel, opera, and painting has been immense, although the poet was widely _____ on moral grounds by his contemporaries.

**4** The notorious smuggler was ultimately caught and _____ to the nation where his criminal activities originated..

**5** The desolate landscape with its barren fields and empty horizon seemed hauntingly _____ under the pale moonlight.

**6** The film director had to meticulously _____ any scenes that could potentially offend the audience's sensibilities before the movie's release.

**7** Despite the critics' relentless attempts to _____ the author's work, the novel continued to garner praise and admiration from readers worldwide.

**8** I had a good chance of getting the job but I'm afraid I _____ the interview by saying all the wrong things.

**9** The school administration's decision to implement _____ disciplinary measures surprised everyone with its severity.

**10** You might suffer from _____, a disease caused by vitamin C deficiency.

[3] Choose the one which is different from the others.

| 11 | ① aplomb | ② equanimity | ③ singularity | ④ serenity |
|----|----------|--------------|---------------|------------|
| 12 | ① fickle | ② lurid | ③ ghastly | ④ hideous |
| 13 | ① bedlam | ② paragon | ③ chaos | ④ tumult |
| 14 | ① eccentric | ② gruff | ③ blunt | ④ brusque |
| 15 | ① stupid | ② insensitive | ③ crass | ④ barren |
| 16 | ① hatred | ② approbation | ③ approval | ④ consent |
| 17 | ① sympathize | ② commiserate | ③ mesmerize | ④ condole |
| 18 | ① uneven | ② rough | ③ bumpy | ④ smooth |
| 19 | ① fiddle | ② hunch | ③ fraud | ④ scam |
| 20 | ① grumble | ② glimmer | ③ flicker | ④ shimmer |

## ✓ Answers

**1** ⑥ ｜ 현재의 상황에 대한 불만으로 일어난 반란군은 파격적인 수단을 통해 기존 권력 구조를 전복하려고 했다.

**2** ⑮ ｜ 갑작스러운 밤 12시 통행금지 부과가 늦은 시간에 생계를 위해 일하는 많은 야간 노동자들의 계획을 좌절시켰다.

**3** ⑳ ｜ 비록 시인 바이런(Byron)은 도덕적인 이유 때문에 동시대 사람들에 의해 널리 비난받았지만, 유럽의 시, 음악, 소설, 오페라 그리고 그림 등에 미친 그의 영향은 지대했다.

**4** ④ ｜ 그 악명 높은 밀수업자는 결국 체포되어 그의 범죄 행위가 일어난 국가로 송환되었다.

**5** ⑩ ｜ 황량한 들판과 텅 빈 지평선이 펼쳐진 황량한 풍경은 창백한 달빛 아래서 잊을 수 없을 만큼 쓸쓸해 보였다.

**6** ⑬ ｜ 영화감독은 영화가 개봉되기 전에 관객들의 감정을 해칠 수 있는 장면을 꼼꼼히 삭제해야 했다.

**7** ② ｜ 작가의 작품을 폄하하려는 비평가들의 가치없는 시도에도 불구하고, 그 소설은 전 세계 독자들로부터 계속해서 칭찬과 존경을 받았다.

**8** ⑱ ｜ 나는 취직할 가능성이 충분했지만, 엉뚱한 것만을 대답하여 인터뷰를 망쳐버렸던 것 같다.

**9** ① ｜ 엄중한 징계 조치를 시행하기로 한 학교측의 결정은 그 엄정함으로 인해 모두를 놀라게 했다.

**10** ⑤ ｜ 당신은 비타민C 결핍으로 인한 질병인 괴혈병에 걸릴 수도 있다.

| | | | | | | | | | |
|---|---|---|---|---|---|---|---|---|---|
| **11** ③ | **12** ① | **13** ② | **14** ① | **15** ④ | **16** ① | **17** ③ | **18** ④ | **19** ② | **20** ① |

# ☑ DAILY CHECKUP

**[1]** Write the meaning of the following words.

| | |
|---|---|
| ☐ frail | ☐ fever |
| ☐ soporific | ☐ armchair |
| ☐ ethics | ☐ cosmetic |
| ☐ defalcate | ☐ grouse |
| ☐ hyperbole | ☐ knot |
| ☐ confess | ☐ riveting |
| ☐ indenture | ☐ chill |
| ☐ strut | ☐ pulverize |
| ☐ reverse | ☐ altercation |
| ☐ plank | ☐ exude |
| ☐ dialectic | ☐ veterinarian |
| ☐ alimony | ☐ obsequious |
| ☐ bustle | ☐ mass |
| ☐ structure | ☐ sweeping |
| ☐ protean | ☐ wean |
| ☐ latch | ☐ bandage |
| ☐ myopic | ☐ turbulent |
| ☐ gauntlet | ☐ overture |
| ☐ shred | ☐ putrid |
| ☐ capitulate | ☐ drain |
| ☐ treason | ☐ accost |
| ☐ buzzword | ☐ ecumenic |
| ☐ nubile | ☐ freak |
| ☐ criterion | ☐ purvey |
| ☐ scour | ☐ circumlocution |

[2] Select <u>the most</u> appropriate word from the box below. Each word should be used only once.

| | | | |
|---|---|---|---|
| ① scour | ② defalcate | ③ armchair | ④ ecumenic |
| ⑤ turbulent | ⑥ capitulate | ⑦ shred | ⑧ hyperbole |
| ⑨ soporific | ⑩ reverse | ⑪ circumlocution | ⑫ confess |
| ⑬ obsequious | ⑭ chill | ⑮ structure | ⑯ dialectic |
| ⑰ knot | ⑱ pulverize | ⑲ grouse | ⑳ myopic |

**1**   Throughout history, periods of significant change often result in a(n) _____ societal landscape fraught with tension and discord.

**2**   He is still as addicted to _____ as he was two decades ago, and still as obsessed with the notion that everything he touches is unparalleled in its greatness.

**3**   The monotonous lecture delivered by the professor was so _____ that several students struggled to stay awake.

**4**   In the courtroom, the defendant was urged by his lawyer to _____ to the crime in order to seek a plea bargain.

**5**   It is a(n) _____ and instant-gratification solution in the fight against air pollution. Governments must invest in infrastructure for clean air as a long term solution.

**6**   The general ultimately had to _____ when he realized further resistance would lead to unnecessary casualties.

**7**   During imperial times, the Roman Senate was little more than a collection of _____ yes men intent on preserving their own lives by gratifying the Emperor's every whim.

**8**   Her knack for expressing ideas in a circuitous manner showcased her mastery of artful _____.

**9**   The disgruntled customer started to _____ about the poor service at the restaurant.

**10**   Recognizing their love's strength, they resolved to tie the _____ and begin a new chapter together.

[3] Choose the one which is different from the others.

**11** ① frail　　　② delicate　　　③ feeble　　　④ solid

**12** ① protean　　② contumacious　　③ ever-changing　　④ kaleidoscopic

**13** ① dally　　　② bustle　　　③ hurry　　　④ rush

**14** ① betrayal　② allegiance　③ treason　④ perfidy

**15** ① engrossing　② captivating　③ shifting　④ riveting

**16** ① quarrel　② bicker　③ altercation　④ perjury

**17** ① overall　② broad　③ sweeping　④ superficial

**18** ① prop　　② strut　　③ default　　④ brace

**19** ① exude　② implode　③ emanate　④ ooze

**20** ① partake　② purvey　③ provide　④ supply

## ✔ Answers

**1** ⑤　｜ 역사상 중대한 변화의 시기에는 긴장과 불화로 가득 찬 격동의 사회 환경을 초래하는 경우가 많다.

**2** ⑧　｜ 그는 20년 전에 그랬던 것과 마찬가지로 여전히 과장하는 것에 중독되어 있으며, 여전히 그가 손을 대는 모든 것이 중요한 면에서 비할 데 없다는 생각에 사로잡혀 있다.

**3** ⑨　｜ 교수님의 단조로운 강의는 너무 졸려서 몇몇 학생들은 자지 않고 깨어있기 위해 애를 썼다.

**4** ⑫　｜ 법정에서 피고인은 변호인으로부터 양형 거래를 위해 죄를 자백하라는 촉구를 받았다.

**5** ⑳　｜ 그것은 대기오염과의 전쟁에서 근시안적이고 즉각적인 만족을 주는 해결책이다. 정부는 장기적인 해결책으로서 맑은 공기를 위한 인프라에 투자해야 한다.

**6** ⑥　｜ 장군은 더 이상의 저항이 불필요한 사상자를 낳게 된다는 것을 깨닫고 결국 항복해야만 했다.

**7** ⑬　｜ 제국시대 로마의 원로원은 황제의 갖가지 변덕을 충족시켜 줌으로써 자신들의 목숨 보전에 열중하는 아첨하는 예스맨 집단에 불과했다.

**8** ⑪　｜ 우회적인 방식으로 생각을 표현하는 그녀의 재주는 기교 있는 완곡한 표현에 정통한 것을 보여주었다.

**9** ⑲　｜ 언짢은 고객은 식당의 서비스가 형편없다고 불평을 늘어놓기 시작했다.

**10** ⑰　｜ 사랑의 힘을 깨닫고 그들은 결혼해서 새로운 장을 함께 시작하기로 결심했다.

- - - - - - - - - - - - - - - - - - - - - - - - - - - - - - - - - - - - - - - - - - - - - - - - - - - - - -

**11** ④　　**12** ②　　**13** ①　　**14** ②　　**15** ③　　**16** ④　　**17** ④　　**18** ③　　**19** ②　　**20** ①

[1] Write the meaning of the following words.

| | |
|---|---|
| ☐ zenith | ☐ educe |
| ☐ exemplary | ☐ unison |
| ☐ declaim | ☐ putative |
| ☐ armament | ☐ ingratiate |
| ☐ intangible | ☐ puppet |
| ☐ shoddy | ☐ volant |
| ☐ progeny | ☐ crusade |
| ☐ rejoice | ☐ leapfrog |
| ☐ cornucopia | ☐ hive |
| ☐ outmoded | ☐ engulf |
| ☐ barb | ☐ benison |
| ☐ exchequer | ☐ overcast |
| ☐ consign | ☐ blockade |
| ☐ invincible | ☐ rugged |
| ☐ dawdle | ☐ ledge |
| ☐ swashbuckle | ☐ transplant |
| ☐ compass | ☐ forte |
| ☐ naughty | ☐ dilapidated |
| ☐ modicum | ☐ stipend |
| ☐ grumble | ☐ minister |
| ☐ tergiversation | ☐ pellucid |
| ☐ bosom | ☐ constituency |
| ☐ coeval | ☐ twig |
| ☐ fret | ☐ anneal |
| ☐ radiation | ☐ infatuation |

[2] Select <u>the most</u> appropriate word from the box below. Each word should be used only once.

| | | | |
|---|---|---|---|
| ① exemplary | ② shoddy | ③ modicum | ④ intangible |
| ⑤ volant | ⑥ stipend | ⑦ naughty | ⑧ leapfrog |
| ⑨ ingratiate | ⑩ cornucopia | ⑪ anneal | ⑫ engulf |
| ⑬ infatuation | ⑭ blockade | ⑮ invincible | ⑯ fret |
| ⑰ rejoice | ⑱ overcast | ⑲ outmoded | ⑳ consign |

**1**     The allure of the unknown often lies in its _____ essence beyond the reach of palpable perception or measurement.

**2**     The annual Thanksgiving feast boasted a(n) _____ of delectable dishes ranging from traditional roasted turkey to an assortment of gourmet desserts.

**3**     After a series of setbacks, the sudden breakthrough made them _____ with relief.

**4**     Despots tend to appear _____ while they rule, and then laughably weak when they fall.

**5**     His sly smirk revealed a(n) _____ side to his personality that often caught others by surprise.

**6**     Despite his attempts to remain calm, he couldn't help but _____ over the looming deadline for his project.

**7**     The ambitious intern tried hard to _____ herself with the company's top executives during the conference.

**8**     Drought leads to extremely favorable conditions for wildfires, and winds aid a wildfire's progress — weather can spur the fire to move faster and _____ more land.

**9**     Despite working part-time, Jennifer struggled to cover her tuition until she received a generous _____ from the university.

**10**    The traveler's mood dampened as the sky grew increasingly _____.

**[3] Choose the one which is different from the others.**

**11**  ① progress    ② progeny    ③ descendant    ④ offspring

**12**  ① zenith    ② acme    ③ stint    ④ apex

**13**  ① loiter    ② idle    ③ dawdle    ④ hasten

**14**  ① unison    ② stake    ③ accord    ④ harmony

**15**  ① sacrosanct    ② putative    ③ alleged    ④ suppositional

**16**  ① blessing    ② benediction    ③ execration    ④ benison

**17**  ① specialty    ② strength    ③ forte    ④ unction

**18**  ① dilapidated    ② jaunty    ③ ramshackle    ④ tumble-down

**19**  ① riveting    ② pellucid    ③ lucid    ④ clear

**20**  ① orate    ② harangue    ③ preen    ④ declaim

## ✓ Answers

**1** ④ | 미지의 것이 가진 매력은 명백한 지각이나 측정의 범위를 넘어서는 무형의 본질에 있는 경우가 많다.

**2** ⑩ | 매년 열리는 추수감사절 축제는 전통 칠면조 구이부터 갖가지 고급 디저트에 이르기까지 다양한 맛있는 요리가 풍성했다.

**3** ⑰ | 연이은 좌절 끝에, 갑작스러운 돌파구로 그들은 안도감에 크게 기뻐했다.

**4** ⑮ | 독재자는 권좌에 있는 동안은 무적처럼 보이다가 몰락하면 우스울 정도로 나약해지는 경향이 있다.

**5** ⑦ | 그의 음흉한 억지웃음은 종종 다른 사람들을 놀라게 하는 그의 성격의 짓궂은 측면을 드러냈다.

**6** ⑯ | 침착함을 유지하려는 그의 노력에도 불구하고, 그는 자신의 프로젝트 마감일이 다가오는 것에 대해 초조해하지 않을 수 없었다.

**7** ⑨ | 야심 많은 인턴은 학회가 진행되는 동안 회사 최고 경영진에게 잘 보이도록 열심히 노력했다.

**8** ⑫ | 가뭄은 산불이 나기에 매우 유리한 환경을 만들며 바람은 산불의 진행을 돕는다. 날씨는 불을 더 빠르게 이동시켜 (불이) 더 많은 땅을 집어삼키게 할 수 있다.

**9** ⑥ | 제니퍼(Jennifer)는 아르바이트를 했음에도 불구하고 대학에서 넉넉한 장학금을 받기 전까지 학비를 충당하기 위해 고생했다.

**10** ⑱ | 하늘이 점점 흐려지자, 여행자의 기분이 한풀 꺾였다.

- - - - - - - - - - - - - - - - - - - - - - - - - - - - - - - - - - - - - - - - - - -

**11** ①   **12** ③   **13** ④   **14** ②   **15** ①   **16** ③   **17** ④   **18** ②   **19** ①   **20** ③

# ACTUAL TEST

[01-100] Choose the one that is closest in meaning to the underlined part.

**01** The open-air garden is accessible to the public and will most likely establish itself as a convenient gathering place in midtown in <u>clement</u> weather.
① abrupt ② circuitous
③ moderate ④ prodigious

**02** While Hitler comes across as pure evil, Mussolini is often indicted on the lesser charge of <u>buffoonery</u>.
① resurgence ② clowning
③ detraction ④ embezzlement

**03** He as a philosopher has a more <u>stringent</u>, demanding notion of freedom.
① indigenous ② stubborn
③ rigorous ④ superficial

**04** In recent manifestations, Western civilization has tended to <u>exalt</u> science and its technological applications at the expense of the arts.
① recall ② weaken
③ promote ④ aggravate

**05** More than fifty years ago, the United States was <u>roiled</u> by the feminist and sexual revolutions, which brought women out of their household isolation.
① devastated ② rectified
③ agitated ④ disparaged

**06** The causes of the global economic downturn in 2008 have been hotly debated. While experts and academics agree the downturn was the result of a credit crunch, the causes of this credit crunch are more <u>contentious</u>.
① debatable ② competitive
③ satisfactory ④ troublesome

**07** George Washington, in his farewell address, advised fellow citizens to "guard against the <u>impostures</u> of pretended patriotism."
① predators ② temptations
③ collisions ④ deceits

**08** To be parsimonious is to be <u>niggardly</u>.
① avid ② vacillating
③ stingy ④ reluctant

**09** The recent poll figures <u>deviated</u> from those of earlier polls to a significant extent.
① ranged ② originated
③ departed ④ separated

**10** Politics is a source of <u>friction</u> in our family because we all have different views.
① infirmity ② distortion
③ conflict ④ creed

11 Despite the persistence of <u>sultry</u> weather conditions that seems as if it will never end, the season has already changed while no one noticed.
① protean        ② erratic
③ resplendent    ④ sweltering

12 <u>Promiscuous</u> use of drugs is making psychological cripples out of millions of people.
① Chronic        ② Hazardous
③ Increased      ④ Indiscriminate

13 His plan has the <u>virtue</u> of being the most economical to put into practice.
① advantage      ② truth
③ handicap       ④ possibility

14 A study conducted by political scientists at the University of Chicago showed that 25 percent of Americans believe that the financial crisis of 2008 was secretly orchestrated by a small <u>clique</u> of bankers.
① boycott        ② coterie
③ enterprise     ④ number

15 During the frontier days, settlers <u>bartered</u> goods with one another.
① consumed       ② produced
③ exchanged      ④ distributed

16 No doubt the president's <u>florid</u> narcissism explains part of his reaction.
① tempestuous    ② ornate
③ arbitrary      ④ capricious

17 The congressman was such an <u>articulate</u> speaker that even his political opponents admired his way with words.
① gratuitous     ② evasive
③ eloquent       ④ solemn

18 Others are <u>quiescent</u> cases of supermassive objects — probably black holes — having long ago ceased to form new stars.
① mutable        ② inactive
③ slovenly       ④ slack

19 They were <u>expatriated</u> because of their political beliefs.
① demoralized    ② deported
③ excruciated    ④ manipulated

20 In the early stages of the conflict, the company <u>prevaricated</u>, choosing to remain in Russia while other international brands were leaving.
① masticated     ② equivocated
③ hibernated     ④ swerved

21 The terms of your insurance policy that you have purchased last September clearly state that any false information in your application <u>invalidates</u> the policy. We recently made a decision that the medical history you provided us was not accurate. Accordingly, with this email, we inform you that, as of Dec. 2, 2020, your policy is cancelled.
① diminishes     ② upgrades
③ prolongs       ④ repeals

22 Often under the guise of upholding community values, censors attack books for profane or obscene language.

① profligate      ② impious

③ bromidic      ④ courteous

23 Harvard became one of the most prominent universities to reckon with its own complicity in slavery, acknowledging that university presidents, faculty, and staff enslaved more than 70 people in the years from 1636 to 1783.

① collusion      ② repentance

③ controversy      ④ resilience

24 As researchers grapple with these questionable results, theorists are asking why man domesticated dogs and cats.

① struggle      ② wriggle

③ believe      ④ talk over

25 Everything has to be in perfect order to please my father; he is very fussy.

① fascinating      ② hardworking

③ fastidious      ④ altruistic

26 The presidential campaign has also moved online, where its presence, like its candidate, is more sedate and traditional.

① uproarious      ② sporadic

③ serene      ④ sullen

27 They began to tumble to the problem.

① remain oblivious to

② take their places

③ avoid

④ become aware of

28 You can never eliminate risk, but preparation and training could attenuate it.

① overcome      ② reduce

③ aggravate      ④ prolong

29 Police swooped on the house after a two-week surveillance operation.

① ransacked thoroughly

② attacked suddenly

③ surrounded tightly

④ exploded completely

30 There is a time in the history of many great civilizations when they begin to retrogress.

① regress      ② ascend

③ trespass      ④ flourish

31 The bank of the stream was a fathom from the water which was brackish at high tide and sweet at low.

① distilled      ② opaque

③ saline      ④ aquatic

32 The tide of history can sweep away many things, but it can't whitewash China's collective memory of the Japanese invasion in the 1930s.

① revive      ② memorialize

③ beautify      ④ erase

33 My uncle is punctilious about using the right tool for each job.

① meticulous      ② stressed

③ punctual      ④ casual

34 The sewer system needs significant upgrades, and city streets have potholes galore.
① obvious          ② reparable
③ pliable          ④ abundant

35 The West African country has been seen as a bastion of democratic stability in the region.
① bulwark          ② haven
③ harbinger        ④ terrain

36 We can easily extrapolate a much higher increase in lower socioeconomic classes that have really been hit economically..
① skimp            ② interrupt
③ infer            ④ precipitate

37 Korean exporters have been meeting with cutthroat competition in European market.
① hypothetical     ② unfettered
③ reciprocal       ④ fierce

38 We have been forced to believe that Africans were somehow benighted, that they had created no great civilizations.
① excluded         ② uncivilized
③ belligerent      ④ refractory

39 When planning military strategy, a nation's leader might convoke her trusted advisors and top generals.
① convene          ② dissemble
③ rectify          ④ savor

40 Many Old World places — Venice — have been largely despoiled by this mass tourism.
① ignored          ② illuminated
③ monopolized      ④ ravaged

41 The more isolated the government feels, the more it justifies its draconian policies, and the less it feels obliged to temper its responses.
① temperate        ② merciful
③ oppressive       ④ customary

42 When the revolt broke out, the government ordered its troop to arrest the insurgents.
① novices          ② rebels
③ negotiators      ④ reckoners

43 The ruthless general killed the innocent people of the hamlet.
① merciless        ② powerful
③ vehement         ④ generous

44 The mother of eleven boys viewed the mudball fight with equanimity; at least they weren't shooting bullets at one another.
① avarice          ② enormity
③ apprehension     ④ composure

45 Some governments started using terrorist groups as surrogates to fight for their political aims.
① scapegoats       ② substitutes
③ mediators        ④ patrons

46 It took a long time for the earth to create the Alps — a lot longer than it's taking humans to wreck them.
① conquer          ② exploit
③ ruin             ④ sustain

47  "Fundamental" is the most over-used word in the debate. There is nothing more fundamental than the markets, which had sound reasons to <u>precipitate</u> the crisis.
① prevent         ② pacify
③ foretell        ④ accelerate

48  The appetite for <u>lurid</u> distraction is especially robust as the COVID-19 pandemic forces hundreds of millions of people to stay home.
① deliberate      ② gruesome
③ blithe          ④ casual

49  The Supreme Public Prosecutors' Office found that about two out of every 10 crimes are committed while the perpetrator is <u>inebriated</u>.
① intoxicated     ② inflamed
③ sulphurous      ④ emollient

50  Certain interest groups were already <u>primed</u> for battle.
① generous        ② indulged
③ prepared        ④ secured

51  At the end of the enthusiastic performance, the audience responded immediately to Tocco's artistically courageous program with shouts of <u>approbation</u>.
① commendation    ② opprobrium
③ tolerance       ④ prohibition

52  Her first performance at the Metropolitan Opera House was a <u>milestone</u> in American music.
① windmill        ② landmark
③ skyscraper      ④ stepping-stone

53  Perhaps an <u>expurgated</u> edition of the novel would be more appropriate for the less sophisticated students.
① easy            ② shortened
③ censored        ④ explicit

54  Some people were shocked by a loudmouthed jerk's rude jokes and <u>crass</u> comments.
① careless        ② clueless
③ redefined       ④ nasty

55  In 1958, Professor Charles David Keeling began to measure an odorless, colorless gas — carbon dioxide — high up on a mountain in Hawaii. Carbon dioxide has been measured there every day since, and the <u>telltale</u> curve illustrates the undeniable: The composition of the air is changing. In his first year of measurements, Professor Keeling recorded an average carbon dioxide level of 315 parts per million (ppm). This May, the recorded average was nearly 408 ppm.
① deceptive       ② equivocal
③ contradictory   ④ revealing

56  To express her <u>sympathy</u>, she sent a bouquet of flowers to the funeral parlor.
① condolence      ② abomination
③ observance      ④ punctuation

57  In a Cervantes' novel *Don Quixote*, main characters make a long <u>peregrination</u>.
① liberation      ② explanation
③ discipline      ④ excursion

58 This hope becomes increasingly <u>forlorn</u> as time passes.
① desperate        ② chaste
③ frail            ④ feasible

59 Russian propaganda <u>denigrating</u> Ukraine is spreading through internationally popular online video games.
① disguising       ② disparaging
③ provoking        ④ cajoling

60 A <u>precipitous</u> decline in exports is likely to be more than offset by a decline in imports.
① steady          ② gradual
③ cyclical         ④ steep

61 Although my grandmother is old and <u>frail</u>, she still enjoys playing cards and listening to dance tunes.
① deaf            ② unhappy
③ unpleasant       ④ weak

62 Everyone was respectful towards him, listening carefully to his <u>soporific</u> explanations.
① profound        ② sedative
③ exciting         ④ erudite

63 Poets sometimes use <u>hyperbole</u> for special effect.
① opposition       ② exaggeration
③ refusal          ④ deletion

64 The motorist decided to <u>reverse</u> his car when he saw an accident ahead.
① turn out         ② turn off
③ turn around      ④ turn on

65 Too tired to think, I <u>bustled</u> into the stone hut and burnt my lips on a steaming cup of hot chocolate.
① exhausted        ② lashed
③ rushed          ④ squatted

66 Like his colleague in Japan, the missionary credited Buddhism's popularity in East Asia with its <u>protean</u> ability to recast itself in the form of Chinese indigenous religious traditions.
① mutable         ② compelling
③ inherited        ④ moored

67 Their <u>myopic</u> refusal to act now will undoubtedly cause problems in the future.
① nearsighted      ② intense
③ regretful        ④ imminent

68 He <u>capitulated</u> under the weight of internal pressure; he was overwhelmed by the media and by the politicians.
① discharged       ② succumbed
③ contested        ④ conceded

69 It is not a completely unwelcome change, but there are bound to be some who will <u>grouse</u> about the bands, no matter who plays.
① praise          ② complain
③ worry           ④ meditate

70 Their report on the plans for nuclear war is a <u>chilling</u> document.
① long            ② frightening
③ confidential      ④ questionable

71 Instead of openness and transparency, the scheme exudes an air of deceptive damage limitation.
① deters ② evades
③ placates ④ emanates

72 Helen valued people who behaved as if they respected themselves; nothing irritated her more than an excessively obsequious salesclerk.
① fawning ② austere
③ mercenary ④ contentious

73 Science probably has never demanded a more sweeping change in a traditional way of thinking about a subject, nor has there ever been a more important subject.
① overall ② regional
③ smooth ④ impressive

74 And as this turbulent summer for the market draws to a close, it will be interesting to see on an almost real-time basis what insiders are doing.
① initial ② prosperous
③ wild ④ lackluster

75 It is indeed a hopeful sign that the terrorist country has begun peace-making overtures, but these gestures have yet to yield anything substantive and lasting.
① suggestions ② pacts
③ conventions ④ clauses

76 I saw five cop cars pull into the driveway. I thought they got freaked by women laughing at them.
① illiterate ② gratuitous
③ upset ④ impudent

77 Aphasic patients sometimes mis-name things, or they use circumlocutions to replace difficult words.
① proclaims ② periphrases
③ swears ④ blasphemes

78 Astronomers discovered the putrid gas lurking within a layer of clouds on Venus, where temperatures are pretty close to those on our planet.
① anaesthetic ② rotten
③ eccentric ④ saturated

79 The teacher halted the altercation by separating the two opponents before they could come to blows.
① assault ② argument
③ threat ④ menace

80 Words from a teacher or actor have a riveting effect when they're full of impact and interest.
① garrulous ② deterrent
③ frugal ④ captivating

81 She is known for her outstanding personal career and her exemplary contributions to the local and national organizations.
① convincing ② commendable
③ unforgettable ④ uproarious

82 It's an intangible yet very real part of our daily life.
① an intelligible ② a transient
③ an impalpable ④ a concrete

83 David was never loquacious on the subject of his progeny.
① offspring ② inheritance
③ predicament ④ ailment

84 One out of five bridges in the United States is outmoded.
① narrow ② reinforced concrete
③ illegal ④ old-fashioned

85 The idea has been fascinating astronomers since the late 18th century, suggesting images of unimaginably strong cosmic whirlpools sucking up space matter and consigning it to oblivion.
① comparing ② committing
③ compiling ④ conserving

86 The Boston team this season was invincible.
① uncomfortable ② unmanageable
③ unbelievable ④ unconquerable

87 The children won't dawdle over their homework if they know they'll be getting ice cream and cookies as soon as they finish.
① molt ② falter
③ pore ④ loiter

88 That student is discourteous; he grumbles no matter how one tries to please him.
① giggles ② scolds
③ complains ④ brags

89 It's no use fretting your life away because you can't have everything you want.
① wandering ② asserting
③ accumulating ④ fussing

90 Although there are some doubts, the putative author of the book is Jennifer H. Johnson.
① assumed ② confirmed
③ imaginative ④ acknowledged

91 The headwaiter, with an ingratiating smile on his false face, came up to us bearing a large basket full of huge peaches.
① a revengeful ② a flattering
③ a dissident ④ a betrothed

92 He continued through the streets and slowed when he reached a dilapidated, boarded-up church on a corner.
① ruined ② desiccated
③ sanctified ④ excavated

93 Thus, sand or pounded glass, which is white to the naked eye, is pellucid in a microscope.
① indecent ② transitory
③ filthy ④ transparent

94 A man described as having an infatuation with Nazi ideology was charged with murder.
① tumult ② humility
③ animosity ④ absorption

95 Riots over the weekend engulfed major U.S. cities on Saturday night.
① undulated ② dissipated
③ overwhelmed ④ disseminated

96 The beauty of scientific inquiry is that when we quickly <u>leapfrog</u> the pace of discovery we uncover an entirely new way of thinking.

① surpass      ② countervail

③ scrutinize      ④ switch

97 At its <u>zenith</u>, the British Empire stretched over one-fourth of the earth's surface.

① vista      ② sovereign

③ heyday      ④ fiasco

98 Republicans solidly opposed the legislation, calling it a <u>cornucopia</u> of wasteful liberal daydreams that would raise taxes and families' living costs.

① arrogance      ② abundance

③ vanity      ④ coterie

99 The international community must act in <u>unison</u> if we are to find a lasting resolution to this problem.

① harmony      ② creed

③ collusion      ④ obedience

100 Most people know me as a science geek, but besides science, math is my <u>forte</u>.

① strength      ② boundary

③ foible      ④ patent

[1] Write the meaning of the following words.

| | |
|---|---|
| ☐ blatant | ☐ greed |
| ☐ primordial | ☐ besmirch |
| ☐ explicate | ☐ apothegm |
| ☐ coronation | ☐ livid |
| ☐ roar | ☐ irrupt |
| ☐ humility | ☐ peroration |
| ☐ stack | ☐ oath |
| ☐ mollusk | ☐ gossamer |
| ☐ outlandish | ☐ duck |
| ☐ sedition | ☐ frontier |
| ☐ construe | ☐ monstrous |
| ☐ introspective | ☐ bayonet |
| ☐ psalm | ☐ piscatorial |
| ☐ den | ☐ aver |
| ☐ twinkle | ☐ evident |
| ☐ cryptic | ☐ snub |
| ☐ macrocosm | ☐ pavilion |
| ☐ insolent | ☐ catapult |
| ☐ fulminate | ☐ affliction |
| ☐ subservient | ☐ jostle |
| ☐ court | ☐ willful |
| ☐ plenitude | ☐ retract |
| ☐ tug | ☐ votary |
| ☐ venial | ☐ encroach |
| ☐ sterling | ☐ disheveled |

[2] Select the most appropriate word from the box below. Each word should be used only once.

| | | | |
|---|---|---|---|
| ① introspective | ② cryptic | ③ fulminated | ④ blatant |
| ⑤ encroach | ⑥ outlandish | ⑦ primordial | ⑧ disheveled |
| ⑨ subservient | ⑩ besmirched | ⑪ catapult | ⑫ snub |
| ⑬ irrupted | ⑭ greed | ⑮ plenitude | ⑯ gossamer |
| ⑰ aver | ⑱ humility | ⑲ retracted | ⑳ roar |

**1**   Her fashion sense was characterized by a(n) _____ combination of colors and styles that always stood out in a crowd.

**2**   Old as the continents are, they are apparently not _____ features of the earth but rather secondary features that have formed and evolved during the earth's lifetime.

**3**   The sage's writings reflected his _____ approach as he constantly examined the intricacies of the human mind and soul.

**4**   The politician's attempt to cover up the truth was so _____ that even the most naive citizens could see through the deception.

**5**   Because of its outspoken support of the president, the news network was accused of being _____ to the government.

**6**   The insatiable desire for more possessions and wealth revealed his unbridled _____ for material gain.

**7**   Adam Smith _____ against the injustice of slavery in *The Theory of Moral Sentiments*, speaking of the slave traders as the refuse of the jails of Europe.

**8**   Her dress, made of the finest silk, was so sheer and light that it resembled a(n) _____ veil floating in the air.

**9**   Four of the five men confessed to the crime, but later _____ their confessions, saying they were coerced.

**10**   As urban development continued, high-rise buildings started to _____ upon the skyline.

[3] Choose the one which is different from the others.

**11** ① sedition     ② rebellion     ③ submission     ④ mutiny

**12** ① render     ② embellish     ③ construe     ④ interpret

**13** ① impudent     ② insolent     ③ arrogant     ④ intrepid

**14** ① reprehensible     ② venial     ③ excusable     ④ pardonable

**15** ① lavish     ② outraged     ③ furious     ④ livid

**16** ① dodge     ② avoid     ③ duck     ④ encounter

**17** ① oath     ② ebullience     ③ pledge     ④ promise

**18** ① misery     ② affliction     ③ integrity     ④ suffering

**19** ① intentional     ② petulant     ③ willful     ④ deliberate

**20** ① explicate     ② elucidate     ③ expound     ④ exculpate

## ✓ Answers

**1** ⑥ ㅣ 그녀의 패션 감각은 사람들 속에서도 항상 눈에 띄는 색과 스타일의 화려한 조합으로 특징지어졌다.

**2** ⑦ ㅣ 대륙들은 오래되긴 했지만 명백히 지구의 원시적(근본적) 특성은 아니며, 지구가 형성되고 진화하면서 생긴 이차적인 특징들이다.

**3** ① ㅣ 그 현자는 인간의 정신과 영혼의 복잡함을 끊임없이 탐구했기 때문에 그의 글은 자기 성찰적인 접근 방식이 반영되어 있다.

**4** ④ ㅣ 진실을 은폐하려는 정치인의 시도는 너무나 노골적이어서 가장 순진한 시민들도 그 속임수를 간파할 정도였다.

**5** ⑨ ㅣ 대통령을 노골적으로 지지했기 때문에 그 뉴스 방송사는 정부에 굴종한다는 비난을 받았다.

**6** ⑭ ㅣ 더 많은 재산과 부를 얻기 위한 만족할 줄 모르는 욕망은 그의 물질적 이익에 대한 억제되지 않는 탐욕을 드러냈다.

**7** ③ ㅣ 애덤 스미스(Adam Smith)는 『도덕감정론』에서 노예 상인을 유럽 감옥의 인간쓰레기라고 말하면서 노예 제도의 부당성에 대해 격렬히 비난했다.

**8** ⑯ ㅣ 최고급 실크로 만든 그녀의 드레스는 너무나 얇고 가벼워서 공중에 떠있는 아주 얇은 베일처럼 보였다.

**9** ⑲ ㅣ 다섯 명 중 네 명이 범죄를 자백했지만, 나중에 그들의 자백을 철회하고 (자백을) 강요받았다고 말했다.

**10** ⑤ ㅣ 도시 개발이 계속되면서 고층 빌딩이 스카이라인을 잠식하기 시작했다.

**11** ③    **12** ②    **13** ④    **14** ①    **15** ①    **16** ④    **17** ②    **18** ③    **19** ②    **20** ④

☑ **DAILY CHECKUP**

[1] Write the meaning of the following words.

| | |
|---|---|
| ☐ explicit | ☐ tricky |
| ☐ subjugate | ☐ melee |
| ☐ corollary | ☐ enthrone |
| ☐ prim | ☐ unrest |
| ☐ blandish | ☐ bulwark |
| ☐ diatribe | ☐ graft |
| ☐ horrible | ☐ diurnal |
| ☐ protégé | ☐ verse |
| ☐ repress | ☐ knowingly |
| ☐ skirmish | ☐ textile |
| ☐ adventitious | ☐ syllogism |
| ☐ contour | ☐ banal |
| ☐ stodgy | ☐ alight |
| ☐ demarcate | ☐ foil |
| ☐ mirage | ☐ gene |
| ☐ chaste | ☐ cull |
| ☐ imbibe | ☐ would-be |
| ☐ consanguinity | ☐ limbo |
| ☐ emeritus | ☐ page |
| ☐ anguish | ☐ stunt |
| ☐ outshine | ☐ roster |
| ☐ clip | ☐ forthright |
| ☐ defray | ☐ ignition |
| ☐ ragged | ☐ presage |
| ☐ non sequitur | ☐ iniquitous |

[2] Select <u>the most</u> appropriate word from the box below. Each word should be used only once.

| | | | |
|---|---|---|---|
| ① subjugated | ② blandished | ③ forthright | ④ stodgy |
| ⑤ adventitious | ⑥ defray | ⑦ foiled | ⑧ ignition |
| ⑨ unrest | ⑩ demarcated | ⑪ ragged | ⑫ outshine |
| ⑬ chaste | ⑭ graft | ⑮ cull | ⑯ bulwark |
| ⑰ enthrone | ⑱ banal | ⑲ non sequitur | ⑳ imbibe |

**1** The director chose to portray the characters in a(n) _____ manner that highlighted their virtuous qualities rather than their sensuality.

**2** Despite his initial reluctance, she _____ him with compliments until he finally agreed to help with her project.

**3** The traveler's shoes, after months of rugged exploration, appeared worn and _____ from the extensive journey.

**4** His final remark seemed like a(n) _____ as it had no logical connection to the preceding discussion.

**5** The two nations' borders were unmistakably _____ with each side visibly delineated by distinct signposts.

**6** The ancient walls, weathered but resilient, stood tall as a formidable _____ against the encroaching forces.

**7** My elder brother often found his friend's conversations about celebrities and fashion _____; he was more interested in politics and science.

**8** The elaborate scheme devised by the detective effectively _____ the robber's attempt to steal the priceless artifact.

**9** Just as religion has fettered the human mind, so has the State _____ his spirit, dictating every phase of conduct.

**10** His _____ nature earned him respect among his peers due to his honesty and directness in expressing his opinions.

[3] Choose the one which is different from the others.

11  ① diatribe      ② dichotomy      ③ denunciation   ④ harangue
12  ① mimicry       ② skirmish       ③ conflict       ④ dispute
13  ① grief         ② sobriety       ③ anguish        ④ agony
14  ① forthright    ② crafty         ③ tricky         ④ sly
15  ① ambiguous     ② explicit       ③ clear          ④ definite
16  ① fracas        ② brawl          ③ melee          ④ bayonet
17  ① discretely    ② deliberately   ③ knowingly      ④ wittingly
18  ① stunt         ② heap           ③ hamper         ④ hinder
19  ① wicked        ② iniquitous     ③ nascent        ④ vicious
20  ① presage       ② augur          ③ bode           ④ punctuate

## ✔ Answers

1  ⑬  | 감독은 등장인물들의 관능미보다 도덕적인 특성을 강조하는 품위 있는 방법으로 등장인물을 묘사하기로 했다.

2  ②  | 그가 처음에는 주저했지만, 그녀가 칭찬으로 그를 구슬리자 마침내 그는 그녀의 프로젝트를 돕기로 동의했다.

3  ⑪  | 수개월간 이어진 험난한 탐험 끝에 그 여행자의 신발은 그 긴 여정으로 인해 낡고 다 해져 보였다.

4  ⑲  | 그의 마지막 발언은 앞서 논의된 것과 아무런 논리적 연관성이 없었기 때문에 관련 없는 이야기처럼 보였다.

5  ⑩  | 두 나라의 국경은 명확한 표지물로 눈에 띄게 그려져 있어 분명히 경계가 표시되어 있었다.

6  ⑯  | 풍화되었지만 튼튼한 고대 성벽은 침입하는 적에 맞서는 강력한 보루로서 우뚝 서 있었다.

7  ⑱  | 나의 형은 종종 친구의 유명인사와 패션에 대한 대화를 따분하게 여겼다. 오히려 그는 정치와 과학에 더 관심이 많았다.

8  ⑦  | 형사가 생각한 치밀한 계획은 귀중한 유물을 훔치려 한 도둑의 시도를 사실상 좌절시켰다.

9  ①  | 종교가 인간 지성을 구속해 왔듯이 국가도 인간 정신을 예속시켜 행동의 모든 면을 지시했다.

10  ③  | 그의 솔직한 성격은 자신의 의견을 표현하는 데 있어서 정직하고 단순 명쾌해서 그는 동료들 사이에서 존경받았다.

- - - - - - - - - - - - - - - - - - - - - - - - - - - - - - - - - - - - - - - - - - - - - - - - - - - - - - - - - - - - - -

11 ②   12 ①   13 ②   14 ①   15 ①   16 ④   17 ①   18 ②   19 ③   20 ④

**[1] Write the meaning of the following words.**

| | |
|---|---|
| ☐ judicious | ☐ avalanche |
| ☐ chicanery | ☐ rub |
| ☐ siphon | ☐ erratic |
| ☐ preemptive | ☐ deign |
| ☐ behead | ☐ travesty |
| ☐ spree | ☐ bountiful |
| ☐ efficacy | ☐ interlope |
| ☐ diaphanous | ☐ warp |
| ☐ contort | ☐ hush |
| ☐ subsidiary | ☐ carouse |
| ☐ invidious | ☐ ornate |
| ☐ promontory | ☐ leviathan |
| ☐ belittle | ☐ foment |
| ☐ sonorous | ☐ notion |
| ☐ repartee | ☐ revitalize |
| ☐ glutton | ☐ privation |
| ☐ assay | ☐ turgid |
| ☐ complimentary | ☐ dope |
| ☐ murmur | ☐ expound |
| ☐ fetid | ☐ bugaboo |
| ☐ aggregate | ☐ provision |
| ☐ crumble | ☐ gloat |
| ☐ stagger | ☐ vine |
| ☐ inflection | ☐ devolve |
| ☐ combustible | ☐ smudge |

[2] Select <u>the most</u> appropriate word from the box below. Each word should be used only once.

| | | | |
|---|---|---|---|
| ① judicious | ② preemptive | ③ carouse | ④ leviathan |
| ⑤ foment | ⑥ privation | ⑦ combustible | ⑧ devolve |
| ⑨ fetid | ⑩ complimentary | ⑪ ornate | ⑫ provision |
| ⑬ diaphanous | ⑭ aggregate | ⑮ travesty | ⑯ invidious |
| ⑰ subsidiary | ⑱ contort | ⑲ chicanery | ⑳ turgid |

1    His reputation as a fair and prudent judge was built on his consistent ability to render _____ decisions that balanced the law with compassion.

2    The politician's _____ comparison between the two communities incited tensions rather than fostering unity.

3    The amenities provided to guests may include such things as the availability of a gym or swimming pool, and _____ meals.

4    Though he is usually good at detecting _____, that swindler cheated him out of a month's pay.

5    The _____ odor emanating from the garbage bin was enough to make anyone cringe in disgust.

6    Spontaneous fire may occur when _____ matter such as hay or coal is stored in bulk.

7    The company's dominance in the industry was often described as a(n) _____ due to its immense size and influence.

8    To _____ an uprising, Chinese rebels used lotus-seed mooncakes with messages written on rice paper hidden inside to successfully overthrow the Mongols.

9    The military commanders launched a(n) _____ strike to disable the enemy's capabilities before their enemy initiated an attack.

10    The palace's grandeur was accentuated by its lavish decorations and _____ designs.

**[3] Choose the one which is different from the others.**

**11** ① spree          ② temperance       ③ binge        ④ orgy

**12** ① belittle      ② disparage       ③ downplay     ④ flatter

**13** ① resonant     ② orotund        ③ oblivious     ④ sonorous

**14** ① shriek       ② murmur        ③ grouse      ④ grumble

**15** ① bizarre      ② eccentric      ③ erratic       ④ steadfast

**16** ① tranquility   ② hush         ③ disturbance   ④ stillness

**17** ① expound    ② exasperate    ③ expatiate    ④ explicate

**18** ① smear       ② smudge       ③ adhesive    ④ blot

**19** ① totter       ② stumble      ③ stagger     ④ crumble

**20** ① protrude    ② interlope    ③ kibitz      ④ meddle

---

**✓ Answers**

**1** ① | 공정하고 신중한 판사라는 그의 평판은 법과 동정심의 균형을 이루는 현명한 결정을 내릴 수 있는 그의 일관된 능력에 바탕을 두었다.

**2** ⑯ | 그 정치인의 두 지역사회에 대한 불공평한 비교는 통합을 촉진하기보다는 오히려 긴장을 유발했다.

**3** ⑩ | 투숙객에게 제공되는 편의 서비스에는 헬스클럽이나 수영장의 이용과 무료 식사와 같은 것들이 포함될 수 있다.

**4** ⑲ | 그는 대개 교묘한 속임수를 간파하는 것에 능했지만, 그 사기꾼은 그를 속여서 한 달 치 월급을 가로챘다.

**5** ⑨ | 쓰레기통에서 풍기는 고약한 악취는 누구라도 물러서게 하기에 충분했다.

**6** ⑦ | 자연발생적인 화재는 건초나 석탄과 같이 불이 붙기 쉬운 물질이 대량으로 저장되어 있을 때 일어날 수 있다.

**7** ④ | 업계 내에서 회사의 지배력은 엄청난 규모와 영향력으로 인해 종종 리바이어던(거대한 바다 동물)으로 묘사되었다.

**8** ⑤ | 봉기를 선동하기 위해, 중국인 반란군들은 메시지를 적은 쌀 종이가 안에 숨겨져 있는 연꽃 씨 월병(月餠)을 사용했으며, 결국 성공적으로 몽고인들을 전복시켰다.

**9** ② | 군 지휘관들은 적이 공격을 개시하기 전에 적의 능력을 무력화하기 위해 선제공격을 감행했다.

**10** ⑪ | 호화로운 장식과 화려한 디자인은 궁전의 웅장함을 더욱 돋보이게 했다.

- - - - - - - - - - - - - - - - - - - - - - - - - - - - - - - - - - - - - - - - -

**11** ②   **12** ④   **13** ③   **14** ①   **15** ④   **16** ③   **17** ②   **18** ③   **19** ④   **20** ①

## ☑ DAILY CHECKUP

[1] Write the meaning of the following words.

| | |
|---|---|
| ☐ quiver | ☐ hang-up |
| ☐ overt | ☐ mutilate |
| ☐ anathema | ☐ ambulatory |
| ☐ stint | ☐ wholesale |
| ☐ convulsion | ☐ epicenter |
| ☐ suffocate | ☐ bereave |
| ☐ equestrian | ☐ gallows |
| ☐ propensity | ☐ luminous |
| ☐ discredit | ☐ infancy |
| ☐ inexorable | ☐ crotchety |
| ☐ assuage | ☐ engrave |
| ☐ cupidity | ☐ prudish |
| ☐ rattle | ☐ nuance |
| ☐ preamble | ☐ chasm |
| ☐ sacrosanct | ☐ debauch |
| ☐ meteor | ☐ gruesome |
| ☐ inveigle | ☐ reservation |
| ☐ snob | ☐ badger |
| ☐ bush | ☐ sophistry |
| ☐ expedient | ☐ tyranny |
| ☐ apparition | ☐ full-fledged |
| ☐ unravel | ☐ curator |
| ☐ tier | ☐ rummage |
| ☐ crush | ☐ plumb |
| ☐ flare | ☐ voyeur |

[2] Select <u>the most</u> appropriate word from the box below. Each word should be used only once.

| | | | |
|---|---|---|---|
| ① rattle | ② unraveling | ③ mutilate | ④ discredit |
| ⑤ sophistry | ⑥ overt | ⑦ debauch | ⑧ prudish |
| ⑨ suffocating | ⑩ full-fledged | ⑪ reservation | ⑫ luminous |
| ⑬ chasm | ⑭ bereave | ⑮ inexorable | ⑯ rummage |
| ⑰ sacrosanct | ⑱ snob | ⑲ anathema | ⑳ plumb |

**1** The unexpected turn of events left him with a lingering sense of uncertainty and a profound feeling of _____ regarding the future outcome.

**2** In contrast to the euphemistic, socially critical songs of the 1970s and 1980s, what differentiates the rebellious songs of the 1990s is the latter's _____ cynicism.

**3** Nitrogen hypoxia is a method of _____ prisoners on death row by forcing them to breathe pure nitrogen, starving them of oxygen until they die.

**4** Science teaches theories must be tested against reality, but some religious beliefs don't stand such a test. People with these beliefs would _____ science.

**5** The economic downturn seemed _____ as every effort to reverse its course yielded no tangible results.

**6** Some people consider desecration of the American flag to be treasonous or even an act of terrorism, but others refuse to treat what they consider a mere symbol as _____.

**7** The sudden loss of his friend seemed to _____ him of friendship and comfort.

**8** The conservative upbringing instilled in her a deeply _____ attitude toward anything deemed too provocative or suggestive.

**9** Science and liberal arts have been separated from each other for so long in history that now there exists a deep _____ between the two.

**10** After misplacing his keys, he began to _____ through the drawers and cabinets in search of them.

[3] Choose the one which is different from the others.

**11**　① tendency　　② impotence　　③ disposition　　④ propensity

**12**　① alleviate　　② assuage　　③ evaporate　　④ relieve

**13**　① avarice　　② greed　　③ cupidity　　④ hypocrisy

**14**　① quiver　　② swell　　③ vibrate　　④ tremble

**15**　① expedient　　② advantageous　　③ convenient　　④ providential

**16**　① infiltrate　　② inveigle　　③ coax　　④ wheedle

**17**　① petulant　　② cranky　　③ crotchety　　④ sedulous

**18**　① macabre　　② gruesome　　③ precocious　　④ ghastly

**19**　① ambulatory　　② iconoclastic　　③ shifting　　④ vagabond

**20**　① voyeur　　② apparition　　③ specter　　④ phantom

✔**Answers**

**1** ⑪　｜ 예상치 못한 사태의 전환으로 인해 그는 미래의 결과에 대한 좀체 사라지지 않는 불확실성과 깊은 의구심을 갖게 되었다.

**2** ⑥　｜ 1970~1980년대의 완곡한 사회 비판 노래들과 달리, 1990년대의 반체제 노래들을 구분 짓는 것은 후자가 냉소를 공공연하게 드러낸다는 점이다.

**3** ⑨　｜ 질소 저산소증(질소 사형)은 사형수에게 질소만을 흡입하게 하여 사형수가 죽을 때까지 산소를 차단해서 이들을 질식시키는 방법이다.

**4** ④　｜ 과학은 이론이 반드시 현실에 비추어 검증되어야 한다고 가르치지만, 몇몇 종교적 믿음은 그러한 검증을 받지 못한다. 이런 믿음이 있는 사람들은 과학을 불신할 것이다.

**5** ⑮　｜ 경기 침체는 그것을 반전시키려는 모든 노력이 가시적인 성과를 거두지 못하자 불가항력적으로 보였다.

**6** ⑰　｜ 일부 사람들은 성조기에 대한 신성모독 행위를 반역적이거나 심지어는 테러 행위로 간주하지만, 다른 사람들은 단순한 상징물로 생각되는 것을 신성한 것으로 취급하는 것에 반대한다.

**7** ⑭　｜ 친구를 갑자기 잃은 것은 그에게 우정과 위안을 앗아간 것처럼 보였다.

**8** ⑧　｜ 보수적인 교육은 그녀에게 너무 자극적이거나 선정적이라고 여겨지는 것에 대해 매우 신중한 태도를 갖게 해주었다.

**9** ⑬　｜ 과학과 인문학은 역사적으로 너무나도 오랫동안 서로 분리되어 있었기 때문에, 지금은 그 둘 사이에 큰 간극이 존재한다.

**10** ⑯　｜ 열쇠를 엉뚱한 곳에 잘못 둔 후에 그는 열쇠를 찾기 위해 서랍과 캐비닛을 뒤지기 시작했다.

**11** ②　**12** ③　**13** ④　**14** ②　**15** ④　**16** ①　**17** ④　**18** ③　**19** ②　**20** ①

[1] Write the meaning of the following words.

| | |
|---|---|
| ☐ oscillate | ☐ stab |
| ☐ mischance | ☐ benevolent |
| ☐ superannuated | ☐ vertigo |
| ☐ affinity | ☐ holistic |
| ☐ rusty | ☐ quell |
| ☐ inveigh | ☐ statute |
| ☐ contumacious | ☐ thoroughfare |
| ☐ squint | ☐ mordant |
| ☐ precedent | ☐ rendition |
| ☐ awry | ☐ lumber |
| ☐ extort | ☐ aperture |
| ☐ fugacious | ☐ blurt |
| ☐ consort | ☐ inextricable |
| ☐ prehensile | ☐ arraign |
| ☐ subterfuge | ☐ deranged |
| ☐ dumbfound | ☐ fail-safe |
| ☐ wound | ☐ gouge |
| ☐ practitioner | ☐ overbearing |
| ☐ careen | ☐ beat |
| ☐ treacherous | ☐ prurient |
| ☐ internment | ☐ clan |
| ☐ gush | ☐ swoon |
| ☐ euphemism | ☐ emollient |
| ☐ doctor | ☐ nomenclature |
| ☐ contraband | ☐ reverberate |

[2] Select <u>the most</u> appropriate word from the box below. Each word should be used only once.

| | | | |
|---|---|---|---|
| ① oscillated | ② inveighed | ③ dumbfounded | ④ holistic |
| ⑤ prehensile | ⑥ subterfuge | ⑦ euphemism | ⑧ inextricable |
| ⑨ treacherous | ⑩ consort | ⑪ doctored | ⑫ internment |
| ⑬ emollient | ⑭ prurient | ⑮ arraign | ⑯ deranged |
| ⑰ vertigo | ⑱ beat | ⑲ extorted | ⑳ affinity |

1    The artist felt a deep _____ with nature, often drawing inspiration from the beauty of the natural world..

2    The journalist boldly _____ against the censorship imposed on free speech.

3    The corrupt official was caught red-handed as evidence surfaced of how he _____ bribes from various contractors in exchange for government contracts.

4    We never believed that he would resort to _____ in order to achieve his goal; we always regarded him as an honest man.

5    The bond between the twins was so strong that it seemed their thoughts and emotions were _____.

6    Despite the scientist's reputation for integrity, suspicions arose when it was revealed that the research findings had been _____ to support a specific conclusion.

7    The dizzying sensation and disorienting feeling of spinning while looking down from a tall building caused a sudden onset of _____.

8    An MTV series that includes explicit scenes might be considered _____ and have censors screaming to have it taken off the air.

9    _____ thinking refers to a big picture mentality in which a person recognizes the interconnectedness of various elements that form larger systems and patterns.

10    In a constant see-saw from one state of mind to another, she _____ between wanting to believe the story he had told her about himself and wondering whether he had deceived her about a fundamental part of his life.

**[3] Choose the one which is different from the others.**

**11** ① contumacious ② defiant ③ tractable ④ mutinous

**12** ① fleeting ② ephemeral ③ fugacious ④ vigorous

**13** ① diverse ② benevolent ③ benign ④ charitable

**14** ① suppress ② surrender ③ quell ④ subdue

**15** ① scathing ② acerbic ③ mordant ④ bland

**16** ① gap ② aperture ③ juncture ④ orifice

**17** ① arrogant ② haughty ③ overbearing ④ enchanting

**18** ① keel ② faint ③ appeal ④ swoon

**19** ① reverberate ② refine ③ echo ④ resound

**20** ① commensurate ② fail-safe ③ infallible ④ foolproof

---

## ✔Answers

**1** ⑳  | 그 화가는 자연과 깊은 친밀감을 느꼈고, 종종 자연 세계의 아름다움으로부터 영감을 받았다.

**2** ②  | 그 기자는 언론의 자유에 가해진 검열에 대해 대담하게 맹렬히 비난했다.

**3** ⑲  | 부패한 공무원은 정부와의 계약을 대가로 다양한 계약자로부터 뇌물을 갈취했다는 증거가 드러나 현행범으로 붙잡혔다.

**4** ⑥  | 우리는 그가 자신의 목적을 성취하기 위해 속임수를 쓸 줄은 몰랐다. 우리는 항상 그를 정직한 사람으로 생각했던 것이다.

**5** ⑧  | 쌍둥이 사이의 유대감은 너무 강해서 그들의 생각과 감정이 떼려야 뗄 수 없을 것처럼 보였다.

**6** ⑪  | 그 과학자가 정직하다는 평판에도 불구하고, 연구 결과가 특정한 결론을 뒷받침하기 위해 조작된 것으로 드러나자 의혹이 불거졌다.

**7** ⑰  | 높은 건물에서 내려다보자 아찔한 느낌과 방향 감각 상실로 인해 갑자기 현기증을 일으켰다.

**8** ⑭  | 노골적인 장면이 포함된 MTV 시리즈는 외설적인 것으로 간주되어 검열관들이 그것을 방송되지 못하게 하려고 큰소리로 외쳐댈 수도 있다.

**9** ④  | 전체론적 사고는 더 큰 시스템과 패턴을 형성하는 다양한 구성요소들의 상호연관성을 인식하는, 전체를 보는 정신구조이다.

**10** ①  | 마음의 상태가 끊임없이 동요하는 가운데 그녀는 그가 자신에 대해 그녀에게 해준 이야기를 믿고 싶어 하는 것과 그가 자신의 인생의 근본적인 한 부분에 대해 그녀를 속이지 않았나 의심하는 것 사이에서 갈피를 못 잡았다.

---

**11** ③  **12** ④  **13** ①  **14** ②  **15** ④  **16** ③  **17** ④  **18** ③  **19** ②  **20** ①

[01-100] Choose the one that is closest in meaning to the underlined part.

**01** Such <u>blatant</u> advertising within the bounds of the school drew protest from parents.
① assimilative      ② inconspicuous
③ monotonous      ④ obtrusive

**02** In the <u>primordial</u> stage, everything except this part did not work properly due to erosion.
① beginning      ② ending
③ critical      ④ peaked

**03** He has often been criticized for offering ideas that seem a little too <u>outlandish</u>.
① ambitious      ② superficial
③ regressive      ④ eccentric

**04** Winston acknowledged that his comments could be <u>construed</u> as racist.
① understood      ② criticized
③ laughed at      ④ reported

**05** Scorpion fishes, which live on coral or on rocky bottoms, possess a remarkable degree of <u>cryptic</u> coloration and shape. Numerous fleshy lappets adorn the head, fin membranes, and body scales, rendering the fish virtually invisible against a background of rocks covered with marine organisms.
① eligible      ② caustic
③ exuberant      ④ concealing

**06** Yet it must be owned that England has pursued her magnificent career in a policy often <u>insolent</u> and brutal, and generally selfish.
① impertinent      ② capricious
③ ludicrous      ④ detrimental

**07** In his inaugural speech, the newly elected president <u>fulminated</u> against the Republicans' plan to cut Medicare fund.
① stormed      ② cajoled
③ lampooned      ④ careened

**08** The scandalous remarks in the newspaper <u>besmirched</u> the reputations of every member of the society.
① defiled      ② supplemented
③ misled      ④ disorganized

**09** Mom was <u>livid</u> when she found out we used her dress to clean up the Coke we spilled on the floor.
① anguished      ② appalled
③ furious      ④ disappointed

**10** France is the only other country to offer congratulations, although it <u>retracted</u> the statement within 24 hours.
① confirmed      ② revised
③ announced      ④ withdrew

11 It was <u>evident</u> that the animals would not survive the winter.
① myriad  ② receptive
③ apparent  ④ muddy

12 John's behaviour caused <u>affliction</u> to Jane as she did not expect such a wild behaviour.
① utility  ② anguish
③ feature  ④ capability

13 Claude S. Fisher focuses less on formal institutions and laws than on the <u>gossamer</u> tissue of attitudes, values, and beliefs — what a scholar referred to as "habits of the heart" — that compose what moderns might call the national psyche.
① grisly  ② delicate
③ porous  ④ reticent

14 The settlers' steady <u>encroachment</u> on the Indians' territory ultimately left the Indians homeless.
① endearment  ② infringement
③ enchantment  ④ enforcement

15 The government was accused of being <u>subservient</u> to the interests of the pro-life campaigners.
① accountable  ② uninterested
③ impetuous  ④ submissive

16 He <u>ducked</u> the first few blows then started to fight back.
① threw  ② clenched
③ dodged  ④ smashed

17 Kakar described the Israeli strikes on Gaza "as deplorable and <u>willful</u> acts of Israeli aggression against innocent Palestinians."
① intentional  ② vengeful
③ malleable  ④ reckless

18 One of the goals of psychoanalysis is to bring <u>repressed</u> conflicts to the level of consciousness.
① inexplicable  ② suppressed
③ unending  ④ troublesome

19 A lot of us can be embarrassed to say what we want, and we spend our entire lives learning how to be <u>forthright</u>.
① whimsical  ② outspoken
③ flamboyant  ④ courteous

20 The New York Times is widely respected for its serious journalism and occasionally kidded for its <u>stodgy</u> traditions.
① insouciant  ② vainglorious
③ premonitory  ④ dull

21 The law is very <u>explicit</u> regarding the use of and standards for child safety seats in automobiles.
① brief  ② new
③ firm  ④ clear

22 She is confident and smart and she can stand up for herself. She is not <u>subjugated</u> by her husband.
① disgraced  ② infatuated
③ persuaded  ④ dominated

23 The corollary is that classic psychoanalysis does not work as well as behavioral therapy in restoring confidence.
① catch
② axiom
③ result
④ perception

24 We must kill a man who blandishes another person into doing something.
① forces
② flatters
③ urges
④ compels

25 Here's another thing Ingraham addresses in her diatribe, and that many Republicans will not admit to: The violence actually was about disrupting the election's outcome.
① accolade
② warning
③ castigation
④ commentary

26 Competition for precious resources resulted in disputes and general unrest between neighboring states. Skirmishes sometimes broke out as tensions mounted and people looked to military leaders for protection.
① Clashes
② Erosions
③ Conciliations
④ Exaltations

27 Gokhale wanted Indians to imbibe the western idea of secular progress.
① pigeonhole
② extol
③ criticize
④ absorb

28 Theresa had been a nurse in the emergency room for twenty years, but she had never gotten used to the anguish of accident victims.
① happiness
② spirit
③ abundance
④ suffering

29 The teacher tried to ascertain the cause of the melee which had broken out among the students.
① mishap
② gamut
③ mien
④ turmoil

30 It sounds almost banal to stress the difference, but that is vital to understanding liberal democracy.
① smart
② trite
③ priceless
④ detrimental

31 In "Star Wars," dark, evil Darth Vader is a perfect foil for fair-haired, naive Luke Skywalker.
① metal
② contrast
③ pair
④ avatar

32 In the impetuous youth of humanity, we can make grave errors that can stunt our growth for a long time.
① postpone
② exaggerate
③ overstretch
④ hinder

33 The dark clouds growing on the horizon presaged the start of a violent storm.
① subsumed
② portended
③ maligned
④ expedited

34 In this country you had at one time iniquitous and merciless laws which sent boys and girls to the scaffold for pocket-picking and other minor offences.
① invalid
② bilious
③ waspish
④ unfair

35 The former president has continued to say fraud and ballot chicanery caused his loss to the current president.
① trickery
② initiative
③ provision
④ betterment

36 Assigning jobs by the type of personality may be a popular management practice, but it is also a good way to belittle people.
① dismantle
② disparage
③ interrogate
④ subdue

37 Hydrogen is colourless, odourless, and highly combustible.
① furtive
② transparent
③ flammable
④ ethereal

38 Those good for nothing scalawags fomented the rebellion.
① necessitated
② instigated
③ quelled
④ conspired

39 Macron's efforts at projecting progressive modernity were belied by the turgid underlying realities.
① fickle
② discreet
③ bloated
④ frivolous

40 In a climate of political unrest, a dictator can often seize power.
① humbug
② allegory
③ exile
④ insecurity

41 Insecticides must be used judiciously in order to maximize the effect of the natural control agents.
① cooperatively
② wisely
③ impartially
④ legally

42 The reporter made invidious comparisons between the company's claims and its performance.
① agreeable
② malign
③ practical
④ meticulous

43 Rooftop pool access is complimentary for hotel guests and $15 per day for outside visitors.
① luxurious
② discounted
③ free
④ unlimited

44 Of all the calamities that befell tourists as the coronavirus took hold, those involving cruise ships stood apart. Contagion at sea inspired a special horror, as pleasure palaces turned into prison hulks, and rumors of infection on board spread between fetid cabins via WhatsApp.
① cozy
② messy
③ clean
④ rotten

45 In some southern regions, like Hudson Bay, bears aggregate on land during the ice-free summer and autumn months.
① are approximate
② amount to
③ abound
④ gather into a group

46 Renowned curator Jacques Sauniere staggered through the vaulted archway of the museum's Grand Gallery.
① ran　　　　② stumbled
③ rolled down　④ fell down

47 On Wednesday, the Ninth Circuit touched off an avalanche of criticism by pronouncing the Pledge of Allegiance unconstitutional.
① gusty wind
② nippy cold
③ gushing water
④ massive snow

48 The erratic dance moves and catchy electronic sounds from the title song have captivated every listener.
① errant　　　② mercurial
③ erroneous　④ typical

49 If he couldn't prepare his case properly, the trial would be a travesty.
① parody　　② tragedy
③ comedy　　④ romance

50 Forests provided bountiful resources for the early North American colonies.
① beautiful　② hidden
③ artificial　　④ abundant

51 Several theories of evolution had historically preceded that of Charles Darwin, although he expounded upon the stages of development.
① elucidated　② detested
③ substantiated　④ rebuffed

52 This syllabus is provisional and subject to amendment without notice.
① concise　　② reliable
③ inflexible　④ temporary

53 She was startled to realize that what she was actually doing was gloating over the fact that the drunken man had specified the Chinese as the unwanted.
① eluding　　② disregarding
③ exaggerating　④ grinning at

54 On occasion, mail pieces may be delivered with some smudges on them due to the automated postal sorting equipment.
① dents　　② blots
③ traces　　④ cracks

55 To explicate the nature of so-called the dark energy, astronomers need to observe billion-year old supernovae.
① enchant　　② extricate
③ eliminate　④ elucidate

56 Critics accuse Modi's Hindu nationalist government of seeking to suppress dissenters and activists using sedition laws and other legal weapons.
① asylum　　② reciprocity
③ mutiny　　④ extradition

57 Lying is regarded as a venial sin, yet the Bible says that unrepentant liars end up in hell.
① pardonable　② besetting
③ inexpiable　④ improbable

58 Democrats say the workers are victims of corporate greed, while Republicans claim workers were brushed aside because of the Biden administration's push toward electric vehicles.

① annexation  ② diversification

③ avarice  ④ invigoration

59 No matter what the circumstances are, swearing an oath is serious business.

① query  ② credit

③ feast  ④ vow

60 The glass started to quiver with the rain hitting it, because it wasn't so much rain as hail. The hail smashed against everything, including my faith.

① get wet  ② fog up

③ tinkle  ④ vibrate

61 People in the village showed overt hostility to the strangers.

① obvious  ② wavering

③ onerous  ④ defensive

62 He is returning to this country after a five-year stint in Hong Kong.

① exile  ② journey

③ service  ④ parole

63 The patient repeatedly had convulsions until he was given the medicine to calm him down.

① condemnations  ② spasms

③ aversions  ④ contritions

64 "But we will destroy the planet eventually if we don't stop hating," Bninski added. The United States is guilty of supplying arms to "all sides in the Middle East conflict," she said. "We have the largest store of nuclear, chemical and biological weapons in the world. We don't see our own propensity for evil when we're dropping thousands of tons of bombs on another country."

① indifference from

② preposterousness in

③ involvement with

④ penchant for

65 Feeling dislocated in the face of the inexorable forces of globalization, such workers lash out against immigrants and free trade.

① repulsive  ② subversive

③ tremendous  ④ relentless

66 Obar's fears about being the first pregnant woman to use her own stem cells in a study to treat her baby's alpha thalassemia in utero were quickly assuaged when she watched the blood transfusions take place smoothly.

① dismissed  ② accelerated

③ relieved  ④ surfaced

67 He got so rattled when he saw the policeman that he drove the car up over the curb.

① became enthusiastic

② became confused

③ got disappointed

④ got angry

**68** You need not <u>beat about the bush</u>. Come to the point at once.
① wander about the bush
② probe the bush
③ say indirectly
④ consult with others

**69** We thought it <u>expedient</u> not to pay the builder until he finished the work.
① unfitting          ② impolite
③ detrimental        ④ useful

**70** We are learning to live in virtual worlds. We may find ourselves alone as we navigate virtual oceans, <u>unravel</u> virtual mysteries, and engineer virtual skyscrapers.
① create             ② solve
③ fold               ④ entangle

**71** It became apparent to me how intertwined the lives of her and her brothers had become in the wake of their <u>bereavement</u>.
① death              ② crisis
③ atrocity           ④ resentment

**72** Charles Lamb's works reveal profound scholarship and are written in <u>a luminous</u> style which is unsurpassed in English prose.
① a lubricious       ② an assiduous
③ a circumscribed    ④ a clear

**73** Only a few students expected to receive feedback from their <u>crotchety</u> old professor.
① petulant           ② virtuous
③ egalitarian        ④ callous

**74** Inspired by psychoanalysis and various "life reform" movements, exposing inner lives, psychological <u>chasms</u> and passions became a central concern to artists.
① narratives         ② characteristics
③ allusions          ④ gaps

**75** The <u>gruesome</u> details of Edgar Allen Poe's stories often stick in people's minds.
① exhilarating       ② fiery
③ horrible           ④ wistful

**76** There were mutters and murmurs and <u>reservations</u>, but when the mayor made his persuasive speech, everyone seemed to forget about their protests and cheered him on.
① bookings           ② reasons
③ doubts             ④ instigations

**77** New York's fashion industry has not fully escaped the <u>tyranny</u> of French design.
① domination         ② bossiness
③ importance         ④ evilness

**78** South Korea has publicized its goal of attaining <u>full-fledged</u> normalization of the economy beyond the pandemic crisis in 2022.
① superlative        ② relative
③ comprehensive      ④ tentative

79 When his back was turned, mother let me get a chair and rummage through his treasures.
① to refuse as wrong
② to arrange the colors
③ to gather together
④ to search a place diligently

80 There is an affinity among the Scandinavian languages.
① daintiness
② queerness
③ closeness
④ peculiarity

81 This decision sets a precedent for future cases of a similar nature.
① controversy
② preview
③ guide
④ record

82 He extorted from his daughter the names and conditions of the men whom she had met.
① forged
② obtained
③ wrested
④ rechristened

83 We frequently judge people by the company whom they consort with.
① abide by
② associate with
③ interfere with
④ stand for

84 To disguise their invasion plans, the Allies engaged in a campaign of subterfuge prior to the Normandy landings.
① deception
② warfare
③ hostility
④ persuasion

85 Over the past year we have seen the rise of a new kind of warfare: microterrorism, which can be defined as small-scale terrorism, driven from the local level, whose practitioners choose not the largest or most spectacular operations but those that are likely to succeed.
① professionals
② proprietors
③ precursors
④ personnel

86 For the next eight months, Oliver was the victim of a systematic course of treachery and deception.
① faith
② malice
③ violence
④ disloyalty

87 The deceitful investigator was accused of doctoring data in his research paper, which is ethically problematic.
① mastering
② stipulating
③ extrapolating
④ fabricating

88 He was happy to live in a peaceful land ruled by a benevolent king.
① unkind
② generous
③ malevolent
④ vulgar

89 The arch was at least 50 meters above me, and for the first time in years I felt vertigo.
① curiosity
② dizziness
③ invigoration
④ vestige

90 Ecological problems usually require holistic solutions.
① notable
② impartial
③ complete
④ concrete

91 The government's reassurances have done nothing to <u>quell</u> the doubts of the public.

① arouse      ② fathom

③ saturate      ④ suppress

92 Responding to a flood of sexual abuse accusations against priests nationwide, Illinois extended the <u>statute</u> of limitations in such cases, giving prosecutors 20 years after a victim turns 18 to bring charges.

① limit      ② law

③ license      ④ list

93 He proved himself a <u>mordant</u> critic with far-reaching influence.

① impartial      ② sarcastic

③ prudent      ④ formidable

94 Calvin Klein's ad for Calvin Klein fragrance for men is a perfect contemporary <u>rendition</u> of the classical myth of Narcissus.

① interpretation      ② example

③ criterion      ④ reference

95 Although the question of gender and the question of sexuality are <u>inextricable</u> in that each can be expressed only in terms of the other, they are nonetheless not the same question.

① unseparable      ② problematic

③ inevitable      ④ deep-rooted

96 Sudden illness <u>deranged</u> our plan for a trip.

① delayed      ② duplicated

③ disturbed      ④ influenced

97 As exciting as a surgery sounds, I was eager not to <u>swoon</u> while photographing such a surgery.

① come up      ② pass out

③ fall down      ④ set in

98 Taiwan, like Ukraine, has long lived in the shadow of a large and <u>overbearing</u> neighbor.

① unreliable      ② heinous

③ negligible      ④ domineering

99 The country's uneasy relationship with Islam was highlighted by testimonies that <u>oscillated</u> between lingering prejudice and calls for tolerance.

① vacillated      ② duplicated

③ authenticated      ④ perpetuated

100 Some <u>prurient</u> scenes in the movie were ended up being cut because people would watch it for the wrong reasons.

① gauche      ② protean

③ brutal      ④ salacious

[1] Write the meaning of the following words.

| | |
|---|---|
| ☐ grisly | ☐ fustian |
| ☐ stupor | ☐ quip |
| ☐ maverick | ☐ banish |
| ☐ dislodge | ☐ heyday |
| ☐ artifice | ☐ irenic |
| ☐ sully | ☐ constrain |
| ☐ plangent | ☐ repository |
| ☐ imprecate | ☐ vituperative |
| ☐ amnesty | ☐ adumbrate |
| ☐ ecclesiastical | ☐ stern |
| ☐ fritter | ☐ usury |
| ☐ apocryphal | ☐ goof |
| ☐ prostrate | ☐ fluke |
| ☐ squarely | ☐ bleed |
| ☐ charter | ☐ exodus |
| ☐ truant | ☐ contrived |
| ☐ seismology | ☐ droop |
| ☐ overrule | ☐ propriety |
| ☐ detonation | ☐ culinary |
| ☐ countermand | ☐ incarnation |
| ☐ reverend | ☐ resuscitate |
| ☐ weed | ☐ sinuous |
| ☐ lineal | ☐ nugget |
| ☐ evoke | ☐ moot |
| ☐ custody | ☐ premiere |

[2] Select <u>the most</u> appropriate word from the box below. Each word should be used only once.

| | | | |
|---|---|---|---|
| ① maverick | ② reverend | ③ apocryphal | ④ repository |
| ⑤ stupor | ⑥ banish | ⑦ amnesty | ⑧ moot |
| ⑨ contrived | ⑩ sinuous | ⑪ exodus | ⑫ fritter |
| ⑬ adumbrated | ⑭ overruled | ⑮ fustian | ⑯ heyday |
| ⑰ prostrate | ⑱ resuscitate | ⑲ sully | ⑳ evoke |

1    Given the absence of substantiated proof or documented evidence within historical records, the historian assessed the tale as _____.

2    The legal team presented compelling evidence, yet the judge firmly _____ their motion for a retrial.

3    His independent spirit and refusal to adhere to conventional methods marked him as a(n) _____ in the realm of contemporary art.

4    The malicious intent behind the gossip was evident, yet it failed to _____ his standing among his loyal supporters.

5    The company's _____ occurred during the economic boom of the 1980s when its innovative products captured the market's attention.

6    The king's decree was to _____ all those who dared to speak against the kingdom in order to maintain absolute control.

7    The Tax Office's _____ on the declaration of undisclosed assets resulted in many people coming forward.

8    The introductory chapter of the novel only briefly _____ the intricate plot that would later unfold in surprising ways throughout the book.

9    The looming threat of war prompted an urgent _____ as people sought refuge in neighboring countries.

10    It's become important for people to learn CPR so that they might _____ someone who loses consciousness.

[3] Choose the one which is different from the others.

**11**　① plangent　② priggish　③ sonorous　④ resonant

**12**　① beseech　② imprecate　③ curse　④ execrate

**13**　① annul　② rescind　③ countermand　④ sanction

**14**　① maneuver　② artifice　③ effrontery　④ ruse

**15**　① grisly　② gullible　③ gruesome　④ hideous

**16**　① irreverent　② irenic　③ peaceful　④ pacific

**17**　① restrain　② curb　③ constrain　④ complement

**18**　① defamatory　② putative　③ vituperative　④ abusive

**19**　① strict　② rigid　③ stern　④ lenient

**20**　① courtesy　② decorum　③ ambiguity　④ propriety

## ✔ Answers

**1** ③ ｜ 역사 기록에 입증되거나 문서화된 증거가 없다는 점을 고려하여 그 역사가는 그 이야기가 출처가 불분명한 것으로 평가했다.

**2** ⑭ ｜ 법률팀은 강력한 증거를 제시했지만, 판사는 그들의 재심 청구를 단호하게 기각했다.

**3** ① ｜ 그의 독립적인 정신과 종래의 방법을 고수하는 것에 대한 거부는 그를 현대 미술 영역에서 이단아로 만들었다.

**4** ⑲ ｜ 그 험담 뒤에 숨겨진 악의적인 의도는 분명했지만, 그것이 그의 충실한 지지자들 사이에서 그의 입지를 훼손하지는 못했다.

**5** ⑯ ｜ 이 회사의 전성기는 자사의 혁신적인 제품이 시장의 주목을 끌던 1980년대 경제 호황기에 일어났다.

**6** ⑥ ｜ 왕의 명령은 절대적인 지배를 유지하기 위해 감히 왕국에 반대하는 말을 하는 모든 사람들을 추방하는 것이었다.

**7** ⑦ ｜ 비공개 자산을 신고하는 것에 대한 국세청의 사면조치는 많은 사람들이 나서는 결과로 이어졌다.

**8** ⑬ ｜ 소설의 첫 장은 나중에 책 전반에 걸쳐 놀라운 방식으로 전개될 복잡한 줄거리를 간략하게만 설명했다.

**9** ⑪ ｜ 다가오는 전쟁의 위협은 사람들이 이웃 나라로 피난처를 찾아 나서자 긴급한 탈출을 촉발시켰다.

**10** ⑱ ｜ 의식을 잃은 사람을 소생시키기 위해 심폐소생술(CPR)을 배우는 것이 중요해졌다.

- - - - - - - - - - - - - - - - - - - - - - - - - - - - - - - - - - - - - - - - - - - - - - - -

**11** ②　**12** ①　**13** ④　**14** ③　**15** ②　**16** ①　**17** ④　**18** ②　**19** ④　**20** ③

# ☑ DAILY CHECKUP

[1] Write the meaning of the following words.

| | |
|---|---|
| ☐ brandish | ☐ trinket |
| ☐ puerile | ☐ debonair |
| ☐ spinster | ☐ originate |
| ☐ disabuse | ☐ mealy-mouthed |
| ☐ all-out | ☐ swagger |
| ☐ promenade | ☐ artisan |
| ☐ stoke | ☐ lagniappe |
| ☐ cocoon | ☐ yield |
| ☐ risque | ☐ exuberant |
| ☐ provident | ☐ prelude |
| ☐ immure | ☐ disarm |
| ☐ suspense | ☐ notch |
| ☐ animus | ☐ whet |
| ☐ clinch | ☐ vein |
| ☐ resolution | ☐ grill |
| ☐ grope | ☐ fragment |
| ☐ crib | ☐ enshrine |
| ☐ smug | ☐ prig |
| ☐ annals | ☐ baleful |
| ☐ momentum | ☐ cadet |
| ☐ implacable | ☐ accrete |
| ☐ excise | ☐ rouse |
| ☐ refulgent | ☐ supple |
| ☐ countenance | ☐ troupe |
| ☐ jolly | ☐ interdict |

[2] Select <u>the most</u> appropriate word from the box below. Each word should be used only once.

| | | | |
|---|---|---|---|
| ① countenance | ② exuberant | ③ brandish | ④ enshrined |
| ⑤ animus | ⑥ grope | ⑦ disarmed | ⑧ puerile |
| ⑨ clinch | ⑩ provident | ⑪ whet | ⑫ interdicted |
| ⑬ implacable | ⑭ grilled | ⑮ resolution | ⑯ rouse |
| ⑰ disabuse | ⑱ mealy-mouthed | ⑲ accrete | ⑳ troupe |

1  Electronic games are often criticized as _____, but research has shown that the young people who play them develop useful daily skills.

2  Recognized for his thoughtful and careful handling of finances, he was widely regarded as a(n) _____ individual.

3  The speaker's _____ was palpable as he vehemently expressed his disdain for the opposing viewpoint during the debate.

4  Despite numerous attempts to negotiate, her _____ resolve made it clear that she wouldn't yield to any compromise.

5  After receiving the exciting news, her face broke into a(n) _____ smile that could brighten anyone's day.

6  The diplomat's ability to defuse volatile discussions and promote dialogue ultimately _____ potential conflicts.

7  The government _____ the distribution of counterfeit goods by intensifying customs inspections and tightening trade regulations.

8  The professor sought to _____ his students' misguided notions by presenting them with compelling evidence and reasoned arguments.

9  Her _____ apology failed to convey genuine remorse because it was filled with vague and evasive language.

10  At a funeral, the minister said that the deceased will forever be _____ in the memories of those who loved him.

**[3] Choose the one which is different from the others.**

**11**  ① risque    ② lewd    ③ salacious    ④ solitary

**12**  ① excise    ② exempt    ③ delete    ④ expunge

**13**  ① refractory    ② refulgent    ③ radiant    ④ shining

**14**  ① jocund    ② jovial    ③ jolly    ④ jejune

**15**  ① harmful    ② evil    ③ auspicious    ④ baleful

**16**  ① lurid    ② supple    ③ elastic    ④ resilient

**17**  ① suspense    ② regret    ③ anxiety    ④ apprehension

**18**  ① complacent    ② humble    ③ smug    ④ self-satisfied

**19**  ① courteous    ② affable    ③ debonair    ④ strong-willed

**20**  ① brag    ② swagger    ③ writhe    ④ vaunt

---

## ✓Answers

1 ⑧ ｜ 전자 게임은 종종 유치하다는 비판을 받지만, 연구 결과 전자 게임을 하는 젊은이들이 유용한 일상 기술들을 발달시킨다는 사실이 드러났다.

2 ⑩ ｜ 사려 깊고 신중한 재정 관리로 인정받은 그는 검소한 사람으로 널리 간주되었다.

3 ⑤ ｜ 토론 중에 반대 의견에 대해 경멸감을 격렬하게 표현하면서 그 연사의 반감이 뚜렷이 드러났다.

4 ⑬ ｜ 수많은 협상 시도에도 불구하고 그녀의 완강한 결심은 그녀가 어떠한 타협에도 양보하지 않을 것임을 분명히 했다.

5 ② ｜ 기분 좋은 소식을 들은 후, 그녀의 얼굴에는 누구의 하루라도 밝게 만들어줄 수 있는 활기 넘치는 미소가 번졌다.

6 ⑦ ｜ 격하기 쉬운 토론을 완화하고 대화를 촉진하는 외교관의 능력은 궁극적으로 잠재적인 갈등을 해소했다.

7 ⑫ ｜ 정부는 세관검사를 강화하고 무역규제를 강화함으로써 위조 상품의 유통을 차단했다.

8 ⑰ ｜ 교수님은 학생들에게 설득력 있는 증거와 합리적인 주장을 제시함으로써 학생들의 잘못된 생각을 깨닫게 하려고 노력했다.

9 ⑱ ｜ 듣기 좋게 말하는 그녀의 사과는 모호하고 얼버무리는 말로 가득 차 있어서 진정한 반성을 전하지 못했다.

10 ④ ｜ 장례식에서 목사님은 고인이 자신을 사랑했던 사람들의 기억 속에 소중히 남을 것이라고 말했다.

- - - - - - - - - - - - - - - - - - - - - - - - - - - - - - - - - - - - - - - - - - -

11 ④    12 ②    13 ①    14 ④    15 ③    16 ①    17 ②    18 ②    19 ④    20 ③

[1] Write the meaning of the following words.

| | | | |
|---|---|---|---|
| ☐ propitiate | | ☐ impunity | |
| ☐ evanescent | | ☐ mellifluous | |
| ☐ squabble | | ☐ comity | |
| ☐ beleaguer | | ☐ hoist | |
| ☐ coward | | ☐ iffy | |
| ☐ swarthy | | ☐ upstart | |
| ☐ dovetail | | ☐ muse | |
| ☐ amenity | | ☐ ergonomics | |
| ☐ trifle | | ☐ reprobate | |
| ☐ provenance | | ☐ viand | |
| ☐ choke | | ☐ disgruntle | |
| ☐ austere | | ☐ greasy | |
| ☐ restraint | | ☐ primogeniture | |
| ☐ intercept | | ☐ consummate | |
| ☐ lugubrious | | ☐ tirade | |
| ☐ febrifuge | | ☐ oust | |
| ☐ glare | | ☐ apotheosis | |
| ☐ strip | | ☐ branch | |
| ☐ contraception | | ☐ superimpose | |
| ☐ disown | | ☐ polyglot | |
| ☐ rife | | ☐ enjoin | |
| ☐ nonentity | | ☐ yummy | |
| ☐ de facto | | ☐ astringent | |
| ☐ appurtenance | | ☐ spasm | |
| ☐ extemporize | | ☐ corral | |

[2] Select <u>the most</u> appropriate word from the box below. Each word should be used only once.

| | | | |
|---|---|---|---|
| ① impunity | ② dovetail | ③ intercept | ④ glare |
| ⑤ swarthy | ⑥ mellifluous | ⑦ extemporize | ⑧ propitiate |
| ⑨ lugubrious | ⑩ mused | ⑪ austere | ⑫ cowardly |
| ⑬ consummate | ⑭ evanescent | ⑮ greasy | ⑯ iffy |
| ⑰ ousted | ⑱ superimposed | ⑲ disgruntled | ⑳ comity |

**1**    The former general led his civilian life as he had his military life with simplicity and _____ dignity.

**2**    The mournful melody played by the violinist filled the concert hall with a(n) _____ resonance, evoking a profound sense of sorrow among the audience.

**3**    When faced with unexpected questions during the interview, the candidate was able to _____ responses that impressed the interviewers with her quick thinking and adaptability.

**4**    We humans live singularly _____ lives. Our consciousness is like the moth: Done in the flicker of candlelight on a summer night. Gone in an instant.

**5**    The corrupt politician behaved with a sense of _____ as if laws didn't apply to him.

**6**    The passengers were visibly _____ when the flight was delayed for the third time without any clear explanation from the airline staff.

**7**    After being defeated in a vote of no confidence, the CEO was _____ by the board from the company.

**8**    Her attempts to calm the situation and ease tensions seemed to _____ the growing skepticism among the group members.

**9**    The soldier's decision to abandon his post during the battle was seen as an act of _____ behavior rather than strategic retreat.

**10**    The coastguard patrol's main duty is to _____ drugs from Latin America.

[3] Choose the one which is different from the others.

11  ① choke          ② smother        ③ repel            ④ suffocate

12  ① squabble       ② concur         ③ quarrel          ④ wrangle

13  ① beguile        ② beleaguer      ③ beset            ④ besiege

14  ① reprobate      ② corrupt        ③ degenerate       ④ recondite

15  ① department     ② branch         ③ administration   ④ section

16  ① astringent     ② astute         ③ harsh            ④ severe

17  ① amend          ② enjoin         ③ command          ④ order

18  ① origin         ② provenance     ③ propensity       ④ source

19  ① renounce       ② attest         ③ disown           ④ repudiate

20  ① replete        ② abundant       ③ rife             ④ restive

## ✓ Answers

1  ⑪  | 그 전직 장군은 그가 군대에서 했던 것처럼 민간인이 되어서도 소박하고 엄격한 위엄을 갖춘 그런 생활을 했다.

2  ⑨  | 바이올리니스트의 애절한 선율은 공연장을 애처로운 울림으로 가득 채웠고, 관객들에게 깊은 슬픔을 자아냈다.

3  ⑦  | 면접 도중 예상치 못한 질문을 받았을 때, 그 지원자는 빠른 사고력과 융통성이 있다는 인상을 면접관들에게 주는 답변을 즉흥적으로 할 수 있었다.

4  ⑭  | 우리 인간은 유난히 덧없이 짧은 삶을 산다. 우리의 의식은 나방과 같다. 한여름 밤에 흔들리는 촛불에 끝장나 순식간에 사라진다.

5  ①  | 그 부패한 정치인은 마치 법이 자신에게 적용되지 않는 것처럼 처벌받지 않는다는 생각을 가지고 행동했다.

6  ⑲  | 항공사 직원의 명확한 설명 없이 비행기가 세 번째 지연되자 승객들은 확실히 불만을 표했다.

7  ⑰  | 그 최고경영자는 불신임 투표에서 패배한 후, 회사의 이사회에 의해 축출되었다.

8  ⑧  | 상황을 진정시키고 긴장을 완화하려는 그녀의 시도는 구성원들 사이에서 점점 커지는 회의감을 달래는 것처럼 보였다.

9  ⑫  | 전투 중 주둔지를 포기한 그 병사의 결정은 전략적 후퇴라기보다는 비겁한 행동으로 비쳤다.

10 ③  | 해안경비 순찰대의 주된 임무는 라틴 아메리카로부터 들어오는 마약을 차단하는 것이다.

- - - - - - - - - - - - - - - - - - - - - - - - - - - - - - - - - - - - - - - - - - - - - - - - - - - - - - - - - -

11 ③    12 ②    13 ①    14 ④    15 ③    16 ②    17 ①    18 ③    19 ②    20 ④

[1] Write the meaning of the following words.

| | |
|---|---|
| ☐ outstanding | ☐ innuendo |
| ☐ espouse | ☐ suavity |
| ☐ atrocity | ☐ humdrum |
| ☐ vernacular | ☐ confectionery |
| ☐ sumptuary | ☐ apocalypse |
| ☐ lance | ☐ proclivity |
| ☐ recompense | ☐ yelp |
| ☐ excrescence | ☐ crook |
| ☐ decrepit | ☐ manure |
| ☐ tycoon | ☐ fortitude |
| ☐ ball-park | ☐ nook |
| ☐ aspersion | ☐ quotidian |
| ☐ fast | ☐ consecrate |
| ☐ spoliation | ☐ incinerate |
| ☐ immanent | ☐ adipose |
| ☐ protrude | ☐ strangle |
| ☐ crabbed | ☐ guise |
| ☐ muddle | ☐ douse |
| ☐ gargantuan | ☐ suture |
| ☐ rustle | ☐ repulsive |
| ☐ baptism | ☐ trek |
| ☐ dissemble | ☐ slate |
| ☐ ablution | ☐ phantom |
| ☐ curmudgeon | ☐ execrable |
| ☐ elegant | ☐ bristle |

[2] Select <u>the most</u> appropriate word from the box below. Each word should be used only once.

| | | | |
|---|---|---|---|
| ① apocalypse | ② consecrate | ③ dissembled | ④ guise |
| ⑤ recompense | ⑥ sumptuary | ⑦ crabbed | ⑧ incinerated |
| ⑨ humdrum | ⑩ spoliation | ⑪ slated | ⑫ decrepit |
| ⑬ innuendo | ⑭ curmudgeon | ⑮ elegant | ⑯ yelp |
| ⑰ crook | ⑱ bristle | ⑲ repulsive | ⑳ tycoon |

**1**    The use of the rare and expensive color purple was restricted by Roman _____ laws, which penalized ostentatious clothing and jewelry.

**2**    In India, where millions of families look to education to break the cycle of poverty, public schools have long had a reputation for _____ buildings, mismanagement, and even poor instruction.

**3**    He _____ his motives for asking me to lunch, but I noticed that he wanted to get information out of me.

**4**    The elderly neighbor, often seen scowling at passersby, was regarded in the neighborhood as a(n) _____ due to his grumpy attitude.

**5**    The novel's protagonist is a young accountant who has grown weary of her _____ life and longs for adventure and world travels.

**6**    The prophet's dire warnings about the impending _____ were met with skepticism until natural disasters and societal unrest began to unfold globally.

**7**    The authorities were determined to apprehend the notorious _____ who had been masterminding the series of financial frauds.

**8**    The stagnant pond, filled with algae and debris, emitted a(n) _____ smell that made visitors cover their noses in disgust.

**9**    After years of dedication and hard work, she finally received the _____ she deserved for her achievements.

**10**    Amid the chaos of the explosion, the ancient artifacts were irreversibly _____.

[3] Choose the one which is different from the others.

| 11 | ① timidity | ② atrocity | ③ brutality | ④ savagery |
|---|---|---|---|---|
| 12 | ① calumny | ② defamation | ③ aspersion | ④ gambit |
| 13 | ① outstanding | ② distinguished | ③ established | ④ eminent |
| 14 | ① intrinsic | ② inherent | ③ immanent | ④ invalid |
| 15 | ① gargantuan | ② garrulous | ③ enormous | ④ immense |
| 16 | ① amiability | ② benignity | ③ suavity | ④ temerity |
| 17 | ① bravery | ② fortitude | ③ apathy | ④ perseverance |
| 18 | ① quotidian | ② unquestionable | ③ commonplace | ④ trivial |
| 19 | ① esoteric | ② execrable | ③ abominable | ④ detestable |
| 20 | ① uphold | ② advocate | ③ espouse | ④ corroborate |

## ✔ Answers

1 ⑥ ｜ 진귀하고 값비싼 보라색의 사용은 로마의 사치금지법에 의해 제한되었는데, 이 법은 호사스러운 의류와 보석을 처벌했다.

2 ⑫ ｜ 수백만 가구가 빈곤의 고리를 끊기 위해 교육에 기대를 거는 인도에서 공립학교는 오랫동안 낡은 건물, 그릇된 관리, 심지어 열악한 교육으로 악명을 떨쳐왔다.

3 ③ ｜ 그는 점심을 같이하자고 요청하는 동기를 숨겼지만 나는 그가 나에게서 정보를 얻어내기를 원한다는 것을 알아차렸다.

4 ⑭ ｜ 행인들에게 찌푸린 얼굴을 종종 보이던 노인은 그의 심술궂은 태도 때문에 동네에서 심술쟁이로 여겨졌다.

5 ⑨ ｜ 그 소설의 주인공은 젊은 회계사인데, 그녀는 자신의 단조로운 생활에 염증을 느끼고 있으며 모험과 세계여행을 갈망한다.

6 ① ｜ 임박한 종말에 대한 예언자의 끔찍한 경고는 자연재해와 사회 불안이 전 세계적으로 펼쳐지기 시작할 때까지 회의론에 부딪혔다.

7 ⑰ ｜ 당국은 일련의 금융 사기를 배후에서 주도해 온 악명 높은 사기꾼을 체포하기로 결심했다.

8 ⑲ ｜ 녹조와 쓰레기로 가득 찬 고인 연못은 방문객들이 혐오감에 코를 막게 만드는 역겨운 냄새를 풍겼다.

9 ⑤ ｜ 수년간의 헌신과 노력 끝에 그녀는 마침내 자신이 이룬 것에 대한 합당한 보상을 받았다.

10 ⑧ ｜ 폭발의 혼란 속에서 고대 유물들이 되돌릴 수 없을 정도로 소실되었다.

11 ①　12 ④　13 ③　14 ④　15 ②　16 ④　17 ③　18 ②　19 ①　20 ④

## ☑ **DAILY CHECKUP**

[1] Write the meaning of the following words.

| | |
|---|---|
| ☐ exacerbate | ☐ turpitude |
| ☐ resurgence | ☐ moribund |
| ☐ ultimatum | ☐ splice |
| ☐ maraud | ☐ cult |
| ☐ prank | ☐ immolate |
| ☐ daredevil | ☐ stricken |
| ☐ steppingstone | ☐ query |
| ☐ beneficent | ☐ desiccate |
| ☐ alacrity | ☐ celibate |
| ☐ rebel | ☐ insurance |
| ☐ pungent | ☐ envisage |
| ☐ crumb | ☐ lump |
| ☐ salve | ☐ fraught |
| ☐ ineffable | ☐ sobriety |
| ☐ breed | ☐ overhaul |
| ☐ compendium | ☐ volley |
| ☐ gung-ho | ☐ drone |
| ☐ fusion | ☐ animadversion |
| ☐ summon | ☐ concatenate |
| ☐ prescience | ☐ ribald |
| ☐ lucubrate | ☐ equinox |
| ☐ hydrophobia | ☐ pounce |
| ☐ ostentatious | ☐ anodyne |
| ☐ atrophy | ☐ token |
| ☐ dingy | ☐ supernumerary |

[2] Select <u>the most</u> appropriate word from the box below. Each word should be used only once.

| | | | |
|---|---|---|---|
| ① alacrity | ② ineffable | ③ ostentatious | ④ sobriety |
| ⑤ pounce | ⑥ breed | ⑦ summon | ⑧ prescience |
| ⑨ rebellious | ⑩ dingy | ⑪ overhaul | ⑫ immolate |
| ⑬ resurgence | ⑭ turpitude | ⑮ exacerbate | ⑯ desiccate |
| ⑰ supernumerary | ⑱ stricken | ⑲ fraught | ⑳ moribund |

1    The firefighter's training and _____ allowed her to respond swiftly and effectively to the emergency situation.

2    Her remarkable ability to predict future events demonstrated an uncanny _____ that left others in awe of her foresight.

3    The community was shocked to discover the depths of the mayor's ethical _____, which tainted their once-respected leader's legacy irreversibly.

4    Fortunately, I happen to be _____ in nature and enjoy the challenge of disproving assumptions made about me.

5    His procrastination only served to _____ the stress he felt about meeting the deadline.

6    The designer's use of expensive materials was _____; every piece of furniture was covered with silk or velvet, and every piece of hardware was made of silver or gold.

7    As streaming videos over the Internet becomes a more and more popular way to watch movies and television shows, the DVD has become a(n) _____ medium.

8    I knew by the _____ look on father's face that the letter had brought some bad news.

9    The authorities should _____ the project in order to avoid the same mistake again.

10    After years of struggling with alcohol, his newfound _____ brought clarity and stability to his life.

[3] Choose the one which is different from the others.

| 11 | ① acrid | ② pungent | ③ blunt | ④ piquant |
|----|---------|-----------|---------|-----------|
| 12 | ① envisage | ② disregard | ③ imagine | ④ visualize |
| 13 | ① amity | ② criticism | ③ censure | ④ animadversion |
| 14 | ① maraud | ② ransack | ③ despoil | ④ rescind |
| 15 | ① brackish | ② ribald | ③ lewd | ④ obscene |
| 16 | ① superficial | ② perfunctory | ③ token | ④ intact |
| 17 | ① prank | ② levity | ③ joke | ④ trick |
| 18 | ① benevolent | ② beneficent | ③ misanthropic | ④ charitable |
| 19 | ① ardent | ② tepid | ③ gung-ho | ④ zealous |
| 20 | ① hex | ② cult | ③ rite | ④ ritual |

## ✓ Answers

1 ① | 그 소방관은 훈련과 민첩성을 통해 긴급 상황에서 신속하고 효과적으로 대응할 수 있었다.

2 ⑧ | 미래의 사건을 예측하는 그녀의 놀라운 능력은 다른 사람들에게 그녀의 선견지명에 경외심을 갖게 하는 놀라운 예지력을 보여주었다.

3 ⑭ | 그 지역사회는 시장의 윤리적 비열함의 깊이를 발견하고 깊은 충격을 받았고, 이로 인해 한때 존경받던 지도자의 유산이 돌이킬 수 없을 정도로 더럽혀졌다.

4 ⑨ | 나는 공교롭게도 천성이 반항적이어서, 나에 대해 내린 가정이 틀렸음을 입증하는 도전을 즐긴다.

5 ⑮ | 그의 미루는 버릇은 마감일을 지키는 것에 대해 느끼는 스트레스를 악화시킬 뿐이었다.

6 ③ | 그 디자이너가 비싼 재료를 사용한 것은 과시하기 위함이었다. 모든 가구는 비단이나 벨벳으로 덮여 있었고, 모든 장비는 은이나 금으로 만들어졌다.

7 ⑳ | 인터넷을 통한 동영상 스트리밍 서비스가 영화와 TV 프로그램을 시청하는 방법으로 점점 더 대중화됨에 따라, DVD는 소멸해가는 매체가 되었다.

8 ⑱ | 나는 아버지의 괴로운 얼굴 표정을 통해 그 편지가 뭔가 나쁜 소식을 전해왔음을 알았다.

9 ⑪ | 관련 당국은 똑같은 실수를 반복하지 않기 위해 그 프로젝트를 철저히 검토해야 한다.

10 ④ | 수년 동안 알코올 문제로 씨름한 후, 최근의 절주는 그의 삶에 명료함과 안정감을 가져다주었다.

---

11 ③  12 ②  13 ①  14 ④  15 ①  16 ④  17 ②  18 ③  19 ②  20 ①

**ACTUAL TEST**   문항수/시간 100문항 ⏱60분

▶▶▶ ANSWERS P.414

[01-100] Choose the one that is closest in meaning to the underlined part.

01 The workman used a crowbar to dislodge a heavy stone from the wall.
① derange
② dislocate
③ disillusion
④ collaborate

02 The argument that the mayor exploited his position to discriminate against the Arabs was meant to sully his reputation.
① blemish
② sneer
③ distend
④ bolster

03 Debt problems must be faced squarely and brought under control through using appropriate bankruptcy tools.
① rapidly
② bravely
③ directly
④ comprehensively

04 The weeding out of the weak members of animal populations in nature appeared to some Victorians sufficient excuse for imperialism.
① selection
② separation
③ conversion
④ elimination

05 She did everything to evoke sympathy from her parents.
① elicit
② validate
③ vaunt
④ evade

06 During their heyday, showboats were popular and generally prosperous.
① infancy
② revival
③ summer voyage
④ golden age

07 Trying to become unconstrained and gain control of one's life at an early age is difficult.
① prosperous
② independent
③ renowned
④ tolerant

08 The architect Norman Foster adumbrated his idea for subway entrances.
① outlined
② amended
③ revealed
④ contrived

09 A strange stone figure stands on a cliff, his back to the ocean. His stern tight-lipped expression reveals nothing as he surveys the barren land before him.
① strange
② serious
③ pedantic
④ vulnerable

10 The exodus of the country's brightest high school students has renewed discussions in the media about the ongoing problem of higher education reform.
① dash
② menace
③ surge
④ escape

11 What we see from Russia is an illegal and illegitimate effort to destabilize a sovereign state and create a <u>contrived</u> crisis with paid operatives across an international boundary.
① potential    ② concocted
③ random    ④ unexpected

12 The other is a low square window protected by medieval iron bars cut roughly into stems with <u>drooping</u> leaves.
① glittering    ② weary
③ dry    ④ soaring

13 Even though he knew that his mother had been ill, he did not have the <u>propriety</u> to write to her.
① apathy    ② eulogy
③ posterity    ④ decency

14 The <u>grisly</u> murder scene made even seasoned detectives' hair stand on end.
① inextricable    ② knotty
③ gruesome    ④ truculent

15 The reviewer's <u>vituperative</u> comments about the new film were so biting that they sparked a heated debate among movie enthusiasts.
① vitriolic    ② putative
③ parlous    ④ equivocal

16 I saw several young men <u>brandishing</u> their knives on the street.
① sharpening    ② waving
③ selling    ④ breaking

17 In light of the facts we have emphasized, these statements are <u>puerile</u> and are accepted only in ignorance.
① innate    ② inane
③ intricate    ④ incompatible

18 After reading Samuel Beckett's works, our students were thoroughly <u>disabused of</u> any residual belief in happy endings.
① nonchalant regarding
② adamant on
③ disenchanted with
④ converted into

19 The workers' declaration of <u>an all-out</u> strike forced management to improve working conditions.
① an overall    ② a hard-up
③ a run-down    ④ an opposed

20 There is a lot of work to do but it is expected that by probably the end of the second quarter of this year we should have <u>clinched</u> the deal.
① decided    ② inclined
③ depended    ④ suspended

21 The comedian's <u>risque</u> humor pushed the boundaries.
① garrulous    ② incessant
③ atypical    ④ lewd

22 People generally feel pretty pleased with themselves when they've paid less for something. You've seen that <u>smug</u> expression on people's faces when they tell you they paid less than you did.
① modest    ② provocative
③ shabby    ④ complacent

23 Digital images have such precision that they are practically underline{implacable}.
① inexorable  ② commutable
③ distinguished  ④ rhythmic

24 I don't think the Prime Minister would ever countenance a referendum on the constitution.
① disavow  ② obviate
③ sanction  ④ terminate

25 Mr. Smith refused to yield to the requirement of the opposite party.
① receive  ② answer
③ give in to  ④ respond to

26 The city responded with a growing chorus of car horns. Along the street, I saw people pouring out of stores and apartment buildings with a flag, a banner, or a bullhorn in their hands. Karim and his friends were exuberant. "That was the best match of the World Cup!" Karim exclaimed.
① exhilarated  ② abstemious
③ pedantic  ④ mendacious

27 The seizure of the airplane by the hijacker was a prelude to disaster.
① a victimization
② an alliance
③ a foreshadowing
④ a sacrifice

28 After many years of backbreaking toil on the family farm, Polo began to whet his craft as artist and performer.
① hone  ② ballyhoo
③ connive  ④ garner

29 Humankind possesses only a fragmentary history of ancient times.
① incomplete  ② incomparable
③ indispensable  ④ invaluable

30 We must interdict the use of weapons of mass destruction for global security and safety.
① designate  ② interrogate
③ forbid  ④ announce

31 When voters grow tired of mealy-mouthed politicians and wasteful bureaucracy, the allure of a pragmatic, efficient, no-nonsense executive in the Oval Office is strong.
① talkative  ② capable
③ imitative  ④ indirect

32 His parents were characters out of a Fitzgerald novel: his father was Jewish, debonair and domineering.
① refined  ② reckless
③ contemptuous  ④ impervious

33 Santa Claus might be the mythical figure best known for being jolly.
① generous  ② jovial
③ penitent  ④ perfunctory

34 Sunny weather might cause you to break into a refulgent smile.
① disillusioned  ② radiant
③ inscrutable  ④ insightful

35 The former president has tried to blame the incumbent, accusing him of wielding the justice system against him out of partisan animus.
① fervor
② levity
③ chicanery
④ animosity

36 Immured in a dark airless cell, the hostages waited six moth for their release.
① incarcerated
② nauseated
③ titillated
④ expropriated

37 In his usual provident manner, he had insured himself against this type of loss.
① prudent
② precious
③ predatory
④ pronounced

38 Previous technological advances have rendered moot a number of jobs that were once essential to the journalism industry.
① indispensable
② irresponsible
③ irrelevant
④ inevitable

39 Ever since Mr Prigozhin was banished to Belarus, there have been questions over Wagner's future.
① sneered
② exiled
③ emigrated
④ deliberated

40 This story has an evanescent touch of whimsy that is lost in translation.
① evaporating
② stifling
③ conjectural
④ lethargic

41 The gods had to be propitiated, and a vast industry of priests and oracles arose to make the gods less angry.
① appeased
② humiliated
③ assimilated
④ converted

42 He had a broad swarthy face.
① dark
② cute
③ healthy
④ silly

43 Additionally, links and extra information are provided on our website to further acquaint you with each hall's features and amenities.
① facilities
② canteens
③ installations
④ deficits

44 Presented first at the conference at Hong Kong University on "New Evidence on China, Southeast Asia and the Vietnam War", the document created considerable controversy among some of the Chinese and Vietnamese participants as to its provenance and significance.
① copyright
② origin
③ relevance
④ authenticity

45 The interior of the church, although sober and austere, is very fine.
① plain
② splendid
③ ominous
④ decorative

46 Harry's lugubrious eulogy at the funeral of his dog eventually made everyone start giggling.
① uncertain
② excessively sad
③ threatening
④ repulsive

**47** There is the increasing glare of the moon's growing crescent, which causes a loss of visibility by irradiation.

① cloud cover ② wave frequency
③ bright light ④ dark sphere

**48** Unchecked, disgruntled workers can shape colleagues' views of the workplace negatively, creating an environment in which even more workers may hate their jobs.

① dull ② discontented
③ incoherent ④ indigent

**49** He was the consummate educator, for that was his greatest joy and passion. But he was also a philosopher, a polymath, and a student of human nature and thinking.

① respectful ② discrete
③ perfect ④ impaired

**50** The African dictator's oppression became so extreme that a popular uprising began with everyone wishing to oust him from power.

① depose ② designate
③ deduce ④ denigrate

**51** The knight in the Middle Ages was the apotheosis of chivalry.

① quintessence ② remnant
③ confirmation ④ antiquity

**52** The child is outstanding in many respects.

① distinguished ② standing outside
③ outgoing ④ outcome

**53** To wake each morning with the goal of doing something wonderful for other people is an attitude we can all espouse to one degree or another.

① uphold ② forsake
③ assume ④ presage

**54** A group of Serbian expatriates staged a demonstration in Berlin last week to protest news coverage that pins all the blame for atrocities in Bosnia on Serbs.

① sanctions ② starvation
③ brutalities ④ hospitalities

**55** The poor old man is so decrepit that he can scarcely walk along the road.

① energetic ② crude
③ calorific ④ infirm

**56** By casting aspersions on the ability and character of others, you reveal the misgivings you have about yourself.

① offshoots ② slanders
③ pretexts ④ spells

**57** Terms like "liberal" and "conservative" do more to muddle than to clarify.

① smother ② confuse
③ enlighten ④ standardize

**58** The gargantuan corruption scandal within the ruling party was first disclosed by a righteous young reporter of a small newspaper company.

① huge ② putrid
③ abominable ④ suspicious

59 They were in their late seventies and their lives were as quiet outside as one could imagine — as quiet as the snow or the rain or the rustle of trees in midsummer.
① echo
② movement
③ incident
④ soft sound

60 After his years of adventure, he could not settle down to a humdrum existence.
① an interesting
② a sultry
③ a repetitious
④ an uncomfortable

61 Because of the patient's proclivity for drug abuse, the doctor did not want to prescribe even a mild sedative.
① reluctance
② inaptitude
③ rashness
④ tendency

62 After a long investigation, it was revealed the crooked cop had received the money from the accused.
① deformed
② bent
③ dishonest
④ winding

63 He suffered all his life from bad health but learned to endure it with great fortitude.
① tenacity
② conception
③ understanding
④ inspiration

64 His discourse theory of citizenship recognizes the fluid, multimodal, and quotidian enactments of citizenship in a multiple public sphere.
① reclusive
② everyday
③ quarterly
④ dictated

65 A doctor's life is consecrated to curing poor and sick people.
① limited
② dedicated
③ subjected
④ depended

66 Prosecutors say the police turned the students over to a drug gang, which allegedly killed them and incinerated their bodies.
① cremated
② interred
③ dumped
④ incised

67 He spoke to us under the guise of friendship.
① with a desire for
② in pretense of
③ in rejection of
④ for the purpose of

68 There is something morally repulsive about modern activistic theories which deny contemplation and recognize nothing but struggle.
① disgusting
② exhausted
③ dominating
④ enormous

69 Scientists and engineers get angry and bristle when industries and politicians don't understand the need to protect our water and wetlands.
① become isolated
② feel obliged
③ get discouraged
④ become irritated

70 These <u>execrable</u> gun-toting racists have received too much tacit encouragement from the former president.

① horrible      ② diligent

③ patriotic      ④ shrewd

71 To abandon the zero covid policy "would require the Communist Party to <u>countermand</u> an order that it has repeatedly and unequivocally given for more than two years.

① amend      ② promulgate

③ revoke      ④ propagate

72 The monsoon failure in parts of India brought severe famine, which was <u>exacerbated</u> by a simultaneous outbreak of plague.

① made worse      ② lessened

③ brought about      ④ stripped

73 The <u>resurgence</u> of religion is nothing but a desperate and mostly futile attempt to regain what has been lost.

① representation      ② reliance

③ reaction      ④ rebirth

74 Senegal responded <u>with alacrity</u> to its Ebola outbreak.

① expeditiously      ② lethargically

③ yieldingly      ④ with caution

75 Since it can easily absorb flavors from food situated nearby, chocolate should be stored away from <u>pungent</u> odors.

① tangy      ② holistic

③ lethargic      ④ inexorable

76 This book contains a <u>compendium</u> of climatic data assembled from several sources.

① segment      ② summary

③ comparison      ④ critique

77 The murderer was <u>summoned</u> to appear in the court yesterday.

① revoked      ② provoked

③ convoked      ④ invoked

78 The remarkable <u>prescience</u> was called "ridiculous" by one of the most knowledgeable experts of the day.

① foresight      ② discovery

③ invention      ④ superstition

79 The government should <u>lucubrate</u> on the shortcomings unveiled by the recent evaluation.

① moil      ② perambulate

③ eke out      ④ quieten down

80 Saint Laurent sought a radical shift from current trends. He wanted pure, graphic black-and-white designs. The designer says, "I worked on the volumes, proportions and colors. Nothing <u>ostentatious</u>: just pure, simple lines. I wanted to send a very clear message: No jewels, no accessories."

① lucid      ② fastidious

③ flamboyant      ④ discernible

81 Linguists can study <u>moribund</u> languages and seek to preserve the components of the language: the sounds, the vocabulary, the grammar, and the traditions.

① dying      ② dominant

③ extant      ④ eloquent

82 Many diseases develop very quickly and do their damage before people even realize they have been <u>stricken</u>.

① impressed      ② attacked

③ warned      ④ depressed

83 If you have any <u>queries</u> about this topic, please get in touch with me.

① questions      ② problems

③ proposals      ④ ideas

84 I find it very difficult to <u>envisage</u> the kind of society that the Greek philosopher Plato once dreamt of creating.

① discredit      ② contradict

③ conceive      ④ sanction

85 Economist Laursen of the World Bank cautions that restructuring and privatization of some economic sectors have stalled and that the entitlement system inherited from the communist era has yet to be fully <u>overhauled</u>.

① yielded      ② cast aside

③ scrutinized      ④ emulated

86 He, as a leader of the union, was criticized for making a <u>token</u> resistance to the company.

① huge      ② nominal

③ serious      ④ talkative

87 The fuel crisis has pushed the <u>beleaguered</u> Cuban people to the brink of desperation.

① frightened      ② segregated

③ besieged      ④ isolated

88 Your own family members often hold opposing opinions, but you don't <u>disown</u> them for that.

① repudiate      ② persuade

③ encourage      ④ tease

89 A year after he became the Republicans' <u>de facto</u> leader, there was a growing view that the party had succumbed to his nationalist populism.

① powerful      ② legal

③ despotic      ④ actual

90 Since the speaker had not prepared his speech, he had to <u>extemporize</u> one.

① provide      ② duplicate

③ improvise      ④ visualize

91 Cybercriminals operate with <u>impunity</u> in some countries.

① incarceration      ② exemption

③ discretion      ④ breach

92 Her criticism was so <u>astringent</u> that it left everyone feeling a bit uncomfortable.

① arcane      ② equivocal

③ trite      ④ harsh

93 The volunteers tackled the community project with a truly <u>gung-ho</u> spirit.

① kindred      ② impetuous

③ enthusiastic      ④ scrupulous

94 Philosophers might debate about whether generosity is an <u>immanent</u> trait or something that people are taught.
① immature  ② invalid
③ inherent  ④ immortal

95 Politicians frequently have to <u>dissemble</u> so as not to admit that mistakes have been made.
① palpitate  ② pretend
③ overstate  ④ seduce

96 The company offered a substantial bonus as <u>recompense</u> for the exceptional performance of its employees.
① requital  ② refinement
③ windfall  ④ solicitude

97 Corrupt politicians get booted out of office for acts of <u>turpitude</u>.
① wickedness  ② bravado
③ decency  ④ obstinacy

98 His commitment to maintaining <u>sobriety</u> was evident in his daily routine.
① promptness  ② abstinence
③ frugality  ④ probity

99 His articulate arguments were met with an unexpected wave of <u>animadversion</u> from the audience.
① criticism  ② amity
③ affinity  ④ vigilance

100 <u>Ribald</u> humor is generally considered to be inappropriate around children.
① belligerent  ② intriguing
③ vulgar  ④ dismissive

# MVP

Vol.2 워크북

# ACTUAL TEST
# 정답

| 01 ② | 02 ③ | 03 ④ | 04 ① | 05 ④ | 06 ① | 07 ② | 08 ② | 09 ② | 10 ① |
|------|------|------|------|------|------|------|------|------|------|
| 11 ③ | 12 ① | 13 ④ | 14 ① | 15 ① | 16 ③ | 17 ③ | 18 ② | 19 ④ | 20 ② |
| 21 ② | 22 ① | 23 ③ | 24 ① | 25 ① | 26 ② | 27 ④ | 28 ③ | 29 ② | 30 ④ |
| 31 ① | 32 ④ | 33 ③ | 34 ④ | 35 ④ | 36 ① | 37 ③ | 38 ② | 39 ③ | 40 ① |
| 41 ④ | 42 ③ | 43 ① | 44 ② | 45 ④ | 46 ① | 47 ① | 48 ④ | 49 ③ | 50 ③ |
| 51 ② | 52 ③ | 53 ② | 54 ② | 55 ③ | 56 ④ | 57 ③ | 58 ④ | 59 ② | 60 ① |
| 61 ② | 62 ② | 63 ④ | 64 ② | 65 ③ | 66 ② | 67 ② | 68 ② | 69 ① | 70 ① |
| 71 ④ | 72 ④ | 73 ② | 74 ④ | 75 ④ | 76 ② | 77 ④ | 78 ① | 79 ③ | 80 ④ |
| 81 ④ | 82 ② | 83 ② | 84 ④ | 85 ② | 86 ④ | 87 ④ | 88 ④ | 89 ① | 90 ② |
| 91 ③ | 92 ④ | 93 ① | 94 ③ | 95 ① | 96 ③ | 97 ② | 98 ③ | 99 ④ | 100 ① |

## 01 ②

☐ go to ~에 의지하다　☐ accountant n. 공인회계사　☐ proficient a. 익숙한, 숙달한(=skillful)　☐ troubleshoot v. 문제를 해결하다　☐ muggy a. (날씨가) 후텁지근한　☐ gibberish n. 알아들을 수 없는 말, 횡설수설　☐ ephemeral a. 수명이 짧은, 단명하는

그는 IT 관련 문제가 생길 때 모두가 의지하는 사람이다. 비록 회계사지만, 그는 소프트웨어 및 하드웨어 문제를 해결하는 데 매우 능숙하다.

## 02 ③

☐ whim n. 변덕, 일시적인 생각(=caprice)　☐ cater v. 요구에 응하다, 만족을 주다; 영합하다(to)　☐ want n. 필요, 소용; 원하는 것, 욕구　☐ satisfy v. 만족시키다; (희망 등을) 충족시키다　☐ hesitation n. 주저, 망설임　☐ sloth n. 마음이 내키지 않음; 게으름, 나태　☐ rubbish n. 쓰레기, 폐물, 잡동사니　☐ gratitude n. 감사, 보은의 마음

당신이 아무리 변덕을 부려도 그것에 맞춰주고, 당신이 무엇을 원하든다 충족시켜주며, 당신이 무엇을 요구하든 주저 없이 들어주는 레스토랑을 상상해 보라.

## 03 ④

☐ formidable a. 무서운, 만만찮은, 어려운(=daunting)　☐ opponent n. (경기의) 적, 상대　☐ malevolent a. 악의 있는, 심술궂은　☐ insolent a. 거만한, 무례한　☐ lecherous a. 호색적인, 음란한

그 레슬링 선수는 몸집이 그다지 크지 않았지만, 기술과 스피드가 그를 만만찮은 상대로 만들었다.

## 04 ①

☐ drastically ad. 급격하게, 격심하게(=violently)　☐ adopt v. 입양하다, 양자로 삼다　☐ forcefully ad. 강제로　☐ against one's will 본의 아니게; 억지로　☐ gradually ad. 점진적으로, 서서히　☐ elastically ad. 유연하게, 융통성 있게　☐ incessantly ad. 끊임없이, 계속적으로

내가 10살이었을 때, 나의 인생은 급격하게 바뀌었다. 나는 강제로 그리고 우리 부모님의 뜻과 다르게 입양이 되었다.

## 05 ④

☐ usurp v. 찬탈하다, 강탈하다(=seize)　☐ divide v. 나누다, 분할하다　☐ provoke v. 야기하다, 자극하다　☐ deteriorate v. 타락시키다, 나쁘게 하다

히틀러(Hitler)와 스탈린(Stalin) 정권의 사례는 인간이 신의 역할을 빼앗을 때 무슨 일이 발생할 수 있는지를 우리에게 끔찍할 정도로 명확하게 보여준다.

## 06 ①

☐ esteem v. 존경하다, 존중하다(=respect)　☐ contribution n. 기여, 공헌　☐ botany n. 식물학　☐ overlook v. 간과하다, 대충 보다; 내려다 보다　☐ criticize v. 비판하다; 비난하다　☐ compensate v. 보상하다, 배상하다

조지 W. 카버(George W. Carver)는 식물학과 화학 분야에서의 공헌으로 존경받았다.

## 07 ②

☐ hedgehog n. 고슴도치 ☐ shrew n. 뒤쥐(=shrewmouse) ☐ mole n. 두더지 ☐ beneficial a. 유익한, 이로운(=helpful) ☐ distressing a. 괴로움을 주는, 비참한 ☐ forgiving a. 관대한, 용서하는 ☐ careful a. 조심스러운, 신중한

고슴도치, 뒤쥐, 두더지 같은 동물들은 곤충을 먹고 살기 때문에, 그들은 인간에게 매우 이롭다.

## 08 ②

☐ outspoken a. 거리낌 없이 말하는, 솔직한, 노골적인(=forthright) ☐ mince v. 완곡하게 이야기하다, 돌려서 말하다 ☐ exemplary a. 본이 되는, 모범적인; 훌륭한 ☐ arbitrary a. 임의의, 자의적인; 독단적인 ☐ agitative a. 선동적인

그는 매우 솔직한 사람이다. 말을 돌려서 하지 않는다.

## 09 ②

☐ laudable a. 칭찬[감탄]할 만한(=commendable) ☐ laughable a. 웃기는, 터무니없는 ☐ regrettable a. 유감스러운, 후회되는 ☐ dependable a. 믿을[신뢰할] 수 있는

크리스틴(Kristin)의 업무에 대한 헌신은 칭찬할 만하지만, 그녀는 훌륭한 임원이 되는 데 필요한 역량은 갖추고 있지 못하다.

## 10 ①

☐ squalid a. 더러운, 지저분한(=filthy) ☐ stewardship n. steward의 직[일]; (한 개인으로서의 사회적·종교적) 책무 ☐ unsullied a. 더럽혀지지 않은 ☐ despotic a. 독재적인; 횡포한 ☐ lofty a. 고상한, 고결한

미국인들은 클린턴(Clinton)의 추잡한 개인적인 행동을 그의 공식적인 책무와 분리해서 보았다.

## 11 ③

☐ depict v. 묘사하다, 기술하다 ☐ bubbling a. 졸졸 흐르는, 거품이 부글부글 이는 ☐ rigidified a. 경화된, 굳어져 버린(=formalistic) ☐ scholasticism n. (중세) 스콜라 철학 ☐ overwhelmed a. 압도당한 ☐ religious a. 종교적인, 신앙의 ☐ peripheral a. 주변의, 지엽적인

우리는 대개 르네상스를 중세의 경직된 스콜라 철학의 댐을 무너뜨린 맑고 졸졸 흐르는 참신함의 강으로 묘사한다.

## 12 ①

☐ brochure n. 소책자, 팸플릿 ☐ circuitous a. (말 따위가) 에두르는, 완곡한; 우회하는(=roundabout) ☐ congested a. 붐비는, 혼잡한 ☐

makeshift a. 임시변통의, 일시적인 ☐ steadfast a. 확고부동한, 고정된, (신념 등이) 불변의 ☐ easygoing a. 태평한, 게으른; 안이한

여행안내 책자에서는 여행객들이 혼잡한 도로를 피하는 데 도움이 되도록 그 호텔로 가는 다소 우회로를 추천하고 있다.

## 13 ④

☐ crafty a. 교활한, 간교한, (나쁜) 꾀가 많은(=cunning) ☐ artistic a. 예술적인, 미술적인 ☐ humanistic a. 인문학의; 인도주의적인 ☐ capable a. 유능한, 능력 있는

모든 문화에 있어서 다른 동물들은 지능이 떨어지는 것으로 여겨지는 반면 하나 혹은 두 종류의 동물이 꾀가 많은 동물로 간주된다.

## 14 ①

☐ treaty n. 조약, 협정, 맹약 ☐ buttress v. 지지하다, 보강하다 (=support) ☐ post-Cold war 냉전 후의 ☐ transparency n. 투명(성) ☐ arsenal n. 무기고; 군수품 비축 ☐ terminate v. 끝나다 ☐ envision v. 마음에 그리다, 상상하다 ☐ design v. 설계하다 ☐ build v. 건설하다

냉전 후 세계의 안보 구조를 지탱하고 있는 두 개의 조약 — 미국과 러시아 양측의 군수품 비축에 대해 엄격한 제한을 가하고 투명성을 강제하는 것 — 이 곧 종료될 것이다.

## 15 ①

☐ disappointment n. 실망, 낙담 ☐ inadequacy n. 부적당; 결점 ☐ reproduction n. 재현, 복원; 번식 ☐ irksome a. 지루한; 성가신, 귀찮은(=deadening) ☐ irreparable a. 회복할[바로잡을] 수 없는 ☐ integral a. 필수적인; 완전한 ☐ irresistible a. 억누를[저항할] 수 없는

재현에 대한 낙담과 불충분함은 점점 더 무기력하게 만드는 것으로 드러났다.

## 16 ③

☐ modify v. 수정하다, 변경하다(=change); 완화하다 ☐ agreement n. 협정, 조약 ☐ congressional a. (종종 C-) <미국> 의회의, 국회의 ☐ approval n. 승인, 찬성 ☐ improve v. 개선하다, 개량하다, 진보시키다 ☐ discard v. 버리다; 해고하다 ☐ renew v. 일신하다; 갱신하다

의회의 승인을 필요로 할 것이기 때문에, 서명되고 난 후에 협정을 수정하기는 어려울 것이다.

## 17 ③

☐ stationary a. 움직이지 않는, 정지한(=motionless) ☐ printed a. 인쇄된, 출판된 ☐ related a. 관계가 있는; 동족의 ☐ introduced a. 소개된; 도입된

영화 촬영의 원리는 행동이 빠르게 연속으로 투사된 일련의 정지된 이미지에 기록되는 것이다.

## 18 ②

☐ altruistic a. 이타주의적인, 애타적인(=unselfish) ☐ egoistic a. 이기적인, 제멋대로의 ☐ eccentric a. 별난, 기이한 ☐ mysterious a. 설명하기 힘든, 불가사의한

적이 나타나면, 땅다람쥐는 이타적인 태도를 보인다. 그들은 자신의 목숨을 걸고서 가까이 있는 동족들에게 경고음을 낸다.

## 19 ④

☐ transition n. (위치·지위·상태·단계 따위의) 변천; 과도기 ☐ occasion n. (특정한) 경우; (~할) 기회, 호기(好機) ☐ tackle v. (일 등에) 부딪치다, (문제 등을) 다루다 ☐ impasse n. 교착상태; 난국(=deadlock) ☐ defiance n. 도전; 반항 ☐ praise n. 칭찬 ☐ retard n. 지체

정부는 미국에서의 권력 이동을 한반도 문제의 난국을 타개할 수 있는 호기로 보고 있다.

## 20 ②

☐ volitional a. 의지의; 의욕적인(=willing) ☐ violent a. 폭력적인, 난폭한 ☐ disheartening a. 낙심시키는, 기를 꺾는 ☐ unconscious a. 의식을 잃은; 무의식적인

진정한 사랑은 감정적이라기보다 의지에 관한 것이다.

## 21 ②

☐ evaporate v. 증발하다; 사라지다(=disappear) ☐ increase v. 늘다, 증가하다; 커지다, 강해지다 ☐ transform v. 변형시키다; 바꾸다, 전환하다 ☐ sharpen v. 날카롭게 하다, 갈다

오늘날에는 이러한 열정의 대부분은 사라졌을 뿐만 아니라 반감으로 변해버렸다.

## 22 ①

☐ expertly ad. 훌륭하게, 전문적으로 ☐ hand-made a. 수제의 ☐ epitome n. 전형, 축도, 요약(=summary) ☐ intelligence n. 지능; 기밀 ☐ fortitude n. 인내, 꿋꿋함 ☐ indigence n. 극심한 곤궁, 극빈

멋지게 자른 검은 머리부터 수제 구두에 이르기까지 그는 새로운 젊은이의 전형이었다.

## 23 ③

☐ conventional a. 관습적인, 극히 평범한(=banal) ☐ catchphrase n. 캐치프레이즈, 사람의 주의를 끌만한 문구, 표어 ☐ feasible a. 실행할 수 있는, 가능한 ☐ superficial a. 피상[표면]적인 ☐ original a. 원래의, 본래의

우리는 상투적인 문구로는 사람들의 관심을 끌 수 없다.

## 24 ①

☐ dispel v. 쫓아버리다, 없애다(=disperse) ☐ depression n. 의기소침, 우울; 불경기 ☐ entangle v. 뒤얽히게 하다; (함정 등에) 빠뜨리다 ☐ coincide v. 동시에 일어나다; 부합[일치]하다 ☐ hurl v. 집어[세게] 던지다

그 경제학자는 불황에 대한 모든 두려움을 쫓아버리려 애썼다.

## 25 ①

☐ prodigal a. 낭비하는, 방탕한(=lavish) ☐ expenditure n. 지출, 소비 ☐ military budget 국방 예산 ☐ time of peace 평시(平時) ☐ create a stir 파문[물의]을 일으키다 ☐ cabinet n. 내각 ☐ various a. 여러 가지의, 각양각색의, 다양한 ☐ tangible a. 분명히 실재하는, 유형(有形)의 ☐ sporadic a. 산발적인, 이따금 일어나는

평시(平時)에 국방예산을 방탕하게 지출한 것이 내각에 큰 파문을 일으켰다.

## 26 ②

☐ ostensible a. 겉치레의; 표면의; 외관상의(=seeming) ☐ Crusade n. 십자군 ☐ cite v. 인용하다, 인증하다; 열거하다 ☐ propel v. 추진하다, 몰아대다 ☐ offensive a. 불쾌한; 무례한 ☐ feasible a. 실행할 수 있는; 가능한 ☐ genuine a. 진짜의; 진심에서 우러난

십자군 전쟁 때 표면적으로 나타났던 종교적 갈등에 더하여, 중세 로마 가톨릭교회 자체 안의 내부적 압력들이 성전(聖戰)을 일으키도록 몰아가는 데 이바지한 것으로 꼽을 수 있을 것이다.

## 27 ④

☐ distribute v. 분배하다, 유통하다 ☐ involved in ~에 관련된 ☐ surplus n. 과잉(=excess); 흑자 ☐ efficiency n. 효율(성), 능률 ☐ cultivation n. 경작, 재배 ☐ nourishment n. 음식물, 영양(분)

지구상에는 모든 사람들을 먹일 수 있는 충분한 식량이 있지만, 모든 사람들이 충분히 먹는 것은 아니다. 이는 주로 식량의 유통 방식에도 기인하고 남아도는 지역에서 크게 부족한 지역으로 식량을 이동시키는 것과 관련된 문제에도 기인한다.

## 28 ③

□ introverted a. 내성적인, 내향적인(=shy) □ outspoken a. 솔직한, 기탄없는 □ life-changing a. 인생을 변화시키는 □ talkative a. 수다스러운, 말수가 많은 □ candid a. 정직한, 솔직한 □ vocal a. 목소리의; 의견을 말하는

내성적인 그 학생은 인생을 바꾸는 경험을 한 후에 솔직해졌다.

## 29 ②

□ anomalous a. 변칙의, 예외의, 이례적인(=atypical) □ anorexic a. 식욕이 없는; 식욕을 감퇴시키는 □ aspiring a. 포부를[야심을] 가진 □ anxious a. 걱정스러운, 근심[염려]하는

에이미(Amy)는 광장공포증이 발생하기까지 몇 주 동안 예상치 못한 이례적인 어떤 경험을 하게 된다.

## 30 ④

□ seizure n. 체포; 압류, 강탈(=capture) □ detection n. 발견, 탐지, 간파 □ consumption n. 소비, 소비량; 소모 □ disruption n. 붕괴; 분열; 중단

그 객실에 대한 불시 단속으로 25kg의 순수한 헤로인을 압류하게 되었다.

## 31 ①

□ congenial a. 마음이 맞는[통하는](=kindred) □ virtuous a. 도덕적인, 고결한 □ romantic a. 로맨틱한, 애정을 표현하는 □ immortal a. 죽지 않는, 불멸의

그러한 젊은이들이 대학에 가면 아마도 마음이 통하는 사람들을 발견하고 몇 년 동안 커다란 행복을 누릴 것이다.

## 32 ④

□ adduce v. (이유, 증거 등을) 제시하다, 인용하다(=present) □ misuse v. 오용하다; 학대하다 □ abolish v. 폐지하다, 철폐하다 □ memorize v. 기억하다, 암기하다

그는 자신의 이론을 뒷받침하기 위해 여러 가지 사실들을 제시했다.

## 33 ②

□ fraud n. 사기(=deceit) □ be on the rise 증가하고 있다 □ credit n. 신용; 영예 □ charge n. 책임; 비난; 고발, 고소; 요금 □ deposit n. 퇴적물, 침전물; 보증금

금융사기는 실직과 개인 금융의 감소로 인하여 증가하고 있다.

## 34 ④

□ syllabus n. 강의 요강 □ provisional a. 일시적인, 임시의 (=temporary) □ amendment n. 변경, 개선 □ concise a. 간결한, 간명한 □ reliable a. 의지가 되는, 믿음직한; 확실한 □ inflexible a. 불굴의; 강직한

이 강의 요강은 임시적이며 공지 없이 수정될 수도 있다.

## 35 ④

□ ally n. 동맹국[자], 연합국 □ abide by 따르다, 지키다(=follow) □ govern v. 통치하다, 다스리다 □ disturb v. 방해하다; 저해하다; 불안하게 하다 □ restrict v. 제한하다, 한정하다

중국은 대만을 중국의 일부로 여기며 동맹국들에게 그 입장을 따르도록 강요한다.

## 36 ①

□ intrinsically ad. 본질적으로 □ belligerent a. 교전 중인; 호전적인 (=combative) □ by nature 선천적으로; 본래 □ harmonious a. 조화된, 균형 잡힌 □ common a. 공통의; 보통의, 일반적인 □ neutral a. 중립의; 공평한, 중용의

세상과 땅은 본질적으로 그리고 근본적으로 항상 충돌을 빚고 있으며, 본래부터 호전적이다.

## 37 ③

□ humidity n. 습기 □ stagnant a. 고여 있는, 정지된(=static) □ endemic n. 풍토병 □ epidemic n. 전염병, 유행병 □ mobile a. 움직이기 쉬운, 가동성의 □ warm a. 따뜻한, 따스한 □ tepid a. 미지근한, 열의 없는

중국 전통에서 습기와 고인 물은 풍토병과 전염병의 근원으로 간주된다.

## 38 ③

□ demeaning a. 품위를 떨어뜨리는, 모욕적인(=degrading) □ status n. 지위 □ run for public office 공직에 입후보하다 □ detain v. 지체하게 하다; 구금하다 □ sustaining a. 떠받치는, 유지하는 □ emerging a. 신생의, 최근에 만들어진

그 결과, 그들은 '비시민'이라는 그들의 품위를 손상시키는 법적 지위를 갖게 되었는데, 이로 인해 투표할 권리 및 공직에 입후보할 권리 등 수많은 권리를 상실하게 된다.

## 39　③

☐ aftermath n. 결과, 여파, 영향(=consequence)　☐ symptom n. 증상; 징조　☐ reason n. 이유, 동기　☐ influence n. 영향(력); 세력

가난과 병은 대개 전쟁의 여파이다.

## 40　①

☐ downgrade v. (중요성·가치를) 떨어뜨리다　☐ protagonist n. 주인공　☐ culprit n. 범인(=offender)　☐ plaintiff n. 원고　☐ suspect n. 용의자　☐ witness n. 증인

의식적으로든 무의식적으로든, 우리는 새로운 아시아계 여자 친구가 우리가 사랑하는 백인 주인공의 격하된 버전이라는 것을 이해하게 된다. 범인에는 '프렌즈' 시즌 2도 포함된다(로스는 중국계 미국인인 새 여자 친구가 생긴다).

## 41　④

☐ resume v. 재개하다, 다시 시작하다(=recommence)　☐ recollect v. 회상하다, 기억해 내다　☐ resolve v. 해결하다; 결심하다　☐ restrict v. 제한하다, 한정하다

블루라인은 거의 정상 스케줄로 서비스를 재개할 것으로 예상되었다.

## 42　③

☐ replicate v. 복사하다; 재현하다(=duplicate)　☐ create v. 창조하다, 만들다　☐ analyze v. 분석하다, 검토하다　☐ modify v. 수정하다, 고치다

원고를 꼼꼼하게 읽고 난 뒤에, 연구원들은 처음에 했던 실험을 재현하려고 노력했다.

## 43　①

☐ apparently ad. 명백히; 겉보기에, 외관상으로(=ostensibly)　☐ loaf v. 놀고 지내다, 빈둥거리다　☐ pigeon n. 비둘기　☐ irreversibly ad. 취소[폐지, 변경]할 수 없게　☐ utterly ad. 완전히　☐ impassably ad. 지나갈[통행할] 수 없게

매일 식사 시간에 당신은 밖으로 나가서 겉보기에는 식당으로 향하지만 한 시간 동안 룩셈부르크 정원에서 비둘기들을 보며 빈둥거린다.

## 44　②

☐ disparate a. 다른, 공통점이 없는(=different)　☐ astronomy n. 천문학　☐ complementary a. 상호 보완적인　☐ compatible a. 양립할 수 있는, 모순이 없는　☐ original a. 최초의, 원시의; 독자적인

과학자들은 천문학에서 서로 다른 여러 사상들을 하나로 통합하고자 노력하고 있다.

## 45　④

☐ gingerly ad. 조심조심, 매우 신중하게(=carefully)　☐ boldly ad. 대담하게; 뻔뻔스럽게　☐ quietly ad. 조용히, 고요히　☐ awkwardly ad. 어색하게, 서투르게

맨발로 가구에 세게 부딪힐까 두려워서 나는 캄캄한 방을 조심조심 걸었다.

## 46　①

☐ lineage n. 혈통, 가계, 계보(=ancestry)　☐ dimension n. 치수; 규모, 범위　☐ qualification n. 자격, 능력; 조건, 제한　☐ genetic trait 유전 형질

모든 사람들은 나름의 특별한 혈통이 있는데, 그것이 그들의 일상생활에서 가지는 중요성의 정도는 서로 다르다.

## 47　①

☐ scornful a. 경멸하는, 멸시하는(=disdainful)　☐ respectful a. 경의를 표하는, 공손한　☐ protective a. 보호하는　☐ negligent a. 태만한, 소홀한

그가 회사의 부사장으로 승진한 후에, 그는 예전의 친구들을 멸시하게 되었다.

## 48　④

☐ pseudonym n. 익명, 필명(=pen name)　☐ synonym n. 동의어; 별명, 별칭　☐ feminine name 여성적인 이름　☐ eponym n. 이름의 시조

19세기에 많은 여성 작가들은 '숙녀답지 않은' 것으로 낙인찍히는 것이 두려웠기 때문에 필명을 사용했다.

## 49　③

☐ turn n. 순번, 차례　☐ nonchalant a. 무관심한, 태연한(=indifferent)　☐ indecorous a. 버릇없는, 예의 없는　☐ nonessential a. 비본질적인, 중요하지 않은　☐ undignified a. 품위가 없는, 위엄이 없는

그 여배우는 태연해 보이려 최선을 다하면서 주연을 뽑는 오디션에서 자신의 차례를 기다렸다.

## 50
③

□ cardinal a. 기본적인, (가장) 중요한(=principal) □ religious a. 종교의; 독실한 □ gigantic a. 거대한, 거창한 □ potential a. 가능성이 있는, 잠재적인

세일즈맨으로서, 가장 중요한 원칙은 고객 만족을 위해 할 수 있는 모든 일을 한다는 것이다.

## 51
②

□ engaged a. (~을 하느라) 바쁜[열심인], ~하고 있는 □ interminable a. 끝없이 계속되는, 한없는; 지루하게 긴(=unceasing) □ intolerable a. 견딜 수 없는, 참을 수 없는 □ pointless a. 적절치 못한

우리는 예술과 문학에 대한 끝없는 논쟁을 하면서 밤늦게까지 머무르곤 했다.

## 52
③

□ susceptible a. 민감한; (~에) 걸리기[영향받기] 쉬운(=prone) □ available a. 이용할 수 있는, 입수할 수 있는 □ digressive a. 여담의, 지엽적인 □ invincible a. 정복할 수 없는, 무적의

간 질환을 앓고 있는 환자들은 세균에 감염되기 쉽다.

## 53
②

□ adroit a. 손재주가 있는, (솜씨가) 능숙한; 교묘한(=dexterous) □ erudite a. 박학한, 학식이 있는 □ tangible a. 유형의; 확실한, 명백한 □ inherent a. 타고난, 고유의

그녀는 보트를 능숙하게 조종함으로써 암초에 좌초되는 것으로부터 우리를 구해냈다.

## 54
②

□ chronicle v. 기록에 남기다, 열거하다(=recount) □ ephemeralize v. 단축하다 □ diarize v. 일기에 쓰다 □ ingerminate v. 싹트게 하다

그 그림들은 로마제국의 멸망에 대해 꼼꼼히 열거하고 있다.

## 55
③

□ turn out ~임이 밝혀지다 □ distortion n. 찌그러뜨림; 왜곡된 이야기; 왜곡, 곡해(=misrepresentation) □ agenda n. 의사일정, 협의 사항 □ routine n. 판에 박힌 일, 일상의 일; 관례 □ mishap n. 사고, 불운

사고에 대한 목격자의 설명은 완전히 왜곡된 것으로 드러났다.

## 56
④

□ eulogy n. 찬미, 칭송, 찬양; 찬사(=praise); (고인에 대한) 송덕문 □ prayer n. 기도, 소원; 기도하는 사람 □ hatred n. 증오, 원한 □ speech n. 말, 이야기, 연설

이(Lee) 씨의 장례식에서 낭독된 김(Kim) 씨의 송덕문은 청중을 사로잡았고 감동적이었다.

## 57
③

□ brazen-faced a. 철면피의, 뻔뻔스러운(=insolent) □ appreciate v. 진가[좋은 점]를 알다 □ distracted a. 산만[산란]해진 □ stubborn a. 완고한 □ jealous a. 질투심이 많은 □ punctual a. 시간을 엄수하는

뻔뻔한 사람은 일반적으로 자신에게 너무 몰입하여 다른 사람들과 세상의 아름다움을 알아볼 수 없다.

## 58
④

□ slash v. (예산·급료 등을) (대폭) 삭감하다 □ capacity n. 수용량; (최대) 수용 능력 □ shutter v. 창에 덧문[겉문]을 달다, ~을 덧문[겉문]으로 닫아 놓다 □ venue n. (경기·회의 등의) 개최지 □ company n. 단체, 협회; 극단 □ improvise v. (축사·연설 따위를) 즉석에서 하다; 임시변통으로 만들다(=extemporize) □ postpone v. 연기하다, 미루다 □ obliterate v. (흔적을) 없애다, 지우다 □ nullify v. 무효로 하다

대유행병으로 인해 최대 수용 관객이 2/3 줄어들거나 극장이 완전히 폐쇄됐을 때, 극단들은 임시변통으로 해내는 것을 배워야 했다. 캘거리 극장은 <로미오와 줄리엣>의 하계 온라인 연출로 그 길을 보여주었다.

## 59
②

□ momentous a. 중대한, 중요한(=tectonic) □ sudden a. 돌연한, 갑작스러운 □ momentary a. 일시적인, 순식간의 □ ominous a. 불길한, 나쁜 징조의

산업혁명은 인류 역사에 중요한 변화를 기록했다.

## 60
①

□ feat n. 위업; (뛰어난) 솜씨(=accomplishment) □ tedium n. 싫증, 지루함 □ engrossment n. 열중; 독점 □ practice n. 실행, 실천

절반가량의 아이들은 주로 유혹적인 보상에서 딴 데로 관심을 돌림으로써 15분이나 기다리는 위업을 달성했다.

## 61
②

□ contemporary a. 동시대의, 같은 시대의, 그 당시의; 최근의, 현대의(=modern) □ critical a. 비평의, 평론의; 비판적인, 흠을 잘 잡는; 위기

의, 아슬아슬한, 위험한; 결정적인, 중대한 ☐ unknown a. 알려지지 않은, 무명의, 미지의; 알 수 없는, 셀 수 없는, 헤아릴 수 없는, 막대한 ☐ productive a. 생산적인; 다산의, 다작의; 풍부한; (땅이) 비옥한

그녀는 19세기의 작가들보다 현대 작가들을 연구하는 것이 더 쉽다는 것을 알았다.

## 62 ②

☐ loquacious a. 말이 많은, 수다스러운; 떠들썩한(=verbose) ☐ lenient a. 관대한, 너그러운 ☐ amicable a. 우호적인, 원만한 ☐ conceited a. 자부심이 강한; 우쭐한, 뽐내는

그 두 남자는 서로 잘 협조하고 있지만 너무 판이한 사람이다. 다시 말해 헨리(Henry)가 느긋하고 말이 많은 반면 제임스(James)는 대체로 신경이 날카롭고 말이 없는 편이다.

## 63 ④

☐ go-it-alone a. 독립한, 자립한 ☐ vindicate v. ~의 정당함을 입증하다; 주장하다(=prove) ☐ crushing defeat 참패 ☐ blame v. 나무라다, 비난하다 ☐ blacken v. 검게 하다; 누명을 씌우다 ☐ acquit v. 무죄로 하다, 면제해주다

아라파트(Arafat)의 독립적인 전략은 1967년 전쟁에서의 아랍국가 정부들의 참패에 의해 정당함이 입증되었다.

## 64 ②

☐ have no (other) choice but to do ~하지 않을 수 없다 ☐ magnify v. 과장하다; 확대하다(=enlarge) ☐ budget n. 예산, 예산안 ☐ obliterate v. 지우다, 말살하다 ☐ assess v. (특성, 자질 등을) 재다; (가치, 양을) 평가하다 ☐ distribute v. 분배하다, 배포하다

그들은 예산을 확대할 수밖에 없었다.

## 65 ④

☐ promote v. 진전시키다, 증진하다; 장려하다(=put forward) ☐ art for art's sake 예술을 위한 예술, 예술지상주의 ☐ fight v. 싸우다, 전투하다 ☐ get through 통과하다; 합격하다; 종료하다, 완수하다 ☐ disprove v. 반증을 들다, 논박하다

제임스 휘슬러(James Whistler)는 예술지상주의 이념을 장려했다.

## 66 ②

☐ conformity n. 유사, 부합, 일치; (관습, 법 등의) 준거, 동조(=agreement with customs or rules) ☐ dread v. 두려워하다, 염려[걱정]하다 ☐ pursuit of individuality 개성의 추구 ☐ state of being poised 침착한 상태 ☐ flexibility in judgement 융통성 있는 의견

비록 동조에 대한 태도가 역사적으로 확립되어 있지 않고 시간이 흐르면서 변해왔지만, 일반적으로 미국인들은 주변의 다른 사람들처럼 행동하고 그들과 같아 보인다는 생각을 두려워하는 것 같다.

## 67 ②

☐ hazard n. 위험; 모험(=danger) ☐ fortune n. 운, 우연; 운명; 행운; 재산 ☐ hope n. 희망, 소망, 바람 ☐ prejudice n. 편견, 선입관; 침해, 손상

가끔 이것은 개인에게 어떤 위험을 안겨줄 수도 있다.

## 68 ②

☐ abstain v. 삼가다, 절제하다, 그만두다(=refrain) ☐ support v. 지지하다; 유지하다 ☐ resist v. ~에 저항하다, 반항하다 ☐ interfere v. 방해하다, 훼방하다

그들은 평화 협상 과정을 위태롭게 할지도 모르는 어떤 행동도 삼가는 데 동의했다.

## 69 ①

☐ unwittingly ad. 자신도 모르게, 부지불식간에 ☐ furtive a. 은밀한, 내밀한, 남몰래 하는(=elusive) ☐ ghost n. 유령, 망령 ☐ inhumane a. 몰인정한; 잔인한, 무자비한, 비인도적인 ☐ languid a. 무감동한, 흥미 없는; 활기 없는, 나른한 ☐ harrowing a. 마음 아픈, 비참한

나의 움직임은 나도 모르는 사이에 은밀하게 느껴진다. 나는 다소 귀신 같은 것으로 변한다.

## 70 ③

☐ conviction n. 유죄 선고[판결]; 확신, 신념 ☐ lazy a. 게으른, 나태한 ☐ impulse n. 충동, 자극 ☐ innate a. 타고난, 생득의(=natural) ☐ conflicting a. 서로 싸우는, 모순되는 ☐ deliberate a. 고의의, 의도적인 ☐ ultimate a. 궁극[최종]적인, 최후의

정치적 신념은 우리를 나태한 생각으로 이끈다. 그러나 훨씬 더 근본적인 충동이 작용하고 있다. 그것은 쉬운 답을 원하는 우리의 타고난 욕망이다.

## 71 ④

☐ measure n. (보통 pl.) 방책; 조처 ☐ stimulate v. 자극하다; 북돋우다(=promote) ☐ domestic consumption 국내 소비 ☐ endorse v. 배서하다; 승인하다 ☐ impose v. 지우다, 부과하다; 강요하다 ☐ affect v. 영향을 주다; 감동시키다

국내 소비와 해외 투자를 장려하기 위해 더 강력한 조치가 취해져야만 한다.

## 72 ④

□ exhaustively ad. 남김없이, 속속들이, 철저하게(=thoroughly) □ tiredly ad. 피로하여, 지쳐서; 싫증 난, 물린 □ enthusiastically ad. 열광적으로, 열중하여, 매우 열심히 □ descriptively ad. 서술적으로, 설명적으로

조이스(Joyce)는 『율리시스(Ulysses)』에서 우리의 삶에 대한 참여가 어떠한지, 또는 우리가 매 순간 살아갈 때 그것이 우리에게 어떻게 보이는가를 언어로 표현할 수 있는 한 철저하고, 정밀하고, 정확하게 표현하려 했다.

## 73 ②

□ archaic a. 고풍의; 오래된; 예스러운(=old) □ confusing a. 혼란시키는; 당황케 하는 □ foreign a. 외국의; 이질적인 □ learned a. 학식이 있는, 박학한

우리는 고어를 판독하는 데 애를 먹었다.

## 74 ④

□ prevail v. 우세하다, 이기다; 널리 보급되다(=predominate) □ exist v. 존재하다, 실재하다, 현존하다 □ preserve v. 보호하다, 지키다; 보존하다 □ continue v. 계속하다, 지속하다; 연장하다

영어가 운송업과 대중 전달 매체에서도 우위를 점하고 있다.

## 75 ④

□ affluent a. 부유한, 풍요한(=wealthy) □ sympathetic a. 동정적인, 공감하는 □ progressive a. 진보[혁신]적인 □ radical a. 급진적인, 과격한 □ insensible a. 둔감한, 무감각한 □ selfish a. 이기적인, 제멋대로인

연구는 근로자들이 더 부유해질수록, 그들이 진보적인 정당에 덜 공감하는 경향이 있다는 것을 보여주고 있다.

## 76 ②

□ descry v. 어렴풋이 알아보다, 발견하다(=discern) □ in full sail 돛을 모두 올리고 □ lose sight of ~이 더 이상 안 보이게 되다 □ understand v. 이해하다, 알아듣다; 깨닫다 □ purify v. 깨끗이 하다, 정화하다 □ ride v. 타다; 타고 가다

나는 돛을 모두 올린 배를 겨우 알아볼 수 있었는데, 아주 멀리에 있어 시야에서 곧 사라졌다.

## 77 ④

□ senator n. 상원 의원 □ insinuate v. 암시하다, 넌지시 말하다

(=suggest) □ qualified a. 자격이 있는, 적임의 □ elucidate v. 밝히다, 명료하게 하다 □ intimidate v. 겁을 주다, 위협하다 □ denounce v. 비난하다, 고발하다

토론회에서 그 상원 의원은 자신의 상대가 공직을 맡을 자격이 없다는 것을 암시하려 애썼다.

## 78 ①

□ discrepancy n. (같아야 할 것들 사이의) 차이, 불일치(=difference) □ protest n. 항의; 주장 □ falsity n. 허위, 기만 □ indignation n. 분개, 분함

그 호텔의 청결도에 관한 후기들에는 큰 차이가 있다.

## 79 ③

□ editorial n. (신문의) 사설, 논설 □ contradict v. 반박하다, 부인하다 (=deny) □ reject v. 거절하다, 거부하다 □ support v. 받치다, 유지하다; 지지하다 □ praise v. 칭찬하다, 찬미하다

오늘 아침 사설은 수상이 어제 경제에 대해 말했던 내용을 반박하는 글이었다.

## 80 ④

□ imperious a. 거만한, 고압적인(=authoritarian) □ demanding a. 너무 많은 것을 요구하는, 부당한 요구를 하는 □ chary a. 조심스러운, 신중한 □ imperturbable a. 침착한, 태연한 □ implacable a. 달래기 어려운, 화해할 수 없는; 용서 없는, 무자비한

왕은 인정 있는 지도자였지만, 그의 딸은 그녀의 통치기간 동안 고압적이었고 부당하게 요구하는 것이 많았다.

## 81 ④

□ cease-fire n. 정전(停戰) (명령), 휴전 □ preclude v. 막다, 방해하다; 제외하다(=prevent) □ retaliatory a. 보복적인, 앙갚음의 □ presume v. 추정하다, 가정하다 □ prescribe v. 규정하다; (약을) 처방하다 □ precede v. ~에 선행하다, 앞서다

일시적인 휴전 협정은 후에 있을 수 있는 보복공격을 저지하지 못한다.

## 82 ②

□ frantic a. 광란의, 극도로 흥분한; 제정신이 아닌(=frenzied) □ speculation n. 사색, 심사숙고; 투기, 투기 매매 □ stock n. 주식 □ real estate 부동산 □ unauthorized a. 권한이 없는, 허가받지 않은, 독단적인 □ concealed a. 숨겨진, 감춰진 □ prohibited a. 금지된

건전한 투자 가능성을 훨씬 넘어서 증가되고 있던 부유층과 중산층의 저축 자금은, 주식이나 부동산의 광적인 투기 자금으로 넘어가고 있었다.

## 83 ④

☐ flow n. 흐름; 유입 ☐ refugee n. 피난자, 난민 ☐ border n. 경계, 국경 ☐ precarious a. 불확실한; 위험한, 위태로운(=perilous) ☐ hampered a. 훼방을 받은; 장애[방해]가 된 ☐ rugged a. 바위투성이의; 기복이 심한; 단호한 ☐ ambiguous a. 애매한, 모호한

태국 국경을 넘어 들어오는 버마 난민들의 최근 유입으로 인하여 아이들의 상황이 점점 위태로워지고 있다.

## 84 ④

☐ comprehensive a. 이해가 빠른; 포괄적인, 종합적인(=extensive) ☐ useful a. 쓸모 있는, 유용한 ☐ understandable a. 이해할 수 있는 ☐ magic a. 마술의; 신비한

어느 나라도 포괄적인 에이즈 경고 프로그램이나 적절한 의료 서비스를 시행하고 있지 않다.

## 85 ②

☐ revile v. 매도하다, 욕설을 퍼붓다, 헐뜯다(=criticize) ☐ memorize v. 기억하다, 암기하다 ☐ obfuscate v. 몽롱하게 하다, (판단 등을) 흐리게 하다 ☐ misunderstand v. 오해하다, 잘못 생각하다

데카르트(Descartes)는 정신과 육체의 엄격한 분리에 대한 주장으로 가장 널리 기억되고 있고 동시에 가장 크게 비난받고 있다.

## 86 ④

☐ second house 별장 ☐ tidy a. 깔끔한, 잘 정돈된 ☐ all year round 1년 내내 ☐ laborious a. 힘든, 어려운(=onerous) ☐ unnatural a. 부자연스러운, 이상한 ☐ industrious a. 근면한, 부지런한; 열심인 ☐ enjoyable a. 즐거운, 유쾌한

별장과 정원을 1년 내내 깔끔하게 유지하는 것은 고된 일이 될 수 있다.

## 87 ④

☐ civilization n. 문명 ☐ manifestation n. 표현, 표시, 표명 ☐ wrath n. 격노, 분노(=anger) ☐ spirit n. 정신, 마음 ☐ voice n. 목소리 ☐ power n. 힘, 체력

고대 그리스 로마 문명에서는, 천둥을 신의 분노가 드러난 것으로 믿었다.

## 88 ④

☐ celebrated a. 유명한, 저명한 ☐ distinctive a. 특유의, 특이한, 독특한, 특색 있는; 차이를 나타내는(=distinguishing) ☐ restrained a. 자제된, 억제된, 차분한 ☐ exquisite a. 아주 아름다운; 최고의; 정교한 ☐ painstaking a. 노고를 아끼지 않는, 근면한; 공들인 ☐ mediocre a. 보통의, 평범한 ☐ ornamented a. (글자체가) 화려한, 장식체의

그 이탈리아의 대가가 1921년 캔버스에 그린 유화는 독특한 붓놀림, 우아하지만 곧은 실루엣 선, 차분하지만 아름다운 색상의 쓰임으로 유명하다.

## 89 ①

☐ mesmerize v. ~에게 최면술을 걸다; 매혹시키다(=hypnotize) ☐ the heart of the matter 문제의 핵심, 핵심적인 사실 ☐ reconcile v. 화해시키다; (논쟁 따위를) 조정하다 ☐ persuade v. 설득하다, 권유하여 ~시키다 ☐ influence v. ~에게 영향을 미치다, 감화하다

또다시 그 단어가 있었다. 'deal'이라는 단어였다. 림보(Limbaugh)는 문제의 핵심을 갑작스럽게 발견한 사실에 매료되어 그 단어를 수없이 되뇌었다.

## 90 ②

☐ cautious a. 주의 깊은, 신중한(=discreet) ☐ awkward a. 거북한, 어색한 ☐ urgent a. 긴급한, 시급한 ☐ aggressive a. 침략적인, 호전적인; 적극적인 ☐ optimistic a. 낙관적인, 낙천적인 ☐ sensitive a. 민감한, 예민한

그의 신중한 접근법이 잠재적인 이점이 있긴 하지만, 이런 긴급한 상황에서는 다소 거북하게 보인다.

## 91 ③

☐ mishap n. 불운한 일; 불운(=misfortune) ☐ misunderstanding n. 오해, 잘못 생각하기; 의견 차이 ☐ accident n. 사고; 재해, 우연 ☐ incidental n. 부수적인 일, 우발적인 일

비록 많은 과학의 발전이 불행에서 비롯되었을지라도 발전의 가능성을 인식하는 데에는 뛰어난 사상가가 필요했다.

## 92 ④

☐ condemn v. 비난하다 ☐ give birth to 낳다 ☐ abject a. 비참한, 절망적인(=miserable) ☐ exquisite a. 정교한, 절묘한; 강렬한, 격렬한 ☐ sophisticated a. 복잡한, 정교한 ☐ sublime a. 숭고한, 장엄한

나는 이 비참한 사회 정책의 실패를 낳은 사람들의 훌륭한 의도를 비난하지는 않는다.

## 93       ①

☐ prophet n. 예언자 ☐ foresee v. 예견하다, 예지하다, 내다보다 (=predict) ☐ famine n. 기근; 흉작 ☐ worry v. 걱정하다, 근심하다, 고민하다 ☐ outspeak v. ~보다 말을 잘하다; 솔직하게 말하다 ☐ overestimate v. 과대평가하다; 지나치게 어림하다

그 예언자는 그 나라에서의 격심한 기근을 예견했다.

## 94       ③

☐ uncompromising a. 양보[타협]하지 않는; 강경한, 완고한 ☐ modernity n. 현대[근대]성 ☐ uplifting a. 희망[행복감]을 주는; 고양시키는(=inspiring) ☐ unconventional a. 관습에 얽매이지 않은; (태도, 복장이) 독특한 ☐ unmistakable a. 오해의 여지가 없는, 틀림없는 ☐ exaggerating a. 과장하는

그 새로운 글 속의 강력한 근대성은 또한 고무적이다.

## 95       ①

☐ epoch n. 시대; 신기원; 획기적인 사건(=long period of time) ☐ termination n. 종료, 마침; 결말 ☐ brief moment 짧은 순간 ☐ cessation n. 중지, 중단, 휴지

조산 운동의 시기는 그저 진화의 과정에 속도를 더해주는 역할을 했을 뿐이다.

## 96       ③

☐ hostile a. 적의가 있는, 적대하는(=antagonistic) ☐ sublimate v. 바람직한 방향으로 돌리다[승화시키다] ☐ delicate a. 연약한; 예민한 ☐ hospitable a. 대접이 좋은; 환대하는 ☐ undefined a. 한정되지 않은, 확실하지 않은

적대적 감정과 폭력적 반응은 종종 스포츠 활동과 같이 바람직한 방향으로 승화되는 것처럼 보인다.

## 97       ②

☐ exert v. 쓰다, 행사하다(=exercise) ☐ fatigued a. 심신이 지친, 피로한 ☐ preserve v. 지키다, 보호하다 ☐ maintain v. 유지하다, 지키다 ☐ ameliorate v. 개선하다

피로감을 느끼고 몸이 쇠약해졌을 때 자제력을 발휘하는 것은 훨씬 더 어렵다.

## 98       ③

☐ vanquish v. 정복하다, 이기다(=defeat) ☐ replicate v. 모사[복제]하다 ☐ mutate v. 돌연변이를 만들다 ☐ precipitate v. 촉발시키다

암세포들을 죽이는 약은 불행하게도 좋지 않은 부작용을 남길 수 있다.

## 99       ④

☐ recession n. 경기 후퇴, 불경기 ☐ quixotic a. 돈키호테식의; 비현실적인(=impractical) ☐ hackneyed a. 진부한 ☐ affirmative a. 긍정[동의]하는 ☐ plausible a. 이치에 맞는, 그럴듯한

경기 침체와 높은 실업률 속에서 직장을 그만두고 쉽게 다른 일자리를 찾을 수 있다고 상상하는 것은 비현실적이다.

## 100       ①

☐ interminable a. 끝없이 계속되는(=endless) ☐ queue n. 줄, 대기 행렬 ☐ sumptuous a. 값비싼, 호화스러운 ☐ inconceivable a. 상상[생각]도 할 수 없는 ☐ cohesive a. 화합[결합]하는

새 정부는 식량 부족 사태와 기초 생활용품을 구하기 위한 끝없는 행렬에 종지부를 찍으리라고 약속했다.

| | | | | | | | | | |
|---|---|---|---|---|---|---|---|---|---|
| 01 ④ | 02 ③ | 03 ① | 04 ② | 05 ① | 06 ④ | 07 ④ | 08 ① | 09 ② | 10 ② |
| 11 ① | 12 ④ | 13 ② | 14 ④ | 15 ④ | 16 ② | 17 ④ | 18 ③ | 19 ① | 20 ④ |
| 21 ② | 22 ② | 23 ④ | 24 ③ | 25 ④ | 26 ④ | 27 ④ | 28 ① | 29 ① | 30 ④ |
| 31 ③ | 32 ④ | 33 ③ | 34 ④ | 35 ① | 36 ② | 37 ① | 38 ③ | 39 ① | 40 ③ |
| 41 ④ | 42 ① | 43 ④ | 44 ① | 45 ① | 46 ① | 47 ③ | 48 ② | 49 ④ | 50 ① |
| 51 ② | 52 ③ | 53 ① | 54 ④ | 55 ④ | 56 ① | 57 ② | 58 ① | 59 ④ | 60 ② |
| 61 ② | 62 ③ | 63 ① | 64 ② | 65 ④ | 66 ④ | 67 ① | 68 ② | 69 ③ | 70 ① |
| 71 ② | 72 ② | 73 ③ | 74 ② | 75 ① | 76 ① | 77 ③ | 78 ① | 79 ③ | 80 ① |
| 81 ④ | 82 ① | 83 ① | 84 ④ | 85 ③ | 86 ① | 87 ② | 88 ③ | 89 ④ | 90 ① |
| 91 ③ | 92 ① | 93 ③ | 94 ① | 95 ① | 96 ③ | 97 ① | 98 ④ | 99 ② | 100 ③ |

## 01 ④

□ outweigh v. ~보다 무겁다; 능가하다, 보다 중대하다(=exceed) □ maximize v. 극대화하다; 최대값을 구하다 □ minimize v. 최소로 하다; 경시하다, 얕보다 □ promote v. 증진하다, 진행시키다

우리는 일부 약의 부작용에 주의해야 하는데 그것은 종종 잠재적인 이익보다 더 중요하다.

## 02 ③

□ flippant a. 경박한, 천박한(=frivolous) □ detention n. 구류; (학생을 벌로서) 방과 후에 남게 하기 □ restrained a. 억제된, 절제하는 □ enraged a. 화가 난 □ immoral a. 부도덕한, 도의에 어긋나는

그의 경박한 언행들이 몇 차례 그의 동료들의 웃음을 샀지만, 그 언행들은 또한 그에게 며칠간 방과 후 남는 벌을 가져다주었다.

## 03 ①

□ sporadic a. 산발적인, 산재하는(=intermittent) □ outburst n. 폭발, 분출; 격발 □ ethnic a. 인종의, 민족의 □ continuous a. 계속되는, 지속적인 □ frequent a. 잦은, 빈번한 □ distant a. 먼, 떨어져 있는

100명이 넘는 사람들이 올해 산발적으로 터진 민족 간의 폭력사태에서 목숨을 잃었다.

## 04 ②

□ infringement n. (법규) 위반, 위배(=violation) □ copyright n. 판권, 저작권 □ plaintiff n. 원고, 고소인 □ pretense n. 구실, 핑계; 겉치레 □ infliction n. (고통·벌·타격을) 가함; 형벌 □ nuisance n. 성가심, 귀찮음; 난처한[성가신, 골치 아픈] 것

법원은 저작권 침해가 심각하다고 보고 원고 승소 판결을 내렸다.

## 05 ①

□ tolerance n. 관용; 아량 □ chronic a. 만성적인, 고질적인; 상습적인(=habitual) □ tardiness n. 지각 □ conventional a. 전통적인; 인습적인, 관습적인 □ reckless a. 무모한, 신중하지 못한 □ incompetent a. 무능한; 부적당한

상습적인 지각에 대해서는 경영진이 거의 관용을 베풀지 않는다는 점이 직원 수칙에 분명하게 설명돼 있다.

## 06 ④

□ exposure n. 노출, 드러남 □ motivation n. 자극; 동기부여 □ crucial a. 결정적인, 중대한(=vital) □ final a. 최후의; 결정적인 □ drastic a. 격렬한, 철저한 □ meager a. 메마른; 빈약한, 결핍한

언어 학습 상황에서는, 언어에 노출되는 것과 동기부여가 중요한 요소이다.

## 07 ④

□ ink v. (서약서 따위에) 서명하다 □ lucrative a. 이익이 되는, 수익성이 좋은(=remunerative) □ smooth a. 매끄러운; 부드러운; 순조로운 □ perceptive a. 지각하는; 통찰력이 있는 □ decremental a. 점감[감소]하는, 감소의

그 예술가는 떠오르는 여성 사업가이기도 해서, 지난 1년 동안 펩시, 리복, 그리고 다른 유명 브랜드들과 수익성 좋은 거래 계약을 체결한 바 있다.

## 08 ①

☐ disregard v. 무시하다, 경시하다(=ignore) ☐ deplore v. 비탄하다, 개탄하다 ☐ explore v. 탐험하다; 탐구하다 ☐ implore v. 간청하다, 애원하다

클라크(Clark) 교수는 그의 연구를 계속하고 동료의 충고는 무시했다.

## 09 ②

☐ trait n. 특성 ☐ consensus n. 의견 일치, 합의(=accord) ☐ inquiry n. 연구, 탐구; 조사 ☐ objectivity n. 객관성 ☐ candor n. 솔직, 성실

인종은 생물학적인 특성이 아니라 사회적인 구성이다. 이것이 과학적 합의인데, 왜 많은 사람들이 여전히 그것을 논박하는가?

## 10 ②

☐ podium n. 지휘대, 연단 ☐ tax audit 세무 감사 ☐ prolong v. 길게 하다, 연장하다(=elongate) ☐ enforce v. 실시하다, 시행하다, 집행하다 ☐ consolidate v. 합병하다, 통합하다 ☐ guarantee v. 보증하다, 보장하다

고위직 당 간부들은 연단을 점거하고, 정부의 세무 감사는 내년도 대통령 선거에서 정권을 연장하는 데 목적을 두고 있다고 주장했다.

## 11 ①

☐ collaborate on ~와 공동으로 일하다(=work together on) ☐ purchase v. 사다, 구입하다 ☐ gather together with ~과 함께 모으다 ☐ complete v. 완료하다, 끝마치다

수전 밀러(Susan Miller)는 그녀의 오빠와 공동 작업하여 소설 한 편을 썼다.

## 12 ④

☐ peer n. 동료; (사회적·법적으로) 동등한 사람(=colleague) ☐ collage n. 콜라주 (기법) ☐ conductor n. 지휘자, 안내원, 승무원 ☐ college n. 대학, 단과 대학

새로운 연구는 로봇이 권위자가 아니라 동료로 제시될 때 더 설득력이 있다는 것을 보여준다.

## 13 ②

☐ transient a. 일시적인, 순간적인(=temporary) ☐ be free of ~에서 자유롭다, ~가 없다 ☐ flagrant a. 노골적인, 명백한 ☐ arduous a. 몹시 힘든, 고된 ☐ causal a. 원인이 되는, 인과 관계의

소음 공해는 여러 가지 면에서 다른 형태의 공해와 다르다. 소음은 일시적이다. 소음 공해가 일단 멈추고 나면, 환경에는 소음 공해가 없다.

## 14 ④

☐ mantra n. 진언(眞言); 슬로건 ☐ equitable a. 공정한, 공평한; 정당한(=impartial) ☐ divergent a. 분기하는; 갈라지는; 일탈한; (의견 등이) 다른 ☐ allowable a. 허락할 수 있는; 정당한 ☐ agreeable a. 기호나 취미에 맞는, 상쾌한

다양성은 이 사회에서, 특히 우리 사회를 인종차별이 덜하고 더욱 공평하게 만들 권한을 갖고 있다고 생각하는 계몽된 학문 및 교양 집단에서 하나의 원칙으로 통하는 말이다.

## 15 ④

☐ foreboding n. (불길한) 예감, 전조(=presentiment) ☐ hypocrisy n. 위선, 위선적 행위 ☐ nonchalance n. 무관심, 냉담, 태연 ☐ barrenness n. 불모, 열매를 맺지 못함

포우(Poe)는 이야기에 전조(前兆)와 비밀스러운 느낌을 부여하기 위해 죽음의 개념과 등장인물의 악화되어가는 정신 상태를 이용한다.

## 16 ②

☐ sociable a. 사교적인(=gregarious) ☐ empathetic a. (다른 사람과) 공감할 수 있는, 감정 이입의 ☐ cautious a. 주의 깊은, 신중한 ☐ loner n. 주로 혼자 지내는 사람, 혼자 있기를 더 좋아하는 사람 ☐ moody a. 변덕스러운; 성미가 까다로운 ☐ reckless a. 분별없는, 신중하지 못한 ☐ withdrawn a. 내성적인, 내향적인 ☐ timorous a. 소심한, 겁 많은 ☐ bashful a. 수줍어하는, 부끄럼 타는

그들은 비록 쌍둥이지만 똑같지 않다. 한 명은 사교적이고, 공감능력이 있으며, 신중하다. 나머지 한 명은 늘 외톨이이며 성미가 까다롭고 신중하지 못하다.

## 17 ④

☐ custom n. 관습, 풍습; (~s) <단수취급> 세관, 통관 ☐ blunder n. 큰 실수, 대실책(=mistake) ☐ commitment n. 범행, 실행; 위임; 공약 ☐ enemy n. 적, 적대자, 경쟁 상대 ☐ injury n. 상해, 손상, 손해

관습에 익숙해 있지 않을 때는 큰 실수를 저지르기 쉽다.

## 18 ③

☐ conspiracy n. 음모(=plot) ☐ fealty n. 충성, 신의 ☐ loyalty n. 충실 ☐ treachery n. 배반, 위약

위원회에서 나를 제거하려는 음모가 있었다고 생각한다.

## 19 ①

☐ inscribe v. 적다, 새기다(=write)  ☐ read v. 읽다, 낭독하다  ☐ translate v. 번역[통역]하다  ☐ remove v. 제거하다; 옮기다, 움직이다

그들은 벽에 글씨들을 새겼다.

## 20 ④

☐ peculiar a. 기묘한, 이상한, 별난, 색다른; 특이한(=odd)  ☐ furry a. 털로 덮인  ☐ curved a. 굽은, 곡선 모양의  ☐ beak n. 부리  ☐ particular a. 특별한, 특유의, 특수한; 특정한  ☐ solemn a. 엄숙한, 근엄한; 장엄한  ☐ awkward a. 어색한, 거북한; 서투른

키위새는 털로 덮인 깃털과 길고 굽은 부리를 가진 특이하게 날지 못하는 동물이다.

## 21 ②

☐ dissolution n. (결혼 생활의) 파경, (사업상 관계의) 해소, (의회의) 해산  ☐ partnership n. 협력, 제휴  ☐ amicable a. 우호적인, 친화적인(=friendly)  ☐ on good terms 친밀한 사이로, 친근하게  ☐ historic a. 역사적으로 유명한, 역사에 남는  ☐ leisurely a. 느긋한, 유유한  ☐ efficient a. 능률적인

사업적 제휴관계의 해소가 상당히 우호적이었기 때문에, 이전의 협력 업체들은 좋은 관계를 유지했다.

## 22 ②

☐ destitute a. 빈곤한, 궁핍한(=indigent)  ☐ anguished a. 괴로워하는  ☐ desperate a. 자포자기의; 필사적인  ☐ exhausted a. 고갈된; 기진맥진한

수백만 명의 빈곤한 이주민들이 흡수되어 홍콩은 지구상에서 가장 성공적인 사회 중의 하나를 만들어냈다.

## 23 ④

☐ swell v. 부풀다; 증대하다(=burgeon)  ☐ retract v. 쑥 들어가게 하다; 취소하다, 철회하다  ☐ acquiesce v. 묵인하다, 마지못해 따르다; 동의하다  ☐ curtail v. 줄이다; 삭감하다; 억제하다

1848년에 캘리포니아에서 금이 발견된 이후 그곳의 인구가 팽창했다.

.

## 24 ③

☐ fanatic n. 열광자, 광신자(=zealot)  ☐ incumbent n. 현직자, 재임자  ☐ candidate n. 후보자; 지원자, 지망자  ☐ jealousy n. 질투, 시기

정치적 광신도인 그는 전 세계에서 혁명가들과 함께 싸워 왔다.

## 25 ④

☐ monotonous a. 단조로운; 변화 없는, 지루한(=tedious)  ☐ critical a. 비평의; 위기의, 위급한  ☐ intriguing a. 음모를 꾸미는; 흥미를 자아내는  ☐ questioning a. 의심스러운, 수상한

그녀의 지루한 목소리 톤(어조) 때문에 학생들은 그녀의 강의를 듣는 것에 대해 다시 생각하게 되었다.

## 26 ④

☐ fractious a. 성마른, 까다로운; 다루기 힘든(=irritable)  ☐ amenable a. 순종하는, 쾌히 받아들이는  ☐ frivolous a. 경솔한, 들뜬; 하찮은  ☐ ambivalent a. 상반하는 감정을 품은; 양면가치의

기저귀를 갈 때 짜증을 내는 예민한 아기들의 경우, 자극을 주는 것이 관심을 다른 곳으로 돌리게 하는 데 매우 효과적이다.

## 27 ④

☐ compel v. 강요[강제]하다(=obligate)  ☐ enrichment n. 풍부하게 함, 농축  ☐ reserve v. 떼어두다, 비축하다  ☐ enumerate v. 열거하다  ☐ meddle v. 쓸데없이 참견하다, 간섭하다

국제 사회가 이란에게 우라늄 농축을 중지하도록 강요하기 위해 할 수 있는 일은 아무것도 없다.

## 28 ①

☐ nullify v. 무효로 하다, 폐기하다(=invalidate)  ☐ join legally 합법적으로 가입하다  ☐ examine carefully 면밀하게 관찰하다, 실험하다  ☐ enforce v. 실시하다, 시행하다, 집행하다

학생회는 이전 학생회들이 통과시킨 몇 가지 규칙들을 무효화하기로 가결했다.

## 29 ①

☐ travail n. 고통, 고뇌; 노고, 수고(=drudgery)  ☐ upside n. 위쪽, 윗면, 상부; 상승 경향  ☐ perusal n. 정독, 숙독  ☐ vanity n. 허영, 자만심

문을 닫아야 하는 의무가 물리적인 접촉이나 그만한 감정적인 고통 없이 충족되었다.

## 30 ③

☐ reprehensible a. 괘씸한, 비난할 만한(=blameworthy)  ☐ flattery n. 아첨, 아부, 듣기 좋은 칭찬  ☐ amiable a. 호감을 주는; 붙임성 있는; 상냥한  ☐ ignoble a. 성품이 저열한, 비열한; 비천한  ☐ commonplace a. 평범한, 개성이 없는; 진부한

아첨을 기꺼이 받아들이려고 하는 것은 우리의 비난받을 만한 본성이다.

## 31 ③

☐ deference n. 복종; 존경, 경의(=respect) ☐ interest n. 관심, 흥미; 중요성; 이익 ☐ fright n. 공포, 경악 ☐ doubt n. 의심, 의혹, 회의, 불신

그들은 주인에게 존경심을 보이지 않았으며 그가 내리는 모든 명령을 무시했다.

## 32 ④

☐ competent a. 유능한, 능력이 있는(=able) ☐ gullible a. 남을 잘 믿는, 잘 속아 넘어가는 ☐ valuable a. 귀중한, 가치 있는; 값비싼 ☐ conspicuous a. 눈에 띄는, 잘 보이는

나는 제이슨(Jason)이 그의 새로운 일에서 성공하리라 생각하지 않는데, 그가 그런 종류의 일에 능숙하지 않기 때문이다.

## 33 ③

☐ release n. 해방, 석방, 면제; 공개, 개봉 ☐ erode v. (서서히) 약화시키다, 무너뜨리다(=destroy) ☐ confidence n. 신용, 신뢰; 확신 ☐ judicial system 재판제도, 사법제도 ☐ restore v. 복원하다, 회복하다 ☐ enhance v. 향상하다, 강화하다 ☐ adjust v. 조절하다, 조정하다

불과 3일 만에 그녀가 석방된 것은 사법제도에 대한 신뢰를 무너뜨린다.

## 34 ④

☐ irrespective of ~와 상관없이, ~와 관계없이 ☐ emit v. (빛, 열, 소리 따위를) 내다, 발하다, 방출하다 ☐ absorb v. 흡수하다, 빨아들이다 ☐ atmosphere n. 대기; 공기; 분위기 ☐ consequence n. 결과, 결말; 중요성 ☐ uniform a. 한결같은, 균일한 ☐ adverse a. 불리한; 해로운; 불운[불행]한 ☐ unilateral a. 일방적인, 한쪽만의; 한쪽에만 제한된(=one-sided) ☐ unauthorized a. 월권의; 공인[승인]되지 않은 ☐ zero-sum a. (게임, 관계 등이) 쌍방 득실(得失)의 차가 없는 ☐ conventional a. 전통적인, 인습적인, 관습적인

기후변화가 전 지구적인 성격을 갖는 것은 지구에서 온실가스는 배출되는 곳과 관계없이 대기 중으로 급속히 흡수되어 지구의 이곳저곳으로 확산된다는 사실에서 비롯된다. 그러나 그로 인해 초래되는 전 지구적 기후변화의 결과는 결코 획일적이지 않을 것으로 예상되어서, 몇몇 국가는 다른 국가들에 비해 나쁜 영향을 훨씬 더 크게 받을 것으로 보인다. 그뿐만 아니라, 어느 한 국가의 일방적인 조치로는 이러한 상황에 의미 있는 변화를 가져올 수 없다. 따라서 그 문제를 해결하기 위해서는 개선을 위한 국제적 차원에서의 합치된 협력이 반드시 필요하다.

## 35 ①

☐ penultimate a. 끝에서 두 번째의 ☐ grueling a. 기진맥진하게 하는, 힘든(=exhausting) ☐ cast oneself in ~에 뛰어들다, 떠맡다 ☐ parliament n. 의회 ☐ enjoyable a. 재미있는, 즐거운, 유쾌한 ☐ extravagant a. 화려한, 낭비하는 ☐ empowering a. 동기를 부여하는

3주에 이르는 매우 고된 유럽 관광이 끝나기 전날이다. 그 관광기간 동안 그녀는 영국과 유럽연합 의회 앞에서 교육자의 역할을 떠맡았다.

## 36 ②

☐ police record 전과(前科), 범죄 경력 ☐ apprehend v. 체포하다(=seize); 파악하다, 이해하다 ☐ witness v. 목격하다; 증언하다 ☐ discover v. 발견하다; 알다, 깨닫다 ☐ blame v. 나무라다, 비난하다

뉴스 보도에 의하면, 전과 기록이 없는 어떤 여자가 관공서 공원에서 그녀 할머니의 무덤에 놓을 꽃을 따다가 체포되었다.

## 37 ①

☐ contagious a. 전염성의, 옮기 쉬운(=transmittable) ☐ variant n. 변형, 변이체 ☐ pop up 갑자기 나타나다 ☐ identify v. (본인·동일물임을) 확인하다 ☐ valid a. 근거가 확실한, 정당한 ☐ strong a. 강한, 유력한 ☐ spoiled a. 손상된, 상한

잠재적으로 더 전염성이 강한 오미크론 코로나바이러스 변종이 남아프리카 공화국에서 확인된 지 불과 며칠 만에 더 많은 유럽 국가들에서 갑작스럽게 나타났다.

## 38 ③

☐ justify v. 옳다고 하다, 정당화하다(=validate) ☐ revenge n. 보복, 복수(=vengeance) ☐ criticize v. 비평하다, 평론하다; 비판하다 ☐ encourage v. 격려하다; 장려하다 ☐ determine v. 결심하다, 결의하다; 결정하다

영화에서 아이의 죽음은 폭력적 복수의 심각한 행위와 심각한 연기의 폭력적 표현을 정당화한다.

## 39 ①

☐ sumptuous a. 사치스러운, 화려한, 값진(=luxurious) ☐ croon n. (낮은 소리로 부르는) 감상적인 유행가 ☐ eggshell a. 얇고 부서지기 쉬운 ☐ chippy a. 화를 잘 내는, 성마른; 무미건조한 ☐ inexpensive a. 비용이 들지 않는, 값싼; 값에 비하여 품질이 좋은 ☐ infectious a. 전염하는, 옮기 쉬운

그들은 사랑이라는 돌에 의해 부서지기 쉬운 연인들의 마음에 대한 그의 화려한 낮은 목소리의 감상적인 유행가를 좋아한다.

## 40 ③

□ bring about 일으키다, 초래하다  □ restriction n. 제한; 제약, 구속  □ nothing short of 아주 ~한, 거의 ~이나 마찬가지인  □ profound a. 난해한; (충격·변화 따위가) 큰, 심각한(=seismic)  □ explosive a. 폭발성의, 폭발적인  □ catastrophic a. 파멸의, 비극적인  □ divisive a. 구분하는; 분열을 일으키는

코로나바이러스와 정부의 관련 조치와 제한으로 초래된 사회 변화는 매우 컸다.

## 41 ④

□ magniloquent a. 호언장담하는, 허풍떠는; 과장한(=grandiloquent)  □ berserk a. 미쳐 날뛰는, 길길이 뛰는  □ sedulous a. 공을 들이는, 정성을 다하는  □ prosaic a. 평범한, 단조로운

그 재판에 대한 기사에서 기자들은 피고측 변호사의 과장된 변론을 조소했다.

## 42 ①

□ stalwart a. 꿋꿋한, 타협하지 않는(=steadfast)  □ tacit a. 암묵적인, 무언의  □ adroit a. 교묘한, 솜씨 좋은  □ ascetic a. 금욕주의의; 고행의  □ coherent a. 일관성 있는, 논리[조리] 정연한

FTA를 가장 완강하게 반대하는 자들 사이에서 마저도, 세계화와 그 밖의 다른 요인들이 그 나라의 경제를 불가피하게 변화시키고 있다는 암묵적인 인식이 존재하고 있다.

## 43 ④

□ apprise v. 알리다, 통지하다, 통고하다(=inform)  □ intransigence n. 비타협적 태도  □ with reference to ~에 관하여  □ suspension n. 중지, 미결정  □ deprive v. ~을 빼앗다, 허용치 않다  □ accuse v. 고발하다; 비난하다  □ relieve v. 경감하다; 안심시키다

그는 파키스탄과 인도 사이의 회담이 중지된 것과 관련하여 인도 측의 비타협적인 태도를 그들에게 알릴 것이다.

## 44 ①

□ ludicrous a. 우스운, 익살맞은(=laughable)  □ lubricating a. 매끄럽게 하는; 원활히 하는  □ negligible a. 하찮은, 사소한  □ luminant a. 빛나는, 빛을 발하는

나는 심각하다. 이것은 우스운 문제가 아니다.

## 45 ①

□ impromptu a. 준비 없이, 즉석에서의, 즉흥적인(=extemporaneous)

□ thoughtful a. 생각이 깊은, 신중한  □ unthoughtful a. 생각이 깊지 못한, 부주의한  □ well-designed a. 잘 설계된, 계획된

그 교수는 그 학급 학생들에게 이야기할 준비가 되어 있지 않았지만, 아무 원고 없이 즉석 강연을 아주 잘했다.

## 46 ①

□ hinge v. ~에 달려있다(on)(=depend on)  □ depart v. 떠나다, 출발하다  □ look on 구경하다, 방관하다  □ let on 폭로하다, 누설하다

그의 주장의 몇몇 부분들은 기억해 낸다는 의식 없이도 기억이 드러날 수 있다는 생각의 실행 가능성에 달려있었다.

## 47 ③

□ demeaning a. 품위를 떨어뜨리는(=degrading)  □ status n. 지위  □ run for public office 공직에 입후보하다  □ detain v. 지체하게 하다; 구금하다  □ sustain a. 떠받치는, 유지하는  □ emerging a. 신생의, 최근에 만들어진

그 결과, 그들은 '비시민'이라는 그들의 품위를 손상시키는 법적 지위를 갖게 되었는데, 이로 인해 투표할 권리 및 공직에 입후보할 권리 등 수많은 권리를 상실하게 된다.

## 48 ②

□ cite v. 인용하다; 예증하다; 열거하다(=quote)  □ read v. 읽다; 해독하다  □ bring v. 가져오다, 데려오다  □ discuss v. 토론하다, 논의하다

우주의 기원에 관한 그의 유명한 책은 전 세계 과학자들과 학자들에 의해 인용되고 있다.

## 49 ④

□ gloomy a. 어두운, 음침한; 우울한(=dark)  □ promising a. 장래성이 있는, 전도유망한  □ precise a. 정확한, 정밀한  □ delicate a. 섬세한, 고운; 연약한

올해 그 회사의 매출 상황은 어둡다.

## 50 ④

□ enigmatic a. 수수께끼 같은, 난해한, 알기 어려운(=puzzling)  □ enlightening a. 계몽적인, 밝혀주는  □ disturbing a. 불안하게 하는; 교란시키는  □ entertaining a. 재미있는, 유쾌한

그 교수의 강의는 그리스 시(詩)에 대한 알기 어려운 언급으로 가득 차 있었다.

## 51 ②

☐ taboo n. 금기 ☐ anxiety n. 불안 ☐ originate v. 기원하다 ☐ transpire v. 발산하다; 일어나다(=occur) ☐ forgo v. 포기하다 ☐ vanish v. 사라지다 ☐ resort v. 잘 가다, 의지하다(to)

금기는 여러 상황에서의 불안을 사람이 하지 않는 행동을 통해 줄일 수 있다. 금기는 특정 행동을 하면 어떤 비극이나 불행이 일어날 것이라는 믿음에서 비롯되는 경우가 많다.

## 52 ③

☐ curtail v. 줄이다, 삭감하다(=reduce) ☐ abolish v. 폐지하다; 파괴하다 ☐ discourage v. 단념시키다, 낙담하게 하다 ☐ target v. 목표로 삼다, 겨냥하다

많은 주(州)가 레스토랑과 술집에서 흡연하는 것을 금지함으로써 공공장소에서의 흡연을 줄여왔다.

## 53 ①

☐ tense a. 팽팽한; 긴장한 ☐ relation n. 관계; 연관 ☐ nomadic a. 유목민의; 방랑의(=wandering) ☐ fierce a. 치열한, 격렬한 ☐ nocturnal a. 야행성의 ☐ pristine a. 초기의, 원시 시대[상태]의

중국의 여러 왕조 국가들은 과거에 유목민들과의 긴장 관계를 경험했다.

## 54 ④

☐ surrealism n. 초현실주의 ☐ omnipotence n. 전능, 무한한 힘 ☐ disinterested a. 공평무사한; 무관심한(=detached) ☐ flustered a. 허둥거리는, 당황하는 ☐ tedious a. 지루한, 진저리나는; 장황한 ☐ mundane a. 이승의, 현세의; 세속적인; 평범한

초현실주의는 이전에 간과되었던 어떤 연상 형태의 월등한 실재성에 대한 믿음, 꿈의 무한한 힘에 대한 믿음, 그리고 사고의 무심한 작용에 대한 믿음에 있다.

## 55 ④

☐ forestall v. 미연에 방지하다(=prevent) ☐ retaliatory a. 보복의 ☐ mass rally 대중 집회 ☐ scold v. 꾸짖다 ☐ investigate v. 조사[연구, 수사]하다 ☐ endure v. 견디다

보복적인 폭력행위가 발생하는 것을 미연에 방지하기 위해, 우리는 전국에서 일주일간 이어지는 대중 집회와 시위를 준비했다.

## 56 ①

☐ capacity n. 능력; 수용력[량]; 용량(=volume) ☐ ship v. 배로 보내다; 수송하다; 적재하다 ☐ equipment n. 장비, 설비, 비품; 준비 ☐ possibility n. 가능성 ☐ employee n. 직원, 종업원

그 터미널은 일 년에 약 1,600만 톤의 석탄을 선적할 수용량을 갖추고 있다.

## 57 ②

☐ visceral a. 내장의; 노골적인; 본능적인(=instinctive) ☐ efficacious a. 효과 있는; (약이) 잘 듣는 ☐ sycophantic a. 아첨하는; 중상적인 ☐ responsive a. 바로 반응하는; 민감한

그 반응은 분석적이기보다 본능적이었다.

## 58 ①

☐ notorious a. 악명 높은 ☐ tendentious a. 편향적인(=biased); 과격한, 극단적인 ☐ account n. (자세한) 이야기 ☐ affair n. 사건 ☐ wholeheartedly ad. 진정으로, 전적으로 ☐ trendy a. 유행을 따르는 ☐ sensational a. 세상을 놀라게 하는 ☐ exaggerated a. 과장된

그 신문은 사건에 대한 편향된 이야기로 악명이 높아서, 사람들은 그 신문을 전적으로 믿지는 않는다.

## 59 ④

☐ exorbitant a. (가격이) 엄청난, 과도한(=expensive) ☐ stage v. 개최하다 ☐ funeral n. 장례식 ☐ cheap a. (값이) 싼, 염가의 ☐ negotiable a. 절충 가능한 ☐ sparse a. (밀도가) 희박한

일부 국가에서는, '적절한' 장례식을 치르는 데 드는 과도한 비용이 가정을 재정적인 파탄상태에 이르게 할 수 있다.

## 60 ②

☐ corroborate v. 확실하게 하다, 보강하다, 확증하다(=confirm) ☐ report v. 보고하다; 공표하다 ☐ collect v. 모으다, 수집하다 ☐ refute v. 논박하다, 반박하다

이 견해를 확증해 주는 윤리적이고, 실질적인 사실들이 많이 있고, 그 견해에 반대되는 사실은 약간뿐인 것 같다.

## 61 ②

☐ strikingly ad. 현저하게, 두드러지게(=remarkably) ☐ effectively ad. 유효하게; 효과적으로 ☐ certainly ad. 확실히, 꼭; 의심 없이, 반드시 ☐ unquestionably ad. 의심할 바 없이, 논의할 여지없이, 확실히

낮은 기온과 풍속의 조합인 풍속냉각지수는 옥외에 있는 사람이 느끼는 추위의 정도를 엄청나게 증가시킨다.

## 62 ③

☐ hallmark n. 특징, 특질 ☐ procrastination n. 미루는 버릇; 지체 (=stalling) ☐ action n. 행동, 조치 ☐ change n. 변화, 변경 ☐ excess n. 초과, 과잉

주의력 결핍 및 과잉 행동 장애(ADHD)의 특징적인 증상 중 하나는 지체하는 것이다.

## 63 ②

☐ atom n. 원자 ☐ discrete a. 따로따로의, 별개의(=distinct) ☐ proton n. 양자 ☐ neutron n. 중성자 ☐ electron n. 전자 ☐ transferable a. 이동[양도, 전이] 가능한 ☐ derived a. 유래된, 파생된 ☐ absolute a. 완전한, 완벽한

원자는 양자와 중성자 그리고 전자라 불리는 서로 다른 구성 단위로 이루어져 있다.

## 64 ②

☐ antibiotic n. 항생제, 항생물질 ☐ alleviate v. 완화시키다, 경감하다 (=soothe) ☐ pneumonia n. 폐렴 ☐ provoke v. 자극하다, 일으키다 ☐ eliminate v. 없애다, 제거하다 ☐ aggravate v. 악화시키다

유감스럽게도, 치료용으로 처음 사용했던 항생제는 지역 사회성 폐렴으로 추정되고 있던 질병을 완화시키지 못했다.

## 65 ④

☐ dedicated a. 헌신적인, 전념하는(=devoted) ☐ stout a. 뚱뚱한; 단호한, 완강한 ☐ capable a. 유능한, 능력 있는 ☐ tranquil a. 조용한, 고요한; 편안한

데이비스(Davis) 씨는 대단히 헌신적이고 재능 있는 팀원이다.

## 66 ④

☐ ingredient n. (혼합물의) 성분, 재료 ☐ subsequently ad. 그 뒤에, 나중에(=later) ☐ elastic a. 탄력 있는, 신축성 있는 ☐ bulkily ad. 거대하게, 엄청나게 크게 ☐ exceedingly ad. 대단히, 매우 ☐ oppressively ad. 가혹하게, 포악하게, 압제적으로

빵을 만드는 과정에서 그 두 가지 재료가 혼합되면, 작은 기포로 이루어진 말랑말랑한 스펀지 같은 덩어리가 형성된다. 이 혼합물이 그 뒤에 가열되면, 글루텐 성분이 말랑말랑해지지 않고 단단해진다.

## 67 ①

☐ bedrock n. 기반; 근본 원리(=foundation) ☐ impasse n. 막다른 골목; 난국 ☐ viewpoint n. 견해, 견지, 관점 ☐ bias n. 선입관, 편견

정신분석학이 기초를 두고 있는 근본 원리는 무의식에 대한 믿음이다.

## 68 ②

☐ conceal v. 숨기다, 비밀로 하다 ☐ inquisitive a. 호기심이 많은, 알고 싶어 하는(=curious) ☐ apathetic a. 냉담한, 무관심한 ☐ sorrowful a. 슬픈, 비탄에 잠긴 ☐ attractive a. 사람의 마음을 끄는, 매력적인

무대 커튼의 주된 기능은 호기심 어린 눈길들로부터 관객을 숨겨주는 것이다.

## 69 ③

☐ landlord n. 지주, 주인 ☐ enclose v. 에워싸다, 둘러싸다; (농지 등을) 둘러막다 ☐ evict v. 퇴거시키다, 축출하다(=exclude) ☐ peasant n. 농부, 소작농 ☐ cultivation n. 경작, 재배; 양식, 배양 ☐ foster v. 육성[촉진, 조장]하다; 양육하다 ☐ enroll v. 명부에 올리다, 등록하다; 기록하다 ☐ tempt v. 유혹하다

지주들은 농토에 울타리를 치고 양을 기르기 위해 농민들을 쫓아냈다.

## 70 ①

☐ precursor n. 선구자, 선봉(=forerunner) ☐ navigator n. 항해자, 항행자 ☐ recipient n. 수납자, 수령인 ☐ mortician n. 장의사

그레이(Gray)와 번즈(Burns)는 영문학에서 낭만주의 운동의 선구자들이었다.

## 71 ②

☐ migrate v. 이주하다, 이동하다(=move from one place to another) ☐ grow new feathers 새로운 깃털이 자라다 ☐ feel death is near 죽음이 임박했음을 느끼다 ☐ search for food and water 먹이와 물을 찾다

새들이 철따라 이동할 때는, 때때로 편대를 이루어 날아간다.

## 72 ②

☐ undermine v. 약화시키다 ☐ brittle a. 부서지기 쉬운, 깨지기 쉬운 (=fragile) ☐ truce n. 정전, 휴전 ☐ indissoluble a. 서로 떼어놓을 수 없는, 불가분의 ☐ long-term a. 장기적인 ☐ mutual a. 서로의, 상호의, 공동의

이번 사건은 어쩌면 두 나라 사이의 존재하는 취약한 정전 상태를 손상시킬 수도 있다.

## 73 ③

□ constitute v. 구성하다, 조직하다, 만들어내다 □ corporal a. 육체의, 신체의(=physical); 개인적인 □ punishment n. 형벌, 처벌; 징계 □ wide-ranging a. 광범위한, 폭넓은 □ slap n. 손바닥으로 (뺨을) 때림 □ whipping n. 채찍질, 태형, 매질 □ paddle n. (아동 체벌용의 손잡이가 달린) 회초리 □ intangible a. 무형의; 만질 수 없는, 만져서 알 수 없는 □ excessive a. 과도한, 과대한; 지나친 □ rude a. 버릇없는, 무례한

체벌을 구성하는 것은 또한 광범위하다. 손을 가볍게 찰싹 때리는 것에서부터 벨트나 회초리로 온 힘을 다해 때리는 것에 이르기까지 온갖 것들이 있다.

## 74 ①

□ blackmail n. 공갈, 갈취 □ kidnapping n. 유괴, 납치 □ detest v. 혐오하다, 몹시 싫어하다(=abhor) □ adore v. 숭배하다, 동경하다; 열애하다 □ desire v. 몹시 바라다, 원하다 □ disguise v. 변장시키다, 숨기다

공갈과 유괴는 우리 모두가 혐오하는 것들이다.

## 75 ①

□ wage v. (전쟁 따위를) 수행하다, 행하다(=conduct) □ guard v. 경계하다 □ campaign v. 종군하다 □ cease v. 멈추다, 중지하다 □ cement v. 결합하다; (우정 따위를) 굳게 하다

이스라엘의 나프탈리 베네트(Naftali Bennett) 총리는 아랍에미리트와 유대관계를 구축하고 이란을 경계하는 한편, 자국에서는 코로나19와의 전쟁을 수행한다.

## 76 ①

□ primarily ad. 주로 □ highlight v. 강조하다 □ superfluous a. 필요치 않은, 불필요한; 여분의, 과잉의(=redundant) □ decoration n. 장식 □ superior a. (~보다) 위의, 상급의, 상위의; 뛰어난 □ inferior a. 하위의, 낮은; 열등한 □ superlative a. 최상의, 최상급의

그 당시에는 텍스트를 강조하거나 잉여적인 영화장식을 추가하기 위해 주로 색조가 사용되었다.

## 77 ③

□ nocturnal a. 밤의; 야행성의(=night) □ busy a. 바쁜, 교통이 빈번한; 통화 중인 □ gathered a. 눈살을 찌푸린, 주름을 잡은 □ wild a. 야만의, 황량한, 거친

랭던(Langdon)은 소수의 공원 야간 거주자들이 이미 어둠 속에서 나타나고 있었기 때문에 집중하는 데 애를 먹고 있었다.

## 78 ①

□ inimical a. 적의가 있는; 해로운, 불리한(=hostile) □ infrared a. 적외선의 □ pervasive a. 만연하는 □ beneficial a. 유리한, 이로운

이 목표는 제인(Jane)에게 불리한데, 그녀가 지금 프랑스에 있기 때문이다.

## 79 ③

□ pivotal a. 중추적인, 요긴한 □ pundit n. 전문가, 권위자(=expert) □ judge n. 판사 □ fan n. (영화·스포츠 등의) 팬 □ player n. 참가자, 선수

알파고(AlphaGo)의 승리는 나뿐만 아니라 대부분의 바둑 전문가들에게 중요한 순간이었다.

## 80 ①

□ frostbitten a. 동상에 걸린; 상해를 입은 □ lukewarm a. 미적지근한, 미온적인(=tepid) □ boiling a. 끓는; 찌는 듯한, 무더운 □ frigid a. 추운, 극한의, 혹한의 □ steamy a. 증기의; 김이 자욱한

동상에 걸린 손가락과 발가락은 미지근한 물로 치료해야 한다.

## 81 ④

□ condone v. 묵과하다, 용서하다(=overlook) □ substance n. 물질, 구성 요소; (유해한) 약물 □ prevent v. 막다, 방해하다; 예방하다 □ concur v. 일치하다; 동시에 일어나다 □ detain v. 감금하다; 보류하다

중독성 약물을 합법화한다고 해도 어떤 중독성 물질을 사용하도록 눈감아주지는 않을 것이다.

## 82 ①

□ inhibit v. 억제하다, 제지하다(=reduce) □ satisfy v. 만족시키다, 충족시키다 □ sustain v. 살아가게[존재하게] 하다 □ deprive v. 박탈하다, 허용치 않다

파란색은 식욕을 억제하는 것 같다. 만약 체중을 감량할 계획이라면, 냉장고에 파란색 등을 더 달아보도록 해라.

## 83 ①

□ anxious a. 불안한, 걱정스러운 □ beseeching a. 간청하는, 탄원[애원]하는 듯한(=begging) □ fearful a. 걱정하는, 무서운 □ aggressive a. 공격적인 □ depressed a. 침울한

찬(Chan)은 예전에도 내가 많이 보았던 불안하고 애원하는 표정을 그에게 지었을 뿐이다.

## 84 ④

☐ veteran n. 참전 용사, (전쟁에 참전했던) 재향 군인 ☐ supplant v. 대체하다, 대신하다(=supersede) ☐ subsequent a. 다음의, 그 후의 ☐ follow v. 뒤를 잇다; 따르다 ☐ support v. 유지하다, 지지하다 ☐ flank v. 측면에 서다, 옆에 있다, 접하다

2006년 의회에 선출된 3명의 민주당 소속 참전용사들은 그다음 선거에서 7명의 공화당 소속 참전용사들에 의해 대체되었다.

## 85 ③

☐ spur v. 원동력[자극제]이 되다, 자극하다(=provoke) ☐ annihilate v. 전멸시키다; 무효로 하다 ☐ inaugurate v. 취임시키다 ☐ release v. 풀어놓다, 석방하다; (영화를) 개봉하다

이것은 그 병원이 그 지역 가정에 무료 카시트와 자동차 안전 교육을 제공하는 서비스를 확대하게 만드는 자극제가 되었다.

## 86 ①

☐ unprecedented a. 전례가 없는, 유례없는 ☐ predicament n. 곤경, 궁지(=quandary) ☐ post-war a. 전후(戰後)의 ☐ era n. 시대 ☐ discourse n. 대화, 담화; 논의; 강연, 설교 ☐ liberation n. 해방, 해방운동 ☐ proliferation n. 급증, 확산 ☐ fluctuation n. 변동, 오르내림; (pl.) 성쇠 ☐ apex n. 꼭대기, 정점; 절정

전후(戰後) 시대의 유례없는 세계적 곤경으로 인해 해방운동에 관한 새로운 논의가 필요하다.

## 87 ②

☐ take action ~에 대해 조치를 취하다 ☐ curb v. 억제하다, 제한하다 (=restrain) ☐ alarming a. 놀라운, 걱정스러운 ☐ ransom n. 몸값을 지불하다 ☐ promote v. 홍보하다, 증진하다 ☐ exterminate v. 근절하다, 전멸시키다

한 유력 인권단체는 아시아와 아프리카 출신의 사람들에 대한 공격이 크게 늘어나는 추세를 억제할 수 있는 조치를 조속히 취하도록 그리스의 새 정부에 촉구하고 있다.

## 88 ③

☐ mural n. 벽화(=painting) ☐ coral n. 산호 ☐ annals n. 연대기, 연보 ☐ pyramid n. 피라미드

그 벽화의 여러 부분들이 훼손되었는데, 이는 마치 마야인들이 그 벽화가 드러내는 역사를 지워버리기를 원하기라도 했듯이, 마야인들 스스로가 훼손한 것이 분명했다.

## 89 ④

☐ instrumental a. 도구적인; 도움이 되는(=useful) ☐ mechanical a. 기계적인; 자동적인 ☐ susceptible a. 예민한, 민감한; 허용하는 ☐ obsolete a. 한물간, 구식의

심리학자 골드(Gold)는 유용한 도움을 위해 형제자매가 더 서로에게 의지하지 않는 데는 몇 가지 이유가 있다고 믿고 있다.

## 90 ③

☐ conduct n. 행동 ☐ vexing a. 짜증나게 구는, 애태우는; 성가신, 귀찮은(=annoying) ☐ administration n. 행정부, 통치 ☐ serious a. 진지한, 진담의; 중대한 ☐ notorious a. 악명 높은; 소문난, 유명한 ☐ unsolvable a. 해결할 수 없는

아이젠하워(Eisenhower) 대통령의 첫 임기 동안, 조셉 매카시(Joseph R. McCarthy) 상원의원의 행동은 행정부가 직면한 가장 성가신 문제들 중 하나였다.

## 91 ③

☐ unprecedented a. 전례 없는, 미증유의(=exceptional) ☐ road salt 제설용 소금 ☐ abundant a. 풍부한, 다량의 ☐ temporary a. 일시적인, 임시의 ☐ excessive a. 지나친, 과도한

올겨울 폭설로 인해 제설용 소금(염화나트륨)의 전례 없는 수요가 발생했다.

## 92 ①

☐ immaculate a. 결점[약점]이 없는, 완전한; 깨끗한(=impeccable) ☐ correspondence n. 서신, 편지 ☐ constructive a. 건설적인, 적극적인 ☐ streaming a. 나부끼는, 펄럭이는; 흘러드는 ☐ monumental a. 기념비적인; 엄청난, 대단한

그 사이트에서, 여러분은 디지털로 완벽하게 재현해 낸 쇤베르크(Schoenberg)의 서신들을 읽으실 수 있습니다.

## 93 ③

☐ turmoil n. 소란, 혼란; 분투(=commotion) ☐ terror n. 공포, 두려움 ☐ liberation n. 해방; 석방, 방면 ☐ emergency n. 비상사태, 위급

지진으로 인한 발생한 도시의 혼란으로 인해 소방관과 경찰관 모두가 출동했다.

## 94 ①

☐ stalk v. (공격 대상에게) 몰래 접근하다; 쫓아다니며 괴롭히다 ☐ ferocious a. 사나운, 흉포한 ☐ denizen n. 주민, 거주자; 서식 동식물

(=dweller) □ scavenger n. 썩은 고기를 먹는 동물; 청소 동물 □ host n. 주인 (노릇), 숙주 □ conservator n. 보호자, 관리인, 후견인

사파리에서 사냥꾼들은 사자나 호랑이, 그리고 다른 정글의 맹수들에게 몰래 접근했다.

## 95 ①

□ offend v. 성나게 하다, 감정을 상하게 하다 □ brusque a. 퉁명스러운, 무뚝뚝한(=abrupt) □ candid a. 솔직한, 숨김없는; 공평한 □ concise a. 간결한, 간명한 □ gentle a. 온화한, 친절한, 다정한, 온순한

그녀는 그의 무뚝뚝한 답변에 기분이 상했다.

## 96 ③

□ beatific a. 더없이 행복한, 기쁨에 찬(=blissful) □ sardonic a. 냉소적인, 냉소하는 □ perfunctory a. 형식적인, 마지못한 □ convincing a. 설득력 있는

그 그림 속의 천사들은 행복한 웃음을 지녔다.

## 97 ①

□ quagmire n. 수렁, 곤경, 궁지(=predicament) □ be on the horizon 곧 본격화되다, 곧 일어날 것이다 □ plateau n. 고원, 대지 □ perspective n. 전망; 시각 □ frugality n. 검약

그럼에도 불구하고 우리 경제를 수렁에서 끌어내기 위한 특단의 대책은 보이지 않는다.

## 98 ④

□ revoke v. 취소하다, 폐지하다(=repeal) □ execute v. 실행하다, 실시하다 □ postpone v. 연기하다, 미루다 □ demand v. 요구하다

당국은 이 시골 지역의 개발을 허용하기로 한 원래 결정을 취소했다.

## 99 ②

□ defunct a. 죽은; 없어져 버린, 현존하지 않는(=nonexistent) □ fraudulent a. 사기의, 부정한 □ indigent a. 가난한, 곤궁한 □ autonomous a. 자치권이 있는, 자치의

변호사들은 파산한 회사의 장부를 조사하려고 했다.

## 100 ③

□ mutable a. 변하기 쉬운; 변덕스러운(=capricious) □ impudent a. 뻔뻔스러운, 철면피의 □ meticulous a. 지나치게 세심한, 매우 신중한 □ tentative a. 시험적인; 머뭇거리는, 자신 없는

그의 의견은 변덕스러워서 설득력이 있는 사람의 영향을 쉽게 받았다.

| | | | | | | | | | |
|---|---|---|---|---|---|---|---|---|---|
| **01** ① | **02** ③ | **03** ① | **04** ① | **05** ① | **06** ② | **07** ④ | **08** ① | **09** ④ | **10** ① |
| **11** ③ | **12** ④ | **13** ④ | **14** ① | **15** ② | **16** ② | **17** ① | **18** ① | **19** ② | **20** ② |
| **21** ② | **22** ① | **23** ① | **24** ① | **25** ① | **26** ① | **27** ② | **28** ③ | **29** ④ | **30** ③ |
| **31** ① | **32** ③ | **33** ④ | **34** ④ | **35** ③ | **36** ① | **37** ③ | **38** ① | **39** ④ | **40** ③ |
| **41** ① | **42** ④ | **43** ④ | **44** ④ | **45** ① | **46** ① | **47** ② | **48** ① | **49** ③ | **50** ② |
| **51** ② | **52** ③ | **53** ② | **54** ④ | **55** ③ | **56** ② | **57** ③ | **58** ① | **59** ④ | **60** ③ |
| **61** ④ | **62** ④ | **63** ④ | **64** ④ | **65** ④ | **66** ① | **67** ② | **68** ④ | **69** ④ | **70** ① |
| **71** ③ | **72** ① | **73** ④ | **74** ④ | **75** ④ | **76** ③ | **77** ① | **78** ④ | **79** ③ | **80** ③ |
| **81** ② | **82** ④ | **83** ④ | **84** ② | **85** ② | **86** ① | **87** ① | **88** ④ | **89** ③ | **90** ④ |
| **91** ④ | **92** ① | **93** ① | **94** ① | **95** ④ | **96** ① | **97** ④ | **98** ② | **99** ③ | **100** ① |

## 01 ①

☐ rage n. 격노, 분노 ☐ fling v. 던지다, 팽개치다 ☐ virtually ad. 사실상, 거의(=practically) ☐ prosaically ad. 단조롭게, 평범하게 ☐ sporadically ad. 산발적으로 ☐ specifically ad. 명확하게, 특히

그는 화가 나서 손이 닿는 곳에 있는 거의 모든 것을 벽으로 내던졌다.

## 02 ③

☐ mainstream n. 주류; 대세 ☐ staunchly ad. 지조가 굳게; 확고하게 (=steadfastly) ☐ abortion n. 낙태; 임신중절 ☐ conspire v. 공모하다, 음모를 꾸미다 ☐ infanticide n. 유아[영아] 살해 ☐ tactfully ad. 재치 있게, 약삭빠르게 ☐ arbitrarily ad. 독단적으로; 제멋대로 ☐ cogently ad. 설득력 있게; 강제적으로

10년 전만 하더라도, 비록 그들이 낙태에 확고히 반대했다고 하더라도, '주류' 공화당원들은 여성과 의사들이 유아 살해를 공모했다고 주장하는 것을 피했다.

## 03 ①

☐ infinitesimal a. 극소의, 극미의; 무한소의(=minute) ☐ prescribed a. 규정된, 미리 정해진 ☐ limited a. 한정된, 유한의, 좁은 ☐ restricted a. 한정된, 제한된

극소량의 코발트는 생활에 꼭 필요한 금속 가운데 하나이다.

## 04 ①

☐ expire v. 끝나다, 만기가 되다; 소멸하다(=cease) ☐ negotiate v. 교섭하다, 협상하다 ☐ amend v. 고치다, 개선하다 ☐ adopt v. 채용하다, 채택하다

두 나라 간의 무역 협정은 3년이 지나면 만료될 것이다.

## 05 ①

☐ suffrage n. 투표권, 선거권(=voting right) ☐ freedom n. 자유; 자유로운 상태 ☐ monogamy n. 일부일처제 ☐ divorce right 이혼권

여성 참정권 운동은 참정권을 여성에게까지 확대하려는 사회적, 경제적, 정치적 개혁 운동이었다.

## 06 ②

☐ gorge on ~을 실컷 먹다, 가득 채우다(=fill oneself with) ☐ relish n. 맛, 풍미; 흥미, 재미 ☐ chase v. 뒤쫓다, 추격하다 ☐ get along well with ~와 잘 지내다 ☐ hate to ~을 싫어하다, 질색하다

곰은 식성이 까다롭지 않다. 그들은 곤충, 딸기류 열매, 견과류, 작은 포유동물, 햄샌드위치, 그리고 그와 같은 맛이 나는 음식 찌꺼기도 게걸스럽게 먹어 치운다.

## 07 ④

☐ brilliantly ad. 찬란히, 번쩍번쩍하게(=brightly) ☐ delicately ad. 섬세하게 ☐ harmoniously ad. 조화롭게 ☐ sensibly ad. 현저히

화려한 색채의 꽃들이 곤충을 유인한다.

## 08 ①

☐ ameliorate v. 개선하다, 개량하다(=improve) ☐ provoke v. (감정 따위를) 일으키다; 성나게 하다; 유발시키다 ☐ remove v. 옮기다; 제거하다 ☐ spread v. 펼치다, 전개하다; 유포하다

그 지방정부는 계속되는 가뭄으로 인한 힘든 여건을 개선하기 위해 노력하고 있다.

## 09 ④

□ neural a. 신경의 □ reinforce v. 강화하다, 보강하다(=buttress) □ atrophy v. 위축되다 □ encompass v. 에워싸다, 포위하다 □ contemplate v. 심사숙고하다 □ absolve v. 용서하다; 면제하다

가장 많이 사용되는 신경망은 강화되는 반면, 혹 사용된다고 하더라도 거의 사용되지 않는 신경망은 위축되어 시간이 지남에 따라 사라진다.

## 10 ①

□ influx n. 유입; 쇄도(=rush) □ drop n. 방울, 물방울; 소량; 낙하 □ income n. 수입, 소득 □ inflation n. 통화팽창; 자만심

케네디 국제공항에 새로이 건설된 제3터미널은 몰려드는 관광객들에게 편의를 도모하는 데 매우 유용하다.

## 11 ③

□ docile a. 유순한, 고분고분한(=obedient) □ aggressive a. 공격적인 □ intelligent a. 총명한, 똑똑한 □ stubborn a. 완고한, 고집스러운

인간의 주변에서는 유순하지만, (사실) 독일산 셰퍼드는 자신들의 영역을 몹시 사납게 지키는 개다.

## 12 ④

□ anthropologist n. 인류학자 □ inhabit v. 살다, 거주하다, 서식하다(=live in) □ threaten v. 협박하다, 으르다 □ fight over ~에 관하여 싸우다 □ dominate v. 지배하다, 복종시키다

인류학자들은 16세기에 수천 여 명의 이누이트족들이 북부 캐나다에 살았다고 믿는다.

## 13 ④

□ frank a. 솔직한, 숨김없는(=honest) □ false a. 그릇된, 틀린; 거짓의, 위조의 □ patient a. 인내심이 강한; 끈기 있는 □ loyal a. 충성스러운; 성실한, 충실한

나는 당신이 내게 무척 솔직하게 대했다고 생각한다.

## 14 ①

□ cordially ad. 진심으로, 정성껏(=in a friendly manner) □ in a hostile manner 적대적인 태도로 □ in an indifferent manner 무관심한 태도로 □ in a loyal manner 충성스러운 태도로

제인(Jane)의 아버지는 화내는 대신 마크(Mark)를 진심으로 환영했고, 그를 편안하게 해주었다.

## 15 ②

□ restive a. 침착성이 없는, 들떠 있는(=restless) □ remorseful a. 후회하는, 양심의 가책을 받는 □ reminiscent a. 연상시키는, 회상하게 하는; 추억의 □ regressive a. 후퇴하는, 회귀하는, 퇴보하는

우리는 저렇게 다루기 힘든 동물을 잡기 위해 더 효율적인 계획을 세웠어야 했는데 그러지 못했다.

## 16 ②

□ enchant v. 매혹하다; 호리다(=attract) □ nicety n. 정확, 정밀; 미세한 차이 □ embarrass v. 어리둥절하게 하다, 난처하게 하다 □ imprison v. 교도소에 넣다, 수감하다, 구속하다 □ impute v. (죄 등을) ~에게 돌리다, 씌우다, 전가하다

이 사건에서 그를 매료시킨 것은, 사기로 시작해서 살인으로 끝난 그 수법의 정밀함이었다.

## 17 ①

□ acrimonious a. 통렬한, 신랄한; 험악한(=bitter) □ discouraging a. 낙담시키는; 실망적인; 비관적인 □ amicable a. 우호적인, 친화적인, 평화적인 □ enlightening a. 계몽적인, 밝혀주는, 깨우치는

새로 개정된 노동법을 둘러싸고 두 당 사이에 신랄한 토론이 있었다.

## 18 ①

□ override v. 짓밟다, 유린하다; 무시하다(=reject) □ laud v. 칭송하다, 찬미하다 □ scold v. 꾸짖다, 잔소리하다 □ praise v. 칭찬하다

내가 직장에서 제안을 할 때마다 사장은 내 말을 무시한다.

## 19 ②

□ arrange v. 정하다; 조정하다 □ coincide v. 동시에 일어나다; 부합하다, 일치하다(=synchronize) □ adjourn v. 연기하다; 휴회하다 □ succeed v. 성공하다; 뒤를 잇다 □ interrupt v. 방해하다, 중단하다

그의 생일 파티는 우리의 여행과 겹치게 정해졌다.

## 20 ②

□ revere v. 존경하다; 숭배하다, 경외하다(=respect) □ implicate v. 관련시키다, 휩쓸려들게 하다, 함축하다 □ condescend v. 겸손하게 굴다; 양보하다, 동의하다 □ agitate v. 동요시키다, 선동하다

이 사회에는 존경할 만한 이들이 많지 않다.


## 21 ②

☐ battle royal 대혼전, 난투극  ☐ staple n. 주요 산물, 주성분, 주[핵심] 요소  ☐ relegate v. 지위를 떨어뜨리다; (어떤 종류, 등급에) 속하게 하다, 분류하다  ☐ clandestine a. 비밀의, 은밀한(=surreptitious)  ☐ exasperating a. 화가 나게 하는, 분통 터지는  ☐ hyperbolic a. 과장법의; 과장된  ☐ licentious a. 방탕한; 음탕한

"대혼전"이라 불리는 형태의 싸움은 오늘날 프로레슬링에서 필수적인 요소이지만, 1950년대에는 밀실에서 이뤄지는 보다 은밀한 역할을 맡고 있었다.


## 22 ①

☐ farce n. 소극(笑劇), 익살극  ☐ provoke v. 불러일으키다; 성나게 하다; 유발시키다, 야기하다(=cause)  ☐ portray v. 묘사하다, 표현하다  ☐ appreciate v. 평가하다; 진가를 인정하다  ☐ reward v. 보답하다, 보상하다  ☐ ridicule v. 비웃다, 조롱하다, 놀리다

주된 목적이 웃음을 자아내는 것인 연극의 한 형태인 소극(笑劇)은 인생을 사실적으로 묘사하려고 하지는 않는다.


## 23 ①

☐ investment n. 투자, 투자대상  ☐ industrious a. 근면한, 부지런한(=diligent)  ☐ liable a. 법적 책임이 있는; ~하기 쉬운  ☐ vicissitude n. 변화, 변천  ☐ occasional a. 때때로의  ☐ various a. 여러 가지의, 다양한  ☐ endless a. 끝없는, 무한한

개인적으로 부지런히 주의를 기울여야 할 필요도 없고 정치 변화에 쉽게 영향받지도 않는 다른 투자대상을 찾는 데는 최근까지 어려움이 많았다.


## 24 ①

☐ dissident a. 의견을 달리하는; 반체제의(=opposing)  ☐ topple v. 끌어 내리다, 몰락시키다  ☐ loyal a. 충성스러운  ☐ fashionable a. 유행하는; 사교계의  ☐ notorious a. 유명한, 악명 높은

소련의 후원을 받은 공산주의를 전복시킨 1989년 무혈의 벨벳 혁명을 통해 나라를 이끌었던 반체제 극작가를 위한 금요일의 국가적인 행사를 위해 외국의 지도자들이 체코 공화국으로 몰려들 것으로 예상된다.


## 25 ①

☐ preside v. 의장이 되다, 사회하다(=direct)  ☐ goof up 실수를 하다  ☐ mess up 망치다  ☐ confuse v. 혼동하다, 헛갈리게 하다

의장이 부재인 상태에서, 부의장이 회의를 주재하도록 요청받았다.


## 26 ①

☐ hospitable a. 대접이 좋은; 쾌히 받아들이는(=amenable)  ☐ clinical a. 진료소의, 임상의  ☐ antagonistic a. 적대의, 반대하는, 상반되는  ☐ parsimonious a. 인색한, 지나치게 알뜰한

공정한 사회를 이룩하기 위해서 우리는 진정한 삶의 의미에 대해서 함께 논의하고 불가피하게 생기게 되는 의견 충돌을 쾌히 받아들일 수 있는 공공의 문화를 만들어야만 한다.


## 27 ②

☐ delineate v. 윤곽을 그리다, 묘사하다(=portray)  ☐ differentiate v. 구별 짓다, 식별하다, 차별하다  ☐ disregard v. 무시하다, 경시하다, 소홀히 하다  ☐ embellish v. 아름답게 하다, 미화하다

전 인류가 하나의 '인종'이라고 가정한다면, 하얗거나 검은 피부색이라든가, 넓거나 좁은 코와 같은 신체적인 차이점들을 어떤 말로 표현할 수 있을까?


## 28 ③

☐ escalate v. 상승하다, 강화되다(=intensify)  ☐ stagnate v. 침체되다, 부진해지다  ☐ resume v. 재개하다, 다시 시작하다  ☐ dwindle v. (점점) 줄어들다

국무총리와 야당 대표는 새로운 법안에 대한 그들의 논쟁이 추악하고 파괴적인 수준으로 치닫도록 내버려 두었다.


## 29 ④

☐ intricate a. 얽힌, 복잡한; 난해한(=complicated)  ☐ vague a. 막연한, 모호한, 애매한  ☐ unusual a. 이상한, 보통이 아닌; 유별난  ☐ routine a. 일상의; 판에 박힌

복잡한 사용법은 이해하기 어려웠다.


## 30 ③

☐ vie v. 다투다, 경쟁하다(=compete)  ☐ rally v. 결집[단결]하다, 규합하다  ☐ wait v. 기다리다, 대기하다  ☐ search v. 찾다, 살펴보다

1880년대, 뉴욕과 시카고 구간에 운영되고 있던 다섯 개의 철도가 승객과 화물 운송을 놓고 경쟁하였고, 두 개의 철도가 더 건설 중에 있었다.


## 31 ①

☐ flamboyance n. 화려[현란]함  ☐ sublimity n. 웅장, 고상, 숭고  ☐ staggering a. 어마어마한, 놀라운(=astonishing)  ☐ athleticism n. (전문가로서의) 운동 경기; 운동의 기량  ☐ masculine a. 남자 같은, 사내다운  ☐ dazzling a. 눈부신  ☐ intense a. 극심한, 강렬한

화려함에서 고상함까지, 놀라운 운동신경에서 은반 위의 예술성까지, 피겨 스케이팅은 진정으로 그 모든 것을 갖추고 있다.

## 32 ③

☐ stereotype n. 고정 관념 ☐ prejudice n. 편견, 선입관(=bias) ☐ unanimity n. 동의, 만장일치 ☐ friction n. 마찰, 불화 ☐ hierarchy n. 계급, 계층

인종에 대한 고정 관념은 모든 문화에 존재하며 때때로 편견으로 이어질 수 있다.

## 33 ④

☐ conciliatory a. 달래는 (듯한), 회유적인, 유화적인(=peacemaking) ☐ confronting a. 직면하는, 마주 대하는 ☐ indistinct a. (형체, 소리 따위가) 불분명한, 희미한 ☐ definite a. (윤곽, 한계가) 뚜렷한

그의 인내와 유화적인 기질조차도 그 좌익단체를 한데 뭉치도록 만들지 못했다.

## 34 ④

☐ accompaniment n. (노래나 다른 악기를 지원하는) 반주(伴奏) ☐ tepid a. 미지근한; 열의 없는(=lukewarm) ☐ induce v. 유도하다; 유발하다 ☐ drowsy a. 나른하게 만드는; 졸리는 ☐ reverie n. 몽상 ☐ hot a. 더운, 고온의 ☐ luxurious a. 아주 편안한, 호화로운 ☐ stylish a. 유행을 따른; 멋진, 우아한

음악을 사용하는 또 다른 방법은 나른한 몽상을 불러일으키는 미지근한 목욕처럼, 배경 반주로 활용하는 것이다.

## 35 ③

☐ incidence n. 범위, 발생(률), 빈도(=occurrence) ☐ treatment n. 취급, 대우; 치료(법) ☐ result n. 결과, 결말, 성과 ☐ expansion n. 팽창, 신장; 확장, 확대

충치 발생이 줄어드는 데서 볼 수 있듯이, 한국인들은 이제 더 나은 치아 건강을 누리고 있다.

## 36 ①

☐ pulse n. 맥박, 고동 ☐ detect v. 발견하다; 탐지하다(=perceive) ☐ monitor v. (기기(機器)로) 감시하다, 모니터하다 ☐ mend v. 수선하다, 고치다; 개선하다 ☐ elude v. 피하다, 벗어나다 ☐ suspend v. 매달다; 보류하다, 중지하다

맥박이 탐지될 수 있는 주요 위치들을 아는 것은 도움이 되는데, 왜냐하면 맥박을 체크하는 것은 임상적으로 중요하기 때문이다.

## 37 ①

☐ burgeoning a. 급증하는, 급성장하는(=developing) ☐ confine v. 제한하다 ☐ weaken v. 약해지다 ☐ decline v. 기울다, 쇠하다

급증하는 시장 자유와 더불어 교육적, 상업적인 압박의 증가가 발생한다.

## 38 ①

☐ implication n. 함축, 내포, 암시(=suggestion) ☐ split up 분열시키다, 분할하다 ☐ supply n. 공급, 지급 ☐ indictment n. 고발, 기소

그녀가 한 말에 담긴 암시는 그들이 갈라선다는 것이었다.

## 39 ④

☐ dawn n. 새벽, 여명; (일의) 시초, 조짐 ☐ bigwig n. 중요 인물, 거물 ☐ opine v. 의견을 밝히다(=observe) ☐ jeer v. 조롱하다, 비웃다 ☐ praise v. 칭찬하다 ☐ brood v. 알을 품다; 곰곰이 생각하다

이들 영화와 몇 편의 다른 영화의 성공으로 인해, 『뉴욕 타임스(New York Times)』는 고액 예산 영화에서의 새로운 독창성 시대의 시작을 환영하는 특집기사를 썼다. 할리우드 거물들은 앞으로는 '독창성'과 '품질'이 중요하다는 의견을 밝혔다.

## 40 ③

☐ conceal v. 숨기다, 감추다; 비밀로 하다(=dissemble) ☐ disaster n. 천재; 재난; 큰 실패 ☐ grumble v. 투덜거리다, 불평하다 ☐ despise v. 경멸하다, 멸시하다, 혐오하다 ☐ applaud v. 박수치다, 갈채를 보내다

정부는 공공 의료보험 제도가 완전한 실패였다는 사실을 숨겼다.

## 41 ①

☐ antagonistic a. 반대의, 상반되는, 대립하는, 적대하는(=opposed) ☐ ignorant a. 무지한, 무식한 ☐ charitable a. 자비로운; 관대한; 자선의 ☐ curious a. 호기심 있는, 알고 싶어 하는

그녀는 교회 신도들에게 다소 적대적이다.

## 42 ④

☐ stingy a. 인색한(=frugal) ☐ resent v. 분개하다; 원망하다 ☐ upright a. 강직한 ☐ discreet a. 분별 있는, 생각이 깊은; 신중한 ☐ strict a. 엄격한, 철저한

나의 아버지는 우리에게 쓰는 동전 한 푼까지도 원망하는 인색한 노인이었다.

## 43 ④

☐ absolve v. 용서하다; 면책하다(=forgive) ☐ villain n. 악인, 악한, 범인 ☐ languish v. (강요를 받아 어디에서) 머물다; (오랫동안 불쾌한 일을) 겪다 ☐ torture v. 고문하다, 괴롭히다 ☐ encourage v. 격려[고무]하다, 용기를 북돋우다 ☐ maintain v. 지속하다, 유지하다

왕은 역사적인 결단의 일환으로, 탑에서 비참하게 지내고 있던 모든 죄수들을 사면하기로 결정했다.

## 44 ④

☐ glowing a. 백열[작열]하는; 열렬한; 격찬하는 ☐ pedestrian a. 평범한(=uninteresting) ☐ exaggerated a. 과장된, 부풀린 ☐ officious a. 참견하는, 거들먹거리는 ☐ embellished a. 재미있는

이 영화는 영화 평론가들로부터 호평을 받았지만, 내가 보기에는 평범했다.

## 45 ①

☐ biography n. 전기(傳記) ☐ detrimental a. 유해한, 손해가 되는(=harmful) ☐ influential a. 영향을 미치는; 유력한 ☐ ineffective a. 효과 없는, 쓸모없는 ☐ advantageous a. 유리한, 형편이 좋은

친한 친구가 쓴 그의 전기는 그의 명성에 해가 되었다.

## 46 ①

☐ intractable a. 말을 듣지 않는, 고집 센; 다루기 힘든(=unruly) ☐ tragic a. 비극의; 비참한, 비장한 ☐ terrible a. 무서운, 가공할, 소름끼치는 ☐ scandalous a. 소문이 나쁜; 명예롭지 못한, 수치스러운

클린턴(Clinton)은 닉슨(Nixon)만큼이나 다루기 힘든 법적인 악몽을 맞이할 수도 있다.

## 47 ②

☐ freshly ad. 갓[막] ~한 ☐ shed v. (피, 눈물 등을) 흘리다; 발산하다 ☐ perspiration n. 발한; 땀(=sweat) ☐ whisper n. 속삭임 ☐ inspiration n. 영감, 고무, 격려 ☐ respiration n. 호흡

방금 흘린 땀 냄새가 작은 방을 채웠다.

## 48 ①

☐ feud n. 적의, 불화 ☐ in earnest 본격적으로 ☐ requite v. 보답하다; 앙갚음하다, 보복하다(=avenge) ☐ slaying n. 학살, 살인, 살해 ☐ compensate v. ~에게 보상하다, 변상하다 ☐ reimburse v. (빚 따위를) 갚다; 상환하다 ☐ accentuate v. 강조하다, 두드러지게 하다

악명 높은 햇필드-멕코이(Hatfield-McCoy) 분쟁은 햇필드 집안에서 멕코이 가의 세 형제를 처형함으로써 엘리슨 햇필드(Ellison Hatfield)의 학살에 보복했던 1882년 본격적으로 시작되었다.

## 49 ③

☐ esoteric a. 소수만 이해하는, 난해한(=recondite) ☐ querulous a. 불평하는, 짜증내는 ☐ acerbic a. 가혹한, 신랄한 ☐ inverse a. 역(逆)의, 반대의

『뉴요커(New Yorker)』지에 실린 단편소설들에는 세상에 알려지지 않은 사람들과 사건들에 대한 난해한 암시가 종종 포함되어 있다.

## 50 ②

☐ knack n. 기교, 재주, (경험으로 익힌) 요령(=skill) ☐ keen a. 간절히 ~하고 싶은, ~을 열망하는 ☐ conversation n. 담화, 대화 ☐ communication n. 의사소통, 연락 ☐ reputation n. 평판, 명성

그들은 거리에서 사람들이 하는 이야기에 편안해하지 못했다. 물론 아무도 그들에게 그 요령을 가르쳐주지 않았고, 그들도 배우려는 열의가 없었다.

## 51 ②

☐ renegade n. 탈당자, 배신자; 배교자(=apostate) ☐ supporter n. 지지자, 후원자, 옹호자 ☐ descendant n. 자손, 후예 ☐ sycophant n. 아첨꾼, 추종자, 알랑쇠 ☐ patron n. 보호자, 후원자, 지지자; 단골손님, 고객

미국 독립전쟁을 이끌었던 위대한 사람들이 영국 왕을 지지하는 사람들에 의해 배반자로 여겨진 것은 이해하기 어려운 일이다.

## 52 ③

☐ presumptuous a. 염치없는, 뻔뻔스러운, 주제넘은(=impertinent) ☐ creditable a. 명예가 되는; 칭찬할 만한, 평판이 좋은 ☐ foolish a. 바보 같은, 어리석은 ☐ aggressive a. 침략적인, 공세의; 진취적인

그가 그녀에게 결혼하자고 하는 것은 그의 입장에서는 다소 염치없는 짓이었다.

## 53 ②

☐ pesticide n. 살충제, 농약 ☐ wither v. 시들다, 말라죽다(=dry up) ☐ grow v. 성장하다, 생장하다; 증대하다 ☐ condense v. 응축하다; 요약하다 ☐ float v. 뜨다, 떠오르다; 떠돌다

농부들은 농작물을 보호하기 위해 농약을 쓰지만, 일부 농약은 너무 많은 생물체를 죽일 수 있어서 자연 그 자체가 시들어 죽을 수 있다.

## 54     ②

☐ pullout n. 철퇴, 철수; (자금의) 회수 ☐ embolden v. 대담하게 하다 ☐ vent v. (감정 등을) 드러내다 ☐ grievance n. 불만, 불평거리 (=complaint) ☐ remorse n. 후회, 양심의 가책 ☐ misfortune n. 불운, 불행; 불행한 일 ☐ condolence n. 조의, 애도의 말

한때 경제에 집중하기를 원했던 중국의 정치 지도자들은 놀라운 정치적 도전에 직면해 있다. 구글이 철수할 수도 있는데, 그렇게 되면 중국 국민들은 분노하고, 다른 회사들도 대담해져 불평을 쏟아낼 수도 있는 것이다.

## 55     ③

☐ foster v. 기르다, 양육하다(=nurture); 조장하다 ☐ self-direction n. 스스로에 의한 방향 결정 ☐ assert oneself 자기의 권리를 주장하다 ☐ avert v. 비키다; 피하다, 막다 ☐ incriminate v. ~에게 죄를 씌우다; 고발하다, 고소하다 ☐ dispatch v. 급송하다, 급파하다; 신속히 처리하다

여자아이는 부모와 어느 정도 마찰이 있는 경우 스스로 방향을 정하는 능력과 독립심을 키울 수가 있는데, 이는 어쩌면 그러한 마찰이 아이로 하여금 그 환경에서 자신의 주장을 내세우게 만들어주기 때문일 것이다.

## 56     ②

☐ adolescent n. 청년, 젊은이 ☐ escape v. 피하다, 모면하다 ☐ barrage n. 연발, 집중 공세(=blast) ☐ exaggeration n. 과장, 과장 표현 ☐ gust n. 세찬바람, 돌풍 ☐ infiltration n. 침입, 침투

청소년들은 텔레비전과 라디오, 잡지와 신문에 끊임없이 나오는 광고의 집중 공세를 피할 수 없다.

## 57     ③

☐ abolish v. 폐지하다; 파괴하다 ☐ death sentence 사형 선고 ☐ rule v. (법정 등이) 규정하다, 판결하다 ☐ arbitrary a. 임의의, 자의적인 ☐ capricious a. 변덕스러운, (마음이) 변하기 쉬운(=changeable) ☐ incompatible a. 양립하지 않는, 모순된 ☐ invariable a. 불변의, 변화 없는; 일정한 ☐ dependable a. 의존할 수 있는, 신뢰할 수 있는

1972년 미 대법원이 사형제도가 임의적이고 변칙적이라고 판결하면서 미국은 사형제도를 폐지했다.

## 58     ①

☐ execute v. 실행하다, 수행하다; 집행하다(=carry out) ☐ carry on 경영하다, 관리하다; 계속하다, 속행하다 ☐ put on 입다, 쓰다 ☐ put out 내쫓다, 해고하다; (불을) 끄다

대통령의 의무는 최선을 다해 그 법들을 실행하는 것이다.

## 59     ④

☐ mulish a. 노새 같은; 고집이 센(=obstinate) ☐ concession n. 양보; 용인 ☐ malicious a. 악의 있는, 심술궂은 ☐ impeccable a. 결점 없는, 죄 없는 ☐ solicitous a. 걱정하는, 염려하는; 열심인

그들의 토론에서 그 두 명의 상원의원은 똑같이 고집불통이었는데, 둘 다 최소한의 양보의 기미도 없었다.

## 60     ③

☐ service member 군 요원, 군인 ☐ toddler n. 걸음마 배우는 아이 ☐ deployment n. 전개, 배치(=arrangement) ☐ institution n. 제도; 기관 ☐ trench n. 참호; (깊은) 도랑 ☐ proposition n. 제안, 제의

20년 전, 이 군인들 중 다수는 아장아장 걷는 아기에 불과했다. 일부는 태어나지도 않았다. 그러나 공격으로 인해 그들은 배치 명령을 받기 전에 지도상에서 찾을 수 있는 사람이 거의 없었을 나라로 가게 되었다.

## 61     ④

☐ felicitous a. (행동, 표현이) 적절한, 들어맞는(=apt) ☐ satire n. 풍자 ☐ mainstream n. 주류; 대세 ☐ comedic a. 희극적인; 우스꽝스러운 ☐ clumsy a. 서투른; 꼴사나운 ☐ fallacious a. 거짓의, 논리적으로 옳지 않은

그 영화는 현재 주류 영화에서 제시하는 내용에 대한 적절한 풍자로 간주할 수 있다.

## 62     ④

☐ abrogate v. 폐지하다, 철폐하다(=repeal) ☐ foster v. 촉진하다, 조장하다 ☐ resolve v. 해결하다; 결의하다 ☐ pass v. (의안을) 가결하다, 승인하다 ☐ observe v. 지키다, 준수하다

대통령의 임무는 국민들 사이에서 불평등을 조장하는 어떠한 법도 폐지하는 것이다.

## 63     ④

☐ claim n. 요구, 청구; 주장 ☐ incontestable a. 논의의 여지가 없는, 명백한 ☐ externalist a. 형식주의자의, 외재론자의 ☐ conclusion n. 결론 ☐ ineluctable a. 면할 길 없는, 불가피한(=inescapable) ☐ externalism n. 형식주의; 현상론 ☐ flamboyant a. 현란한, 화려한; 대담한 ☐ reductionistic a. 환원주의의 ☐ indulgent a. 멋대로 하게 하는; 관대한

일부 철학자들은 전통적인 주장을 너무나도 명백한 것으로 간주하고 형식주의적 결론은 너무나도 불가피한 것으로 간주해서, 그 결과 그들은 형식주의를 배척하도록 내몰리고 있다.

## 64 ④

☐ streamline v. 유선형으로 하다; 간소화[능률화]하다(=simplify) ☐ revolutionize v. 혁명을 일으키다; 혁명 사상을 고취하다 ☐ bypass v. 우회하다; 회피하다; 무시하다 ☐ invent v. 발명하다; 날조하다

1914년 존 R. 브레이(John R. Bray)는 만화를 제작하는 데 일관된 작업 기술을 이용함으로써 만화영화 제작 과정을 단순화했다.

## 65 ④

☐ frugal a. 절약하는, 검소한(=thrifty) ☐ ingenuous a. 순진한, 천진한 ☐ creative a. 창조적인, 창의적인 ☐ predictable a. 예측[예견]할 수 있는

퀼트는 전통적으로 낡은 옷을 이용하는 검소한 방법이었다.

## 66 ①

☐ drop a hint 힌트를 주다, 암시를 주다 ☐ accomplice n. 공범자, 연루자; 협력자(=collaborator) ☐ decoy n. 유인하는 사람, 바람잡이 ☐ interrogator n. 질문자, 심문자 ☐ bait n. 미끼; 유혹(물)

그는 또한 '즐기면서 게임을 하는 것'에 대해 더 많은 암시를 주었고, 보웬(Bowen)은 그것이 자기를 아이들을 찾아다니는 일의 협력자로 고용하는 것을 의미하는 것으로 간주했다.

## 67 ②

☐ mortifying a. 분한, 원통한; 굴욕적인(=humiliating) ☐ be obliged to 어쩔 수 없이 ~하다 ☐ surprising a. 놀라운, 의외의; 불시의 ☐ disturbing a. 교란시키는, 불안하게 하는 ☐ complacent a. 자기만족의, 마음에 흡족한

내가 10프랑이 부족해서 어쩔 수 없이 손님에게 빌려야 한다면 굴욕적일 것이다.

## 68 ②

☐ launch v. (상품을) 출시[출간]하다 ☐ disseminate v. 퍼뜨리다, 전파하다(=diffuse) ☐ recant v. 취소하다; 철회하다 ☐ deteriorate v. 나쁘게 하다; 열등하게 하다, (가치를) 저하시키다 ☐ intercept v. 가로막다

그는 훨씬 더 많은 청중에게 버밍엄 접근법을 전파하는 일련의 교과서와 안내서를 출간했다.

## 69 ②

☐ stigma n. 치욕, 오점, 불명예(=disgrace) ☐ purpose n. 목적; 용도; 요점 ☐ illness n. 병, 불쾌; 발병 ☐ honor n. 명예, 영예; 경의

네가 지금 하고 있는 일에는 치욕이 따르지는 않는다.

## 70 ③

☐ impetus n. 힘, 추진력(=stimulus) ☐ esteem n. 존중, 존경 ☐ favorite n. 마음에 드는 것, 좋아하는 것 ☐ destination n. 목적지

환경보호주의의 추진력은 상당 부분 독일인 빌헬름 하인리히 릴(Wihelm Heinrich Riehl)로부터 온 것이었는데, 그는 19세기 중엽에 유럽 보수주의의 토대를 마련한 인물이었다.

## 71 ③

☐ arrange v. 정돈하다, 배열하다; 준비하다, 정하다(=set up) ☐ set forth 출발하다; 진술하다; 발표하다 ☐ set out 출발하다; 말하다, 제시하다 ☐ set to 착수하다, 본격적으로 시작하다

다음 달 회의 계획을 짜볼까요?

## 72 ①

☐ vilify v. 비방하다, 헐뜯다; 욕하다(=accuse) ☐ hound v. 끈덕지게 괴롭히다 ☐ force somebody into exile 유배를 보내다 ☐ arrest v. 체포하다; 막다 ☐ chase v. 쫓다, 추적하다; 추격하다 ☐ interrogate v. 질문하다; 심문하다

그는 정부기관으로부터 비난받고, 박해받다가 추방당했다.

## 73 ④

☐ remote a. 먼, 멀리 떨어진, 외딴(=distant) ☐ small a. 작은, 소형의, 비좁은; 적은; 하찮은 ☐ beautiful a. 아름다운, 고운, 예쁜 ☐ strange a. 이상한, 야릇한, 기묘한; 낯선

그는 외딴 마을에서 산다.

## 74 ④

☐ tout v. 선전[권장]하다, 격찬하다(=trumpet) ☐ define v. 정의하다, 규정하다 ☐ criticize v. 비판하다 ☐ mystify v. 어리둥절하게 하다, 미혹하다

1920년대 미국의 소비문화는 젊음을 사람이 실제로 구입할 수 있는 상품으로 선전했다.

## 75 ④

☐ confer v. 수여하다, 주다(=accord) ☐ tax v. 과세하다; 무거운 짐을 지우다 ☐ consult v. ~의 의견을 듣다, ~의 충고를 구하다 ☐ revoke v. 철회하다, 무효로 하다

죽은 자의 시신을 처리하는 것은 살아 있는 자들에게 힘든 일의 마침을 가져오고 고인에게 존경심을 표하는 것이다.

## 76 ③

☐ cater to ~에게 만족을 주다, ~에 영합하다(=indulge) ☐ blame v. 비난하다 ☐ challenge v. 이의를 제기하다, 도전하다 ☐ preach v. 설교하다, 전도하다

"스타워즈: 라스트 제다이"의 감독 라이언 존슨(Rian Johnson)은 그저 팬들을 즐겁게 만족시키려고만 하는 것은 "잘못"이라고 말했다.

## 77 ①

☐ retain v. 유지하다, 보유하다, 간직하다(=maintain) ☐ sacrifice v. 바치다, 희생하다 ☐ dispense with ~없이 지내다; ~을 덜다, 필요 없게 하다 ☐ distract v. 산만하게 하다; 혼란시키다; 즐겁게 하다

텔레비전은 능동적이기보다 오히려 수동적인 듣기를 조장한다. 당신이 텔레비전을 시청할 때 당신은 당신에게 어떤 것도 간직하도록 요구하지 않는 방식으로 듣는다.

## 78 ①

☐ supervise v. 관리하다, 감독하다, 지휘하다(=oversee) ☐ estimate v. 어림잡다, 견적하다, 산정하다 ☐ undertake v. 떠맡다, 의무를 지다, 약속하다 ☐ aid v. 원조하다, 돕다, 거들다

관리자가 그의 직원들의 업무를 감독하는 것은 중요하다.

## 79 ③

☐ dour a. 기분이 언짢은, 시무룩한(=sullen) ☐ strong a. 힘센, 튼튼한; 강경한, 강력한 ☐ faithful a. 충실한, 성실한; 헌신적인 ☐ calm a. 고요한, 잔잔한; 평온한

영향력 있는 연설자인 짐(Jim)은 실제로 알려진 것보다는 성미가 덜 까다롭다.

## 80 ③

☐ gullible a. 남을 잘 믿는, 잘 속아 넘어가는(=naive) ☐ debt n. 빚, 부채, 채무 ☐ distress n. 고통, 곤경 ☐ unconventional a. 색다른, 독특한 ☐ starve v. 굶주리다 ☐ stabilize v. 안정시키다 ☐ entire a. 전체의, 완전한

그들은 잘 속아 넘어가는 젊은이들을 붙잡아 매우 일찍이 부채에 시달리게 하고 회사들은 그들이 돈을 갚지 못하면 독특한 방법을 사용하여 그들을 망신시킨다.

## 81 ②

☐ enormously ad. 엄청나게, 대단히(=immensely) ☐ conveniently ad. 편리하게, 알맞게 ☐ politely ad. 공손하게 ☐ slightly ad. 약간

우리의 사회적 행동에서 언어가 굉장히 중요한 역할을 한다는 것을 깨닫기란 어렵다.

## 82 ④

☐ Secretary of State <미국> 국무장관 ☐ despicable a. 야비한, 비열한(=abominable) ☐ bloodshed n. 유혈참사; 살육 ☐ disparate a. 다른, 공통점이 없는 ☐ complacent a. 만족한, 자기만족의; 사근사근한 ☐ ingenious a. 교묘한, 독창적인, 정교한; 영리한

미(美) 국무장관 힐러리 클린턴(Hillary Clinton)은 시리아의 유혈사태를 막기 위한 UN 제재에 반대한 것을 두고 러시아와 중국을 비열하다고 했다.

## 83 ④

☐ naïveté n. 소박; 단순; 순진한 말[행위](=naivety) ☐ trample on ~을 짓밟다, 무시하다, 유린하다(=crush) ☐ weigh v. 무게를 달다; 숙고하다 ☐ vindicate v. 정당성을 입증하다; 변호하다 ☐ advocate v. 옹호하다, 지지하다

대학은 당신의 순진함이 비워지고, 격렬한 토론을 하며, 마음 깊은 곳에 자리했던 당신의 확신들이 짓밟혀 뭉개지는 소리를 들을 수 있는 곳이다.

## 84 ②

☐ criticize v. 비평하다, 비판하다; 비난하다 ☐ focus on ~에 초점을 맞추다 ☐ morbid a. 병적인, 불건전한; 음울한; 무서운, 무시무시한(=dismal) ☐ abstruse a. 난해한, 심오한 ☐ invariable a. 불변의; 일정한 ☐ indecent a. 버릇없는, 점잖지 못한; 음란한

현대의 고스 문화 운동은 그 추종자들이 음울한 주제에 초점을 맞추기 때문에 종종 비난을 받는다.

## 85 ②

☐ insatiable a. 만족할 줄 모르는, 그칠 줄 모르는(=bottomless) ☐ suitable a. 적합한, 알맞은 ☐ abrupt a. 돌연한, 갑작스러운 ☐ absurd a. 우스꽝스러운, 불합리한

이 여성은 시각적인 세계에 대한 만족을 모르는(끝없는) 욕구와 그것을 영상으로 포착해 낼 수 있는 재능을 가진 여성이었다.

## 86 ①

☐ harsh a. 거친; 난폭한; 가혹한(=cruel) ☐ humid a. 습기 있는, 눅눅한 ☐ spacious a. 넓은; 광활한; 광범위한 ☐ poisonous a. 유독한, 유해한

작년 10월 이후로 323명의 사람들이 미국으로 넘어가려다가 애리조나의 험하고 고립된 사막에서 종종 목숨을 잃었다.

## 87 ①

☐ ostracize v. 추방하다; 배척하다(=banish) ☐ nurture v. 양육하다, 기르다 ☐ decapitate v. 목을 베다, 참수하다 ☐ appraise v. 평가하다; 감정하다

그 신문 칼럼니스트가 바바리아 도시의 과거 나치시절에 관하여 글을 쓰기 시작했을 때 그 도시의 많은 시민들이 그녀를 추방했다.

## 88 ④

☐ fledgling a. 신출내기인, 초보인(=inexperienced) ☐ prestigious a. 명성 있는, 일류의, 유명한 ☐ unknown a. 알려지지 않은, 미지의, 무명의 ☐ experimental a. 실험적인; 경험에 의한

이러한 신출내기 시인들에게 그들의 작품을 발표할 기회를 제공하는 것이 필요하긴 하지만 그들의 모든 작품을 우리가 칭찬해야 할 필요는 없다.

## 89 ③

☐ seek v. 추구하다 ☐ ye pron. (옛글투 또는 방언) 그대들, 너희들 (=you) ☐ admonish v. 훈계하다; 충고하다(=advise) ☐ appeal v. 호소하다 ☐ transform v. 변형시키다 ☐ rebuke v. 질책하다, 꾸짖다

베이컨(Bacon)은 "정신의 좋은 것들을 먼저 구하라"라고 권고한다.

## 90 ②

☐ clout n. 힘, 영향력(=influence) ☐ investment n. 투자, 출자 ☐ burden n. 부담; 걱정 ☐ ambition n. 대망, 야심, 야망

메리(Mary)는 아버지가 사장이기 때문에 그 회사에서 영향력이 엄청나다.

## 91 ④

☐ indulge oneself in ~에 빠지다, 탐닉하다 ☐ extravagant a. 낭비하는, 사치스러운; 기발한, 엄청난(=profuse) ☐ peculiar a. 기묘한, 이상한, 별난, 색다른 ☐ probable a. 있음직한, 충분히 가능한, 거의 확실한 ☐ provident a. 신중한, 조심스러운; 검약한, 절약하는

그는 사치스러운 취미와 습관에 젖어 있다.

## 92 ①

☐ sleazy a. 지저분한; 보잘것없는 ☐ tattered a. (옷 등이) 해진; 누더기를 두른(=ragged) ☐ stained a. (보통 복합어로 쓰여) 얼룩진 ☐ dirty a. 더러운, 불결한 ☐ desolate a. 황폐한; 황량한; 쓸쓸한, 외로운 ☐ savaged a. 야만적인, 야만인의, 미개한

몇 년 전 신시내티에 있는 싸구려 모텔에서 태풍을 피하고 있는 동안 나는 공중전화 위에 있는 너덜거리는 맥주 자국으로 얼룩진 공고문을 봤다. 그 공고문에는 그저 다음과 같이 쓰여 있었다. "이것은 예행연습이 아니다. 이것이 인생이다. 놓치지 마라."

## 93 ①

☐ wholesome a. 건강에 좋은; 건전한, 유익한(=worthy) ☐ reaction against ~에 대한 반발 ☐ facile a. 손쉬운, 안이한 ☐ pernicious a. 유해한, 치명적인; 파괴적인 ☐ imposing a. 인상적인; 눈길을 끄는; 당당한 ☐ impressive a. 인상에 남는, 인상적인

모든 예술 작품의 개성과 심지어 특유함을 강조하는 것은 안이한 일반화에 대한 반작용으로서 유익하다.

## 94 ①

☐ genetic mutation n. 유전자 변이 ☐ circumstance n. 환경, 상황 ☐ noxious a. 유독한, 유해한(=deleterious) ☐ decrepit a. 노후한, 노쇠한 ☐ onerous a. 아주 힘든 ☐ odious a. 끔찍한, 혐오스러운

일부 유전자 변이는 어떤 상황에서는 유용하지만, 대부분은 기존의 모든 환경에서 무조건 해롭다.

## 95 ④

☐ idiosyncrasy n. 특이함, 특징; (개인의) 특유한 체격(=peculiarity) ☐ skull n. 두개골, 머리 ☐ coin slot (자동판매기의) 동전 투입구 ☐ discovery n. 발견; 발견물 ☐ phenomenon n. 현상; 사건 ☐ image n. 상; 이미지, 인상

존(John)의 두개골이 특이했기 때문에 그 의사는 관심이 생겼다. 그의 뒤통수에 동전 투입구가 있는 것처럼 보였다.

## 96 ①

☐ balk v. 방해하다, 좌절시키다(=block) ☐ reverse v. 거꾸로 하다, 반대로 하다; 전환하다 ☐ monitor v. 감시하다, 조정하다 ☐ emulate v. (우열을) 다투다, 겨루다

제2차 세계대전 이후 미국 외교정책의 주요 목표 중 하나는 제3세계에 공산주의를 전하려는 소련의 시도를 저지하는 것이었다.

## 97　④

☐ defy v. 무시하다, 문제삼지 않다 ☐ augury n. 전조, 조짐(=portent)
☐ attention n. 주의, 유의 ☐ supervision n. 관리, 감독, 지휘 ☐
assistance n. 원조, 도움

그의 놀라운 회복은 모든 의학적인 예언을 무색하게 했다.

## 98　②

☐ abeyance n. 중지, 정지(=cessation) ☐ charge n. 비난; 고발 ☐
dissent n. 불찬성, 이의 ☐ practice n. 실행, 실시

거래 위원회가 주가 조작을 조사하는 동안 주식 시장의 거래가 일시적으
로 중단되었다.

## 99　③

☐ unnerve v. 불안하게 만들다, 무기력하게 하다(=enervate) ☐
indulge v. 빠지다, 탐닉하다 ☐ sanction v. 인가[재가]하다; 시인하다
☐ discriminate v. 식별[구별]하다; 차별하다

일본이 다른 나라를 공격할 수 있는 잠재적인 새로운 방법은 주변국들을
불안하게 만들고 있다.

## 100　①

☐ apathy n. 냉담; 무관심(=indifference) ☐ resentment n. 침범,
위반 ☐ delusion n. 망상; 착각 ☐ consent n. 동의, 허가

이 나라에는 자동차 사고에 대한 대중의 무관심이 팽배해 있다.

| 01 ③ | 02 ④ | 03 ① | 04 ③ | 05 ② | 06 ④ | 07 ④ | 08 ① | 09 ② | 10 ① |
|-------|-------|-------|-------|-------|-------|-------|-------|-------|-------|
| 11 ④ | 12 ④ | 13 ② | 14 ① | 15 ② | 16 ④ | 17 ① | 18 ② | 19 ④ | 20 ④ |
| 21 ② | 22 ② | 23 ① | 24 ① | 25 ④ | 26 ① | 27 ① | 28 ③ | 29 ④ | 30 ④ |
| 31 ④ | 32 ④ | 33 ② | 34 ① | 35 ③ | 36 ③ | 37 ④ | 38 ② | 39 ① | 40 ③ |
| 41 ④ | 42 ③ | 43 ② | 44 ① | 45 ④ | 46 ② | 47 ② | 48 ① | 49 ② | 50 ① |
| 51 ③ | 52 ③ | 53 ③ | 54 ③ | 55 ① | 56 ① | 57 ④ | 58 ④ | 59 ② | 60 ② |
| 61 ④ | 62 ① | 63 ④ | 64 ③ | 65 ④ | 66 ③ | 67 ④ | 68 ① | 69 ② | 70 ④ |
| 71 ② | 72 ② | 73 ② | 74 ① | 75 ② | 76 ① | 77 ④ | 78 ③ | 79 ③ | 80 ④ |
| 81 ③ | 82 ① | 83 ③ | 84 ③ | 85 ③ | 86 ④ | 87 ④ | 88 ① | 89 ① | 90 ④ |
| 91 ③ | 92 ③ | 93 ④ | 94 ② | 95 ① | 96 ③ | 97 ② | 98 ① | 99 ③ | 100 ② |

## 01 ③

☐ orthodox a. 전통적인; 흔히 있는(=conventional) ☐ alternative a. 대안적인, 대체의(전통적인 방식과 다른) ☐ meticulous a. 지나치게 세심한, 매우 신중한 ☐ innovative a. 혁신적인 ☐ ingenious a. 기발한, 독창적인

사람들은 그들의 병이 전통적인 방법으로 치료될 수 없다는 것을 알게 되면, 대체 치료법으로 눈을 돌린다.

## 02 ④

☐ debase v. 떨어뜨리다, 저하시키다(=lower) ☐ alter v. 바꾸다, 변경하다, 개조하다 ☐ discard v. 버리다, 처분하다 ☐ exalt v. 높이다; 올리다; 승진시키다; 칭찬하다

그는 회원의 가치를 저하시키는 많은 실수를 저질렀다.

## 03 ①

☐ swindle v. 사취하다, 사기치다(=defraud) ☐ abolish v. 폐지하다 ☐ ruin v. 망치다, 엉망으로 만들다 ☐ render v. (어떤 상태가 되게) 만들다

그 부유하고 잔인한 독재자는 국민들을 사취한 죄로 결국 유죄판결을 받았고 국가를 파산하게 만들었다.

## 04 ③

☐ milieu n. 환경(=environment) ☐ visually ad. 시각적으로 ☐ custom n. 관습, 풍습 ☐ property n. 재산, 소유물 ☐ perspective n. 전망; 시각

뉴스와 소셜 미디어를 포함한 우리의 문화적 환경은 점점 시각 지향적으로 변화하고 있다.

## 05 ②

☐ equivocally ad. 애매하게, 분명하지 않게, 모호하게(=ambiguously) ☐ quickly ad. 빠르게, 급히; 곧 ☐ aggressively ad. 공격적으로, 정력적으로 ☐ loudly ad. 큰 소리로; 눈에 띄게

분명하지 않게 말하는 선생님은 학생들을 혼란에 빠뜨릴 수 있다.

## 06 ④

☐ clog v. 방해하다, 막다(=obstruct); (마음을) 무겁게 하다, 괴롭히다 ☐ waterway n. 수로 ☐ impede v. 방해하다, 지연시키다 ☐ drain v. 배수하다, 방수하다; (물을) 빼서 말리다 ☐ grow along ~을 따라 자라다 ☐ float on ~위에 뜨다; 떠돌아다니다

잡초들은 수로를 막고, 야생 생물의 서식지를 파괴하며, 농업을 방해한다.

## 07 ④

☐ conversant a. 밝은, 정통한; 친교가 있는(with)(=familiar) ☐ well-mannered a. 예의 바른, 점잖은 ☐ argumentative a. 논쟁적인, 토론적인; 논쟁을 좋아하는 ☐ talkative a. 이야기하기 좋아하는, 말이 많은, 수다스러운

그는 모형제작에서 주조기술에 이르기까지 조각의 전 분야에 정통하다.

## 08 ①

☐ intercede v. 중재하다, 조정하다(=mediate)  ☐ intercept v. 도중에서 빼앗다, 가로막다  ☐ organize v. 조직하다, 편제하다, 구성하다  ☐ participate v. 참가하다, 관여하다, 관계하다

한 중립 국가가 평화를 이룩하기 위해 중재하겠다고 자원했다.

## 09 ②

☐ scheme n. 계획; 음모; 체계(=contrivance)  ☐ necessity n. 필수품; 필요성; 필연성  ☐ document n. 문서, 서류, 조서  ☐ forfeit n. 벌금; 몰수; 상실, 박탈

역사상 가장 위대한 우편 업무원 로우랜드 힐(Rowland Hill)은 그렇게 기록했는데, 그는 1837년에 우편요금을 내리면서 표준화하고 요금 지불 부담을 수취인에서 발송인으로 바꾸는 체계를 고안했다.

## 10 ①

☐ half-hearted a. 성의가 없는, 냉담한  ☐ desultory a. 산만한; 일관성이 없는; 변덕스러운(=unmethodical)  ☐ misguided a. 오도된, 미혹된  ☐ disguised a. 변장한; 속임수의  ☐ systematic a. 조직적인, 질서 있는, 계획적인

오늘날 이러한 주제들은 성의 없고 일관성 없는 방식으로 여전히 논의되고 있다.

## 11 ④

☐ contretemps n. 공교롭게 일어난 사건, 사소한 언쟁(=argy-bargy)  ☐ curmudgeon n. 심술궂은 구두쇠, 까다로운 사람  ☐ conundrum n. 어려운 문제, 수수께끼  ☐ hame n. 멍에, 불유쾌한 일, 허드렛일, 단조로운 일

발렌티(Valenti)는 이번의 사소한 언쟁으로 인해 거의 은퇴할 지경이 되었다.

## 12 ④

☐ parallel n. 유사점; 필적하는 것  ☐ abstruseness n. 난해함, 심오함(=reconditeness)  ☐ obvious a. 분명한, 명백한  ☐ purity n. 맑음, 청순; 순수함  ☐ vulgarity n. 저속함, 야비함  ☐ abdication n. (권리) 포기, 퇴임

현대예술의 난해함과 현대과학의 난해함 사이의 유사점은 너무나 명백해서 누구나 알아볼 수 있다.

## 13 ②

☐ dub v. (~을 …이라고) 부르다, 이름을 붙이다(=name)  ☐ replace v. 제자리에 놓다; 대신하다  ☐ precede v. 앞서다, 선행하다  ☐ create v. 창조하다, 창작하다; 야기하다

최초의 대형 컴퓨터들은 곧 '전자두뇌'라고 이름이 붙여졌다.

## 14 ①

☐ prognosis n. 예지, 예측; 예후(=prospect)  ☐ tuberculosis n. 결핵  ☐ symptom n. 징후, 조짐; 증상  ☐ deterioration n.악화, (질의) 저하  ☐ operation n. 수술; 작전

환자가 진단과 치료를 받을 수 있을 때는 결핵 환자들의 예후가 상당히 양호해서 대부분이 완치를 기대할 수 있다.

## 15 ②

☐ unceremoniously ad. 격식을 차리지 않고; 허물없이, 버릇없이, 갑작스럽게(=abruptly)  ☐ drop out of ~에서 중도하차하다  ☐ stand a chance of ~의 가능성이 있다  ☐ conscientiously ad. 양심적으로, 성실히, 공들여  ☐ deliberately ad. 고의로, 의도[계획]적으로  ☐ meticulously ad. 너무 세심하게, 꼼꼼히

그는 자신이 당선될 가능성이 없다는 것을 알았기 때문에 갑작스럽게 대통령 경선에서 중도하차했다.

## 16 ④

☐ edify v. 교화하다, 계발하다(=instruct)  ☐ simulate v. 흉내 내다, 가장하다  ☐ divert v. ~을 전환하다; 기분 전환을 시키다  ☐ scold v. 꾸짖다, 나무라다

그의 목적은 즐기는 것이 아니라 교화하는 것이었다.

## 17 ①

☐ vigilant a. 경계하는, 방심하지 않는(=watchful)  ☐ indolent a. 나태한, 게으른; (병리) 무통의  ☐ drowsy a. 졸음이 오는, 졸리게 하는  ☐ imprudent a. 경솔한, 무분별한, 조심하지 않는

관리자는 안전에 대해서라면 방심해서 안 된다. 사원들을 계속 교육시켜야 한다.

## 18 ②

☐ organism n. 유기체, (극도로 작은) 생물  ☐ succumb v. 굴복하다(=yield)  ☐ oxygen n. 산소  ☐ unnoticed a. 눈에 띄지 않는  ☐ stick v. ~을 고수하다  ☐ impose v. 부과하다  ☐ transfer v. 옮기다

어떤 유기체는 산소 부족에 굴복할 것이고 그 죽음은 눈에 띄지 않고 쉽게 지나갈지 모른다.

## 19 ④

☐ conductor n. 안내자; 지휘자  ☐ poised a. 침착한, 위엄 있는  ☐ animated a. 힘찬; 활기찬, 활발한  ☐ distinctive a. 독특한, 특이한  ☐ requiem n. 위령곡, 진혼가  ☐ tempo n. 박자 (pl. tempi)  ☐ exquisite a. 정교한, 매우 훌륭한, 최고의(=sublime)  ☐ shading n. 명암법; 농담(濃淡); (빛깔, 명암 따위의) 미세한 변화  ☐ lackadaisical a. 활기 없는, 열의 없는  ☐ profuse a. 아낌없는, 마음이 후한; 풍부한  ☐ querulous a. 불평하는, 흠잡는

이 지휘자의 위엄 있고 활기찬 지휘 하에서 "레퀴엠(Requiem)"이 독특하게 연주되었다. 박자는 물 흐르듯 했고, 역동적인 음의 변화는 매우 훌륭했으며, 오케스트라는 더할 나위 없이 완벽했다.

## 20 ④

☐ evacuation n. 소개(疏開), 피난, 대피  ☐ precedence n. (순서·중요성 등에서) 선행, 우위, 우선(=priority)  ☐ approval n. 인정, 찬성, 승인  ☐ procession n. 행진, 행렬  ☐ relocation n. 재배치, 배치전환

대부분의 비상 대피 계획은 부상자들에게 우선권이 주어져야 한다고 명시하고 있다.

## 21 ②

☐ advisor n. 조언자, 고문  ☐ upbraid v. 질책하다, 호되게 나무라다, 비난하다(=reprimand)  ☐ stockpile n. (많은) 비축량  ☐ alienate v. 멀리하다, 소원하게 하다  ☐ overawe v. 위압하다; 겁을 주어 ~하게 하다  ☐ scavenge v. 쓰레기 더미를 뒤지다; 죽은 고기를 먹다

군사 고문들은 핵 비축량의 전 세계적인 감소를 진전으로 설명하여 비난을 받았다.

## 22 ②

☐ flat a. 평평한; 부진한, 활기 없는(=inactive)  ☐ reluctance n. 마지못해함, 꺼림  ☐ diversify v. 다각[다양]화하다  ☐ exuberant a. 풍부한; 왕성한; 열광적인  ☐ insatiable a. 만족을 모르는, 탐욕스러운  ☐ extravagant a. 낭비하는, 사치스러운; 지나친

국제 상품가격의 하락과 국내 투자가들이 새로운 사업 분야로 사업을 다양화하기를 꺼림으로 인해 필리핀의 교역은 올해 부진했다.

## 23 ①

☐ aloof from ~으로부터 멀리 떨어져 있는; ~에 초연한, 무관심한(=separated from)  ☐ upward of (수, 양이) ~이상  ☐ bored with ~때문에 지루한, ~에 싫증나는  ☐ exhausted from ~로 인해 지쳐버린; 고갈된

그의 아버지는 그의 가정의 일상적인 일에 초연한 상태이다.

## 24 ①

☐ transitional a. 변하는 시기의, 과도적인  ☐ phase n. 단계, 국면; 양상(=stage)  ☐ notion n. 관념, 개념; 생각, 의견  ☐ pattern n. 모범, 본보기, 귀감; 모형  ☐ alternative n. 대안; 양자택일

미국의 교육 제도에 있어서 중학교는 초등학교와 고등학교 사이의 과도적 단계이다.

## 25 ④

☐ benign a. 인자한, 친절한, 상냥한(=gentle)  ☐ intense a. 격렬한, 심한, 격앙된  ☐ ordered a. 정연한; 질서 바른  ☐ weak a. 약한, 무력한, 연약한, 둔한

실비아(Sylvia)는 상냥한 성격을 가졌다. 그녀와 함께 있는 것이 전혀 싫지 않다.

## 26 ①

☐ withdrawal n. 철수, 철퇴  ☐ tension n. 긴장상태  ☐ mollify v. 달래다, 진정시키다(=appease)  ☐ coerce v. 강제하다, 위압하다  ☐ persuade v. 설득하다, 납득시키다  ☐ encourage v. 용기를 돋우다, 격려하다

병력을 철수하더라도 러시아와 조지아 사이의 긴장상태를 종식시키거나 서방세계를 완전히 진정시키지는 못할 것이다.

## 27 ①

☐ intrepid a. 두려움을 모르는, 용맹한, 대담한(=fearless)  ☐ reckless a. 분별없는, 무모한; 개의치 않는  ☐ calm a. 고요한, 조용한; 침착한  ☐ stable a. 안정된; 견고한, 고정된

그들의 지도자는 큰 어려움 앞에서도 대담함을 보였다.

## 28 ③

☐ sustained a. 지속된, 한결같은, 일관된(=continuous)  ☐ fastidious a. 세심한, 꼼꼼한  ☐ aggressive a. 공격적인; 적극적인  ☐ decent a. 괜찮은, 품위 있는

문제를 효과적으로 해결하려면 지속적인 노력이 필요하다. 당신은 너무 빨리 포기해서는 안 된다.

## 29 ④

☐ enumerate v. 열거하다(=list)  ☐ dreadful a. 끔찍한, 지독한; 무시무시한  ☐ rampant a. (병·소문 등이) 유행하는; 만연하는  ☐ allot v. 할당[배당]하다  ☐ incarnate v. 구현하다  ☐ validate v. 입증하다; 승인하다

보건부 소속 의사가 그 수상공원에서 유행하는 무시무시하게 들리는 모든 질병들을 열거한 후 나는 결국 그곳에 가지 않기로 결정했다.

## 30 ③

☐ stupendous a. 엄청난; 굉장한(=monumental) ☐ unintelligent a. 무지한; 우둔한 ☐ strenuous a. 분투적인; 활발한 ☐ energetic a. 활기찬; 강력한

자전거로 에베레스트산을 오르는 것은 대단한 업적이 될 것이다.

## 31 ④

☐ puritanical a. 청교도적인; 금욕적인, 근엄한, 엄격한(=moralistic) ☐ profligate a. 품행이 나쁜; 방탕한, 부도덕한 ☐ penurious a. 가난한, 극빈한; 인색한 ☐ salacious a. 외설스러운, 음란한, 호색의

그녀는 전혀 근엄하지 않다. 그리고 그녀는 동료들을 재미있게 해주려고 한다.

## 32 ④

☐ pronouncement n. 선언, 발표 ☐ scrutinize v. (면밀하게) 검토하다(=examine) ☐ ascertain v. (조사 등으로) 확인하다, 규명하다 ☐ methodology n. 방법론 ☐ utilize v. 이용하다, 활용하다 ☐ select v. 선택하다, 고르다 ☐ systemize v. 체계화하다, 조직화하다

교육 공학에 관한 모든 발표는 기계, 소프트웨어, 방법론 등, 프로세스의 어떤 부분이 관련돼 있는지를 확인하기 위해 매우 신중하게 검토되어야 한다.

## 33 ②

☐ glut n. 차고 넘침, 과다(=excess) ☐ pool n. 물웅덩이; 합동자금; 기업연합 ☐ demand n. 요구; 수요 ☐ trade n. 거래, 무역

시장에 변호사들이 넘쳐나고 있어서, 많은 로스쿨 졸업생들이 좋은 일자리를 얻을 수 없다.

## 34 ①

☐ trivial a. 하찮은, 대단치 않은(=frivolous) ☐ prodigious a. 엄청난, 굉장한 ☐ remorseful a. 후회하는, 양심의 가책을 받는 ☐ insolvent a. 채무를 이행할 수 없는

자신은 하찮다고 여기는 인생을 살았음에도 불구하고, 조지(George)는 그가 아는 모든 사람들에게 실제로는 엄청난 영향을 미쳤다.

## 35 ③

☐ famine n. 기근; 굶주림 ☐ relief n. 구호, 구조 ☐ struggle v. 노력하다, 분투하다 ☐ dauntless a. 용감한, 불굴의, 겁 없는(=intrepid) ☐ optimism n. 낙천주의, 낙관론 ☐ haughty a. 오만한, 거만한 ☐ ill-advised a. 경솔한, 문제의 소지가 있는 ☐ feeble a. 연약한; 나약한

엄청난 규모의 기근에도 불구하고 구호요원들은 불굴의 낙관주의를 갖고 악전고투를 계속했다.

## 36 ③

☐ condone v. 묵과하다, 용서하다 ☐ knavery n. 불량배 같은 행위; 속임수, 부정, 사기(=iniquity) ☐ conjecture n. 추측, 억측; (사본 따위의) 판독 ☐ frailty n. 무름, 약함; 덧없음 ☐ complaint n. 불평, 불만; 신체적 고통, 병

우리는 공무원들의 그런 부정을 묵과할 수 없다.

## 37 ④

☐ faintly ad. 희미하게, 어렴풋이 ☐ reproach n. 비난, 질책, 책망(=reprimand) ☐ ridiculous a. 우스꽝스러운 ☐ cravat n. 넥타이 ☐ collar n. 옷깃; 목걸이; 목에 거는 훈장 ☐ conscious of ~을 의식하는 ☐ dignity n. 위엄; 존엄성; 품위 ☐ approbation n. 승인; 칭찬 ☐ prohibition n. 금지 ☐ tolerance n. 관용, 포용력

조(Joe)는 나를 약간 질책하는 듯이 잠깐 동안 쳐다보았다. 비록 그의 넥타이와 목에 걸린 훈장들은 완전히 우스꽝스러웠지만, 나는 그런 모습에서 일종의 위엄을 의식했다.

## 38 ②

☐ aplomb n. 침착, 태연(자약)(=collectedness) ☐ malaise n. 불쾌(감), 불안감 ☐ cacophony n. 불협화음; 소음 ☐ idiosyncrasy n. (어느 개인의) 특이성, 특이한 성격

당시 사람들의 설명으로는, 그 오케스트라는 그 음악을 점점 더 침착하게 연주했다고 한다.

## 39 ①

☐ cross v. (가로질러) 건너다 ☐ torrid a. 몹시 더운(=scorching) ☐ fertile a. (땅이) 비옥한 ☐ habitable a. 거주하기에 적당한 ☐ northern hemisphere 북반구 ☐ benign a. 상냥한, 유순한; <의학> 양성의 ☐ equatorial a. 적도의 ☐ connecting a. 연결하는

오랫동안 인간의 생존이 불가능하다고 여겨져 왔던 몹시 더운 지역을 일단 건너고 나면, 북반구 지역과 같이 비옥하고 거주하기에 적합한 땅을 발견하게 될 것이다.

## 40 ③

□ proverbial a. 유명한, 잘 알려진(=well-known) □ magnify v. 확대하다 □ despair n. 절망; 자포자기 □ provable a. 증명할 수 있는 □ illuminating a. 밝히는, 계몽적인 □ controversial a. 논쟁의 여지가 있는

결코 가져본 적이 없는 것을, 또는 참으로 존재한 적이 없었던 것을 그리워할 수는 없다는 것은 주지의 사실이지만, 과거 흑인들의 단합과 투쟁에 대한 낭만적 사고들은 현실의 절망을 더욱 크게 한다.

## 41 ④

□ pupil n. 동공 □ dilate v. 팽창[확장]하다(=expand) □ paralyze v. 마비시키다; 무력[무능]하게 만들다 □ recoil v. 움찔하다[흠칫 놀라다] □ focus v. 초점을 맞추다

우리 눈의 동공은 조도가 낮아지면 팽창한다.

## 42 ③

□ jute n. 황마; (황마로 만든) 황저포, 삼베 □ flourish v. 번성하다, 무성하게 자라다(=thrive) □ humid a. 습기 있는, 눅눅한 □ amplify v. 확대하다, 증대하다; 증폭하다 □ swell v. 부풀다, 붓다, 팽창하다 □ prolong v. 늘이다, 길게 하다; 연장하다

참피나무의 일종인 황마는 따뜻하고 습기 있는 기후에서 무성하게 자란다.

## 43 ②

□ understudy n. 대역(代役), 대행하는 사람; 임시 대역 배우 □ hoarse a. 목이 쉰, 귀에 거슬리는(=rough) □ fatigued a. 피로한, 지친 □ thin a. 얇은, 두껍지 않은; 드문드문한, 희박한 □ famous a. 유명한, 이름난, 잘 알려진, 소문난

리드싱어의 목이 쉬게 되면 대타 가수가 공연한다.

## 44 ①

□ slaughterhouse n. 도축장(=abattoir) □ gallow n. 교수대 □ penitentiary n. 주[연방] 교도소 □ arboretum n. 수목원

그 지역의 3곳의 도축장에서는 2년 동안 10만 마리 미만의 당나귀들을 처리했다고 보고하였다.

## 45 ④

□ catholic a. 보편적인, 일반적인; 너그러운(=universal) □ bounded a. 경계가 있는; 한계가 있는 □ official a. 공무상의, 공식의 □ religious a. 종교(상)의, 종교적인

이것은 편협한 생각이 아니다. 보편적인 것이다.

## 46 ②

□ propitious a. 좋은, 알맞은; 상서로운(=auspicious) □ voluntary a. 자발적인, 임의적인 □ conducive a. 공헌하는, 도움이 되는 □ perspicacious a. 통찰력 있는, 명민한

다른 소유자들은 자신들이 받게 될 판매 가격이 실망스럽다는 것을 알고, 좀 더 적절한 판매시기를 기다리기를 선호한다.

## 47 ②

□ interim a. 중간의; 잠정의, 임시의(=temporary) □ solid a. 고체의, 고형의; 단단한; 견고한 □ desirable a. 바람직한, 탐나는, 호감이 가는 □ unreflected a. 사려(思慮) 부족의; 반성하지 않는

정부는 당면한 곤궁에 처해 있는 사람들을 도울 임시 조처를 취하고 있다.

## 48 ②

□ dismiss v. 해고하다, 면직하다 □ culpable a. 비난할 만한, 과실이 있는(=blameworthy) □ chronic a. 상습적인, 만성적인, 장기간에 걸친 □ felicitous a. 적절한, 들어맞는; 표현을 잘하는 □ trustworthy a. 신뢰할 수 있는, 신용할 수 있는

그 경찰관은 비난받을 만한 근무태만으로 해고되었다.

## 49 ②

□ collector n. 수집가; 수금원; 징세관 □ lax a. 느슨한; 태만한, 부주의한(=loose) □ deliver v. 배달하다, 전하다; 넘겨주다 □ accountable a. 책임이 있는; 설명할 수 있는 □ firm a. 굳은; 확고한, 단호한 □ resilient a. 되튀는, 원상으로 돌아가는, 탄력 있는 □ careful a. 주의 깊은, 조심스러운

실질적인 부기 시스템의 부재 상황에서 세관원들은 세입을 왕립 재무부에 전달하는 것을 태만히 했다.

## 50 ②

□ tight-fitting a. 몸에 딱 붙는 □ voluptuousness n. 관능의 만족에 젖음; 관능적임, 요염함(=seductiveness) □ distract v. 집중이 안 되게 하다, 주의를 딴 데로 돌리다 □ awkwardness n. 어색함, 거북함 □ carelessness n. 부주의, 경솔 □ pleasance n. (대저택에 부속된) 유원지; 기쁨

브라질의 상파울루에서 로마에 도착한 33세의 여성은 자신의 외모가 국경 경찰들의 주의를 산만하게 만들기를 바라며 그녀의 요염함을 돋보이게 하기 위해 꽉 끼는 옷을 입고 있었다.

## 51  ③

□ transgress v. (법률, 계율 등을) 어기다, 범하다(=violate); (한계를) 넘다 □ disagree with ~과 일치하지 않다, 의견이 다르다 □ disperse v. 흩뜨리다, 흩어지게 하다, 뿔뿔이 헤어지게 하다 □ interfere with ~을 방해하다, 간섭하다

사회법규를 위반하는 사람들은 처벌받을 수 있다.

## 52  ③

□ drab a. 칙칙한 황갈색의; 단조로운(=colorless) □ plumage n. (조류의) 깃털, 깃; 좋은 옷 □ variegated a. 잡색의, 얼룩덜룩한; 변화 많은 □ enticing a. 유혹적인, 마음을 끄는 □ distinct a. 별개의, 전혀 다른; 뚜렷한, 명료한

온난한 지역의 많은 명금은 겨울 동안에 칙칙한 색의 깃털을 보여준다.

## 53  ③

□ lucid a. 맑은, 투명한; 명쾌한(=clear) □ short a. 짧은, 단기간의 □ compact a. 조밀한, 빽빽한; 간결한 □ enlightening a. 계몽적인, 깨우치는

그가 했던 연설은 균형 잡힌 말이 많아서 명료했다.

## 54  ③

□ recollect v. 생각해내다; 회상하다(=remember) □ repeat v. 되풀이하다, 반복하다 □ understand v. 이해하다, 알아든다 □ change v. 바꾸다, 변경하다, 고치다

그는 노력했지만 그 이야기를 기억해 낼 수 없었다.

## 55  ①

□ chary a. 조심하는, 신중한, ~을 (하기를) 꺼리는(=apprehensive) □ quiescent a. 정지한, 무활동의; 조용한 □ facetious a. 익살맞은, 우스운 □ obdurate a. 완고한, 고집 센

이론가들은 음악의 정신적인 역할을 분석하길 꺼려 왔다.

## 56  ①

□ aging a. 노화의, 늙어가는, 고령화의 □ burden v. ~에 무거운 부담을 지우다[안기다] □ strenuous a. 막대한 노력이 필요한, 고생스러운 (=arduous) □ prolong v. 연장시키다 □ senior citizen 고령자, 노인 □ efficient a. 능률적인, 효과적인 □ continuing a. 연속적인, 계속적인 □ controversial a. 논쟁의, 논란이 많은

고령화되고 있는 한국은 젊은 노동자들에게 부담이 될 것이다. 정부는 노인들의 일자리를 창출함으로써 개개인들이 경제활동 기간을 연장시

키는 것을 돕기 위해 부단한 노력을 해야 할 필요가 있다.

## 57  ④

□ gradually ad. 차츰, 서서히 □ raucous a. 목이 쉰; 무질서하고 소란한(=boisterous) □ erroneous a. 잘못된, 틀린 □ mellifluous a. 감미로운, 부드럽게 흘러나오는 □ sanctimonious a. 신성한 체하는, 신앙심이 깊은 체하는

직장에서 열린 크리스마스 파티는 점점 더 소란스러워졌다.

## 58  ④

□ muster up ~을 모으다, 소집하다(=gather) □ finance v. 자금을 조달하다; 투자하다 □ convince v. 납득시키다, 깨닫게 하다, 확신시키다 □ disguise v. 변장하다, 가장하다, 꾸미다; 숨기다

혁명군은 영국군에 대항하기 위한 충분한 수의 사람들을 모아야 했다.

## 59  ②

□ unequivocal a. 명백한, 분명한 □ controvertible a. 논쟁의 여지가 있는, 논쟁할 만한(=ambiguous) □ eyewitness n. 목격자 □ lucid a. 명쾌한, 명료한 □ infallible a. 틀림없는, 절대 확실한 □ theoretical a. 이론(상)의

증인들이 제공한 분명한 설명들과는 다르게, 비행 기록 장치에서 얻은 증거는 오히려 논쟁의 여지가 있었고 이로 인해 추락 사고를 설명하는 서로 다른 여러 이론들이 생겨났다.

## 60  ②

□ profitable a. 수익성이 있는, 이득이 되는(=lucrative) □ retailer n. 소매업자 □ up front 선불로 □ redeem v. 만회하다; (주식, 상품권 등을) 현금[상품]으로 바꾸다[교환하다] □ convenient a. 편리한, 사용하기 좋은 □ productive a. 생산적인; 다산의 □ responsible a. 책임이 있는, 책임을 져야 할

상품권은 미국에서 가장 인기가 많은 선물이다. 상품권은 수익성이 좋은데, 소매업자들이 상품권에 대한 돈을 선불로 지급받고, 또한 상품권 중 약 10%는 상품으로 교환되지 않기 때문이다.

## 61  ④

□ acutely ad. 강렬히, 절실히; 몹시(=strongly) □ abstractly ad. 추상적으로, 관념적으로, 이론적으로 □ reasonably ad. 합리적으로; 꽤, 상당히 □ commonly ad. 일반적으로, 보통

나는 내 신념이 개인적인 경험에 의해 결코 평가받은 적이 없다는 것을 강하게 인식하고 있다.

## 62 ①

☐ fortuitous a. 우연의, 뜻밖의; 운이 좋은, 행운의(=lucky) ☐ rational a. 이성적인; 합리적인 ☐ careful a. 조심스러운, 주의 깊은 ☐ sensible a. 분별 있는, 현명한

그 남자가 광산 회사에 투자한 시점은 운이 좋았던 것으로 드러났고, 그래서 예상외로 빠른 수익을 얻게 되었다.

## 63 ④

☐ refugee n. 피난자, 난민 ☐ wretched a. 가엾은, 불쌍한, 비참한(=miserable) ☐ convincing a. 설득력 있는 ☐ trivial a. 하찮은, 평범한 ☐ decent a. 괜찮은

난민 수용소의 상황은 인도주의 단체들의 대단한 노력에도 불구하고 비참하다.

## 64 ③

☐ trepidation n. 전율, 공포; 걱정, 불안(=fright) ☐ dexterity n. 솜씨 좋음; 기민함, 빈틈없음 ☐ fortitude n. 용기, 불굴의 정신, 강한 참을성 ☐ avarice n. 탐욕, 허욕

나는 캐럴(Carol)이 연설할 때 불안해할 거로 생각했으나, 그녀는 두려움 없이 연설을 했다.

## 65 ③

☐ fortress n. 요새; 성채 ☐ besiege v. 포위하다, 에워싸다(=blockade) ☐ starve v. 굶주리다, 배고프다 ☐ desert v. 버리다, 유기하다 ☐ construct v. 건설하다; 조립하다 ☐ occupy v. 차지하다, 점유하다

그 요새는 주민들이 굶어죽을 때까지 적군에 의해 포위되어 공격당했다.

## 66 ③

☐ amphibian n. 양서류 ☐ to date 지금까지 ☐ excrete v. 배설하다, 분비하다(=let out) ☐ compound n. 혼합물, 화합물 ☐ make up 이루다, 구성하다 ☐ set out 출발하다; 착수하다 ☐ give in 제출하다; 공표하다

지금까지 발견된 의학적으로 가장 흥미로운 양서류는 중미와 남미에 사는 독화살 개구리인데, 그것의 피부는 여러 가지 유용한 화합물을 분비한다.

## 67 ④

☐ chromosome n. 염색체 ☐ overturn v. 뒤집다, 전복시키다; 타도하다(=revoke) ☐ longstanding a. 오랫동안[여러 해]에 걸친 ☐

☐ reaffirm v. 다시 확인하다, 다시 단언하다 ☐ reclaim v. 교정하다, 개선하다; 개간하다 ☐ redeem v. 되찾다, 회복하다, 상환하다

인간의 Y염색체에 관한 새로운 고찰은 그것의 진화 역사에 관한 오랜 관점들을 뒤집었다.

## 68 ①

☐ divulge v. 누설하다, 폭로하다(=disclose) ☐ conceal v. 감추다, 숨기다 ☐ contradict v. 부정하다, 반박하다 ☐ recognize v. 인정하다, 인지하다; 승인하다

그 피고인은 자신의 범죄 연관성을 밝히려 하지 않았다.

## 69 ②

☐ allegation n. 주장 ☐ irascible a. 성난, 성마른, 화를 잘 내는(=choleric) ☐ inclement a. 냉혹한 ☐ desperate a. 절박한 ☐ genial a. 친절한

누군가에게 밤늦게 전화를 걸어오는 수화기 너머의 성난 의사의 주장만 있을 뿐 명확한 것은 아무것도 없다.

## 70 ④

☐ odorous a. 향기로운; 냄새 나는(=fragrant) ☐ mundane a. 현세의, 세속적인 ☐ stingy a. 물건을 너무 아끼는, 인색한 ☐ oblique a. 비스듬한, 기울어진

이 하이브리드 티 장미는 당신이 당신 정원에서 재배하는 장미보다 더 향기롭다.

## 71 ②

☐ grandiloquent a. 말을 거창하게 하는; 과장된(=bombastic) ☐ orator n. 연설자, 웅변가 ☐ magnanimous a. 관대한, 너그러운 ☐ prosaic a. 평범한, 지루한 ☐ discursive a. 두서없는, 산만한

그 상원의원은 시대에 뒤떨어진 웅변가의 과장된 스타일로 말한다.

## 72 ②

☐ compatriot n. 동포 ☐ benignity n. 다정함, 자비로움 ☐ spurn v. 쫓아내다, 버리다; 일축하다, 퇴짜 놓다(=reject) ☐ kinsfolk n. 친척, 일가 ☐ quadruped n. 네발짐승 ☐ hate v. 미워하다, 싫어하다, 증오하다 ☐ save v. 구하다; 지키다 ☐ leave v. 떠나다, 출발하다

그의 동포인 스위프트(Swift)는 보편적인 자비로움에 대한 혐오감을 가지고 있었는데, 제정신이 아닌 걸리버(Gulliver)로 하여금 한걸음 더 나아가 그의 친척을 내쫓고 다른 종족의 네발 동물과 사랑에 빠지도록 했다.

## 73                                    ②

□ exacerbate v. 악화시키다  □ arid a. 건조한, 메마른; 불모의(=dry)
□ hot a. 뜨거운, 더운  □ insipid a. 무미건조한, 재미없는; 맛없는
□ torrent n. 급류; 연발, 속출

지구온난화는 특히 가난하고, 건조한 지역의 나라에서 그 문제를 악화
시킬 것이다.


## 74                                    ①

□ evident a. 분명한, 명백한  □ depose v. 물러나게 하다, 폐하다,
찬탈하다(=dethrone)  □ thaw v. (눈, 얼음 등이) 녹다  □ melt v.
(고체가) 녹다, 용해하다  □ cope v. 대항하다, 맞서다; 처리하다

질서를 확립하기 위해 그들이 국왕을 폐할 수밖에 없었다는 것은 명백한
사실이었다.


## 75                                    ②

□ consternation n. 섬뜩 놀람, 당황(=dismay)  □ impatience n. 성급
함; 조급  □ contest n. 경쟁, 겨루기; 논쟁  □ anomaly n. 변칙, 이례

당황할 필요는 없다. 모든 것이 통제하에 있다.


## 76                                    ①

□ abysmal a. 심연의, 나락의; 지독히 나쁜(=awful)  □ barrage v.
~에 탄막 포화를 퍼붓다; (질문 등으로) 공격하다  □ hype n. 과대광고
□ glitzy a. 현란한, 화려한  □ terrific a. 빼어난, 대단한, 아주 좋은
□ comforting a. 격려가 되는, 기운을 돋우는  □ agreeable a. 기분
좋은, 유쾌한, 마음에 드는, 호감을 주는

인터넷이 기업의 중역들 사이에서 악명을 얻을 만한 이유가 충분하다.
그들에게 월드와이드웹에 관한 과대광고와 현란한 영화 장면들과 가상
쇼핑몰이 들어 있는 멀티미디어 플래시 영상이 매일 매일 쏟아지기 때문
이다.


## 77                                    ④

□ prominent a. 현저한, 두드러진; 저명한, 걸출한(=eminent)  □ silent
a. 조용한, 소리 없는  □ indulgent a. 멋대로 하게 하는, 관대한, 눈감아주
는  □ imminent a. 긴급한, 임박한, 절박한

대통령 선거 첫 라운드에서 탈락한 다른 대통령 후보자들을 지지했던
여러 정당과 당원 중 수많은 저명한 인물들이 그 사람을 지지할 것으로
예상된다.


## 78                                    ③

□ three-dimensional a. 3차원의  □ muscle n. 근육  □ tissue n.
직물; (세포) 조직  □ evaluate v. 평가하다, 판단하다(=determine)
□ remove v. 제거하다; 치우다; 옮기다  □ prescribe v. 규정하다;
처방하다  □ treat v. 다루다, 대우하다; 치료하다

컴퓨터는 다친 근육의 주변을 의사들이 볼 수 있도록 해주는 3차원 영상
을 제공하며, 그 결과 상처가 주변 조직에 미친 영향을 판단할 수 있다.


## 79                                    ③

□ drought n. 가뭄; (장기간에 걸친) 부족, 결핍  □ devastate v. 황폐화
시키다, 파괴하다(=destroy)  □ trigger v. 유발하다, 촉발시키다  □
enhance v. 향상하다, 강화하다  □ manipulate v. 조작하다, 조종하다

스테이크 전문점의 메뉴 가격들이 3년 전보다 오르고, 미국 중서부의 옥
수수작물을 황폐화시켰던 가뭄이 가격 인상을 더욱 부추길 것이다.


## 80                                    ③

□ protagonist n. 주역, 주인공; 수령; 주창자(=principal)  □ bondman
n. 남자 노예, 농노  □ antagonist n. 적대자, 경쟁자  □ subordination
n. 예속시킴, 종속, 하위; 복종, 순종

그녀는 우리 부서에서 변화의 주역이다.


## 81                                    ③

□ mull over ~에 대해 숙고하다(=ponder over)  □ suggest v. 제안하
다; 암시하다  □ criticize v. 비판하다, 비난하다  □ be wary of ~을
경계하다

한편, 유일하게 이스라엘을 승인했던 아랍국가인 이집트와 요르단이 관
계의 단절을 공개적으로 숙고했는데, 그러한 조치는 회복하는 데 여러
해가 걸리는 것이었다.


## 82                                    ①

□ aghast a. 깜짝 놀라서, 넋이 나가서, 어안이 벙벙하여(at)(=alarmed)
□ wise a. 슬기로운, 현명한  □ lavishing a. 풍부한; 호화로운  □
discouraged a. 낙담한, 낙심한

적어도 200파운드 하는 자동차를 살 여유가 있으면서도 때때로 책 사는
데 0.5기니를 쓴다는 생각에 깜짝 놀랄 사람들이 많이 있다.


## 83                                    ③

□ conjecture n. 추측; 추측한 내용(=surmise)  □ merge n. (조직체,
사업체의) 합병  □ assiduity n. 근면, 부지런함  □ ignorance n. 무지,
무식  □ indigestion n. 소화 불량; 이해 부족

합병 가능성에 대한 몇 가지 추측이 있어왔다.

## 84     ③

☐ tenable a. 견딜 수 있는; 주장[지지]할 수 있는, 조리 있는(=logical) ☐ redundant a. 여분의, 과다한 ☐ tolerable a. 참을 수 있는, 웬만한, 꽤 좋은 ☐ efficient a. 능률적인, 효과적인; 유능한

많은 동료들은 브라운(Brown) 박사의 이론이 조리 있는 타당한 이론이라고 결국 동의했다.

## 85     ③

☐ nugatory a. 무가치한(=worthless) ☐ tentative a. 잠정적인 ☐ subtle a. 미묘한, 포착하기 힘든 ☐ vulnerable a. 취약한, 연약한

이 양탄자가 빨간색인지 녹색인지는 색맹인 사람에게 중요하지 않다.

## 86     ④

☐ vitriolic a. 신랄한, 통렬한, 독설에 가득찬(=acerbic) ☐ shield v. 감싸다, 보호하다 ☐ cowardly a. 겁이 많은; 비겁한 ☐ tactful a. 요령[눈치] 있는 ☐ discreet a. 신중한, 조심스러운

그는 총리가 부패한 친구들을 감싸고 있다고 비난하면서 총리에 대한 통렬한 공격을 시작했다.

## 87     ④

☐ fulcrum n. (지렛대의) 받침점, 지렛목; 주축이 되는 것, 지주, 버팀대 (=pivot) ☐ pride n. 자부심, 긍지 ☐ attraction n. 명소, 매력(적인 요소) ☐ caliber n. 역량, 자질

대부분의 시민들이 그곳에서 일하기 때문에 그 공장은 우리 마을의 중심이다.

## 88     ①

☐ intrinsic a. 고유한, 본질적인(=inherent) ☐ obsolete a. 쓸모없게 된, 진부한, 시대에 뒤진 ☐ exquisite a. 최고의, 절묘한; 정교한 ☐ uncertain a. 불확실한, 불안정한

과거를 연구하는 것은 우리 자신에 대한 호기심을 충족시키는 본질적인 가치를 가지고 있다.

## 89     ①

☐ lull n. 중간 휴식; 잠잠함; 일시적 불경기(=pause) ☐ clamor n. 떠들썩함; 소란, 아우성 ☐ agitation n. 뒤흔들기; 동요; 선동; 들썩임 ☐ commotion n. 동요, 소동; 폭동

그 어떤 휴식시간 중에라도 마실 것이 필요하다거나 다른 사람들에게 인사를 하고 싶다고 말하며 양해를 구하고 자리를 떠라.

## 90     ④

☐ chide v. 꾸짖다, 책망하다(=scold) ☐ soothe v. 달래다, 위로하다 ☐ compliment v. 칭찬하다; 아첨의 말을 하다 ☐ threaten v. 협박하다, 위협하다

그는 자신과 함께 그 선생님이 훈련시키기 시작했던 어린아이들을 꾸짖었다.

## 91     ③

☐ pay tribute to ~를 칭찬하다; ~에게 경의를 표하다(=honor) ☐ redeem v. 되사다, 되찾다; 벌충하다, 채우다 ☐ spawn v. 알을 낳다, 산란하다 ☐ reimburse v. 갚다, 상환하다; 변상하다

헬렌 켈러(Helen Keller)와 그녀의 선생님인 앤 설리번(Anne Sullivan)을 기리는 우표가 발행되었다.

## 92     ③

☐ perennial a. 여러 해 계속되는, 영구적인, (샘 따위가) 연중 마르지 않는 ☐ ephemeral a. 덧없는; 단명한; 순식간의, 덧없는(=temporary) ☐ chronic a. 장기간에 걸친, 만성적인 ☐ inveterate a. 상습적인; 고질적인 ☐ contaminated a. 오염된, 더럽혀진

주(州) 관리들에 따르면, 뉴멕시코주에 있는 강 가운데 7%에 약간 못 미치는 강이 영구적인 강이며 나머지 93%는 일시적인 강이라고 한다.

## 93     ④

☐ a slap on the wrist 경고, 가벼운 꾸지람(=a soft punishment) ☐ antitrust a. 독점 금지의 ☐ a slap on the back 등을 두드리기; 칭찬, 찬사 ☐ a slap in the face (고의적인) 모욕 면박 ☐ a severe punishment 엄벌, 가혹한 처벌

이것이 독점 금지에 관한 가장 큰 수사 중의 하나인 한 미국 기업에 관한 수년간의 수사가 목요일에 가벼운 경고로 끝이 난 이유인데, 연방 통상 위원회는 구글 검색 실행에 대한 수사를 한 건의 고소 없이 마무리 지었다.

## 94     ②

☐ bond market 채권 시장 ☐ revive v. 부활하다, 되살아나다 ☐ doldrums n. 우울, 의기소침; 침체(=depression) ☐ humidity n. 습기, 습윤 ☐ venture n. 모험, 투기

채권 시장은 여름철 침체기가 지나면 보통 되살아난다.

## 95     ①

☐ predatory a. 포식성의; 약탈하는(=plundering) ☐ fastidious a.

세심한, 꼼꼼한  □ beleaguered a. 사면초가에 몰린  □ whimsical
a. 마음이 잘 변하는, 변덕스러운

악덕 고리업자들은 교육 수준이 낮은 사람들을 먹잇감으로 삼는다.


## 96 ③
□ abyss n. 심연, 깊은 구렁(=gulf)  □ dawn n. 새벽, 동틀녘; 발단
□ cult n. 숭배, 예찬  □ usher n. 안내인, 접수원

윈스턴 처칠(Winston Churchill)은 영국 국민들이 나치에 굴복한다면
"새로운 암흑시대의 심연으로 빠져들 것"이라고 경고했다.


## 97 ②
□ counteract v. (무엇의 악영향에) 대응하다, 꺾다(=offset)  □
strengthen v. 강화되다, 강력해지다  □ pursue v. 뒤쫓다; 추구하다
□ commence v. 시작하다, 개시하다

정부는 원화 가치 상승의 영향에 맞서기 위한 많은 대책방안을 실시
했다.


## 98 ①
□ sacred a. 성스러운, 종교적인  □ inviolable a. 범할 수 없는, 불가침
의(=sacrosanct)  □ blithe a. 즐거운, 유쾌한; 쾌활한  □ phlegmatic
a. 차분한, 침착한  □ mercurial a. 쾌활한; 재치 있는; 변덕스러운

모든 인간의 삶은 그 시작에서 자연스러운 죽음에 이르기까지 신성하고
불가침하다.


## 99 ③
□ bait n. 미끼, 유혹물(=decoy)  □ substitute n. 대리; 대용물  □
precedent n. 선례, 전례  □ resort n. 의지; 수단, 방책

그 상점은 새 고객을 끌어들이는 미끼로 무료 선물을 이용했다.


## 100 ②
□ windfall n. 습득물, (유산 등의) 예기치 않았던 횡재(=bonanza)  □
makeshift n. 임시변통의 수단  □ stopgap n. 미봉책  □ setback
n. 방해, 정지

그 불법적인 정책이 상품권 발행업자들에게 하루 밤새 엄청난 이익을
가져다주었다.

# MVP 21-25 ACTUAL TEST

| | | | | | | | | | |
|---|---|---|---|---|---|---|---|---|---|
| 01 ④ | 02 ② | 03 ② | 04 ③ | 05 ① | 06 ③ | 07 ④ | 08 ④ | 09 ① | 10 ④ |
| 11 ③ | 12 ③ | 13 ① | 14 ② | 15 ① | 16 ① | 17 ② | 18 ② | 19 ① | 20 ① |
| 21 ④ | 22 ③ | 23 ③ | 24 ④ | 25 ② | 26 ② | 27 ① | 28 ② | 29 ④ | 30 ③ |
| 31 ② | 32 ③ | 33 ④ | 34 ② | 35 ② | 36 ④ | 37 ② | 38 ② | 39 ③ | 40 ④ |
| 41 ③ | 42 ④ | 43 ④ | 44 ② | 45 ① | 46 ② | 47 ③ | 48 ④ | 49 ③ | 50 ③ |
| 51 ① | 52 ① | 53 ② | 54 ④ | 55 ② | 56 ③ | 57 ② | 58 ① | 59 ① | 60 ② |
| 61 ③ | 62 ② | 63 ① | 64 ③ | 65 ① | 66 ③ | 67 ④ | 68 ① | 69 ② | 70 ② |
| 71 ③ | 72 ④ | 73 ④ | 74 ② | 75 ③ | 76 ④ | 77 ① | 78 ① | 79 ③ | 80 ④ |
| 81 ① | 82 ① | 83 ④ | 84 ① | 85 ① | 86 ② | 87 ④ | 88 ④ | 89 ④ | 90 ① |
| 91 ④ | 92 ④ | 93 ② | 94 ① | 95 ③ | 96 ① | 97 ④ | 98 ③ | 99 ④ | 100 ② |

## 01 ④

□ opinion poll 여론 조사 □ robustness n. 억셈, 강건함, 튼튼함 (=power) □ randomness n. 우연성, 무작위 □ interpretation n. 설명; 통역 □ irrelevance n. 부적절; 무관함 □ testimony n. 증거, 증언

여론 조사를 시행할 때, 여론 조사가 갖는 힘은 표본의 크기와 무작위성에 따라 증가한다.

## 02 ②

□ paralyze v. 마비시키다; 무력하게 하다(=disable) □ despise v. 경멸하다, 멸시하다 □ displace v. 대신하다, 바꾸어놓다 □ degrade v. 강등시키다, 떨어뜨리다

택시기사들이 공무를 마비시켰다.

## 03 ②

□ voter n. 투표자, 선거인; 유권자 □ impress v. ~에게 감명을 주다 □ stately a. 당당한, 위엄 있는(=dignified) □ election n. 선거 □ national a. 국가의, 전국적인 □ spontaneous a. 자발적인, 임의의 □ well-planned a. 잘 계획된

선거일을 겨우 이틀 앞두고 행해진 그의 위엄 있는 연설에 유권자들이 감명받았다.

## 04 ③

□ confiscate v. 몰수하다, 압류하다(=impound) □ draft v. 초안을 작성하다; 선발하다 □ donate v. 기부하다, 기증하다 □ dispatch v. 급송하다, 급파하다, 파병하다

한국예금보험공사는 올해 한국에 있는 거래 정지된 저축은행들로부터 몰수한 예술작품을 해외 경매에서 판매할 것이다.

## 05 ①

□ sovereignty n. 주권, 통치권 □ duress n. 구속, 속박(=coercion) □ under duress 협박당하여, 강압하에 □ quarantine n. 격리 □ exuberance n. 풍부 □ surveillance n. 감시, 감독

우리는 우리나라의 주권을 지키기 위해 최선을 다할 것이며 절대로 강압하에 굴복하지 않을 것이다.

## 06 ③

□ intimidate v. 으르다, 겁주다, 위협하다, 협박하다(=frighten) □ encourage v. 용기를 돋우다, 격려하다, 고무하다 □ discourage v. 용기를 잃게 하다, 실망시키다 □ cox v. ~의 키잡이가 되다

사람들을 협박해서 여당에 투표하게 하려 했으나, 아무 소용이 없었다.

## 07 ④

□ conceive v. (생각·계획 등을) 마음속으로 하다 □ bold a. 용감한, 대담한 □ arduous a. 고된, 힘이 드는, 분투적인, 끈기 있는(=strenuous) □ averse a. ~을 싫어하는 □ fastidious a. 세심한, 꼼꼼한, 까다로운 □ austere a. 꾸밈없는, 소박한

이 무렵 나는 도덕적 완벽에 이르는 대담하고 고된 프로젝트를 구상했다.

## 08      ④

☐ evangelist n. 복음 전도자, 선교사 ☐ exhort v. 타이르다, 권하다, 훈계하다(=advise) ☐ sinner n. 죄인 ☐ exasperate v. 성나게 하다, 격분시키다 ☐ obliterate v. 지우다, 말소하다; 없애다 ☐ cast away ~을 물리치다, 제거하다, 없애다

그 복음 전도사는 청중 가운데 있는 모든 죄인들에게 회개하라고 권할 것이다.

## 09      ①

☐ traverse v. 가로지르다, 횡단하다(=cross) ☐ conquer v. 정복하다; 공략하다; 극복하다 ☐ survey v. 측량하다; 조사하다 ☐ witness v. 목격하다; 증언하다

이븐 바투타(Ibn Battuta)가 탕헤르(Tangier)로 돌아왔을 때 이미 그는 걷고, 당나귀를 타고, 낙타를 타고, 배를 이용해서 지식과 경험을 찾아 이슬람 세계 거의 전체와 그 이상의 거리를 횡단한 셈이었다.

## 10      ④

☐ unprecedented a. 전례[선례]가 없는 ☐ accuracy n. 정확성 ☐ cutting-edge a. 최첨단의(=innovative) ☐ scientific a. 과학적인; 체계적인 ☐ extensive a. 대규모의, 광범위한 ☐ in-depth a. 철저하고 상세한, 면밀한

오늘날 생물학 연구는 최첨단 기술을 사용하여 전례 없는 수준의 정확성을 성취할 수 있는 흥미진진한 새로운 시대로 접어들고 있다.

## 11      ③

☐ revelation n. (비밀 등을) 드러냄, 폭로 ☐ brace oneself 대비하다, 준비하다(=prepare) ☐ turbulent a. 떠들썩한, 소란스러운; 몹시 거친, 사나운 ☐ mounting a. 증가하는, 커져 가는 ☐ mayhem n. 대혼란, 아수라장 ☐ anticipate v. 기대하다, 예상하다 ☐ head v. 지휘하다; ~으로 향하게 하다 ☐ stand v. 서다, 기립하다

중앙은행이 경제 침체를 초래하는 시장의 대혼란을 막기 위해 금리를 곧 낮출 수도 있다는 높아지는 기대감과 함께 증권업자들이 또 한 번의 혼란스러운 한 주에 대비하고 있을 때 그 폭로가 나왔다.

## 12      ③

☐ itinerant a. 순회하는, 이동하는(=travelling) ☐ ply v. 바쁘게 움직이다, 열심히 하다 ☐ ply one's trade 일[사업]을 하다 ☐ sickly a. 병약한 ☐ temporary a. 일시적인 ☐ proficient a. 능숙한

내가 보기에 누가(Luke)는 드로아와 빌립보 같은 곳에서 일했던 순회 의사였다.

## 13      ①

☐ delve into ~을 탐구하다; 꼼꼼히 조사하다(=examine) ☐ recruit v. (새 회원을) 모집하다; 징집하다; 보충하다 ☐ divide v. 나누다, 분할하다, 쪼개다 ☐ dissolve v. 녹이다, 용해시키다; 분해시키다

우리가 그것들의 이름을 붙일 수 있건 없건 간에, 우리 모두는 두 가지 기본적인 방식으로 사고한다. 즉, 우리는 어떤 대상을 탐구하여 그것을 부분들로 나누려고 하거나, 또는 분리된 것처럼 보이는 두 가지 이상의 대상들을 보고 그것들을 함께 맞추려 한다.

## 14      ②

☐ prolific a. 다산(多産)의, (토지가) 비옥한; (화가·작가 등이) 다작하는 (=productive) ☐ detective novel 탐정소설 ☐ original a. 최초의; 독창적인, 창의성이 풍부한 ☐ tolerant a. 관대한, 아량 있는; 내성이 있는 ☐ celebrated a. 유명한, 세상에 알려진

아가사 크리스티(Agatha Christie)는 다작하는 작가여서, 작품 활동을 하는 동안 66권의 탐정소설과 14권의 단편소설 모음집을 출판했다.

## 15      ①

☐ sluggish a. 게으른, 나태한; 동작이 느린(=slow) ☐ weak a. 약한, 무력한 ☐ quick a. 신속한, 빠른 ☐ swift a. 신속한, 빠른

노화되어가는 내 면역계는 의심할 여지없이 예전보다 더 느리다.

## 16      ①

☐ unmistakable a. 오해의 여지가 없는, 틀림없는 ☐ backlash n. 역회전; 반동; 반발(=negative reaction) ☐ handheld a. 손에 들고 사용하는 ☐ physical violence 신체적인 폭력 ☐ political controversy 정치적인 논쟁 ☐ religious discrimination 종교적인 차별

아직 조직적인 소비자 운동으로까지 발전하지는 않았지만, 오늘날 미국에 7,500만 대나 되는 휴대용 통신장비에 대한 반발의 기미가 있다는 데에는 의심의 여지가 없다.

## 17      ②

☐ voracious a. 폭식하는; 열렬히 탐하는(=enthusiastic) ☐ cozy a. 아늑한, 편안한 ☐ dot v. 점을 찍다, 여기저기 흩어져 있다 ☐ considerable a. 중요한; 상당한 ☐ imaginative a. 상상의, 공상적인 ☐ speedy a. 급속한, 신속한

열렬한 독서광이었던 나의 이모는 그녀가 살았던 대학가에 산재해 있던 매우 아늑한 서점들을 자주 들렀다.

## 18 ②

☐ intransigent a. 고집스러운, 완고한, 비타협적인(=flatfooted) ☐ noncommittal a. 언질을 주지 않은, 애매한 ☐ squalid a. 지저분한, 불결한 ☐ amicable a. 우호적인, 원만한

나는 그 지배인이 왜 그렇게 비타협적인 입장을 유지했는지 모르겠어.

## 19 ①

☐ stigma n. 치욕, 오명 ☐ discrimination n. 차별 ☐ dissuade v. 단념시키다, 만류하다(=deter) ☐ convince v. 확신시키다, 납득시키다; 설득하다 ☐ bar v. 금하다; 제외하다 ☐ prescribe v. 규정하다, 명하다

후천성면역결핍증과 관련된 치욕과 차별 그리고 때때로 지역 사회나 혹은 심지어 정부에서 그 병에 대한 불인정으로 인해, 개인들이 검사를 받거나 혹은 치료를 받는 것을 자주 그만두게 된다.

## 20 ①

☐ abdicate v. (권리 등을) 버리다, 포기하다; 퇴위하다(=renounce) ☐ reverberate v. 반향하다; 울려 퍼지다; 반사하다, 굴절하다 ☐ restitute v. 원상으로 되돌리다; 반환하다 ☐ resonate v. 공명(하게)하다, 울리다

권리 포기에 관한 지침서는 없다. 그러나 오프라 윈프리(Oprah Winfrey)는 조용히 물러나고 싶지 않은 많은 군주들(거물급 인사들)에게 아주 훌륭한 모델을 제시했다.

## 21 ④

☐ ingredient n. 원료, 성분 ☐ hand sanitizer 손 세정제 ☐ volatile a. 휘발성의; 불안정한(=unstable) ☐ commodity price 물가, 상품 가격 ☐ elastic a. 신축성 있는; 융통성 있는 ☐ unreliable a. 신뢰할 수 없는 ☐ immobile a. 움직이지 않는

요즘에는 손 세정제의 원료가 저렴하지 않은데, 왜냐하면 에틸알코올과 글리세린의 상품 가격이 불안정하기 때문이다.

## 22 ③

☐ figure n. 인물, 사람 ☐ humility n. 겸손, 겸양 ☐ down-to-earth a. 현실적인, 실제적인(=practical) ☐ alternative a. 대체 가능한, 대안이 되는 ☐ conciliatory a. 달래는, 회유하기 위한 ☐ holistic a. 전체론의

그럼에도 불구하고, 사벨라(Sabella)는 여전히 축구계에서 사랑받는 인물이었으며 겸손함과 현실적인 생활방식으로 존경받았다.

## 23 ③

☐ principal n. 교장 ☐ promulgate v. 널리 알리다, 공포하다, 발표하다(=announce) ☐ pupil n. 학생, 제자 ☐ conduct n. 처신, 품행 ☐ instigate v. 선동하다, 부추기다 ☐ procure v. 손에 넣다, 획득하다 ☐ retract v. 철회하다, 취소하다

교장은 학생의 품행을 규정하는 질서를 중히 여기는 규칙들을 발표했다.

## 24 ④

☐ promising a. 가망 있는, 유망한, 믿음직한 ☐ donation n. 기증, 기부 ☐ drive n. (기부, 모집 등의 조직적인) 운동 ☐ auspicious a. 길조의, 상서로운(=favorable) ☐ irreparable a. 고칠 수 없는, 회복할 수 없는 ☐ false a. 그릇된, 틀린 ☐ preliminary a. 예비의; 임시의

100명의 사람들이 각각 100달러를 기부할 것을 약속하면서 모금 운동은 매우 기분 좋은 출발을 했다.

## 25 ②

☐ demagogue n. (민중) 선동자; 선동 정치가(=agitator) ☐ appeal v. 호소하다; 간청하다 ☐ prejudice n. 편견, 선입관 ☐ crowd n. 군중; (the ~) 대중 ☐ tyrant n. 폭군, 전제 군주, 압제자 ☐ critic n. 비평가, 평론가 ☐ pedagogue n. 학자인 체하는 사람, 현학자; 교사

그 선동가는 대중의 격정과 편견에 호소하기 위해 모든 수단을 다 썼다.

## 26 ②

☐ flummox v. 어리둥절하게 하다(=baffle) ☐ weigh down ~을 무겁게 누르다 ☐ marginalize v. 사회적으로 무시[과소평가]하다 ☐ brace v. 버티다, 떠받치다 ☐ summon v. 소환하다

투자자들은 경제를 압박하는 이례적인 일련의 상황에 당황했다.

## 27 ①

☐ insidious a. 교활한, 음흉한; (병 등이) 잠행성(潛行性)의(=furtive) ☐ obvious a. 명백한, 분명한; 알기[이해하기] 쉬운 ☐ unilateral a. 한편(만)의, 일면(적)인; 단독의 ☐ meaningless a. 목적 없는, 무의미한

그는 의사들이 그가 아프다는 사실을 알아내기 전에 잠행성 질환으로 사망했다.

## 28 ②

☐ stipulate v. 규정하다; 명기하다(=specify) ☐ material prosperity 물질적 번영 ☐ insinuate v. 넌지시[돌려서] 말하다 ☐ negate v. 무효로 하다; 부인하다 ☐ reverse v. 되돌리다; 거꾸로 하다

체르노빌(Chernobyl) 원전사고의 충격을 목격한 독일의 사회학자 울리히 벡(Ulrich Beck)은 『위험사회(Risk Society)』를 발표했다. 이 책은 위험에 관한 이론으로, 산업화 및 현대화가 기술 발전과 물질적 번영을 가져다주긴 하지만, 보다 거대한 위험 또한 초래한다고 규정하고 있다.

## 29 ④
□ frost n. 서리 □ bud v. 싹을 틔우다 □ limp a. 나긋나긋한; 야무지지 못한; 무기력한, 생기 없는(=lifeless and drooping) □ lanky a. (손발, 사람이) 홀쭉한, 호리호리한 □ stiff and firm 경직되고 굳은 □ burnt a. 탄, 눋은, 불에 덴; 태워서 만든

늦봄의 서리가 수목이 무성한 지역에 영향을 미치면, 삼림에 심각한 상처를 남길 수 있다. 막 싹이 튼 어린잎은 검게 되고 축 처지게 된다.

## 30 ③
□ monumental a. 기념비의, 불후의; 대단한, 엄청난(=outstanding) □ archaic a. 고풍의, 낡은, 오래된 □ degrading a. 품위를 떨어뜨리는, 불명예스러운, 창피스러운 □ entire a. 전체의; 완전한; 흠 없는, 온전한

1974년에 행크 아론(Hank Aaron)은 714개의 홈런을 친 베이브 루스(Babe Ruth)의 불후의 기록을 깨뜨렸다.

## 31 ②
□ nuclear reactor n. 원자로 □ substantial a. 상당한, 실질적인(=considerable) □ radioactive a. 방사의 □ ignorable a. 무시할 만한 □ dangerous a. 위험한 □ essential a. 본질적인; 필수불가결한

가장 최근에는 일본의 후쿠시마 원자력 발전소에서 볼 수 있듯이, 원자력 발전의 안전성에 대한 우려는 여전히 남아있다. 그 원자력 발전소가 쓰나미의 타격을 받고, 그 결과 상당한 양의 방사능 물질을 유출하기 시작했을 때, 일본은 원자로를 폐쇄해야 했다.

## 32 ②
□ legislature n. 입법부, 국회 □ convene v. 소집되다, 모이다(=gather) □ bill n. 법안 □ draft v. 초안을 작성하다 □ intervene v. 개입하다, 끼어들다 □ adjourn v. 중단하다, 휴정하다 □ dissemble v. 숨기다; ~인 체하다

입법부(국회)는 빨라도 1월까지는 소집되지 않을 것이기 때문에, 얼마나 많은 법안이 어느 주제에 대하여 초안 작성되고 있는지는 불분명하다.

## 33 ④
□ turbid a. 혼탁한; 혼란스러운(=confused) □ decisive a. 결정적인

□ be set to ~하도록 예정되어 있다 □ fearless a. 무서워하지 않는; 용감한 □ adamant a. 단호한, 완강한 □ morose a. 성미가 까다로운; 시무룩한

그 시(詩)는 결전이 시작되기 전날 밤 그 병사의 혼란스러운 심적 상태를 묘사한다.

## 34 ②
□ prohibitively ad. 엄두를 못 낼 만큼, 엄청나게(=extraordinarily) □ momentarily ad. 잠시, 잠깐(동안), 곧, 금방 □ strangely ad. 이상하게 □ tolerably ad. 참을 수 있을 만큼; 어지간히

식민지 시대에, 애팔래치아(Appalachian) 산맥을 가로질러서 어떠한 물건을 실어 나르는 일이 엄청나게 비싼 일이었다.

## 35 ②
□ surmount v. 오르다; (곤란 등을) 이겨내다; 극복하다, 타파하다(=overcome) □ devour v. 게걸스럽게 먹다; 탐독하다 □ decline v. 거절하다; 감소하다 □ denude v. 발가벗기다; (껍질을) 벗기다, 노출시키다; 박탈하다(of)

게임 후반의 반이 지났을 때는 원정팀이 18점이나 앞서 우리 팀이 도저히 따라갈 수 없었다.

## 36 ④
□ resort to ~에 호소하다, 의지하다(=make use of) □ put up with 참다, 참고 견디다 □ suffer from ~으로 괴로워하다, 고생하다; ~을 앓다 □ find fault with ~의 흠을 잡다, ~을 비난하다, 나무라다

불행한 사람들은 종종 자신의 고통을 표현하는 수단으로 폭력에 의지한다.

## 37 ②
□ nurture v. 양육하다; 양성하다(=promote) □ hold back 취소하다, 제지하다 □ disregard v. 무시하다, 문제시하지 않다; 경시하다 □ discipline v. 훈련하다, 단련하다; 훈계하다

한국은 발전하고 성공을 거둘 수 있도록 자금과 특혜를 제공함으로써 중소기업을 육성해왔다.

## 38 ②
□ fault n. 과실; 결점, 결함 □ object n. 물체, 사물 □ mist n. 안개, 연무 □ hunger n. 배고픔 v. 갈망하다(for) □ thirst n. 갈증 v. 갈망하다(for) □ chastise v. 응징하다; 질책하다, 비난하다(=upbraid) □ vindicate v. 정당함을 입증하다; 변호하다 □ commend v. 칭찬하다; 추천하다, 권하다 □ succor v. 돕다, 구제하다

분노를 통해 보이는 결점은 안개를 통해 보이는 물체와 같다. 그것들은 더 크게 보인다. 배가 고프면(음식을 갈망하면) 음식을 먹게 하라. 그러나 (결점을) 비난할 생각이라면, 결코 분노를 갈망해서는 안 된다(결점이 더 커 보일 테니까).

## 39 ③

□ predilection n. 편애, 좋아함(=liking) □ provision n. 예비, 준비; 공급 □ probability n. 있음직함; 가망 □ prospect n. 전망; 예상

정치가들은 흔히 단기적인 정치적 이익을 얻기 위한 말을 많이 하는데, 그 내용은 그들이 취했던 과거의 입장에 비하면 말도 안 되거나 모순되는 것들이다.

## 40 ④

□ mired a. 수렁에 빠진, 곤경에 빠진(=stagnant) □ exotic a. 이국적인; 외래의 □ pure a. 순수한, 순전한 □ essentialize v. 요점을 말하다

시간적으로 아득하고 정지된 과거라는 수렁에 빠져 있는 아시아의 익숙한 모습 대신, 일본은 갑자기 근대성이나 심지어 탈근대성을 상징하게 되었다.

## 41 ③

□ amulet n. 부적(=talisman) □ trinket n. 값싼[자질구레한] 장신구 □ totem n. 토템 □ tartan n. 타탄, 격자무늬 모직물

부적은 전형적으로 민속 신앙이나 토속 신앙의 일부이다.

## 42 ④

□ notorious a. 악명 높은; 유명한, 소문난(=infamous) □ exciting a. 흥분시키는, 자극적인 □ unbearable a. 견딜 수 없는, 참기 어려운 □ expecting a. 임신한; 기대하는

프로 하키 팀들은 경기 중에 선수들 사이에서 벌어지는 몸싸움으로 악명이 높다.

## 43 ④

□ sin n. (종교상, 도덕상의) 죄, 죄악; 과실, 잘못 □ penitence n. 후회, 참회, 속죄(=contrition) □ resume v. 다시 시작[계속]하다 □ free will 자유의지 □ penalty n. 형벌, 처벌; 벌금 □ salvage n. 해난구조, 구조 □ grudge n. 악의, 원한

이곳에 그녀의 죄가 있었다. 이곳에 그녀의 슬픔이 있었다. 그리고 이곳에 이윽고 그녀의 참회가 있을 것이었다. 그래서 그녀는 돌아왔고, 우리가 너무나 암울하게 이야기해 온 그 상징을 자신의 자유의지에 따라 다시 시작했다.

## 44 ②

□ instigate v. 유발시키다, 조장하다(=provoke) □ project v. 계획하다; 발사하다 □ instruct v. 지시하다, 가르치다 □ investigate v. 조사하다, 연구하다

그 선장은 성난 여인의 행동에 대한 응답으로서 예상치 못한 반응을 유발했다.

## 45 ①

□ reticent a. 입이 무거운, 과묵한, 신중한(=reserved) □ quarrel n. 말다툼, 언쟁 □ querulous a. 불만이 많은, 화를 잘 내는 □ hilarious a. 아주 재미있는, 명랑한, 즐거운 □ dogmatic a. 독단적인, 독선적인; 교리상의

그는 말다툼을 하는 이유에 대해 말이 없었다.

## 46 ②

□ deplete v. (세력, 자원 등을) 고갈[소모]시키다; 빼앗다(=exhaust) □ give up 포기하다, 그만두다 □ disprove v. 반증을 들다, 논박하다 □ malinger v. 꾀병을 부리다 □ appease v. 달래다, 진정시키다

물이 고갈되자마자 그 탐험가들은 희망을 버려야만 했다.

## 47 ③

□ prosaic a. 단조로운, 평범한(=mundane); 산문(체)의 □ exuberant a. 활기[생동감] 넘치는; 풍부한 □ consonant a. 일치하는, 조화로운 □ pastoral a. 목가적인; 전원생활의

잠시 후 그들에게는 응접실과 일상생활의 단조로운 일과 속으로 돌아가야 한다는 생각이 떠오른다.

## 48 ④

□ superficial a. 깊이 없는, 피상적인(=shallow) □ passing grade 합격점 □ redundant a. 여분의, 과다한 □ superfluous a. 남은, 여분의 □ wide-spread a. 널리 퍼진, 광범위한

그녀의 연구는 그 문제에 대해 피상적인 분석만 했기 때문에 교수님은 그녀에게 합격점 이상을 줄 수 없었다.

## 49 ③

□ solid a. 튼튼한 □ vault n. 금고; 둥근 천장, 둥근 천장 비슷한 것 □ fragile a. 취약한, 허술한(=frail) □ grotesque a. 터무니없는; 기괴한 □ refined a. 정제된; 세련된 □ formidable a. 가공할, 어마어마한

허술해 보이는 그 집을 둘러싼 아파트 건물들의 견고한 둥근 지붕이 보인다.

## 50 ③

□ mumble v. 중얼거리다(=mutter); 우물우물 씹다　□ rant v. 폭언을 하다, 고함치다; 호언장담하다　□ ramble v. (이리저리) 거닐다; 두서없이 이야기하다　□ baffle v. 좌절시키다, 곤란케 하다

그 아이가 너무 심하게 중얼거려서 나는 그 아이가 말하는 것을 한마디도 이해할 수 없었다.

## 51 ①

□ lurking a. 숨어[잠복해] 있는　□ predator n. 포식자　□ eavesdrop on 엿듣다(=overhear)　□ chatter n. (동물의) 재잘거림[깩깩거림]　□ gaze v. 지켜보다, 응시하다　□ camouflage n. 위장하다　□ mimic v. 흉내 내다

야생 동물들은 숨어있는 포식자들에 대한 단서를 찾기 위해 서로의 말에 귀를 기울이며, 다른 종들의 대화를 사실상 엿듣는 것으로 알려져 있다.

## 52 ①

□ acquaint v. 숙지시키다, 익히 알게 하다, 알리다(=familiarize)　□ under discussion 심의[토의]중인　□ explain v. 설명하다, 밝히다　□ question v. 질문하다, 묻다　□ acquire v. 취득하다, 얻다

이런 종류의 책을 쓸 때, 나의 주된 목적은 독자들에게 논의 중인 저자들과 시대들에 대한 일반적으로 인정되는 견해를 숙지시키기 위한 것이었다.

## 53 ③

□ consolidate v. 합병하다, 통합하다(=merge)　□ lavish v. 아낌없이 후하게 주다; 낭비하다　□ prevent v. 막다, 방해하다　□ impress v. ~에게 (깊은) 인상을 주다; 감동시키다

마침내 그들은 두 회사를 하나로 합병하기로 결정했다.

## 54 ④

□ glimpse n. 흘끗 봄(=looking)　□ opportunity n. 기회, 호기; 가망　□ extension n. 확대, 확장; 신장　□ meaning n. 의미, 뜻, 취지; 중요성

이 데이터를 통해 가정 내에서 실제로 일어나고 있는 일을 독특하게 엿볼 수 있게 될 것이라는 생각인데, 이러한 것은 스스로 보고하는 전통적인 방법을 통해서는 얻을 수 없었던 것이다.

## 55 ②

□ surmise v. 추측하다, 짐작하다(=suppose)　□ assess v. 재다, 가늠하다; 평가하다, 사정하다　□ decide v. 결심하다, 결정하다; 해결하다　□ confess v. 자백하다, 고백하다, 인정하다

우리는 교통 체증이 간선 도로에서 발생한 몇몇 교통사고 때문이라고 추측했다.

## 56 ②

□ diffident a. 조심스러운, 소심한(=modest)　□ wanton a. 방자한, 방종한; 변덕스러운　□ hidebound a. 완고한, 편협한　□ propathetic a. 호감을 느끼는, 본래부터 좋아하는

사라(Sara)는 그 교수의 강의에 대해 논평할 때 조심스러웠다.

## 57 ①

□ kindle v. 불붙이다; 밝게 하다, 빛내다; 자극하다(=inspire)　□ dampen v. 축축하게 하다; 기를 꺾다　□ discourage v. 용기를 잃게 하다, 낙담시키다　□ confuse v. 혼동하다; 혼란시키다, 어지럽히다

선생님의 칭찬은 그녀의 마음속에 희망의 불꽃을 타오르게 했다.

## 58 ①

□ shift n. 변천, 추이, 변화　□ potential n. 잠재력, 가능성　□ equilibrium n. 평형상태, 균형(=balance)　□ agitation n. 동요, 흥분; 선동　□ desertion n. 버림, 유기; 도망　□ frustration n. 좌절, 차질, 실패

북한에 대한 중국의 그 어떤 입장 변화도 아시아의 정치적인 균형을 크게 바꿀 수 있는 잠재력을 갖고 있다.

## 59 ①

□ contradiction n. 부인; 모순　□ allegiance n. 충성, 충절; 충실(=dedication)　□ sympathy n. 동정; 동조, 지지　□ define v. 규정짓다, 한정하다; (입장 따위를) 분명히 하다; ~을 설명하다　□ identity n. 동일성; 독자성, 정체성　□ deterioration n. 악화; 타락　□ fertility n. (토지가) 기름짐; 다산(多産), 풍부　□ delinquency n. 의무불이행, 직무태만

국가적인 충성과 국제적인 동조 사이의 강력한 모순은 아인슈타인(Einstein)의 유대인 정체성 찾기의 성격을 잘 나타내었다.

## 60 ②

□ pretext n. 구실, 핑계(=excuse)　□ insult n. 모욕　□ pretension n. 허세, 가식; 요구　□ engagement n. 약속, 맹세; 약혼　□ prestige n. 위신, 명성, 신망

그들이 이것을 핑계로 댄다면 그건 나를 모욕하는 것이다.

## 61 ③

☐ pretentious a. 거만한, 젠체하는; 과시적인(=showy) ☐ brag v. 자랑하다(about) ☐ tremendous a. 굉장한, 엄청난 ☐ prominent a. 두드러진, 뚜렷한; 주목을 끄는 ☐ explicable a. 설명할 수 있는, 납득할 수 있는 ☐ exponential a. <수학> 지수의; 기하급수적인; 해설자의

모두가 불쾌하게도, 존(John)은 자신의 고액 급료와 엄청난 특전에 대해 자랑할 때 허세를 부렸다.

## 62 ④

☐ compelling a. 강제적인, 어쩔 수 없는; 설득력 있는(=unavoidable) ☐ controversial a. 논쟁의 소지가 많은 ☐ illusionary a. 환영의; 환상의, 착각의 ☐ doubtful a. 의심스러운, 분명치 않은; 확신이 없는

연설에서, 그녀는 자신의 생각을 뒷받침해 줄 몇 가지 설득력 있는 실례들을 제시했다.

## 63 ①

☐ exotic a. 외래의, 이국적인; 색다른(=unusual) ☐ expensive a. 값비싼; 사치스러운 ☐ common a. 공통의, 공동의; 일반의 ☐ beautiful a. 아름다운, 고운, 예쁜

김(Kim)은 색다른 식물(외래식물)을 수집하기를 좋아한다.

## 64 ④

☐ sturdy a. 튼튼한, 건장한(=stalwart) ☐ attractive a. 매력적인, 마음을 끄는 ☐ unfriendly a. 비우호적인, 불친절한 ☐ friendly a. 친한, 우호적인

이 튼튼해 보이는 소녀들은 이 문제에 연루되는 것을 두려워한다.

## 65 ③

☐ monastic a. 수도원의; 수도사의 ☐ property n. 재산, 자산 ☐ at one's disposal ~의 뜻대로 되는 ☐ discretion n. 신중; 판단[선택]의 자유, 결정권, (자유) 재량(=inclination) ☐ piety n. 경건; 신앙심 ☐ sagacity n. 총명, 명민 ☐ avarice n. 탐욕

수도원장이 뜻대로 할 수 있는 다양한 수도원의 재산과 수입에서 이것들을 어떻게 공급할지에 관한 결정은 전적으로 수도원장의 재량에 맡겨져 있었다.

## 66 ③

☐ dutiful a. 의무[본분]에 충실한; 순종하는(=obedient) ☐ virtuous a. 도덕적인, 고결한 ☐ surrogate a. 대리의, 대용의 ☐ freewheeling a. (구속·책임 등에) 구속당하지 않는, 자유분방한

처음에는 충실한 딸로서, 그다음에는 아내, 어머니, 교사로서 낸시(Nancy)는 평생 자신의 욕망을 억눌러왔다.

## 67 ④

☐ dinosaur n. 공룡 ☐ promptly ad. 신속히; 재빠르게, 즉시 ☐ scrutinize v. 자세히 조사하다, 음미하다 ☐ regale v. 향응하다; 기쁘게 해주다(=entertain) ☐ triceratops n. 트리케라톱스(중생대 공룡) ☐ velociraptor n. 벨로키랍토르(백악기 공룡) ☐ bore v. 지루하게 하다, 따분하게 하다 ☐ relate v. 관계시키다, 관련시키다 ☐ inspire v. 고무하다, 격려하다

루크(Luke)의 선생님들은 아이들에게 공룡 모형 세트를 처음 선보였는데, 루크는 즉시 그것을 자세히 살펴보았다. 차를 타고 학교에서 집으로 돌아오는 길에, 루크는 트리케라톱스, 티라노사우루스, 벨로키랍토르에 대한 이야기로 엄마를 즐겁게 해주었다.

## 68 ①

☐ indiscriminate a. 무차별의, 닥치는 대로의, 분별없는(=haphazard) ☐ decry v. 비난하다, 깎아내리다 ☐ pesticide n. 살충제, 농약 ☐ innovative a. 혁신적인, 창조적인 ☐ unpleasant a. 불쾌한, 기분 나쁜, 싫은 ☐ indispensable a. 불가결의, 없어서는 안 될, 절대 필요한

『고요한 봄(Silent Spring)』이라는 소설에서, 레이첼 카슨(Rachel Carson)은 살충제의 무분별한 사용을 강력히 비난했다.

## 69 ②

☐ case n. (특별한 대우나 관심이 필요한) 사람 ☐ corporeal a. 형체를 가진; 물질적인(=palpable) ☐ bilious a. 담즙질의; 화를 잘 내는; 불쾌한 ☐ impervious a. 영향받지 않는; 침투하지 않는 ☐ intuitable a. 직감으로 알 수 있는

영화『비너스(Venus)』는 노인들이 마술과 같은 능력을 지닌 성자도 아니요, 비극의 주인공도 아닌, 다만 우리와 같은 몸을 지닌 존재라는 것을 보여주는 드문 영화다.

## 70 ②

☐ conjugal a. 부부간의, 혼인상의(=spousal) ☐ legal a. 법률(상)의, 법정의, 합법의 ☐ conjuring a. 요술의, 마술의 ☐ performative a. 수행을 나타내는, 수행적인

그 영화는 부부 동거권을 빼앗긴 한 남자의 모습을 보여주었다.

## 71 ③

☐ run-of-the-mill a. 흔해빠진, 평범한, 보통의(=average) ☐ New Russians 노브이 루스키(시장개방으로 인해 재벌로 급부상하면서 돈을

물 쓰듯이 쓰는 러시아의 재벌계층) □ tasty a. 맛있는; 재미있는, 흥미를 끄는 □ native a. 출신의, 태생의, 원주민의 □ envious a. 샘하는, 시기하는

일전에 모스크바(Moscow)에 있는 한 이탈리아 레스토랑에 근무하는 어떤 웨이터는 왜 메뉴판에 있는 흔해빠진 토스카나(Tuscan) 와인이 그렇게 비싼지를 한 고객에게 설명하려 했다. "만일 우리가 토스카나 와인을 메뉴판에 싸게 기재해 놓으면, 신흥재벌 러시아인들은 그것을 사지 않을 겁니다."라고 그 웨이터는 말했다.

## 72 ④

□ Igbo n. 이그보우 부족; 이그보우어(나이지리아 서남부에서 거주하는 민족 또는 그 언어) □ work out ~을 계획해[생각해] 내다 □ canvass v. 조사하다, 검토하다(=scrutinize) □ geopolitical a. 지정학의 □ botch v. (서투른 솜씨로) 망치다 □ prattle v. (쓸데없이 마구) 지껄이다 □ emaciate v. 여위게[쇠약하게] 하다

다양한 분야에 걸친 15개 이상의 이그보우(Igbo) 족 단체들이 남동부의 지정학적 지대에 의해 검토될 수 있는 입장을 내놓기 위해 모임을 가졌다.

## 73 ④

□ grotesque a. 기괴한, 터무니없는, 말도 안 되는(=dreadful) □ emotional a. 감정의, 정서의 □ beautiful a. 아름다운, 예쁜, 고운 □ original a. 최초의; 본래의, 고유의, 독창적인

그 정치가의 연설은 내가 이제껏 들은 연설 중에 가장 괴상한 것이었다.

## 74 ②

□ watershed a. 분수계[분기점]를 이루는; 획기적인(=significant) □ destructive a. 파괴적인; 해로운 □ upsetting a. 소란을 일으키는, 엉망으로 만드는 □ humiliating a. 면목 없는, 치욕이 되는

애플에서 해고당하고 실직 상태에 있었던 것은 스티브 잡스(Steve Jobs)에게 하나의 분기점이 되는 순간이었다.

## 75 ③

□ stentorian a. 목소리가 큰, 우렁찬(=deafening) □ tranquil a. 조용한, 평온한 □ delightful a. 매우 기쁜, 즐거운 □ twisted a. 비틀린, 꼬인

그녀는 마흔 살 가량의 쾌활해 보이는 여인으로, 목소리가 깊고 거의 남자 같은 크고 우렁찬 음색이었고, 크고 다부진 체격이었으며, 큰 음성과 큰 체격에 어울리는 두 발에는 두툼하고 멋진 부츠를 신고 있었다.

## 76 ④

□ mundane a. 현세의; 세속적인(=worldly) □ quotation n. 인용; 시세, 시가 □ global a. 지구의, 세계적인 □ futile a. 쓸데없는, 무익한; 하찮은 □ spiritual a. 정신의, 정신적인, 신성한

그는 단지 세속적인 일들, 특히 매일의 주식시장 시세에만 관심을 가졌다.

## 77 ①

□ exasperated a. 몹시 화가 난, 격분한(=irritable) □ drowsy a. 졸리는, 나른하게 만드는 □ forlorn a. 버림받은, 외로운, 쓸쓸한 □ dizzy a. 어지러운, 현기증을 일으키는

화가 나는 것은 약물 과다복용의 부작용일지도 모른다.

## 78 ①

□ apogee n. 정점(=zenith) □ mesmerize v. 매료시키다 □ nadir n. <천문> 천저(天底); (역경, 운명 등의) 밑바닥, 최악의 순간 □ perigee n. <천문> 근지점(달이나 인공위성이 궤도상에서 지구에 가장 가깝게 접근하는 점) □ longitude n. 경도, 경선

비엔나 음악 스타일의 정점인 모차르트(Mozart)의 음악은 21세기에도 계속해서 청중을 매료시키고 있다.

## 79 ③

□ happen v. 일어나다, 발생하다 □ account for ~을 설명하다, 해명하다(=explain) □ accident n. 사고, 재해; 사건 □ maintain v. 유지하다, 지속하다 □ recollect v. 회상하다, 생각해 내다 □ deny v. 부인하다, 부정하다

그때 갑자기 다른 일이 발생했고, 그는 그 사건을 해명해야 했다.

## 80 ④

□ preposterous a. 말도 안 되는, 터무니없는, 가당찮은(=ridiculous) □ embarrass v. 당황하게 하다, 난처하게 하다 □ rude a. 버릇없는, 무례한 □ prospective a. 예상된, 기대되는 □ ambiguous a. 애매모호한, 알쏭달쏭한

그녀의 터무니없는 말은 동료들을 당황하게 했다.

## 81 ①

□ surveillance n. 감시, 감독; 사찰(=observation) □ manipulation n. 교묘히 다루기, 조작 □ protection n. 보호, 보안 □ recovery n. 회복, 복구; 쾌유; 되찾음, 만회

그 남자가 여전히 치료에 반응을 보이지 않았기 때문에, 보험 사정원은 그를 감시 상태에 두기로 결정했다.

## 82 ①

☐ obscure v. 어둡게 하다; 덮어 감추다, 가리다 ☐ downplay v. ~을 중시하지 않다, 경시하다 ☐ tailor v. 맞추다, 조정하다(=adjust) ☐ self-understanding n. 자각(自覺), 자기 인식 ☐ abandon v. (지위 등을) 버리다; 단념하다 ☐ improve v. 개량하다, 개선하다 ☐ curtail v. 짧게 줄이다; 생략하다

그들은 더 큰 문화에서 요구하는 바를 따르기 위해 종종 자신들이 가진 인종적 자각을 감추거나, 무시하거나, 맞추려 노력했다.

## 83 ④

☐ steadfastly ad. 확고부동하게, 고정되게, 불변으로(=tenaciously) ☐ insurgent n. 반란[내란]을 일으킨 사람 ☐ rebel n. 반역자, 저항 세력 ☐ stealthily ad. 몰래, 은밀히 ☐ capriciously ad. 변덕스럽게, 불규칙적으로 ☐ petulantly ad. 건방지게, 성마르게

반정부주의자는 정통성을 주장하는 정부에 대항하는 반역자인 반면, 자유의 투사는 외국 침략자를 확고부동하게 받아들이기를 거부하는 이상주의적인 사람들로서 긍정적으로 정의된다. 그러나 사실상 이 두 단어는 반대쪽 입장에서 보면 똑같은 사람들을 나타낸다.

## 84 ①

☐ shatter v. 산산이 부수다, 박살내다; 파괴하다 ☐ yellow-fever n. 황열병 ☐ epidemic n. 유행병, 전염병; 역병(=pestilence) ☐ epoch n. (중요한 사건이 일어났던) 시대; (역사, 정치 등의) 신기원, 새시대 ☐ incidence n. (사건의) 발생, 발생 정도 ☐ villainy n. 나쁜 짓, 악행

아내와 어머니로서 메리 해리스(Mary Harris)가 가지고 있던 기대는 1867년에 황열병이라는 역병으로 전 가족, 즉 남편과 네 자녀를 잃었을 때 산산조각 났다.

## 85 ①

☐ cataclysm n. 대변동, 격변(=upheaval) ☐ aristocracy n. 귀족, 귀족 사회 ☐ culmination n. 최고점 ☐ barometer n. 기압계; 표준, 척도 ☐ milepost n. 획기적 사건

미국 남북전쟁은 실제로 북부와 서부의 자본가와 노동자와 농민들이 남부의 농장경영 귀족들을 국가정부의 권력에서 몰아낸 사회적 격변이었다.

## 86 ②

☐ verbal a. 말에 의한, 구두의 ☐ pugnacious a. 싸움하기 좋아하는,

호전적인(=truculent) ☐ break with 관계를 끊다, 절교하다 ☐ ebullient a. 비등하는, 끓어 넘치는 ☐ effervescent a. 흥분한, 활기 있는 ☐ unruffled a. 어지럽지 않은; 조용한, 냉정한

그들이 결별한 후에, 더글러스(Douglas)에 대한 개리슨(Garrison)의 언어 공격은 그가 그 운동에서 관계를 끊은 다른 사람들에 대한 공격만큼이나 호전적이었다.

## 87 ③

☐ impression n. 인상, 감명 ☐ malaise n. (상황·집단 내에 존재하는 설명·규명하기 힘든) 문제들[불안감]; (특정한 문제로 표출되지는 않지만 전반적으로 존재하는) 불만감[불쾌감](=unease) ☐ supremacy n. 최고, 최상위; 우월 ☐ misbehavior n. 무례, 나쁜 행실 ☐ temperament n. 기질, 성미

그 이해는 그들의 불안감에 대한 단순한 인상 이상을 근거로 하고 있었다.

## 88 ④

☐ nominate v. 지명하다; 임명하다(=name) ☐ refuse v. 거절하다; (제의를) 받아들이지 않다 ☐ keep v. 보유하다, 간직하다 ☐ change v. 바꾸다; 교환하다; 잔돈으로 바꾸다

미국에서는 한 정당이 공직을 위해 단 한 명의 후보자를 지명할 수 있다.

## 89 ④

☐ unbeatable a. 패배시킬 수 없는, 맞겨룰 수 없는 ☐ juggernaut n. (통제할 수 없는) 비대한 힘[조직](=leviathan) ☐ steamroll v. 압도하다, 분쇄하다; 끝까지 밀고 나아가다 ☐ competitor n. 경쟁자, 경쟁상대 ☐ relentless a. 가차 없는, 잔인한 ☐ maverick n. 독립 입장을 취하는 지식인; 비동조자 ☐ machination n. 교묘한 책략[술책] ☐ largess n. 아낌없이 줌; (아낌없이 주어진) 선물

중국은 부(富)와 권력을 끈질기게 추구하는 데 있어 경쟁국들을 강압적으로 밀고 나갈 무적의 산업 최강국이다.

## 90 ①

☐ occult a. 신비스러운, 불가사의한; 비밀의(=mystical) ☐ rite n. 의례, 의식 ☐ facile a. 손쉬운, 용이한, 간편한 ☐ devious a. 우회한; 정도를 벗어난 ☐ peculiar a. 독특한, 고유의, 달리 없는

그 조직의 신비로운 의식은 회원에게만 공개되었다.

## 91 ④

☐ dispatch v. (특히 특별한 목적을 위해) 보내다, 파견하다 ☐ retrieve v. 만회하다, 회복하다; 구출하다, 구하다(=salvage) ☐ hurl v. 집어던지

다, 세게 던지다 ☐ revive v. 소생하게 하다; 회복시키다; 재상연하다 ☐ forfeit v. 상실하다; 몰수되다

해군 잠수팀은 침몰된 배를 구하기 위해 급파되었다.

## 92 ④

☐ sage n. 현자, 철인; 경험이 풍부한 현자, 박식한 사람 ☐ askance ad. 의심하여, 미심쩍은 눈으로(=skeptically) ☐ look askance at ~을 곁눈질로[의심쩍은 눈으로] 보다 ☐ forgive v. (빚 따위를) 탕감하다 ☐ spontaneously ad. 자발적으로, 자연스럽게 ☐ stringently ad. 용서 없이, 가혹하게 ☐ relentlessly ad. 가차없이

정치, 문화, 경제 전문가들은 일부 학자금 대출을 탕감해 주려는 바이든 (Biden) 대통령의 비용이 많이 드는 계획에 여전히 의구심을 품고 있다.

## 93 ②

☐ sleight n. 능숙한 솜씨; 술책(=dexterity) ☐ sleight of hand 날랜 손재주; 교묘한 속임수 ☐ competitiveness n. 경쟁력 ☐ splendor n. 훌륭함, 뛰어남; 탁월 ☐ agility n. 민첩; 명민함

마술사들은 그들의 날랜 손재주를 강화하기 위해 (사람들의) 시선과 주의를 돌리는 능력을 이용한다.

## 94 ①

☐ impudent a. 염치없는, 무례한(=impertinent) ☐ attentive a. 주의 깊은, 세심한; 정중한 ☐ nebulous a. 불투명한; 애매한, 모호한 ☐ bureaucratic a. 관료주의적인, 요식적인

일본의 고위 외교관이 두 나라 사이의 신뢰를 언급한 것은 지나치게 무례한 행동이다.

## 95 ③

☐ precept n. 가르침, 교훈(=teaching) ☐ preference n. 선호(도), 애호 ☐ pride n. 자랑, 자존심 ☐ dignity n. 존엄, 위엄

그들은 반성하지 않은 삶은 한 개인에게 무가치하다는 그의 가르침에 따라 살려고 노력했다.

## 96 ①

☐ opprobrium n. 불명예, 오명; 욕설, 비난(=vilification) ☐ artifice n. 교묘한 솜씨; 책략 ☐ tenacity n. 고집; 끈기 ☐ impetus n. 자극(제), 기동력

대통령은 수치심에 대해 특이하게도 영향을 받지 않는 것처럼 보이지만, 우리의 나머지 정치인들은 여전히 비난에 취약하다.

## 97 ④

☐ outrageous a. 아주 별난, 터무니없는(=preposterous) ☐ from cover to cover (책의) 처음부터 끝까지 ☐ far-sighted a. 미래를 내다볼 줄 아는, 선견지명이 있는 ☐ effusive a. 감정이 넘쳐나는 듯한; 과장된 ☐ eclectic a. 절충적인; 다방면에 걸친

그 책은 터무니없는 내용 때문에 잘 팔렸지만, 많은 사람이 그 책을 처음부터 끝까지 읽는다고 믿기 어렵다.

## 98 ③

☐ bear the brunt of ~에 정면으로 맞서다; 견디다 ☐ stalemate n. 교착상태(=impasse) ☐ dispute n. 토론, 논쟁 ☐ breach n. 어김, 위반, 불이행 ☐ libel n. 명예 훼손(죄), 비방

해결책이 보이지 않는 상황에서 정치적 교착상태로 큰 타격을 받고 있는 것은 상인들이다.

## 99 ④

☐ honorary professor 명예교수 ☐ speculative a. 사색적인, 명상적인; 투기적인(=risky) ☐ capitalist n. 자본가, 자본주의자 ☐ take advantage of ~을 이용하다 ☐ reflective a. 반영하는; 반사적인 ☐ ablaze a. (활활) 타오르는, 화염에 휩싸인 ☐ sentient a. 지각이 있는

그 명예교수는 한국 기업들이 스스로를 보호할 수단이 없는 상황에서 투기적인 외국 자본가들이 그 새로운 법안을 기회로 활용할 것이라고 또한 언급했다.

## 100 ②

☐ invective n. 욕설, 악담(=denunciation) ☐ tolerance n. 관용; 아량 ☐ consent n. 동의, 허가 ☐ interference n. 방해, 간섭

여야 간의 상호 비방이 그칠 기미가 보이지 않는다.

| | | | | | | | | | |
|---|---|---|---|---|---|---|---|---|---|
| 01 ① | 02 ② | 03 ③ | 04 ② | 05 ② | 06 ③ | 07 ① | 08 ④ | 09 ② | 10 ① |
| 11 ③ | 12 ③ | 13 ① | 14 ② | 15 ④ | 16 ③ | 17 ④ | 18 ③ | 19 ① | 20 ③ |
| 21 ④ | 22 ① | 23 ④ | 24 ② | 25 ① | 26 ① | 27 ④ | 28 ③ | 29 ④ | 30 ② |
| 31 ② | 32 ① | 33 ④ | 34 ④ | 35 ② | 36 ③ | 37 ② | 38 ③ | 39 ④ | 40 ③ |
| 41 ① | 42 ④ | 43 ② | 44 ④ | 45 ④ | 46 ③ | 47 ① | 48 ③ | 49 ④ | 50 ③ |
| 51 ④ | 52 ① | 53 ② | 54 ② | 55 ③ | 56 ① | 57 ② | 58 ③ | 59 ① | 60 ① |
| 61 ① | 62 ③ | 63 ① | 64 ② | 65 ③ | 66 ① | 67 ① | 68 ④ | 69 ③ | 70 ③ |
| 71 ③ | 72 ① | 73 ① | 74 ③ | 75 ② | 76 ③ | 77 ④ | 78 ① | 79 ③ | 80 ② |
| 81 ④ | 82 ④ | 83 ③ | 84 ② | 85 ② | 86 ④ | 87 ③ | 88 ④ | 89 ② | 90 ④ |
| 91 ③ | 92 ④ | 93 ④ | 94 ④ | 95 ② | 96 ① | 97 ④ | 98 ② | 99 ③ | 100 ① |

## 01 ①

☐ contempt n. 경멸; 모욕, 창피; 치욕(=scorn) ☐ humility n. 겸손, 겸양 ☐ dignity n. 위엄, 존엄성 ☐ reverence n. 숭배, 존경, 경의

우리는 영어 수업 시간에 "미움은 가슴에서 나오고 경멸은 머리에서 나오는데 이 두 감정 모두 잘 통제되지 않는다"라는 쇼펜하우어 (Schopenhauer)의 인용문에 대한 글을 썼다.

## 02 ②

☐ inordinate a. 지나친, 과도한, 엄청난(=excessive) ☐ assignment n. 연구 과제; 숙제 ☐ onerous a. 부담이 되는; 번거로운, 성가신 ☐ designated a. 지명된, 지정의; 관선의 ☐ exhaustive a. 고갈시키는, 소모적인

매우 열심히 공부한다는 사실을 교수에게 보여주기 위해, 그는 과제에 엄청난 시간을 들였다.

## 03 ③

☐ vociferous a. (의견, 감정을) 소리 높여 표현하는 ☐ moniker n. 인명, 별명, 별칭(=nickname) ☐ certificate n. 증명서, 면허장 ☐ medal n. 메달, 훈장 ☐ honor n. 명예, 영예; 영광

프랑스 대통령이었을 때 자크 시라크(Jacques Chirac)는 온갖 이름으로 욕을 들었는데, 특히 미국 주도의 이라크 전쟁에 대해 큰 소리로 반대한 것으로 욕을 많이 먹었다. 현재 그는 없어지지 않을 별명을 갖고 있는데, 그것은 바로 유죄판결을 받은 범죄자이다.

## 04 ②

☐ release v. 풀어놓다; 해방하다; 개봉하다; 발매하다(=distribute) ☐ pay for ~의 대금을 치르다; 빚을 갚다 ☐ overturn v. 뒤집어엎다, 전복시키다 ☐ itemize v. 조목별로 쓰다, 항목별로 나누다

음악 사업에서 성공하기란 매우 어렵다. 첫 음반을 발매한 열 중 아홉 밴드는 두 번째 음반을 제작하지 못한다.

## 05 ②

☐ adore v. 흠모하다, 숭배하다(=esteem) ☐ find v. 찾아내다, 발견하다 ☐ obtain v. 얻다, 획득하다 ☐ reject v. 거절하다, 거부하다

새뮤얼 존슨(Samuel Johnson) 박사는 그 여자 간호사를 흠모했으며, 그녀가 가진 치유의 힘에 놀랐다.

## 06 ③

☐ splenetic a. 화를 잘 내는, 성질을 잘 부리는(=peevish) ☐ eccentric a. 괴짜인, 별난, 기이한 ☐ vibrant a. 활기찬, 강렬한 ☐ effusive a. 정을 토로하는; 과장된

외국인에 대한 그의 언짢은 트윗은 그의 이민 발의안을 막는 법정 의견에 인용되었다.

## 07 ①

☐ frost n. 서리; 추위 ☐ blight v. 말라죽게[시들게] 하다; 망치다 (=damage) ☐ fertilize v. 기름지게[비옥하게] 하다 ☐ sanitize v. 살균하다, ~을 위생적으로 만들다 ☐ cultivate v. 경작하다; 기르다

농부들은 간밤의 서리로 인해 감자 농작물이 완전히 망가진 것을 우려하고 있다.

## 08     ④

☐ take a nosedive 자빠지다; 급하강하다; 폭락하다(=plummet) ☐ hype n. 과대 선전[광고] ☐ flourish v. 번창하다; 무성하게 자라다 ☐ finish v. 끝내다, 완료하다, 완성하다 ☐ remain v. 남다, 잔존하다, 존속하다

그 쇼 프로그램은 너무 지나친 과대 선전과 반복적인 형식 때문에 이번 시즌에 (인기가) 대폭락했다.


## 09     ②

☐ fugitive a. 도망치는; 변하기 쉬운, 일시적인, 순간적인(=temporary) ☐ melodious a. 선율이 아름다운, 곡조가 좋은 ☐ awe-inspiring a. 경외케 하는, 장엄한 ☐ of real value 진정한 가치의

음악가의 머릿속에 일시적으로 떠올랐던 일련의 음표들이 천천히 어떤 곡조로 변하기 시작했다.


## 10     ①

☐ worship n. 숭배 ☐ belief n. 믿음, 생각, 신념 ☐ value n. 가치, 가치관 ☐ measure v. 측정하다, 평가하다 ☐ in terms of ~의 관점에서 ☐ ultimate a. 궁극적인; 최고의; 최종의 ☐ touchstone n. 기준, 시험, 표준(=test) ☐ source n. 근원, 근본, 원천 ☐ challenge n. 도전, 시합의 신청 ☐ objective n. 목표, 목적

내가 고려키길 원하는 것은 바로 돈의 숭배인데, 즉 모든 가치들이 돈의 관점에서 평가될 수 있으며 돈이 인생에 있어 성공의 궁극적인 기준이라는 생각이다.


## 11     ③

☐ punctuate v. 구두점을 찍다; 강조하다(=emphasize) ☐ routinely ad. 일상적으로 ☐ memorable a. 기억할 만한, 잊기 어려운 ☐ repeatable a. 되풀이할 수 있는, 반복할 수 있는 ☐ describe v. 묘사하다, 기술하다 ☐ articulate v. 똑똑히 발음하다, 분명히 말하다 ☐ address v. 이야기하다, 발언하다

그러한 모든 의사소통 사건들은 기억할 만하고 반복할 만한 여러 다양한 단위의 전통적인 자료들에 의해 일상적으로 강조되고 있다.


## 12     ③

☐ buttercup n. 미나리아재비(작은 컵 모양의 노란색 꽃이 피는 야생식물) ☐ cursory a. 서두르는; 대충 하는(=casual) ☐ glance n. 한 번 봄, 일견 ☐ staring a. 응시하는; 돋보이는 ☐ probing a. 엄밀히 조사하는 ☐ precise a. 정확한, 정밀한

토끼, 벌, 사과, 솔방울, 미나리아재비의 공통점은 무엇일까? 대충 봐서는 공통점이 그다지 많아 보이지 않는다.


## 13     ①

☐ inspire v. 고무하다, 격려하다; 영감을 주다 ☐ indoctrinate v. (사상 등을) 주입[세뇌]하다(=inculcate) ☐ seminal a. 정액의; 생식의; 발전성 있는; 독창성이 풍부한 ☐ incarnate v. 육체를 갖게 하다; 구체화하다 ☐ inflect v. (안쪽으로) 구부리다, 굴곡시키다 ☐ inseminate v. (씨앗을) 뿌리다; (인공)수정시키다

소쉬르(Saussure)의 1916년 저서 『일반언어학 강의』는 야콥슨 (Jakobson)에게 그랬듯이 기욤(Guillaume)에게도 영감을 주어, 그가 세뇌된 추종자가 되지 않고 소쉬르의 독창적인 사상을 뛰어넘게 만들었다.


## 14     ②

☐ hubris n. 자만, 오만(=hauteur) ☐ indecency n. 예절[버릇] 없음; 외설 ☐ blandishment n. 감언이설, 유혹 ☐ larceny n. 절도, 도둑질

잘못 돼 갔던 점은 폭풍이 나쁜 시기에 닥쳤다는 점과 자신들은 악천후의 현실에 영향을 받지 않는다고 생각한 주민들의 오만함이 겹친 것이었다.


## 15     ④

☐ prerogative n. 특권, 특혜(=privilege) ☐ preserve v. 지키다, 보호하다 ☐ at the expense of ~을 희생하면서 ☐ prejudice n. 편견, 선입관 ☐ prediction n. 예측, 예견 ☐ project n. 안(案), 계획

자유는 영국인의 특권이다. 따라서 우리는 우리의 삶을 희생해서라도 그것을 지켜야 한다.


## 16     ③

☐ hate v. 싫어하다 ☐ unkempt a. 헝클어진, (정원 따위가) 손질이 되지 않은(=disheveled) ☐ detrimental a. 해로운 ☐ property n. 재산; 부동산 ☐ truncated a. 끝을 자른 ☐ redolent a. 냄새가 나는 ☐ unwitting a. 자신도 모르는

제레미(Jeremy)는 이웃의 정리되지 않은 잔디를 싫어했다. 그는 잔디가 방치된 모습이 동네 부동산 가치에 해로운 영향을 미친다고 생각했다.


## 17     ④

☐ compile v. 엮다, 편집[편찬]하다(=edit) ☐ summary n. 요약, 개요 ☐ scan v. 자세히 조사하다; (신문 등을) 대충 훑어보다 ☐ copy v. 복사[복제]하다, 베끼다 ☐ remit v. 보내다; (죄를) 용서하다 ☐ deliver v. 배달하다; 해방시키다

우리 웹사이트는 다른 출처의 뉴스 헤드라인과 요약들을 편집해서 당신이 그것들을 한 곳에서 모두 훑어볼 수 있게 해준다.

## 18 ③

☐ succinct a. 간결한, 간명한(=brief)  ☐ tedious a. 지루한; 장황한; 끈덕진  ☐ tardy a. 느린, 완만한; 늦은, 더딘  ☐ final a. 마지막의, 최후의; 종국의, 궁극적인

노동조합의 메시지는 간결했다. 노동자들 중 아무도 다음날 출근하지 않겠다는 것이다.

## 19 ①

☐ wield v. (칼, 무기 등을) 사용하다, 휘두르다; 행사하다(=use)  ☐ hide v. 감추다, 숨기다; 가리다, 은닉하다  ☐ cover v. 덮다, 싸다, 씌우다  ☐ want v. 원하다, 바라다; 필요하다

미사일과 대량 살상 무기를 휘두르는 예측불허의 독재정권으로부터의 위협을 잘 알고 있었지만, 그는 취임 1년이 채 지나지 않아 전쟁을 할 것이라고는 예상하지 못했다.

## 20 ③

☐ laid back a. 느긋한, 태평스러운  ☐ easygoing a. 태평한, 마음 편한  ☐ captious a. 흠잡기 잘하는, 말꼬리를 잡고 늘어지는(=quibbling)  ☐ arduous a. 몹시 힘든, 고된; 분투적인  ☐ complacent a. 현실에 안주하는, 자기만족적인  ☐ supercilious a. 거만한, 건방진, 남을 얕보는

존(John)은 과거에는 성격이 느긋하고 태평스러운 편이었는데, 부모님의 이혼 이후로 모든 것에 대해 트집을 잡는 성격이 되었다.

## 21 ④

☐ replete a. 가득 찬, 충만한(=filled)  ☐ villain n. 악인, 악한  ☐ conflict n. 충돌, 대립, 갈등  ☐ resolution n. 결심; 해결, 해답  ☐ related a. 관계가 있는, 관련된  ☐ construct v. 조립하다, 건설하다, 건조하다

호모사피엔스(인류)는 숫자와 그래프가 아니라 이야기로 생각하는 이야기하는 동물이다. 우리는 우주 자체가 이야기처럼 움직이며, 영웅과 악당, 갈등과 해결, 절정과 해피엔딩으로 가득 차 있다고 믿는다.

## 22 ①

☐ stupefy v. 마취시키다; 깜짝 놀라게 하다; 멍하게 하다(=stun)  ☐ elate v. 기운을 돋우다; 의기양양하게 하다  ☐ enjoy v. 즐기다; 맛보다; 누리다  ☐ beam v. 빛나다; 빛을 발하다, 비추다

아내가 울음을 터뜨리려는 것을 봤을 때, 그는 깜짝 놀라고 매우 당황해서 그 자리에 멈춰 섰다.

## 23 ④

☐ boisterous a. 활기가 넘치는, 떠들썩한, 시끄러운(=rowdy)  ☐ to say the least 조금도 과장하지 않고  ☐ be in no mood for ~할 기분이 아니다  ☐ somber a. 어두컴컴한; 음산한  ☐ bizarre a. 기이한, 특이한  ☐ flamboyant a. 이색적인, 화려한

도심에 모여든 군중들은 아무리 좋게 보아도 시끄러운 편이었다. 그들은 공휴일 기념식을 거행할 기분이 아니었다.

## 24 ④

☐ unsightly a. 보기 흉한, 볼품없는(=repulsive)  ☐ inject v. 주사하다, 주입하다  ☐ solution n. 해결; 용액, 물약  ☐ shrink v. 줄어들다, 오그라들다; 수축하다  ☐ normalize v. 정상화하다  ☐ faint a. 어렴풋한, 희미한  ☐ clogged a. 방해받은, 막힌  ☐ invisible a. 눈에 보이지 않는, 감추어진

의사들은 화학용액이 든 가는 주삿바늘을 보기 흉한 정맥에 찔러 넣어 정맥이 수축했다가 다시 정상이 되게 한다.

## 25 ①

☐ catastrophe n. 대참사, 큰 재앙; 대단원(=disaster)  ☐ blessing n. 축복, 은총  ☐ surprise n. 놀람, 경악; 기습  ☐ disappointment n. 실망, 기대에 어긋남

국민 기금의 동결은 빈곤층 여성들과 그 자녀들에게는 하나의 큰 재난이었다.

## 26 ①

☐ grudge n. 원한, 악의, 유감, 앙심(=unfriendly feelings)  ☐ bad conscience 떳떳지 못한 마음  ☐ material loss 물질적 손실  ☐ secret suspicion 남모르는 의심

나에 대해 원한을 품지 않기를 바랍니다.

## 27 ④

☐ overweening a. 자부심이 강한, 잘난 체하는, 거만한(=immoderate)  ☐ persuasive a. 설득력 있는, 설득을 잘하는  ☐ elegant a. 품위 있는, 우아한, 세련된  ☐ categorical a. 절대적인, 무조건의; 단언적인; 범주에 속하는

지나칠 정도의 개인적 야심은 미덕이 되지 못한다. 그러나 그동안 내가 그것을 품었다면 나는 바늘방석 위에서도 춤을 추었을 것이다.

## 28 ③

☐ inoculate v. 접종하다, 예방 접종하다(=vaccinate) ☐ transform v. 변형시키다; (성질·기능·용도 등을) 바꾸다 ☐ extricate v. 구출하다, 해방하다 ☐ impinge v. 영향을 주다; 침범[침해]하다

이것은 쿠루병으로 죽은 사람들의 뇌에서 나온 물질을 세 마리의 암컷 침팬지의 뇌에 접종함으로써 이루어졌다.

## 29 ④

☐ oncology n. 종양학 ☐ relapse v. 병이 도지다[재발하다] ☐ refractory a. 말을 안 듣는, 고집 센; 난치의, 잘 낫지 않는(=intractable) ☐ mutable a. 변할 수 있는, 잘 변하는 ☐ manipulative a. 조종하는 ☐ inevitable a. 불가피한, 필연적인

정밀 종양학은 재발된 난치성 고형 종양 환자의 약 1.5%에 도움이 될 것이다.

## 30 ②

☐ didactic a. 교훈적인, 설교조의(=preachy) ☐ dialectic a. 변증법적인; 방언의 ☐ nebulous a. 흐릿한, 모호한 ☐ discerning a. 통찰력이 있는, 분별 있는

『The Idea of North』라는 기록물이 가진 교훈적 목적이 "North"와 음악적 구성 사이의 주요 차이점들 중 하나이다.

## 31 ②

☐ misdemeanor n. 경범죄, 비행, 못된 행동(=wrong doing) ☐ sickness n. 병, 건강치 못함; 멀미 ☐ mistake n. 잘못, 틀림, 오해 ☐ rude word 무례한 말

그 아이의 비행은 그의 부모에게 결코 심각하게 받아들여지지 않았다.

## 32 ①

☐ racist n. 인종 차별주의자 a. 인종 차별주의자의 ☐ incident n. 사건, 분쟁 ☐ obloquy n. 욕설, 비방; 악평, 오명, 불명예(=disgrace) ☐ eulogy n. 칭송, 찬양 ☐ soliloquy n. 혼잣말(하기), 독백 ☐ oblivion n. 망각, 잊기 쉬움, 건망

지난봄 인종차별적인 물의를 일으킨 그 두 학생은 이미 공개적으로 비난을 받았다.

## 33 ④

☐ estrangement n. 이간, 소외, 소원(=distancing) ☐ errand n. 심부름, 용건 ☐ establishment n. 설립, 창설 ☐ reconciliation n. 화해, 조화

가족 갈등은 대부분의 경우 회복이 가능하고 사이가 멀어지는 것보다는 더 낫다.

## 34 ④

☐ solidarity n. 연대, 결속 ☐ volunteer v. 자진하여 떠맡다, 자청하다 ☐ forgo v. ~없이 지내다, 삼가다, 보류하다; 그만두다(=waive) ☐ renege v. 딴 패를 내다; 손을 떼다, 취소하다 ☐ bestow v. 주다, 수여하다, 증여하다 ☐ dole v. 나누어주다, 베풀다

동료 직원들과의 결속을 보여주기 위해 그 회사의 사장은 자진하여 봉급을 포기하기로 했다.

## 35 ②

☐ potentiality n. 가능성; (발전의) 가망(=possibility) ☐ learnability n. 학습 용이성 ☐ likeness n. 비슷함, 닮음; 외관 ☐ quantity n. 양, 다량, 다수

모든 행동은 유전되지만, 엄격히 말해서 유전되는 것은 잠재성일 뿐이다.

## 36 ③

☐ vicarious a. 대신하는, 대리의(=substitute) ☐ precious a. 귀중한, 값비싼 ☐ vigorous a. 원기 왕성한 ☐ indispensable a. 불가결의

그는 대리 만족을 위해 TV로 스포츠 경기를 보는 것을 즐기는데, 젊은 시절에 그는 유명한 축구선수가 되고 싶어 했기 때문이다.

## 37 ②

☐ proclaim v. 공표하다, 선언하다(=declare) ☐ loyalty n. 충의, 충성; 충실 ☐ forsake v. 저버리다, 버리다; 단념하다 ☐ declaim v. 낭독하다, 암송하다, 연설하다 ☐ provoke v. 화나게 하다; 자극하다, 유발하다

모든 나라들은 동맹에 대한 충성을 선언했다.

## 38 ③

☐ reprimand v. 견책하다, 징계하다; 호되게 꾸짖다(=admonish) ☐ undermine v. (명성 따위를) 음험한 수단으로 훼손하다, 몰래 손상시키다 ☐ ridicule v. 비웃다, 조롱하다 ☐ discharge v. 해임[해고]하다

지속적으로 지각하는 직원들은 관리자로부터 공식적으로 질책 받을 수 있다.

## 39 ④

☐ give voice to ~을 말로 나타내다 ☐ facet n. 양상, 국면(=aspect)

□ affirm v. 확언하다; 확인하다 □ vantage point 견해, 관점 □ restoration n. 회복; 복원 □ embellishment n. 장식; 수식, (이야기 등의) 윤색 □ decadence n. 쇠미; 타락

그녀의 작품이 미국 흑인 문화의 이러한 거의 언급되지 않은 측면을 표현한 것과 마찬가지로, 그것은 흑인 여성의 독특한 관점을 확인시켜 주었다.

## 40 ③

□ indulgence n. 탐닉, 방자, 방종(=luxury) □ frugality n. 절약, 검소 □ discipline n. 훈련; 수양; 자제 □ complaint n. 불평, 불평거리

"즐거운 삶"으로 잘못 불리고 있는 방종의 삶은 행복을 불쌍하게 흉내 내고 있는 것이다.

## 41 ①

□ demise n. 사망; 소멸(=death); 권리 양도 □ fame n. 명성, 명망; 평판 □ heritage n. 유산; 세습 재산 □ vanity n. 덧없음, 공허; 허영심

팝 문화는 사람들이 그들 자신의 죽음을 상상하는 것을 가장 좋아한다는 사실을 알고 있다.

## 42 ④

□ germ-line 생식계열 □ gene manipulation 유전자 조작 □ frivolous a. 경솔한; 하찮은, 보잘 것 없는(=imprudent) □ personal a. 개인의; 사적인 □ experimental a. 실험의; 시험적인 □ fallacious a. 잘못된, 틀린

최초의 생식계열 유전자 조작이 경솔한 이유로 시도될 것 같지는 않다.

## 43 ②

□ secure v. 안전하게 하다; 보증하다, 책임지다; 확보하다(=obtain) □ lock v. 자물쇠를 채우다, 잠그다 □ tighten v. (바짝) 죄다, 단단하게 하다; 강화하다 □ keep v. 보유하다, 계속 가지고 있다

영국의 무역회사 허드슨베이 컴퍼니(Hudson Bay Company)는 알래스카 모피 무역시장에서의 발판을 확보하고자 했다.

## 44 ④

□ mince v. 잘게 저미다; 조심스럽게 말하다, 완곡하게 말하다 (=mitigate) □ do not mince words 솔직히[곧이곧대로] 말하다 E. coli n. 대장균(=Escherichia coli) □ manure n. 퇴비, 거름 □ coin v. 만들다, 주조하다 □ experiment v. 실험하다; 시도하다 □ emphasize v. 강조하다, 역설하다

슐로서(Schlosser)는 대장균 오염에 관해서 솔직하게 말한다. 그는 그것을 "배설물이 고기와 섞인 것"이라고 있는 그대로 말한다.

## 45 ④

□ murky a. 어두운; 음산[우울]한 □ overlook v. 못 보고 지나치다, 간과하다; 봐주다(=pass over) □ witness v. 목격하다; 증언하다 □ foot-binding n. (옛날 중국의) 전족(纏足) □ scrutinize v. 조사하다, 철저히 검사하다 □ glance at ~을 힐끗 보다 □ recollect v. 회상하다, 생각해 내다

이 어두운 역사는 그 책이 그 베네치아 사람이 아마도 볼 수 없었던 것을 묘사하면서도 중국에 가는 어떤 여행자라도 보았음에 틀림없는 만리장성이나 전족 그리고 젓가락과 같은 광경들은 간과하고 있는 이유를 설명하는 데 도움을 준다.

## 46 ③

□ abstemious a. 절제하는, 삼가는, 금욕적인(=abstinent) □ typical a. 전형적인 □ inconsistent a. 일치하지 않는, 조화되지 않는 □ indulgent a. 제멋대로 하게 하는, 관대한

더 오래 살기 위해서, 금욕적인 습관을 지녀야 한다.

## 47 ①

□ dire a. 무서운; 비참한; 지독한(=terrible) □ beneficial a. 유익한, 이로운 □ desirable a. 바람직한, 호감이 가는 □ tangible a. 유형의; 만질 수 있는, 실체적인

상승하는 연료 가격이 가난한 사람들에게 끔찍한 영향을 미칠 것이다.

## 48 ③

□ accessible a. 접근[가까이]하기 쉬운; 이용할 수 있는 □ establish oneself 자리 잡다 □ convenient a. 편리한, 형편 좋은 □ gathering n. 모임, 회합, 집회 □ clement a. (기후가) 온화한, 온난한(=moderate) □ abrupt a. 돌연한, 갑작스러운 □ circuitous a. 우회로의; (말 따위가) 에두르는 □ prodigious a. 거대한, 막대한; 비범한

그 야외정원은 일반인들이 이용할 수 있으며 날씨가 온화할 때 도심지에서 편리한 모임 장소로 자리 잡게 될 것이다.

## 49 ④

□ exonerate v. 무죄를 증명하다, 혐의를 벗겨주다; 석방하다(=acquit) □ infuriate v. 격노하게 하다; 격분시키다 □ denounce v. 공공연히 비난하다; 고발하다 □ condemn v. 비난하다, 힐난하다

한 죄수의 고백이 다른 용의자들의 결백을 증명했다.

## 50          ③

☐ stadium n. 육상 경기장 ☐ gradually ad. 차차, 서서히(=by degrees) ☐ in general 일반적으로 ☐ at once 즉시, 동시에 ☐ for good 영원히, 영구히

경기장에 사람들이 점점 많아지고 있다.

## 51          ④

☐ coagulate v. 응고시키다; 굳히다(=congeal) ☐ consecrate v. (종교 의식을 통해) 축성하다 ☐ contaminate v. 오염시키다, 더럽히다 ☐ constrain v. 강요하다; 감금하다

벌어져 있는 상처에 약물을 충분히 발라 혈액을 응고시켰다.

## 52          ①

☐ undertake v. 떠맡다, 착수하다; 약속하다 ☐ restitution n. 상환, 보상, 배상(=reparation) ☐ verify v. 입증하다 ☐ restraint n. 규제, 억제 ☐ repentance n. 후회, 회개 ☐ replacement n. 교체

그녀가 전액 배상하겠다고 약속하고 그녀가 그렇게 하고 있음을 당신이 입증할 수 있으면 당신의 문제는 해결된 것이다.

## 53          ②

☐ marine ecologist 해양생태학자 ☐ great white shark 백상아리 ☐ inevitably ad. 불가피하게, 필연적으로 ☐ dwindle v. 줄어들다, 작아지다 ☐ prudent a. 신중한, 세심한; 분별 있는(=sensible) ☐ legal a. 법률의; 합법적인 ☐ massive a. 부피가 큰; 육중한; 대량의 ☐ timely a. 적시의, 때에 알맞은

해양생태학자들은 신중한 억제 수단을 법으로 정하지 않으면 백상아리의 개체수가 반드시 줄어들 것이라고 주장하고 있다.

## 54          ②

☐ insipid a. (음식 등이) 맛없는; 재미없는, 진부한(=boring) ☐ turn away 물리치다; 외면하다, 돌보지 않다 ☐ incipient a. 시작의, 발단의, 초기의 ☐ impudent a. 뻔뻔스러운, 주제넘은 ☐ rash a. 무모한; 성급한

당신 회사의 긍정적인 이미지를 반드시 유지해라. 분별없고 진부한 광고는 고객들을 외면하게 만들 수 있다.

## 55          ③

☐ assimilate v. 동화되다, 흡수하다(=absorb) ☐ infuse v. 불어 넣다, 주입하다, 고취하다 ☐ imbue v. (~에) 듬뿍 스며들게 하다; (감정, 사상 등을) 불어넣다, 고취하다

이들 청년들 중 높은 비율의 사람들이 자신들이 태어난 나라에 대한 지식이 거의 혹은 전혀 없는 상태로 미국 사회에 동화되고 있다.

## 56          ④

☐ authorize v. 권한을 부여하다, 위임하다 ☐ dictate v. 구술하다; 지령하다, 명령하다(=decree) ☐ policy n. 정책, 방침; 수단, 방법 ☐ underscore v. 강조하다, 분명히 나타내다 ☐ deposit v. 두다; 침전[퇴적]시키다; (돈을) 맡기다, 예금하다 ☐ dispatch v. 급파하다, 특파하다; 발송하다

대통령은 정책을 명령할 권한을 부여받은 유일한 사람이다.

## 57          ②

☐ subversive a. 전복하는, 파괴적인(=rebellious) ☐ cult n. 추종[숭배]; 광신적[사이비] 종교 집단 ☐ lukewarm a. 미온의; 열의가 없는 ☐ sinister a. 사악한, 해로운; 불길한 ☐ vicious a. 사악한, 악덕한; 악의 있는

베이징 당국은 그 집단을 체제 전복 의도를 지닌 '사악한 사교집단'으로 묘사하고 있다.

## 58          ③

☐ acrid a. 매운, 쓴; 아리는; 가혹한, 신랄한(=pungent) ☐ imperialism n. 제국주의, 영토 확장주의 ☐ complete a. 전부의, 완벽한 ☐ undeniable a. 부정하기 어려운, 명백한 ☐ vigorous a. 정력적인, 원기 왕성한; 격렬한

그는 미국의 제국주의적 태도를 신랄하게 공격했다.

## 59          ①

☐ under the weather 몸이 좀 안 좋은(=unwell) ☐ anxious a. 걱정스러운, 불안한 ☐ isolated a. 고립된 ☐ uplifting a. 희망[행복감]을 주는, 정신이 고양되는

당신이 몸이 좋지 않다면 따뜻한 음료를 마시고 잠자리에 드는 것보다 더 좋은 것은 없다.

## 60          ①

☐ punctual a. 시간을 잘 지키는; 기한을 엄수하는(=on time) ☐ prepared a. 준비된, 각오가 되어 있는 ☐ anxious a. 걱정하는, 불안한; 열망하는 ☐ anticipating a. 예상하는, 예측하는, 기대하는

성공적인 판매원은 언제나 약속 시간을 잘 지킨다.

## 61 ①

☐ distract v. (주의를) 딴 데로 돌리다  ☐ rigour n. 근엄함, 엄숙함
☐ importunate a. 성가신(=troublesome)  ☐ disdain n. 경멸  ☐
brutal a. 잔인한  ☐ condescending a. 거들먹거리는, 잘난 체하는
☐ disrespectful a. 무례한

일찍부터 귀구(Guigou) 부인은 진지함과 엄격함, 그리고 성가신 남성
들에 대한 냉담한 경멸로 그녀의 외모에 대한 주변의 관심을 딴 데로 돌
리려고 했다.

## 62 ③

☐ withstand v. 저항하다; 견디다, 지탱하다(=endure)  ☐ subsidiary
a. 보조의, 부차적인  ☐ project v. 입안하다, 안출하다, 설계하다  ☐
array v. 치장하다; 정렬시키다  ☐ ignite v. 불을 붙이다; 작열케 하다;
흥분시키다

이 새 건물은 주 건물과 다른 부속 지원 설비의 전체 무게를 지탱할 수
있을 만큼 견고하진 않다.

## 63 ①

☐ exposure n. 노출  ☐ relive v. (특히 상상 속에서) 다시 체험하다
☐ traumatic a. (어떤 경험이) 잊을 수 없을 정도로 큰 정신적 충격을
준(=painful)  ☐ puerile a. 유치한, 미숙한  ☐ hallucinatory a. 환각의,
환영의  ☐ drastic a. 강렬한; 철저한, 과감한

가상현실은 '노출치료'의 흥미로운 가능성을 갖고 있는데, 그 치료에
서는 환자들이 충격적인 기억들을 상상 속에서 다시 체험하도록 권
장한다.

## 64 ②

☐ schism n. 분리, 분열(=split)  ☐ deviation n. 벗어남, 탈선  ☐
encroachment n. 침입, 침해  ☐ mediation n. 중개; 조정

이러한 분열은 보수적이고 독실한 사람이 많은 것으로 알려진 예루살렘
에서 극명하게 감지된다.

## 65 ③

☐ collude v. 공모하다, 결탁하다(=connive)  ☐ myth n. 사회통념 ☐
superiority n. 우위  ☐ finish first 1등을 하다, 우승하다  ☐ collide
v. 충돌하다, 상충하다  ☐ confer v. 수여하다, 부여하다  ☐ convert
v. 전환시키다, 개조하다

얼마나 많은 여성들이 여전히 남성이 우월하다는 사회통념과 공모해,
소년들과 남성들이 1등하는 것이 '더 낫다고' 믿고 있는가?

## 66 ①

☐ pristine a. 본래의; 아주 깨끗한; 자연 그대로의(=immaculate)  ☐
barren a. 척박한, 불모의  ☐ mellow a. (과실이) 익은; 부드러운; 원숙한
☐ stale a. 신선하지 않은; 진부한

아직 오염되지 않은 자연 그대로의 구성물인 빙붕은 가장 흔히 연구되는
빙하 형성물인 경향이 있다.

## 67 ①

☐ acquiesce v. 묵묵히 따르다, (마지못해) 동의하다(=consent)  ☐
disagree v. 일치하지 않다, 의견이 다르다  ☐ compliment v. 경의를
표하다, 칭찬하다; 아첨의 말을 하다  ☐ revise v. 개정하다, 교정하다,
바꾸다

그녀가 고용주의 제안에 동의하고 난 후에 일이 훨씬 더 순조롭게 진행
되었다.

## 68 ①

☐ leap v. 뛰어오르다  ☐ harpoon n. (고래잡이용) 작살  ☐ standoff
n. 고립, 냉담, 교착상태(=deadlock)  ☐ piracy n. 해적 행위, 해적질
☐ equilibrium n. 평형, 균형; 평형상태  ☐ decisiveness n. 결정적임,
단호함  ☐ tranquility n. 고요, 평온

일본은 차가운 남극해의 포경선으로 뛰어든 뒤 붙잡힌 두 명의 고래
잡이 반대 운동가를 넘겨주겠다고 수요일에 약속했다. 그러나 양편이
공해상에서 해적 행위를 했다고 서로를 비난함에 따라 곧바로 교착
상태에 빠졌다.

## 69 ③

☐ intermittently ad. 간헐적으로(=periodically)  ☐ abundantly ad.
충분히, 많이  ☐ steadily ad. 착실하게; 꾸준히, 끊임없이  ☐ daily
ad. 매일, 날마다

미국 북동부에서는 봄 내내 비가 오락가락한다.

## 70 ③

☐ sentence v. 판결을 내리다, (형을) 선고하다  ☐ imprisonment n.
투옥, 구금, 금고  ☐ perjury n. 위증(죄)  ☐ pervert v. 왜곡하다; 오용
[악용]하다(=distort)  ☐ delay v. 미루다, 연기하다  ☐ resolve v. 해결
하다  ☐ modify v. 수정하다, 변경하다

그 전직 장관은 위증과 재판 과정을 왜곡하려 한 혐의로 18개월의 징역
형을 선고받았다.

## 71 ③

□ heterogeneous a. 이종(異種)의; 이질적인; 잡다한(=diverse) □ subdiscipline n. (어떤) 학문 분야의 하위 구분 □ ubiquitous a. (동시에) 도처에 있는, 편재하는 □ genealogical a. 족보의; 가계의; 계통을 표시하는 □ logical a. 논리적인; 필연의

담화 분석은 언어학의 많은 하위 구분 중에서 유례없이 이질적인 것이다.

## 72 ①

□ convivial a. 즐거운, 쾌활한(=jolly) □ acquaintance n. 면식; 아는 사람, 아는 사이 □ complicated a. 복잡한, 풀기[알기] 어려운 □ moody a. 변덕스러운; 뚱한, 언짢은 □ enigmatic a. 수수께끼의, 불가해한

연회를 좋아하는 호스트인 드류(Drew)는 자신의 파티에 온 모든 친구들 및 지인들과 교류했다.

## 73 ①

□ deploy v. 배치하다; 효율적으로 활용하다 □ conventional a. 틀에 박힌; 전통적인 □ referent n. 지시대상 □ voluble a. 유창한, 달변의 (=glib) □ sumptuous a. 사치스러운, 호화로운 □ taciturn a. 말수가 적은, 무뚝뚝한 □ wily a. 약삭빠른, 교활한

그녀는 말 잘하는 여자라는 상투적인 문화적 지시대상을 만화 컷 안에 배치시켜 넣을 수 있다.

## 74 ③

□ proclaim v. 선언하다, 공포하다 □ frenzied a. 광적인, 미쳐 날뛰는; 흥분한, 열광한 □ entrepreneurialism n. 기업가 정신[주의] □ prowess n. 용감함, 용감한 행위; 훌륭한 솜씨(=skill) □ rock v. 뒤흔들다 □ affordability n. 감당할 수 있는 능력; 입수 가능함 □ diversity n. 차이, 변화, 다양성 □ individuality n. 개성; 특성, 인격

21세기는 이미 '중국의 세기'라고 선언되었다. 중국의 열광적인 기업주의, 대량 생산기술, 저임금 노동으로부터 비롯되는 충격파는 세계 곳곳의 산업을 뒤흔들고 있다.

## 75 ②

□ blankly ad. 멍하니, 우두커니(=vacantly) □ easily ad. 쉽게, 수월하게, 용이하게 □ shortly ad. 곧, 이내, 즉시; 간략하게 □ perfidiously ad. 불신하여; 불성실하게; 배반하여

그는 매우 지친 얼굴로 멍하니 나를 쳐다보았고, 그다음에는 자신의 걱정을 누군가와 나누고 싶다고 말했다.

## 76 ③

□ grimly ad. 잔인하게; 엄하게, 무섭게, 단호하게(=sternly) □ microscope n. 현미경 □ wisely ad. 슬기롭게; 현명하게(도); 빈틈없이 □ kindly ad. 친절하게, 상냥하게 □ drily ad. 냉담하게; 무미건조하게

"인간에게 알려져 있는 모든 현미경을 조정해서라도 우리는 그것을 시도해 볼 것이야"라고 그 교수는 내게 단호하게 말했다.

## 77 ④

□ elicit v. 도출하다, 이끌어 내다 □ malediction n. 악담, 험담, 중상, 비방(=slander) □ contumacy n. 완강한 불복종; 법정 모독 □ acclamation n. 환호, 갈채 □ acclimation n. 새 환경[풍토] 순응

일부 설문 조사의 질문들은 그 추종자들로부터 험담을 이끌어내도록 고안되어 있다.

## 78 ①

□ conservative n. 보수주의자 □ forsake v. 버리다, 포기하다 (=abandon) □ embrace v. 채택하다 □ interpret v. 해석하다; 이해하다 □ impose v. 강요하다

보수주의자들은 자신들의 이데올로기 목적에 부합하지 않는다면 주(州)의 권리에 대한 원칙을 종종 포기한다.

## 79 ③

□ turnaround n. 부실 기업 회생 (작업); 결손으로부터의 흑자 전환 □ astute a. 기민한, 빈틈없는(=shrewd) □ amicable a. 우호적인, 친화적인 □ inert a. 활발하지 못한, 생기가 없는 □ speculative a. 투기의; 투기적인

워런 버핏(Warren Buffett)은 어려움을 겪고 있는 회사에 투자하여 결국에 그 기업이 흑자 전환하면, 기민한 투자자라는 찬사를 받으며 수십억 달러의 수익을 거둔다.

## 80 ②

□ drudgery n. 힘들고 단조로운 일, 고된 일(=toil) □ contemplation n. 숙고, 심사 □ agility n. 민첩, 기민 □ strife n. 투쟁, 다툼

인공지능(AI)은 사무 관리와 같은 일상적인 힘들고 고된 업무를 덜어 줄 수 있다.

## 81 ④

□ interlocutor n. 대화[대담]자(=conversationalist) □ spectator n. 구경꾼, 관찰자 □ speculator n. 사색가, 이론가; 공론가; 투기꾼 □ efficient clerk 유능한 사무원

디드로(Diderot)는 그 시대 지성인의 집회를 만드는 데 있어 대화자로서 여성의 역할에 경의를 표했다.

## 82 ④

□ firm n. 기업 □ requisite a. 필수적인 □ pedigree n. (훌륭한) 혈통, 가문(=breed) □ kingdom n. 왕국 □ asset n. 자산, 장점 □ condition n. 조건; 환경 □ honour n. 명예, 존경

그가 고등학교 졸업 후 곧바로 입사하여 지금은 사장으로 있는 그 기업은 (사업하는 데) 필수적인 훌륭한 혈통을 갖고 있는데, 그 기업이 바로 '자전거 왕국'에서 가장 역사가 오래된 자전거 제조업체라는 것이다.

## 83 ③

□ stymie v. 방해하다; 좌절시키다(=thwart) □ worry v. 걱정시키다, 괴롭히다 □ amaze v. 몹시 놀라게 하다 □ motivate v. 동기를 주다, 자극하다

일반적인 감기의 원인은 과학자들을 끊임없이 좌절시켜왔다.

## 84 ②

□ discursive a. 산만한, 만연한, 종잡을 수 없는(=incoherent) □ ebullient a. 패기만만한, 사기가 충천한 □ somnolent a. 졸린, 최면의 □ obdurate a. 억지센, 완고한

그는 뉴스 매체에 책임을 돌리면서, 그가 왜 미국인들을 분열시키는 데 책임이 없는지에 대해 두서없고 방어적인 분석을 내놓았다.

## 85 ②

□ ingrate n. 은혜를 모르는 사람, 배은 망덕자(=ungrateful person) □ libertine n. 방탕자, 난봉꾼 □ enemy n. 적, 원수; 적수 □ betrayer n. 배반자, 배신자

당신은 절대로 부모님께 배은망덕한 사람이 되어서는 안 된다.

## 86 ④

□ diverse a. 다양한 □ vast a. 광대[거대]한 □ encompass v. 포함[망라]하다, 아우르다 □ myriad a. 무수한; 막대한 □ suspend v. 중지하다(=stop) □ dismiss v. 묵살[일축]하다 □ postpone v. 연기하다, 미루다 □ prevent v. 막다

광대한 만큼 다양하기도 한 중국은 수많은 지형과 문화를 아우르고 있다. 중국의 초현대적이고 초연결된(첨단인터넷을 갖춘) 대도시들이 미래로 나아가고 있는 동안, 전통에 뿌리를 두고 머물러 있는 탁 트인 시골에서의 시간은 정지된 느낌이다.

## 87 ③

□ convergence n. 한 점에의 집합, 집중성; 수렴(=union) □ congregation n. 모임, 회합; 집회 □ optimum n. 최적 조건 □ renovation n. 수선, 수리; 혁신, 쇄신

디지털 기술, 특히 방송과 원격 통신의 통합을 가속화하기 위한 서비스와 장치 부문에 대한 보다 강한 지원 노력이 약속되었다.

## 88 ④

□ contagious a. (접촉을 통해) 전염되는, 전염성의 □ cluster v. 모이다 □ quarantine v. 검역(檢疫)하다, 격리하다(=segregate) □ coalesce v. 합체하다; 합동하다 □ curtail v. 단축하다, 삭감하다 □ protract v. ~을 연장하다, 오래 끌게 하다

전염병을 옮기는 그 환자들을 모아서, 다른 환자들로부터 격리시켰다.

## 89 ②

□ infuriate v. 격앙시키다, 화나게 만들다(=enrage) □ amuse v. 즐겁게[재미나게] 하다 □ summon v. 소환하다, 호출하다 □ motivate v. 동기를 주다, 자극하다

아베크롬비앤피치(Abercrombie & Fitch)의 노출이 심한 광고와 나이트클럽의 진동(소음)은 미국의 십대들을 열광시켰지만 부모들을 화나게 했다.

## 90 ④

□ extraordinary a. 보기 드문, 비범한; 대단한 □ repudiate v. ~을 거부하다, 부인하다(=renounce) □ reinterpret v. 재해석하다 □ revise v. 변경하다, 개정하다 □ rejuvenate v. 도로 젊게 하다

초서(Chaucer)는 자신의 특별한 작품의 가치를 의심하게 됐을 뿐만 아니라 그 가치를 부인했다.

## 91 ③

□ vivacious a. 활기 있는; 활발한, 쾌활한(=lively) □ tired a. 피곤한, 지친 □ gloomy a. 어두운; 우울한 □ easily ad. 용이하게, 쉽게

그 커플들은 매우 쾌활한 음악에 맞춰 춤을 추면서 즐거운 시간을 보냈다.

## 92 ④

□ affirmative action 차별 철폐 조처(미국의 소수집단 우대 정책) □ minority group 소수집단 □ proliferate v. 급증하다, (빠르게) 확산되다(=multiply) □ decline v. 감소하다; 거절하다 □ improve v. 개량하다, 개선하다 □ deteriorate v. 악화되다, 저하하다

여성과 소수 집단의 교육 기회를 향상시키기 위한 차별 철폐 조처 프로그램이 1970년대 초 이래로 확산돼 왔다. 초·중등 공교육에서 차별 철폐 조처는 가장 먼저 교육 프로그램과 교과서를 수정하는 결과를 가져왔다.

## 93 ④

☐ convict v. 유죄를 선언하다, 유죄를 입증하다 ☐ thief n. 도둑 ☐ counterfeiter n. 위조자, 화폐 위조자 ☐ death penalty 사형 ☐ deterrent n. 억제하는 것, 억제책(=hindrance) ☐ beacon n. 횃불; 등대 ☐ amphibian n. 양서류 동물 ☐ eminence n. 높음, 고귀함

유죄판결을 받은 절도범들과 화폐 위조범들은 종종 사형을 선고받았는데, 이는 다른 범죄자들을 억제하는 대책으로 여겨졌다.

## 94 ④

☐ scrupulous a. 빈틈없는, 꼼꼼한; 양심적인(=meticulous) ☐ unrelenting a. 용서[가차] 없는, 엄한, 무자비한 ☐ obsessive a. 사로잡혀 있는, 강박적인 ☐ escalating a. 단계적으로 확대[증대, 강화, 상승]하는

자신의 업무에 세심한 주의를 기울인 덕분에 그는 회사에서 승진할 수 있었다.

## 95 ②

☐ tremulous a. 전율하는; (기쁨으로) 몸이 떨리는 듯한(=trembling) ☐ fleeting a. 순식간의; 덧없는, 무상한 ☐ traumatic a. 외상의; 대단히 충격적인 ☐ facetious a. 익살맞은, 우스운; 농담의

동굴 속에서 그 지도를 발견했을 때, 그는 떨리는 흥분 상태에 있었다.

## 96 ①

☐ luster n. 광택, 윤(=sheen) ☐ immortality n. 불멸, 불후 ☐ vanity n. 덧없음, 허영 ☐ rapture n. 큰 기쁨, 환희, 황홀

사람 안에 있는 영혼은 거친 다이아몬드 원석과도 같아, 반드시 갈고 닦아 윤을 내야 한다. 그렇지 않으며 그 영혼의 광택은 절대 나타나지 않을 것이다.

## 97 ④

☐ unwittingly ad. 자신도 모르게, 부지불식간에(=involuntarily) ☐ thoroughly ad. 대단히, 철저히 ☐ sternly ad. 엄격하게, 준엄하게 ☐ punctiliously ad. 격식에 치우쳐; 꼼꼼하게

부동산 소유자는 농사나 주택 건설과 같은 일반적인 활동을 하는 것에 대한 허가를 받지 않아 자신도 모르게 때때로 민형사상 처벌을 받는 경우가 있다.

## 98 ②

☐ wishy-washy a. 우유부단한(=indecisive) ☐ liberal a. 진보적인 ☐ apathetic a. 냉담한; 무관심한 ☐ conclusive a. 결정적인, 확실한

정치에 대해 다소 "우유부단한" 태도를 보였던 많은 사람들이 이제 진정한 민주주의라는 목표를 향해 더욱 헌신하고 있다.

## 99 ③

☐ nuisance n. 성가신[귀찮은] 사람[것, 일], 골칫거리(=annoyance) ☐ impasse n. 막다름; 곤경 ☐ barrier n. 장벽 ☐ grievance n. 불만; 불평하기

정부 기관에 빚을 갚을 능력이 있는 미국인들에게는 몇 달러에서 수백 달러에 이르는 그러한 벌금이 성가신 일이다.

## 100 ①

☐ abet v. 선동하다, 교사하다(=incite) ☐ burglar n. 강도 ☐ getaway n. 도망, 도주 ☐ imitate v. 모방하다, 흉내내다 ☐ chase v. 쫓다, 추적하다 ☐ defraud v. 속여서 빼앗다, 횡령하다

그녀는 도주 차량을 운전했다는 이유로 강도를 돕고 선동한 혐의로 기소되었다.

| | | | | | | | | | |
|---|---|---|---|---|---|---|---|---|---|
| **01** ④ | **02** ① | **03** ② | **04** ① | **05** ② | **06** ① | **07** ① | **08** ① | **09** ① | **10** ④ |
| **11** ④ | **12** ③ | **13** ① | **14** ② | **15** ④ | **16** ④ | **17** ④ | **18** ① | **19** ④ | **20** ① |
| **21** ② | **22** ① | **23** ④ | **24** ③ | **25** ② | **26** ④ | **27** ① | **28** ④ | **29** ② | **30** ④ |
| **31** ③ | **32** ① | **33** ② | **34** ② | **35** ① | **36** ④ | **37** ③ | **38** ④ | **39** ② | **40** ② |
| **41** ③ | **42** ④ | **43** ② | **44** ④ | **45** ④ | **46** ③ | **47** ② | **48** ③ | **49** ② | **50** ① |
| **51** ② | **52** ② | **53** ② | **54** ② | **55** ③ | **56** ④ | **57** ④ | **58** ② | **59** ④ | **60** ④ |
| **61** ③ | **62** ③ | **63** ① | **64** ② | **65** ② | **66** ① | **67** ④ | **68** ② | **69** ① | **70** ③ |
| **71** ③ | **72** ② | **73** ④ | **74** ④ | **75** ② | **76** ② | **77** ④ | **78** ② | **79** ① | **80** ② |
| **81** ③ | **82** ② | **83** ③ | **84** ① | **85** ① | **86** ② | **87** ② | **88** ① | **89** ① | **90** ③ |
| **91** ① | **92** ② | **93** ① | **94** ④ | **95** ④ | **96** ④ | **97** ① | **98** ① | **99** ③ | **100** ④ |

## 01     ④

☐ inscrutable a. 헤아릴 수 없는, 불가해한(=enigmatic) ☐ bizarre a. 기이한; 특이한 ☐ shoddy a. 조잡한, 질이 떨어지는 ☐ insipid a. 싱거운; 김빠진, 재미없는

데이지(Daisy)는 그것이 다소 이해할 수 없는 예술작품이라고 말했지만 그는 그것이 마음에 들었다.

## 02     ①

☐ preeminence n. 걸출, 탁월, 우위(=supremacy) ☐ setback n. (진보 따위의) 방해; 역행, 퇴보; 패배 ☐ inception n. 처음, 시작, 개시 ☐ failure n. 실패

독일은 대부분의 동유럽을 지배하고 나서 군대를 서부 전선으로 옮겼는데, 그곳에서 대부분의 전투가 벌어졌기 때문이다. 유감스럽게도, 미군이 연합군을 지원하기 위해 매일 수천 명씩 도착함에 따라 그들의 우위는 지속되지 않았다.

## 03     ②

☐ pilot n. 시험적으로 행하는 것 ☐ shed light on ~을 명백히 하다, ~을 분명히 하다 ☐ with no stings attached 아무런 조건 없이; 무조건으로(=unconditionally) ☐ charitably ad. 자비롭게, 너그럽게 ☐ impartially ad. 편견 없이; 공명정대하게 ☐ bountifully ad. 아낌없이

시카고에서 시험적으로 행해질 조치는 아무런 조건 없이 저소득층 가족에게 현금을 주는 것의 잠재적인 영향을 보다 분명하게 해줄 수 있다.

## 04     ①

☐ contend v. 주장하다, 논쟁하다 ☐ depraved a. 사악한; 타락한, 부패한(=corrupt) ☐ secluded a. 한적한, 외딴 ☐ dejected a. 실의에 빠진, 낙담한 ☐ unpopulated a. 사람이 살지 않는

일부 범죄 전문가들은 부패한 지역에서 자라는 십대들이 범죄와 마약 남용에 빠질 가능성이 훨씬 높다고 주장한다.

## 05     ②

☐ consistent a. 일치하는; 불변한, 시종일관된 ☐ vociferous a. 소란한, 시끄러운(=loud) ☐ advocate n. 옹호자; 주장자 ☐ preemptory a. 선매권이 있는; 선제적인 ☐ prescient a. 선견지명[예지력]이 있는 ☐ dislodge v. 제거하다; 몰아내다; (적을 진지로부터) 격퇴하다 ☐ twisted a. 뒤틀린 ☐ conscientious a. 양심적인, 성실한 ☐ positive a. 확신하는; 단정적인

국내에서는, 일관된 양상으로, 선제적 전쟁을 가장 큰 소리로 옹호하는 사람들이 대개, 미군이 탈레반과 사담 후세인을 신속하게 몰아냈을 때처럼, 자신들이 예지력 있는 총명함을 가졌다고 주장했다.

## 06     ①

☐ prod v. 찌르다; 자극하다(=push) ☐ leap v. 뛰다, 뛰어오르다 ☐ build v. 짓다; 쌓아올리다 ☐ hit v. 때리다, 치다; 맞히다

그녀는 긴 막대기를 찾아서 통나무 더미를 찔러댔다.

## 07     ①

☐ simulation n. 모의실험; 가장, 속임(=imitation) ☐ destruction n. 파괴 ☐ authentic a. 믿을만한, 확실한; 진정한 ☐ discourse n.

강연, 설교; 담론 □ quantum leap 비약적인 발전, 약진 □ recognize v. 알아보다; 인지하다; 인정하다 □ milestone n. 이정표, 획기적인 사건 □ hyper-reality n. 초현실성, 과잉현실 □ colonization n. 식민지 건설, 식민지화 □ quasi-political a. 유사 정치적인 □ affinity n. 친밀감; 관련성 □ originality n. 독창성 □ difference n. 차이

진짜 담론을 가장(假裝)하는 것(따라서 파괴시키는 것)은 미국에서 가장 먼저 일어나서 나머지 세계로 퍼져나간 것으로, 기 드보르(Guy Debord)는 이것을 "스펙터클의 사회"로의 최초의 비약적인 발전이라 부를 것이고 장 보드리야르(Jean Baudrillard)는 이것을 세계가 과잉 현실로 돌입했다는 이정표로 여길 것이다. 대중매체가 시민사회를 식민지화한 것은 TV의 이미지 메이킹 기술이 등장하자 기술 자체를 홍보하는 유사(類似) 정치 캠페인으로 바뀌었다.

## 08 ①

□ intimacy n. 친교, 친밀함(=friendliness) □ currency n. (화폐의) 통용, 통화, 화폐; 세상의 평판 □ identity n. 일치, 동일성; 개성, 독자성 □ hinge on ~여하에 달려있다, ~에 따라 정해지다 □ hired-gun n. 청부살인업자; 난국 타개를[사업 추진을] 위해 고용된 사람 □ airbrush v. 에어브러시로 착색하다; (사진을) 에어브러시로 수정하다 □ photo shoot (유명인, 패션모델 등에 대한) 사진 촬영 □ popularity n. 인기; 대중성 □ resemblance n. 닮음, 유사함 □ similarity n. 유사점

아티스트의 정체성과 이미지가 돈이 되면 뭐든지 하는 히트곡 가수들, 에어브러시로 수정된 사진, 소셜미디어의 게시물에 좌우되는 때에, 친밀감이 있다는 것은 매우 귀중한 평판이다.

## 09 ①

□ sweltering a. 더위에 지친, 찌는 듯한(=very hot) □ tiring a. 피로하게 하는, 힘이 드는; 지루한 □ pretty a. 예쁜, 귀여운 □ smoothing a. 매끈매끈한, 반드러운

3월의 어느 찌는 듯이 더운 늦은 오후에 나는 나무를 모으기 위해 걸어 나갔다.

## 10 ④

□ bombardier n. (폭격기의) 폭격수 □ exculpate v. 무죄로 하다; ~의 무죄를 증명하다(=acquit) □ praise v. 칭찬하다 □ familiarize v. 친하게 하다; 익숙하게 하다 □ exaggerate v. 과장하다

폭격수들이 사우디아라비아 사람들이라는 사실이 좀체 미국을 무죄로 만들지는 않는다.

## 11 ④

□ resort to ~에 의지하다 □ mudslinging n. (정치 운동 등에서의) 중상(中傷), 인신공격(=slander) □ veracity n. 진실을 말함, 정직 □ gimmick n. 술책, 장치 □ precursor n. 선구자

선거가 다가올수록 상호 비방하는 후보가 점점 늘고 있다.

## 12 ③

□ foolproof a. 잘못될 수가 없는, 아주 간단한; 절대 확실한(=fully reliable) □ wholly operational 제 기능을 다하는 □ entirely serviceable 매우 쓸모 있는 □ completely safe 아주 안전한

비록 오래된 물건들의 연대를 측정하는 탄소 14를 이용한 연대측정법이 완전히 믿을 수 있는 방법은 아닐지라도, 그것은 현재 이용 가능한 최고의 방법이다.

## 13 ①

□ indecency n. 예절[버릇] 없음; 외설 □ blasphemy n. 신성모독(=impiety) □ brutality n. 잔인, 무자비 □ assault n. 강습, 습격 □ derision n. 조롱, 조소

제이콥 엡스타인(Jacob Epstein)의 일부 상징적인 조각품들은 외설과 신성모독이라는 비난을 받았다.

## 14 ②

□ contraption n. 장치(=device); 새로운 고안 □ conception n. 개념, 생각; 구상, 착상 □ plaything n. 장난감, 노리개 □ replica n. 복사(품), 복제(품)

최초의 스케이트보드와 같이 생긴 장치는 1950년대 경에 캘리포니아 남부 해변의 지역사회에서 선보였던 것으로 여겨진다.

## 15 ④

□ allude to ~을 암시하다, 넌지시 비추다(=speak indirectly about) □ avoid speaking about ~에 관해 말하는 것을 피하다 □ concentrate on ~에 집중하다, 전력을 기울이다 □ be proud of ~을 자랑스럽게 여기다

그녀는 "저는 지난 몇 년 동안 매우 바쁘게 지냈어요."라고 말하며, 자신의 업무 경험을 넌지시 비췄다.

## 16 ④

□ intact a. 온전한, 본래대로의, 손대지 않은(=untouched) □ inactive a. 활동치 않는; 움직이지 않는 □ obsolete a. 쇠퇴한, 시대에 뒤진 □ struggling a. 노력하는, 분투[고투]하는

1950년~1953년의 한국전쟁은 대부분의 도시를 파괴했고, 일제 식민지 시기 내내 대체로 온전히 유지되었던 전통적인 사회를 뒤흔들어 놓았다.

## 17 ④

☐ squander v. (시간, 돈을) 낭비하다, 탕진하다(=waste) ☐ evade v. 피하다, 비키다, 면하다, 벗어나다 ☐ compile v. 편집하다; 수집하다 ☐ manipulate v. 조종하다; 조작하다; 능숙하게 다루다

형편없는 계획으로 그는 전 재산을 탕진하게 되었다.

## 18 ①

☐ trenchant a. 통렬한, 신랄한; 명쾌한(=incisive) ☐ negative a. 부정의; 부정적인; 소극적인 ☐ fulsome a. 억척스러운, 집요한; 아첨이 지나친 ☐ cagey a. 빈틈없는, 조심성 있는; 태도를 분명히 하지 않는

그녀의 변호사의 주장은 예리한 관찰이 특징이었다.

## 19 ④

☐ repellent a. (사람에게) 혐오감을 주는, 불쾌한(=unpleasant) ☐ reserved a. 보류된, 따로 치워둔; 예약의; 수줍어하는 ☐ insincere a. 불성실한, 언행 불일치의, 위선적인 ☐ aggressive a. 침략적인, 공세의; 싸우기 좋아하는; 진취적인

납치범의 행동들은 너무나 혐오스러워서 그녀에게 어떤 동정심도 얻기 어려웠다.

## 20 ①

☐ affront n. 모욕, 무례한 언동(=insult) ☐ vanity n. 자만(심), 허영(심) ☐ disagree with 동의하지 않다 ☐ damage n. 손해, 피해, 손상 ☐ contempt n. 경멸, 모욕, 멸시 ☐ ignorance n. 무지, 무식

네가 그에게 동의하지 않은 것은 그의 자만심에 대한 모욕이었다.

## 21 ②

☐ betrothed a. 약혼한(=engaged) ☐ suspect v. (어렴풋이) 알아채다; 의심하다 ☐ segregated a. 분리된, 격리된 ☐ hospitalize v. 입원시키다 ☐ fabled a. 전설적인

그들이 약혼했다는 발표는 사랑의 기운을 전혀 알아채지 못했던 친구들을 놀라게 했다.

## 22 ①

☐ fraudulently ad. 속여서, 부정하게, 사기를 쳐서(=deceitfully) ☐ aggressively ad. 공격적으로; 정력적으로 ☐ violently ad. 격렬하게, 맹렬히 ☐ actively ad. 활발하게; 적극적으로

보고서는 그가 부정직하거나 부적절한 행동을 하지 않았다고 결론내렸다.

## 23 ④

☐ eradicate v. 뿌리째 뽑다, 근절하다, 박멸하다(=exterminate) ☐ tetanus n. 파상풍(균) ☐ proliferate v. 증식하다, 급격히 늘어나다 ☐ decline v. 줄어들다, 감소하다; 거절하다 ☐ degenerate v. 나빠지다, 퇴보하다

의사들은 말라리아나 파상풍과 같은 질병을 근절하기 위해 싸우고 있다.

## 24 ③

☐ dispassionate a. 침착한, 냉정한, 감정적이 아닌(=unemotional) ☐ shocked a. 충격을 받은, 어안이 벙벙한 ☐ competent a. 유능한, 능력 있는; 충분한 ☐ gallant a. 용감한, 용맹한

톰(Tom)은 그녀의 행방에 대한 소식을 들었을 때에도 대체로 냉정했다.

## 25 ②

☐ substantive a. 현실의, 실제의; 중요한, 가치 있는(=important) ☐ excursive a. 지엽적인, 본제를 벗어난; 두서없는 ☐ instinctive a. 본능적인, 직감적인; 천성의 ☐ obstructive a. 방해하는; 의사 방해의

심각한 문제들에 대한 실질적인 논의가 이루어지지 않아 그 계획을 늦추고 있다.

## 26 ④

☐ goad v. 뾰족한 막대기로 찌르다; 격려하다, 부추기다(=urge) ☐ put down a deposit 계약금을 걸다[치르다] ☐ guide v. 안내하다, 인도하다; 지도하다 ☐ ask v. 묻다, 물어보다 ☐ force v. ~에게 강제하다, 억지로 ~시키다

그 부동산 중개업자는 그 부부를 부추겨 계약금을 치르도록 했다.

## 27 ①

☐ undoubtedly ad. 의심할 여지없이, 틀림없이, 확실히 ☐ convict v. 유죄를 입증하다, 유죄를 선고하다(=condemn) ☐ culprit n. 범죄자, 죄인, 범인 ☐ larceny n. 절도(죄), 도둑질 ☐ extend v. 뻗다, 내밀다; 연장하다 ☐ scorch v. 태우다, 그슬리다 ☐ supplant v. 대신 들어앉다, 탈취하다; 대신하다

배심원단은 틀림없이 그 범인에게 중(重) 절도죄에 대해 유죄판결을 내릴 것이다.

## 28 ④

☐ swathe n. 베어낸 한 구획 ☐ cut off ~을 차단하다, 가로막다 ☐ inundate v. 범람시키다, 침수시키다; 쇄도하다(=engulf) ☐ parch v.

바짝 마르게 하다; 목타게 하다 ☐ destroy v. 파괴하다, 훼손하다 ☐ conserve v. 보존하다, 유지하다; 절약하다

거대한 퀸즐랜드주 내의 20개가 넘는 도시들이 연락이 끊기거나 홍수 피해를 당했고 20만 명 이상이 피해를 입었다. 남쪽에 있는 세인트 조지 시에서는 기상청이 그 도시의 80퍼센트가 침수될 것이라는 첨두홍수량(flood peak)을 예보한 후 주민들이 최고의 경계 태세를 하고 있다.

## 29 ②

☐ resilient a. 탄력있는; 쾌활한(=buoyant) ☐ attentive a. 주의 깊은, 세심한 ☐ chimerical a. 공상의, 망상의 ☐ erratic a. 일정하지 않은, 변하기 쉬운, 불규칙적인

어떤 사람들은 선천적으로 다른 사람들보다 쾌활한데, 아마도 그들이 낙관적으로 생각하는 경향이 있기 때문이다.

## 30 ④

☐ belt-tightening n. 긴축경영, 긴축재정 ☐ dampen v. (물에) 적시다; (기세를) 약화시키다(=attenuate) ☐ as it is 사실, 실제로는, 현 상황에서는 ☐ incite v. 선동하다, 조장하다 ☐ saddle with ~에게 짐을 지우다; ~을 부과하다 ☐ distend v. ~을 넓히다, 부풀게 하다, 팽창시키다; 과장하다

이 모든 긴축재정은 한층 더 수요를 약화시킨다. 사실, 소비자들은 힘겹게 버텨나가고 있다.

## 31 ③

☐ grasp v. 납득하다, 이해[파악]하다 ☐ gist n. 요점, 요지(=essence) ☐ axis n. 굴대, 축(軸) ☐ jest n. 농담, 익살 ☐ mettle n. 기개, 용기

언어 학습자들은 듣고 있는 것을 완전히 파악할 수는 없지만, 종종 그것의 요지는 이해할 수 있다.

## 32 ①

☐ provincial a. 지방의; 편협한(narrow-minded) ☐ patriotic a. 애국의 ☐ prosaic a. 평범한 ☐ middle-of-the-road a. 중도의, 온건한

많은 펜실베이니아 사람들은 매우 편협해서 또 다른 세상이 있다는 사실조차 인정하지 않는다.

## 33 ②

☐ addle v. 혼란스럽게 만들다(=muddle) ☐ demesmerize v. ~의 최면 상태를 풀다, 각성시키다 ☐ dulcify v. 누그러뜨리다, 달래다 ☐ meddle v. 간섭하다, 건드리다

그의 마음을 혼란에 빠뜨렸던 것은 아마도 눈부신 햇살이었던 것 같다.

## 34 ②

☐ mole n. 두더지 ☐ devour v. 게걸스럽게 먹다, 먹어 치우다; 집어삼키다(=consume) ☐ worm n. 벌레; 기생충 ☐ larva n. 유충, 애벌레 (pl. larvae) ☐ disturb v. 방해하다, 어지럽히다; 폐를 끼치다 ☐ carry v. 운반하다, 나르다; 이끌다 ☐ discover v. 발견하다; 알다, 깨닫다

매일 두더지는 거의 자기 몸무게만큼의 연충과 곤충 애벌레를 먹어 치운다.

## 35 ①

☐ nimble a. 재빠른, 민첩한; 재치 있는(=quick-moving) ☐ hasty a. 급한; 경솔한 ☐ delicious a. 맛 좋은; 유쾌한, 즐거운 ☐ ridiculous a. 우스운, 어리석은

회색 토끼를 잡았던 그 소년은 대략 여우 크기만 한 대단히 영리하고 민첩한 개를 갖고 있었다.

## 36 ②

☐ gratuitous a. 불필요한, 쓸데없는(=unnecessary) ☐ potent a. 강력한, 유력한 ☐ uncivilized a. 예의 없는, 점잖지 못한 ☐ disastrous a. 처참한, 형편없는

TV에 너무 많은 범죄와 불필요한 폭력이 나오는데, 이는 청소년들과 젊은이들에게 나쁜 영향을 끼친다.

## 37 ③

☐ reprisal n. 앙갚음, 보복(=revenge) ☐ defect n. 결점, 결함 ☐ digression n. 본제를 벗어나 지엽으로 흐름, 여담, 탈선 ☐ recess n. (통상의 일·활동의 일시적인) 쉼, 휴식, 휴게; (의회의) 휴회

경영진의 보복을 두려워했기 때문에, 근로자들 중에 회사를 비판하는 공개서한에 서명한 사람은 거의 없었다.

## 38 ②

☐ instantaneous a. 즉시의, 순간적인; 동시에 일어나는(=immediate) ☐ serious a. 진지한, 엄숙한, 심각한, 중대한 ☐ expected a. 예기된, 기대된 ☐ desired a. 바랐던, 희망했던; 훌륭한

심장을 맞힌 탄환이 하나도 없었으므로 즉사한 것은 아니었다.

## 39 ②

☐ communism n. 공산주의 ☐ incentive n. 장려책, 유인책 ☐ deteriorate v. 악화되다, 더 나빠지다(=degenerate) ☐ isolate v. 고립시키다 ☐ transfer v. 이동하다 ☐ change v. 변화하다

공산주의 아래에서는 유인책들이 약해서, 근로 습관이 더 나빠진다.

## 40      ②

☐ strike off 제명하다 ☐ find guilty of ~에게 유죄판결을 내리다 ☐ practice n. (의사, 변호사 등 전문직 종사자의) 업무 ☐ circumvent v. 피하다, 모면하다(=evade) ☐ impose v. 시행하다; 부과하다 ☐ repeal v. 폐지하다 ☐ castigate v. 크게 책망하다 ☐ circumscribe v. 제한하다

변호사 협회(Law Society)가 요구하는 조건들을 회피하기 위해 그런 영업을 한 것으로 유죄판결을 받으면 세 명 모두 제명될 위기에 처해 있다.

## 41      ③

☐ extraneous a. 외래의, 외부의; 이질적인; 관계없는(=irrelevant) ☐ banal a. 따분한, 평범한, 시시한 ☐ exemplary a. 모범적인, 본이 되는 ☐ complicated a. 복잡한, 뒤얽힌, 풀기 어려운

글 속에 무관한 내용들이 너무 많아 필자의 메시지를 이해하기 어려웠다.

## 42      ④

☐ supercilious a. 거만한, 사람을 깔보는(=haughty) ☐ submissive a. 복종적인, 순종하는 ☐ talkative a. 수다스러운, 이야기하기 좋아하는 ☐ superfluous a. 남는, 여분의; 불필요한

그는 사람들과 만날 때 거만한 태도를 보였으며, 그 때문에 자신의 동료들 사이에서 인기가 없었다.

## 43      ②

☐ wistfully ad. 열망하는 듯이, 동경하는 듯이(=yearningly) ☐ wantonly ad. 방자하게, 제멋대로 ☐ dreadfully ad. 몹시, 굉장히; 끔찍하게 ☐ pleasantly ad. 즐겁게, 유쾌하게

교실에 틀어박혀서 그는 창문을 통해 밖에서 축구를 하는 소년들을 동경하는 듯이 바라본다.

## 44      ④

☐ examine v. 검사하다, 조사하다, 검토하다(=look over) ☐ look in 잠깐 들여다보다; 들르다 ☐ look on 관찰하다, 방관하다, 지켜보다 ☐ look out 밖을 보다, 얼굴을 내밀다; 경계하다

어떤 것에 서명하기 전에 계약서를 신중하게 검토하십시오.

## 45      ④

☐ prophecy n. 예언 ☐ strengthen v. 강화되다 ☐ apposite a. 아주 적절한(=pertinent) ☐ quotation n. 인용; 인용구 ☐ drift n.
일반적인 경향[추세] ☐ diametric a. 직경의; 정반대의 ☐ conjecture v. 추측하다 ☐ extant a. 현존[잔존]하는

이 예언은 기존의 여론 동향을 보여주는 적절한 인용문에 의해 강화되었다.

## 46      ③

☐ devote v. (시간·노력을) ~에 바치다, 쏟다 ☐ youthful a. 젊을 때의; 기운찬 ☐ advancement n. 발전, 촉진(=promotion) ☐ principle of utility 공리의 원리 ☐ establishment n. 설립, 창설 ☐ abolishment n. 폐기, 철폐; 무효화 ☐ clarification n. 설명, 해명

J. S. 밀(Mill)은 젊었을 때 대부분의 에너지를 공리의 원리를 발전시키는 데 바쳤다.

## 47      ②

☐ dogged a. 완강한, 집요한, 끈질긴(=tenacious) ☐ perseverance n. 인내, 인내력, 참을성, 끈기 ☐ poignant a. 매서운, 날카로운, 통렬한 ☐ drowsy a. 졸음이 오는, 졸리게 하는 ☐ zealous a. 열심인, 열광적인

개선할 수 있는 유일한 방법은 노력과 끈기를 통해서이다.

## 48      ③

☐ fleetingly ad. 일순간, 일시적으로, 잠시; 덧없이(=temporarily) ☐ easily ad. 쉽게, 수월하게, 용이하게 ☐ haphazardly ad. 우연히, 제멋대로 ☐ fundamentally ad. 근본적으로, 본질적으로

감각 기억은 당신의 마음에 일시적으로 들어온 일종의 이미지나 기억이다.

## 49      ②

☐ outbreak n. (전쟁·사고·질병 등의) 발생[발발], 창궐(=breakout) ☐ quarantine n. 격리 ☐ visitor n. 방문자, 내객 ☐ subsidence n. 침하, 침강

경제가 전 세계적인 유행병에서 회복되면서 지역적인 발병과 단속(제한 조치)이 오락가락하기 때문에 그 회복은 고르지 못할 것이다.

## 50      ①

☐ bump n. 충돌; 장애물 ☐ bruise n. 타박상, 멍; 흠; 상처(=damage) ☐ remedy n. 치료; 구제책 ☐ comfort n. 위로, 위안 ☐ compassion n. 연민, 동정심

우리가 서로 사랑한다는 것에 대해서는 내 마음에 전혀 의심이 없었지만, 우리 사이엔 많은 충돌과 상처가 있었다.

## 51　②

□ catchy a. 인기를 끌 것 같은, 매력적인, 사람의 마음을 끄는 (=pleasant) □ melancholic a. 우울한; 우울증의; 우울하게 하는 □ melodious a. 선율이 아름다운, 음악적인 □ gloomy a. 어둑어둑한; 울적한, 우울한; 비관적인

그녀는 피아노로 사람의 마음을 끄는 곡을 연주했다.

## 52　②

□ premise n. 전제, 가정(=assumption) □ obscurity n. 애매한 상태; 불명료 □ exalt v. 높이다, 찬양하다 □ impalpable a. 쉽사리 이해할 수 없는, 미묘한 □ promise n. 약속; 기대, 희망; 징후 □ assignment n. 할당, 지정; 지령, 담당 □ prompt n. 자극하는 것, 고무하는 것; 주의

그의 전제는 단순했다. 그에 따르면 20세기의 모더니즘이 모호함에서 시작했거나 모호함으로 귀착되었다면 19세기의 낭만주의는 우리가 잘 알 수 없고 비이성적인 것을 신주 모시듯이 했다는 점이다.

## 53　②

□ fearsome a. 무서운, 무시무시한 □ predator n. 육식동물 □ roam v. 걸어다니다, 돌아다니다, 배회하다(=wander) □ help oneself to (음식물 따위를) 마음대로 집어먹다; ~을 마음대로 쓰다 □ pursue v. 추구하다; 추격하다; 수행하다 □ stalk v. 몰래 접근하다; 만연하다 □ haunt v. 자주 가다; 자주 나타나다

인간과 늑대와의 관계는 항상 골칫거리였다. 100년 전만 해도 십만 마리가 넘는 사나운 육식동물들이 서부를 돌아다니면서, 인간이 그곳에서 찾은 풍부한 먹이와 드넓은 땅을 마음껏 누렸다.

## 54　②

□ vapid a. 맛없는; 생기 없는, 활기 없는(=inane) □ unkempt a. 흐트러진, 단정치 못한 □ urbane a. 세련된, 점잖은 □ inbred a. 타고난, 천부적인

우리 수상은 활기 없는 연설을 했다.

## 55　③

□ cul-de-sac n. 막다른 골목; 궁지, 곤경(=impasse) □ derision n. 조롱, 조소 □ pillar n. 기둥; 표주 □ delirium n. 정신착란, 헛소리하는 상태

우리는 지난 정부가 우리를 막다른 골목에 몰아넣은 후 그 곤경에서 나라를 구하기 위해 노력하고 있다.

## 56　④

□ fortify v. 요새화하다; 강화하다, 튼튼히 하다(=strengthen) □ resolve n. 결심, 결의 □ ease v. 진정시키다, 덜다, 완화하다 □ lower v. 낮추다, 내리다; 떨어뜨리다 □ decrease v. 줄다, 감소하다; 축소되다

이것의 결과는 정당을 구하기 위해 노력하려는 그들의 결의로 그들을 강화시키려는 것이었다.

## 57　④

□ lend v. 빌려주다 □ imbecile a. 저능한; 우둔한, 어리석은(=absurd) □ superimpose v. 위에 놓다, 겹쳐 놓다; 덧붙이다, 첨가하다 □ transportable a. 수송[운송]할 수 있는 □ checked a. 바둑판[체크]무늬의

다른 사람에게 당신의 여권을 빌려주는 것은 어리석은 일이다.

## 58　②

□ allegedly ad. 소문에 의하면, 주장하는 바에 따르면 □ supersede v. 대신[대리]하다(=replace); 경질하다 □ predicate v. 단언하다, 단정하다; 서술하다 □ antedate v. (시기적으로) ~에 앞서다, ~보다 먼저 일어나다 □ accumulate v. 모으다, 축적하다

몇 분마다, 시장에 나와 있는 기존의 모든 제품을 대신한다고 하는 새로운 노화방지 크림이 출시되어 나오고 있다.

## 59　④

□ celebrated a. 유명한, 저명한 □ distinctive a. 특유의, 특이한, 독특한 차이를 나타내는(=distinguishing) □ restrained a. 자제된; 억제된, 차분한 □ exquisite a. 아주 아름다운; 최고의; 정교한 □ painstaking a. 노고를 아끼지 않는, 근면한; 공들인 □ mediocre a. 보통의, 평범한; 2류의 □ ornamented a. (글자체가) 화려한, 장식체의

그 이탈리아의 대가가 1921년 캔버스에 그린 유화는 독특한 붓놀림, 우아하지만 곧은 실루엣 선, 차분하지만 아름다운 색상의 쓰임으로 유명하다.

## 60　④

□ craven a. 겁 많은, 비겁한(=cowardly) □ versatile a. 재주가 많은; 융통성 있는 □ tentative a. 시험적인; 주저하는, 자신 없는; 모호한 □ hard-bitten a. 완고한, 고집 센

정치인들이 선거를 앞두고 표를 잃지 않기 위해서 비겁한 행동들을 하고 있다.

## 61 ③

□ accede v. (높은 지위, 왕위 등에) 오르다(=succeed) □ throne n. 왕좌, 옥좌; 왕위; 군주 □ abdicate v. 버리다, 포기하다 □ proceed v. 나아가다; 계속하다, 속행하다 □ precede v. 앞서다, 먼저 일어나다; ~보다 우월하다

왕이 사망하면서 왕자가 왕위를 이어받았다.


## 62 ③

□ astronomer n. 천문학자 □ detect v. 발견하다; 탐지하다 □ emit v. (빛·열·냄새·소리 따위를) 내다, 방출하다(=release) □ radiation n. 방사선; 복사에너지 □ interstellar a. 별과 별 사이의, 항성(恒性)간의 □ expand v. 확장하다, 팽창시키다 □ condense v. 응축하다, 압축하다 □ exhaust v. 다 써버리다, 고갈시키다

천문학자들은 블랙홀을 탐지하는 데 어려움을 겪는데, 이는 블랙홀이 전자 방사선을 전혀 방출하지 않기 때문이다. 따라서 블랙홀의 존재 여부는 그러한 방사선의 부재에 의해서나 부근에 있는 성간(星間) 물질 구름으로부터 블랙홀을 향해 물질이 끌어당겨지는 것에 의해 추론된다.


## 63 ①

□ disparaging a. 깔보는, 얕잡아 보는; 비난하는(=belittling) □ equitable a. 공정한, 공평한, 정당한 □ incisive a. 날카로운, 통렬한, 신랄한 □ unfair a. 공정치 못한, 부정한, 부당한

그들의 깔보는 듯한 비평에도 불구하고, 그는 아들의 그림을 자랑스러워했다.


## 64 ②

□ prolix a. 지루한, 장황한(=verbose) □ suffice v. 충분하다, 족하다 □ pithy a. (표현 등이) 힘찬, 함축성 있는; 간결한 □ sententious a. 간결한, 금언적인; 교훈적인 □ sacrilegious a. 신을 모독하는; 벌받을

그는 글이 너무 장황하다. 그는 한 문장이면 충분할 때도 한 페이지를 쓴다.


## 65 ②

□ celebrity n. (유명) 연예인; 유명인 □ be involved in ~에 개입되다, 관계[연루]되다 □ cosmetic n. 화장품 □ rescind v. (법률·행위 등을) 폐지하다; (계약 등을) 취소하다(=revoke) □ endorsement n. 배서; 보증; (유명인이 광고에 나와 하는 상품에 대한) 보증[홍보] □ contract n. 계약 □ renew v. 새롭게 하다; (계약 등을) 갱신하다 □ rectify v. 개정하다, 수정하다 □ redraft v. 다시 쓰다, 다시 기초하다

그 유명 연예인이 스캔들에 연루된 후에 화장품 회사는 광고홍보 계약의 제안을 취소했다.


## 66 ①

□ covert a. 비밀의, 은밀한(=clandestine) □ crafty a. 교활한; 간악한 □ ruthless a. 무자비한 □ impetuous a. 격렬한, 맹렬한; 성급한

독재정권을 전복시키려는 그 단체의 비밀 계획은 실패했다.


## 67 ④

□ sacrifice v. 희생하다; 제물로 바치다 □ avaricious a. 탐욕스러운, 욕심 많은(=greedy) □ blatant a. 떠들썩한, 시끄러운; 뻔뻔스러운 □ fable n. 우화, 교훈적인 이야기 □ honest a. 정직한, 성실한; 진실한

그는 자신의 출세를 희생하면서까지 그의 탐욕스러운 형이 성공할 수 있도록 했다.


## 68 ②

□ infraction n. 위반, 침해(=breach) □ divergence n. 분기; 일탈; 상이 □ discrimination n. 구별, 식별(력), 판별(력) □ depreciation n. 가치 하락, 가격의 저하

때때로 사회관습을 습관적으로 어기는 행위는 단지 사회적 비난이나 소문들에 의해서만 처벌된다.


## 69 ④

□ outgoings n. 경비, 지출(=expenditure) □ dividend n. 배당금 □ dependent n. 의지하는 사람; 부양 가족 □ draft n. 원고, 초안

메리(Mary)는 당신이 먼저 경비 지출을 평가한 다음 그에 따라 재정 계획을 세워야 한다고 제안한다.


## 70 ③

□ individualist n. 개인주의자; 이기주의자 □ extol v. 칭찬하다, 격찬하다(=praise) □ environmentalist n. 환경보호론자, 환경문제 전문가 □ dome v. 둥근 지붕으로 덮다, 반구형으로 만들다 □ oppose v. 반대하다 □ support v. 지탱하다; 지지하다 □ downplay v. 경시하다

그는 대량생산을 크게 칭찬한 개인주의자였으며, 북극을 둥근 지붕으로 덮길 원했던 환경보호론자였다.


## 71 ③

□ homage n. 존경, 경의(=respect) □ personify v. ~의 화신이다, ~을 전형적으로 보여주다 □ fame n. 명성, 평판 □ reward n. 보수, 보상 □ contribution n. 기부; 기여; 기고

벤저민 프랭클린(Benjamin Franklin)은 미국의 특별한 천재성을 상징하는 사람으로서 유럽과 북미 양측으로부터 존경을 받았다.

## 72 ②

☐ cede v. 양도하다, 양보하다(=yield) ☐ territory n. 영토, 영지 ☐ stabilization n. 안정 ☐ cease v. 그만두다, 그치다 ☐ terminate v. 끝내다, 종결시키다; 해고하다 ☐ procrastinate v. 지연시키다, 꾸물거리다

베트남에서 게릴라들은 흔히 낮에는 영토에 대한 지배권을 양도했다가 밤에는 되돌아와 정치적인 안정을 방해했다.

## 73 ④

☐ venture n. 모험적 사업, 벤처 사업 ☐ remunerative a. 보수가 있는; 수지맞는(=lucrative) ☐ untenable a. 지지할 수 없는, 옹호할 수 없는 ☐ detrimental a. 해로운, 불리한 ☐ chancy a. 불확실한, 위험한; 우연한

그 벤처 사업은 사업 투자자들에게 돈벌이가 되는 것으로 판명되었다.

## 74 ④

☐ cast n. 깁스; 붕대 ☐ fracture n. 골절; 부러짐, 파손, 균열(=crack) ☐ hypocrisy n. 위선 (행위) ☐ affectation n. 가장; 허식, 으스댐 ☐ blotch n. 큰 얼룩; 반점; 부스럼

매우 작은 골절상에 깁스를 하는 것은 불필요할 수도 있다.

## 75 ②

☐ destabilize v. 불안정하게 하다, ~을 동요시키다 ☐ sovereign a. 주권을 갖는, 자치의, 독립의 ☐ contrived a. 부자연스러운, 꾸며낸(=concocted) ☐ boundary n. 경계, 영역 ☐ potential a. 잠재적인, 가능성 있는 ☐ random a. 되는 대로의, 임의의 ☐ unexpected a. 예기치 않은, 돌발적인

러시아로부터 우리가 목격하는 것은 한 독립 국가를 불안정하게 하고 고용된 첩보원들을 이용하여 국경선 건너편에 작위적인 위기를 만들어내려는 불법적이고 비합법적인 노력이다.

## 76 ②

☐ legislation n. 입법, 법률제정; 법률 ☐ malicious a. 악의 있는, 심술궂은 ☐ vindictive a. 복수심이 있는, 원한을 품은(=vengeful) ☐ hysterical a. 히스테리 상태의; 병적으로 흥분한 ☐ compelling a. 강한 흥미를 돋우는 ☐ shameless a. 파렴치한

이 법률은 악의적이고 앙심을 품은 사람들이 옆집에서 강아지나 개를 키울지도 모르는 이웃 사람들의 트집을 잡는 데 이용될 수 있다.

## 77 ④

☐ ad hoc a. 특별한; 임시의(=provisional) ☐ posse n. 무리; 보안대, 수색대 ☐ labyrinthine a. 미로와 같은; 복잡한 ☐ rapid a. 신속한 ☐ adhesive a. 점착성의; ~에 집착하는 ☐ non-violent a. 비폭력적인

그 사무실 관리자는 경비를 불렀고, 임시 수색대와 함께 미로 같은 집회 장들을 지나, 거의 편집장 사무실까지 나를 추격했다.

## 78 ④

☐ instill v. 스며들게 하다, 서서히 주입시키다(=implant) ☐ ignore v. 무시하다, 모르는 체하다, 묵살하다, 상대하지 않다 ☐ practice v. 연습하다; 실행하다 ☐ moderate v. 절제하다, 완화하다

부모의 모범이야말로 아이들에게 사회적 책임감을 주입시키는 최고의 방법이다.

## 79 ②

☐ defile v. 더럽히다, 부정하게 하다; 모독하다(=contaminate) ☐ purify v. 깨끗이 하다, 정화하다; 다듬다, 순화하다 ☐ ridicule v. 비웃다, 조롱하다, 놀리다 ☐ discipline v. 훈련하다, 단련하다

폭력과 섹스로 가득 차 있는 혐오스러운 비디오 영화는 젊은이들의 정신을 더럽힐 것이다.

## 80 ②

☐ repugnant a. 비위에 거슬리는, 불유쾌한, 싫은(=disgusting) ☐ mediocre a. 보통의, 평범한, 범용한 ☐ tasteless a. 맛없는; 무미건조한 ☐ sumptuous a. 사치스러운, 호사스러운

식사는 완벽하게 준비되었지만, 손님들은 그 식사가 비위에 거슬렸다.

## 81 ③

☐ milk v. 젖을 짜다; (정보 등) 짜내다, 끌어내다, 착취하다(=extract money by guile from) ☐ insurance company 보험 회사 ☐ draw milk from a cow 소에게서 우유를 짜다 ☐ take advantage of ~을 이용하다; 속이다 ☐ render measures to develop 발전을 위한 방안을 제공하다

많은 사람들이 보험 회사로부터 돈을 뜯어내기 위해 수작을 부린다고 한다.

## 82 ②

☐ cerebellum n. 소뇌 ☐ coordinate v. 조정하다(=integrate) ☐ voluntary a. 자발적인; 수의(隨意)의 ☐ execute v. 실행하다, 집행하다 ☐ differentiate v. 구별하다, 식별하다 ☐ activate v. 활동적으로 하다

소뇌는 수의근(隨意筋) 운동을 조정하는 뇌의 한 부분이다.


## 83 ③

☐ mule n. 노새(수나귀와 암말과의 잡종) ☐ sterile a. 메마른; 아이를 못 낳는, 불임의(=barren) ☐ donkey n. 당나귀 ☐ obnoxious a. 밉살스러운, 불쾌한; 미움받고 있는 ☐ shabby a. 초라한; 누더기를 걸친 ☐ forsaken a. 버려진; 의지가 없는, 고독한

노새는 말과 당나귀 사이에서 나온, 새끼를 못 낳는 동물이다.


## 84 ①

☐ futile a. 쓸데없는; 무익한; 하찮은(=vain) ☐ tragic a. 비극의, 비극적인 ☐ excessive a. 과도한, 과다한, 지나친 ☐ depressed a. 의기소침한, 우울한; 불경기의

배를 구조하기 위한 몇 차례의 헛된 시도 끝에 선장은 그 배를 포기하라고 명령했다.


## 85 ①

☐ geographical a. 지리학(상)의, 지리(학)적인 ☐ conundrum n. 수수께끼, 어려운 문제(=riddle) ☐ terrain n. 지형 ☐ distribution n. 분배, 배분, 분포 ☐ barrier n. 장애, 장벽

전문가들은 바다의 한가운데를 찾는 지리학적인 수수께끼를 오랫동안 논의해 왔지만, 완전한 해답을 찾는 데는 현대적인 기술을 사용해야 했다.


## 86 ②

☐ shyly ad. 수줍게, 부끄러워하며; 겁내어 ☐ gregarious a. 남과 어울리기 좋아하는, 사교적인(=sociable) ☐ noisy a. 시끄러운, 떠들썩한 ☐ distracting a. 마음을 산란케 하는 ☐ unashamed a. 부끄러워하지 않는, 뻔뻔스러운

에밀리(Emily)는 새로운 사람들을 만났을 때 수줍게 엄마 뒤에 숨었지만, 그녀의 남자 형제인 키스(Keith)는 사람들과 어울리기를 좋아했다.


## 87 ②

☐ want ad 구직[구인] 광고 ☐ broach v. 말을 꺼내다, (화제 따위를) 끄집어내다(=bring up) ☐ look after 보살피다, 감독하다 ☐ find out 발견하다, 깨닫다 ☐ diverge from (진로 등을) 벗어나다; (의견 따위가) 갈라지다

기본적으로, 구직광고에서 지시하지 않으면, 급여에 관한 주제를 꺼내지 않는 게 가장 좋다.


## 88 ④

☐ precocious a. 조숙한, 어른다운(=advanced) ☐ studious a. 학구적인; 신중한 ☐ aggressive a. 공격적인, 호전적인 ☐ presumptive a. 추정의, 가정의

미국식품의약국은 30년 전 성조숙증 어린이들을 치료하기 위해 사춘기 차단제를 승인했다.


## 89 ②

☐ distill v. 증류하다; (주지, 요점 따위를) 뽑다, 추출하다(=extract) ☐ implicate v. 관련[연루]시키다 ☐ endorse v. (어음 따위에) 배서(背書)하다; (계획 등을) 승인하다 ☐ paraphrase v. (쉽게) 바꿔 쓰다, 말을 바꿔서 설명하다

대부분의 학생들은 그녀의 강의에 당황스러워하지만, 톰(Tom)은 항상 그녀의 강의에서 중요한 개념을 뽑아낼 수 있다.


## 90 ③

☐ sublime a. 기품 있는, 고상한(=lofty) ☐ esoteric a. 비밀의, 내밀한 ☐ epoch-making a. 신기원을 이루는, 획기적인 ☐ unconventional a. 관습에 의하지 않은, 인습에 얽매이지 않은

모차르트(Mozart)는 그의 시대의 대중적인 음악 스타일을 기품 있는 스타일로 바꿀 수 있는 능력이 있었다.


## 91 ①

☐ high-handed a. 고압적인, 독단적인(=overbearing) ☐ prescient a. 앞을 내다보는, 선견지명이 있는 ☐ solicitous a. 열심인; 간절히 ~하려 하는 ☐ fastidious a. 꾀까다로운, 세심한

중요한 직위를 갖는다는 것은 사람들을 갑자기 권위적으로 만드는 것처럼 보인다.


## 92 ②

☐ burlesque n. 패러디; 풍자극(=parody) ☐ dystopia n. 반(反)이상향, 디스토피아 ☐ soliloquy n. 혼잣말 ☐ intrigue n. 음모

뮤지컬 "캣츠"는 인간의 본성을 우회적으로 표현한 유명한 풍자극이다.


## 93 ①

☐ truncated a. 짧게 된, 너무 생략된, 불완전한(=shortened) ☐ anthem n. 축가(祝歌), 찬가 ☐ patriotic a. 애국적인, 애국의 ☐ metrical a. 운율의, 운문의 ☐ solemn a. 엄숙한, 근엄한

그의 발언이 끝나자마자 짧게 만든 러시아 국가가 흘러나왔다.

## 94 ④

☐ wheedle v. 감언이설로 유혹하다, (듣기 좋은 말로) 구슬리다, 꾀다 (=coax) ☐ wheedle one's way 남의 비위를 맞추어 출세하다[나아가다] ☐ plunge v. 빠지게 하다, 몰아넣다 ☐ convert v. 전환하다 ☐ galvanize v. 갑자기 활기를 띠게 하다, 기운이 나게 하다

어떤 사람들은 종종 상사의 비위를 맞추어 출세한다.

## 95 ④

☐ stolid a. 둔감한(=dull); 완강한(=stubborn) ☐ embattled a. 궁지에 몰린, 공세에 시달리는 ☐ indefatigable a. 지칠 줄 모르는, 끈질긴 ☐ outspoken a. 노골적으로[거침없이] 말하는 ☐ orthodox a. 전통적인; 인습적인

그녀는 현재 궁지에 몰린 유럽연합과 서구 자유주의 가치의 굳건한 수호자이다.

## 96 ④

☐ have no choice but to ~할 수밖에 없다 ☐ surrender v. 포기하다; 항복하다(=succumb) ☐ edge n. 끝, 가장자리 ☐ pursue v. 뒤쫓다, 추적하다 ☐ confess v. 고백하다, 실토하다 ☐ intervene v. 사이에 들다, 방해하다

그는 벼랑 끝에 몰리자 항복할 수밖에 없었다.

## 97 ①

☐ plaudit n. (pl.) 갈채, 박수, 칭찬(=acclaim) ☐ curb v. 억제하다, 구속하다 ☐ impunity n. 처벌되지 않음; 무사 ☐ graft n. 일, 힘든 일; 뇌물 수수; 뇌물 ☐ serenity n. 고요함; 평온 ☐ concord n. 일치, 화합, 조화 ☐ haven n. 안식처, 피난처

과테말라는 지난 10년 동안 면책과 뇌물 수수를 억제하려는 노력으로 찬사를 받았다.

## 98 ①

☐ wrangle v. 말다툼하다, 논쟁하다(=quarrel) ☐ trudge v. (지쳐서) 터덜터덜 걷다 ☐ ingratiate v. 마음에 들도록 하다, 영합하다 ☐ mock v. 조롱하다, 놀리다

그들은 법안을 만드는 것보다 끝없는 논쟁을 하는 국회에 지쳐버렸다.

## 99 ③

☐ static a. 고정된; 변화가 없는(=stationary) ☐ fluctuating a. 변동이 있는, 동요하는 ☐ resilient a. 되튀는; 탄력 있는 ☐ impending a. 임박한

변화가 없던 주가가 이제 다시 오르고 있다.

## 100 ④

☐ finicky a. 지나치게 까다로운(=fastidious) ☐ revolutionary a. 혁명적인, 대개혁을 일으키는 ☐ fast-moving a. 고속의; (연극·소설 등이) 전개가 빠른 ☐ volatile a. 격하기 쉬운; 변하기 쉬운

그 기술의 까다로운 특성으로 인해 예상치 못한 문제가 발생했다.

| | | | | | | | | | |
|---|---|---|---|---|---|---|---|---|---|
| 01 ④ | 02 ③ | 03 ④ | 04 ④ | 05 ④ | 06 ② | 07 ① | 08 ④ | 09 ④ | 10 ① |
| 11 ② | 12 ① | 13 ① | 14 ③ | 15 ② | 16 ① | 17 ③ | 18 ① | 19 ④ | 20 ① |
| 21 ③ | 22 ④ | 23 ② | 24 ① | 25 ② | 26 ④ | 27 ② | 28 ④ | 29 ③ | 30 ① |
| 31 ④ | 32 ③ | 33 ④ | 34 ④ | 35 ④ | 36 ③ | 37 ④ | 38 ③ | 39 ① | 40 ② |
| 41 ③ | 42 ① | 43 ④ | 44 ① | 45 ④ | 46 ④ | 47 ③ | 48 ④ | 49 ④ | 50 ③ |
| 51 ③ | 52 ① | 53 ② | 54 ⑤ | 55 ③ | 56 ③ | 57 ② | 58 ② | 59 ② | 60 ③ |
| 61 ② | 62 ③ | 63 ④ | 64 ② | 65 ④ | 66 ① | 67 ② | 68 ② | 69 ① | 70 ① |
| 71 ③ | 72 ① | 73 ① | 74 ① | 75 ③ | 76 ① | 77 ① | 78 ① | 79 ② | 80 ① |
| 81 ② | 82 ④ | 83 ① | 84 ① | 85 ① | 86 ③ | 87 ① | 88 ③ | 89 ③ | 90 ② |
| 91 ④ | 92 ① | 93 ③ | 94 ① | 95 ② | 96 ③ | 97 ④ | 98 ② | 99 ② | 100 ① |

## 01 ④

☐ disconcerted a. 당혹한, 당황한(=embarrassed) ☐ prevail v. 우세하다, 이기다, 극복하다; 널리 보급되다 ☐ exult v. 크게 기뻐하다, 기뻐날뛰다 ☐ vigorous a. 정력적인, 원기 왕성한; 활기 있는

메리(Mary)는 글을 잘 쓰려면 열심히 공부해야 한다는 주장에 무척 당황했다.

## 02 ③

☐ raucous a. 목이 쉰, 쉰 목소리의, 귀에 거슬리는; 요란하고 거친, 시끌벅적한 ☐ strain v. 긴장시키다; 뒤틀리게 하다, 상하게 하다 ☐ decorum n. 단정; 예의 바름(=propriety) ☐ vigor n. 활기, 정력 ☐ pinnacle n. 정점, 절정 ☐ commotion n. 소란, 소동

그 나라의 시끌벅적한 팬들은 탁구와 같이 정숙함을 중시하는 스포츠 경기의 예절을 망치고 있다.

## 03 ④

☐ proscribe v. 금지하다(=ban) ☐ amplification n. 증폭 ☐ permit v. 허락하다, 허가하다 ☐ process v. 가공하다; 처리하다 ☐ demand v. 요구하다; 필요로 하다; 묻다

몇몇 지휘자들은 자신의 연주회에서 소리를 증폭하는 것을 금지한다.

## 04 ④

☐ spurious a. 거짓된, 위조의, 겉으로만 그럴싸한(=counterfeit) ☐ complaisant a. 친절한; 붙임성 있는; 정중한 ☐ superordinate a. 상위의, 높은, 고위의 ☐ spruce a. 말쑥한, 단정한

비록 그 정치인에 대한 고발은 그럴싸한 거짓말이었지만, 많은 유권자들이 그 고발을 믿어서 그의 공직에 대한 도전은 심대한 타격을 입었다.

## 05 ④

☐ ebb v. 서서히 사그라지다, 줄어들다(=recede) ☐ even v. 평평하게 하다, 평등하게 하다 ☐ bounce v. 되튀다, 튀어 오르다 ☐ stop v. 멈추다, 정지하다

1990년대 중반 이후로, 에이즈 위기가 남자 동성애자들 때문이라는 문화적 묘사가 줄어들기 시작했다.

## 06 ②

☐ daylight saving time 일광 절약 시간, 서머타임 ☐ institute v. 세우다, 설립하다, 제정하다; 시작하다(=start) ☐ organize v. 조직하다; 체계화하다 ☐ encourage v. 용기를 북돋우다, 격려하다 ☐ teach v. 가르치다, 교육하다; 훈련하다

일광 절약 시간은 생산성을 향상시키기 위하여 시작되었다.

## 07 ①

☐ preliminary a. 예비적인, 준비의; 서문의; 시초의(=preparatory) ☐ religious a. 종교(상)의; 신앙의 ☐ sympathetic a. 동정적인 ☐ thorough a. 철저한, 완전한

기도와 노래의 예비의식 후에, 그날의 연사가 강연을 했다.

## 08 ④

☐ revamp v. 쇄신하다, 개정하다(=overhaul) ☐ curriculum n. 교과과정 ☐ integrate v. 통합하다, 접목하다 ☐ globalize v. 세계화하다 ☐ publicize v. 공표하다, 선전하다 ☐ downplay v. 얕보다, 경시하다

지금 많은 대학들은 국제적인 사례들을 강좌에 통합시키는 방식으로 기존의 교과과정을 쇄신할 계획이다.

## 09 ④

☐ horrid a. 무시무시한; 지독한, 불쾌한(=nasty) ☐ horrified a. 겁에 질린, 오싹한, 섬뜩한 ☐ arrogant a. 거만한, 건방진, 오만한 ☐ cynical a. 냉소적인, 비꼬는

그녀는 그녀의 진저리나는 친구들에게 한 번 더 기회를 주기로 했다.

## 10 ①

☐ brochure n. 소책자, 팸플릿 ☐ circuitous a. (말 따위가) 에두르는, 완곡한; 우회하는(=roundabout) ☐ congested a. 붐비는, 혼잡한 ☐ makeshift a. 임시변통의, 일시적인 ☐ steadfast a. 확고부동한, 고정된, (신념 등이) 불변의 ☐ easygoing a. 태평한, 게으른; 안이한

그 여행안내 책자는 여행객들이 혼잡한 도로를 피하는 데 도움이 되도록 그 호텔로 가는 다소 우회적인 경로를 추천하고 있다.

## 11 ②

☐ effective a. 효과적인(=efficacious) ☐ effluent a. 유출하는 ☐ feasible a. 실현 가능한 ☐ available a. 이용할 수 있는, 쓸모 있는

대부분의 사람들은 가장 효과적인 치료는 회복과정 초기에 시작된다고 믿는다.

## 12 ①

☐ converse with ~와 이야기하다, 대화를 나누다 ☐ effectively ad. 효과적으로 ☐ extensive a. 광범위한 ☐ arcane a. 신비로운; (그 분야에 정통한) 소수만 알고 있는(=esoteric) ☐ inclusive a. 일체를 포함한, 포괄적인, 총괄적인 ☐ systematic a. 체계적인, 조직적인 ☐ comprehensive a. 종합적인

다른 사람들과 효과적으로 대화하기 위해, 우리는 광범위한 어휘와 소수만이 알고 있는 문법규칙 이상의 수단이 필요하다.

## 13 ①

☐ gorgeous a. 호화스러운, 화려한; 멋진(=beautiful) ☐ disturbed a. 정신 장애의, 불안한 ☐ gloomy a. 우울한, 음침한 ☐ perplexed a. 당황한, 난처한, 어찌할 바를 모르는

내가 바라는 집은 산에 있는 집이다. 그 집은 나무로 둘러싸여 있고, 아름다운 호수가 내다보이는 그런 집이다.

## 14 ③

☐ exhume v. 발굴하다, (묻힌 명작 등을) 햇빛을 보게 하다, 발견하다 (=excavate) ☐ music hall n. 보드빌(노래와 춤을 섞은 대중적인 희가극) ☐ disrupt v. 붕괴시키다; 혼란시키다 ☐ render v. ~하게 하다; 표현하다; 양도하다 ☐ compose v. 조립하다, 구성하다; 만들다

그 악단은 몇몇 오래된 영국의 보드빌 노래들을 찾아내어 그것으로 오늘날의 청중들을 기쁘게 했다.

## 15 ②

☐ clamp down on ~을 엄하게 단속하다 ☐ rambunctious a. 난폭한, 제멋대로의, 다루기 어려운(=unruly) ☐ prescient a. 선견지명[예지력]이 있는 ☐ obsequious a. 아부하는 ☐ pedantic a. 현학적인

다루기 어려운 영국 언론을 규제하려던 정부의 시도는 새로운 왕실 스캔들을 불러일으켰다.

## 16 ①

☐ exaggerate v. 과장하다; 지나치게 강조하다 ☐ downright ad. 철저히, 완전히(=thoroughly) ☐ plausibly ad. 그럴싸하게 ☐ promptly ad. 지체 없이 ☐ tepidly ad. 미지근하게; 열의[박력, 생기]가 없이

많은 기업들이 그들의 식품과 약초로 만든 제품에 대해 과장하거나 완전히 거짓말하고 있다.

## 17 ③

☐ uphold v. 지지하다, 옹호하다, 유지시키다(=defend) ☐ amend v. 수정하다, 개정하다 ☐ ratify v. 비준하다 ☐ transcend v. 초월하다; 능가하다

경찰관으로서 당신은 그 법을 찬성하든 하지 않든 간에, 그 법을 준수해야 한다.

## 18 ①

☐ infirm a. 허약한; 쇠약한(=feeble) ☐ insolvent a. 지급불능의, 파산한 ☐ disabled a. 장애를 가진 ☐ restless a. 침착하지 못한, 들떠있는

몸이 쇠약한 사람들이 자립할 수 있는 국가가 운영하는 주거 시설은 거의 없다.

## 19 ④

☐ omen n. 전조, 징조(=portent)  ☐ confession n. 고백, 자백  ☐ vigor n. 활기  ☐ artifice n. 책략, 술책  ☐ portent n. 징조, 전조

나는 그것이 좋은 징조인지 아니면 나쁜 징조인지 확실하지 않았기 때문에 꿈에 대해서 어느 누구에게도 말하지 않았다.

## 20 ①

☐ novice n. 풋내기, 신참자(=learner)  ☐ expert n. 숙달자, 전문가, 숙련가, 달인  ☐ genius n. 천재; 비상한 재주  ☐ preacher n. 설교자, 전도사

영화 연출에 관한 한 존 톰슨(John Thompson)은 아직도 풋내기이다.

## 21 ③

☐ expunge v. 지우다, 삭제하다(=remove)  ☐ shame n. 수치심; 치욕, 불명예  ☐ flee v. 달아나다, 도망하다  ☐ entrench v. 참호로 에워싸다; 확립하다; 정착시키다  ☐ insert v. 끼워 넣다, 삽입하다  ☐ prevail v. 우세하다; 널리 보급되다, 유행하다

그는 적으로부터 도망쳐야 했던 치욕을 결코 마음속에서 지우지 않았다.

## 22 ④

☐ dismiss v. 묵살[일축]하다  ☐ profligate a. 방탕한, 품행 불량의, 부도덕한; 낭비하는(=wasteful)  ☐ autocrat n. 전제 군주, 독재자  ☐ progressive a. 전진하는; 진보하는  ☐ stingy a. 인색한, 너무 아끼는  ☐ frugal a. 검소한, 절약하는

얼마 전까지 빈곤한 국가의 대기업들은 부유한 족벌이나 방탕한 독재자들이 경영하는 이류기업으로 여겨져 일반적으로 외면당했다.

## 23 ②

☐ assailant n. 공격자; 가해자(=attacker)  ☐ assistant n. 조수, 보좌역, 보조자, 보조물  ☐ smoke n. 연기; 매연  ☐ ship n. 배, 함(선)

가해자의 고향이 어디였습니까?

## 24 ①

☐ prerequisite n. 필요조건; 기초 필수과목(=requirement)  ☐ disadvantage n. 불이익; 불리한 사정, 손해  ☐ permission n. 허가, 면허; 허용  ☐ disappointment n. 실망, 기대에 어긋남

스미스(Smith) 교수님의 이탈리안 르네상스 과목을 듣기 위해서 먼저 들어야 할 선수과목이 없는 거 맞지?

## 25 ②

☐ shrewd a. 빈틈없는, 약삭빠른  ☐ sidestep v. 회피하다(=avoid)  ☐ capitalize on ~을 이용하다  ☐ enforce v. 집행하다, 강요하다  ☐ adhere to ~을 고수하다  ☐ stipulate v. ~을 규정하다

약삭빠른 인터넷 사용자들은 다른 사람들의 개인 정보를 사용하거나 해외 서버로 운영되는 사이트를 이용함으로써 실명제 규정을 피할 수 있다.

## 26 ④

☐ despondent a. 낙담한, 의기소침한(=dejected)  ☐ nostalgic a. 향수를 불러일으키는  ☐ responsible a. 책임 있는  ☐ elated a. 의기양양한, 우쭐대는

많은 아프가니스탄 사람들은 탈레반에게 나라가 넘어간 상황에 대해 깊은 실망감을 느끼고 있다.

## 27 ②

☐ strident a. (소리가) 귀에 거슬리는, 거친(=severe)  ☐ divergent a. (의견 등이) 다른  ☐ consoling a. 위안이 되는  ☐ stereotyped a. 판에 박은, 진부한  ☐ aristocratic a. 귀족의, 귀족적인

소셜 미디어에 대해 그들이 공유하는 거친 비판은 서로 다른 정치적 견해들로부터 나온 것이다.

## 28 ④

☐ festering a. 지겨운, 싫증이 나는(=suppurating)  ☐ dreary a. 음울한  ☐ festive a. 축제의, 기념일의  ☐ fetching a. 멋진, 매력적인

1860년 에이브러햄 링컨(Abraham Lincoln)의 대통령 당선은 연방 정부와 주 정부의 상대적 권력에 대한 오래 곪아온 논쟁을 절정에 달하게 했다.

## 29 ③

☐ circulatory system (혈액이나 림프액이 흐르게 하는) 순환계  ☐ dispose of ~을 배열하다; 처리하다; 매각하다; 제거하다(=get rid of)  ☐ intake n. 받아들이는 곳; 빨아들임, 흡입  ☐ bear up under ~을 견디다  ☐ run over 넘치다; ~을 대충 훑어보다

순환계는 축적되면 몸에 해를 줄 수도 있는 노폐물을 제거하는 데 도움을 준다.

## 30 ①

☐ timidity n. 겁 많음(=fearfulness); 수줍음, 소심  ☐ try somebody/something out ~을 (~에게) 테스트해[시험적으로 사용해] 보다  ☐

reverence n. 숭상, 존경; 경의, 경외 ☐ inclination n. 경향, 기질, 성향 ☐ impulse n. 추진(력); 자극; 충동; 욕구

그 수줍은 아이의 타고난 겁이 많은 성격은 그녀가 그 팀에 들어가기 위한 적격 시험을 보는 것을 두려워하게 만들었다.

## 31 ④

☐ addiction n. 중독 ☐ failure to V ~하지 않음, 불이행 ☐ inhibit v. 억제하다 ☐ euphoria n. 행복감, 희열(=exhilaration) ☐ disruption n. 분열; 혼란 ☐ realization n. 자각, 인식 ☐ frustration n. 좌절감, 불만

중독은 사실 한번 보상받은 행동을 억제하지 못하는 것이지, 생겨나는 행복감의 정도를 말하는 것이 아니다.

## 32 ③

☐ compress v. 압축하다, 압착하다(=condense) ☐ expand v. 넓히다, 펼치다; 확장하다 ☐ commemorate v. 기념하다, 축하하다 ☐ spend v. (돈을) 쓰다, 소비하다

그 여행객은 자신의 모든 운동복을 하나의 여행 가방에 밀어 넣으려 애썼다.

## 33 ④

☐ influence v. 영향을 미치다 ☐ agenda n. 안건, 의제 ☐ stand out 눈에 띄다, 두드러지다 ☐ exigency n. 긴급성, 위급(=urgency) ☐ provocative a. 성나게 하는; 도발적인, 자극적인 ☐ accuracy n. 정확, 정밀 ☐ factuality n. 사실에 입각함, 사실성 ☐ ingenuity n. 창의력, 재간; 교묘함

사회적 의제 설정과 여론 형성에 큰 영향을 미치는 인기 검색어들은 눈에 잘 띄도록 배치돼 있으며, 검색어 리스트는 실시간으로 바뀌면서 긴박감을 더해준다. 그러나 그 검색어들의 상당수는 부정확하고 또한 나쁜 정보나 도발적인 주제로 이어지기도 한다.

## 34 ④

☐ subterranean a. 지하에 있는; 숨은, 비밀의(=underground) ☐ reservoir n. 저수지; 저장소 ☐ naval a. 해군의, 해군에 의한 ☐ rainwater a. 빗물의 ☐ unpolluted a. 오염되지 않은

미국의 지하에 있는 저수지에는 지표상에 있는 저수지와 호수를 모두 합친 것보다 훨씬 더 많은 용수가 있다.

## 35 ④

☐ mercurial a. 변덕스러운(=capricious) ☐ think things out 이것저것 다 따져보다 ☐ dogmatic a. 독단적인; 고압적인 ☐ parsimonious

a. 인색한 ☐ unscrupulous a. 비양심적인

변덕스러운 사람은 이것저것 다 따져보면서 미래에 대해 계획 세우는 것을 꺼려한다는 측면에서 극적이고 특별히 모험을 즐기는 사람과 비슷하다.

## 36 ④

☐ glean v. 얻다, 모으다(=garner) ☐ remove v. 없애다, 제거하다 ☐ amend v. 개정하다, 수정하다 ☐ quote v. 인용하다, 전달하다

링컨(Lincoln)은 독립선언서에서 얻은 가치로 노예제도의 종식을 주장했다.

## 37 ④

☐ stoical a. 금욕의; 태연한, 냉철한 ☐ tumultuous a. 떠들썩한, 소란스러운; 사나운, 거친(=violent) ☐ emotional a. 감정적인, 정서의 ☐ pertinent a. 타당한, 적절한 ☐ sarcastic a. 빈정대는, 비꼬는

그들의 냉철한 모습에도 불구하고, 그들의 모든 몸짓은 격정적인 과거의 기억에 의해 여전히 불안정하다.

## 38 ③

☐ mete out (벌, 가혹 행위 등을) 가하다, 부과하다 ☐ retribution n. 보답; 징벌; 응보, 보복(=vengeance) ☐ transgression n. 위반, 범죄 ☐ reticence n. 과묵, (입을) 조심함 ☐ lawsuit n. 소송, 고소 ☐ discord n. 불화, 불일치, 내분

자연은 늘 자연의 법칙을 위반한 것에 대해 징벌을 가한다.

## 39 ①

☐ crux n. 중요점, 핵심(=heart) ☐ identification n. (사람·물건의) 신원[정체]의 확인; 동일하다는 증명[확인]; 식별 ☐ cuneiform a. 쐐기문자의, 설형문자의 ☐ passage n. (책의) 구절 ☐ appropriateness n. 적합, 적절성 ☐ solution n. 해결, 해법 ☐ fascination n. 매혹; 매력

문제의 핵심은 설형문자로 쓴 글의 저자가 사용한 독특한 식별 수단이다.

## 40 ②

☐ divergent a. (사상 따위가) 다른, 일치하지 않는(=dissimilar) ☐ realistic a. 현실적인, 사실적인 ☐ untruthful a. 진실이 아닌, 거짓의 ☐ profound a. 엄청난; 심오한

부모와 자녀는 종종 삶에 대해 서로 다른 신념을 가지고 있다.

## 41 ③

☐ dwarf v. 작게 하다; ~의 성장을 방해하다 ☐ ornamental a. 장식(용)의, 장식적인(=decorative) ☐ medicinal a. 의약의, 약용의, 약효 있는, 병을 고치는 ☐ diverse a. 다양한, 가지각색의; 다른 ☐ constructive a. 건설적인, 적극적인; 구조상의

어떤 소나무들은 장식을 목적으로 일부러 작게 만든다.

## 42 ①

☐ amorphous a. 일정한 형태가 없는, 무정형(無定形)의(=formless) ☐ eccentric a. 괴짜의 ☐ mobile a. 이동하기 쉬운 ☐ transient a. 일시적인

그 사진작가는 구름, 엎질러진 밀크셰이크, 텐트 같은 옷을 입은 여인 등, 일정한 형태가 없는 피사체를 좋아했다.

## 43 ④

☐ prowl v. 배회하다, 어슬렁거리다; 기웃거리다(=move around) ☐ open early 일찍 열다 ☐ clean up 깨끗이 청소하다, 지우다 ☐ feel proud of ~을 자랑스럽게 여기다

하루에 커피를 다섯 잔 마시는 51세의 그는 사무실을 배회하며 그 모든 일이 어떻게 시작되었는지 생각하면서 집중한 모습을 보이고 있다.

## 44 ①

☐ immortal a. 불멸의, 영원한; 불변의, 끊임없는(=imperishable) ☐ counterfeit a. 위조의, 가짜의; 허위의 ☐ disreputable a. 평판이 좋지 않은, 창피한; 초라한 ☐ ostensible a. 표면상의, 허울만의, 겉치레의

사실, 그는 소설에서 죽지 않는 인물들 중의 하나다.

## 45 ④

☐ subordinate a. 부수적인; 하위의(=subsidiary) ☐ superior a. 뛰어난, 보다 나은; 우수한 ☐ tedious a. 지루한, 지겨운 ☐ temporary a. 일시적인, 잠시의; 임시의

당신은 젊고 경험이 부족한 직원이기에, 대기업에서 보조적인 일 이상의 것을 맡을 것이라고 기대할 수는 없을 것이다.

## 46 ④

☐ board a plane 비행기에 탑승하다 ☐ exterior n. 외부, 외면 ☐ ritual n. (종교적) 의식, 예배식; 의식적 행사(=ceremony) ☐ game n. 놀이, 경기 ☐ hazard n. 위험, 모험 ☐ scheme n. 계획, 설계; 책략

비행기를 탈 때, 나는 항상 문 오른쪽의 비행기 외벽을 반드시 만져야 한다. 이것은 내가 여행할 때 하는 개인적인 의식인데, 이렇게 하면 웬일인지 마음이 편해진다.

## 47 ③

☐ edifice n. 건물; 조직, 체계(=structure) ☐ facade n. 정면; 외관 ☐ menace n. 위협, 협박 v. 위협하다 ☐ plethora n. 과다, 과잉

틀림없이 이것은 국제시장을 지배하는 규칙들의 또 다른 취약한 구조다.

## 48 ④

☐ bamboozle v. 속이다(=cheat) ☐ saloon n. 큰 홀, 술집 ☐ confuse v. 혼동케 하다; 당황하게[난처하게] 하다 ☐ benumb v. 마비시키다 ☐ intimidate v. 위협하다, 협박하다

시프티 샐리(Shifty Sally)는 술집에서 술 취한 카드놀이꾼들을 속이고 게임을 이기기가 쉽다는 것을 알게 되었다.

## 49 ④

☐ exploit v. 이용하다; 착취하다(=utilize) ☐ census n. 인구 조사 ☐ procedure n. 절차 ☐ to one's advantage ~에게 유리하게 ☐ seek v. 찾다; 추구[탐구]하다 ☐ explain v. 설명하다, 해명하다 ☐ explore v. 탐험하다

정치인들은 인구 조사 절차를 자신들에게 유리하게 이용하려고 하였다.

## 50 ③

☐ contingent a. ~에 부수하는; ~을 조건으로 하는(=dependent) ☐ clear a. 맑은; 분명한; 명백한 ☐ advisable a. 권할 만한, 바람직한 ☐ proper a. 적당한, 타당한, 알맞은

결과는 성공하기 위해 쏟은 노력에 좌우됐다.

## 51 ③

☐ equality n. 같음; 평등, 대등 ☐ antecedent n. 선행사건, 전례(=precedent) ☐ aspiring a. 출세 지향적인, 포부[야심]가 있는 ☐ element n. 요소, 성분 ☐ procedure n. 과정, 절차, 순서 ☐ justification n. 정당화, 타당한 이유

평등 추구권을 위한 운동에는 야심 있는 여성들의 대의명분에 도움을 준 몇몇 전례들이 있었다.

## 52     ①

☐ purport n. 의미; 취지, 요지(=meaning) ☐ thesis n. 논제, 주제; 제목; 논문; 학위 논문 ☐ contradistinction n. 대조, 대비 ☐ flaw n. 흠; 금; 결점, 결함 ☐ rectitude n. 정직, 청렴; 정확

왓슨(Watson)은 홈즈(Holmes)가 쓴 논문의 취지를 알고 싶었다.

## 53     ②

☐ derelict a. 유기된; 의무 태만의, 무책임한(=careless) ☐ deserted a. 인적이 끊긴; 사람이 살지 않는; 버림받은 ☐ unprecedented a. 선례가 없는; 새로운, 신기한 ☐ deteriorating a. 악화 중인

그 경비원은 직장에서의 태만한 직무 태도로 인해 해고당했다.

## 54     ④

☐ precipitate v. 거꾸로 떨어뜨리다; 촉진시키다(=accelerate) ☐ prevent v. 막다, 방해하다; 예방하다 ☐ pacify v. 진정시키다, 가라앉히다 ☐ foretell v. 예언하다; 예고하다

'중요한'이란 말은 토론에서 가장 남발하는 말이다. 시장보다 더 중요한 것은 없는데, 이것이 위기를 촉진했다고 해도 무리가 아니다.

## 55     ③

☐ erudite a. 학식 있는, 박학한(=scholarly) ☐ boring a. 지루한, 따분한 ☐ heated a. 뜨거워진; 흥분한; 성난 ☐ epoch-making a. 획기적인, 신기원을 이루는

영국 소설의 기원과 그 전통에 관한 회의에서 학술 토론이 이뤄졌다.

## 56     ③

☐ exceedingly ad. 대단히, 매우, 몹시 ☐ like-minded a. 같은 생각[의견, 취미]의 ☐ ordinarily ad. 보통(은), 대개; 보통으로 ☐ dissolve v. (환영·공포 따위가) 점점 사라지다(=dissipate) ☐ emerge v. 나타나다 ☐ increase v. 증가하다 ☐ oscillate v. 동요하다

인터넷 덕분에 우리 각자가 생각이 맞는 유형의 사람을 찾는 것은 매우 쉬운 일이다. 단순히 사회적 지지가 없어서 대개는 사라지고 말 견해들을 인터넷에서는 매우 많이 찾아볼 수 있다.

## 57     ②

☐ instantly ad. 당장에, 즉시 ☐ connive v. 묵인하다; 공모하다(=conspire) ☐ liquidation n. 청산, 정리, 상환; 살해 ☐ prolong v. 늘이다, 연장하다 ☐ embezzle v. 착복하다; 횡령하다 ☐ annihilate v. 전멸시키다

비서가 그 스파이의 살해를 공모했다는 소문이 즉시 퍼져나갔다.

## 58     ②

☐ divisive a. 불화를[분열을] 일으키는 ☐ herald v. 알리다; 예고하다(=foreshadow) ☐ polarization n. (주의·경향 등의) 대립, 양극화 ☐ divulge v. (비밀을) 누설하다; 폭로하다 ☐ solicit v. 간청하다, 청구하다 ☐ decompress v. ~의 압력을 줄이다

분열을 일으키는 시장의 선출은 그 도시에 정치적 양극화의 어려운 시기를 예고했다.

## 59     ②

☐ inured a. 익숙한, 단련된(=hardened) ☐ catastrophe n. 대참사, 큰 재앙 ☐ vulnerable a. 취약한, 연약한 ☐ resurgent a. 소생하는, 부활하는 ☐ irrevocable a. 취소할 수 없는

환경 저널리즘 분야에서 아주 오랫동안 일하게 되면, 당신은 결국 참사에 익숙해져 버릴 수 있다.

## 60     ③

☐ fluorescent a. 형광성의; 빛을 내는(=luminous) ☐ microscopic a. 현미경으로밖에 보이지 않는; 현미경의 ☐ poisonous a. 유독한, 유해한 ☐ aquatic a. 수생(水生)의, 물의

빛이 나는 균류의 종류는 50가지가 넘는다.

## 61     ②

☐ testament n. 유언; (사실, 정당성 등의) 입증, 증거(=evidence) ☐ bullying n. 집단 괴롭힘 ☐ curriculum n. 교육과정 ☐ elementary school 초등학교 ☐ question n. 질문; 의문, 의심 ☐ will n. 유언장

여학생들이 아무도 어른 앞에서 '뚱뚱한'과 같은 단어를 사용하지 않을 것이라는 것이 초등학교에서 시행되는 집단 괴롭힘 방지 교육과정에 대한 증거인데, 그것은 3, 4년 전에도 사실이 아니었다.

## 62     ③

☐ off-the-cuff a. 즉석의, 준비 없이 바로 하는(=impromptu) ☐ ruffle feather 신경을 건드리다 ☐ provocative a. 성나게 하는, 약올리는 ☐ tactful a. 재치 있는, 꾀바른 ☐ humble a. 시시한, 변변찮은

그의 즉흥적인 발언들은 국내와 해외에서 분노를 샀다.

## 63     ④

☐ laid-back a. 느긋한, 태평스러운 ☐ jocular a. 익살스러운, 유머러스한(=humorous) ☐ snappy a. 딱딱거리는, 퉁명스러운 ☐ oracular a. 신탁[탁선]의; 신비적인 ☐ obstinate a. 완고한, 고집 센, 집요한 ☐ affectionate a. 애정 깊은

보통 느긋하고 유머러스한 존스는 기자회견에서 퉁명스러웠다.

## 64 ②

☐ upright a. 직립한, 똑바로[곧추]선 ☐ vestige n. 자취, 흔적; 표적 (=trace) ☐ pattern n. 모범, 본보기; 양식; 도안 ☐ version n. 번역(문); 각색, 변형 ☐ proof n. 증명, 증거

이 똑바로 서 있는 돌들은 어떤 고대 종교의 흔적이다.

## 65 ④

☐ dissent v. 의견을 달리하다, 이의를 말하다, 반대하다(=oppose) ☐ bolster v. 지지하다, 강화하다; 기운을 북돋우다 ☐ contrive v. 고안하다, 연구하다; 설계하다 ☐ initiate v. 시작하다, 일으키다, 창시하다

수단 정부는 그 생각에 반대해 왔다.

## 66 ①

☐ excruciating a. 몹시 고통스러운, 참기 어려운, 극심한(=pestersome) ☐ abstruse a. 심원한, 난해한 ☐ denunciatory a. 비난의, 탄핵적인 ☐ dilatory a. 미적거리는; 지체시키는

웬디(Wendy)가 낯설고 종종 위협적인 세계를 극복해 나가는 것은 지켜보기에 고통스러울 것이다.

## 67 ①

☐ folly n. 어리석음, 우둔; 어리석은 행위(=stupidity) ☐ danger n. 위험 (상태); 위험한 것 ☐ difficulty n. 곤란; 어려움; 수고; 난국; 곤경 ☐ advantage n. 유리, 이익; 우월; 이점, 장점

그들은 그의 생각의 우둔함을 깨닫지 못하고 있다.

## 68 ②

☐ roundabout a. (말 따위가) 에두르는, 완곡한, 간접적인(=circuitous) ☐ rudimentary a. 기본의, 초보의 ☐ sporadical a. 때때로 일어나는, 산발적인 ☐ audible a. 들리는, 청취할 수 있는

그것은 우리에게 떠나라고 말하는 완곡한 방법이었다.

## 69 ①

☐ derivative a. 유도된; 파생적인(=unoriginal) ☐ throughout ad. 두루, 도처에 ☐ disingenuous a. 솔직하지 않은; 부정직한; 음흉한 ☐ foreign a. 외국의; 대외적인 ☐ speculative a. 사색적인; 투기적인

세계 시장 도처에서 실물 경제와 동떨어진 복잡한 파생 상품들이 무분별하게 유통되어 세계 금융 시장을 위기에 빠뜨렸다.

## 70 ①

☐ protract v. 오래 끌다, 길게 하다, 연장하다; 뻗다(=lengthen) ☐ befuddle v. 정신을 잃게 하다; 어리둥절하게 하다 ☐ illuminate v. 조명하다, 밝게 하다, 비추다; 설명하다 ☐ distend v. 넓히다, 팽창하다; 과장하다

그들의 엇갈린 견해로 인해 배심원단의 심의가 길어졌다.

## 71 ③

☐ cumbersome a. 성가신, 귀찮은, 번거로운(=burdensome) ☐ equivalent n. 동등한 것, 등가물; 상당하는 것 ☐ unparalleled a. 비할 데 없는 ☐ sluggish a. 게으른, 나태한 ☐ compulsory a. 강제적인, 의무적인 ☐ coarse a. 조잡한, 조악한

아날로그 방식은 동등한 디지털 방식에 비해 성가시지만, 화면에서 전달되는 그 무엇과도 비할 데 없는 풍부한 경험을 제공한다.

## 72 ①

☐ assiduous a. 끊임없는; 근면한, 부지런한(=diligent) ☐ rare a. 드문, 진기한 ☐ exhibition n. 전시회, 박람회 ☐ sufficient a. 충분한, 흡족한; 역량이 있는 ☐ flattered a. 우쭐해진, 기분 좋은 ☐ insufficient a. 불충분한, 부족한; 부적당한

일본 내 주요 박물관에서의 끈기 있는 연구 작업을 통해, 몇 점의 매우 희귀한 그림들이 2004년 봄 전시회를 위해 복원되고 있다.

## 73 ①

☐ credulous a. (남의 말을) 쉽사리 믿는, 잘 속는(=gullible) ☐ delusive a. 기만적인, 오해를[착각을] 일으키는 ☐ credible a. 믿을 수 있는, 신뢰할 수 있는 ☐ skeptical a. 의심 많은, 회의적인

일부 사람들은 신문에서 읽는 것이면 뭐든지 믿을 정도로 잘 속는다.

## 74 ①

☐ eschew v. 피하다, 멀리하다; 삼가다(=elude) ☐ stick with ~을 고수하다 ☐ strategy n. 전략, 책략 ☐ eradicate v. 근절하다, 박멸하다 ☐ execute v. 처형하다; 실행하다 ☐ elucidate v. 밝히다, 설명하다

그는 팔레스타인인들이 쉽게 협상을 피하고 그들의 유엔 전략을 고수할 수 있도록 해주었다.

## 75 ③

□ live up to ~을 이행하다; ~의 기대에 부응하다 □ make full use of 충분히 활용하다 □ mechanism n. 방법, 메커니즘 □ augment v. 늘리다, 증가시키다(=ratchet up) □ mitigate v. 완화시키다, 경감시키다 □ gripe at ~에 대해 불평하다 □ abominate v. 증오하다

만약 약속대로 그 협정이 이행된다면, 관련 국가들은 향후 수십 년 동안 배출량 감축을 늘려가면서 적응을 앞당기기 위해 그 방법을 최대한 활용해야 할 것이다.

## 76 ①

□ benediction n. 축복; 감사기도(=blessing) □ be informed 통지를 받다 □ donation n. 증여, 기증, 기부 □ attendance n. 출석, 출근; 출석자

잭(Jack)과 질(Jill)은 그들 부모님의 축복 없이 결혼했다.

## 77 ①

□ proximity n. 가까움, 근접(=adjacency) □ dispel v. 쫓아버리다; (근심 등을) 없애다 □ aloofness n. 무관심, 초연해 있는 것 □ complacency n. 자기만족, 안주 □ visibility n. 눈에 보임, 가시성, 시야

당신은 어디에서든 외로울 수 있지만, 도시에서 수많은 사람들에 둘러싸여 사는 것에서 비롯되는 고독에는 특별한 묘미가 있다. 단순한 물리적 근접성은 내적인 고립감을 떨쳐버리기에 충분하지 않다.

## 78 ①

□ assertion n. 단언, 주장 □ empirical a. 경험적인 □ evidence n. 증거, 증언 □ desuetude n. 폐지, 불용(不用)(=abolition) □ cease v. 그만두다 □ activation n. 활성화 □ beatitude n. 더없는 행복, 지복 □ vitality n. 생명력, 활력

정치·경제적 주장을 경험적 증거에 견주어 검증하는 것이 폐지되었고, 과학적 모델에 대한 공개적인 논의가 중단되었다.

## 79 ②

□ flee v. 달아나다, 도망치다(=run away) □ hide oneself 숨다, 몸을 감추다 □ protect oneself 보호하다, 막다 □ stay away 떨어져 있다, 거리를 두다

모든 위험에서 피하려고 해봐야 소용없다. 몇 가지 위험은 감수해야만 한다.

## 80 ①

□ neatnik n. 깔끔한 사람 □ messiness n. 혼란스러움, 뒤범벅 □ intentional a. 의도적인, 고의적인 □ provocative a. 도발적인, 자극적인(=irritating) □ seductive a. 마음을 끄는, 유혹적인 □ soothing a. 달래는, 위로하는 □ voluntary a. 자발적인, 임의적인

두 룸메이트가 있는 상황에서, 청결함을 유지하려는 깔끔한 사람의 열정은 그녀로 하여금 상대방의 지저분함이 단순히 생활방식의 차이가 아니라 의도적이고 심지어 도발적이라고 여기게 만들지도 모른다.

## 81 ②

□ ruminate v. 심사숙고하다(=brood) □ synthesize v. 종합하다; 합성하다 □ modify v. 수정하다 □ reminisce v. 회상하다 □ vault v. 도약하다

다윈(Darwin)은 자신이 모은 특별한 자료에 대해 25년 동안 연구하고 숙고한 후에 진화에 대한 자신의 생각을 종합했다.

## 82 ④

□ moratorium n. 지불 유예; (활동의) 일시적 연기(=postponement) □ prime minister 국무총리 □ put off 연기하다 □ refusal n. 거절, 거부 □ liability n. 책무; (pl.) 부채, 채무 □ increment n. 임금 인상, 증가

1월 1일 자로 시행 예정이었던 연료세 인상이 6개월 동안 연기될 것이라고 국무총리가 언급한 다음날 연료세 인상이 1년간 유예될 것이라고 발표되었다.

## 83 ①

□ blunt a. 무딘; 둔감한(=dull) □ instrument n. 기구, 도구 □ pick up 포착하다, 찾아내다 □ distinction n. 구별, 차별; 대조, 대비; 특성 □ efficient a. 능률적인, 효과적인; 유효한 □ keen a. 날카로운, 예리한; 열심인 □ outdated a. 구식의

시장 조사가 가진 문제점은 나쁜 점과 단순히 다른 점 사이의 차이를 포착하기에는 그것이 너무나도 무딘 도구라는 점이다.

## 84 ①

□ claim v. 공언하다, 주장하다 □ extrinsic a. 비본질적인, 부대적인; 무관한(=extraneous) □ agitated a. 흥분한; 동요한 □ fictive a. 가공의, 허위의 □ frenetic a. 열광적인

회의 관리자는 "비록 그 사실들이 주목할 만큼 흥미롭긴 하지만, 논의 중인 문제와 무관합니다."라고 주장했다.

## 85      ①

☐ fishy a. 의심스러운, 수상한(=suspicious) ☐ obvious a. 분명한, 확실한 ☐ placid a. 평온한, 조용한 ☐ helpless a. 무력한, 난감한

폐점 시간 이후에 그 가게 안에서 불빛을 보았을 때, 경비원은 뭔가 수상한 일이 일어나고 있는 것 같은 느낌이 들었다.

## 86      ③

☐ rally n. 집회 ☐ advisor n. 조언자, 보좌관 ☐ supplicate v. 탄원하다, 간청하다(=implore) ☐ mandate v. 명령하다, 요구하다 ☐ convince v. 납득[확신]시키다; 설득하다 ☐ expedite v. 촉진하다

그는 그의 보좌관들이 모두 그에게 그만두라고 간청할 때까지 거의 모든 집회에서 폭력을 조장했다.

## 87      ①

☐ collateral a. 부수[부차]적인, 이차적인 ☐ raid n. 급습, 습격 (=attack) ☐ decree n. 법령, 포고 ☐ sight n. 시각, 시력 ☐ disposal n. 처분, 처리

정부는 그 폭탄 공격 당시 어떤 부수적 피해가 있었다는 것을 부인했다.

## 88      ③

☐ virulent a. 치명적인, 맹독의; 매서운, 맹렬한(=destructive) ☐ nagging a. 성가시게 잔소리하는 ☐ unextinguished a. 꺼지지 않은, 소멸되지 않은 ☐ exorbitant a. 터무니없는, 과대한

스페인은 기후 변화로 인해 점점 더 맹렬해지는 산불에 대비하기 위해 더 많은 노력을 기울여야 한다.

## 89      ③

☐ anonymity n. 익명(사용) ☐ imbroglio n. (정치적) 분규, 뒤얽힌 오해(=quandary) ☐ reluctance n. 마음이 내키지 않음, 마지못해 함 ☐ recitation n. 암송, 낭독 ☐ truancy n. 무단결석, 등교 거부

그 관리는 익명을 전제로 하원 지도부의 분규에 대해 솔직한 답변을 내놨다.

## 90      ②

☐ refrain from ~을 삼가다 ☐ worldly a. 세속적인, 속세의(=secular) ☐ furious a. 성난, 격노한 ☐ unbridled a. 구속이 없는, 억제할 수 없는 ☐ unsullied a. 더럽혀지지 않은; 오점 없는

성직자들은 세속적인 욕망을 자제함으로써 행복해지려 하는 사람들이다.

## 91      ④

☐ stifle v. 억누르다, 억압하다(=suppress) ☐ clarify v. 명확하게 하다, 분명히 말하다 ☐ glean v. 얻다, 모으다 ☐ atone v. 속죄하다

보수주의자들은 소셜 미디어 회사들이 보수적인 의견을 억압하려고 한다고 비난해 왔다.

## 92      ①

☐ roundup n. (범인 일당 등의) 검거, ~몰이 ☐ vagrant n. 방랑자, 부랑자(=vagabond) ☐ beautify v. 아름답게 하다, 미화하다 ☐ detain v. 구금[억류]하다 ☐ dissident n. 의견을 달리하는 사람, 불찬성자 ☐ pervert n. 배교자; 변절자 ☐ lunatic n. 미치광이

1960년대에서 1980년대에 군부 독재자들은 거리를 미화하기 위해 부랑자들을 검거하라고 명령했고, 수천 명의 노숙자, 장애인, 어린이들을 구금시키고 강제 노동을 하는 시설로 보냈다.

## 93      ③

☐ skyrocketing a. 치솟는, 급등하는 ☐ bonanza n. 대성공, 뜻밖의 행운(=windfall) ☐ solace n. 위안, 위로 ☐ allocation n. 할당, 배당 ☐ collusion n. 공모

급등하는 세계 밀 가격은 무역업자들에게 대성공을 의미했다.

## 94      ①

☐ authoritarian state 권위국가(절대적인 권한을 가진 지도자를 중심으로 하는 통치형태) ☐ leery a. (~을) 미심쩍어하는, 조심스러워하는 (=wary) ☐ brutal a. 잔인한 ☐ mercurial a. 재치 있는; 변덕스러운 ☐ trifling a. 하찮은, 시시한 ☐ reprehensible a. 비난하는, 질책하는 ☐ indifferent a. 무관심한

중국과 러시아와 같은 권위국가들조차 북한의 김정은과 같은 잔인하고 변덕스러운 지도자를 상대하는 것을 조심스러워한다.

## 95      ②

☐ retaliate v. 보복하다, 앙갚음하다(=revenge) ☐ temper v. 누그러뜨리다[완화시키다] ☐ agonize v. 번민하다, 괴로워하다 ☐ hesitate v. 주저하다, 망설이다

그 병사는 선임병들의 괴롭힘에 복수한 것이었다고 말했다.

## 96      ③

☐ air raid 공습 ☐ ghastly a. 무서운(=horrible), 소름 끼치는 ☐ slight a. 가벼운; 사소한 ☐ corporal a. 육체의, 신체의 ☐ strenuous a. 정력적인, 열심인

공습 사이렌이 현재 하루에도 몇 번씩 울리고 현지 군 병원은 무서운 부상을 입은 채 최전방에서 들어오는 병력으로 가득 차 있다.

## 97　④

☐ battery n. 구타 ☐ lascivious a. 호색의, 음탕한; 색정을 돋우는, 선정[도발]적인(=lewd) ☐ unctuous a. 상냥한 ☐ propitiatory a. 달래는; 화해의 ☐ disruptive a. 파괴적인

오클라호마 법에 따르면, 성폭력은 누군가의 동의 없이 "선정적인 방식으로" 누군가의 몸을 의도적으로 만지는 것이라고 한다.

## 98　②

☐ inevitably ad. 필연적이다시피, 아니나 다를까 ☐ scrutiny n. 감시, 감독, 뚫어지게 봄 ☐ forfeit v. 상실하다; 몰수되다(=lose) ☐ infringe v. 어기다, 침해하다 ☐ trespass v. 침입하다 ☐ uphold v. 유지시키다, 옹호하다

유명 인사들은 필연적으로 감시를 당하며, 따라서 사생활에 대한 권리를 잃게 된다.

## 99　②

☐ phlegmatic a. 차분한, 침착한(=unemotional) ☐ fortuitous a. 생각밖의, 뜻밖의, 우연한 ☐ nefarious a. 못된, 사악한 ☐ affirmative a. 긍정의, 확언적인

컴퓨터 과학자들과 공학자들은 양자우위(양자 컴퓨터가 슈퍼컴퓨터의 성능을 넘어서는 현상)의 개념에 대해 논평가들보다 침착하다.

## 100　①

☐ presentiment n. 예감(=foreboding) ☐ stupor n. 무감각, 인사불성 ☐ attachment n. 부착, 접착; 애착 ☐ antipathy n. 반감, 혐오

그는 독살당할 것 같은 예감을 갖고 있다.

| | | | | | | | | | |
|---|---|---|---|---|---|---|---|---|---|
| 01 ③ | 02 ④ | 03 ② | 04 ② | 05 ③ | 06 ② | 07 ③ | 08 ① | 09 ③ | 10 ① |
| 11 ④ | 12 ① | 13 ④ | 14 ③ | 15 ④ | 16 ② | 17 ① | 18 ① | 19 ② | 20 ① |
| 21 ① | 22 ③ | 23 ① | 24 ④ | 25 ② | 26 ④ | 27 ① | 28 ② | 29 ③ | 30 ② |
| 31 ④ | 32 ④ | 33 ③ | 34 ② | 35 ④ | 36 ③ | 37 ③ | 38 ① | 39 ③ | 40 ② |
| 41 ③ | 42 ③ | 43 ③ | 44 ③ | 45 ② | 46 ① | 47 ② | 48 ① | 49 ① | 50 ① |
| 51 ① | 52 ① | 53 ② | 54 ④ | 55 ② | 56 ① | 57 ③ | 58 ① | 59 ④ | 60 ① |
| 61 ② | 62 ④ | 63 ③ | 64 ② | 65 ③ | 66 ① | 67 ② | 68 ③ | 69 ④ | 70 ③ |
| 71 ② | 72 ③ | 73 ② | 74 ④ | 75 ① | 76 ④ | 77 ① | 78 ① | 79 ④ | 80 ① |
| 81 ③ | 82 ② | 83 ④ | 84 ② | 85 ② | 86 ① | 87 ③ | 88 ② | 89 ① | 90 ② |
| 91 ② | 92 ③ | 93 ① | 94 ③ | 95 ③ | 96 ③ | 97 ① | 98 ② | 99 ③ | 100 ① |

## 01 ③

□ avid a. 욕심 많은, 탐욕스러운; 열심인(=eager) □ watchful a. 주의 깊은, 경계하는 □ skillful a. 숙련된, 솜씨 좋은, 능숙한 □ elementary a. 기본의, 초보의

열렬한 축구 팬으로서 나는 제츠(Jets) 팀이 하는 모든 경기를 보려고 한다.

## 02 ④

□ stampede v. 우르르 도망치다; 재촉하여 어떤 행동을 취하게 하다 (=force) □ mislead v. 오도하다, 잘못 인도하다 □ lull v. 달래다, 어르다 □ embarrass v. 어리둥절하게 하다

그 여인숙 주인들은 우리가 과식하도록 했다.

## 03 ②

□ hilarious a. 즐거운, 유쾌한, 몹시 재미있는(=amusing) □ account n. 설명, 기술; 이야기 □ absurd a. 불합리한; 어리석은, 바보 같은 □ dubious a. 수상쩍은; 모호한 □ obvious a. 명백한, 분명한

그녀는 선생님으로서 첫발을 내딛던 날에 대한 재미있는 이야기를 우리에게 해주었다.

## 04 ②

□ eclipse n. (일식, 월식의) 식(蝕) □ portentous a. 전조의; 불길한 (=threatening) □ omen n. 징조, 조짐 □ usher in 예고하다; 안내하다 □ fated a. 운명이 정해진 □ import n. 수입(품); 중요성; 의미 □ oblivious a. 잘 잊어버리는, 망각의 □ obese a. 비만의, 뚱뚱한 □ tantalizing a. 감질나게 하는, 애타는

고대에는 (일식, 월식의) 식(蝕)이 불길한 전조, 즉 역사적으로 중요한 일의 예정된 시작이나 종말을 예고하는 사건으로 여겨졌다.

## 05 ③

□ extinction n. 멸종, 절멸; 단절(=extermination) □ class n. (동식물 분류상의) 강(綱) □ subsidence n. 함몰; 가라앉음, 침전; 침전물 □ augmentation n. 증가, 증대; 증가율 □ propagation n. (동식물의) 번식, 증식; 선전, 보급

동물의 한 강(綱) 전체의 멸종을 목격하는 것은 드문 일이다.

## 06 ②

□ delirious a. 정신이 착란한, 헛소리를 하는(=demented) □ vivid a. 활발한, 발랄한 □ excruciating a. 몹시 고통스러운, 참기 어려운 □ hollow a. 속이 빈, 공허한

"오즈의 마법사"의 이야기는 도로시가 토네이도가 발생하는 동안 머리를 부딪친 후 그녀가 꾸는 혼미한 꿈에 바탕을 두고 있다.

## 07 ③

□ undeniable a. 부인[부정]할 수 없는 □ compunction n. 양심의 가책(=scruple) □ drastic a. 과감한, 극단적인; 급격한 □ extirpation n. 근절, 박멸 □ quip n. 경구, 명언 □ proclivity n. 경향, 성벽, 기질

부정할 수 없는 것은 빌(Bill)이 극단적인 조치들에 대해 전혀 양심의 가책을 느끼지 않았다는 사실이다.

## 08 ①

☐ bespoke a. 주문품의, 맞춤으로 한(=tailor-made) ☐ genetic a. 유전의 ☐ infusion n. (정맥에의) 주입 ☐ state-of-the-art a. 최신의, 최근의, 최신 기술의 ☐ over-the-top a. 과장된, 정도가 지나친 ☐ down-to-earth a. 실제적인, 견실한

이러한 맞춤형 유전자 치료제 기술이 2018년에 출시된 이후, 약 24명의 환자들이 다양한 신경 증후군을 치료하기 위한 약물을 투여받았다.

## 09 ③

☐ vicissitude n. 갑작스러운 변화, 변천(=unexpected change); (pl.) 흥망, 성쇠 ☐ wheel n. 수레바퀴; (자동차의) 핸들 ☐ exchange n. 교환, 주고받기; 언쟁, 논쟁 ☐ prophecy n. 예언; 예언 능력

비록 적응하려고 무척 애썼지만, 그는 결국 운명의 예기치 않은 변화에 의해 파멸되었다.

## 10 ①

☐ curse n. 저주, 악담, 독설(=bane) ☐ symbol n. 상징, 표상, 기호 ☐ vanguard n. 선봉, 선도; 지도자 ☐ advantage n. 유리; 편의; 이점

인류의 가장 큰 저주는 가난이다.

## 11 ④

☐ jeremiad n. 넋두리, 한탄(=lamentation) ☐ initiative n. 발의 ☐ amendment n. 수정 ☐ extremity n. 끝, 말단; 극한

샌더스(Sanders) 씨는 여전히 의료 산업에 대해 즉흥적으로 한탄을 하는 경향이 있으며, "모두를 위한 의료보험"과 같은 중요한 정책 제안을 논하는 것만큼 그를 행복하게 하는 것은 없다.

## 12 ①

☐ cellular a. 휴대전화의 ☐ outstrip v. ~을 능가하다, 추월하다 (=exceed) ☐ power line 송전선 ☐ deactivate v. 정지시키다, 비활성화 시키다 ☐ intensify v. 심화시키다, 강화하다 ☐ unveil v. (비밀을) 밝히다, 공표하다

휴대전화 기술은 시골지역을 연결하는 데 있어 송전선과 인터넷을 능가했다.

## 13 ④

☐ mind-blowing a. 몹시 자극적인, 매우 놀라운, 압도적인 ☐ dwarf v. 작아보이게 하다(=overshadow) ☐ Black Friday 블랙 프라이데이(미국 추수감사절(11월 넷째 주 목요일) 다음날인 금요일로, 1년 중 쇼핑센터가 가장 붐비는 날) ☐ Cyber Monday 사이버 먼데이(미국 추수감사절 연휴가 끝난 첫 월요일로 온라인 쇼핑몰의 판매량이 급증하는 날) ☐ aggravate v. 악화시키다; 화나게 하다 ☐ perpetuate v. 영구화하다, 끊이지 않게 하다 ☐ reinstate v. 원상태로 회복시키다

중국의 광군제(光棍節, 독신자의 날)는 세계 최대 규모의 쇼핑 행사가 되었으며, 올해 매출기준으로 압도적인 250억 달러를 달성해, 블랙 프라이데이와 사이버 먼데이 둘을 합친 것을 작아 보이게 만들었다.

## 14 ③

☐ transitory a. 일시적인, 덧없는(=fleeting) ☐ transcendental a. 선험적인, 초월적인 ☐ deceptive a. 현혹시키는, 거짓의, 사기의 ☐ translucent a. 반투명의; 명백한

스코틀랜드의 겨울은 다른 나라에 비해 더 길고 어둡기 때문에 비록 일시적이나마 독하고 따뜻한 술이 빛과 휴식을 제공한다.

## 15 ④

☐ evenly ad. 공평하게 ☐ match v. 맞붙게 하다 ☐ foretell v. 예언하다(=predict); 예고하다 ☐ outcome n. 결과 ☐ endorse v. (어음 따위에) 배서(背書)하다; (계획 등을) 승인[확인·시인]하다, 찬성하다 ☐ hinder v. 방해하다, 훼방하다 ☐ negate v. 부정하다, 부인하다

만약 전력이 매우 대등한 팀들끼리 맞붙게 되지 않는다면, 리그 시합의 결과를 예측하기가 더 쉬워질 것이다.

## 16 ②

☐ surreptitiously ad. 몰래, 은밀히, 비밀스럽게(=secretly) ☐ nest n. 보금자리, 둥지 ☐ quickly ad. 빠르게, 급히, 곧 ☐ occasionally ad. 가끔, 이따금 ☐ forcefully ad. 격렬하게, 힘차게

그 연구원은 새의 둥지에서 하루에 한 개의 알을 몰래 옮겼다.

## 17 ①

☐ adulterated a. 섞음질을 한; 불순한, 불량한; 상한(=spoiled) ☐ expensive a. 돈이 드는, 값비싼; 사치스러운 ☐ warm a. 따뜻한, 온난한; 열렬한, 열심인 ☐ leaking a. 새는, 새어나오는

이 그릇들 속에 담긴 우유는 상했다.

## 18 ①

☐ prognosticate v. 예지하다, 예언[예측]하다(=forecast) ☐ truncate v. 잘라 줄이다 ☐ quash v. 가라앉히다, 진압하다 ☐ polarize v. 양극화하다

일부 금융 지표들을 검토한 이후에, 소수의 비관적인 경제학자들이 경기 침체를 예측하기 시작했다.

## 19 ②

☐ considerate a. 사려 깊은, 신중한, 남을 배려하는(=thoughtful) ☐ considerable a. 상당한, 많은 ☐ peevish a. 짜증을 잘 내는, 성마른 ☐ dominant a. 우세한, 지배적인

많은 사람들이 그들 중 잭슨(Jackson)을 가장 사려 깊은 사람이라고 생각한다.

## 20 ①

☐ substantiate v. 실체화하다, 구체화하다, 실증하다(=affirm) ☐ overturn v. 뒤집다, 전복하다 ☐ propose v. 제의하다, 제안하다 ☐ reject v. 거절하다, 거부하다

많은 새로운 연구가 텔레비전이 가족 활동과 가족 관계의 형성을 방해한다는 가정을 확인해 주고 있다.

## 21 ①

☐ inveterate a. 뿌리 깊은, 상습적인(=habitual) ☐ curiosity n. 호기심 ☐ impoverished a. 가난한 ☐ superstitious a. 미신적인

이 상습적인 여행자들은 임금노동을 찾아서뿐만 아니라 단순히 다른 민족들과 장소들에 대한 호기심에서 종종 다른 집단들을 방문한다.

## 22 ③

☐ platitude n. 평범한 의견, 상투어(=banality) ☐ empirical a. 경험적인 ☐ dogmatism n. 독단주의; 독단론 ☐ gloss over ~에 대해 얼버무리고 넘어가다 ☐ plethora n. 과다, 과잉 ☐ glitch n. 사소한 결함; 작은 기술상의 문제 ☐ trapping n. 덫 놓기; 개입 중단

중요한 문제들을 진지하게 논의하지 않고 아무렇게나 얼버무림으로써 우리에게는 경험적으로 되는 것, 미묘한 차이를 띠게 되는 것, 독단주의를 피하는 것 등에 관한 진부한 말들만 남게 된다.

## 23 ①

☐ revise v. 개정[수정, 교정]하다(=amend) ☐ estimate n. 견적, 어림 ☐ annual expenditure 세출 ☐ transact v. 집행하다, 행하다; 처리하다 ☐ dispose of ~을 처분[처리]하다 ☐ bleach v. 표백하다, 희게 하다

인플레이션으로 인해 정부는 세출(歲出) 예산을 수정해야 했다.

## 24 ④

☐ extricate v. (위험·곤경에서) 구출하다; 해방하다(=remove) ☐ barbed-wire n. 가시철사 ☐ vaunt v. 자랑하다, 허풍떨다, 뽐내다 ☐ rankle v. 괴롭히다; 짜증나게 하다 ☐ scrutinize v. 자세히 조사하다

농부는 그 개를 철조망 울타리에서 구해냈다.

## 25 ②

☐ mettle n. 기질; 기개, 혈기, 용기, 열의, 근성(=courage) ☐ test v. (순도, 성능, 정도 등을) 검사하다, 시험하다; (가치 등을) 판단하다 ☐ adversity n. 역경; 불행 ☐ cleverness n. 영리함 ☐ insight n. 통찰(력), 간파 ☐ promise n. 약속; 계약; 기대, 희망

사람의 용기는 역경 속에서 시험되며 자신의 신념에 변함이 없는 사람은 결국 빛나게 된다.

## 26 ④

☐ browbeat v. 위협하다; 위협하여 ~하게 하다(=threaten) ☐ advise v. 충고하다, 조언하다; 권하다 ☐ acknowledge v. 인정하다, 시인하다; 승인하다 ☐ beg v. 간청하다, 구걸하다

그들은 끈기 있게 집주인을 위협하여 난방 시설을 고치고 배관 공사를 하게 했다.

## 27 ①

☐ lead poisoning 납중독 ☐ unremitting a. 간단없는, 끊임[그칠 새] 없는(=incessant) ☐ abdominal a. 배의, 복부의 ☐ nausea n. 메스꺼움, 욕지기 ☐ obtuse a. 둔한, 무딘 ☐ indelible a. 지울 수 없는

납 중독 환자는 계속되는 복부 통증과 현기증을 일으킬 수 있다.

## 28 ②

☐ probity n. 정직, 성실(=integrity) ☐ care for ~를 보살피다[돌보다] ☐ misconduct n. 비행, 부정행위, 직권 남용 ☐ privilege n. 특권; 특전 ☐ surveillance n. 감시, 감독

어디에서나 시민들은 더 나은 정부, 공직에서의 정직, 그리고 국민을 돌보는 국가를 원하는 것 같다.

## 29 ②

☐ in contrast 그에 반해서 ☐ appreciate v. 진가를 인정하다, 높이 평가하다 ☐ coalition n. 연합; 제휴(=alliance) ☐ obsession n. 강박관념, 집착, 망상 ☐ nomination n. 지명, 임명; 추천 ☐ nullification n. 무효화, 폐기

그에 반해서, 비폭력은 모든 사람의 인간성과 노력을 높이 평가하고 가치 있게 여기려 하며, 더 나은 삶을 추구하는 모든 사람들과 연대를 구축하고자 한다.

## 30 ②

☐ routine a. 판에 박힌, 일상의(=regular) ☐ temporary a. 일시의, 잠깐 동안의, 순간의, 덧없는 ☐ special a. 특별한, 특수한; 독특한, 특유의 ☐ important a. 중요한, 의미 있는; 유력한

면접은 채용 선발 과정의 일상적인 부분이다.

## 31 ④

☐ dissect v. 상세히 분석하다(=analyze), 비평하다; 해부하다 ☐ woe n. 고민, 문제, 재난 ☐ run across ~와 우연히 만나다, 발견하다 ☐ dissolve v. 녹이다, 용해하다; 분해하다; 해산하다 ☐ exact v. ~을 요구하다, 강요하다 ☐ dilute v. 묽게 하다; 희박하게 하다; 강도를 약하게 하다

사회적, 정치적 문제를 분석하는 것 대신에, U.S. News의 기자들은 크든 작든 여러 문제들에 대해 최근 몇 달간 우연히 알게 된 해결책에 대한 여러 가지 견해를 제공한다.

## 32 ④

☐ guts n. 용기, 결단력(=determination) ☐ raise a riot 폭동을 일으키다 ☐ bazaar n. 시장, 상점가 ☐ spit v. (침 등을) 뱉다 ☐ betel n. 구장나무 ☐ juice n. 즙 ☐ apprehension n. 우려, 불안; 체포 ☐ intervention n. 중재, 간섭 ☐ intransigence n. 비타협적인 태도

어느 누구도 폭동을 일으킬 결단력은 없었지만, 유럽의 어떤 여성이 시장을 혼자서 돌아다닌다면, 누군가는 아마도 구장나무 잎(잎담배)을 잘근잘근 씹어 나온 즙을 그녀의 옷에다 뱉을 것이었다.

## 33 ④

☐ desecrate v. (신성한 것을) 훼손하다(=defile) ☐ beleaguer v. 에워싸다; 포위 공격하다 ☐ adulterate v. 불순물을 섞다 ☐ sanctify v. 신성하게 하다

외국 점령을 준비할 때, 그 군대는 병력들에게 성스러운 장소를 모독하지 말고 지역 주민들을 불쾌하게 하지 말라고 지시한다.

## 34 ②

☐ chasten v. (잘 되게 하기 위하여) 혼내다, 징벌하다(=discipline) ☐ sully v. 더럽히다, 오손하다 ☐ empower v. ~에게 권력[권한]을 주다 ☐ coax v. 감언으로 설득하다, 달래다

법정에서 판사는 아마도 상습범을 훈계와 가혹한 선고로 징벌할 것이다.

## 35 ②

☐ devious a. 우회하는, 에두르는, 구불구불한(=indirect) ☐ route n. 길, 노선, 항로 ☐ scenic a. 경치의, 풍경의 ☐ straight a. 곧은, 똑바른; 직립의, 수직의 ☐ short a. 짧은; 불충분한, 모자라는

그들은 우회로로 갔다.

## 36 ③

☐ mallow n. 아욱 ☐ taxonomic a. 분류학[법]의 ☐ Malvaceae n. 아욱과(科) ☐ profusely ad. 아낌없이, 풍부하게(=abundantly) ☐ marsh n. 습지, 소택지, 늪 ☐ wildly ad. 격렬하게, 사납게; 야생상태로 ☐ preciously ad. 비싸게, 까다롭게; 매우, 대단히 ☐ profoundly ad. 깊이; 심오하게

아욱은 분류학상 아욱과에 속하는 일종의 화훼식물로, 숲과 습지에서 많이 자란다.

## 37 ③

☐ robe v. ~을 입다 ☐ bearer n. (메시지 등의) 전달자 ☐ communal a. 자치단체의, 공공의 ☐ block party 주민 파티, 거리행사 ☐ gathering n. 모임, 회합, 집회 ☐ infiltrate v. 스며들게 하다; ~에 잠입[침입]하다(=permeate) ☐ simulate v. ~을 가장하다, 흉내내다 ☐ adulterate v. ~에 섞음질을 하다 ☐ evacuate v. 피난시키다; (군대를) 철수시키다

텔레비전은 공동체적 유대감의 전달자의 모습을 하고서 우리의 삶 속에 들어왔으며, 일련의 새로운 공통적인 경험, 거리 행사, 아이들과 어른들 모두가 함께하는 즐거운 모임을 제공해 주었다. 텔레비전이 가져다주는 상상들이 우리 자신의 상상 안으로 서서히 스며들고 있다.

## 38 ③

☐ celerity n. (행동의) 신속, 기민, 민첩함(=very quick and swift in action) ☐ determination n. 결심; 결단(력); 결정 ☐ independent spirit 독립심; 자립심 ☐ reluctance n. 마음이 내키지 않음

톰(Tom)은 재빨리 그 일을 하겠다고 했다. 부탁이 채 끝나기 전에 그는 이미 식탁을 치우고 있었다.

## 39 ①

☐ forge v. 위조하다, 날조하다; 구축하다; (계획을) 세우다(=construct) ☐ dismantle v. 해체하다, 부수다, 폐지하다 ☐ solitary a. 고독한, 혼자의 ☐ disassemble v. 해체하다, 분해하다 ☐ condemn v. 비난하다; 유죄 판결을 내리다 ☐ discard v. 버리다, 포기[폐기]하다

우리는 우리 주변 사람들과 협력관계를 구축해야 하고 혼자만의 완벽이라는 잘못된 통념을 버리기 시작해야 한다.

## 40
② 

☐ point out 지적하다 ☐ highrise n. 고층건물 ☐ contravene v. (법률 등을) 위반하다, 범하다; 반대하다(=violate) ☐ submit v. 복종하다, 종속시키다 ☐ assure v. 보증하다, 보장하다; 납득하다 ☐ obey v. 복종하다, 순종하다; (명령을) 준수하다

고층건물을 건설하는 것은 건축법을 위반하게 될 것이라는 지적이 있었다.

## 41
③

☐ agitation n. 선동; 동요, 흥분(=nervousness) ☐ swelling n. 증대; 팽창, 혹, 종기 ☐ infection n. 감염; 전염병 ☐ clumsiness n. 서투름, 솜씨 없음

나는 피터(Peter)가 안절부절못하는 모습으로 자신의 시계를 힐끗 쳐다보는 것을 목격했다.

## 42
③

☐ like no other 그 어떤 것과도 다른, 남다른 ☐ colossal a. 거대한; 굉장한 ☐ millennium n. 천년(간)(pl. millennia) ☐ replenish v. (원래처럼) 다시 채우다, 보충하다(=restore) ☐ monsoon n. (계절풍이 부는) 계절, 우기, 몬순 ☐ smother v. 질식시키다; (연기, 안개 등으로) 덮어버리다; 휩싸다 ☐ recycle v. 다시 이용하다 ☐ remove v. 치우다 ☐ revolve v. 회전하다; 자전하다; 순환하다

히말라야산맥의 거대한 빙하는 지구상 그 어디에서도 찾아볼 수 없는 경관인데, 수천 년 동안 매년 여름 새로운 눈으로 산맥을 덮어버리는 몬순에 의해서 계속 채워져 왔다.

## 43
③

☐ abandon v. (돌볼 책임이 있는 사람을) 버리다, 떠나다, 유기하다 ☐ whiny a. 불평하는, 투덜대는, 짜증내는 ☐ toddler n. 유아, 아장아장 걷는 아이 ☐ sullen a. 부루퉁한, 시무룩한, 기분이 언짢은(=morose) ☐ wary a. 조심성 있는, 경계하는 ☐ unfriendly a. 비우호적인, 불친절한 ☐ remote a. 외진, 외딴

징징대는 어린아이나 뚱해 있는 십대아이를 그대로 내버려 두는 것은 그리 쉬운 일이 아니다.

## 44
③

☐ flimsy a. 무른; (근거·이론 따위가) 박약한, 설득력이 없는(=feeble) ☐ heavy a. 무거운, 비중이 큰 ☐ civil a. 시민의; 문명의; 예의 바른 ☐ false a. 허위의, 그릇된

아프리카에서든, 인도에서든, 심지어 키프로스에서든, 영국인들은 민족주의 지도자들을 종종 근거가 약한 혐의로 투옥하는 것을 주저하지 않았다.

## 45
②

☐ befuddled a. 당황스러운, 정신이 없는(=confused) ☐ beguiled a. 기만당한, 현혹된 ☐ weird a. 기묘한, 이상한; 불가사의한, 수상한 ☐ hilarious a. 유쾌한, 즐거운

서커스단의 광대들은 어색하거나 당혹스럽게 보일 수도 있다. 그러나 훌륭하게 어릿광대 노릇을 하는 것은 유연한 신체와 재치를 필요로 한다.

## 46
①

☐ trite a. 흔해 빠진, 진부한, 케케묵은(=hackneyed) ☐ exhausted a. 소모된; 고갈된; 기운이 빠진 ☐ vacant a. 공허한; 비어 있는 ☐ tepid a. 미지근한; 열의 없는

하객들이 늘어선 줄이 끝나갈 무렵엔, 신랑과 신부의 감사 인사가 진부하고 지친 듯이 들렸다.

## 47
②

☐ evacuate v. (건물을) 비우다, 대피시키다(=desert) ☐ construct v. 건설하다; 구성하다 ☐ rent v. 임차하다, 빌리다 ☐ decorate v. 꾸미다, 장식하다; (훈장을) 수여하다

그는 배터리 공원(Battery Park)에 있는 그의 건물을 비우라고 명령받았다.

## 48
③

☐ serene a. 고요한, 잔잔한(=calm) ☐ romantic a. 낭만적인; 몽상적인; 허구의 ☐ hot a. 뜨거운, 열이 있는; 열렬한 ☐ exciting a. 흥분시키는, 자극적인

그 소녀가 바닷가를 걷던 때는 고요한 여름밤이었다.

## 49
①

☐ revulsion n. 혐오감; 격변, 급변(=repulsion) ☐ revelry n. 야단법석; 흥청대는 술잔치, 환락 ☐ reprisal n. 보복, 앙갚음 ☐ rescission n. 폐지, 취소

독재를 찬미했던 이 나라의 많은 국민들은 대통령이 시행하려고 하던 바를 이해했을 때 극도의 혐오감을 경험했다.

## 50
①

☐ diverting a. 재미나는, 즐거운(=entertaining) ☐ platitudinous a. 평범한, 하찮은 ☐ prosaic a. 평범한, 산문의 ☐ tiresome a. 성가신, 짜증스러운

이러한 프로그램을 발견하는 것은 프로그래머들에게 즐거운 퍼즐이었다.

## 51 ①

☐ purge v. 정화하다; 추방하다(=extirpate) ☐ panhandler n. 거지, 걸인 ☐ succor v. 구조하다, 원조하다 ☐ contort v. 비틀어버리다; 곡해하다 ☐ abet v. 부추기다, 선동하다, 교사하다

몽고메리 카운티의 지도자들은 번잡한 거리에서 걸인들을 추방하기 위한 값비싼 노력을 기울이겠다고 발표했다.

## 52 ①

☐ gimmick n. 비밀 장치, 속임수(=trick) ☐ delight n. 기쁨, 즐거움 ☐ tidbit n. 맛있는 가벼운 음식 ☐ confectionary n. 과자류

우리는 초콜릿이 그냥 또 하나의 상술이 아니라, 피부에 정말로 이롭다고 생각한다.

## 53 ②

☐ nitty-gritty n. 핵심, 요체(=kernel) ☐ liability n. 책임, 의무 ☐ waiver n. 포기, 기권 ☐ disclaimer n. 포기, 기권

우리가 진짜 핵심에 들어가기도 전에 시간이 다 되었다.

## 54 ④

☐ bypass v. 우회하다; 회피하다(=avoid) ☐ grasp v. 납득하다, 이해하다 ☐ modify v. 수정하다 ☐ manipulate v. 조종하다, 조작하다

공무원은 이미 대가를 받고 있는 일을 하거나 법령을 피하기 위해 뇌물을 요구할 수도 있다.

## 55 ②

☐ enormity n. 중대한 범죄; 심각함(=villainy) ☐ insincerity n. 불성실, 위선 ☐ demise n. 종말, 죽음

그들은 자신들이 저지른 극악무도한 범죄에 대해 혹독하게 처벌을 받아야 한다.

## 56 ①

☐ extermination n. 근절, 멸종, 몰살(=annihilation) ☐ extraction n. 뽑아냄, 추출; 혈통, 태생, 계통 ☐ dejection n. 낙담, 실의; 우울 ☐ ferocity n. 사나움, 잔인성

우리는 이런 동물들의 멸종을 막을 수 있는 방법을 찾아야 한다.

## 57 ③

☐ resplendent a. 빛나는, 눈부시게[빤짝빤짝] 빛나는(=dazzling) ☐ haughty a. 오만한, 거만한 ☐ prodigal a. 낭비하는; 방탕한 ☐ spurious a. 가짜의, 위조의

다이애나 왕세자빈은 화려한 삶을 산 것 같지만 그녀의 아름다움과 부는 외로움으로부터 보호해 주지 않았다.

## 58 ①

☐ rivalry n. 경쟁 ☐ hatred n. 증오, 미움, 원한 ☐ intrigue n. 음모 ☐ cease v. 그치다, 멎다, 끝나다 ☐ animosity n. 증오, 악의 ☐ amity n. 우호, 친목, 친선(=friendship) ☐ enmity n. 적의, 적개심, 악의 ☐ amenity n. 기분 좋음, 쾌적함 ☐ dignity n. 위엄, 품의

국가적인 경쟁, 원한, 음모는 끝나고 인종간의 원한과 편견은 인종간의 우호, 이해, 협력으로 대체될 것이다.

## 59 ④

☐ spoil v. 망치다, 상하게 하다; (손님에게) 대대적으로 서비스하다(=treat too well) ☐ supply beverage free to ~에게 무료음료를 제공하다 ☐ take a decisive step for ~에 대해 중대한 조치를 취하다 ☐ offer free parking to ~에게 무료 주차장을 제공하다

이 호텔은 손님들에게 최고의 서비스를 제공한다고 광고한다.

## 60 ③

☐ forbearance n. 삼가기, 조심; 인내, 참음(=patience) ☐ affinity n. 유사; 친족; 좋아함 ☐ negligence n. 태만; 부주의 ☐ transparency n. 투명(성); 명료

그가 여전히 병으로 쇠약하기 때문에 당신은 그를 대할 때 인내심을 발휘해야 한다.

## 61 ②

☐ genealogist n. 계보학자 ☐ traceable a. (기원·자취 등을) 추적할 수 있는 ☐ progenitor n. 조상, 선조(=forebear) ☐ root n. 근원 ☐ successor n. 상속자, 후계자 ☐ descendant n. 자손, 후예

칼라(Carla)는 뛰어난 아마추어 계보학자였으며, 그녀의 가문 전체가 적어도 1638년까지 거슬러 올라가는 그 책에 들어 있었는데, 그때는 그 가문의 추적 가능한 최초의 조상이 이름 모를 떠돌던 사람들의 무리로부터 나온 때였다.

## 62 ④

☐ commitment n. 약속; 전념  ☐ rectitude n. 정직, 청렴(=integrity)
☐ imperative n. 의무, 책임  ☐ uplift n. 향상  ☐ fortitude n. 용기

도덕적 올바름에 대한 우리의 헌신은 대학생활 동안 그리고 일생을 통해
변함없이 책임감 있고 충실하게 행동하는 것이다.

## 63 ②

☐ prone a. ~하기 쉬운, ~의 경향이 있는(=disposed)  ☐ infallible
a. 틀림없는, 절대 확실한  ☐ pronounced a. 뚜렷한, 현저한; 명백한;
확고한  ☐ lay down 아래에 놓다, 내리다; 놓다; 세우다  ☐ averse
a. 싫어하는; 반대하는

인간은 비록 자신은 전혀 틀림이 없다고 생각하고 싶어 하지만, 과오를
저지르기 쉽다.

## 64 ②

☐ grandiose a. 웅장[웅대]한, 숭고한(=magnificent)  ☐ compatible
a. 호환이 되는, 양립될 수 있는  ☐ eccentric a. 괴짜인, 별난, 기이한
☐ rudimentary a. 가장 기본[기초]적인

어떤 의미에서, 인터넷이라는 거대한 파도는 전통적인 미디어 산업과
그들의 단기 수익 전망치를 완전히 바꿔 놓았다.

## 65 ③

☐ detain v. 구금하다  ☐ abscond v. 무단이탈하다, 도주하다(=flee)
☐ deport v. 강제 추방하다  ☐ infringe v. 위반하다  ☐ trudge v.
터벅터벅 걷다  ☐ settle v. 해결하다; 정착하다

유럽연합의 국가들은 강제 추방되기 전에 도주할지도 모르는 이민자들
을 구금해야 한다.

## 66 ①

☐ incensed a. 몹시 화난, 격분한(=irate)  ☐ timid a. 소심한, 용기[자신
감]가 없는  ☐ doleful a. 서글픈, 슬픈  ☐ euphoric a. 행복감의; 도취
(감)의

커트(Kurt)는 내 실수를 발견하고 너무 화가 나서 5분 내내 나에게 고함
을 질렀다.

## 67 ②

☐ unruly a. 다루기 힘든, 제멋대로 구는(=restive)  ☐ phlegmatic a.
차분한, 침착한  ☐ obsequious a. 아부하는  ☐ onerous a. 번거로운,
귀찮은

다루기 힘든 시위 군중은 경찰이 나타나자 갑자기 폭동 태세로 변했다.

## 68 ③

☐ burnish v. 닦다, 갈다; 빛나게 하다(=enhance)  ☐ tarnish v. (명예
등을) 더럽히다, 손상시키다; 녹슬게 하다  ☐ restore v. 복구하다, 복원하
다  ☐ distort v. 왜곡하다, 그릇 전하다

그가 사업을 해 온 방식은 틀림없이 그의 전반적인 이미지를 쇄신해 줄
것이다.

## 69 ④

☐ punishment n. 벌, 형벌, 처벌  ☐ expulsion n. 배제, 제명, 추방
(=ejection)  ☐ harsh a. 거친, 난폭한; 가혹한, 엄한  ☐ nomination
n. 지명, 추천; 임명  ☐ injection n. 주입, 주사(액)  ☐ emancipation
n. 해방, 이탈, 벗어남

조직에서 제명되는 처벌은 너무 가혹한 것으로 여겨졌다.

## 70 ③

☐ demonstrate v. 입증하다  ☐ deprecate v. 비난하다, 반대하다
(=condemn)  ☐ disabuse v. 바로 잡다  ☐ adulate v. 아첨하다  ☐
redress v. 고치다, 시정하다

사회 개혁의 전체 역사는 악에 대항하는 실질적인 행동을 취하기보다는
악을 비난하는 것이 훨씬 더 쉽다는 사실을 보여준다.

## 71 ②

☐ defect n. 흠, 결함(=blemish)  ☐ befriend v. ~의 편을 들다, 돕다;
~의 친구가 되다  ☐ default n. 채무 불이행  ☐ merit n. 가치, 훌륭함
☐ mediocrity n. 보통, 평범함

인간으로서 그의 결점들이 무엇이었던지 간에, 그리고 그것들이 그와
친구가 되려고 했던 모든 이들에게 분명했던지 간에, 루소(Rousseau)
는 천재였다.

## 72 ③

☐ brevity n. 간결(성); (시간, 기간의) 짧음, 덧없음(=briefness)  ☐
humor n. 유머, 해학; (일시적) 기분, 변덕  ☐ description n. 기술,
묘사, 서술  ☐ magnificence n. 장려, 웅장, 장엄; 호화

그 수필은 놀랄 만큼 간결하게 쓰였다.

## 73 ②

□ compound v. 악화시키다, 더 심각하게 만들다(=aggravate) □ murky a. 어두운; 음산한 □ decrease v. 감소하다, 저하하다 □ cause v. ~의 원인이 되다; 일으키다 □ camouflage v. 위장하다; 속이다

이와 같은 정치적 난제들은 주 정부의 암울한 재정 상태로 인해 악화되고 있다.

## 74 ④

□ in retrospect 회고해보니, 되돌아보면(=looking back) □ speaking honestly 솔직하게 말하자면 □ recently ad. 최근에, 요즈음, 근래 □ surprisingly ad. 놀랍게도, 의외로

돌이켜보면 공학을 배우기로 결심하길 잘한 것 같다.

## 75 ①

□ veteran a. 경험이 많은 n. 퇴역군인 □ jaded a. 몹시 지친, 지겨워진(=bored) □ awe n. 경외심 □ pristine a. 자연[원래] 그대로의, 오염되지 않은 □ versatile a. 다재다능한 □ impressed a. 인상 깊게 생각하는, 감명을 받은 □ confident a. 자신감 있는; 확신하는

그 퇴역군인으로 구성된 단체 관광객은 여행 초에는 조금 지겨워하는 것 같았지만, 경외심을 자아내는 야생동물과 원시적인 자연환경이 모든 사람의 기분을 바꿔놓는 것 같았다.

## 76 ④

□ stultify v. 망쳐놓다, 무의미하게 하다, 엉망으로 만들다(=have an inhibiting effect on) □ firmly reinforce 견고하게 강화시키다 □ provide entertainment for ~를 위한 오락거리를 제공하다 □ effectively facilitate 효과적으로 촉진시키다

쉴라(Sheila)는 대화를 엉망으로 만드는 경향이 있는 단정적이고 독선적인 말을 하는 습관이 있다.

## 77 ①

□ prying a. 응시하는, 흘끔흘끔 보는; 캐묻기 좋아하는(=inquisitive) □ candid a. 정직한, 솔직한; 노골적인; 공정한 □ naive a. 천진난만한, 순진한; 우직한 □ verbose a. 말이 많은, 다변의

사람들은 다른 사람의 일에 관해 너무 많은 것을 알려고 드는 캐기 좋아하는 사람을 좋아하지 않는다.

## 78 ①

□ acquisitive a. 탐내는; 욕심내는(=avaricious) □ intrusive a. 강제하는 □ attentive a. 주의 깊은 □ disobedient a. 순종치 않는; 불효의

우리는 성공을 우선적으로 물질적 소유의 관점에서 바라보는 탐욕스러운 사회에 살고 있다.

## 79 ④

□ detached a. 분리된, 떨어진(=separated) □ damage v. 손해를 입히다; 손상시키다 □ fix v. 고정시키다; 결정하다; 고치다 □ fasten v. 묶다, 죄다, 고정하다

그 트레일러는 그것을 끌고 가던 트럭에서 분리됐다.

## 80 ①

□ insouciant a. 무관심한, 부주의한, 태평한, 걱정 없는(=indifferent) □ sarcastic a. 빈정대는, 비꼬는, 풍자적인 □ impeccable a. 흠잡을 데 없는, 나무랄 데 없는 □ impassioned a. 열정적인, 간절한

그런 중요한 순간에 너의 무관심한 태도는 그 상황의 심각성을 네가 이해하지 못하고 있다는 것을 의미한다.

## 81 ③

□ revert to 되돌아가다; 복귀하다, 귀속하다(=return) □ deposit v. 예금하다 □ due a. 지불 기일이 된, 당연히 치러야 할 □ available a. 이용할 수 있는, 쓸모 있는

돈은 6개월 후에 은행에 상환될 것이다.

## 82 ②

□ brash a. 성마른, 경솔한; 무모한(=reckless) □ start-up n. 신규 업체(특히 인터넷 기업) □ established a. 인정받는, 확실히 자리를 잡은 □ laudable a. 칭찬할 만한, 훌륭한 □ latent a. 보이지 않는; 잠재적인 □ baleful a. 재앙의, 해로운

과거의 무모한 신규 기술 업체들이 지금은 인정받는 대기업들이 되었다.

## 83 ④

□ pressing a. 긴급한, 절박한(=urgent) □ important a. 중요한, 의미 있는 □ confidential a. 기밀의, 은밀한 □ sensitive a. 민감한, 예민한

나의 가장 절박한 문제들의 목록을 편지에 동봉한다.

## 84 ②

□ forage v. 마구 뒤지며 찾다; 식량을 징발하다(=search for) □ plant v. 심다, 뿌리다, 이식하다 □ cook v. 요리하다, 조리하다 □ foster v. 기르다, 양육하다, ~을 돌보다, 육성하다

그의 가족들은 들판에서 식량을 찾아다녔으며, 먹을 수 있는 것이면 무엇이든 찾았다.

## 85 ②

☐ infuse v. 붓다; 주입하다, 불어넣다, 고취하다(=inspire) ☐ tempt v. 유혹하다, 꾀다, 부추기다 ☐ regard v. ~으로 여기다, ~라고 간주하다

선배 남자 승무원은 신입 여승무원들에게 용기를 불어넣어 주었다.

## 86 ②

☐ nest n. 둥지 ☐ young n. (새 등의) 새끼 ☐ predator n. 천적, 포식동물 ☐ feral a. 야생의, 길들여지지 않은(=untamed) ☐ mutant a. 돌연변이의 ☐ aboriginal a. 원주민의, 토착의 ☐ wicked a. 못된, 사악한

도도새는 날 수가 없었기 때문에 부득이하게 땅에다 둥지를 틀었다. 도도새의 새끼들은 선원들이 두고 간 들개와 멧돼지 같은 천적들로부터 거의 보호를 받지 못했다.

## 87 ③

☐ duplicity n. 표리부동, 일구이언; 불성실(=deceit) ☐ creativity n. 창조력, 독창성 ☐ congruence n. 일치, 합치; 조화(성); 합동 ☐ ingenuity n. 발명의 재주, 독창력; 교묘함

그가 자신의 과거 세부사항들을 날조했다는 사실을 알았을 때, 프랭크(Frank)의 친구들은 그의 속임수에 간담이 서늘해졌다.

## 88 ②

☐ evince v. 분명히 나타내다, 명시하다(=draw out) ☐ anger n. 화, 분노 ☐ repress v. 억제하다, 억누르다; 저지[제지]하다; 진압하다 ☐ conform v. (모범, 범례에) 따르게 하다, 맞게 하다 ☐ override v. 우위에 서다; 무시하다

그는 분노를 드러낼 의도가 없었으나, 그것은 그의 행동 속에서 분명히 드러나 보였다.

## 89 ③

☐ rudimentary a. 원시적인; 근본의, 기본의, 초보의(=primitive) ☐ penetrate v. 꿰뚫다; 침투하다, 영향을 미치다 ☐ repetitive a. 반복적인, 되풀이하는 ☐ productive a. 생산적인; 다산의, 다작의 ☐ derivative a. 모방한, 독창적인 것이 아닌

5천 년 내지 6천 년 전에 문명은 나일강 계곡까지 확장되어 가면서, 여러 시기에 걸쳐 목축업과 원시농업이 아프리카 지역으로 더욱더 퍼져나갔다.

## 90 ②

☐ dissipate v. 흩뜨리다; 없애다; 낭비하다(=disappear) ☐ waste v. 헛되이 하다, 낭비하다 ☐ come along 함께 가다; 잘해나가다; 동의하다 ☐ use up foolishly 어리석게도 다 써버리다

대체로 구름은 싣고 있던 비를 쏟아버리고는 흩어져 없어진다.

## 91 ②

☐ nominal a. 명목상의, 이름뿐인(=insignificant) ☐ in comparison with ~과 비교하면, ~에 비하여 ☐ enormous a. 막대한, 매우 큰 ☐ reasonable a. 이치에 맞는, 분별 있는 ☐ manageable a. 관리할 수 있는; 다루기 쉬운 ☐ substantial a. 실질적인; 상당한

네가 받은 것의 막대한 가치에 비하면 그 비용은 아주 적은 것이었다.

## 92 ③

☐ converse a. (의견이) 반대의; (방향이) 정반대의(=opposite) ☐ convergent a. 한 점으로 향하는, 한데 모이는, 집중적인 ☐ parallel a. 평행인, 일치하는 ☐ optimize v. 낙관하다, 최적화하다

그 후보자의 연설은 그녀가 늘 하던 형식과는 정반대였고, 이것이 그녀의 정치 경력에 있어 일대 전환점이 되었다.

## 93 ①

☐ lampoon v. 풍자하다(=satirize) ☐ romanticize v. 낭만적으로 묘사하다 ☐ obfuscate v. 당황[난처]하게 하다 ☐ reprimand v. 질책하다

만화영화 "사우스 파크"의 제작자들은 새로운 영화에서 대통령의 쌍둥이 십대 딸들을 풍자하지 않겠다고 약속했다.

## 94 ③

☐ choleric a. 성마른, 화를 잘 내는(=irascible) ☐ outrageous a. 지나친, 터무니없는 ☐ absurd a. 불합리한; 부조리한 ☐ abstruse a. 심원한, 난해한

그의 리더십 스타일은 화를 잘 내는 것일 수도 있지만, 그것이 그가 끔찍한 운명에 이르게 한 것은 아니다.

## 95 ③

☐ impose v. 부과하다[지우다] ☐ stricture n. 심한 비난; 제한[제약](=restriction) ☐ proceeds n. 수입 ☐ covenant n. 계약, 맹약 ☐ countermeasure n. 대응책

중국 정부는 지난 1년간 거대 인터넷 기업들에게 새로운 규제를 가하기 위해 빠르게 움직였다.

## 96　　③

□ rabid a. 과격한, 난폭한, 맹렬한(=fanatical)　□ sizable a. 상당한 크기의, 꽤 큰　□ innovative a. 혁신적인　□ dexterous a. 솜씨 좋은, 교묘한

iPod과 후에 iPhone으로 주류가 되기까지, 수십 년 동안 애플은 작지만, 광적인 팬층의 지원을 받았다.

## 97　　①

□ parasite n. 기생 동물[식물]　□ wily a. 약삭빠른, 교활한(=sly)　□ pathogen n. 병원균, 병원체　□ exotic a. 외국의, 이국적인　□ atypical a. 전형적이 아닌, 부정형(不定型)의　□ susceptible a. 민감한

말라리아를 일으키는 이 작은 기생충은 아마도 가장 복잡하고 인류에게 알려진 가장 교활한 병원체 가운데 하나이다.

## 98　　②

□ resolution n. 결의, 결의안　□ back v. 지지하다, 보증하다　□ binding n. 속박[구속]하는; 구속력 있는(=obligatory)　□ amorphous a. 확실한 형태가 없는, 무정형의　□ factual a. 사실에 기반을 둔　□ statutory a. 법으로 명시된

그 결의안은 국제사법재판소의 판결을 뒷받침하는 것이지만 법적 구속력은 없다.

## 99　　③

□ wry a. 비꼬는, 풍자적인; (일시적으로) 찡그린(=frowning)　□ wan a. 창백한, 파랗게 질린　□ perfunctory a. 형식적인, 마지못한　□ reluctant a. 마음 내키지 않는, 꺼리는

그의 쓴웃음은 그가 이미 무엇인가를 알고 있다는 것을 의미하고 있다.

## 100　　①

□ non-binding a. 구속력이 없는, 강제적이 아닌　□ referendum n. 국민투표　□ expropriate v. (남에게서 토지 따위를) 수용(收用)[징수]하다; (재산을) 몰수하다(=confiscate)　□ bequeath v. 물려주다, 유증하다　□ contribute v. 기부하다, 기증하다　□ transfer v. 옮기다, 이동하다

베를린 시민들은 지방정부가 대기업 지주들의 재산을 몰수해야 한다는 요구에 대한 구속력이 없는 국민투표를 할 것이다.

| | | | | | | | | | |
|---|---|---|---|---|---|---|---|---|---|
| 01 ③ | 02 ② | 03 ③ | 04 ③ | 05 ③ | 06 ① | 07 ④ | 08 ③ | 09 ③ | 10 ③ |
| 11 ④ | 12 ④ | 13 ① | 14 ② | 15 ③ | 16 ② | 17 ③ | 18 ② | 19 ② | 20 ② |
| 21 ④ | 22 ② | 23 ① | 24 ① | 25 ③ | 26 ③ | 27 ④ | 28 ② | 29 ② | 30 ① |
| 31 ③ | 32 ④ | 33 ① | 34 ④ | 35 ④ | 36 ③ | 37 ④ | 38 ② | 39 ① | 40 ④ |
| 41 ③ | 42 ② | 43 ① | 44 ④ | 45 ② | 46 ③ | 47 ④ | 48 ② | 49 ① | 50 ③ |
| 51 ① | 52 ② | 53 ② | 54 ④ | 55 ④ | 56 ① | 57 ④ | 58 ① | 59 ② | 60 ④ |
| 61 ④ | 62 ② | 63 ② | 64 ③ | 65 ③ | 66 ① | 67 ④ | 68 ② | 69 ② | 70 ② |
| 71 ④ | 72 ① | 73 ③ | 74 ③ | 75 ① | 76 ③ | 77 ② | 78 ② | 79 ② | 80 ④ |
| 81 ② | 82 ③ | 83 ① | 84 ④ | 85 ② | 86 ④ | 87 ④ | 88 ③ | 89 ④ | 90 ① |
| 91 ② | 92 ① | 93 ④ | 94 ④ | 95 ③ | 96 ① | 97 ③ | 98 ② | 99 ① | 100 ① |

## 01 ③

☐ accessible a. 접근[가까이]하기 쉬운; 이용할 수 있는 ☐ establish oneself 자리 잡다 ☐ convenient a. 편리한, 형편 좋은 ☐ gathering n. 모임, 회합, 집회 ☐ clement a. (기후가) 온화한, 온난한(=moderate) ☐ abrupt a. 돌연한, 갑작스러운 ☐ circuitous a. 우회로의; (말 따위가) 에두르는 ☐ prodigious a. 거대한, 막대한; 비범한

그 야외정원은 일반인들이 이용할 수 있으며 날씨가 온화할 때 도심지에서 편리한 모임 장소로 자리 잡게 될 것이다.

## 02 ②

☐ come across (특정한) 인상을 주다 ☐ indict v. 기소하다; ~의 (죄·악행 등을) 비난하다, 나무라다 ☐ buffoonery n. 어릿광대, 익살꾼(=clowning) ☐ resurgence n. 소생하는 사람 ☐ detraction n. 욕, 비난 ☐ embezzlement n. 착복

히틀러(Hitler)는 순전히 악으로 여겨지지만, 무솔리니(Mussolini)는 익살꾼으로 종종 덜 비난 받는다.

## 03 ③

☐ stringent a. 절박한; 엄중한, 엄격한(=rigorous) ☐ indigenous a. 토착적인, 원산의, 그 고장 특유의 ☐ stubborn a. 완고한, 고집 센; 완강한 ☐ superficial a. 표면상의, 피상적인; 천박한

철학자인 그는 자유에 대해 좀 더 엄격하고 까다로운 생각을 갖고 있다.

## 04 ③

☐ manifestation n. 징후 ☐ exalt v. 높이다; 칭찬하다; 강화하다(=promote) ☐ at the expense of ~을 희생하여 ☐ recall v. 상기시키다, 생각나게 하다 ☐ weaken v. 약화시키다, ~의 힘을 빼다 ☐ aggravate v. 악화시키다, 심화시키다

최근 징후를 보면, 서구 문명은 인문학을 희생시킨 채 과학과 기술의 응용을 숭상하는 경향이 있어 왔다.

## 05 ③

☐ roil v. 마음을 휘젓다, 혼란[산란]하게 하다(=agitate) ☐ feminist n. 여성권리 주장자 ☐ sexual revolution 성혁명 ☐ isolation n. 고립, 분리 ☐ devastate v. 황폐시키다; 비탄에 빠뜨리다 ☐ rectify v. 바로잡다, 고치다, 수정하다 ☐ disparage v. 비난하다, 폄하하다

50여 년 전에, 미국은 여권주의 혁명과 성 혁명에 의해서 동요되었고, 그것이 여성을 가정의 고립으로부터 벗어나게 했다.

## 06 ①

☐ downturn n. (경기의) 침체 ☐ academic n. (대학) 교수 ☐ credit crunch 신용 경색 ☐ contentious a. 논쟁적인, 논쟁의 여지가 있는(=debatable) ☐ competitive a. 경쟁력 있는 ☐ satisfactory a. 만족스러운 ☐ troublesome a. (오랫동안) 골칫거리인

2008년의 세계 경제침체의 원인에 대해 열띤 논쟁이 있어 왔다. 전문가들과 대학교수들이 (당시의) 세계 경제침체가 신용 경색의 결과였다는 것에는 의견을 같이 하는 반면, 이 신용 경색의 원인에 대해서는 훨씬 더 의견이 분분하다.

## 07 ④

☐ farewell address 고별 연설 ☐ imposture n. 사기 행위; 사기, 협잡(=deceit) ☐ predator n. 약탈자; 육식동물 ☐ temptation n. 유혹 ☐ collision n. 충돌

고별 연설에서 조지 워싱턴(George Washington)은 국민들에게 "애국심을 가장한 사기 행위를 경계해야 한다."라고 조언했다.

## 08 ③

☐ parsimonious a. (돈에 지독히) 인색한 ☐ niggardly a. 인색한, 쩨쩨한(=stingy) ☐ avid a. 탐욕스러운, 열심인 ☐ vacillating a. 망설이는, 우유부단한 ☐ reluctant a. 꺼리는, 마음 내키지 않는

지나치게 인색한 것은 쩨쩨하게 구는 것이다.

## 09 ③

☐ deviate v. 벗어나다, 빗나가다(=depart) ☐ poll n. 투표; 여론조사 ☐ figure n. 수치 ☐ range v. 분포하다, 범위에 걸쳐있다 ☐ originate v. 비롯되다, 유래하다 ☐ separate v. 분리하다, 나뉘다

최근의 여론조사 수치는 이전의 여론조사들의 수치에서 상당한 정도로 벗어났다.

## 10 ③

☐ friction n. 불화, 갈등(=conflict) ☐ infirmity n. (장기적인) 병약[질환] ☐ distortion n. 왜곡, 곡해 ☐ creed n. 교의(敎義), 신조

우리 식구는 모두 다른 견해를 가지고 있기 때문에 정치는 우리 가족들에게 있어 불화의 근원이다.

## 11 ④

☐ sultry a. 무더운, 찌는 듯이 더운(=sweltering) ☐ protean a. 변화무쌍한; 다방면의 ☐ erratic a. 일정하지 않은, 변하기 쉬운, 불규칙한 ☐ resplendent a. 눈부신

끝날 것 같지 않은 무더위가 기승을 부리고 있지만, 아무도 미처 깨닫지 못한 사이에 계절이 이미 바뀌었다.

## 12 ④

☐ promiscuous a. 난잡한; 뒤죽박죽인, 무차별한(=indiscriminate) ☐ cripple n. 신체[정신] 장애자, 불구자 ☐ chronic a. 만성의, 상습적인 ☐ hazardous a. 위험한; 모험적인; 운에 맡기는 ☐ increased a. 증대된

무차별한 마약의 사용이 수백만의 사람들을 정신적 장애자로 만들고 있다.

## 13 ①

☐ virtue n. 미덕, 덕행; 장점, 가치(=advantage) ☐ put into practice ~을 실행하다 ☐ truth n. 진실, 사실; 진리 ☐ handicap n. 불리한

조건, 곤란, 불이익 ☐ possibility n. 가능성; 실현성

그의 계획은 실행하기에 가장 경제적이라는 이점을 가지고 있다.

## 14 ②

☐ clique n. (배타적인) 도당(徒黨), 파벌(=coterie) ☐ conduct v. 수행하다, 처리하다 ☐ orchestrate v. 조직화하다; 획책하다 ☐ boycott n. 불매 동맹[운동] ☐ enterprise n. 기업(체), 회사 ☐ number n. 수, 숫자

시카고대학의 정치학자들이 시행한 연구는 미국인들의 25%가 2008년 금융위기가 작은 한 무리의 은행가들에 의해 비밀리에 획책된 것으로 믿고 있다는 것을 보여주었다.

## 15 ③

☐ barter v. 물물 교환하다, 교역하다(=exchange) ☐ consume v. 소비하다, 다 써버리다 ☐ produce v. 생산하다, 제조하다 ☐ distribute v. 분배하다; 배포하다

변경지역을 개척하던 시대에, 정착민들은 서로 물건을 물물 교환했다.

## 16 ②

☐ florid a. 화려한, 찬란한, 현란한(=ornate) ☐ narcissism n. 자기애; 자기중심주의 ☐ tempestuous a. 소란스러운, 광포한 ☐ arbitrary a. 임의적인, 제멋대로인 ☐ capricious a. 변덕스러운

의심할 여지 없이 대통령의 화려한 나르시시즘이 그의 반응의 일부를 설명한다.

## 17 ③

☐ articulate a. 명료한; 말[생각]을 또렷하게 표현할 수 있는(=eloquent) ☐ gratuitous a. 무료의; 불필요한 ☐ evasive a. 회피적인, 포착하기 어려운 ☐ solemn a. 엄숙한; 장엄한

그 하원의원은 너무나 논리정연하게 말하는 연설가였기 때문에 정적들조차도 그의 말솜씨를 감탄해 마지않았다.

## 18 ②

☐ quiescent a. 조용한, 정지한, 움직이지 않는(=inactive) ☐ mutable a. 변하기 쉬운, 변덕스러운 ☐ slovenly a. 단정치 못한, 게으른; 부주의한 ☐ slack a. 느슨한, 늘어진, 태만한

다른 것들은 오래전에 새로운 별을 생성하는 것을 멈춘, 아마도 블랙홀인 초대형 천체들의 진행이 중단된 경우이다.

## 19 ②

☐ expatriate v. 국외로 추방하다(=deport) ☐ demoralize v. 사기를 꺾다, 의기소침하게 만들다 ☐ excruciate v. 고문하다; 괴롭히다 ☐ manipulate v. 조종하다

그들은 정치적 신념 때문에 국외로 추방되었다.

## 20 ②

☐ prevaricate v. 얼버무려 넘기다, 발뺌하다(=equivocate) ☐ masticate v. (음식을) 씹다 ☐ hibernate v. 겨울을 지내다, 동면하다 ☐ swerve v. 빗나가다

분쟁의 초기 단계에서, 그 회사는 다른 국제 브랜드 회사들이 떠나는 동안 (회사 철수에 대해) 얼버무리면서 러시아에 남는 선택을 했다.

## 21 ④

☐ terms n. (지급·계약 따위의) 조건, 조항; 약정 ☐ insurance n. 보험 ☐ policy n. 보험 증권[증서] ☐ invalidate v. (서류·계약·선거 등을) 무효화하다(=repeal) ☐ accurate a. 정확한 ☐ diminish v. 줄어들다, 약해지다 ☐ upgrade v. 개선하다 ☐ prolong v. 연장시키다, 연장하다

귀하가 지난 9월 매입한 보험 증권의 약관에는 신청서에 어떤 허위 정보가 있으면 보험 증권을 무효화 한다는 내용이 분명히 명시되어 있습니다. 우리는 귀하가 우리에게 제공한 병력(病歷)이 정확하지 않다는 결정을 최근 내렸습니다. 이에 따라 귀하의 보험 증권이 2020년 12월 2일부로 취소되었음을 이 이메일을 통해 알려드립니다.

## 22 ②

☐ guise n. 외관, 겉모양; 구실, 가장 ☐ profane a. 신성 모독적인, 불경한(=impious); 세속적인 ☐ profligate a. 낭비하는 ☐ bromidic a. 평범한, 흔해 빠진 ☐ courteous a. 공손한, 정중한

종종 지역사회의 가치들을 유지한다는 것을 가장하여, 검열관들은 불경스럽거나 음탕한 말이 나오는 책들을 비난한다.

## 23 ①

☐ prominent a. 중요한, 유명한 ☐ reckon with 청산하다, 처리하다, 처벌하다 ☐ complicity n. 공모(=collusion) ☐ faculty n. 교수단 ☐ enslave v. (사람을) 노예로 만들다 ☐ repentance n. 뉘우침, 회개 ☐ controversy n. 논쟁, 논의 ☐ resilience n. 회복력; 탄성

하버드대학교는 1636년부터 1783년까지 대학교 총장, 교수진, 교직원이 70명이 넘는 사람들을 노예로 만들었다는 사실을 인정하면서 노예제도 공모를 고려한 가장 유명한 대학 중 하나가 되었다.

## 24 ①

☐ grapple with ~과 씨름하다, 해결하려고 노력하다(=struggle) ☐ domesticate v. (동물을) 길들이다, 사육하다 ☐ wriggle v. 꿈틀거리다; 꿈틀거리며 나아가다 ☐ believe v. 믿다, 신용하다 ☐ talk over ~에 관해 의논하다; 설득하다

연구원들이 이런 문제가 되는 결과들을 해결하려 노력할 때, 이론가들은 왜 인간이 개와 고양이를 가축으로 길들였나 하는 질문을 던지고 있다.

## 25 ③

☐ be in perfect order 질서가 정연하다 ☐ fussy a. 소란 떠는, 시끄러운; 까다로운(=fastidious) ☐ fascinating a. 황홀케 하는, 매혹적인 ☐ hardworking a. 근면한 ☐ altruistic a. 이타주의의, 애타적인

나의 아버지의 마음에 들게 하기 위해서는 모든 것이 완벽하게 정돈되어 있어야 한다. 왜냐하면 그분은 매우 까다롭기 때문이다.

## 26 ③

☐ presence n. 존재, 현존; 출석; 주둔; 현장감, 분위기 ☐ sedate a. 차분한, 조용한(=serene) ☐ uproarious a. 시끌벅적한 ☐ sporadic a. 산발적인, 이따금 발생하는 ☐ sullen a. 뚱한, 시무룩한, 침울한

대통령 선거 운동 또한 온라인으로 진행되었는데, 온라인에서는 선거운동을 하는 후보처럼 선거운동 현장도 더 차분하고 전통적이다.

## 27 ④

☐ tumble to ~을 이해하다, 인식하다(=become aware of) ☐ oblivious a. 염두에 없는, 안중에 없는 ☐ take one's place 위치를 차지하다 ☐ avoid v. 회피하다; 무효로 하다

그들은 그 문제를 깨닫기 시작했다.

## 28 ②

☐ eliminate v. 제거하다, 배제하다 ☐ attenuate v. 약하게 하다, 감소하다(=reduce) ☐ overcome v. 이기다; 극복하다 ☐ aggravate v. 악화시키다, 심화시키다 ☐ prolong v. 늘이다, 연장하다

당신은 위험을 없앨 수는 없지만, 준비와 훈련을 통해 위험을 완화시킬 수는 있을 것이다.

## 29 ②

☐ swoop on ~에 달려들다; ~을 급습하다(=attack) ☐ surveillance n. 감시, 감독 ☐ ransack v. 샅샅이 뒤지다; 약탈하다 ☐ surround v. 에워싸다, 둘러싸다 ☐ explode v. 폭발시키다, 파열하다

경찰들은 2주간의 잠복근무 후 그 집을 급습했다.

## 30 ①

☐ civilization n. 문명 ☐ retrogress v. 되돌아가다, 후퇴하다, 역행하다; 하강하다(=regress) ☐ ascend v. 오르다, 올라가다; 높아지다 ☐ trespass v. 침입하다, 침해하다; 폐를 끼치다; 위법 행위를 하다 ☐ flourish v. 번창하다, 번성하다; 활약하다

많은 위대한 문명의 역사에는 문명이 쇠퇴하기 시작하는 시기가 있다.

## 31 ③

☐ bank n. 둑, 제방 ☐ fathom n. 패덤(물의 깊이 측정 단위, 6피트 또는 1.8미터에 해당) ☐ brackish a. 염분이 섞인(=saline) ☐ sweet a. 염분이 없는 ☐ distilled a. 증류한, 증류하여 얻은 ☐ opaque a. 불투명한; 불명료한 ☐ aquatic a. 물속에서 자라는, 수생의

그 개천의 강둑은 수면에서 1.8미터 정도 되는 높이였는데 그 물은 만조(滿潮) 시에는 염분이 섞였다가 저조(低潮) 시에는 염분이 사라졌다.

## 32 ④

☐ whitewash v. 흰 도료를 칠하다; 지워버리다(=erase) ☐ collective memory 집단 기억(흔히 부모 세대에서 자식 세대로 전달되는 한 공동체의 기억) ☐ revive v. 소생하게 하다, 되살리다; 기운나게 하다 ☐ memorialize v. 기념식을 거행하다, 기념하다 ☐ beautify v. 아름답게 하다, 미화하다

역사의 흐름은 많은 것들을 없앨 수 있다. 하지만 1930년대 일본의 침략에 대한 중국의 집단적인 기억을 지워버릴 수는 없다.

## 33 ①

☐ punctilious a. 세심한, 꼼꼼한; 격식을 차리는(=meticulous) ☐ stressed a. 강조된; 압력을 받고 있는 ☐ punctual a. 시간을 잘 지키는, 시간을 엄수하는 ☐ casual a. 우연의, 무심결의; 격식을 차리지 않은

삼촌은 작업마다 알맞은 도구를 사용하는 것에 세심한 주의를 기울인다.

## 34 ④

☐ pothole n. (길 바닥의) 움푹 팬 곳; 깊은 구멍 ☐ galore a. 많은, 풍성한(=abundant) ☐ obvious a. 분명한, 확실한 ☐ reparable a. 수선할 수 있는 ☐ pliable a. 유연한; 순응적인

하수도는 상당한 개선이 필요하고 도로에는 움푹 팬 곳이 많다.

## 35 ①

☐ bastion n. 수호자, 보루(=bulwark) ☐ haven n. 안식처, 피난처 ☐ harbinger n. 선구자; 조짐, 전조(前兆) ☐ terrain n. 지대, 지역

그 서아프리카 국가는 이 지역의 민주적 안정의 보루로 여겨져 왔다.

## 36 ③

☐ extrapolate v. (~을) 추정[추론, 예측]하다(=infer) ☐ skimp v. (돈·시간 등을) 지나치게 아끼다 ☐ interrupt v. 훼방놓다, 방해하다, 차단하다 ☐ precipitate v. 촉진시키다, 몰아대다

우리는 실제로 경제적으로 타격을 입은 하위 사회경제 계층의 훨씬 더 높은 증가를 쉽게 추정할 수 있다.

## 37 ④

☐ cutthroat a. 격렬한, 맹렬한(=fierce) ☐ hypothetical a. 가상적인, 가설[가정]의 ☐ unfetterd a. 제한받지 않는; 구속[속박]을 벗어난 ☐ reciprocal a. 상호간의

한국 수출업체들은 유럽 시장에서 치열한 경쟁을 벌이고 있다.

## 38 ②

☐ benighted a. 무지몽매한, 미개한, 문화가 뒤떨어진(=uncivilized) ☐ excluded a. 제외되는 ☐ belligerent a. 적대적인, 공격적인 ☐ refractory a. 다루기 힘든, (행실이) 불량한

우리는 아프리카 사람들이 왠지 미개하며 위대한 문화를 낳지 못했다고 생각하도록 강요받았다.

## 39 ①

☐ convoke v. (공식적인 회의를) 소집하다(=convene) ☐ dissemble v. (진짜 감정·의도를) 숨기다, 가식적으로 꾸미다 ☐ rectify v. (잘못된 것을) 바로잡다 ☐ savor v. ~을 맛보다, 즐기다

군사 전략을 짤 때, 한 나라의 지도자는 신뢰할 수 있는 고문들과 고위 장군들을 소집할 수도 있다.

## 40 ④

☐ despoil v. (어떤 장소에서 귀중한 것을) 빼앗다[훼손하다](=ravage) ☐ ignore v. 무시하다 ☐ illuminate v. 밝히다, 분명히 하다 ☐ monopolize v. 독점하다; (사람의 관심·시간을) 독차지하다

베니스와 같은 구세계의 많은 장소들은 이러한 단체 관광으로 인해 충분히 훼손되었다.

## 41　③

☐ isolated a. 고립된, 격리된 ☐ draconian a. 매우 엄격한, 가혹한 (=oppressive) ☐ temperate a. 온화한 ☐ merciful a. 자비로운; 다행스러운 ☐ customary a. 관례적인, 습관적인

정부가 고립될수록 엄격한 정책을 정당화할 뿐 아니라 대응을 완화해야 할 의무감도 줄어든다.

## 42　②

☐ revolt n. 반란, 폭동 ☐ break out 발발[발생]하다 ☐ insurgent n. 폭도, 반란자(=rebel) ☐ novice n. 초심자, 풋내기 ☐ negotiator n. 협상자, 교섭자 ☐ reckoner n. 계산하는 사람

폭동이 일어났을 때 정부는 군대에게 반란자들을 체포할 것을 명령했다.

## 43　①

☐ ruthless a. 무정한, 무자비한; 잔인한(=merciless) ☐ hamlet n. 작은 마을, 촌락 ☐ powerful a. 강한, 강력한; 유력한, 우세한 ☐ vehement a. 격렬한, 맹렬한; 열심인, 열렬한 ☐ generous a. 후한; 풍부한; 관대한, 아량 있는

그 무자비한 장군은 그 마을의 무고한 사람들을 죽였다.

## 44　④

☐ equanimity n. 평정; 침착, 냉정(=composure) ☐ avarice n. 탐욕, 허욕 ☐ enormity n. 극악무도; 중대한 범죄 ☐ apprehension n. 염려, 불안; 이해

열한 명의 아들을 둔 그 엄마는 진흙 싸움을 침착하게 바라보았다. 적어도 아이들이 서로를 향해 던지고 있는 것이 총알은 아니었으니까.

## 45　②

☐ surrogate n. 대리, 대행자, 대행인(=substitute) a. 대리의, 대용의 ☐ fight for ~을 위해 싸우다; ~을 얻기 위해 싸우다 ☐ scapegoat n. 희생양, 희생자, 남의 죄를 대신 지는 사람 ☐ mediator n. 중재인, 조정자, 매개자 ☐ patron n. 보호자, 후원자, 지지자; 단골손님, 고객

일부 국가들이 그들의 정치적 목적을 달성하기 위해 테러단체를 대리인으로 이용하기 시작했다.

## 46　③

☐ wreck v. 파괴하다, 부수다(=ruin) ☐ conquer v. 정복하다, 공략하다; 극복하다 ☐ exploit v. 이용하다, 활용하다; 개발하다 ☐ sustain v. 떠받치다, 지탱하다

지구가 알프스산맥을 만들기까지 매우 오랜 시간이 걸렸는데, 이는 인간이 알프스산맥을 파괴하는 데 걸리는 시간보다 훨씬 더 긴 시간이다.

## 47　④

☐ precipitate v. 거꾸로 떨어뜨리다; 촉진시키다(=accelerate) ☐ prevent v. 막다, 방해하다; 예방하다 ☐ pacify v. 진정시키다, 가라앉히다 ☐ foretell v. 예언하다; 예고하다

'중요한'이란 말은 토론에서 가장 남발하는 말이다. 시장보다 더 중요한 것은 없는데, 이것이 위기를 촉진했다고 해도 무리가 아니다.

## 48　②

☐ appetite n. 식욕; 욕구 ☐ lurid a. 소름끼치는, 무서운(=gruesome) ☐ distraction n. 기분 풀이[전환]하기; 기분 풀이, 위락, 오락 ☐ robust a. 원기 왕성한, 팔팔한; (기구 등이) 튼튼한[강력한] ☐ pandemic n. 전국적[세계적]으로 유행하는 병 ☐ deliberate a. 계획적인, 고의의 ☐ blithe a. 즐거운, 유쾌한 ☐ casual a. 우연한, 뜻밖의

코로나-19 대유행 병으로 인해 수억 명의 사람들이 어쩔 수 없이 집에 머무르게 되면서, 섬뜩한 기분전환 거리에 대한 욕구가 특히 강하다.

## 49　①

☐ prosecutor n. 검사 ☐ commit v. (죄, 과실 등을) 저지르다, 범하다 ☐ perpetrator n. 가해자, 범인, 하수인 ☐ inebriated a. 술에 취한(=intoxicated) ☐ inflamed a. (신체 부위에) 염증이 생긴; 흥분한, 격앙된 ☐ sulphurous a. 지옥불의; 지옥 같은; 열렬한, 격한, 흥분한 ☐ emollient a. (피부를) 부드럽게 하는; 진정시키는, 완화시키는

대검찰청은 10건의 범죄 당 약 2건이 가해자가 취한 상태에서 일어난다는 사실을 발견했다.

## 50　③

☐ primed a. 의향이 있는, 준비가 되어 있는(=prepared) ☐ generous a. 후한; 풍부한; 관대한, 아량 있는 ☐ indulged a. 몰두한, 탐닉한 ☐ secured a. 보증하는; 확보한

특정 이익 집단들은 이미 싸울 준비가 되어 있었다.

## 51　①

☐ courageous a. 용기 있는 ☐ approbation n. 허가, (공식) 인가, 재가, 면허; 승인, 시인, 찬동; 칭찬(=commendation) ☐ opprobrium n. 오명, 불명예; 욕설, 비난 ☐ tolerance n. 관용; 내성; 참을성, 관대함 ☐ prohibition n. 금지

열광적인 공연이 끝난 후, 관객들은 예술적으로 대담한 토코(Tocco)의 공연 프로그램에 대해 열렬한 찬사로 즉각 화답했다.

## 52 ②

☐ milestone n. 이정표; 획기적인 사건(=landmark) ☐ windmill n. 풍차; 가상의 적 ☐ skyscraper n. 초고층 빌딩, 마천루 ☐ stepping-stone n. 디딤돌, 발판

메트로폴리탄 오페라 극장에서의 그녀의 첫 공연은 미국 음악계에서 획기적인 사건이었다.

## 53 ③

☐ expurgated a. (불온하여 영화, 책에서) 삭제된, 검열된(=censored) ☐ easy a. 쉬운, 힘들지 않은, 안락한, 마음 편한 ☐ shorten v. 짧게 하다, 적게 하다 ☐ explicit a. 뚜렷한, 명백한, 명시된

아마도 그 소설의 검열 삭제판이 수준이 높지 않은 학생들에게는 더 적절할 것이다.

## 54 ④

☐ loudmouthed a. 큰 목소리의; 시끄러운, 요란한 ☐ jerk n. <속어> 바보 ☐ crass a. 우둔한; 형편없는, 지독한(=nasty) ☐ careless a. 부주의한, 조심성 없는; 경솔한 ☐ clueless a. 단서가 없는; 무지한 ☐ redefined a. 다시 정의된

일부 사람들은 시끄러운 얼간이의 무례한 농담과 지독한 말에 경악했다.

## 55 ④

☐ odorless a. 냄새 없는, 향기 없는 ☐ carbon dioxide 이산화탄소 ☐ telltale a. 고자질하는; 감추려 해도 드러나는(=revealing) ☐ illustrate v. 설명하다, 예증하다 ☐ undeniable a. 부인[부정]할 수 없는, 명백한 ☐ composition n. 구성; 성분; (타고난) 기질 ☐ measurement n. 측량, 측정; 치수 ☐ deceptive a. (사람을) 현혹시키는, 거짓의 ☐ equivocal a. 모호한, 애매한, 불분명한 ☐ contradictory a. 모순된, 양립하지 않는

1958년에 찰스 데이비드 킬링(Charles David Keeling) 교수는 하와이의 어느 산 높은 곳에서 무색무취의 가스 ― 이산화탄소 ― 를 측정하기 시작했다. 그 이후로 그곳에서 매일 이산화탄소를 측정했는데, 있는 그대로를 보여주는 곡선 그래프는 부인할 수 없는 사실을 보여주었다. 공기의 구성이 변하고 있다는 것이다. 킬링 교수는 측정 첫해에 315ppm의 평균 이산화탄소 수치를 기록했다. 올해 5월에, 기록된 평균 수치는 거의 408ppm이었다.

## 56 ①

☐ sympathy n. 동정; 조위, 조문(弔問); 위문(=condolence) ☐ bouquet n. 꽃다발 ☐ funeral a. 장례의 ☐ parlor n. 응접실; ~점(店), 영업실 ☐ abomination n. 혐오, 증오 ☐ observance n. 준수; 관습; 축하 ☐ punctuation n. 구두(句讀); 구두법

애도의 뜻을 표하기 위해, 그녀는 장례식장에 꽃다발을 보냈다.

## 57 ④

☐ peregrination n. 여행, 편력(=excursion) ☐ liberation n. 해방, 석방; 해방운동 ☐ explanation n. 해명, 이유; 설명 ☐ discipline n. 규율, 훈육

세르반테스(Cervantes)의 소설 『돈키호테』에서 주인공들은 긴 여정을 펼친다.

## 58 ①

☐ forlorn a. 희망을 잃은, 절망적인(=desperate) ☐ chaste a. 순결한, 순수한 ☐ frail a. 노쇠한; (허)약한 ☐ feasible a. 실현 가능한

이 희망은 시간이 지날수록 점점 더 절망적이다.

## 59 ②

☐ propaganda n. 선전 ☐ denigrate v. 폄하하다(=disparage) ☐ disguise v. 변장[가장]하다 ☐ provoke v. 유발하다, 화나게 하다 ☐ cajole v. 꼬드기다, 회유하다

우크라이나를 폄하하는 러시아의 선전이 국제적으로 인기 있는 온라인 비디오 게임을 통해 확산되고 있다.

## 60 ④

☐ precipitous a. 가파른, 깎아지른 듯한; 급작스러운(=steep) ☐ steady a. 꾸준한, 변함없는 ☐ gradual a. 점진적인, 서서히 일어나는 ☐ cyclical a. 순환하는, 주기적인

수출의 급격한 감소는 수입의 감소로 상쇄될 가능성이 높다.

## 61 ④

☐ frail a. 여린; 연약한, 허약한(=weak) ☐ deaf a. 귀머거리의, 귀가 먼; 무관심한 ☐ unhappy a. 불행한, 불운한; 비참한 ☐ unpleasant a. 불쾌한, 기분 나쁜, 싫은

비록 나의 할머니는 연세가 많으시고 허약하시지만, 여전히 카드게임과 댄스음악을 즐기신다.

## 62 ②

☐ soporific a. 최면(성)의; 졸린 듯한(=sedative) ☐ profound a. 심오한, 깊은 ☐ exciting a. 흥분시키는, 자극적인 ☐ erudite a. 박식한, 학식 있는

모든 사람이 그를 존경했고, 그의 졸릴 만큼 차분한 설명을 신중하게 경청했다.

## 63      ②

☐ hyperbole n. 과장, 과장어구(=exaggeration) ☐ opposition n. 반대, 반항; 방해 ☐ refusal n. 거절, 거부; 사퇴 ☐ deletion n. 삭제; 삭제 부분

시인들은 때로 특별한 효과를 위해 과장법을 사용한다.

## 64      ③

☐ reverse v. 거꾸로 하다; 뒤집다; 전환하다; 후진시키다(=turn around) ☐ turn out ~을 끄다; ~임이 밝혀지다 ☐ turn off 잠그다, 멎게 하다; ~을 끄다 ☐ turn on ~을 켜다, 틀다

그 자동차 여행자는 앞에서 사고가 발생한 것을 보았을 때 차를 돌리기로 결심했다.

## 65      ③

☐ bustle v. 부산하게 움직이다; 법석 떨다, 서두르다(=rush) ☐ hut n. 오두막 ☐ steaming a. 김을 푹푹 내뿜는 ☐ exhaust v. 다 써버리다, 고갈시키다 ☐ lash v. 채찍질하다; 몹시 꾸짖다, 비꼬다 ☐ squat v. 웅크리다, 쪼그리고 앉다; 땅에 엎드리다

너무 지쳐 생각할 겨를도 없이, 나는 돌로 지어진 오두막에 서둘러 들어갔고 김이 나는 핫초콜릿을 마시다가 컵에 입술을 데었다.

## 66      ①

☐ colleague n. 동료; 동업자 ☐ missionary n. 선교사, 전도사 ☐ credit v. (공적·명예 등을) ~에게 돌리다, ~의 소유자[공로자, 행위자]로 생각하다 ☐ Buddhism n. 불교 ☐ protean a. 다방면의, 변화무쌍한(=mutable) ☐ compelling a. 강제적인; 강한 흥미를 돋우는 ☐ inherited a. 물려받은; 유전의 ☐ moored a. 정박된; 단단히 고정된

일본에 있는 그의 동료와 마찬가지로, 그 선교사는 동아시아에서의 불교의 대중적 인기가 중국의 토착적인 종교 전통의 형태로 스스로 탈바꿈할 수 있는 불교의 변화무쌍한 능력 때문인 것으로 보았다.

## 67      ①

☐ myopic a. 근시(성)의; 근시안적인(=nearsighted) ☐ intense a. 강렬한, 격렬한; 열정적인 ☐ regretful a. 유감스러운, 후회하는 ☐ imminent a. 임박한, 절박한

지금 행동하는 것에 대한 그들의 근시안적인 거부는 의심할 바 없이 미래에 문제들을 야기할 것이다.

## 68      ②

☐ capitulate v. (조건부로) 항복[굴복]하다(=succumb) ☐ discharge v. 짐을 부리다; 배출하다; 해방하다, 면제하다 ☐ contest v. 논쟁하다, 다투다; 겨루다 ☐ concede v. 인정하다, 용인하다

그는 내부의 압력에 짓눌려 굴복했다. 그는 언론과 정치인들에게 압도당했던 것이다.

## 69      ②

☐ unwelcome a. 달갑지 않은 ☐ be bound to do 반드시 ~하다, ~하려고 마음먹다 ☐ grouse v. 불평하다(=complain) ☐ praise v. 칭찬하다 ☐ worry v. 걱정하다 ☐ meditate v. 명상하다

완전히 달갑잖은 변화인 것은 아니지만 누가 연주하든 밴드에 대해 불평할 사람은 있을 수밖에 없다.

## 70      ②

☐ chilling a. 냉기가 스미는; 냉담한; 으스스한(=frightening) ☐ long a. 긴; 장기간에 걸치는 ☐ confidential a. 비밀[기밀]의; 은밀한 ☐ questionable a. 의심스러운; 수상한

핵전쟁 계획에 대한 그들의 보고서는 몸을 오싹하게 하는 문서이다.

## 71      ④

☐ openness n. 개방성, 솔직 ☐ transparency n. 투명(성) ☐ exude v. (냄새·분위기 따위를) 풍기다, 발산시키다(=emanate) ☐ deceptive a. 남을 속이는, 기만적인 ☐ demage limitation 피해 대책(야기될 피해를 최소화하려는 조치) ☐ deter v. 단념시키다, 그만두게 하다 ☐ evade v. 피하다, 모면하다 ☐ placate v. (화를) 달래다

그 계획은 개방성과 투명성 대신 기만적인 피해 대책의 분위기를 풍긴다.

## 72      ①

☐ obsequious a. 아첨하는, 알랑거리는(=fawning) ☐ austere a. 엄격한; 검소한 ☐ mercenary a. 돈 버는 데만 관심이 있는 ☐ contentious a. 논쟁을 좋아하는

헬렌(Helen)은 스스로를 존중하는 것처럼 행동하는 사람들을 높이 평가했다. 지나치게 알랑거리는 판매원보다 더 그녀를 화나게 하는 것은 없었다.

## 73      ①

☐ sweeping a. 일소하는; 포괄적인(=overall) ☐ regional a. 지방의; 지역적인 ☐ smooth a. 매끈한; 잔잔한 ☐ impressive a. 인상적인

아마도 어떤 주제에 관한 전통적인 사고방식에 대해 과학이 지금보다 더 총체적인 변화를 요구한 적은 없었을 것이고, 또한 이보다 더 중요한 주제는 없었을 것이다.

## 74 ③

☐ turbulent a. 휘몰아치는, 사나운, 폭풍우의; 소란스러운(=wild) ☐ draw to a close 끝에 가까워지다 ☐ initial a. 처음의, 최초의 ☐ prosperous a. 번영하는, 부유한 ☐ lackluster a. 광택 없는; 활기 없는

시끌벅적했던 여름 시장이 끝나고 있으므로, 내부자들이 무엇을 하는지 거의 실시간으로 관찰하는 것도 흥미로울 것이다.

## 75 ①

☐ overture n. (보통 pl.) 신청, 제안, 교섭 개시; 자문(=suggestion) ☐ substantive a. 실질[본질]적인; 현실의 ☐ lasting a. 영속적인, 영구적인 ☐ pact n. 계약, 협정, 조약 ☐ convention n. 집회, 대회; 협정 ☐ clause n. 절; 조항, 항목

그 테러 국가가 화평을 제안하기 시작한 것은 참으로 희망적인 신호이지만, 이런 의사표시들은 아직 그 어떤 실질적이고 영속적인 결과도 낳지 못하고 있다.

## 76 ③

☐ freaked a. 충격을 받은; 몹시 지친; 얼룩진(=upset) ☐ illiterate a. 무식한, 문맹의 ☐ gratuitous a. 무료의, 무보수의; 불필요한 ☐ impudent a. 뻔뻔스러운, 철면피의, 염치없는

나는 다섯 대의 경찰차가 차도에 세워지는 것을 보았다. 나는 그들이 자신들을 비웃는 여자들에 의해 충격을 받았다고 생각했다.

## 77 ②

☐ aphasic a. 실어증의 n. 실어증 환자 ☐ circumlocution n. 완곡, 에두른[완곡한] 표현(=periphrasis) ☐ replace v. 대신하다, 대체하다 ☐ proclaim v. 선언하다, 공포하다, 포고하다 ☐ swear n. 저주, 욕설, 독설 ☐ blaspheme v. 모독하다

실어증 환자들은 때때로 사물을 잘못된 이름으로 부르거나, 어려운 단어 대신 완곡한 표현들을 사용한다.

## 78 ②

☐ astronomer n. 천문학자 ☐ putrid a. 부패한; 악취가 나는(=rotten) ☐ lurk v. 숨다, 잠복하다 ☐ anaesthetic a. 마취제가 든 ☐ eccentric a. 보통과 다른 ☐ saturated a. 흠뻑 젖은, 포화된

천문학자들은 지구와 기온이 비슷한 금성의 구름층인 안에 숨어 있는 썩은 가스를 발견했다.

## 79 ②

☐ halt v. 멈추다, 중단시키다 ☐ altercation n. 언쟁, 논쟁(=argument) ☐ come to blow 난투극이 되다 ☐ assault n. 강습, 습격 ☐ menace n. 협박, 위협, 공갈

선생님은 난투극을 벌이기 전에 두 명의 상대를 갈라놓음으로써 말다툼을 중단시켰다.

## 80 ④

☐ riveting a. 황홀케 하는, 매혹적인(=captivating) ☐ garrulous a. 수다스러운, 말많은 ☐ deterrent a. 단념시키는 ☐ frugal a. 검약한, 소박한

선생님이나 배우의 말이 임팩트와 흥미로 가득 차 있을 때 관심을 사로잡는 효과가 있다.

## 81 ②

☐ exemplary a. 본이 되는, 모범적인; 훌륭한(=commendable) ☐ convincing a. 설득력 있는 ☐ unforgettable a. 잊을 수 없는, 언제까지나 기억에 남는 ☐ uproarious a. 떠드는, 법석 떠는; 시끄러운, 떠들썩한

그녀는 뛰어난 개인적인 경력과 지역과 국제기관에 대한 모범적인 공헌으로 잘 알려져 있다.

## 82 ③

☐ intangible a. 만질 수 없는, 무형의; 실체가 없는(=impalpable) ☐ intelligible a. 이해할 수 있는, 알기 쉬운, 명료한 ☐ transient a. 덧없는, 일시적인 ☐ concrete a. 구체적인, 유형의; 현실의, 실제의

그것은 형체는 없지만 우리의 일상생활을 구성하고 있는 매우 실질적인 요소이다.

## 83 ①

☐ loquacious a. 수다스러운, 말이 많은 ☐ progeny n. 자손, 아이들; 제자, 후계자(=offspring) ☐ inheritance n. 상속 재산, 유산; 유전 ☐ predicament n. 곤경, 궁지 ☐ ailment n. 병; 불쾌, 불안

데이비드(David)는 자신의 자식 문제에 대해서 말을 많이 하지 않았다.

## 84 ④

☐ outmoded a. 유행에 뒤떨어진, 구식의(=old-fashioned) ☐ narrow a. 폭이 좁은; 여유가 없는; 한정된 ☐ reinforced concrete 철근 콘크리트 ☐ illegal a. 불법의, 위법의

미국의 다섯 다리 중 한 개는 구식이다.

## 85 ②

□ whirlpool n. 소용돌이 □ consign v. 건네주다, 인도하다; 위탁하다, 위임하다(=commit) □ oblivion n. (완전 파괴되어) 흔적도 없이 사라짐 □ compare v. 비교하다, 견주다; 비유하다 □ compile v. 엮다, 편집하다; 수집하다 □ conserve v. 보존하다, 유지하다; 절약하다

18세기 후반 이래로 그 생각은 상상할 수 없을 정도로 강력한 우주의 소용돌이가 우주의 물질들을 빨아들여 흔적도 없이 없애버리는 모습을 연상시키며 천문학자들을 매료시키고 있다.

## 86 ④

□ invincible a. 정복할[이길] 수 없는, 무적의; (장애 등을) 극복할 수 없는(=unconquerable) □ uncomfortable a. (사람, 물건이) 불유쾌한, 기분이 언짢은 □ unmanageable a. 다루기 힘든; 제어하기 어려운, 힘에 겨운 □ unbelievable a. 믿을 수 없는, 거짓말 같은

이번 시즌 보스턴은 무적의 팀이었다.

## 87 ④

□ dawdle v. 빈둥거리다, 게으름 피우다(=loiter) □ molt v. (허물을) 벗다 □ falter v. 비틀거리다 □ pore v. 숙고하다

숙제를 끝내는 대로 아이스크림과 쿠키를 먹을 것을 안다면 어린이들은 그들의 숙제를 하는 데 빈둥거리지 않을 것이다.

## 88 ③

□ discourteous a. 무례한 □ grumble v. 불평하다, 투덜거리다 (=complain) □ giggle v. 킬킬 웃다, 피식 웃다 □ scold v. 잔소리하다, 꾸짖다 □ brag v. 자랑하다, 뽐내다

저 학생은 버릇이 없다. 그를 기쁘게 해주려고 아무리 노력해도 그는 불평만 한다.

## 89 ④

□ fret v. 안달하다, 초조해하다, 애타다(=fuss) □ wander v. (정처 없이) 떠돌다, 헤매다, 방랑하다 □ assert v. 단언하다; 역설하다; (권리를) 주장하다 □ accumulate v. 모으다, 축적하다

당신이 원하는 것을 모두 가질 수는 없기 때문에 안달하며 인생을 보내 봐야 소용없는 일이다.

## 90 ①

□ putative a. ~으로 추정되는, 추정상의(=assumed) □ confirmed a. 확립된; 확인된; 굳어버린 □ imaginative a. 상상의, 가공의, 허위의 □ acknowledged a. 승인된, 일반적으로 인정된, 공인된

다소 의심스럽긴 하지만, 그 책의 저자는 제니퍼 존슨(Jennifer H. Johnson)으로 추정된다.

## 91 ②

□ ingratiating a. 매력 있는, 싹싹한, 남에게 호감을 주는(=flattering) □ revengeful a. 복수심에 불타는, 앙심 깊은 □ dissident a. 의견이 다른, 반대하는 □ betrothed a. 약혼한, 약혼자의

수석 웨이터는 억지로 꾸민 얼굴에 싹싹한 미소를 지으며, 커다란 복숭아로 가득한 큰 바구니를 들고서 우리에게 다가왔다.

## 92 ①

□ dilapidated a. 황폐한, 다 허물어져 가는(=ruined) □ boarded-up a. (창문, 문 등이) 판자로 덮인 □ desiccated a. (저장을 위해) 건조시킨; 분말의 □ sanctified a. 신성화된; 축성된 □ excavated a. 발굴된

그는 거리를 지나 계속 가다가 모퉁이에 있는 판자로 된 낡은 교회에 다다르자 속도를 줄였다.

## 93 ④

□ pound v. 산산이 부수다, 분쇄하다 □ naked eye (안경 등을 쓰지 않은) 육안 □ pellucid a. (유리 등이) 투명한; 명쾌한(=transparent) □ microscope n. 현미경 □ indecent a. 외설적인; 무례한 □ transitory a. 일시적인, 덧없는 □ filthy a. 아주 더러운; 추잡한

모래나 부서진 유리는 육안으로는 흰색인데, 현미경으로 보면 투명하다.

## 94 ④

□ infatuation n. 열중(하게 함); 심취(=absorption) □ tumult n. 법석, 소동 □ humility n. 겸손, 겸양 □ animosity n. 악의, 원한

나치 이데올로기에 열광하는 것으로 알려진 한 남성이 살인 혐의로 기소되었다.

## 95 ③

□ riot n. 폭동 □ engulf v. 완전히 에워싸다, 휩싸다(=overwhelm) □ undulate v. 물결을 일으키다, 진동시키다 □ dissipate v. 흩뜨리다; 낭비하다 □ disseminate v. (정보·지식 등을) 퍼뜨리다[전파하다]

지난 주말 폭동이 토요일 밤 미국 주요 도시를 휩쓸었다.

## 96 ①

☐ inquiry n. 연구, 탐구  ☐ leapfrog v. (더 높은 위치·등급으로) 뛰어넘다(=surpass)  ☐ uncover v. 알아내다  ☐ countervail v. 상쇄하다, 무효로 하다  ☐ scrutinize v. 자세히 조사하다  ☐ switch v. 전환되다, 바뀌다

과학 탐구의 장점은 발견의 속도를 빠르게 앞설 때 완전히 새로운 사고방식을 알아낼 수 있다는 것이다.

## 97 ③

☐ zenith n. (명성·성공·권세 등의) 정점, 극도, 절정(=heyday)  ☐ stretch v. (어떤 지역에 걸쳐) 뻗어 있다[펼쳐지다, 이어지다]  ☐ vista n. 경치, 풍경; 전망  ☐ sovereign n. 독립국, 주권국  ☐ fiasco n. 대실패, 완패

전성기의 대영제국은 지구 면적의 4분의 1에 달하는 영토를 차지했다.

## 98 ②

☐ solidly ad. 굳게; 견고하게  ☐ cornucopia n. 풍요(豊饒)의 뿔; 풍부, 풍요(=abundance)  ☐ daydream n. 백일몽, 공상  ☐ arrogance n. 거만, 불손, 오만  ☐ vanity n. 자만심, 허영심  ☐ coterie n. 동료, 친구

공화당은 그 법안을 세금과 가족의 생활비를 올리는 많은 낭비적인 자유주의적 공상이라고 부르며 강력하게 반대했다.

## 99 ①

☐ unison n. 조화, 화합, 일치(=harmony)  ☐ resolution n. (문제·불화 등의) 해결  ☐ creed n. 교리, 신념  ☐ collusion n. 공모, 결탁  ☐ obedience n. 복종, 순종

우리가 이 문제에 대한 지속적인 해결책을 찾으려면 국제 사회가 한마음으로 행동해야 한다.

## 100 ①

☐ geek n. 괴짜, 기인  ☐ forte n. 강점(특히 잘하는 것)(=strength)  ☐ boundary n. 경계(선); 한계  ☐ foible n. (성격상의) 약점, 결점, 단점  ☐ patent n. 특허권

많은 사람들이 나를 과학만을 좋아하는 괴짜라고 생각하지만, 과학뿐만 아니라 수학도 나의 장점이다.

| | | | | | | | | | |
|---|---|---|---|---|---|---|---|---|---|
| 01 ④ | 02 ① | 03 ④ | 04 ① | 05 ④ | 06 ① | 07 ① | 08 ① | 09 ③ | 10 ④ |
| 11 ③ | 12 ② | 13 ② | 14 ② | 15 ④ | 16 ③ | 17 ① | 18 ② | 19 ② | 20 ④ |
| 21 ④ | 22 ④ | 23 ③ | 24 ② | 25 ③ | 26 ① | 27 ④ | 28 ④ | 29 ④ | 30 ② |
| 31 ② | 32 ④ | 33 ④ | 34 ④ | 35 ① | 36 ② | 37 ③ | 38 ② | 39 ③ | 40 ④ |
| 41 ② | 42 ② | 43 ③ | 44 ④ | 45 ④ | 46 ② | 47 ④ | 48 ② | 49 ① | 50 ④ |
| 51 ① | 52 ④ | 53 ④ | 54 ② | 55 ④ | 56 ① | 57 ① | 58 ③ | 59 ④ | 60 ④ |
| 61 ① | 62 ② | 63 ④ | 64 ④ | 65 ④ | 66 ③ | 67 ① | 68 ② | 69 ④ | 70 ② |
| 71 ① | 72 ④ | 73 ① | 74 ④ | 75 ③ | 76 ③ | 77 ① | 78 ③ | 79 ④ | 80 ③ |
| 81 ③ | 82 ③ | 83 ② | 84 ① | 85 ① | 86 ④ | 87 ④ | 88 ② | 89 ① | 90 ④ |
| 91 ④ | 92 ② | 93 ④ | 94 ① | 95 ① | 96 ③ | 97 ② | 98 ④ | 99 ① | 100 ④ |

## 01
④

☐ blatant a. 소란스러운; 노골적인(=obtrusive) ☐ assimilative a. 동화하는 힘이 있는, 동화작용의 ☐ inconspicuous a. 눈에 띄지 않는, 주의를 끌지 않는 ☐ monotonous a. 단조로운, 변화가 없는

학교 안에서의 그와 같은 노골적인 광고는 학부모들로부터 항의를 불러일으켰다.

## 02
①

☐ primordial a. 최초의, 본원의, 근본적인(=beginning) ☐ ending n. 끝남, 종결, 결말 ☐ critical a. 결정적인, 중대한; 위기의 ☐ peaked a. 뾰족한, 뾰족한 끝이 있는

최초 단계에서는 이 부분을 제외한 모든 것이 부식으로 인해 제대로 작동하지 않았다.

## 03
④

☐ outlandish a. 이상한, 기이한(=eccentric) ☐ ambitious a. 야심찬, 의욕적인 ☐ superficial a. 피상적인, 표면상의 ☐ regressive a. 역행하는, 퇴행하는

그는 다소 지나칠 정도로 기이하게 보이는 생각을 제안해서 종종 비난을 받아왔다.

## 04
①

☐ construe v. ~의 뜻으로 파악[이해]하다(=understand) ☐ criticize v. 비평하다, 비판하다 ☐ laugh at 비웃다 ☐ report v. 보고하다, 보도하다

윈스턴(Winston)은 자신의 논평이 인종차별적으로 이해될 수 있다는 것을 인정했다.

## 05
④

☐ cryptic a. 숨은, 비밀의; 애매한(=concealing) ☐ fleshy a. 살집이 있는, 살찐 ☐ lappet n. 늘어진 주름 ☐ fin membrane 지느러미막 ☐ scale n. 비늘 ☐ invisible a. 보이지 않는, 볼 수 없는 ☐ eligible a. 적격의, 적임의; 자격이 있는 ☐ caustic a. 부식성의; 신랄한 ☐ exuberant a. 활기 넘치는, 원기 왕성한

산호나 바위 밑에 사는 쏨뱅이들은 놀라울 정도로 몸을 숨기는 데 알맞은 색과 모양을 가지고 있다. 수많은 살찐 주름들은 머리와 지느러미막들과 비늘들을 장식하여 해양유기체들로 덮인 바위를 배경으로 물고기가 보이지 않도록 만들고 있다.

## 06
①

☐ insolent a. 버릇없는, 무례한(=impertinent) ☐ capricious a. 변덕스러운, 잘 변하는 ☐ ludicrous a. 우스운, 익살맞은 ☐ detrimental a. 해로운, 불리한

그러나 영국이 종종 무례하고 잔인하며 전반적으로 이기적인 정책에서 자신의 훌륭한 이력을 추구해 왔다는 사실은 인정해야만 한다.

## 07
①

☐ inaugural a. 취임(식)의 ☐ fulminate v. 맹렬히 비판하다, 야단치다(=storm) ☐ cajole v. 감언이설로 속이다; 부추기다 ☐ lampoon v. 풍자하다, 비방하다 ☐ careen v. (차량이) 위태롭게 달리다

취임 연설에서, 새로 선출된 대통령은 의료보험기금을 삭감하려는 공화당의 계획을 맹렬히 비난했다.

## 08 ①

☐ besmirch v. 더럽히다; 변색시키다; (인격, 명예를) 손상시키다 (=defile) ☐ supplement v. 보충하다; 추가하다 ☐ mislead v. 그릇 인도하다; 오해하게 하다 ☐ disorganize v. ~의 조직을 파괴하다

신문에 실린 수치스러운 소견은 그 협회의 모든 회원들의 명성을 더럽혔다.

## 09 ③

☐ livid a. 몹시 화가 난, 격노한(=furious); (멍든 것처럼) 검푸른 ☐ anguished a. 괴로워하는, 고민의; 고민에 찬 ☐ appalled a. 오싹해진, 얼이 빠진 ☐ disappointed a. 실망한, 낙담한; 실연한

엄마는 우리가 바닥에 쏟은 콜라를 청소하기 위해 자신의 드레스를 이용했다는 것을 알게 되었을 때 몹시 화를 내셨다.

## 10 ④

☐ retract v. (약속, 명령 등을) 취소하다, 철회하다(=withdraw) ☐ confirm v. (결심 등을) 굳게 하다; 확인하다 ☐ revise v. 교정하다, 수정하다 ☐ announce v. 알리다, 발표하다, 공표하다

프랑스가 비록 24시간도 채 지나지 않아 축하의 말을 취소하긴 했지만, 축하를 표한 유일한 나라이다.

## 11 ③

☐ evident a. 분명한, 명백한(=apparent) ☐ myriad a. 무수한, 막대한; 가지각색의 ☐ receptive a. 수용하는, 잘 받아들이는 ☐ muddy a. 진창의, 진흙의; 흐린, 선명치 않은

그 동물들이 겨울을 넘기지 못할 것이 분명했다.

## 12 ②

☐ affliction n. 고통, 고뇌(=anguish) ☐ utility n. 유용성, 실용 ☐ feature n. 특징, 특색; 이목구비 ☐ capability n. 능력, 역량

제인(Jane)은 그런 난폭한 행동을 예상하지 못했기 때문에, 존(John)의 행동은 제인에게 고통을 안겨 주었다.

## 13 ②

☐ gossamer a. 섬세한; 얇고 가벼운(=delicate) ☐ grisly a. 무서운, 불쾌한 ☐ porous a. 흡수성의, 투과성의 ☐ reticent a. 과묵한

클로드 S. 피셔(Claude S. Fisher)는 형식적인 제도나 법률보다는 학자가 '마음의 관습들'이라고 언급했던, 현대인들이 국민적 정서라고 여기는 것들인 태도나 가치, 믿음이라는 섬세한 조직에 초점을 두고 있다.

## 14 ②

☐ encroachment n. 침입, 침해(=infringement) ☐ territory n. 지역, 영토 ☐ ultimately ad. 궁극적으로, 결국 ☐ endearment n. 친애(의 표시) ☐ enchantment n. 매혹, 매력 ☐ enforcement n. 시행, 실시

인디언들의 영토에 대한 정착민들의 끊임없는 침해로 인해 결국 인디언들은 집을 잃게 되었다.

## 15 ④

☐ subservient a. 비굴한, 아첨하는(=submissive) ☐ pro-life a. 낙태[낙태 합법화]에 반대하는 ☐ accountable a. 책임이 있는, 해명할 의무가 있는 ☐ uninterested a. 흥미[관심] 없는, 무관심한 ☐ impetuous a. 성급한, 충동적인

정부는 낙태 합법화에 반대하는 운동가들의 이해관계에 굴종한다는 혐의로 비난받았다.

## 16 ③

☐ duck v. (머리나 몸을 움직여) 피하다(=dodge) ☐ throw v. 던지다 ☐ clench v. (주먹을[이]) 꽉 쥐다 ☐ smash v. 부딪치다[충돌하다]

그가 처음에 주먹을 몇 차례 피하더니 반격을 가하기 시작했다.

## 17 ①

☐ deplorable a. 한탄할; 개탄스러운 ☐ willful a. 고의적인, 의도적인(=intentional) ☐ vengeful a. 복수심에 불타는 ☐ malleable a. 영향을 잘 받는, 잘 변하는 ☐ reckless a. 무모한, 신중하지 못한; 난폭한

카카르(Kakar)는 가자지구에 대한 이스라엘의 공격을 "무고한 팔레스타인인에 대한 이스라엘의 개탄스럽고 의도적인 공격 행위"라고 설명했다.

## 18 ②

☐ psychoanalysis n. 정신 분석(학[법]) ☐ repressed a. 억압된, 억눌린, 억제된(=suppressed) ☐ conflict n. 갈등, 충돌 ☐ consciousness n. 의식, 자각 ☐ inexplicable a. 불가해한, 설명할 수 없는 ☐ unending a. 끝이 없는, 영원한 ☐ troublesome a. 골칫거리인

정신분석학의 목표 중 하나는 억압된 갈등을 의식의 수준으로 이끌어내는 것이다.

## 19 ②

☐ forthright a. 단도직입적인; 솔직한(=outspoken) ☐ whimsical a. 엉뚱한, 기발한 ☐ flamboyant a. 이색적인; 화려한 ☐ courteous a. 공손한, 정중한

우리 중 많은 사람들은 우리가 원하는 것을 말하는 것을 부끄러워할 수 있고, 솔직하게 말하는 법을 배우는 데 평생을 소비한다.

## 20 ④

☐ stodgy a. 따분한, 지루한(=dull) ☐ insouciant a. 무관심한; 태평한 ☐ vainglorious a. 자만심이 강한 ☐ premonitory a. 예고의; 전조의

"뉴욕 타임스"는 진지한 저널리즘으로 인해 크게 존중받고 있으면서도 따분한 전통으로 조롱거리가 된다.

## 21 ④

☐ explicit a. 명백한, 뚜렷한, 명시적인(=clear) ☐ brief a. 짧은, 간결한; 단시간의; 덧없는 ☐ new a. 새로운, 최근의 ☐ firm a. 굳은, 단단한

그 법은 자동차 안에서 어린이용 안전벨트의 사용과 기준에 대해 매우 명확하다.

## 22 ④

☐ stand up for oneself 자립하다, 남에게 좌우되지 않다 ☐ subjugate v. 정복하다, 복종시키다, 종속시키다(=dominate) ☐ disgrace v. 수치가 되다; 욕보이다 ☐ infatuate v. 얼빠지게 하다; 호리다 ☐ persuade v. 설득하다, 권하여 ~시키다; 납득시키다

그녀는 자신감이 넘치고 똑똑하며 혼자서 자립할 수 있는 사람이다. 그녀는 결코 남편한테 예속될 사람이 아니다.

## 23 ③

☐ corollary n. 논리, 추론; 당연한 결과(=result) ☐ catch n. 잡기; 잡은 것; 정지, 중단 ☐ axiom n. 자명한 이치, 원리; 격언 ☐ perception n. 지각; 인식, 인지

고전적인 정신분석이 행동요법과 마찬가지로 자신감을 회복시키는 데 도움이 되지 않는다는 것은 당연한 결과이다.

## 24 ②

☐ blandish v. 아첨하다, 감언으로 설득하다(=flatter) ☐ force v. 강요하다, 억지로 ~시키다 ☐ urge v. 몰아대다; 강요하다 ☐ compel v. 강제하다, 억지로 ~시키다

우리는 다른 사람을 부추겨서 어떤 일을 하도록 하는 사람을 제거해야 한다.

## 25 ③

☐ diatribe n. 통렬한 비난; 비방(=castigation) ☐ disrupt v. 방해하다,

지장을 주다; 혼란스럽게 하다 ☐ outcome n. 결과 ☐ accolade n. 칭찬, 영예 ☐ warning n. 경고 ☐ commentary n. 논평, 비평

잉그래햄(Ingraham)이 자신의 비판에서 다루고 있는, 그리고 많은 공화당원들이 인정하지 않으려 할, 또 다른 것이 있는데, 그것은 바로 폭력이 실제로는 선거 결과를 혼란스럽게 하는 것에 관한 것이었다는 점이다.

## 26 ①

☐ dispute n. 논쟁, 말다툼 ☐ unrest n. (특히 사회적인) 불안 ☐ neighboring a. 이웃의, 인접해 있는 ☐ skirmish n. 전초전, 작은 충돌(=clash) ☐ tension n. 긴장; (국제정세 따위의) 긴장상태 ☐ mount v. (양이나 강도가) 증가하다 ☐ erosion n. 부식, 침식 ☐ conciliation n. 회유; 조정 ☐ exaltation n. 칭찬, 찬양; 승진

귀중한 자원을 얻기 위한 경쟁이 이웃 국가들 사이에 분쟁과 전반적인 불안을 초래했다. 긴장이 고조되면서 때때로 작은 충돌이 벌어졌고 사람들은 보호를 받으려 군사 지도자들에 의지했다.

## 27 ④

☐ imbibe v. (사상 등을) 흡수하다, 받아들이다, 동화하다(=absorb) ☐ pigeonhole v. 분류 정리하다; 뒤로 미루다 ☐ extol v. 극찬[격찬]하다 ☐ criticize v. 비판[비난]하다

고칼레(Gokhale)는 인도인들이 서구의 세속적인 진보 사상을 받아들이기를 원했다.

## 28 ④

☐ anguish n. (심신의) 고통, 괴로움(=suffering) ☐ happiness n. 행복, 만족, 기쁨 ☐ spirit n. 정신, 마음, 영혼 ☐ abundance n. 풍부, 많음

테레사(Theresa)는 20년 동안 응급실에서 간호사로 있었지만, 사고 희생자들의 괴로움에 결코 익숙해지지 않았다.

## 29 ④

☐ ascertain v. 확인하다; 규명하다, 알아보다 ☐ melee n. 혼란, 소동(=turmoil) ☐ mishap n. 불행한 사건, 재난 ☐ gamut n. 전 영역, 전반(全般), 범위 ☐ mien n. 태도, 몸가짐

그 교사는 학생들 사이에서 발생한 그 소란의 원인을 확인하려고 했다.

## 30 ②

☐ banal a. 진부한, 평범한(=trite) ☐ smart a. 재치 있는, 영리한 ☐ priceless a. 아주 귀중한, 값을 매길 수 없는 ☐ detrimental a. 손해를 입히는, 해로운

차이를 강조하는 것은 거의 진부하게 들리지만, 그것은 자유 민주주의를 이해하는 데 필수적이다.

## 31 ②

☐ foil n. 금속박편; (물건을 싸는) 포일; (대조되어) 남을 돋보이게 하는 것(=contrast) ☐ fair-haired a. 머리카락이 옅은 색인, 금발의 ☐ metal n. 금속; 합금 ☐ pair n. 한 쌍, 한 벌 ☐ avatar n. 화신; 구현

"스타워즈(Star Wars)"에서, 악당인 다스 베이더(Darth Vader)는 때 묻지 않은 금발의 순진한 루크 스카이워커(Luke Skywalker)를 대조적으로 돋보이게 하는 역할을 완벽하게 하고 있는 인물이다.

## 32 ④

☐ impetuous a. (기질, 행동이) 성급한, 충동적인 ☐ grave a. 심각한, 엄숙한; 중대한 ☐ stunt v. 성장[발달]을 방해하다, 저해하다(=hinder) ☐ postpone v. 연기하다, 미루다 ☐ exaggerate v. 과장하다; 지나치게 강조하다 ☐ overstretch v. 너무 잡아 늘이다

충동적인 젊은 시절에 우리 인간은 오랫동안 성장을 저해할 수 있는 중대한 실수를 저지를 수 있다.

## 33 ②

☐ presage v. 예언하다, ~의 전조가 되다(=portend) ☐ subsume v. 포함[포괄]하다 ☐ malign v. 중상하다, 비방하다 ☐ expedite v. 촉진하다; (일을) 신속히 처리하다

지평선에서 피어나고 있던 먹구름은 사나운 폭풍의 시작을 알리는 전조였다.

## 34 ④

☐ iniquitous a. 매우 부당한(=unfair) ☐ scaffold n. 교수대, 처형대 ☐ minor offence 경범죄 ☐ invalid a. 효력 없는 ☐ bilious a. 곧 토할 것 같은, 보기 싫은; 화가 잔뜩 난 ☐ waspish a. 성질이 더러운, 화를 잘 내는

이 나라에서 한때 우리는 소매치기를 하거나 다른 경범죄를 저지른 미성년자들을 교수형에 처했던 매우 부당하고 무자비한 법률들을 갖고 있었다.

## 35 ①

☐ fraud n. 사기 ☐ ballot n. 무기명[비밀] 투표 ☐ chicanery n. 발뺌, 속임수(=trickery) ☐ initiative n. 계획 ☐ provision n. 공급, 제공 ☐ betterment n. 개량, 개선

전 대통령은 사기와 투표 속임수(조작)로 인해 현 대통령에게 그가 패배했다고 계속 말해왔다.

## 36 ②

☐ belittle v. 과소평가[경시]하다, 얕보다(=disparage) ☐ dismantle v. 분해[해체]하다 ☐ interrogate v. 심문[추궁]하다 ☐ subdue v. 진압하다

성격 유형에 따라 업무를 할당하는 것이 일반적인 경영 방식일지도 모르지만, 한편으로는 사람들을 얕잡아 보는 방법일 수도 있다.

## 37 ③

☐ hydrogen n. 수소 ☐ combustible a. 불이 잘 붙는, 가연성인(=flammable) ☐ furtive a. 은밀한 ☐ transparent a. 투명한 ☐ ethereal a. 아주 가벼운; 희박한

수소는 무색, 무취, 그리고 가연성이 매우 높다.

## 38 ②

☐ good for nothing 아무짝에도 쓸모없는 ☐ scalawag n. 말썽쟁이 ☐ necessitate v. 필요로 하다 ☐ foment v. (문제·폭력을) 조성[조장]하다(=instigate) ☐ quell v. 진압[평정]하다 ☐ conspire v. 음모[모의]를 꾸미다, 공모하다

아무짝에도 쓸모없는 말썽쟁이들이 반란을 선동했다.

## 39 ③

☐ belie v. 착각하게 만들다, 거짓[허위]임을 보여주다 ☐ turgid a. 복잡하고 따분한[이해하기 힘든](=bloated) ☐ underlying a. 근본적인 ☐ fickle a. 변덕스러운 ☐ discreet a. 신중한, 조심스러운 ☐ frivolous a. 경솔한; 시시한

진보적인 현대성을 투영하려는 마크롱(Macron)의 노력은 이해하기 어려운 근본적인 현실에 의해 허위로 판명되었다.

## 40 ④

☐ unrest n. (사회·정치적인) 불안[불만](=insecurity) ☐ humbug n. 사기, 협잡 ☐ allegory n. 우화, 풍자 ☐ exile n. 망명, 추방

정치적으로 불안한 상황에서 독재자는 종종 권력을 잡을 수 있다.

## 41 ②

☐ insecticide n. 살충제 ☐ judiciously ad. 현명하게(=wisely) ☐ natural agent 자연력 ☐ cooperatively ad. 협력하여, 협조적으로 ☐ impartially ad. 편견 없이, 공정하게 ☐ legally ad. 합법적으로

살충제는 자연 퇴치의 효과를 극대화하기 위해 현명하게 사용되어야 한다.

## 42
②

☐ invidious a. 불공정한, 부당한; 비위에 거슬리는(=malign)  ☐ agreeable a. 기분 좋은, 유쾌한  ☐ practical a. 실제적인; 실용적인; 효과적인  ☐ meticulous a. 지나치게 세심한, 매우 신중한

그 기자는 그 회사의 주장과 성과를 불공정한 방식으로 비교했다.

## 43
③

☐ access n. 접근, 출입; 접근[출입]하는 방법[권리]  ☐ complimentary a. 칭찬의, 찬사의; 무료의(=free)  ☐ luxurious a. 사치스러운, 호사스러운  ☐ discounted a. 할인된  ☐ unlimited a. 무제한적인

옥상 수영장 이용은 호텔 투숙객들에게 무료이며 외부 방문객은 하루 15달러이다.

## 44
④

☐ calamity n. 재난, 재해  ☐ befall v. (~의 신상에) 일어나다, 미치다, 닥치다  ☐ take hold 확고히 자리를 잡다, 효과가 강력해지다  ☐ stand apart 떨어져 있다, 분명히 다르다, 차이가 나다  ☐ contagion n. 전염, 감염  ☐ inspire v. 고무하다, 격려하다; (사상·감정 등을) 일어나게 하다  ☐ hulk n. 노후한 배, 폐선  ☐ fetid a. 악취가 나는, 구린(=rotten)  ☐ cozy a. 아늑한, 포근한  ☐ messy a. 지저분한, 엉망인  ☐ clean a. 깨끗한, 깔끔한

코로나바이러스가 위세를 떨치면서 관광객들에게 들이닥친 모든 재난 중에서도, 유람선과 관련한 재난은 유별났다. 쾌락의 궁전(즐거움으로 가득한 호화로운 배)이 감옥선으로 변함에 따라, 바다에서의 전염은 특별한 공포를 불러일으켰으며, 선상에서의 감염에 대한 소문이 악취가 진동하는 선실 사이에 WhatsApp을 통해 퍼져나갔다.

## 45
④

☐ aggregate v. 모이다(=gather into a group)  ☐ approximate a. 근사한, 대체[대략]의 v. 가까워지다, 가깝다  ☐ amount to (합계가) ~에 이르다[달하다]  ☐ abound v. 많이 있다, 가득하다

허드슨만(灣) 같은 일부 남쪽 지역에서, 곰은 얼음이 없는 여름과 가을 동안 육지로 모여든다.

## 46
②

☐ renowned a. 유명한, 명성 있는  ☐ stagger v. 비틀거리다; 망설이다, 주저하다, 동요하다(=stumble)  ☐ vaulted a. 둥근[아치 모양] 천장으로 된  ☐ archway n. 통로 위의 아치  ☐ run v. 달리다; 경영하다  ☐ roll down 굴러떨어지다, 흘러내리다  ☐ fall down 땅에 엎드리다; 넘어지다; 실패하다, 좌절되다

유명한 박물관장 쟈끄 소니에르(Jacques Sauniere)는 박물관 대화랑의 둥근 아치 모양 통로를 비틀거리며 걸었다.

## 47
④

☐ avalanche n. 눈사태(=massive snow), (산)사태; 쇄도  ☐ gusty wind 돌풍  ☐ nippy cold 매서운 추위  ☐ gushing water 용출수

수요일에, 제9순회 법원은 국기에 대한 맹세를 위헌이라 선언함으로써 눈사태 같은 비판을 유발했다.

## 48
②

☐ erratic a. 불규칙한, 일정치 않은; 변덕스러운(=mercurial)  ☐ catchy a. 재미있고 외기 쉬운; 사람의 마음을 끄는  ☐ electronic a. 전자의, 전자 활동에 의한  ☐ captivate v. ~의 마음을 사로잡다, 매혹하다  ☐ errant a. (정도에서) 벗어난, 잘못된  ☐ erroneous a. 잘못된, 틀린  ☐ typical a. 전형적인, 대표적인

주제곡의 일정치 않은 춤동작과 사람의 마음을 끄는 전자음은 모든 청자들의 마음을 사로잡았다.

## 49
①

☐ travesty n. 원작을 익살맞게 고친 것; 졸렬한 모조품, 서투른 모방(=parody)  ☐ tragedy n. 비극(적인 사건); 비극적인 이야기  ☐ comedy n. 희극; 희극적인 장면  ☐ romance n. 가공적인 이야기, 꿈 이야기; 연애 이야기

그가 소송 준비를 철저하게 하지 않는다면 그 재판은 서투른 모방에 불과할 것이다.

## 50
④

☐ bountiful a. 아낌없이 주는, 관대한, 인심 좋은; 풍부한(=abundant)  ☐ beautiful a. 아름다운, 고운; 훌륭한  ☐ hidden a. 숨은, 숨겨진; 비밀의  ☐ artificial a. 인공의, 인위적인; 부자연스러운

숲은 초창기 북아메리카 식민지에 풍부한 자원들을 제공했다.

## 51
①

☐ evolution n. 진화  ☐ precede v. 앞서다  ☐ expound upon 상세히 설명하다(=elucidate)  ☐ detest v. 몹시 싫어하다  ☐ substantiate v. 입증하다; 구체화하다  ☐ rebuff v. 거절하다

찰스 다윈(Charles Darwin)이 진화의 발달 단계를 상세하게 설명하긴 했지만, 일부 진화이론들은 찰스 다윈의 진화이론보다 역사적으로 앞섰다.

## 52
④

☐ syllabus n. 강의 요강, 개략  ☐ provisional a. 일시적인, 임시의(=temporary)  ☐ amendment n. 변경, 개선  ☐ concise a. 간결한,

간명한 □ reliable a. 의지가 되는, 믿음직한; 확실한 □ inflexible a. 불굴의; 강직한

이 강의 요강은 임시적이며 공지 없이 수정될 수도 있다.

## 53 ④

□ startle v. 깜짝 놀라게 하다 □ gloat over 기쁜[만족스러운] 듯이 바라보다, 혼자 싱글벙글하다(=grin at) □ specify v. 일일이 열거하다; 자세히[구체적으로] 말하다 □ unwanted a. 불필요한, 있으나 마나한, 쓸모없는 □ elude v. 피하다, 벗어나다 □ disregard v. 무시하다; 경시하다 □ exaggerate v. 과장하다, 허풍떨다

그녀는 자신이 실제로 하고 있는 행동이 그 술에 취한 남자가 중국인들을 쓸모없는 사람들이라고 말한 사실에 대해 혼자 히죽거리며 웃고 있는 것임을 깨닫고는 깜짝 놀랐다.

## 54 ②

□ on occasion 때때로 □ deliver v. 배달하다 □ smudge n. 오점; 얼룩(=blot) □ automated a. 자동화된 □ postal a. 우편의 □ sorting n. 분류 □ equipment n. 장비, 설비; 준비 □ dent n. 눌린 자국 □ trace n. 자취, 흔적 □ crack n. 갈라진 금, 균열

때때로 우편물이 자동화된 우편 분류 장비 때문에 얼룩이 묻은 채로 배달될지도 모른다.

## 55 ④

□ explicate v. (어떤 사상·문학 작품을) 설명[해석]하다(=elucidate) □ astronomer n. 천문학자 □ supernova n. 초신성(超新星) (pl.) (pl.-vae) □ enchant v. 황홀하게[넋을 잃게] 만들다 □ extricate v. 구해내다, 탈출시키다 □ eliminate v. 없애다, 제거[삭제]하다

소위 암흑에너지라는 것의 성질을 밝혀내려면 천문학자들은 10억 년 된 초신성들을 관찰해야 한다.

## 56 ③

□ dissenter n. 반대자 □ sedition n. 폭동 선동, 난동 교사(=mutiny) □ asylum n. 망명, 보호소 □ reciprocity n. 상호의존; 상호 관계 □ extradition n. 외국 범인의 인도, 본국 송환

비판론자들은 모디(Modi)의 힌두 국민 정부가 선동법과 다른 법적 무기를 사용하여 반체제 인사와 운동가들을 탄압하려 한다고 비난한다.

## 57 ①

□ venial a. 용서할 수 있는, 가벼운(=pardonable) □ unrepentant a. 뉘우치지 않는 □ besetting a. 끊임없이 붙어 다니는 □ inexpiable a. 속죄할 길 없는, 죄 많은 □ improbable a. 사실[있을 것] 같지 않은

거짓말을 하는 것은 가벼운 죄로서 간주되지만, 성경은 뉘우치지 않는 거짓말쟁이들은 결국 지옥에 가게 된다고 말한다.

## 58 ③

□ greed n. 탐욕, 큰 욕심(=avarice) □ annexation n. 부가; (특히 새 영토의) 합병 □ diversification n. 다양화, 다양성 □ invigoration n. 기운을 돋우기, 격려

민주당 의원들은 노동자들이 기업의 탐욕의 희생자라고 주장하는 반면, 공화당 의원들은 바이든(Biden) 행정부의 전기차 정책을 위한 추진 때문에 노동자들이 외면당했다고 주장한다.

## 59 ④

□ oath n. 맹세, 서약(=vow) □ swear an oath 맹세하다, 선서하다 □ query n. 질문 □ credit n. 신용, 신뢰 □ feast n. 연회, 잔치

어떤 상황이 됐든 맹세를 하는 것은 진지한 일이다.

## 60 ④

□ quiver v. 떨리다, 흔들리다(=vibrate) □ not so much A as B A라기보다는 B인 □ hail n. 우박 □ get wet 비에 젖다, 축축해지다 □ fog up 안개가 자욱이 끼다 □ tinkle v. 딸랑딸랑 소리를 내다

빗방울이 떨어지자 창문이 흔들리기 시작했는데 사실 그것은 비라기보다는 우박에 더 가까웠다. 그 우박은 모든 것을 다 부수어버리는 것 같아서 나의 신념도 부수어버리는 것 같았다.

## 61 ①

□ overt a. 명백한(=obvious) □ hostility n. 적대감, 적개심 □ wavering a. 흔들리는, 주저하는 □ onerous a. 아주 힘든; 부담되는 □ defensive a. 방어적인

마을 사람들은 낯선 사람들에게 명백한 적대감을 보였다.

## 62 ③

□ stint n. 할당된 일, 활동(=service) □ exile n. 망명; 추방 □ journey n. 여행, 여정 □ parole n. 가석방

그는 5년간의 홍콩 근무를 마치고 귀국한다.

## 63 ②

□ convulsion n. 경련, 경기(=spasm); 격동, 변동 □ condemnation n. 심한 비난, 견책, 책망 □ aversion n. 혐오, 반감, 싫음 □ contrition n. 회개; 죄를 뉘우침

그 환자는 그를 진정시키는 약을 먹기까지 반복해서 경련을 일으켰다.

돌려서 말할 필요가 없다. 바로 요점에 들어가라.

## 64 ④

☐ propensity n. 성질, 성향, 경향(=penchant) ☐ indifference n. 무관심한, 냉담한; 중요치 않은 ☐ preposterousness n. 불합리, 비상식 적임, 터무니없음 ☐ involvement n. 말려듦; 연루, 관련

"그러나 만약 우리가 (서로에 대한) 증오를 멈추지 않는다면, 우리는 결국 이 행성(지구)을 파괴하게 될 것입니다."라고 브니스키(Bninski)는 덧붙였다. 그녀는 미국이 '중동 분쟁의 모든 편에' 무기를 공급하는 죄를 범하고 있다고 말했다. "우리는 핵무기와 생화학무기를 세계에서 가장 많이 보유하고 있습니다. 우리는 수천 톤에 달하는 폭탄을 다른 나라에 떨어뜨릴 때도 우리 자신이 악으로 기울어진 성향이 있음을 보지 못하고 있습니다."

## 65 ④

☐ dislocate v. 혼란에 빠지다; 탈구하다, 쫓아내다 ☐ inexorable a. 냉혹한, 무정한, 가차 없는(=relentless) ☐ lash out against ~을 맹렬히 비난하다 ☐ repulsive a. 불쾌한, 혐오감을 일으키는 ☐ subversive a. 전복적인, 파괴적인 ☐ tremendous a. 엄청난, 거대한

세계화의 냉혹한 힘에 직면하여 쫓겨났다고 느끼면서, 그 노동자들은 이민자와 자유무역을 맹렬히 비난한다.

## 66 ③

☐ alpha thalassemia 알파 지중해빈혈 ☐ in utero (태아가 태어나기 전인) 자궁 내의[에] ☐ assuage v. 완화하다, 진정시키다(=relieve) ☐ blood transfusion 수혈 ☐ dismiss v. 묵살하다 ☐ accelerate v. 가속하다 ☐ surface v. 떠오르다, 부상하다, 표면화하다

자궁 안의 태아의 알파 지중해빈혈을 치료하기 위한 한 연구에서 자신의 줄기세포를 이용한 최초의 임신부가 되는 것에 대한 오바르(Obar)의 두 려움은 수혈이 원활히 이루어지는 것을 보자 빠르게 진정되었다.

## 67 ②

☐ rattled a. 당황한; 허둥지둥하는(=confused) ☐ enthusiastic a. 열광적인, 열성적인 ☐ disappointed a. 실망한, 낙담한 ☐ angry a. 성난, 화난

그가 경찰을 보았을 때 너무 당황해서 차를 인도로 향해 몰았다.

## 68 ③

☐ beat about the bush 요점을 피하다, 에둘러 말하다(=say indirectly) ☐ wander about the bush 덤불 속을 헤매다 ☐ probe the bush 덤불을 살피다 ☐ consult with others 다른 사람과 상의하다

## 69 ④

☐ expedient a. 편리한, 적당한(=useful) ☐ unfitting a. 부적당한, 어울리지 않는 ☐ impolite a. 버릇없는, 무례한 ☐ detrimental a. 해로운, 불리한

우리는 건설업자가 그 일을 마칠 때까지 그에게 돈을 지불하지 않는 것을 적절한 것이라고 생각했다.

## 70 ②

☐ unravel v. 풀다, 해명하다, 해결하다(=solve) ☐ create v. 창조하다, 창작하다; 야기하다 ☐ fold v. 접다, 접어 포개다 ☐ entangle v. 뒤얽히게 하다, 걸리게 하다

우리는 가상세계에서 살아가는 법을 배워가고 있다. 우리는 혼자서 가상의 바다를 항해하고, 가상의 미스터리를 밝히고, 가상의 고층건물을 설계할 수 있다.

## 71 ①

☐ intertwine v. 뒤얽히게 하다 ☐ in the wake of ~의 결과로 ☐ bereavement n. 사별, 가족[친지]의 사망(=death) ☐ crisis n. 위기, (흥망의) 갈림길; 중대 국면 ☐ atrocity n. 흉악, 잔인; 잔학 행위 ☐ resentment n. 노함, 분개, 원한

가족들이 사망한 후에 그녀와 그녀의 남동생들의 삶이 어떻게 뒤얽히게 되었는지를 나는 분명하게 알 수 있게 됐다.

## 72 ④

☐ luminous a. 빛나는, 밝은; 명료한; 총명한, 명석한(=clear) ☐ unsurpassed a. 이겨낼 사람 없는, 매우 뛰어난, 탁월한 ☐ lubricious a. 미끄러운; 붙잡기 곤란한; 불안정한 ☐ assiduous a. 부지런한, 근면한; 주도면밀한 ☐ circumscribed a. 한정된, 제한된

찰스 램(Charles Lamb)의 작품들은 심오한 학식을 드러내며, 영국 산문에서 독보적이라 할 만큼 명쾌한 스타일로 쓰여 있다.

## 73 ①

☐ crotchety a. 변덕스러운, 괴벽스러운; 외고집의(=petulant) ☐ virtuous a. 덕망 있는, 고결한; 정숙한 ☐ egalitarian a. 평등주의의 ☐ callous a. 굳은; 무감각한; 냉담한

별나고 나이 든 교수로부터 학업에 대한 평가 의견을 들을 것으로 기대하는 학생은 소수에 불과하다.

## 74        ④

☐ psychoanalysis n. 정신 분석 ☐ expose v. 드러내다; 폭로하다 ☐ chasm n. 틈, 차이, 간극(=gap) ☐ narrative n. 묘사, 서술 ☐ characteristic n. 특징, 특질 ☐ allusion n. 암시, 빗대어 말하기

정신 분석과 다양한 '생활 개혁' 운동에 영감을 받아, 내면의 삶과 심리적인 간극과 열정을 드러내는 것이 예술가들에게 중요한 관심사가 되었다.

## 75        ③

☐ gruesome a. 무시무시한, 소름 끼치는, 섬뜩한(=horrible) ☐ stick in one's mind 마음에 뚜렷이 남아있다 ☐ exhilarating a. 기분을 돋우는, 상쾌한 ☐ fiery a. 불의, 불길의; 불같은; 타는 듯한 ☐ wistful a. 탐내는 듯한; 그리워하는, 동경하는 듯한; 생각에 잠긴

에드거 앨런 포(Edgar Allen Poe)의 소설의 섬뜩한 세부 묘사들은 종종 사람들의 마음에서 사라지지 않는다(오래 남는다).

## 76        ③

☐ mutter n. 중얼거림 ☐ murmur n. 속삭임 ☐ reservation n. 보류; 의혹, 의구심(=doubt) ☐ persuasive a. 설득력 있는 ☐ protest n. 항의, 시위 ☐ cheer v. 응원하다, 환호하다 ☐ booking n. 예약; 장부 기입 ☐ reason n. 이유, 까닭, 사유 ☐ instigation n. 선동, 부추김

이런저런 말들과 의구심들이 있었지만, 시장이 설득력 있는 연설을 했을 때 모두들 그들의 항의는 잊은 듯했고 시장을 응원했다.

## 77        ①

☐ tyranny n. 학대; 폭정, 전제정치; 지배(=domination) ☐ bossiness n. 두목행세, 위세 부림 ☐ importance n. 중요성, 중대성 ☐ evilness n. 악, 불선, 사악

뉴욕의 패션 산업은 프랑스 디자인의 지배에서 완전히 벗어나지 못하고 있다.

## 78        ③

☐ publicize v. (사람들에게) 알리다, 공표하다 ☐ attain v. (노력 끝에) 달성하다 ☐ full-fledged a. (새가) 깃털이 완전히 다 난; (빠짐없이) 완전한(=comprehensive) ☐ normalization n. 정상화 ☐ pandemic n. 세계적인 유행병 ☐ superlative a. 최상의 ☐ relative a. 상대적인 ☐ tentative a. 잠정적인

한국은 2022년에 세계적인 유행병의 위기에서 벗어나 완전한 경제 정상화를 달성하겠다는 목표를 공표하였다.

## 79        ④

☐ rummage v. 뒤지다, 샅샅이 찾다; 샅샅이 조사하다; 검사하다 (=search) ☐ refuse v. 거절하다; 받아들이지 않다 ☐ arrange v. 배열하다, 정리하다; 가지런히 하다 ☐ gather v. 모으다, 거두어들이다; 채집하다

그가 등을 돌렸을 때, 어머니께서는 내게 의자를 가져오게 하고 그의 소장품을 샅샅이 뒤졌다.

## 80        ③

☐ affinity n. 친밀감; (밀접한) 관련성(=closeness) ☐ daintiness n. 우미함, 맛이 좋음 ☐ queerness n. 괴상함, 괴벽 ☐ peculiarity n. 기이한 특징; 기벽

스칸디나비아 언어들 간에는 밀접한 관련성이 존재한다.

## 81        ③

☐ precedent n. 전례, 관례; 판례(=guide) ☐ controversy n. 논쟁, 논의 ☐ preview n. 미리 보기, 사전 검토 ☐ record n. 기록, 등록

이 판결은 앞으로 있을 유사한 성질의 사건들에 전례를 세웠다.

## 82        ③

☐ extort v. 갈취하다; (정보를) 억지로 얻어내다, 강요하다(=wrest) ☐ forge v. 구축하다; 위조하다 ☐ obtain v. 얻다, 구하다 ☐ rechristen v. 다시 명명하다, 개명하다

그는 딸에게 윽박질러 그동안 만났던 남자들의 이름과 신상에 대해 말하게 했다.

## 83        ②

☐ consort with 교제하다, 사귀다, 어울리다(=associate with) ☐ abide by 준수하다, 지키다 ☐ interfere with 간섭하다, 방해하다 ☐ stand for 나타내다, 상징하다

우리는 종종 사람들을 그들이 교제하는 친구를 보고 판단한다.

## 84        ①

☐ disguise v. 변장하다; (사실 등을) 꾸미다, 숨기다; (의도·감정 따위를) 감추다 ☐ invasion n. 침입, 침략 ☐ engage in 착수하다, 시작하다 ☐ campaign n. (일련의) 군사 행동; 출정, 종군 ☐ subterfuge n. 구실, 핑계; 속임수(=deception) ☐ warfare n. 전투, 교전; 전쟁 ☐ hostility n. 적의, 적개심; 적대행위 ☐ persuasion n. 설득, 신념

연합군은 침공 계획을 숨기기 위해 노르망디 상륙에 앞서 기만 작전을 펼쳤다.

## 85      ①

☐ practitioner n. 개업자, 전문가; 개업의(醫), 변호사(=professional) ☐ proprietor n. 소유자, 경영자 ☐ precursor n. 선구자, 선봉 ☐ personnel n. 총인원, 전사원, 전대원

지난 한 해 동안 우리들은 새로운 종류의 전쟁의 발생을 지켜봤다. 즉 소규모 테러인데, 이것은 특정 지역의 수준에서 발발하는 소규모의 테러로 정의할 수 있고, 그것을 수행하는 사람들은 가장 크거나 가장 극적인 작전들 대신 성공할 가능성이 있는 작전들을 선택한다.

## 86      ④

☐ treachery n. 반역, 변절, 배반; 불안정한 것(=disloyalty) ☐ faith n. 신념; 신뢰; 약속 ☐ malice n. 악의, 앙심, 적의 ☐ violence n. 격렬함; 폭력, 난폭; 폭행

이후 8개월 동안 올리버(Oliver)는 배신과 사기의 체계적인 과정의 희생자였다.

## 87      ④

☐ deceitful a. 기만적인, 부정직한 ☐ doctor v. (문서·증거 따위를) 조작하다(=fabricate) ☐ master v. 숙달하다 ☐ stipulate v. 규정[명기]하다 ☐ extrapolate v. 추론하다, 추정하다

부정직한 그 연구자는 자신의 연구 논문에서 데이터를 조작했다는 비난을 받았는데, 이는 윤리적으로 문제가 되는 것이다.

## 88      ②

☐ benevolent a. 자비로운, 인정 많은(=generous) ☐ unkind a. 불친절한 ☐ malevolent a. 악의 있는, 심술궂은 ☐ vulgar a. 저속한

그는 자비로운 왕이 다스리는 평온한 국가에 살게 되어 기뻤다.

## 89      ②

☐ vertigo n. 현기증, 어지러움; 혼란(=dizziness) ☐ curiosity n. 호기심; 진기한 것 ☐ invigoration n. 기운 나게 함, 고무, 격려 ☐ vestige n. 자취, 흔적, 표적

그 아치는 적어도 내 위로 50미터였으며 나는 몇 년 만에 처음으로 현기증을 느꼈다.

## 90      ③

☐ ecological a. 생태학의, 생태학적인 ☐ holistic a. 전체론의, 전체론적인(=complete) ☐ solution n. (문제 등의) 해결; 해법 ☐ notable a. 주목할 만한; 두드러진, 현저한 ☐ impartial a. 치우치지 않은, 공평한 ☐ concrete a. 유형의; 구체적인

생태학적 문제들은 대개 전체론적인 해결책을 필요로 한다.

## 91      ④

☐ quell v. 진압하다, 평정하다, 억누르다(=suppress) ☐ arouse v. 깨우다, 자극하다, 환기하다 ☐ fathom v. (마음을) 통찰하다, 헤아리다 ☐ saturate v. 푹 적시다, 과잉공급하다

정부의 안심시키는 말이 대중의 의심을 가라앉히는 데 아무런 역할을 하지 못했다.

## 92      ②

☐ statute n. 법규, 법령(=law) ☐ statute of limitations 출소기한법, 공소시효 ☐ limit n. 한계(선), 극한, 한도; 제한 ☐ license n. 면허, 인가; 승낙, 허락 ☐ list n. 목록, 명부, 명단, 표, 일람표

사제들에 대한 성희롱 고발이 전국적으로 빗발치고 있는 가운데, 일리노이주는 이러한 사건들의 공소시효를 연장하여, 검사로 하여금 피해자가 18세가 된 후 20년 동안에도 기소할 수 있도록 했다.

## 93      ②

☐ mordant a. 신랄한, 독설적인, 통렬한(=sarcastic) ☐ critic n. 비평가, 평론가 ☐ far-reaching a. 광범위한, 엄청난, 어마어마한 ☐ impartial a. 편견 없는, 공정한 ☐ prudent a. 신중한, 조심성 있는, 세심한 ☐ formidable a. 무서운; 만만찮은, 가공할

그는 자신이 광범위한 영향력을 가진 신랄한 비평가임을 증명해 보였다.

## 94      ①

☐ ad n. 광고 ☐ fragrance n. 향수, 향기 ☐ contemporary a. 현대의; 동시대의 ☐ rendition n. 연출(=interpretation) ☐ classical myth 그리스·로마 신화 ☐ Narcissus n. 나르시소스(샘물에 비친 자기 자신의 모습을 연모하여 수선화가 되었다는 미모의 청년) ☐ example n. 예, 본보기, 전형 ☐ criterion n. 기준, 표준 ☐ reference n. 참고문헌

캘빈 클라인(Calvin Klien)의 캘빈 클라인 남성 향수 광고는 그리스·로마 신화에 나오는 나르시소스(Narcissus)의 완벽한 현대판 해석이다.

## 95      ①

☐ inextricable a. 탈출할 수 없는; 해결할 수 없는; 뒤얽힌; 풀리지 않는(=unseparable) ☐ problematic a. 문제의, 의문의 ☐ inevitable a. 불가피한; 필연적인 ☐ deep-rooted a. 깊이 뿌리박힌, 뿌리 깊은

성(gender)에 관련된 문제와 성적 특성(sexuality)에 관련된 문제는 각각이 다른 나머지 하나의 관점에서만 표현될 수 있다는 점 때문에 서로 분리할 수 없지만, 그럼에도 그 둘은 같은 문제가 아니다.

## 96 ③

□ derange v. 흐트러뜨리다, 어지럽히다(=disturb) □ delay v. 늦추다, 지체시키다 □ duplicate v. 두 배로 하다; 복사하다, 복제하다 □ influence v. 영향을 미치다

갑작스러운 병 때문에 우리의 여행 계획이 흐트러졌다.


## 97 ②

□ eager a. 열망하는, 간절히 바라는 □ swoon v. 기절하다, 졸도하다 (=pass out) □ come up 생기다, 발생하다; 언급하다 □ fall down 부족하다 □ set in 시작하다

수술이 흥미진진하게 들리지만, 나는 그런 수술과정을 사진 촬영하는 동안 기절하지 않기를 간절히 바랐다.


## 98 ④

□ in the shadow of ~에 아주 접근하여, ~의 영향 아래 □ overbearing a. 고압적인, 남을 지배하려 드는(=domineering) □ unreliable a. 믿을[신뢰할] 수 없는 □ heinous a. 악랄한, 극악무도한 □ negligible a. 무시해도 될 정도의

대만은 우크라이나와 마찬가지로 오랫동안 크고 위압적인 이웃국의 영향 아래서 살아왔다.


## 99 ①

□ testimony n. 증거; 공식 선언[발표], 공표 □ oscillate v. 진동하다; 흔들리다, 동요하다(=vacillate) □ lingering a. 질질 끄는, 망설이는 □ duplicate v. 복사[복제]하다, 사본을 만든다 □ authenticate v. 진짜임을 증명하다 □ perpetuate v. 영구화하다, 영속시키다

그 나라의 이슬람과의 불안한 관계는 오래 지속된 편견과 관용을 요구하는 흔들리는 성명에 의해 강조되었다.


## 100 ④

□ prurient a. 호색의, 음란한; 외설한(=salacious) □ gauche a. 서투른 □ protean a. 변화무쌍한 □ brutal a. 잔혹한, 악랄한

그 영화에서 일부 선정적인 장면들은 사람들이 나쁜 동기로 볼 수 있다는 이유에서 결국 삭제되었다.

| | | | | | | | | | |
|---|---|---|---|---|---|---|---|---|---|
| **01** ② | **02** ① | **03** ③ | **04** ④ | **05** ① | **06** ④ | **07** ② | **08** ① | **09** ② | **10** ④ |
| **11** ② | **12** ② | **13** ④ | **14** ③ | **15** ① | **16** ② | **17** ② | **18** ③ | **19** ① | **20** ① |
| **21** ④ | **22** ④ | **23** ① | **24** ③ | **25** ③ | **26** ① | **27** ③ | **28** ① | **29** ① | **30** ③ |
| **31** ④ | **32** ① | **33** ② | **34** ② | **35** ④ | **36** ① | **37** ① | **38** ③ | **39** ② | **40** ① |
| **41** ① | **42** ① | **43** ① | **44** ② | **45** ① | **46** ② | **47** ③ | **48** ② | **49** ③ | **50** ① |
| **51** ① | **52** ① | **53** ① | **54** ③ | **55** ④ | **56** ② | **57** ② | **58** ① | **59** ④ | **60** ③ |
| **61** ④ | **62** ③ | **63** ① | **64** ② | **65** ② | **66** ① | **67** ② | **68** ① | **69** ④ | **70** ① |
| **71** ③ | **72** ① | **73** ④ | **74** ① | **75** ③ | **76** ② | **77** ③ | **78** ① | **79** ① | **80** ③ |
| **81** ① | **82** ② | **83** ① | **84** ③ | **85** ③ | **86** ② | **87** ③ | **88** ① | **89** ④ | **90** ③ |
| **91** ② | **92** ④ | **93** ③ | **94** ③ | **95** ② | **96** ① | **97** ① | **98** ① | **99** ① | **100** ③ |

## 01 ②

☐ crowbar n. 쇠지레 ☐ dislodge v. 이동시키다, 제거하다(=dislocate) ☐ derange v. 흐트러뜨리다, 어지럽히다 ☐ disillusion v. ~의 환영을 깨우치다 ☐ collaborate v. 공동으로 일하다, 합작하다

그 일꾼은 쇠지레를 이용해서 무거운 돌을 벽에서 떨어뜨렸다.

## 02 ①

☐ exploit v. 이용하다 ☐ sully v. 훼손하다, 더럽히다(=blemish) ☐ sneer v. 비웃다, 냉소하다 ☐ distend v. 넓히다 ☐ bolster v. 지지하다, 강화하다

시장이 자신의 지위를 이용해 아랍인들을 차별했다는 주장은 시장의 명성을 더럽히려는 의도에서 나온 것이었다.

## 03 ③

☐ squarely ad. 정면으로, 정확하게(=directly) ☐ bring under control 억누르다, 억제하다 ☐ bankruptcy n. 파산 ☐ rapidly ad. 빠르게, 신속히 ☐ bravely ad. 용감하게; 훌륭히 ☐ comprehensively ad. 포괄적으로

부채 문제는 정면으로 대응해야 하며 적절한 파산 수단을 이용하여 억제되어야 한다.

## 04 ④

☐ weed out 제거하다, 뽑아버리다 ☐ selection n. 선발, 선택, 선정 ☐ separation n. 분리, 떨어짐, 이탈 ☐ conversion n. 변환, 전환 ☐ elimination n. 제거, 배제, 삭제

자연 속의 동물 집단에서 약한 개체들이 제거되는 현상은 일부 빅토리아 시대 사람들에게는 제국주의에 대한 충분한 변명처럼 보였다.

## 05 ①

☐ evoke v. ~를 일으키다, 자아내다(=elicit) ☐ validate v. 입증하다, 인증하다 ☐ vaunt v. 자랑하다, 허풍떨다 ☐ evade v. 피하다, 모면하다

그녀는 부모님으로부터 동정심을 자아내기 위해 뭐든 다 했다.

## 06 ④

☐ heyday n. 절정, 전성기(=golden age) ☐ showboat n. 연예선(船); 남의 이목을 끌려는 사람 ☐ prosperous a. 번영하는, 성공한 ☐ infancy n. 어릴 때, 유년기; 초기 ☐ revival n. 소생, 재생, 부활 ☐ summer voyage 여름철 항해

전성기 동안, 연예선은 인기가 있었고 일반적으로 번창했다.

## 07 ②

☐ unconstrained a. 구속[속박]을 받지 않는, 자발적인(=independent) ☐ prosperous a. 번영하는, 부유한 ☐ renowned a. 유명한, 명성 있는 ☐ tolerant a. 관대한, 아량 있는

어린 나이에 구속받지 않고 자신의 삶을 통제하려 애쓰는 것은 어렵다.

## 08 ①

☐ adumbrate v. ~의 윤곽을 나타내다; 막연히 나타내다; 예시하다 (=outline) ☐ amend v. 고치다, 개선하다; 수정하다 ☐ reveal v. 드러내다, 밝히다; 누설하다 ☐ contrive v. 고안하다, 연구하다; 설계하다

건축가 노먼 포스터(Norman Foster)는 지하철 출입구에 대한 자신의 생각을 개략적으로 말했다.

그는 자신의 어머니가 편찮으셨다는 것을 알았지만, 그녀에게 편지를 쓸 만큼의 예의도 없었다.

## 09 ②

☐ stern a. 엄격한, 근엄한(=serious) ☐ tight-lipped a. 말을 잘 안 하는, 입을 꽉 다문 ☐ survey v. 살펴보다 ☐ barren a. 척박한, 불모의 ☐ strange a. 이상한; 낯선 ☐ pedantic a. 현학적인, 박식한 체하는 ☐ vulnerable a. 취약한, 연약한

낯선 석상 하나가 바다를 등진 채 절벽 위에 서 있다. 눈앞에 있는 척박한 땅을 살펴보면서 근엄하게 입을 굳게 다문 그의 표정은 아무것도 드러내지 않는다.

## 10 ④

☐ exodus n. 탈출, 이동; 출국, 이주(=escape) ☐ renew v. 새롭게 하다, 일신하다; 다시 시작하다 ☐ ongoing a. 전진하는; 진행 중의 ☐ reform n. 개혁 ☐ dash n. 돌진, 돌격; 충돌 ☐ menace n. 위협, 협박 ☐ surge n. 큰 파도; 쇄도, 돌진; 동요, 고조

그 나라의 가장 명석한 고등학생들의 이탈은 고등교육 개혁의 고질적인 문제에 관한 방송매체의 논의를 재개시켰다.

## 11 ②

☐ destabilize v. 불안정하게 하다, ~을 동요시키다 ☐ sovereign a. 주권을 갖는, 자치의, 독립의 ☐ contrived a. 부자연스러운, 꾸며낸 (=concocted) ☐ boundary n. 경계, 영역 ☐ potential a. 잠재적인, 가능성 있는 ☐ random a. 되는 대로의, 임의의 ☐ unexpected a. 예기치 않은, 돌발적인

러시아를 통해 우리가 확인할 수 있는 것은 한 독립 국가를 불안정하게 하고 고용된 첩보원들을 이용하여 국경선 건너편에 인위적인 위기를 만들어내려는 불법적이고 비합법적인 노력이다.

## 12 ②

☐ drooping a. 늘어진; 눈을 내리깐, 고개 숙인; 풀이 죽은(=weary) ☐ glittering a. 번쩍이는, 빛나는, 화려한 ☐ dry a. 마른, 물기 없는; 가문 ☐ soaring a. 급상승하는, 치솟는

나머지 하나는 낮은 곳에 위치한 정사각형의 창문으로 낡은 쇠창살들이 둘러져 있었는데, 그 창살들은 거칠게 깎여 가느다란 대를 이루고 있었으며, 거기에는 축 처진 잎들이 붙어 있었다.

## 13 ④

☐ propriety n. 타당; 교양, 예의 바름(=decency) ☐ apathy n. 냉담; 무관심 ☐ eulogy n. 찬사; 송덕문, 칭송 ☐ posterity n. 자손, 후세

## 14 ③

☐ grisly a. 섬뜩한, 소름 끼치게 하는, 무서운(=gruesome) ☐ make someone's hair stand on end 소름 끼치게 하다, 겁나게 하다, 머리가 쭈뼛하게 하다 ☐ inextricable a. 탈출할 수 없는; 풀 수 없는, 해결할 수 없는 ☐ knotty a. (복잡하게) 얽히고설킨 ☐ truculent a. 반항적인, 약간 공격적인

그 끔찍한 살인 현장에 노련한 형사들조차도 머리카락이 쭈뼛해졌다.

## 15 ①

☐ vituperative a. 악담하는, 욕질하는; 독설을 퍼붓는(=vitriolic) ☐ biting a. 가슴을 후비는[찌르는] 듯한, 통렬한 ☐ enthusiast n. 열광적인 팬 ☐ putative a. 추정되는, 추정상의 ☐ parlous a. 아주 불확실한, 위태로운 ☐ equivocal a. 모호한, 애매한

새 영화에 대한 평론가의 독설은 너무 통렬해서 영화 애호가들 사이에 뜨거운 논쟁을 불러일으킬 정도였다.

## 16 ②

☐ brandish v. 휘두르다; 과시하다(=wave) ☐ sharpen v. 날카롭게 하다; 뾰족하게 하다, 깎다, 갈다 ☐ sell v. 팔다, 매도하다, 판매를 촉진시키다 ☐ break v. 깨뜨리다, 쪼개다, 부수다; 자르다

나는 몇 명의 젊은 남자들이 길에서 칼을 휘두르고 있는 것을 보았다.

## 17 ②

☐ in light of ~에 비추어, ~를 생각하면 ☐ puerile a. 유치한, 바보 같은(=inane) ☐ innate a. 타고난, 선천적인; 내재적인 ☐ intricate a. 뒤얽힌, 얽히고설킨; 복잡한 ☐ incompatible a. 양립하지 않는, 모순된; 조화하지 않는

우리가 강조한 사실들을 생각하면, 이 진술들은 바보 같아서 오직 모르고 있는 경우에만 받아들여진다.

## 18 ③

☐ thoroughly ad. 대단히, 완전히 ☐ disabuse v. 미혹을 풀어주다, 오해를 풀어주다 ☐ residual a. 남은; 잔여의 ☐ nonchalant a. 무관심한, 냉담한; 태연한, 냉정한 ☐ adamant a. 단호한, 물러서지 않는 ☐ disenchant v. ~을 미몽(迷夢)에서 깨어나게 하다; ~의 마법을 풀다 ☐ convert v. 전환하다

사무엘 베케트(Samuel Beckett)의 작품들을 읽은 후, 우리 학생들은 행복한 결말에 대한 일말의 믿음을 완전히 버리게 되었다.

## 19 ①

☐ declaration n. 선언(서), 포고 ☐ all-out a. 온 힘을 다한, 전면적인 (=overall) ☐ strike n. 파업, (노동) 쟁의 ☐ hard-up a. 결핍한; 쪼들리는 ☐ run-down a. 황폐한; 지친, 병든 ☐ opposed a. 반대의, 대항하는; 대립된

노동자들의 총파업 선언은 경영진으로 하여금 근로 조건을 개선하도록 했다.

## 20 ①

☐ clinch v. 끝을 구부리다; 결말을 내다, 매듭짓다(=decide v. 결정하다, 결심하다) ☐ incline v. 기울이다; (마음을) 내키게 하다 ☐ depend v. 의존하다, 의지하다; 믿다, 신뢰하다 ☐ suspend v. 매달다, 중지하다

해야 할 일이 많지만 아마도 올 2/4분기가 끝날 때까지 우리는 거래를 매듭지어야 할 것이다.

## 21 ④

☐ risque a. 외설스러운, 음란한(=lewd) ☐ garrulous a. 수다스러운, 말이 많은 ☐ incessant a. 끊임없는, 쉴 새 없는 ☐ atypical a. 틀에 박히지 않은; 이상한

그 코미디언의 외설스러운 유머는 한계를 뛰어넘었다.

## 22 ④

☐ smug a. 의기양양한, 우쭐해하는(=complacent) ☐ modest a. 겸손한; 점잖은 ☐ provocative a. 도발적인, 자극하는 ☐ shabby a. 초라한; 누더기를 걸친

일반적으로 사람들은 어떤 것에 대해 더 적은 돈을 지불했을 때 스스로에게 상당한 만족감을 느낀다. 당신은 사람들이 당신보다 더 적은 돈을 지불했다고 말하면서 의기양양한 표정을 짓는 것을 본 적이 있을 것이다.

## 23 ①

☐ precision n. 정확, 정밀 ☐ implacable a. 누그러뜨릴 수 없는, 냉혹한; 확고한, 바꿀 수 없는(=inexorable) ☐ commutable a. 교환[전환]할 수 있는; 통근 가능한 ☐ distinguished a. 유명한, 성공한 ☐ rhythmic a. 율동적인, 리드미컬한

디지털 이미지는 너무나 정확해서 그것들은 사실상 바꿀 수 없다.

## 24 ③

☐ countenance v. 지지[동의]하다, 인정하다, 찬성하다(=sanction) ☐ referendum n. 국민투표, 총선거 ☐ constitution n. 헌법 ☐

☐ disavow v. 거부[부인]하다 ☐ obviate v. (문제·필요성을) 제거[배제]하다 ☐ terminate v. 끝나다, 종료되다, 마무리하다

나는 총리가 헌법에 의거한 국민투표를 인정하지 않을 것이라고 생각한다.

## 25 ③

☐ yield to 생기게 하다, 산출하다; 양보하다, 굴복하다, 포기하다(=give in to) ☐ receive v. 받다, 수취하다; 얻다 ☐ answer v. 대답하다, 회답하다 ☐ respond to ~에 대답하다, 응하다; 반응하다

스미스(Smith) 씨는 반대당의 요구에 굴복하기를 거부했다.

## 26 ①

☐ chorus n. 합창 ☐ horn n. (자동차) 경적 ☐ pour v. 마구 쏟아지다, 붓다, 쏟다 ☐ banner n. 현수막 ☐ bullhorn n. 확성기 ☐ exuberant a. 열광적인, 신이 난(=exhilarated) ☐ exclaim v. 소리치다, 외치다 ☐ abstemious a. 자제하는; 검소한 ☐ pedantic a. 현학적인, 박식한 체하는 ☐ mendacious a. 허위인

도시는 점점 커지는 자동차 경적의 합창으로 응답했다. 길을 따라 깃발, 현수막 또는 확성기를 들고 상점과 아파트 건물에서 사람들이 쏟아져 나오는 것이 보였다. 카림(Karim)과 그의 친구들은 한껏 신이 나 있었다. "이번 경기는 월드컵 최고의 경기였어!" 카림이 외쳤다.

## 27 ③

☐ seizure n. 붙잡음; 체포; 몰수, 압류; 강탈 ☐ prelude n. 전주곡, 서곡; 서막(=foreshadowing) ☐ victimization n. 정신적인 피해 ☐ alliance n. 동맹, 연합 ☐ sacrifice n. 희생; 희생적 행위

납치범에 의한 비행기의 나포는 재앙의 서막이었다.

## 28 ①

☐ backbreaking a. 대단히 힘든 ☐ whet v. 갈다, 연마하다(=hone) ☐ craft n. 기능, 솜씨 ☐ ballyhoo v. 요란하게 선전하다 ☐ connive v. 못 본 체하다 ☐ garner v. 모으다

가족농장에서 여러 해 힘들게 수고한 후에 폴로(Polo)는 예술가와 연기자로서의 솜씨를 갈고닦기 시작했다.

## 29 ①

☐ fragmentary a. 파편의; 조각난, 단편적인, 부분적인(=incomplete) ☐ incomparable a. 견줄 데 없는, 비교가 되지 않는 ☐ indispensable a. 불가결의, 없어서는 안 될, 절대 필요한 ☐ invaluable a. 값을 헤아릴 수 없는, 평가할 수 없는, 매우 귀중한

인류는 고대 시대에 대한 단편적인 역사만을 가지고 있을 뿐이다.

## 30 ③

☐ interdict v. 금하다, 막다; 방해하다(=forbid) ☐ designate v. 가리키다, 명시하다; 지명하다 ☐ interrogate v. 질문하다, 심문하다, 문의하다 ☐ announce v. 알리다, 발표하다, 공고하다

우리는 세계 안보와 안전을 위해 대량 살생무기의 사용을 금지해야만 한다.

## 31 ④

☐ mealy-mouthed a. (자신의 생각을) 솔직히 말하지 않는(=indirect) ☐ bureaucracy n. 관료 (체제) ☐ allure n. 매력 ☐ pragmatic a. 실용적인 ☐ no-nonsense a. 간단명료한 ☐ talkative a. 수다스러운 ☐ capable a. 유능한 ☐ imitative a. 모방적인

유권자들이 (자신의 생각을) 솔직히 말하지 않는 정치인들과 소모적인 관료주의에 질려갈 때, 대통령 집무실에서 근무하는 실용적이고 효율적이며 현실적인 관료에 대한 매력은 강해진다.

## 32 ①

☐ debonair a. 멋지고 당당한; 정중한(=refined) ☐ domineering a. 지배[군림]하려 드는 ☐ reckless a. 무모한, 신중하지 못한; 난폭한 ☐ contemptuous a. 경멸하는, 업신여기는 ☐ impervious a. 영향받지 않는, 좌우되지 않는

그의 부모는 피츠제럴드(Fitzgerald)의 소설에 등장하는 인물과 같았다. 그의 아버지는 유대인이었고, 멋지고 당당했으며, 거만했다.

## 33 ②

☐ mythical a. 신화 속에 나오는 ☐ figure n. (언급된 유형의) 인물 ☐ jolly a. 즐거운, 유쾌한, 명랑한(=jovial) ☐ generous a. 후한, 너그러운 ☐ penitent a. 뉘우치는, 참회하는 ☐ perfunctory a. 형식적인, 마지못한

산타클로스는 유쾌한 것으로 잘 알려진 신화 속 인물일지도 모른다.

## 34 ②

☐ refulgent a. 환히 빛나는(=radiant) ☐ disillusioned a. 환멸을 느낀 ☐ inscrutable a. 헤아릴 수 없는, 불가해한 ☐ insightful a. 통찰력 있는, 식견 있는

화창한 날씨는 당신이 빛나는 미소를 짓게 할 수도 있다.

## 35 ④

☐ incumbent n. (공적인 직위의) 재임자 ☐ wield v. (권력·권위 등을) 행사하다 ☐ animus n. 반감, 적대감(=animosity) ☐ fervor n. 열렬, 열정 ☐ levity n. 경솔, 경박 ☐ chicanery n. 교묘한 속임수

전 대통령은 현 대통령이 당파적 적개심으로 자신에게 사법권을 휘두른다고 비난하면서 현 대통령을 탓했다.

## 36 ①

☐ immure v. 감금하다, 투옥하다, 가두다(=incarcerate) ☐ hostage n. 인질 ☐ nauseate v. 역겹게 하다 ☐ titillate v. 자극하다, 흥분시키다 ☐ expropriate v. 수용하다; 도용하다

환기가 안 되는 어두운 쪽방에 감금된 채 인질들은 6개월 동안 석방되기만을 기다렸다.

## 37 ①

☐ provident a. 장래를 준비하는[앞날에 대비하는](=prudent) ☐ insure v. (위험 등에서) 지키다, 안전하게 하다 ☐ precious a. 귀중한, 값비싼 ☐ predatory a. 포식성의 ☐ pronounced a. 확연한; 단호한

그는 늘 미래에 대비하는 신중한 태도로 이런 종류의 손해로부터 자신을 지켰다.

## 38 ③

☐ moot a. (가능성이 적으므로) 고려할 가치가 없는(=irrelevant) ☐ indispensable a. 없어서는 안 될, 필수적인 ☐ irresponsible a. 무책임한 ☐ inevitable a. 불가피한, 필연적인

이전의 기술 발전은 한때 저널리즘 산업에 필수적이었던 수많은 직업을 고려할 가치가 없는 것으로 만들었다.

## 39 ②

☐ banish v. 추방하다, 유형[유배]을 보내다(=exile) ☐ sneer v. 비웃다, 조롱하다 ☐ emigrate v. 이민을 가다 ☐ deliberate v. 숙고[숙의]하다, 신중히 생각하다

프리고진(Prigozhin)이 벨라루스로 추방된 이후 바그너 그룹의 미래에 대한 의문이 제기돼 왔다.

## 40 ①

☐ evanescent a. 사라지는(=evaporating) ☐ touch n. 느낌, 솜씨; 특징 ☐ whimsy n. 기상천외함, 기발함 ☐ stifling a. 숨 막힐 듯한 ☐ conjectural a. 추측의 ☐ lethargic a. 혼수상태의; 무기력한

이 이야기에는 번역에서는 잃게 되는 곧 사라져 버리는 기상천외한 느낌이 있다.

## 41 ①
☐ propitiate v. 달래다; 비위 맞추다(=appease) ☐ oracle n. 신탁 ☐ humiliate v. 굴욕감을 주다 ☐ assimilate v. 동화되다 ☐ convert v. 개종시키다

신들은 달래야 했고, 신들의 노여움을 덜기 위해 사제와 신탁과 관련된 많은 산업이 생겨났다.

## 42 ①
☐ swarthy a. 거무스레한, 가무잡잡한(=dark) ☐ cute a. 귀여운, 매력적인 ☐ healthy a. 건강한, 건강상 좋은 ☐ silly a. 어리석은, 분별없는

그의 얼굴은 넓적하고 거무스레했다.

## 43 ①
☐ acquaint v. ~에게 알려주다, 전하다 ☐ amenity n. (pl.) 쾌적한 오락[문화, 편의] 시설(=facility) ☐ canteen n. 물통; 매점; 간이식당 ☐ installation n. 설치, 설비 ☐ deficit n. 적자, 부족액

또한, 각 홀의 특징과 편의 시설을 더 잘 알 수 있도록 링크와 추가 정보가 우리 웹사이트에서 제공된다.

## 44 ②
☐ document n. 문서, 서류, 기록 ☐ provenance n. 출처, 기원 (=origin) ☐ copyright n. 저작권 ☐ relevance n. 관련성 ☐ authenticity n. 진짜임, 신빙성

홍콩 대학에서 열린 "중국, 동남아시아, 베트남 전쟁에서의 새로운 증거"에 관한 회의에서 처음 제시된 그 문서는 그 문서의 기원(출처)과 중요성에 대해 일부 중국과 베트남 참가자들 사이에 상당한 논란을 불러일으켰다.

## 45 ①
☐ sober a. 수수한, 소박한 ☐ austere a. 엄격한, 준엄한; 간소한; 꾸밈없는(=plain) ☐ splendid a. 빛나는, 화려한; 멋진 ☐ ominous a. 불길한, 나쁜 징조의 ☐ decorative a. 장식(용)의, 장식적인

그 교회의 실내 장식은 수수하고 단조롭지만 매우 훌륭하다.

## 46 ②
☐ eulogy n. 찬사; 송덕문, 추도 연설 ☐ lugubrious a. 가여운, 불쌍한,

우울한(=excessively sad) ☐ giggle v. 낄낄 웃다, 키득거리다 ☐ uncertain a. 불분명한, 모호한 ☐ threatening a. 위협적인, 협박적인 ☐ repulsive a. 역겨운, 쫓아버리는; 냉정한

해리(Harry)가 그의 개의 장례식에서 읽은 우울한 추도문은 모든 이를 결국 웃게 만들었다.

## 47 ③
☐ glare n. 섬광, 눈부신 빛; 현란함(=bright light) ☐ crescent n. 초승달 ☐ irradiation n. 발광(發光), 방열 ☐ cloud cover 운량(雲量) ☐ wave frequency 파동 주파수 ☐ dark sphere 어두운 영역

달의 초승달 부분이 점점 커져 달빛이 더욱 강해지면, 그로 인해 달의 어두운 부분은 더욱 안 보이게 된다.

## 48 ②
☐ disgruntled a. 불만스러워 하는, 언짢은(=discontented) ☐ dull a. 따분한, 재미없는 ☐ incoherent a. 일관되지 않는, 모순된 ☐ indigent a. 가난한, 곤궁한

불만을 품은 근로자들을 저지하지 않으면, 그들은 직장에 대한 동료들의 견해를 부정적으로 형성하여, 훨씬 더 많은 근로자들이 자신들의 직업을 싫어할지도 모르는 환경을 조성할 수 있다.

## 49 ③
☐ consummate a. 완성된, 더할 나위 없는, 완벽한(=perfect) ☐ respectful a. 공손한, 예의바른, 정중한 ☐ discrete a. 별개의, 분리된; 구별된 ☐ impaired a. 손상된, 제 기능을 못 하는

그것이 그에게 가장 큰 기쁨과 열정이었기에, 그는 완벽한 교육자였다. 그러나 그는 또한 철학자요, 박식가이기도 했으며, 인간의 본성과 사고(思考)를 연구하는 학자이기도 했다.

## 50 ①
☐ uprising n. 봉기, 폭동, 반란 ☐ oust v. 몰아내다, 축출하다, 쫓아내다 (=depose) ☐ designate v. 지명하다 ☐ deduce v. 연역[추론]하다 ☐ denigrate v. 모욕하다, 폄하하다

그 아프리카 독재자의 폭압이 너무나 극심해져서 모두가 그를 권좌에서 축출하기를 바라는 가운데 민중 봉기가 시작되었다.

## 51 ①
☐ knight n. 기사 ☐ apotheosis n. 신격화; 신성시; 전형, 극치, 절정기 (=quintessence) ☐ chivalry n. 기사도 ☐ remnant n. 나머지, 잔여; 자투리 ☐ confirmation n. 확인, 확증 ☐ antiquity n. 낡음, 태고

중세 시대의 기사는 기사도 정신의 정수였다.

## 52 ①

□ outstanding a. 눈에 띄는, 현저한, 우수한(=distinguished) □ standing outside 밖에 서 있는 □ outgoing a. 나가는; 떠나가는; 사교적인, 개방적인 □ outcome n. 결과, 성과, 결론

그 아이는 많은 면에서 뛰어나다.

## 53 ①

□ espouse v. 지지하다(=uphold) □ to one degree or another 어느 정도로 □ forsake v. 버리다, 포기하다 □ assume v. 가정하다; 떠맡다 □ presage v. ~의 전조가 되다, 예시하다

매일 아침 다른 사람들을 위해 멋진 일을 한다는 목표를 갖고 잠에서 깨어나는 것은 우리 모두가 어느 정도 지지할 수 있는 삶의 태도이다.

## 54 ③

□ expatriate n. 국외로 추방된 사람, (고국이 아닌) 국외 거주자 □ pin something on somebody ~을 …탓으로 돌리다 □ atrocity n. 흉악, 극악, 잔인; 잔학 행위(=brutality) □ sanction n. 인가, 재가; 제재 □ starvation n. 기아, 아사 □ hospitality n. 환대, 친절히 접대함

지난주 베를린에서 한 무리의 세르비아계 국외 추방자들이 보스니아에서의 잔학 행위에 대한 모든 비난을 세르비아인들에게 돌린 뉴스 보도에 반대하는 시위를 벌였다.

## 55 ④

□ decrepit a. 노후한; 노쇠한(=infirm) □ energetic a. 정력적인, 활동적인 □ crude a. 대충의, 대강의 □ calorific a. 열을 발생하는; 열의

그 불쌍한 노인은 너무 노쇠해서 길을 걸을 수조차도 없다.

## 56 ②

□ cast aspersions on ~을 비방[중상]하다 □ aspersion n. 비방, 중상 (=slander) □ misgiving n. 걱정, 불안 □ offshoot n. 분지; 파생물; 분파 □ pretext n. 구실, 핑계 □ spell n. 주문

다른 사람들의 능력과 인격을 비방함으로써 당신은 자신에 대한 불안을 드러내고 있다.

## 57 ②

□ muddle v. 혼란시키다, 어리둥절케 하다(=confuse) □ smother v. 숨 막히게 하다, 질식시키다 □ enlighten v. 계몽하다, 교화하다

□ standardize v. 표준화하다, 획일화하다

'진보주의자'와 '보수주의자' 같은 용어들은 분명하게 하기보다는 더욱 혼란스럽게 한다.

## 58 ①

□ gargantuan a. 거대한, 엄청난(=huge) □ corruption n. 부패, 타락 □ ruling party 제1당, 여당 □ disclose v. 폭로하다, 드러내다 □ righteous a. 옳은, 의로운, 정의의 □ putrid a. 부패하는; 아주 불쾌한 □ abominable a. 가공할, 심히 끔찍한 □ suspicious a. 의심스러운

여당 내의 엄청난 부패 스캔들은 한 작은 신문사의 정의로운 젊은 기자에 의해 처음으로 폭로되었다.

## 59 ④

□ rustle n. 바스락거리는 소리; 나뭇잎의 살랑거림; 옷 스치는 소리 (=soft sound) □ echo n. 메아리, 반향 □ movement n. 움직임; 운동, 활동; 이동 □ incident n. 사건; 부수적인 사건; 분쟁

그들은 70대 후반이었고, 그들의 삶은 상상하는 것만큼 겉보기에 너무나도 조용했다. 눈과 비, 혹은 한여름에 나무들이 바스락거리는 소리만큼 조용한 삶이었던 것이다.

## 60 ③

□ humdrum a. 평범한, 단조로운(=repetitious) □ interesting a. 흥미 있는, 재미있는 □ sultry a. 무더운, 찌는 듯이 더운; 몹시 뜨거운 □ uncomfortable a. 유쾌하지 않은, 기분이 언짢은

수년간 모험을 한 이후에 그는 단조로운 생활에 정착할 수 없었다.

## 61 ④

□ proclivity n. (흔히 좋지 못한) 성향, 경향(=tendency) □ sedative n. 진정제 □ reluctance n. 마음이 내키지 않음, 마지못해 함 □ inaptitude n. 적합하지 않음; 서투름 □ rashness n. 성급함, 무분별함

환자의 약물을 남용하는 성향 때문에, 의사는 약한 진정제조차 처방하길 원치 않았다.

## 62 ③

□ crooked a. 비뚤어진; 부정직한, 마음이 비뚤어진(=dishonest) □ deformed a. 볼품없는; 불구의, 기형의 □ bent a. 굽은, 뒤틀린; 열중한 □ winding a. 꾸불꾸불한; 둘러 말하는

장기간의 수사 끝에 그 부정직한 경찰관이 피고로부터 돈을 받았다는 사실이 드러났다.

## 63 ①

□ endure v. 견디다, 참다 □ fortitude n. 용기, 불굴의 정신, 강한 참을성, 인내(=tenacity) □ with fortitude 의연하게 □ conception n. 개념, 생각 □ understanding n. 이해; 깨달음, 납득; 지식 □ inspiration n. 영감

그는 건강이 좋지 않아 평생 고생했지만 매우 의연하게 견디어 내는 법을 배웠다.

## 64 ②

□ discourse n. 담론, 담화 □ fluid a. 유동적인 □ multimodal a. 다양한 □ quotidian a. 일상적인, 보통의(=everyday) □ enactment n. (법률의) 제정, (제정된) 법률, 법규 □ reclusive a. 세상을 버린; 은둔한 □ quarterly a. 연(年) 4회의, 분기별의 □ dictate v. 구술하다; 명령하다, 지시하다

시민권에 대한 그의 담론론은 다중 공공 영역에서의 시민권에 대한 유동적이며 다양한 일상적인 법규들을 인정하고 있다.

## 65 ②

□ consecrate v. 신성하게 하다, 정화하다; 바치다(=dedicate) □ limit v. 제한하다, 한정하다 □ subject v. 복종[종속]시키다, 지배하다 □ depend v. 의존[의지]하다

의사의 삶은 가난하고 병든 사람들을 치료하는 데 바쳐진다.

## 66 ①

□ prosecutor n. 검찰관 □ incinerate v. 태워 없애다, 소각하다(=cremate) □ inter v. 매장하다 □ dump v. (쓰레기 등을) 내버리다 □ incise v. 절개하다

검찰은 경찰이 학생들을 마약 범죄조직에 넘겨줬고 마약 범죄조직이 학생들을 살해해서 시신을 화장했다는 소문이 있다고 말한다.

## 67 ②

□ under the guise of ~을 가장하여, ~을 구실로(=in pretense of) □ desire for ~에 대한 열망 □ rejection of ~에 대한 거부 □ purpose of ~의 목적

그는 우정을 빙자하여 우리에게 말했다.

## 68 ①

□ repulsive a. 물리치는, 되쫓아버리는; 불쾌한(=disgusting) □ contemplation n. 사색, 명상; 관조 □ nothing but 오직, 그저 ~일 뿐인 □ exhausted a. 다 써버린, 소모된; 고갈된; 지쳐빠진 □

dominating a. 지배하는, 우세한 □ enormous a. 거대한, 막대한, 매우

관조(觀照)를 부정하고 오직 투쟁만을 승인하는 현대의 운동 이론에는 도덕적으로 불쾌한 데가 있다.

## 69 ④

□ bristle v. 털을 곤두세우다; 벌컥 화내다; 초조해하다(=become irritated) □ become isolated 고립되다 □ feel obliged 의무감을 느끼다 □ get discouraged 낙담하다, 낙심하다

기업 경영자와 정치가들이 우리의 물과 습지를 보호해야 하는 필요성을 이해하지 못할 때 과학자들과 공학자들은 화를 내며 초조해한다.

## 70 ①

□ execrable a. 저주할, 혐오할, 증오스러운(=horrible) □ gun-toting a. (권)총을 휴대하는 □ tacit a. 암묵적인, 무언의 □ diligent a. 근면한, 성실한 □ patriotic a. 애국적인 □ shrewd a. 상황 판단이 빠른; 기민한

이런 혐오할 만한 총을 휴대한 인종차별주의자들은 전 대통령으로부터 너무 많은 암묵적인 격려를 받았다.

## 71 ③

□ abandon v. 버리다, 단념하다 □ countermand v. 철회하다(=revoke) □ unequivocally ad. 모호하지 않게 □ amend v. 개정[수정]하다 □ promulgate v. 널리 알리다 □ propagate v. 선전하다

코로나 제로 정책을 포기하려면 공산당이 2년 넘게 반복적이고 단호하게 내린 명령을 철회해야 할 것이다.

## 72 ①

□ exacerbate v. 악화시키다(=make worse) □ simultaneous a. 동시의, 동시에 일어나는 □ outbreak n. (소동·전쟁·유행병 따위의) 발발, 창궐 □ plague n. 역병, 전염병 □ lessen v. 줄다, 줄이다 □ bring about 야기하다, 초래하다 □ strip v. 벗기다; ~로부터 빼앗다

인도 일부 지역에 장마가 오지 않아 심각한 기근이 초래됐으며, 이는 동시에 발생한 전염병으로 인해 악화되었다.

## 73 ④

□ resurgence n. 소생, 부활(=rebirth) □ desperate a. 자포자기의, 무모한; 필사적인 □ futile a. 쓸데없는, 무익한 □ representation n. 표시, 표현, 묘사 □ reliance n. 의지, 신뢰 □ reaction n. 반응, 반작용; 반발

종교의 부활은 잃어버린 것을 되찾으려는 필사적이고 대개 무익한 시도에 불과하다.

## 74 ①

☐ alacrity n. 기민함, 민첩함 ☐ with alacrity 민첩하게, 기민하게 (=expeditiously) ☐ lethargically ad. 혼수상태로; 둔감하게 ☐ yieldingly ad. 유연하게; 온순하게 ☐ with caution 조심하여, 신중하게

세네갈은 에볼라의 발병에 민첩하게 대응했다.

## 75 ①

☐ pungent a. (코를) 강하게 자극하는; 신랄한(=tangy) ☐ holistic a. 전체론적인 ☐ lethargic a. 혼수상태의, 무기력한 ☐ inexorable a. 무정한, 냉혹한

가까이에 있는 음식 냄새를 쉽게 흡수할 수 있기 때문에 초콜릿은 자극적인 냄새로부터 멀리 보관되어야만 한다.

## 76 ②

☐ compendium n. 개론; 개요, 요약(=summary) ☐ segment n. 단편, 조각; 구획 ☐ comparison n. 비교, 대조 ☐ critique n. 비평, 비판

이 책에는 여러 가지 출처에서 모은 기후 데이터를 요약한 내용이 들어 있다.

## 77 ③

☐ murderer n. 살인자, 살인범 ☐ summon v. 소환하다, 호출하다; (의회 등을) 소집하다(=convoke) ☐ revoke v. 취소하다, 폐지하다, 무효로 하다 ☐ provoke v. 화나게 하다; 유발시키다, 자극하여 ~시키다 ☐ invoke v. 빌다, 기원하다; 호소하다

그 살인범은 어제 법정 출두 명령을 받았다.

## 78 ①

☐ prescience n. 예지, 선견, 통찰(=foresight) ☐ ridiculous a. 웃기는, 말도 안 되는, 터무니없는 ☐ knowledgeable a. 아는 것이 많은, 유식한 ☐ discovery n. 발견 ☐ invention n. 발명; 날조 ☐ superstition n. 미신

그 놀라운 선견지명은 당시 가장 유식한 전문가들 중 한 명에게 '터무니없는' 것이라고 불렸다.

## 79 ①

☐ lucubrate v. 부지런히 일하다, 열심히 갈고닦다(=moil) ☐ shortcoming n. 결점, 단점, 불충분한 점 ☐ unveil v. 밝히다, 공개하다 ☐ evaluation n. 평가; 평가액 ☐ perambulate v. 순회하다, 답사하다 ☐ eke out 이럭저럭 꾸려나가다 ☐ quieten down 조용히 가라앉히다

정부는 최근의 평가에 의해 밝혀진 문제점들에 대해 부지런히 노력해야 한다.

## 80 ③

☐ ostentatious a. 과시하는, 화려한(=flamboyant) ☐ lucid a. 명쾌한, 명료한 ☐ fastidious a. 꼼꼼한, 세심한 ☐ discernible a. 분명한

생 로랑(Saint Laurent)은 현재의 트렌드에서 벗어나는 급진적인 변화를 꾀했다. 그는 순수하고 생생한 흑백의 디자인을 원했다. 이 디자이너는 "나는 부피와 비율과 색깔에 공을 들였어요. 화려한 것은 없고 그저 순수하고 단순한 선만 있을 뿐이죠. 나는 보석도 액세서리도 필요 없다는 아주 분명한 메시지를 전하고 싶었어요."라고 말한다.

## 81 ①

☐ moribund a. 빈사의, 죽어가는; 소멸해가는(=dying) ☐ dominant a. 지배적인, 우세한 ☐ extant a. 현존하는, 지금도 남아 있는 ☐ eloquent a. 웅변의; 감동적인

언어학자들은 사멸위기에 놓인 언어를 연구하면서 그 언어의 구성요소인 음(音), 어휘, 문법, 그리고 전통을 보존하려고 노력할 수 있다.

## 82 ②

☐ stricken a. 시달리는; 병에 걸린(=attacked) ☐ impressed a. 인상 깊게 생각하는, 감명[감동]을 받은 ☐ warn v. 경고하다, 주의를 주다 ☐ depressed a. 우울한

많은 질병은 사람들이 심지어 병에 걸렸다고 깨닫기도 전에 아주 빨리 진전되어 해를 끼친다.

## 83 ①

☐ query n. 질문, 의문(=question) ☐ get in touch with ~와 연락을 취하다 ☐ problem n. 문제, 과제 ☐ proposal n. 신청, 제안 ☐ idea n. 생각, 관념

이 주제와 관련하여 문의사항이 있으시면 저에게 연락주세요.

## 84 ③

☐ envisage v. 관찰하다; 마음에 그리다, 상상하다(=conceive) ☐ discredit v. 신용을 떨어뜨리다, 평판을 나쁘게 하다 ☐ contradict v. 부정하다; 모순되다 ☐ sanction v. 인가하다, 재가하다; 시인하다

그리스 철학자 플라톤(Plato)이 한때 만들기를 꿈꾸었던 그런 사회를 상상하는 것은 나에게 매우 어려운 일이다.

## 85 ③

□ restructuring n. (조직·제도·사업 등의) 재편성, 구조 개혁 □ stall v. 교착 상태에 빠지다, 오도 가도 못하게 되다 □ entitlement n. 자격[권리]; (사회적 약자를 위한 정부의) 사회보장 혜택 □ inherit v. (재산·권리 따위를) 상속하다, 물려받다 □ communist a. 공산주의의 □ era n. 연대; 시기, 시대 □ overhaul v. 철저히 조사하다(=scrutinize) □ yield v. 산출하다; 굴복하다 □ cast aside (물건·습관·불안 따위를) 버리다, 제거하다 □ emulate v. ~와 경쟁하다; 흉내 내다

세계은행의 경제학자 로르슨(Laursen)은 일부 경제 분야의 구조조정과 민영화가 교착상태에 빠졌으며 공산주의 시대에서 물려받은 사회보장 제도도 아직 완전한 조사가 이루어지지 않았다고 경고한다.

## 86 ②

□ token a. 형식적인, 이름뿐인, 명목상의(=nominal) □ huge a. 거대한; 막대한 □ serious a. 심각한, 진지한 □ talkative a. 말하기를 좋아하는, 수다스러운

그는 노조 지도자로서 회사에 대해 시늉에 불과한 저항만 한다는 비판을 받았다.

## 87 ③

□ beleaguered a. 사면초가에 몰린(=besieged) □ frightened a. 겁먹은, 무서워하는 □ segregated a. 분리된, 격리된 □ isolated a. 고립된

연료 위기는 사면초가에 몰린 쿠바인들을 절망의 위기로 몰아넣었다.

## 88 ①

□ disown v. 의절[절연]하다(=repudiate) □ persuade v. 설득하다 □ encourage v. 격려[고무]하다 □ tease v. 놀리다; 못 살게 굴다

당신의 가족은 종종 반대 의견을 갖고 있지만, 그렇다고 해서 당신은 그들과 의절하지 않는다.

## 89 ④

□ de facto a. 사실상의(=actual) □ succumb v. 굴복하다, 지다(to) □ populism n. 대중영합주의 □ legal a. 법적인 □ despotic a. 독재적인; 횡포한

그가 공화당의 사실상의 지도자가 되고 1년이 지난 후 공화당이 그의 국가주의적 대중영합주의에 굴복했다는 견해가 늘어나고 있었다.

## 90 ③

□ extemporize v. (연설, 연주 등을) 즉흥적으로 하다(=improvise) □ provide v. 주다, 공급하다; 준비하다, 대비하다 □ duplicate v. 복사[복제]하다, 사본을 만들다 □ visualize v. 보이게 하다, 마음에 떠오르게 하다

그 연사는 연설을 준비하지 않았기 때문에, 즉석에서 연설해야 했다.

## 91 ②

□ impunity n. 처벌을 받지 않음(=exemption) □ incarceration n. 투옥, 감금 □ discretion n. (자유) 재량(권) □ breach n. 위반

일부 국가에서는 사이버 범죄자들이 처벌받지 않고 활동한다.

## 92 ④

□ astringent a. (표현이) 신랄한, 통렬한(=harsh) □ arcane a. 신비로운, 불가사의한 □ equivocal a. 모호한, 애매한 □ trite a. 진부한, 독창적이지 못한

그녀의 비판은 너무 신랄해서 모두가 약간 불편함을 느꼈다.

## 93 ③

□ gung-ho a. 열렬한, 매우 열성적인(=enthusiastic) □ kindred a. 비슷한, 동류의; 관련된 □ impetuous a. 성급한, 충동적인, 경솔한 □ scrupulous a. 세심한, 꼼꼼한

자원봉사자들은 진정한 열정을 가지고 지역사회 프로젝트에 임했다.

## 94 ③

□ generosity n. 관대, 관용 □ immanent a. 안에 있는, 내재하는(=inherent) □ immature a. 미숙한 □ invalid a. 효력 없는, 근거 없는 □ immortal a. 불후의, 불멸의

철학자들은 관대함이 내재적 특성인지 아니면 사람들이 배우는 것인지에 대한 논쟁을 벌일 수도 있다.

## 95 ②

□ dissemble v. 숨기다, 가식적으로 꾸미다(=pretend) □ palpitate v. 두근거리다 □ overstate v. 과장하다 □ seduce v. 유혹하다, 꾀다

정치가들은 실수를 저질렀다는 것을 인정하지 않기 위해 종종 시치미를 떼야만 한다.

## 96 ①

□ recompense n. 보수, 보상(=requital) □ exceptional a. 비범한, 뛰어난 □ refinement n. 개선, 개량 □ windfall n. 뜻밖의 횡재 □ solicitude n. 배려

회사는 직원들의 뛰어난 성과에 대한 보상으로 상당한 보너스를 제
공했다.


# 97                                                          ①

☐ boot somebody out ~를 쫓아내다  ☐ turpitude n. 대단히 부도덕
한 행위(=wickedness)  ☐ bravado n. 허세  ☐ decency n. 체면, 품위
☐ obstinacy n. 완고함, 고집

부패한 정치인들은 부도덕한 행위로 인해 공직에서 쫓겨난다.


# 98                                                          ②

☐ commitment n. 약속, 전념  ☐ sobriety n. 술에 취하지 않음; 절주,
금주; 맑은 정신(=abstinence)  ☐ promptness n. 재빠름, 신속  ☐
frugality n. 절약, 검소  ☐ probity n. 정직성

금주하려는 그의 의지는 일상생활에서 분명하게 드러났다.


# 99                                                          ①

☐ animadversion n. 비평, 비난, 혹평(=criticism)  ☐ amity n. 우호,
친선  ☐ affinity n. 친밀감, 관련성  ☐ vigilance n. 경계, 조심

그의 분명한 주장은 청중으로부터 예상치 못한 일련의 혹평에 부딪
혔다.


# 100                                                         ③

☐ ribald a. 음란한 말을 하는, (말이) 상스러운(=vulgar)  ☐ belligerent
a. 적대적인, 공격적인  ☐ intriguing a. 아주 흥미로운  ☐ dismissive
a. 무시[멸시]하는

음란한 유머는 일반적으로 아이들 주위에서는 부적절하다고 여겨진다.

# MVP

Vol.2 워크북

# APPENDIX

[01-84] Choose the one that is closest in meaning to the CONTEXTUAL meaning of the underlined word.

01 After the game, the coach blamed the referee's poor calls for the team's loss.
① summonses ② needs
③ options ④ decisions

02 With everyone shouting and complaining about the terms of purchase, she was the only one who came to a level appraisal of the situation.
① horizontal ② rational
③ equal ④ steady

03 Prices are likely to remain cheap, reduced by heavy government issues of new stock for some time.
① topics ② offspring
③ supplies ④ editions

04 The tourist carefully negotiated his way through the crowds on the busy streets of Paris.
① discussed ② moved
③ agreed ④ stipulated

05 The processing of straw mushroom is still at the primary stage and urgently needs further processing technologies.
① foremost ② original
③ dominant ④ initial

06 The new engineer manipulated the dials of the complex machinery in a surprisingly skillful manner.
① swayed ② influenced
③ operated ④ exploited

07 The subcontractor shall be obliged to carry out any outstanding work or rectify any defects as soon as possible.
① excellent ② protruding
③ unpaid ④ incomplete

08 The whole team deserves credit for bringing the project in on time.
① belief ② payment
③ praise ④ asset

09 The disease is not as benign as previously thought and causes future health complications.
① pleasant ② harmless
③ warm ④ benevolent

10 People's immediate response to the terrorist's attack was sheer horror.
① steep ② complete
③ thin ④ transparent

11 The central parliament at Vienna with very extensive powers was grossly <u>partial</u> to the Germans.
① fractional  ② advantageous
③ uncertain  ④ attached

12 The firefighter hopes that the townspeople will <u>hail</u> him as a hero for rescuing the children.
① cheer  ② fall
③ originate  ④ greet

13 Although <u>delicate</u> in structure, spider webs are strong enough to withstand hurricane-force winds.
① intricate  ② fragile
③ sensitive  ④ discreet

14 This can best be done in clearly situated case studies, which <u>yield</u> qualitative findings.
① surrender  ② stop
③ profit  ④ provide

15 The violent movie received an adult-only rating from the film review <u>board</u>.
① plank  ② group
③ stage  ④ meal

16 Fried chicken smothered in hot sauce presents the <u>sport</u> of trying to eat it with anything fewer than four paper napkins.
① athletics  ② mockery
③ companion  ④ entertainment

17 The room was <u>austere</u> and neat, containing only a bed and a rocking chair.
① barren  ② destitute
③ stern  ④ unadorned

18 Many narrators wrote only reluctantly, suspecting that their life stories were too <u>mundane</u> to be of any interest to anybody.
① ordinary  ② secular
③ earthly  ④ material

19 Over the years, they have carefully avoided tapping into their home <u>equity</u> for unnecessary expenses.
① ownership  ② fairness
③ value  ④ stock

20 European countries are increasingly reluctant to grant <u>asylum</u> to refugees from war-torn countries.
① sanatorium  ② institution
③ haven  ④ retreat

21 After the performance, the actors go offstage and come back for the <u>convention</u> of the encore.
① agreement  ② tradition
③ assembly  ④ conference

22 She came a long way to see me, and I really enjoyed her <u>company</u> over the weekend.
① guest  ② companionship
③ enterprise  ④ partner

23 I would never agree to do that even if I were assured of a <u>clean</u> getaway.
① complete
② blank
③ virtuous
④ unsoiled

24 To my surprise, my question provoked a <u>burst</u> of anger from the salesman.
① puncture
② explosion
③ fracture
④ rupture

25 Today no one would accept such a naive explanation for a <u>lapse</u> in security, nor should they.
① breach
② interval
③ respite
④ termination

26 The fact that justice <u>hinges</u> on witnesses telling the truth in court requires serious penalties for those who lie.
① links
② pivots
③ rotates
④ depends

27 His political career ended when he <u>compromised</u> himself by accepting bribes.
① abased
② abandoned
③ settled
④ divulged

28 The old man in front of me in the queue had a really loud voice and spoke in a <u>broad</u> Yorkshire accent.
① liberal
② extensive
③ obvious
④ generous

29 He could barely bring himself to be <u>civil</u> to the guests.
① private
② domestic
③ considerate
④ unarmed

30 My sister's <u>oblique</u> answers to my questions made me suspicious.
① indirect
② unequal
③ slanting
④ diagonal

31 Science is the systematic method by which we <u>apprehend</u> what is true about the world in which we live.
① fear
② arrest
③ seize
④ understand

32 Short-term fluctuations in the trajectory have little or no <u>bearing</u> on how one might view the long-term situation.
① demeanor
② sustaining
③ relevance
④ reproduction

33 We thought of informing you of the event, but we <u>figured</u> that you'd want to rest after your trip.
① computed
② appeared
③ depicted
④ expected

34 The new product occupied a <u>prominent</u> place in the store and was easy to spot.
① noticeable
② renowned
③ protruding
④ creditable

35 Bushfires in Australia have <u>claimed</u> nearly 800 people since 1850.
① asserted
② demanded
③ killed
④ merited

36 After her father passed away, she took over the <u>maintenance</u> of her family.
① repair
② continuance
③ payment
④ livelihood

37 We must <u>appreciate</u> the freedom of people living under tyranny.
① prize      ② admire
③ understand      ④ inflate

38 He put his own liberal <u>slant</u> on the senator's speech.
① lean      ② opinion
③ slope      ④ gradient

39 The security council resolved to invoke <u>sanctions</u> against the parties involved in terrorism.
① authorization      ② penalties
③ patronage      ④ confirmations

40 After the horrific crash, the emergency services workers <u>pronounced</u> the driver dead at the scene of the accident.
① declared      ② vocalized
③ decided      ④ uttered

41 She seemed very <u>cool</u> before her final exam even though she hadn't studied.
① chilly      ② stylish
③ excellent      ④ calm

42 The economic depression has been such that machinery has lain in the factory <u>untouched</u> for years.
① unused      ② unaffected
③ unmoved      ④ unmodified

43 Would you ever <u>entertain</u> the idea of putting a temporary roller coaster in your house?
① amuse      ② consider
③ cheer      ④ treat

44 The <u>depressed</u> sections of the highway under the overpasses constantly get flooded during heavy rainstorms.
① sunken      ② distressed
③ mournful      ④ underprivileged

45 He was <u>positive</u> he'd be lost for life without her.
① optimistic      ② beneficial
③ certain      ④ complete

46 What is the company's <u>account</u> for their great loss in the last quarter?
① advantage      ② version
③ invoice      ④ reason

47 The old man had dark hair, serious brown eyes in a chiseled face, and a form as <u>fit</u> as his son's.
① suitable      ② healthy
③ equipped      ④ right

48 A baby's limbs are relatively <u>plastic</u> when compared to those of an adult.
① malleable      ② molded
③ inorganic      ④ artificial

49 For more than two decades she shot <u>game</u> for food and grew her own vegetables.
① match      ② prey
③ pastime      ④ trick

50 Overly criticizing the <u>establishment</u> can get newspeople thrown in jail.
① business      ② creation
③ households      ④ rulers

**51** The obnoxious child <u>tried</u> everyone's patience to the limit.

① determined     ② attempted

③ stretched     ④ studied

**52** Her acceptance of the unfortunate test results was amazingly <u>positive</u> for a 9-year-old.

① certain     ② beneficial

③ perfect     ④ optimistic

**53** The teacher was not being <u>mean</u> in asking the students to be quiet.

① inferior     ② average

③ cheap     ④ unkind

**54** The <u>sensible</u> thing to do if someone tries to start a fight is to just walk away.

① tangible     ② wise

③ sentient     ④ physical

**55** To the participants, the conference was excellent; however, to the organizers who made little profit, it was a <u>qualified</u> success.

① licensed     ② capable

③ defined     ④ limited

**56** Although he resembles his father, they differ in almost every other <u>respect</u>.

① appreciation     ② courtesy

③ heed     ④ facet

**57** The government is investigating an <u>oversight</u> by the Minister of Education who forgot to submit a report.

① lapse     ② control

③ supervision     ④ indifference

**58** Nobody said a word about impending war, but the atmosphere in the barracks was <u>charged</u> with tension.

① accused     ② attacked

③ permeated     ④ obligated

**59** Prior to the <u>draft</u> ending in 1973, the U.S. sent its military overseas 27 times.

① plan     ② check

③ conscription     ④ blueprint

**60** A thick skin is essential, as colleagues are <u>blunt</u> in their evaluation of your strengths and weaknesses.

① dull     ② round

③ forthright     ④ weak

**61** I am an avid body-builder and work out everyday, yet I am very <u>susceptible</u> to colds and flu.

① responsive     ② suggestible

③ sensitive     ④ vulnerable

**62** The pretty, blue-eyed princess was only fourteen years old, but her bearing was <u>unassuming</u>.

① plain     ② modest

③ simplistic     ④ subservient

**63** Parliament's rejection of the traditional ceremony is evidently the result not of accident, but of <u>design</u>.

① intention     ② drawing

③ ambition     ④ pattern

64 After graduating from an Ivy League school, Alice wants to join the corporate world and become a woman of <u>substance</u>.
① matter      ② density
③ essence      ④ importance

65 After a long investigation, it was revealed the <u>crooked</u> cop had received the money from the accused.
① deformed      ② bent
③ dishonest      ④ winding

66 The legislation was <u>enacted</u> in the aftermath of two high-profile child abuse cases last year.
① enforced      ② dramatized
③ carried out      ④ introduced

67 Any necessary <u>measures</u> we take must have the chance of improving the chaotic situation in that country.
① yardsticks      ② actions
③ merits      ④ instruments

68 The nurse <u>dressed</u> the soldier every morning, but the soldier got the second infection.
① bandaged      ② clothed
③ decorated      ④ aligned

69 If we hurry, there's still an outside <u>chance</u> of catching the plane.
① likelihood      ② risk
③ destiny      ④ luck

70 The government is prepared for an urban development in the outer <u>peripheral</u> areas of large towns.
① secondary      ② marginal
③ superficial      ④ insignificant

71 The <u>initiative</u>, proposed by Congress, to expand preschool will rely largely on the private sector.
① leadership      ② bill
③ ambition      ④ introduction

72 The future depicted in the National Intelligence Council's "Global Trends 2015" report, published in December 2000, contains numerous contemporary <u>echoes</u>.
① imitation      ② sound
③ reflection      ④ noise

73 He is an incurable <u>scamp</u>, and so even when the bits were apolitical, they were hilarious.
① prankster      ② swindler
③ rogue      ④ troublemaker

74 This isn't terribly important and maybe I'm just a bit <u>dense</u>, but if someone could clarify, I'd really appreciate it.
① crowded      ② heavy
③ opaque      ④ stupid

75 The king died without <u>issue</u> and was eventually succeeded by his nephew.
① outcome      ② sequel
③ posterity      ④ contention

76 They led the charge, breaking through the third Union line and following on the heels of the retreating Federal troops.
① sally　　　　② liability
③ indictment　　④ custody

77 In a world ruled by photographic images, all framing borders seem arbitrary: anything can be separated and made discontinuous, from anything else.
① whimsical　　② tyrannical
③ random　　　④ absolute

78 Tess was apprehended by the local police and subsequently accused for her misdemeanor.
① understood　　② appreciated
③ arrested　　　④ concerned

79 The elegant Princess Ingrid has long complained about Duchess Sarah Norton's common accent.
① vulgar　　　　② recognizable
③ trivial　　　　④ frequent

80 The sculpture has been purchased for an undisclosed figure with assistance from the art fund.
① symbol　　　　② sum
③ statue　　　　④ form

81 His biography of Samuel Johnson gains the status of classic through its relentless devotion to social and intellectual descriptions.
① constant　　　② inflexible
③ implacable　　④ brutal

82 A misstep in the resolution of the dispute over tuberculosis control could have serious and unintended side effects in the entire state.
① courage　　　② intention
③ perseverance　④ settlement

83 The stadium can only hold 10,000 people but a monstrous crowd came for the concert.
① villainous　　② colossal
③ grotesque　　④ hideous

84 The earthquake has already claimed more than one hundred lives.
① killed　　　　② alleged
③ maintained　　④ demanded

[01-59] Choose the <u>antonym</u> of the underlined word.

01 Climate change now impacts each and every single country on each continent, affecting the lives of individuals and communities as well as <u>disrupting</u> national economies.
① marginalizing  ② simulating
③ enlivening  ④ enervating
⑤ insinuating

02 The failure to <u>mitigate</u> and adapt to climate change is among the biggest global risks for our planet, with significant environmental, economic and health impacts.
① exacerbate  ② exasperate
③ expiate  ④ exfoliate
⑤ exonerate

03 For some people being faced with a difficult situation, <u>prevarication</u> is a go-to response.
① forbearance  ② forewarning
③ forgoing  ④ forthrightness
⑤ foresight

04 The clamor over the group's second album has precipitated an insatiable fervor for their media, particularly their early recordings, which have been regularly <u>lauded</u> by critics.
① purloined  ② padded
③ penned  ④ pawned
⑤ panned

05 Strong <u>empirical</u> studies that investigate the questions are important in informing the current theoretical debate between serial versus parallel word identification during natural sentence reading.
① conjectural  ② convivial
③ conspiratorial  ④ consanguine
⑤ conjunctive

06 Children identify with a group of others like themselves and <u>take on</u> the norms of the group.
① absorb  ② receive
③ reject  ④ rewrite
⑤ obliterate

07 In adulthood, the pressure gradually <u>lets up</u> and individual differences reassert themselves.
① stops  ② diminishes
③ increases  ④ dies out
⑤ goes down

08 We have already surveyed some of the <u>salient</u> features of the language, focusing on the differences.
① bright  ② influential
③ underscored  ④ non-trivial
⑤ minor

**09** This new and potentially controversial view of women's friendships is <u>amply</u> supported.

① substantially ② insufficiently
③ sufficiently ④ happily
⑤ unambiguously

**10** To find solutions to this misinformation crisis, our society needs a <u>clear-eyed</u> assessment of who and what drives the spread of malicious falsehoods and conspiracy theories.

① empirical ② impartial
③ discerning ④ reasonable
⑤ imperceptive

**11** The excesses of Picasso's artistic endowment, of his will, of his life appetites, and of his character appear to have been <u>idiosyncratic</u> from earliest childhood.

① comical ② conventional
③ incessant ④ eccentric
⑤ electric

**12** In his classicist period, Goethe was so <u>taken</u> with the concept of a single ideal of beauty that he was pleased when people could not distinguish his work from that of Schiller.

① captivated ② obsessed
③ humiliated ④ bored
⑤ displeased

**13** Because Kleist's skeptical statements <u>obscure</u> his thoughts, critics have raised doubts about attempts to interpret his response precisely.

① highlight ② cover
③ reveal ④ emphasize
⑤ darken

**14** To properly assess the situation, you have to carefully <u>weigh</u> planned improvements against anticipated results.

① assess ② debate
③ bypass ④ insist
⑤ estimate

**15** There are questions of the same order as those posed in Lawrence W. Levin's thesis of "cultural <u>bifurcation</u>" to characterize the trajectory of American culture in the nineteenth century.

① exuberance ② mitigation
③ polarity ④ unification
⑤ exhortation

**16** In the opening lines to a section of one of the lengthiest and most <u>enduring</u> poems in the English language, a sage and serious poet wrote of man's first disobedience.

① short-lived ② contingent
③ uninspiring ④ amoral
⑤ sacrilegious

**17** All cats, from the smallest house kitten to the most <u>ferocious</u> lion, share a common feline ancestor who lived about 25 million years ago.

① rampant ② peevish
③ gentle ④ small-sized
⑤ unintelligent

**18** Benoit's foresight to pack an evacuation box and purchase a hefty insurance policy less than two months before the fire proved <u>fortuitous</u>, but they were temporarily homeless.

① auspicious    ② salutary

③ credible    ④ prudent

⑤ inopportune

**19** Abandon that precept, and you <u>undermine</u> the moral basis of our common American citizenship.

① subvert    ② diminish

③ enhance    ④ abhor

⑤ accumulate

**20** At a time of hyper-partisanship, the Senate Intelligence Committee stands out as a rare island of bipartisanship and <u>collegiality</u> — even on the issue of Russian meddling in U.S. elections.

① animosity    ② rapprochement

③ civilization    ④ quandary

⑤ status

**21** Another name that anthropologists regularly use to refer to band hunter-gatherer societies is <u>egalitarian</u> societies.

① traditional    ② elitist

③ populist    ④ secular

⑤ archaic

**22** In an era when scientists, corporations, and governments are learning to hack the human brain, this truism is more <u>sinister</u> than ever.

① judicious    ② benign

③ erroneous    ④ implausible

⑤ prevalent

**23** Their attitude stemmed from the belief that they would <u>acquiesce to</u> any conditions, including the dissolution of the government they had installed.

① reprove    ② concede to

③ exasperate    ④ demur at

⑤ prevail over

**24** In a world where people increasingly retreat to their <u>parochial</u> interests, free trade agreements should be welcomed to encourage economic free movement and global interactions.

① alternative    ② frivolous

③ illiterate    ④ liberal

⑤ monetary

**25** The <u>contrived</u> applause of a TV studio audience that has been told when to clap has become an essential part of a TV show.

① dismissive    ② encouraging

③ genuine    ④ impinging

⑤ incongruous

**26** One of her "most impressive and humorous achievements," Lorna Sage, her friend and cleverest critic, once wrote, "was that she evolved this part to play: How to Be the Woman Writer. Not that she was wearing a mask exactly: it was more a matter of refusing to observe any <u>decorous</u> distinction between art and life."

① enticing    ② wild

③ incorporeal    ④ superlative

⑤ still

27 It was not a very <u>arduous</u> job, but pleasantly remunerative.
① archaic　　② bucolic
③ comfortable　　④ inflammatory
⑤ lineal

28 Black locust and autumn olive trees fix nitrogen, allowing more goldenrods, sunflowers, and white snakeroot to move in along apple trees, their seeds expelled by <u>proliferating</u> birds.
① gratifying　　② exacerbating
③ migrating　　④ plummeting
⑤ fortifying

29 His memories were a stolen, <u>derivative</u>, aesthetically shaped, part of that library of images to which we are exposed.
① dissipated　　② exonerated
③ derogatory　　④ original
⑤ rabid

30 None of the three authors <u>subscribes to</u> the popular theory that mental illness is caused by a chemical imbalance in the brain.
① opposes　　② enlarges
③ lubricates　　④ impedes
⑤ reduces

31 Customers don't line up at a <u>discreet</u> distance, the way city folk do; in Nucla they crowd the counter and talk loudly about health problems.
① shy　　② astute
③ tactless　　④ critical
⑤ inconvenient

32 In the common view, the peddler became a confidence man who gained his goal through <u>guile</u> rather than strength — particularly through a skillful theatricality.
① reserve　　② naivete
③ praise　　④ repudiation
⑤ reprisal

33 Hegemony is not maintained through the <u>obliteration</u> of the opposition but through the articulation of opposing interests into the political affiliations of the hegemonic group.
① annihilation　　② construction
③ revision　　④ oblivion
⑤ infiltration

34 Language does not name an already organized and <u>coherent</u> reality; its role is far more powerful and complex.
① coercive　　② expansive
③ exhilarating　　④ disjointed
⑤ equivalent

35 Cultural Studies soon <u>separated</u> itself from literary studies — despite the close links between its theoretical influences and those of literary studies.
① alleviated　　② extenuated
③ dissociated　　④ upheld
⑤ reconciled

36 <u>Inept</u> handling of the match by the referee ensured that the game would not pass without incident.
① uncanny　　② recalcitrant
③ wholesale　　④ skillful
⑤ pompous

**37** If postcolonial studies is obsessed with the critique of the West and its transgression, the discourses surrounding globalization tend to obscure the relationships between globalization and the imperial and colonial past from which it emerged.

① obedience     ② disparity

③ conscription     ④ revocation

⑤ infusion

**38** The cultural and historical links between the many provinces were seen to be very tenuous.

① obdurate     ② permanent

③ lucid     ④ substantial

⑤ pervasive

**39** New Critics believed a text was complete in and of itself; they adhered to a detached reading of texts, focusing on language and its structures and eschewing any outside contexts, including political and social influences.

① confiscating     ② opposing

③ mitigating     ④ underpinning

⑤ adopting

**40** Clearly we have sporadic outbreaks of violence, but then, we are not unique in that in this world.

① spasmodic     ② continuous

③ staggering     ④ endangered

⑤ destructive

**41** It is quite important to say that the cultural influence of the Japanese animation is closely associated with a palpable, realistic appreciation of "Japanese" lifestyles or ideas.

① tangential     ② exclusive

③ sophisticated     ④ whimsical

⑤ intangible

**42** In their political analyses, pragmatists sought to understand the relative and shifting importance of multiple factors germane to specific questions or goals.

① avaricious     ② extraneous

③ irrepressible     ④ meticulous

⑤ sumptuous

**43** Voters have always indulged a certain amount of hyperbole and rhetorical excess from their politicians.

① appraisal     ② equivocation

③ revulsion     ④ skepticism

⑤ understatement

**44** Politicians have also been unwilling to alienate the electorate by taking any unpopular (albeit necessary) steps.

① abduct     ② antagonize

③ preempt     ④ reunite

⑤ revamp

**45** Avoid pretentious expression. You're trying to get judges to understand a case, not to impress them with your erudition.

① stilted     ② mincing

③ conceited     ④ inculpable

⑤ unassuming

**46** It was suddenly clear how lonely his life has been. Here he was, a man with an <u>insatiable</u> appetite for learning, forced for most of his adult life to live in intellectual isolation.

① voracious     ② avid

③ ravenous     ④ rapacious

⑤ contented

**47** The results were <u>unequivocal</u>. There were clear differences in how the young men responded to being called a bad name.

① ambiguous     ② obnoxious

③ palpable     ④ predictable

⑤ encouraging

**48** Research findings on caregiving continue to <u>corroborate</u> that families caring for Alzheimer's patients experience tremendous burdens and strain.

① controvert     ② concede

③ conflate     ④ complicate

⑤ counterfeit

**49** Those who <u>persevere</u> in science-related careers may find more employment opportunities and job security than their counterparts in other fields.

① take away

② send out

③ put into

④ give up

⑤ bring forward

**50** The report is designed to promote the <u>dubious</u> concept that the nation's economy can gain momentum with a more radical integration into the global economy.

① shabby     ② thoughtless

③ perplexing     ④ convincing

⑤ stringent

**51** In order not to deter whistle-blowing, we should encourage a debate on the need to remain <u>discreet</u> about the identity of informers in high-profile corruption cases.

① intelligent     ② modest

③ secretive     ④ inconsiderate

⑤ suspicious

**52** It is quite likely that science fiction tends to <u>engender</u> logical incongruities.

① provoke     ② mystify

③ clarify     ④ remove

⑤ stimulate

**53** Banks that have been repeatedly successful with mergers have a blueprint for <u>consolidation</u> ready to be used the moment a merger is complete.

① provocation     ② restriction

③ opposition     ④ fragmentation

⑤ instigation

**54** Virtue is measured by one's approximation to proper class appearances. Even a simple adventure story like *Treasure Island* manifests this <u>implicit</u> class perspective.

① noble     ② overt

③ absurd     ④ tacit

⑤ inherent

55 In his recent study of the ethereal aspects of sound, David Toop defines sound as formlessness, a medium that haunts places and people.
① sublime
② divine
③ incorporeal
④ tangible
⑤ spectral

56 The point of the chapter is that the unconscious mind often opposes what the conscious mind wants to do or say, and frequently trips it up with all kinds of evasions, deceits, gags, and kicks in the pants.
① confrontations
② tricks
③ facts
④ quibbles
⑤ blames

57 The ability to voluntarily delay immediate gratification, to tolerate self-imposed delays of reward, is at the core of most concepts of willpower, ego strength, and ego resilience.
① acceptance
② pleasantness
③ gratitude
④ indulgence
⑤ dissatisfaction

58 The alternative mechanism of normative morphogenesis is the accumulation of innovations.
① atypical
② conformist
③ customary
④ preceptive
⑤ abortive

59 An ingredient of resilience is an optimistic orientation and a focus on the positive on oneself and in human nature.
① convalescence
② recovery
③ recuperation
④ retrieval
⑤ stagnation

| | | | | | | | | | |
|---|---|---|---|---|---|---|---|---|---|
| 01 ④ | 02 ② | 03 ③ | 04 ② | 05 ④ | 06 ③ | 07 ④ | 08 ③ | 09 ② | 10 ② |
| 11 ④ | 12 ④ | 13 ② | 14 ④ | 15 ② | 16 ② | 17 ④ | 18 ① | 19 ③ | 20 ③ |
| 21 ② | 22 ② | 23 ① | 24 ② | 25 ① | 26 ④ | 27 ① | 28 ③ | 29 ③ | 30 ① |
| 31 ① | 32 ③ | 33 ④ | 34 ① | 35 ③ | 36 ④ | 37 ① | 38 ② | 39 ② | 40 ① |
| 41 ④ | 42 ① | 43 ② | 44 ① | 45 ③ | 46 ④ | 47 ② | 48 ① | 49 ② | 50 ④ |
| 51 ③ | 52 ④ | 53 ④ | 54 ② | 55 ④ | 56 ③ | 57 ① | 58 ② | 59 ③ | 60 ③ |
| 61 ④ | 62 ② | 63 ① | 64 ④ | 65 ③ | 66 ② | 67 ② | 68 ① | 69 ① | 70 ② |
| 71 ② | 72 ① | 73 ① | 74 ② | 75 ③ | 76 ① | 77 ③ | 78 ③ | 79 ① | 80 ② |
| 81 ① | 82 ④ | 83 ② | 84 ① | | | | | | |

## 01 2023 한국외대 T1 A형 ④

명사 call에는 '소환', '요구', '(심판의) 판정' '선택권' 등 다양한 의미가 있다. 경기와 관련하여 감독이 팀의 패배 원인으로 돌릴 수 있는 것은 심판의 '판정'이다.

☐ blame A for B B를 A의 탓으로 돌리다   ☐ referee n. 심판

경기 후, 감독은 팀의 패배를 심판의 형편없는 판정 탓으로 돌렸다.

## 02 2023 한국외대 T1 A형 ②

형용사 level에는 '수평의', '차분한', '동등한', '분별 있는' 등의 다양한 의미가 있다. 혼란스러운 상황에서 그녀만이 상황을 분별 있게 평가했다는 의미가 되는 것이 적절하므로 ②가 정답이다.

구매 조건에 대해 모두가 큰 소리를 내며 불평하는 상황에서 그녀는 그 상황을 분별 있게 평가한 유일한 사람이었다.

## 03 2023 한국외대 T1 A형 ③

명사 issue에는 '쟁점', '자녀, 자식', '(정기 간행물의) 호', '공급' 등 다양한 의미가 있다. 가격이 저렴하게 유지된다는 것은 공급이 많이 이루어지기 때문이므로 issues의 문맥상 동의어로 적절한 것은 ③ supplies이다.

가격은 한동안 정부의 새로운 비축품의 대규모 공급으로 인해 저렴하게 유지될 가능성이 높다.

## 04 2023 한국외대 T1 A형 ②

동사 negotiate에는 '협상[교섭]하다', '통과하다, 뚫고나가다' 등의 의미가 있는데, 주어진 문장은 관광객이 분주한 거리에서 군중들 사이를 빠져 나왔다는 의미가 되는 것이 적절하므로 ② moved가 문맥상 동의어로 적절하다.

그 관광객은 파리의 분주한 거리에서 군중들 사이를 조심스럽게 통과했다.

## 05 2023 한국외대 T2-1 C형 ④

primary가 '초기의', '처음의'라는 의미로 쓰였으므로, initial이 문맥상의 동의어로 적절하다.

☐ straw mushroom 풀버섯   ☐ primary a. 주요한; 최초의; 본래의
☐ foremost a. 맨 먼저의; 주요한   ☐ original a. 최초의; 독창적인
☐ dominant a. 지배적인   ☐ initial a. 초기의, 시작의

풀버섯의 가공은 여전히 초기 단계에 있으며 추가적인 가공 기술이 시급히 필요하다.

## 06 2023 한국외대 T2-1 C형 ③

manipulate가 '(기계 등을) 능숙하게 다루다[조작(操作)하다]'라는 의미로 쓰였으므로, operate가 문맥상의 동의어로 적절하다.

☐ manipulate v. (사람·여론 등을) (부정하게) 조종하다; (시장·시가 등을) 조작(造作)하다; (기계 등을) 능숙하게 다루다   ☐ sway v. 흔들다; (사람·의견 따위를) 움직이다, 좌우하다   ☐ influence v. ~에게 영향을 미치다   ☐ operate v. 조작(操作)하다, 운전하다, 조종하다; 수술하다   ☐ exploit v. (자원 등을) 개발하다; (이기적인 목적으로) 이용하다

새로 온 엔지니어는 복잡한 기계의 다이얼을 놀라울 정도로 능숙하게 다뤘다.

## 07 2023 한국외대 T2-1 C형 ④

outstanding이 '미해결의'라는 의미로 쓰였으므로, incomplete가 문맥상의 동의어로 적절하다.

☐ subcontractor n. 하도급 업체   ☐ be obliged to 하는 수 없이 ~하다
☐ carry out 수행하다   ☐ outstanding a. 걸출한, 현저한; 돌출한; 미결제

의; 미해결의 □ rectify v. 개정하다; (악습 등을) 교정하다 □ protruding a. 돌출한 □ unpaid a. 지급되지 않은, 미납의 □ incomplete a. 불완전한

하도급 업체는 미해결된 작업을 수행하거나 그 어떤 결함도 가능한 한 신속하게 시정해야 할 것이다.

## 08 2023 한국외대 T2-1 C형 ③

credit이 '칭찬'이라는 의미로 쓰였으므로, praise가 문맥상의 동의어로 적절하다.

□ deserve v. ~할 만하다, 받을 가치가 있다 □ credit n. 신용; 명예, 칭찬; 공적; 믿음 □ bring in (새로운 것을) 받아들이다; (의제 등을) 제출하다 □ belief n. 확신; 신념, 믿음 □ payment n. 지불, 지급 □ praise n. 칭찬 □ asset n. 자산

제시간에 프로젝트를 제출한 것에 대해 팀 전체가 칭찬받을 만하다.

## 09 2022 한국외대 T1 ②

benign은 '상냥한', '친절한', '온화한', '(병리) 양성(良性)의', '무해한'의 의미로 쓰이는 다의어이다. 주어진 문장에서, 이 병이 나중에 합병증을 일으킨다고 했는데, 이는 이 질병이 이전에 생각했던 것만큼 '무해하지 않다'는 것이므로 benign은 ② 무해한(harmless)의 의미로 쓰였다고 볼 수 있다.

□ health complication 합병증

그 병은 이전에 생각했던 것만큼 무해하지 않고 나중에 합병증을 일으킨다.

## 10 2022 한국외대 T1 ②

sheer는 '몹시 가파른', '완전한', '얇은', '투명한'의 의미로 사용되는 다의어이다. 테러범의 공격에 대한 사람들의 반응은 '완전한' 공포였을 것이므로, sheer가 ② 완전한(complete)의 의미로 쓰였다고 볼 수 있다.

테러범의 공격에 대한 사람들의 즉각적인 반응은 완전한 공포였다.

## 11 2022 한국외대 T1 ④

partial은 '부분적인', '불완전한', '불공평한', '편파적인'의 의미로 사용되는 다의어이다. 주어진 문장에서는, 비엔나 중앙 의회가 독일인들에게 매우 편파적이라는(치우쳤다는) 의미로 쓰였다. 따라서 partial은 ④ (~에) 마음이 기울어진(attached)의 의미로 쓰였다고 볼 수 있다.

□ grossly ad. 지독히, 극도로 □ fractional a. 단편적인, 얼마 안 되는

매우 광범위한 권한을 가지고 있는 비엔나(오스트리아)의 중앙 의회는 독일인들에게 매우 편파적이었다.

## 12 2022 한국외대 T1 ④

hail은 '환호하며 맞이하다', '~에게 인사하다', '큰 소리로 부르다'의 의미로 사용되는 다의어이다. 주어진 문장에서, 소방관은 마을 사람들에게 아이들을 구한 영웅으로 환영받길 원할 것이므로, hail은 ④ 환영하다, 맞이하다(greet)의 의미로 쓰였다고 볼 수 있다.

그 소방관은 마을 사람들이 자신을 아이들을 구한 영웅으로 맞이해 주기를 희망한다.

## 13 2022 한국외대 T2 ②

delicate가 '연약한', '허약한'이라는 의미로 쓰였으므로, fragile이 문맥상 동의어로 적절하다.

□ delicate a. 섬세한; 미묘한, (취급에) 신중을 요하는; 허약한 □ intricate a. 뒤얽힌, 복잡한 □ fragile a. 깨지기 쉬운, 허약한 □ sensitive a. 민감한, 예민한 □ discreet a. 분별 있는, 신중한

거미줄은 비록 구조적으로는 허약하지만, 허리케인급 바람을 견딜 수 있을 만큼 튼튼하다.

## 14 2022 한국외대 T2 ④

yield가 '산출하다', '내놓다'라는 의미로 쓰였으므로, provide가 문맥상 동의어로 적절하다.

□ yield v. 굴복하다; 생기게 하다, 산출하다, 내놓다 □ qualitative a. 질적인 □ surrender v. 항복하다, 굴복하다 □ stop v. 멈추게 하다, 중지하다 □ profit v. ~의 이익이 되다 □ provide v. 주다, 공급하다

이것은 상황이 분명한 사례 연구에서 가장 잘 수행될 수 있는데, 이런 사례 연구가 질적 조사 결과를 내놓기 때문이다.

## 15 2022 한국외대 T2 ②

board가 '위원회, 국 (局)'이라는 의미로 쓰였으므로, group이 문맥상 동의어로 적절하다.

□ board n. 판자; 위원회, 원(院), 청(廳), 국(局); 무대; 식사 □ plank n. 두꺼운 판자; 강령 □ group n. 그룹, 집단 □ stage n. 무대 □ meal n. 식사

그 폭력적인 영화는 영화검열국으로부터 성인 등급을 받았다.

## 16 2022 한국외대 T2 ②

sport가 '웃음거리'라는 의미로 쓰였으므로, mockery가 문맥상 동의어로 적절하다.

□ smother v. 숨 막히게 하다; 듬뿍 바르다 □ sport n. 스포츠, 경기; 오락; 장난; 놀림거리, 웃음거리 □ athletics n. 운동경기 □ mockery n. 비웃음, 냉소; 흉내 □ companion n. 동료 □ entertainment n. 대접, 환대; 오락

핫 소스를 듬뿍 바른 프라이드치킨은 (입 주변을 엉망으로 만들므로) 종이 냅킨을 4장도 채 갖지 않고 먹으려 했다가는 웃음거리가 된다.

## 17 2021 한국외대 T1-1 ④

austere는 '(사람이) 근엄한', '금욕적인, 내핍 생활을 하는', '꾸밈없는, 소박한' 등의 의미가 있는데, 여기서는 '꾸밈없는, 소박한'의 의미로 쓰였으므로, '꾸밈없는, 아무런 장식이 없는'이라는 뜻의 unadorned가 정답으로 적절하다.

□ neat a. 정돈된, 깔끔한 □ rocking chair 흔들의자 □ barren a. 척박한, 황량한 □ destitute a. 극빈한, 가난한 □ stern a. 근엄한, 엄격한; 심각한 □ unadorned a. 꾸밈없는, 아무런 장식이 없는

그 방은 꾸밈없고 깔끔했으며, 침대 하나와 흔들의자 하나만 있었다.

## 18 2021 한국외대 T1-1 ①

mundane은 '속세의, 세속적인', '세계의, 우주의', '평범한, 일상적인' 등의 의미가 있는데, 여기서는 '평범한, 일상적인'이라는 의미로 쓰였으므로, '보통의, 평범한'이라는 뜻의 ordinary가 정답으로 적절하다.

□ narrator n. 서술자, 이야기하는 사람 □ suspect v. ~이라고 생각하다 □ of interest 흥미 있는 □ ordinary a. 보통의; 평범한 □ secular a. 세속적인 □ earthly a. 현세의, 속세의 □ material a. 물질의; 구체적인; 육체적인

많은 서술자들은 단지 마지못해 글을 썼을 뿐이며, 그들의 인생 이야기가 너무 평범해서 사람들에게 아무런 흥미도 불러일으키지 못할 것이라고 생각했다.

## 19 2021 한국외대 T1-1 ③

equity는 '공평, 공정', '소유권, 이권', '(한 회사의) 자기 자본', '(자산의) 순수가치' 등의 의미가 있는데, 여기서는 '(자산의) 순수가치'라는 의미로 쓰였으므로, '가치'를 뜻하는 value가 정답으로 적절하다. home equity (주택 순자산)는 주택을 팔 경우, 주택담보 대출 잔고를 빼고 실제로 받게 될 금액을 말한다.

□ over the years 수년간 □ tap into ~을 활용하다 □ expense n. 비용 □ ownership n. 소유권 □ fairness n. 공정 □ value n. 가치 □ stock n. 주식

수년 동안, 그들은 그들의 주택 순자산을 불필요한 경비에 활용하는 것을 조심스럽게 피해왔다.

## 20 2021 한국외대 T1-1 ③

asylum은 '(외국 정치범에게 허락되는) 망명, 피난', '(고아, 노인 등의) 보호소, 수용소', '은신처, 피난처' 등의 의미가 있는데, 여기서는 '피난처'라는 의미로 쓰였으므로, haven이 정답으로 적절하다. retreat에도 '피난처'의 의미가 있으나 주로 도시생활이나 직장생활에서 뒤로 물러나 찾는 '은둔처, 은퇴처'의 의미로 쓰여서 grant retreat to refugees로는 잘 쓰

이지 않고, '난민들에게 피난처를 제공하다'라는 뜻으로 grant asylum to refugees나 grant haven to refugees를 쓴다.

□ grant v. 주다, 승인하다 □ refugee n. 난민, (국외) 망명자 □ war-torn a. 전쟁으로 피폐해진 □ sanatorium n. 요양소; 휴양지 □ institution n. 기관; (고아원 등의) 보호시설 □ haven n. 안식처, 피난처; 항구 □ retreat n. 퇴각, 은퇴, 은신처, 피난처

유럽의 국가들은 전쟁으로 피폐해진 국가에서 온 난민들에게 피난처를 제공하기를 점차 꺼리고 있다.

## 21 2021 한국외대 T2 ②

convention은 '관습, 관례, 합의, 대회' 등 많은 의미를 갖는다. 본문에서는 공연이 끝나고 청중들의 앙코르를 받는 관례, 즉 전통에 따라 무대로 다시 나오는 것이므로 '전통'이나 '관례'의 의미를 갖는 'tradition'이 가장 적절하다.

□ offstage ad. 무대 밖으로 □ encore n. 재청, 앙코르 □ assembly n. 의회; 집회 □ conference n. 회의, 회담

공연이 끝난 후, 배우들은 무대 밖으로 나갔다가 앙코르를 받는 관례에 따라 다시 등장한다.

## 22 2021 한국외대 T2 ②

company는 '회사, 단체, 동석한 사람, 교제' 등 많은 의미를 갖는다. 본문에서는 주말 동안 그녀와 함께 보냈다는 '교제'라는 의미의 'companionship'이 가장 적절하다.

□ enterprise n. 기업, 회사; 사업 □ partner n. 동반자, 동업자 □ over the weekend 주말에

그녀가 나를 보러 먼 길을 왔으며, 나는 주말에 그녀와의 교제를 즐겼다.

## 23 2021 한국외대 T2 ①

형용사 clean은 '깨끗한, 순수한, 단정한, 완전한' 등의 뜻을 가진 다의어이다. 본문에서는 도주(getaway)가 시작부터 끝까지 완전무결하게 진행되는 것을 의미하므로 '완전한'이라는 의미로 'complete'를 뜻하고 있다.

□ getaway n. 도망, 도주 □ blank a. 빈, 그림이 없는 □ virtuous a. 도덕적인, 고결한 □ unsoiled a. 더럽혀지지 않은, 청결한

비록 내가 완전한 도주에 대해 확신이 든다고 하더라도, 나는 결코 그렇게 하기로 동의하지 않을 것이다.

## 24 2021 한국외대 T2 ②

명사 burst는 '파열, 감정의 폭발, 사격' 등의 의미를 갖는다. 본문에서는 '한바탕 화를 내다'는 의미이므로, '감정의 폭발'을 나타내는 'explosion'이 정답으로 적절하다.

□ provoke v. 유발하다, 일으키다　□ puncture n. 펑크, 찔러서 생긴 구멍　□ fracture n. 골절

놀랍게도 내 질문이 판매원의 분노를 폭발시켰다.

## 25　2021 한국외대 T3　①

lapse는 '실책, 경과, 타락, 저하' 등의 의미를 가진 다의어이다. 주어진 문장에서 lapse는 보안상의 '실책'을 의미한다. 따라서 '파괴, 실패, 실책'을 뜻하는 ① breach가 정답으로 적절하다.

□ naive a. 순진한, 천진난만한　□ lapse n. 실책; 경과; 저하　□ breach n. 파괴, 실책　□ interval n. 간격, 휴지기　□ respite n. 연기, 유예, 중간 휴식　□ termination n. 종료

오늘날 그 누구도 보안상의 실책에 대한 그런 순진한 설명을 받아들이지 않을 것이고, 그들 또한 마찬가지일 것이다.

## 26　2021 한국외대 T3　④

hinge는 명사로는 '경첩'을 뜻하고, 동사일 때에는 '의존하다'의 의미이다. 따라서 ④ depends가 정답으로 적절하다.

□ hinge on 의존하다　□ penalty n. 처벌, 형벌　□ pivot v. 선회하다　□ rotate v. 회전하다, 교대로 하다

재판이 법정에서 진실을 말하는 증인들에게 달려있다는 사실로 인해, 거짓말을 하는 사람은 중대한 처벌을 받아야 할 필요가 있다.

## 27　2021 한국외대 T3　①

동사 compromise는 '타협하다, 양보하다; 더럽히다, 손상하다, (체면을) 깎다' 등의 의미를 가진 다의어이다. 주어진 문장에서는 뇌물 수수 혐의로 정치 경력이 끝났다는 점에서, 자신을 '더럽히고 체면을 깎다'는 의미인 ① abased가 정답으로 적절하다.

□ compromise v. 타협하다, 화해하다; (명예·평판·신용 따위를) 더럽히다, 손상하다; 위태롭게 하다　□ bribe n. 뇌물　□ abase v. 깎아내리다, 비하하다　□ divulge v. 누설하다

그의 정치 경력은 뇌물을 받아 자신의 품위를 실추시켰을 때 끝이 났다.

## 28　2021 한국외대 T3　③

broad는 '폭이 넓은, 대강의, 뚜렷한, 명백한' 등의 의미를 가진 다의어이다. 주어진 문장에서는 뚜렷한 요크셔 지방의 악센트를 뜻하고 있다. 따라서 '뚜렷한, 명백한'의 의미인 ③ obvious가 정답으로 적절하다.

□ queue n. 줄, 대열　□ broad a. 폭이 넓은; 관대한; 명료한　□ liberal a. 관대한; 자유주의의　□ extensive a. 광대한; 광범위하게 미치는　□ obvious a. 명백한, 명료한　□ generous a. 관대한

내 앞에서 줄을 서있던 그 노인은 목소리가 아주 컸고 뚜렷한 요크셔 억양으로 말했다.

## 29　2020 한국외대 A형　③

civil은 '시민의', '민간의', '국내의', '예의바른' 등의 의미로 사용되는데, 여기서는 '예의바른, 친절한'의 뜻으로 쓰였으므로, '배려하는, 인정 있는, 친절한'이란 뜻의 ③ considerate이 정답으로 적절하다.

□ bring + O + to부정사 ~할 마음이 들게 하다, ~할 마음이 내키다　□ private a. 민간의　□ unarmed a. 무장하지 않은

그는 손님들에게 친절하게 대할 마음이 거의 내키지 않았다.

## 30　2020 한국외대 A형　①

oblique에는 '기울어진', '비스듬한', '잘못된', '빗면의', '에두른' 등의 의미가 있는데, 여기서는 '간접적인, 완곡한, 빙 둘러 말하는'의 의미로 쓰였으므로 '간접적인, 우회적인'이란 뜻의 ① indirect가 정답으로 적절하다.

□ suspicious a. 의심하는　□ unequal a. 불평등한　□ slanting a. 경사진, 기울어진　□ diagonal a. 대각선의, 사선의

내 질문에 대한 여동생의 우회적인 답변은 나에게 의심이 들게 했다.

## 31　2020 한국외대 A형　④

apprehend에는 '우려하다', '체포하다', '이해하다' 등의 의미가 있는데, 여기서는 '이해하다'라는 의미로 쓰였으므로, ④ understand가 정답으로 적절하다.

□ arrest v. 체포하다; 시선을 끌다　□ seize v. 잡다, 포착하다

과학은 우리가 살고 있는 세상에 대한 진리를 이해하는 체계적인 방법이다.

## 32　2020 한국외대 A형　③

bearing은 '태도', '행동거지', '출산', '관계' 등의 의미로 쓰이는데, 여기서는 '관계, 관련'의 뜻으로 쓰였으므로 ③ relevance가 정답으로 적절하다.

□ trajectory n. 곡선, 탄도; 지나온 경로　□ fluctuation n. 변화, 변동, 동요　□ demeanor n. 행동; 태도　□ sustaining a. 지속성의　□ relevance n. 관련, 적절성　□ reproduction n. 번식; 재현

그 궤도의 단기적 변동은 장기적 형세를 어떻게 보느냐 하는 것과는 거의 혹은 전혀 관련이 없다.

## 33　2020 한국외대 C형　④

figure는 '계산하다', '나타나다', '묘사하다', '생각하다' 등의 뜻이 있는데, figure 뒤에 (that)절이 이어질 경우 '~라고 생각하다, 추측하다'는 뜻으로 쓰이므로, 주어진 문장에서 figured의 문맥상 동의어는 ④ expected이다.

우리는 당신에게 그 행사를 알려주려고 생각했지만, 당신이 여행에서 돌아온 후에 쉬고 싶어 할 것이라 생각했다.

**34** **2020 한국외대 C형** ①

prominent는 '중요한', '저명한', '눈에 잘 띄는', '돌출된' 등의 뜻이 있는데, and 이하에서 쉽게 발견할 수 있었다고 했으므로 신제품이 눈에 잘 띄는 곳에 있었음을 알 수 있다. 따라서 prominent는 ① noticeable의 의미로 쓰였다고 볼 수 있다.

신제품이 가게에서 눈에 띄는 장소를 차지해서 쉽게 발견할 수 있었다.

**35** **2020 한국외대 C형** ③

claim은 '주장하다', '요구하다', '(목숨을) 앗아가다', '가치가 있다' 등의 뜻이 있는데, 주어가 '산불'이고 people이 목적어로 주어져 있으므로, claim은 ③ killed의 의미로 쓰였다고 볼 수 있다.

☐ bushfire n. 삼림[총림지]의 화재

1850년 이후로 호주의 산불은 거의 800명의 목숨을 앗아갔다.

**36** **2020 한국외대 C형** ④

maintenance에는 '유지', '지속', '생계' 등의 뜻이 있는데, 아버지가 세상을 떠난 후라면, 그녀가 가족의 생계를 떠맡았을 것이라고 볼 수 있다. ④ livelihood가 문맥상 동의어로 적절하다.

아버지가 세상을 떠난 후에, 그녀는 가족의 생계를 떠맡았다.

**37** **2019 한국외대 A형** ①

appreciate에는 '진가를 인정하다', '감사하다', '알다, 이해하다', '평가절상하다[되다]' 등의 다양한 뜻이 있지만, 여기서는 폭정에 시달리는 사람들의 자유를 가치 있는 귀중한 것으로 여겨야(value highly, hold dear)한다는 뜻으로 보는 것이 문맥상 적절하므로 appreciate는 ① prize의 의미로 쓰였다. ③ understand와 같은 의미로 쓰이는 경우는 목적어로 that절이나 귀중한 것과 무관한 명사가 올 때이다.

☐ tyranny n. 폭정, 압제, 전제 (정치)

우리는 폭정 하에서 살아가는 사람들의 자유를 귀중한 것으로 여겨야 한다.

**38** **2019 한국외대 A형** ②

slant는 '비스듬함', '의견', '경사', '기울기' 등의 뜻으로 사용되는데, 그가 상원의원의 연설에 대해 의견을 표했다는 것이 문맥상 적절하므로 slant는 ② opinion의 의미로 쓰였다.

☐ lean n. 기울기, 경사; 치우침 ☐ slope n. 경사면, 비탈 ☐ gradient n. 경사도; 비탈, 사면

그는 상원의원의 연설에 대해 자신만의 자유로운 의견을 말했다.

**39** **2019 한국외대 A형** ②

sanction은 '허가', '승인', '인가', '제재' 등의 뜻으로 사용되는데, 안전보장이사회는 국제 평화의 안전을 우선 사항으로 할 것이므로 테러에 연관된 당사국들에 대해서는 제재를 가하는 결정을 내릴 것이다. 따라서 sanctions는 ② penalties의 의미로 쓰였다.

☐ invoke sanctions against ~에 대해 제재를 가하다 ☐ authorization n. 허가, 인가 ☐ patronage n. 보호, 후원, 장려 ☐ confirmation n. 확인

안전보장이사회는 테러에 연관된 당사국들에 대한 제재를 가하기로 결의했다.

**40** **2019 한국외대 A형** ①

pronounce는 '발음하다', '선언하다', '발표하다' 등의 뜻으로 사용되는데, 자동차 사고와 관련하여 긴급 구조대원들은 운전자가 사고 현장에서 사망했다고 발표했을 것이므로 문맥상 pronounced는 ① declared의 의미로 쓰였다.

☐ horrific a. 끔찍한, 무시무시한 ☐ vocalize v. 목소리로 내다 ☐ utter v. 입 밖에 내다; 발언하다

끔찍한 충돌 사고 후에, 긴급 구조대원들은 운전자가 사고 현장에서 사망했다고 발표했다.

**41** **2019 한국외대 C형** ④

cool은 '시원한', '멋진', '근사한', '침착한' 등의 뜻으로 쓰이는데, 주어진 문장에서는 '시험공부를 제대로 하지 않은 사람이 보일 태도나 심리와 상반되는 태도'를 나타내는 의미로 쓰였으므로, ④ calm이 정답으로 적절하다.

☐ chilly a. 쌀쌀한, 추운 ☐ stylish a. 유행을 따른; 멋진

그녀는 공부를 하지 않았음에도 불구하고 기말시험 전에 매우 침착한 듯 보였다.

**42** **2019 한국외대 C형** ①

untouched는 '손대지 않은', '영향을 받지 않은' 등의 뜻으로 쓰이는데, 경기침체가 공장의 생산을 저하시키면 기계가 '사용되지 않고 그대로 있을' 것이므로, ① unused가 문맥상의 동의어로 적절하다.

☐ unaffected a. 영향을 받지 않은 ☐ unmoved a. 흔들리지 않는, 냉정한 ☐ unmodified a. 변경되지 않은

경기침체가 너무나 심해서 기계가 수년 동안 공장에 방치된 채로 있었다.

**43** 2019 한국외대 C형                                      ②

entertain은 '즐겁게 하다', '(생각·감정 등을) 품다', '대접하다' 등의 의미로 쓰이는데, 목적어로 'the idea'가 왔으므로 '(생각·감정 등을) 품다'라는 뜻으로 쓰인 것이다. 따라서 ②가 정답으로 적절하다.

☐ temporary a. 일시의, 잠깐 동안의  ☐ cheer v. 갈채하다; 환영하여 소리치다

당신은 당신의 집에 임시 롤러코스터를 설치할 생각을 해본 적이 있습니까?

**44** 2019 한국외대 C형                                      ①

depressed는 '(노면이) 내려앉은', '낙담한', '부진한' 등의 뜻으로 쓰인다. 폭우가 내릴 때 항상 물에 잠기는 부분은 노면이 '내려앉은' 부분일 것이므로, 주어진 문장에서는 ① sunken의 의미로 쓰였음을 알 수 있다.

☐ overpass n. 고가도로, 육교  ☐ distressed a. 고통스러워하는  ☐ mournful a. 슬픔에 잠긴  ☐ underprivileged a. 혜택을 못 받는

고가도로 아래에 있는 고속도로의 움푹 내려앉은 부분은 폭우가 내리면 항상 물에 잠긴다.

**45** 2018 한국외대 A형                                      ③

positive가 '확신하는'이라는 의미로 쓰였으므로, certain이 문맥상의 동의어로 적절하다.

☐ positive a. 확신하는; 긍정적인; 건설적인; 완전한  ☐ optimistic a. 낙관적인  ☐ beneficial a. 유익한, 이익을 가져오는  ☐ certain a. 확신하는; 확실한  ☐ complete a. 완전한, 완벽한

그는 그녀가 없으면 자신이 평생 방황하게 될 것이라 확신했다.

**46** 2018 한국외대 A형                                      ④

account가 '이유'라는 의미로 쓰였으므로, reason이 문맥상의 동의어로 적절하다.

☐ account n. 계산; 청구서; 답변, 설명; 이유, 근거; 이익  ☐ advantage n. 이익; 우세, 우월  ☐ version n. 번역; 번역문; 해석, 의견, 설명  ☐ invoice n. 송장(送狀); 청구서  ☐ reason n. 이유, 까닭; 근거

지난 분기에 큰 손실이 발생한 것에 대한 그 회사의 이유는 무엇입니까?

**47** 2018 한국외대 A형                                      ②

fit이 '건강한'이란 의미로 쓰였으므로, healthy가 문맥상의 동의어로 적절하다.

☐ chiseled a. 이목구비가 뚜렷한, 잘생긴  ☐ fit a. 알맞은; 적임의; 건강이 좋은  ☐ suitable a. 적당한; 어울리는  ☐ healthy a. 건강한  ☐ equipped a. 갖춰진, 설비된  ☐ right a. 옳은, 적절한

그 노인은 검은 머리카락과 이목구비가 뚜렷한 얼굴에 진지한 갈색 눈을 갖고 있었고, 그의 아들만큼이나 건강한 모습이었다.

**48** 2018 한국외대 A형                                      ①

plastic이 '마음대로 모양을 만들 수 있는, 유연한'이라는 의미로 쓰였으므로, malleable이 문맥상의 동의어로 적절하다.

☐ limb n. (사람·동물의) 수족, 손발  ☐ relatively ad. 비교적; 상대적으로  ☐ plastic a. 마음대로 모양을 만들 수 있는; 유연한; 성형의  ☐ malleable a. 펴서 늘일 수 있는; 유순한  ☐ molded a. 틀에 넣어 만든, 본을 뜬  ☐ inorganic a. 생활기능이 없는, 무생물의  ☐ artificial a. 인공의, 인위적인

아기의 팔다리는 성인의 팔다리와 비교했을 때 상대적으로 유연하다.

**49** 2018 한국외대 C형                                      ②

game에는 '경기', '오락', '계략', '사냥감' 등의 뜻이 있는데, 식량을 얻고자 사냥을 했다고 했으므로 game이 문맥상 뜻하는 것은 ② prey이다.

20년이 넘는 동안 그녀는 식량을 얻고자 먹이를 사냥하고 채소를 재배했다.

**50** 2018 한국외대 C형                                      ④

establishment는 '설립', '시설', '회사', '지배층' 등의 뜻이 있는데, 자신을 비판하는 언론인을 감옥에 보낼 수 있는 것은 언론의 감시대상이면서 언론인에게 위해를 가할 수 있는 권력 계급인 '지배층'이라고 볼 수 있으므로 ④가 정답이다.

지배층을 과도하게 비난하는 경우 언론인은 투옥될 수도 있다.

**51** 2018 한국외대 C형                                      ③

try a person's patience to the limit는 '~의 인내심을 한계에 이르기까지 시험하다'라는 의미로 쓰이는데, stretch a person's patience to the limit이 이와 같은 의미로 사용되므로 ③이 정답이다.

☐ obnoxious a. 밉살스러운, 불쾌한, 싫은  ☐ patience n. 인내(력), 참을성  ☐ determine v. 결심하다

밉살스러운 그 아이는 모든 사람의 인내심을 한계에 이르기까지 시험했다.

**52** 2018 한국외대 C형                                      ④

positive는 '명백한', '확신하는', '완전한', '긍정적인'의 뜻이 있는데, 아이가 나쁜 시험 결과를 받아들인 것을 통해 그 아이가 긍정적인 성격을 지닌 것으로 볼 수 있다. 따라서 positive가 ④ optimistic의 의미로 쓰였음을 알 수 있다.

그녀가 나쁜 시험 결과를 받아들인 것은 9살짜리 아이치고는 놀라울 정도로 긍정적인 행동이었다.

## 53  2017 한국외대 A형                                               ④

mean은 형용사로 쓰일 때 '뒤떨어진', '평범한', '인색한', '무례한' 등의 의미로 쓰이는데, 학생들에게 조용히 할 것을 요구하는 방법 혹은 성향을 설명하는 표현이 문맥상 적절하므로, ④ unkind가 정답이다.

그 선생님은 학생들에게 조용히 할 것을 요구하는 데 있어 무례하지 않았다.

## 54  2017 한국외대 A형                                               ②

누군가가 싸움을 걸려고 할 때 외면해 버린다면 싸움이 일어나지 않을 것이므로, 이런 행동은 '현명한' 행동일 것이다. 따라서 sensible은 문맥상 ② wise의 의미로 쓰였다고 볼 수 있다.

☐ walk away (힘든 상황·관계를 외면하고) 떠나 버리다

누군가가 싸움을 걸려고 할 경우에 할 수 있는 현명한 행동은 그냥 피하는 것이다.

## 55  2017 한국외대 A형                                               ④

qualified는 '자격이 있는', '권한[자격]이 주어진', '제한[한정]된' 등의 뜻으로 쓰인다. '참가자들에게는 훌륭했으나, 주최자들에게는 그다지 이득이 되지 못했다'는 것은 제한적인 성공을 거뒀다는 것을 의미하므로, qualified가 ④ limited(제한된)의 의미로 쓰였음을 알 수 있다.

참가자들에게 그 회의는 훌륭했다. 그러나 이득을 거의 보지 못하는 주최자들에게 그 회의는 제한적인 성공이었다.

## 56  2017 한국외대 A형                                               ④

respect는 '존경', '경의', '측면' 등의 의미로 쓰인다. 겉모습은 아버지와 닮았지만, 다른 모든 면이 다르다는 의미로 쓰였으므로, respect는 문맥상 ④ facet(측면)의 뜻으로 쓰였음을 알 수 있다.

그는 아버지를 닮았음에도 불구하고, 그들은 거의 모든 면에서 서로 다르다.

## 57  2017 한국외대 C형                                               ①

보고서를 제출하지 못했다는 표현을 통해, oversight가 '과실'의 의미로 쓰였음을 알 수 있다.

☐ oversight n. 실수, 과실; 부주의; 감독  ☐ lapse n. 실책, 실수, 잘못; (시간의) 경과  ☐ supervision n. 감독  ☐ indifference n. 무관심

정부는 보고서를 제출하지 못한 교육부 장관의 과실을 조사하는 중이다.

## 58  2017 한국외대 C형                                               ③

charge가 '가득 채우다, 충만하게 하다'는 의미로 쓰였으므로, ③ permeated가 문맥상의 동의어로 적절하다.

☐ impending a. 곧 일어날 것 같은  ☐ barrack n. 막사  ☐ charge v. 가득 채우다; 책망하다, 비난하다; 고발하다  ☐ accused a. 고발된  ☐ permeate v. 스며들다, 충만하다, 가득 채우다  ☐ obligated a. 의무가 있는

임박한 전쟁에 대해 말하는 사람은 없었지만, 막사의 분위기는 긴장으로 가득 찼다.

## 59  2017 한국외대 C형                                               ③

미국 군대의 '해외파병'을 언급한 점에서 볼 때, draft는 '징병'이라는 의미로 쓰인 것이며, 따라서 ③ conscription이 문맥상의 동의어로 적절하다.

☐ draft n. 통풍; 설계도; 징병  ☐ conscription n. 징병제도  ☐ blueprint n. 청사진; 상세한 계획

1973년에 징병제도가 종식되기 전까지, 미국은 자국의 군대를 27번 해외에 파병했었다.

## 60  2017 한국외대 C형                                               ③

blunt에는 도구의 날이 '무딘', 성격이 '무뚝뚝한', 이해가 '둔감한', '솔직한' 등의 의미가 있는데, 주어진 문장에서는 '솔직한'의 뜻으로 쓰였으므로, ③ forthright가 문맥상의 동의어이다.

☐ blunt a. 무딘; (이해가) 둔감한; 솔직한  ☐ thick skin 둔감함; 낯두꺼움, 사람들의 비판을 무시하거나 견뎌낼 수 있는 능력  ☐ forthright a. 솔직한; 털어놓는

동료들은 당신의 강점과 약점을 평가하는 데 솔직하므로, (당신에게는) 낯 두꺼움이 필수적이다.

## 61  2016 한국외대 A형                                               ④

자신이 감기와 독감에 '걸리기 쉬운' 사람이라고 설명하고 있으므로 '취약한'이란 뜻의 ④가 정답이 된다.

☐ avid a. 열렬한; 탐욕스러운  ☐ work out 운동하다, 해결하다, 이끌어내다  ☐ susceptible a. 영향을 받기 쉬운, 감염되기 쉬운; 민감한  ☐ responsive a. 반응하는, 호응하는  ☐ suggestible a. 남의 영향을 받기 쉬운  ☐ vulnerable a. 취약한, 연약한

나는 열렬한 보디빌더이고 매일 운동을 하지만, 감기와 독감에 매우 잘 걸린다.

## 62  2016 한국외대 A형                                               ②

어린 나이와 어울리지 않는 공주의 성품을 이야기하고 있는 흐름이므로, ②가 정답이 된다.

□ bearing n. 관련; 태도, 자세 □ unassuming a. 참견하지 않는, 허세 부리지 않는 □ plain a. 명백한; 평범한 □ modest a. 겸손한 □ simplistic a. 극단적으로 단순한 □ subservient a. 굴종하는; 부차적인

그 예쁘고 눈이 푸른 공주는 14살에 불과했지만, 태도가 겸손했다.

## 63 2016 한국외대 A형 ①

'not A but B'는 'A가 아니라 B이다'라는 의미로, 이때 A와 B에는 대조를 이루는 표현이 온다. 주어진 문장에서 design은 '우연'과 반대되는 의미로 쓰인 것이므로, '의도'의 뜻을 지닌 ①이 정답이다.

□ parliament n. 의회, 국회 □ rejection n. 거절, 배제, 폐기, 각하, 부결 □ ceremony n. 의식, 격식 □ evidently ad. 분명히, 눈에 띄게 □ accident n. 사고; 우연 □ design n. 디자인, 설계; 계획, 의도

의회가 전통 의식을 거절한 것은 틀림없이 우연의 결과가 아니라 의도된 결과이다.

## 64 2016 한국외대 A형 ④

substance에는 '물질', '본질', '핵심', '중요성' 등의 의미가 있는데, 재계에 진출하고 싶어 하는 것은 영향력을 행사할 수 있는 '중요한' 사람이 되고 싶은 것이므로, 주어진 문장에서 substance는 '중요성'의 의미로 쓰였다고 볼 수 있다.

□ corporate a. 법인의, 회사의, 기업의 □ substance n. 물질, 실체, 본질, 핵심, 중요성 □ matter n. 문제, 일, 상황, 물질 □ density n. 밀도, 농도 □ essence n. 본질, 정수, 진수

앨리스(Alice)는 아이비리그에 속한 학교를 졸업한 후에 재계에 참여하여 영향력 있는 여성이 되기를 바라고 있다.

## 65 2016 한국외대 C형 ③

crooked는 '굽은, 구부러진'이라는 뜻 이외에도 사람의 인격에 대한 설명으로 '부정한, 부정직한'의 뜻이 있는데, 주어진 문장에서는 후자의 뜻으로 쓰였다.

□ crooked a. 꼬부라진, 비뚤어진; 부정직한, 마음이 비뚤어진 □ the accused 피고인 □ deformed a. 볼품없는; 불구의, 기형의 □ bent a. 굽은, 뒤틀린; 열중한 □ dishonest a. 부정직한, 불성실한

장기간의 수사 끝에 그 부정직한 경찰관이 피고로부터 돈을 받았다는 사실이 드러났다.

## 66 2016 한국외대 C형 ④

법(legislation, law)을 enact한다(제정한다)는 것은 법을 만드는 것을 의미하고, introduce한다(도입한다)는 것은 법을 처음으로 만들어 받아들이는 것을 의미하므로 문맥상 동의어라 할 수 있다. 한편, enforce한다는 것은 만든 법을 실행[집행]하는 것을 의미하므로, 문맥상으로 동의어가 될 수 없다.

□ aftermath n. (전쟁·사고 등의) 여파, 후유증 □ high-profile a. 세간의 이목을 끄는 □ enforce v. (법률 등을) 집행하다, 실시하다 □ dramatize v. 각색하다; 과장되게 표현하다 □ carry out v. ~을 수행하다, 실시하다 □ introduce v. 창안하다, 도입하다, 소개하다

그 법은 작년에 세간의 이목을 끌었던 두 건의 아동학대 사건의 여파로 제정되었다.

## 67 2016 한국외대 C형 ②

measure는 '측정'이나 '계측' 이외에도 '행동이나 조치'를 의미한다. 주어진 문장의 경우, 우리가 취하는 필요한 '조치'라는 의미이므로, ②가 문맥상 동의어이다.

□ measure n. 측정, 계측; 조치 □ yardstick n. 기준, 척도 □ merit n. 가치, 장점 □ instrument n. 도구; 수단

우리가 취하는 모든 필요한 조치는 그 나라의 혼란스러운 상황을 개선시킬 가능성을 갖고 있어야 한다.

## 68 2016 한국외대 C형 ①

dress는 '옷을 입히다'와 '장식하다'의 의미 이외에도 '(상처를) 치료하다'와 '붕대를 감다(bandage)'라는 의미가 있으며, 주어진 문장에서는 후자의 의미로 쓰였으므로 ①이 정답이 된다.

□ infection n. (병의) 전염, 감염 □ bandage v. 붕대를 감다 □ clothe v. 옷을 입히다 □ decorate v. 장식하다 □ align v. 일직선으로 하다; 조정하다

매일 아침, 그 간호사가 군인의 상처를 치료하고 붕대로 감아주었지만, 그 군인은 2차 세균감염이 되었다.

## 69 2015 한국외대 A형 ①

chance는 '가능성', '기회' 그리고 '우연이나 위험'과 같은 다양한 의미를 갖는데, 주어진 문장에서는 비행기를 탈 수 있는 실낱같은 '가능성'을 의미하므로 likelihood가 동의어가 된다.

□ outside chance 실낱같은 가능성 □ likelihood n. 가능성, 있음직한 일 □ risk n. 위험, 위험성 □ destiny n. 운명

우리가 서두른다면, 아직은 그 비행기를 탈 수 있는 실낱같은 가능성이 있다.

## 70 2015 한국외대 A형 ②

peripheral은 '중요하지 않은', '주변의', '변두리의' 등의 의미를 갖고 있는데, 주어진 문장에서는 '주변의'라는 의미로 쓰였으므로 ② marginal이 동의어이다.

□ peripheral a. 중요하지 않은, 지엽적인; 주변부의 □ secondary a. 부차적인; 종속적인 □ marginal a. 미미한; 주변부의, 가장자리의 □ superficial a. 피상적인; 표면적인 □ insignificant a. 사소한, 하찮은

정부는 대도시의 변두리 지역에 도시 개발을 추진할 준비가 되어 있다.

## 71 2015 한국외대 A형 ②

initiative에는 '주도권', '계획', '진취성', '법안' 등의 의미가 있다. 국회가 발의했다는 내용으로 미루어, 주어진 문장에서는 '법안'의 뜻으로 쓰였음을 알 수 있으며, 따라서 ②가 정답이 된다.

☐ initiative n. 계획; 진취성; 주도권; 주민법안 발의 ☐ propose v. 제안하다, 발의하다 ☐ preschool n. 유치원 ☐ leadership n. 지도, 지도력, 리더십, 통솔력 ☐ bill n. 청구서; 고지서; (국회에 제출된) 법안 ☐ ambition n. 야심, 야망 ☐ introduction n. 도입; 소개

국회에서 발의한 유치원 확대 법안은 대체로 민간 분야에 의해 좌우될 것이다.

## 72 2015 한국외대 A형 ①

명사 echo에는 '메아리', '반향' 외에 '모방', '반영', '흔적'의 의미도 있다. 주어진 문장의 경우, 동시대의 수많은 '유사한 사건'을 의미하므로, ①이 문맥상의 동의어이다.

☐ contemporary a. 동시대의, 현대의 ☐ echo n. 메아리, 반향, 되풀이, 모방; 의견의 공감 ☐ imitation n. 모방; 흉내; 모조품 ☐ reflection n. 반사; 반영; 영상; 숙고

2000년 12월에 국가정보위원회가 발간한 "2015년 세계 동향" 보고서에서 묘사하고 있는 미래는 오늘날의 수많은 유사한 사건들을 담고 있다.

## 73 2015 한국외대 C형 ①

scamp에는 '깡패', '장난꾸러기', '강도' 등의 의미가 있는데, 주어진 문장에서는 '장난꾸러기'라는 의미로 쓰였으므로, prankster가 문맥상의 동의어이다. rogue는 hilarious와 의미적으로 호응하지 않는다.

☐ scamp n. 무뢰한, 깡패; 개구쟁이; 노상강도 ☐ bit n. 짧은 공연물, 행사 ☐ apolitical a. 정치적 관심이 없는, 정치와 무관한 ☐ hilarious a. 재미있는, 즐거운 ☐ prankster n. 장난꾸러기 ☐ swindler n. 사기꾼 ☐ rogue n. 불량배, 깡패 ☐ troublemaker n. 말썽꾸러기

그는 구제불능의 장난꾸러기이다. 그래서 정치색이 없는 공연행사들조차도 재미있었다.

## 74 2015 한국외대 C형 ④

dense가 주어진 문장에서는 '아둔한', '어리석은'이란 의미로 쓰였으므로, stupid가 문맥상의 동의어이다.

☐ dense a. 밀집한; (인구가) 조밀한; 밀도가 높은; 아둔한, 어리석은 ☐ crowded a. 붐비는, 혼잡한, 꽉 찬; 만원의 ☐ opaque a. 불투명한; (전파소리 따위를) 통과시키지 않는 ☐ stupid a. 어리석은, 우둔한, 바보 같은

이것은 대단히 중요한 게 아니고 아마도 제가 조금 아둔한 것일 수도 있습니다만, 누군가 명확하게 밝혀주시면 정말 감사하겠습니다.

## 75 2015 한국외대 C형 ③

issue가 주어진 문장에서는 '자손', '자녀', '후대'의 의미로 쓰였으므로, posterity가 문맥상의 동의어이다.

☐ issue n. 발행; 발행물; 토론; 결과; 자녀, 자손 ☐ outcome n. 결과; 성과 ☐ sequel n. 계속, 후편; 결과 ☐ posterity n. 자손; 후세, 후대 ☐ contention n. 투쟁; 말다툼, 논쟁

그 왕은 후손을 두지 못한 채 죽었다. 그래서 결국 그의 조카가 왕위를 계승했다.

## 76 2015 한국외대 C형 ①

charge가 주어진 문장에서는 '돌격', '진격'의 의미로 쓰였으므로, sally가 문맥상의 동의어이다.

☐ charge n. 책임, 의무; 위탁, 보호; 비난; 고소; 돌격 ☐ Union n. (남북전쟁 당시의) 연방정부를 지지한 북부의 여러 주들, 연방군, 북군 ☐ Federal a. 연방주의자의; (남북전쟁 당시의) 연방 정부 지지의, 북부의 ☐ Federal troop 북부(지상)군 ☐ sally n. 출격, 돌격 ☐ liability n. 책임, 책무, 부담 ☐ indictment n. 기소, 고발 ☐ custody n. 보호, 관리; 감금, 구류

그들은 돌격을 이끌었으며, 북군(北軍)의 세 번째 방어선을 돌파하여 퇴각하는 북군을 바싹 뒤쫓았다.

## 77 2014 한국외대 A형 ③

콜론(:) 이하에서 설명하고 있는 내용으로부터 arbitrary가 주어진 문장에서 어떤 의미로 쓰였는지를 알아보아야 한다. '어떤 것이든 다른 어느 것으로부터도 분리되어 단절되도록 만들 수 있다'는 것의 속뜻은 그 경계가 정해져 있지 않다는 것이므로, arbitrary는 '임의적인'이란 의미로 쓰였음을 알 수 있다.

☐ border n. 테두리, 가장자리; 경계 ☐ arbitrary a. 임의의, 멋대로의; 독단적인 ☐ separate v. 갈라서 떼어놓다, 분리하다 ☐ discontinuous a. 끊어진, 계속되지 않는 ☐ whimsical a. 마음이 잘 변하는, 변덕스러운 ☐ tyrannical a. 폭군 같은; 전제적인 ☐ random a. 닥치는 대로의, 임의의 ☐ absolute a. 절대적인; 순전한; 전적인

사진 이미지가 지배하는 세계에서는, 영상(映像)의 모든 경계가 임의적인 것처럼 보인다. 어떤 것이든 다른 어느 것으로부터도 분리되어 단절되도록 만들 수 있다.

## 78 2014 한국외대 A형 ③

apprehend의 행위 주체가 경찰이고, and 이하에서 테스가 경범죄로 기소되었다고 했으므로, apprehend는 '체포하다'라는 의미로 쓰였음을 알 수 있다.

□ apprehend v. 염려하다; 체포하다; 이해하다 □ subsequently ad. 그 후, 계속해서 □ accuse v. 고발하다; 비난하다 □ misdemeanor n. 경범죄; 비행, 행실이 나쁨 □ appreciate v. 평가하다, 진가를 인정하다; 감상하다 □ arrest v. 체포하다; 저지하다 □ concern v. 관계하다; 염려하다, 걱정하다

테스(Tess)는 지역 경찰에 체포되었으며, 그 후에 경범죄로 기소되었다.

## 79  2014 한국외대 A형                                      ①

기품 있는 사람이 다른 사람의 말투에 대해 불평했다면, 이는 그 사람의 말투가 자신의 기준에 미치지 못했기 때문일 것이다. 따라서 common이 '기품 있는'과 반대되는 의미로 쓰였음을 알 수 있으므로 '저속한'이란 의미의 ①이 정답이다.

□ common a. 공통의; 일반적인, 평범한; 비속한 □ vulgar a. 저속한, 야비한; 통속적인 □ recognizable a. 인지할 수 있는, 알아볼 수 있는 □ trivial a. 하찮은, 사소한; 평범한 □ frequent a. 자주 일어나는, 빈번한; 상습적인

기품 있는 잉그리드(Ingrid) 공주는 사라 노튼(Sarah Norton) 공작부인의 저속한 말투에 관해 오랫동안 불평해 왔다.

## 80  2014 한국외대 A형                                      ②

'펀드의 도움을 받았다'는 부분이 단서가 된다. 이는 곧 figure가 돈과 관련된 의미로 쓰였다는 것을 뜻하며, 따라서 '값', '액수'라는 의미의 ②가 정답이 된다.

□ sculpture n. 조각; 조각 작품 □ undisclosed a. 발표되지 않은, 비밀에 부쳐진 □ figure n. 숫자; 합계, 값; 모양; 인물 □ symbol n. 상징; 기호 □ sum n. 총계, 총액; 액수, 금액 □ statue n. 상(像), 조상(彫像) □ form n. 모양, 형상

그 조각상은 미술품 펀드의 도움을 받아 밝혀지지 않은 액수에 구입되었다.

## 81  2014 한국외대 C형                                      ①

이 문장에서 relentless는 '잔혹한, 가차 없는'의 뜻이 아니라 '집요한, 끊임없는, 부단한, 지속적인(continuing without ever stopping)'의 뜻이므로 constant가 가장 가깝다.

□ relentless a. 엄격한, 가혹한; 끊임없는, 지속적인 □ devotion n. 전념, 헌신 □ constant a. 일정한, 항구적인, 부단한 □ inflexible a. 경직된, 완고한, 강직한 □ implacable a. 무자비한, 앙심 깊은 □ brutal a. 잔인한, 사나운

그가 쓴 새뮤얼 존슨(Samuel Johnson)의 전기(傳記)는 그것이 사회적이고 지적인 기술(記述)에 끊임없이 전념한 것으로 인해 고전의 지위를 갖게 된다.

## 82  2014 한국외대 C형                                      ④

논쟁을 해결하고 풀어간다는 점에서 'resolution'은 'settlement'와 같다.

□ misstep n. 잘못, 과실, 실수 □ resolution n. 결의, 결심; (문제의) 해결, 해답 □ tuberculosis n. 결핵 □ unintended a. 고의가 아닌, 의도된 것이 아닌 □ side effect 부작용, 후유증 □ perseverance n. 인내, 끈기 □ settlement n. 거주; 해결, 확정

결핵 퇴치에 대한 논쟁을 해결하는 데 있어 한 번 실수를 하면 심각하고 의도하지 않은 부작용을 국가 전체에 가져올 수도 있을 것이다.

## 83  2014 한국외대 C형                                      ②

엄청난 관객들이 운집했다는 점에서, 'monstrous'는 '기괴한'의 의미가 아니라 '거대한, 엄청난'의 의미이다.

□ monstrous a. 괴물 같은, 기괴한; 엄청난 □ villainous a. 악당의; 악랄한 □ colossal a. 거대한, 어마어마한 □ grotesque a. 기괴한 □ hideous a. 무서운, 극악한

그 경기장은 불과 10,000명을 수용할 수 있지만, 그 콘서트를 보러 엄청난 관객들이 왔다.

## 84  2014 한국외대 C형                                      ①

지진으로 인한 결과를 생각하면, 'claimed'는 '주장하다'의 의미가 아니라 '생명을 앗아가다'는 의미임을 알 수 있다.

□ claim v. 요구하다, 주장하다; (인명을) 빼앗다 □ allege v. 주장하다, 진술하다 □ maintain v. 지속하다, 유지하다; 주장하다

그 지진으로 인해 이미 100명 이상이 사망했다.

| | | | | | | | | | |
|---|---|---|---|---|---|---|---|---|---|
| 01 ③ | 02 ① | 03 ④ | 04 ⑤ | 05 ① | 06 ③ | 07 ③ | 08 ⑤ | 09 ② | 10 ⑤ |
| 11 ② | 12 ④ | 13 ③ | 14 ③ | 15 ④ | 16 ① | 17 ③ | 18 ⑤ | 19 ③ | 20 ① |
| 21 ② | 22 ② | 23 ④ | 24 ④ | 25 ③ | 26 ④ | 27 ③ | 28 ④ | 29 ④ | 30 ① |
| 31 ③ | 32 ② | 33 ② | 34 ④ | 35 ⑤ | 36 ④ | 37 ① | 38 ④ | 39 ⑤ | 40 ② |
| 41 ⑤ | 42 ② | 43 ⑤ | 44 ④ | 45 ⑤ | 46 ③ | 47 ① | 48 ① | 49 ④ | 50 ④ |
| 51 ④ | 52 ④ | 53 ④ | 54 ② | 55 ④ | 56 ① | 57 ⑤ | 58 ① | 59 ⑤ | |

## 01 2023 이화여대 ③

□ impact v. 영향을 끼치다 □ disrupt v. 방해하다, 지장을 주다 (↔ enliven 활기 있게 만들다, 생기를 주다) □ marginalize v. 하찮게 대하다, 주변화하다 □ simulate v. 모방하다 □ enervate v. 약화시키다 □ insinuate v. 암시하다, 넌지시 말하다

기후변화는 현재 각 대륙 모든 나라에 영향을 미치고 있어서, 국가 경제를 악화시킬 뿐 아니라 개인 및 공동체의 삶에도 악영향을 끼치고 있다.

## 02 2023 이화여대 ①

□ mitigate v. 완화하다(↔ exacerbate 악화시키다) □ exasperate v. 화나게 하다 □ expiate v. 속죄하다 □ exfoliate v. 박피하다 □ exonerate v. 무죄임을 밝히다

기후변화를 완화시켜서 적응하지 못한 것은 가장 커다란 전 지구적 위험으로서, 환경, 경제 및 보건상에 상당한 영향을 끼친다.

## 03 2023 이화여대 ④

□ faced with ~에 직면한 □ prevarication n. 발뺌, 핑계, 변명, 얼버무림(↔ forthrightness 단도직입, 솔직성) □ go-to a. 항상 찾는, 기본적인, 자동적인 □ forbearance n. 관용 □ forewarning n. 경고 □ forgoing n. 포기 □ foresight n. 선견지명

어려운 상황에 직면하는 일부 사람들에게는 발뺌이 늘 찾는 대응(방법)이다.

## 04 2023 이화여대 ⑤

□ clamor n. 아우성 □ precipitate v. 촉진하다 □ insatiable a. 만족을 모르는, 채울 길 없는 □ fervor n. 열정, 열의 □ laud v. 칭송하다 (↔ pan 혹평하다) □ purloin v. 훔치다 □ pad v. 완충재를 대다 □ pen v. 글을 쓰다 □ pawn v. 전당포에 잡히다, ~을 저당잡히다

그 그룹의 두 번째 앨범에 대한 아우성은 이들의 매체, 특히 비평가들이 늘 칭송해 왔던 이들의 초기 앨범에 대한 식을 줄 모르는 열기를 가속화시켰다.

## 05 2023 이화여대 ①

□ empirical a. 경험(주의)적인, 실제적인(↔ conjectural 추측의, 추론의) □ investigate v. 탐구하다, 연구하다 □ theoretical a. 이론적인 □ serial a. 직렬의 □ parallel a. 병렬의, 평행의 □ identification n. 식별 □ convivial a. 유쾌한 □ conspiratorial a. 공모의, 음모의 □ consanguine a. 같은 혈족의 □ conjunctive a. 접속의, 연결의

그 문제들을 연구하는 유력한 경험적 연구들은 자연적으로 문장을 읽고 이해하는 동안 직렬적인(나란히 이루어지는) 단어 식별이 행해지는가 아니면 병렬적인(함께 이루어지는) 단어 식별이 행해지는가에 대한 현재의 이론 논쟁에 정보를 제공하는 데 있어 중요하다.

## 06 2022 이화여대 ③

□ identify with ~와 동일시하다 □ take on ~을 받아들이다, 수용하다 (↔ reject 거부[거절]하다) □ norm n. 규범 □ absorb v. 흡수하다 □ obliterate v. 없애다, 지우다

아이들은 자신과 비슷한 아이들의 집단과 동일시하고 그 집단의 규범을 받아들인다.

## 07 2022 이화여대 ③

□ adulthood n. 성인(임), 성년 □ let up 멈추다, 느슨해지다, 줄어들다 (↔ increase 증가하다) □ reassert oneself 다시 효력을 발휘하다 □ diminish v. 감소하다 □ die out 멸종되다 □ go down 넘어지다

성인기에는 압박이 점차 줄어들고 개인차가 다시 효력을 발휘한다.

## 08 2022 이화여대 ⑤

□ survey v. 조사하다, 살피다 □ salient a. 두드러진, 현저한(↔ minor 사소한, 하찮은) □ feature n. 특징 □ focus on ~에 초점을 맞추다 □ influential a. 영향력이 있는 □ underscore v. 강조하다 □ non-trivial a. 특별한

우리는 그 언어의 두드러진 특징 몇 가지를 차이를 중심으로 이미 조사해 보았다.

**09** 2022 이화여대      ②

☐ potentially ad. 잠재적으로 ☐ controversial a. 논란이 많은, 논쟁의 ☐ amply ad. 충분히, 풍부하게, 넉넉히(↔ insufficiently 불충분하게) ☐ substantially ad. 상당히 ☐ unambiguously ad. 명확히

여성들의 우정에 관한 이 새롭고 논란이 될 수 있는 견해는 충분히 지지받고 있다.

**10** 2022 이화여대      ⑤

☐ misinformation n. 오보, 그릇된 정보 ☐ crisis n. 위기 ☐ clear-eyed a. 눈이 맑은, 총명한, 명민한(↔ imperceptive 감지 못하는, 지각력이 없는) ☐ drive v. 추진하다, 밀어붙이다 ☐ spread n. 확산 ☐ malicious a. 악의적인 ☐ falsehood n. 거짓 ☐ conspiracy theory 음모론 ☐ empirical a. 경험적인 ☐ impartial a. 공정한, 편견이 없는 ☐ discerning a. 안목[식별력] 있는 ☐ reasonable a. 합리적인

이 허위정보 위기의 해결책을 찾기 위해 우리 사회는 누가 그리고 무엇이 악의적인 거짓과 음모론의 확산을 부추기는지 현명하게 평가해야 한다.

**11** 2022 이화여대      ②

☐ endowment n. 재능 ☐ will n. 의지 ☐ appetite n. 욕구 ☐ idiosyncratic a. 특이한, 색다른(↔ conventional 평범한, 상투적인) ☐ comical a. 웃기는, 재미있는 ☐ incessant a. 끝없는, 그칠 새 없는 ☐ eccentric a. 기이한, 색다른 ☐ electric a. 전기의, 열광케 하는

피카소의 예술적 재능과 의지와 삶의 욕망과 인격이 과다한 것은 아주 어린 시절부터 특이했던 것 같다.

**12** 2021 이화여대      ④

☐ taken a. 매혹된(↔ bored 따분해진, 흥미를 잃은) ☐ captivated a. 매혹된 ☐ obsessed a. ~에 집착하는, 사로잡힌 ☐ humiliated a. 창피한 ☐ displeased a. 불쾌한, 불만이 있는

괴테(Goethe)는 고전주의 작품을 쓰던 시기에 아름다움이라는 단일한 이상의 관념에 너무나 매혹되어 있었기 때문에 사람들이 자신의 작품과 실러(Schiller)의 작품을 구별하지 못하자 흡족해했다.

**13** 2021 이화여대      ③

☐ skeptical a. 의심 많은, 회의적인 ☐ obscure v. 숨기다, 가리다 (↔ reveal (보이지 않던 것을) 드러내다) ☐ highlight v. 돋보이게 하다, 강조하다 ☐ emphasize v. (중요성을) 강조하다 ☐ darken v. 어두워[캄캄해]지다

클라이스트(Kleist)의 회의적인 말이 그의 생각을 숨기기 때문에 비평가들은 그의 응답을 정확히 해석하려는 시도에 대해 의문을 제기해 왔다.

**14** 2021 이화여대      ③

☐ properly ad. 올바르게, 제대로 ☐ assess v. 평가하다, 가늠하다, 재다 ☐ weigh v. 저울질하다, 숙고하다(↔ bypass 우회하다, 회피하다, 무시하다) ☐ assess v. 평가[사정]하다

상황을 제대로 평가하려면 당신은 계획상의 개선점들을 실제로 예상되는 결과들에 견주어 주의 깊게 고려해야 한다.

**15** 2021 이화여대      ④

☐ bifurcation n. 갈라짐, 분기(↔ unification 통일) ☐ trajectory n. 궤적 ☐ order n. 등급, 급 ☐ exuberance n. 풍부함 ☐ mitigation n. 완화 ☐ polarity n. 양극성 ☐ exhortation n. 간곡한 권고, 장려

19세기 미국 문화의 궤적을 특징짓기 위한 "문화적 분기"라는 로렌스 W. 레빈(Lawrence W. Levin)의 논문에서 제기된 문제들과 동일한 급의 문제들이 있다.

**16** 2021 이화여대      ①

☐ enduring a. 오래 가는, 영속적인(↔ short-lived 수명이 짧은) ☐ sage a. 현명한 n. 현자 ☐ contingent a. ~을 조건으로 하는, 우발적인 ☐ uninspiring a. 시시한, 흥미롭지 못한 ☐ amoral a. 도덕을 초월한, 도덕과 무관한 ☐ sacrilegious a. 신성을 더럽히는

영어로 된 가장 길고 영속적인 시 한 단락의 첫 몇 행에서 현명하고 진지한 시인은 인간 최초의 불순종에 관해 썼다.

**17** 2021 이화여대      ③

☐ kitten n. 새끼 고양이 ☐ ferocious a. 사나운, 흉포한(↔ gentle 온순한) ☐ feline a. 고양잇과의, 고양이의 ☐ rampant a. 횡행하는 ☐ peevish a. 짜증을 잘 내는 ☐ unintelligent a. 우둔한

가장 작은 집고양이부터 가장 사나운 사자까지 모든 고양잇과 동물들은 약 2500만 년 전에 살았던 공통의 고양잇과 조상을 두고 있다.

**18** 2020 이화여대      ⑤

☐ foresight n. 예지, 예측; 선견지명 ☐ evacuation box 비상대피용 구급함, 피난함 ☐ purchase v. 사다, 구입하다 ☐ hefty a. 무거운; 많은, 큰 ☐ insurance policy 보험증권 ☐ fortuitous a. 뜻밖의, 우연한; 행운의(↔ inopportune 때가 좋지 않은) ☐ temporarily ad. 일시적으로, 임시로 ☐ auspicious a. 길조의, 상서로운; 행운의 ☐ salutary a. 유익한, 건전한, 이로운 ☐ credible a. 신뢰할 수 있는, 확실한 ☐ prudent a. 신중한, 조심성 있는

화재가 발생하기 두 달도 안 남은 시점에 비상용 구급함을 꾸려놓고 두둑한 액수의 보험증권에 가입한 브느아(Benoit)의 선견지명은 어쩌다 운 좋지 않을 때가 맞은 것으로 드러났지만, 그들은 일시적으로 오갈 데 없는 신세였다.

## 19 2020 이화여대 ③

☐ abandon v. 버리다; 단념하다, 그만두다 ☐ precept n. 가르침, 교훈, 훈계 ☐ undermine v. (명성 따위를) 음험한 수단으로 훼손하다, 몰래 손상시키다(↔ enhance 향상시키다) ☐ moral a. 도덕의, 윤리의 ☐ subvert v. (체제·권위 따위를) 뒤엎다, (국가정부 따위를) 전복시키다, (종교·주의 따위를) 타파하다 ☐ diminish v. 줄이다, 감소시키다 ☐ abhor v. 몹시 싫어하다, 혐오하다 ☐ accumulate v. 모으다, 축적하다

그 교훈을 저버리면, 당신은 일반적인 미국 시민의 도덕적 기반을 손상시킬 것이다.

## 20 2020 이화여대 ①

☐ hyper-partisanship n. 과도한 당파주의 ☐ bipartisanship n. 양당주의, 초당파주의 ☐ collegiality n. 동료 간의 협력 관계(↔ animosity 악의, 원한) ☐ meddle v. 쓸데없이 참견하다, 간섭하다(in) ☐ election n. 선거 ☐ rapprochement n. 화해, 친선 ☐ civilization n. 문명 ☐ quandary n. 궁지, 곤경 ☐ status n. 상태, 사정; 지위

과도한 당파주의 시기에, 상원 정보위원회는 심지어 러시아의 미국 선거 개입 문제에 관해서도 초당파주의와 협력관계를 보이는 희귀한 섬(집단)으로 부각되고 있다.

## 21 2020 이화여대 ②

☐ anthropologist n. 인류학자 ☐ hunter-gatherer n. <인류> 수렵채집인 ☐ egalitarian a. 평등주의의(↔ elitist 소수특권주의의) ☐ traditional a. 전통의 ☐ populist a. 포퓰리즘적인 ☐ secular a. 현세의, 세속의 ☐ archaic a. 고풍의, 낡은

인류학자들이 집단 수렵채집 사회를 지칭하는 데 늘 사용하는 또 다른 이름은 평등주의의 사회이다.

## 22 2020 이화여대 ②

☐ era n. 기원, 연대; 시대 ☐ corporation n. 법인, 사단법인, 주식회사 ☐ hack v. 프로그램을 교묘히 변경하다; (컴퓨터 시스템·데이터 따위에) 불법 침입하다, 해킹하다 ☐ truism n. 자명한 이치; 진부한 문구 ☐ sinister a. 불길한, 사악한(↔ benign 상서로운, 길조의) ☐ judicious a. 현명한 ☐ erroneous a. 잘못된 ☐ implausible a. 받아들이기 어려운, 정말 같지 않은 ☐ prevalent a. (널리) 보급된; 유행하고 있는; 우세한

과학자들, 기업들, 정부들이 인간의 뇌를 해킹하는 법을 배우고 있는 시대에, 이러한 진부한 문구는 그 어느 때보다도 사악한 것이다.

## 23 2020 이화여대 ④

☐ attitude n. 태도, 마음가짐 ☐ stem v. 유래하다, 일어나다(from) ☐ acquiesce to 묵인하다, 묵묵히 따르다(↔ demur at 반대하다) ☐ dissolution n. (의회·단체 등의) 해산; 붕괴; 소멸; 사멸 ☐ install v. 설치하다, 가설하다, 설비하다 ☐ reprove v. 꾸짖다, 비난하다 ☐ concede to 양보하다, 용인하다 ☐ exasperate v. 노하게 하다 ☐

prevail over 우세하다, 이기다

그들의 태도는 그들이 세운 정부의 해체를 포함한 그 어떤 조건에도 묵인하겠다는 믿음에서 비롯됐다.

## 24 2019 이화여대 ④

☐ retreat v. 물러가다, 후퇴하다; (더 조용하거나 안전한 곳으로) 빠져나가다[도피하다] ☐ parochial a. 교구의; 지역주의의; 편협한(↔ liberal) ☐ free trade agreement 자유무역협정 ☐ encourage v. 장려하다, 조장하다, 촉진하다 ☐ interaction n. 상호작용 ☐ alternative a. 양자택일의, 대신 할, 대신의 ☐ frivolous a. 경솔한, 들뜬; 하찮은 ☐ illiterate a. 무식한; 문맹의 ☐ monetary a. 화폐의, 통화의

사람들이 점점 더 자신들의 편협한 이익을 추구하는 쪽으로 뒷걸음치고 있는 세상에서, 경제적인 자유로운 이동과 전 세계적인 교류를 촉진시키기 위해 자유무역협정을 기꺼이 받아들여야 한다.

## 25 2019 이화여대 ③

☐ contrived a. 부자연스러운, 인위적인(↔ genuine) ☐ applause n. 박수갈채, 칭찬 ☐ audience n. 청중, 관객 ☐ clap v. 박수치다 ☐ essential a. 근본적인, 필수의 ☐ dismissive a. 퇴거시키는, 그만두게 하는; 거부하는 ☐ encouraging a. 장려하는, 고무하는 ☐ impinge v. 부딪치다, 충돌하다; ~에게 영향을 주다; 침범하다 ☐ incongruous a. 일치하지 않는, 조화하지 않는

언제 박수를 쳐야 하는지를 지시받은 TV 스튜디오 방청객들이 터뜨리는 인위적인 박수갈채가 TV 쇼의 필수적인 부분이 되었다.

## 26 2019 이화여대 ②

☐ impressive a. 인상에 남는, 인상적인 ☐ achievement n. 성취, 달성; 업적, 위업 ☐ critic n. 비평가, 평론가 ☐ evolve v. (이론·의견·계획 따위를) 서서히 발전시키다; (결론·법칙 따위를) 도출하다 ☐ observe v. (법률·풍습·규정 따위를) 지키다; (행위 등을) 유지하다, 계속하다 ☐ decorous a. 예의바른, 점잖은(↔ wild) ☐ distinction n. 구별, 차별; 구별 짓기; 대조, 대비; 특성 ☐ enticing a. 마음을 끄는, 매혹적인 ☐ incorporeal a. 실체 없는, 비물질적인 ☐ superlative a. 최상의, 최고의 ☐ still a. 정지한, 움직이지 않는

그녀의 친구이자 가장 재기 넘치는 비평가인 로나 세이지(Lorna Sage)는 그녀의 "가장 인상적이고 유머러스한 업적들 중 하나는 그녀가 (인생의) 이 부분을 여성 작가가 되는 법이라는 연극으로 발전시켰다는 것이었다. 그것은 그녀가 가면을 꼭 맞게 쓰고 있었다(본모습을 완전히 감추고 있었다)는 것이 아니라 예술과 인생 사이의 점잖은 구별을 지키기를 거부하는 문제에 더 가까웠다."라고 쓴 적이 있다.

## 27 2019 이화여대 ③

☐ arduous a. 힘든, 곤란한(↔ comfortable) ☐ pleasantly ad. 즐겁게, 유쾌하게 ☐ remunerative a. 보수가 많은, 유리한, 수지맞는 ☐

archaic a. 고풍의, 낡은 □ bucolic a. 목가적인; 전원생활의 □ inflammatory a. 열광시키는, 선동적인 □ lineal a. 직계의; 선 모양의

그것은 그리 고된 일이 아니었고 기분 좋을 정도로 수지맞는 일이었다.

## 28　2019 이화여대　　　　　　　　　　　　　　④

□ black locust 아카시아나무 □ autumn olive 보리수나무 □ fix v. 고정시키다, 고착시키다; 응고시키다 □ nitrogen n. 질소 □ goldenrod n. <식물> 메역취 □ sunflower n. 해바라기 □ white snakeroot 등골나물속(屬)의 식물 □ expel v. 쫓아내다, 물리치다 □ proliferate v. 증식하다, 번식하다; 급격히 늘다(↔ plummet) □ gratify v. 기쁘게 하다, 만족시키다 □ exacerbate v. 악화시키다; 노하게 하다 □ migrate v. 이주시키다 □ fortify v. 강화하다; 요새화하다

아카시아나무와 보리수나무는 질소를 고정시켜 더 많은 메역취, 해바라기, 등골나물이 사과나무를 따라 옮겨올 수 있도록 하는데, 이렇게 하여 그것들의 씨앗은 급증하는 새들에 의해 밖으로 방출된다.

## 29　2019 이화여대　　　　　　　　　　　　　　④

□ derivative a. 유도된, 이끌어낸; 파생적[이차적]인; 모방한, 독창적이 아닌(↔ original) □ aesthetically ad. 미학적으로, 심미적으로 □ expose v. 노출시키다, (환경 따위에) 접하게 하다 □ dissipate v. (안개·구름 따위를) 흩뜨리다; (군중 따위를) 쫓아 흩어버리다; (의심·공포 따위를) 일소하다 □ exonerate v. ~의 결백을[무죄를] 증명하다; ~를 (책임·곤란 따위에서) 면제하다 □ derogatory a. (명예·인격 따위를) 손상시키는; 가치를 떨어뜨리는 □ rabid a. 맹렬한, 미친 듯한; 열광적인

그의 기억은 우리가 접하고 있는 이미지들의 일부를 도용하고, 파생시켜, 미적으로 형성시킨 것이었다.

## 30　2018 이화여대　　　　　　　　　　　　　　①

□ author n. 저자, 작가 □ subscribe to ~에 동의하다(↔ oppose 반대하다) □ chemical a. 화학의; 화학적인 □ imbalance n. 불균형 □ enlarge v. 확대하다, 크게 하다 □ lubricate v. ~에 기름을 치다; 미끄럽게 하다 □ impede v. 방해하다 □ reduce v. 줄이다, 감소시키다

세 명의 저자 중 어느 누구도 정신 질환이 뇌의 화학적 불균형에 의해 야기된다는 대중적인 이론에 동의하지 않는다.

## 31　2018 이화여대　　　　　　　　　　　　　　③

□ customer n. 손님, 고객 □ discreet a. 분별 있는(↔ tactless 분별없는) □ crowd v. 밀어닥치다 □ shy a. 소심한, 수줍어하는, 부끄러워하는 □ astute a. 기민한, 빈틈없는 □ critical a. 비판적인, 비평의; 위기의 □ inconvenient a. 불편한; 형편이 나쁜

고객들은 도시 사람들이 하는 식으로 분별 있게 일정한 간격으로 줄을 서지 않는다. 누클라(Nucla)에서는 사람들이 계산대로 한꺼번에 밀어닥치며, 건강 문제에 대해 큰 소리로 이야기를 나눈다.

## 32　2018 이화여대　　　　　　　　　　　　　　②

□ peddler n. 행상인; 마약판매인 □ confidence man 사기꾼 □ guile n. 교활, 간계(↔ naivete 순진) □ skillful a. 능숙한, 숙련된 □ theatricality n. 연극조, 과장된 언동 □ reserve n. 비축; 유보; 자제 □ praise n. 칭찬 □ repudiation n. 거부, 거절; 절연 □ reprisal n. 앙갚음, 보복

일반적인 견해로는, 행상인은 힘보다는 간계를 통해 ─ 특히 능수능란한 연기를 통해 자신의 목적을 달성하는 사기꾼이 되었다.

## 33　2018 이화여대　　　　　　　　　　　　　　②

□ hegemony n. 패권, 주도권, 헤게모니 □ obliteration n. 말살(↔ construction 건설) □ opposition n. 반대; 야당 □ articulation n. 명료한 발음; (사상·감정 따위의) 명확한 표현 □ affiliation n. 가입; 제휴; (pl.) 관계, 우호관계 □ annihilation n. 전멸, 절멸 □ revision n. 개정, 교정 □ oblivion n. 망각 □ infiltration n. 스며듦, 침입

패권은 반대파를 전멸시킴으로써가 아니라 반대 세력을 패권 집단의 정당에 분명하게 가입시킴으로써 유지된다.

## 34　2018 이화여대　　　　　　　　　　　　　　④

□ organized a. 정리된, 규칙 바른; 조직화된 □ coherent a. 일관성 있는, 논리 정연한(↔ disjointed 뒤죽박죽인) □ complex a. 복잡한; (문제가) 어려운 □ coercive a. 강제적인, 위압적인 □ expansive a. 팽창력이 있는; 확장적인; 광대한 □ exhilarating a. 기분을 돋우어 주는, 유쾌하게 하는; 상쾌한 □ equivalent a. 동등한, 같은; (가치·힘 따위가) 대등한

언어는 이미 질서정연하고 일관성 있는 실체에 이름을 붙이지 않는다. 언어의 역할은 훨씬 더 강력하고 복잡하다.

## 35　2018 이화여대　　　　　　　　　　　　　　⑤

□ separate v. 구별하다; 분리하다, 떼어놓다(↔ reconcile 일치시키다) □ theoretical a. 이론의, 이론상의 □ influence n. 영향, 영향력, 세력 □ alleviate v. 경감하다; 완화하다, 누그러뜨리다, (고통 따위를) 덜다 □ extenuate v. (범죄·결점을) 가벼이 보다, 경감하다, (정상을) 참작하다 □ dissociate v. 분리하다, 떼어놓다; 떼어서 생각하다 □ uphold v. 지지하다, 변호하다

문화 연구는 그것의 이론적 영향과 문학 연구의 이론적 영향 사이에 밀접한 연관성이 있음에도 불구하고 얼마 지나지 않아 문학 연구와 분리되었다.

## 36　2017 이화여대　　　　　　　　　　　　　　④

□ inept a. 부적당한; 서투른(↔ skillful 능숙한) □ ensure v. ~을 책임지다, 보증하다 □ without incident 별일 없이, 무사히 □ uncanny a. 엄청난; 초자연적인 □ recalcitrant a. 반항하는, 고집 센 □ wholesale a. 도매의; 대규모의 □ pompous a. 거만한, 건방진

심판의 미숙한 경기 진행은 반드시 경기가 무사히 지나는 법이 없게 만들었다.

## 37 2017 이화여대 ①

☐ be obsessed with ~에 사로잡혀 있다  ☐ critique n. (문예 작품 따위의) 비평; 평론  ☐ transgression n. 범죄, 위반(↔ obedience 복종)  ☐ imperial a. 제국의, 황제의; 위엄 있는  ☐ disparity n. 불균형, 불일치  ☐ conscription n. 징병제도, 모병  ☐ revocation n. 폐지, 취소, 철회  ☐ infusion n. 주입, 불어넣음; 고취

탈(脫)식민주의 연구가 서구와 서구가 저지른 범법행위에 대한 비판에 사로잡혀 있으면, 세계화를 둘러싼 담론은 세계화와 세계화 이전의 제국주의 식민주의 시대 사이의 관계를 모호하게 만드는 경향이 있다.

## 38 2017 이화여대 ④

☐ province n. 지방; 분야  ☐ tenuous a. 희박한, 미약한(↔ substantial 상당한)  ☐ obdurate a. 완고한  ☐ permanent a. 영속하는; 불변의  ☐ lucid a. 맑은, 투명한; 명료한  ☐ pervasive a. 퍼지는, 널리 미치는

그 여러 지역들 사이의 문화적, 역사적 연관은 매우 희박한 것으로 보였다.

## 39 2017 이화여대 ⑤

☐ adhere v. 고수하다, 집착하다, 지지하다  ☐ detached a. 초연한, 편견이 없는, 공평한  ☐ eschew v. 삼가다, 피하다(↔ adopt 받아들이다)  ☐ context n. (글의) 전후 관계, 문맥; (사건 등에 대한) 경위, 배경  ☐ confiscate v. 몰수하다, 압류하다  ☐ oppose v. 반대하다, 이의를 제기하다  ☐ mitigate v. 누그러뜨리다, 가라앉히다, 완화하다  ☐ underpin v. 지지하다, 응원하다

신(新)비평가들은 텍스트(글)는 그 자체로 완전하다고 믿었다. 그래서 그들은 언어와 그 구조에 초점을 맞추고 정치적, 사회적 영향을 비롯한 모든 외부적인 상황을 피하면서, 상황과 분리된 텍스트 읽기를 고수했다.

## 40 2017 이화여대 ②

☐ sporadic a. 산발적인, 이따금 발생하는; 드문(↔ continuous 계속적인)  ☐ outbreak n. (전쟁·유행병 등의) 발발, 돌발; 폭동  ☐ spasmodic a. <의학> 경련의; 발작적[돌발적]인  ☐ staggering a. 비틀거리는, 망설이는; 경이적인  ☐ endangered a. (동식물이) 멸종위기에 처한  ☐ destructive a. 파괴적인

분명 우리는 폭력의 산발적인 발발을 겪고 있지만, 그렇다면 그 점에 있어서 우리가 이 세상에서 유일무이한 것은 아니다.

## 41 2017 이화여대 ⑤

☐ palpable a. 손으로 만질 수 있는; 매우 뚜렷한, 명백한(↔ intangible 실체가 없는, 무형의)  ☐ appreciation n. 평가, 이해  ☐ tangential a. 접선의; 접하는; 별로 관계가 없는  ☐ exclusive a. 배타적인; 독점적인  ☐ sophisticated a. (기계·기술 따위가) 정교한, 고급인; 복잡한; 고도로 세련된  ☐ whimsical a. 마음이 잘 변하는, 변덕스러운

일본 애니메이션의 문화적 영향은 "일본인의" 라이프스타일이나 사상에 대한 명백하고 실질적인 이해와 밀접하게 관련돼 있다고 말하는 것이 대단히 중요하다.

## 42 2016 이화여대 ②

☐ germane a. 적절한; 밀접히 관계있는(↔ extraneous 관계없는, 본질에서 벗어난)  ☐ avaricious a. 탐욕스러운  ☐ irrepressible a. 억누를 수 없는, 억제할 수 없는  ☐ meticulous a. 지나치게 세심한, 매우 신중한  ☐ sumptuous a. 사치스러운, 화려한

그들의 정치 분석에서, 실용주의자들은 특정 문제나 목표와 밀접한 관련이 있는 다중적인 요소들의 상대적이고 가변적인 중요성을 이해하려고 노력했다.

## 43 2016 이화여대 ⑤

☐ hyperbole n. 과장법, 과장어구(↔ understatement 절제된 표현, 삼가는 말)  ☐ appraisal n. 평가, 감정, 견적  ☐ equivocation n. 애매함, 얼버무리기  ☐ revulsion n. (감정 따위의) 격변, 급변; 급격한 반동  ☐ skepticism n. 회의론, 의심

유권자들은 정치인들이 하는 어느 정도의 과장과 수사적인 과잉을 항상 받아주었다.

## 44 2016 이화여대 ④

☐ alienate v. 멀어지게 만들다, 소원(疏遠)하게 하다(↔ reunite 재결합시키다, 화해시키다)  ☐ abduct v. 유괴하다  ☐ antagonize v. 적대하다, 대립하다, 반목하다  ☐ preempt v. ~을 남보다 먼저 손에 넣다; 선수를 쳐서 회피하다  ☐ revamp v. 수선하다; 개편하다, 개혁하다

정치인들은 또한 (반드시 필요함에도 불구하고) 인기가 없는 조처를 취함으로써 유권자들을 멀어지게 만드는 것을 꺼려 왔다.

## 45 2016 이화여대 ⑤

☐ pretentious a. 자만하는; 뽐내는, 허세부리는(↔ unassuming 주제넘지 않은, 젠체하지 않은)  ☐ stilted a. 과장된, 뽐내는, 잘난 체하는  ☐ mincing a. 점잔빼는, 점잔빼며 걷는  ☐ conceited a. 자만심이 강한, 우쭐한  ☐ inculpable a. 나무랄 데 없는

허세부리는 표현을 피하도록 해라. 당신은 판사들이 사건을 이해하게 만들려 하고 있는 것이지, 당신이 가진 학식으로 그들을 감동시키려 하고 있는 것이 아니다.

**46** 2016 이화여대      ⑤

☐ insatiable a. 탐욕스러운, 만족을 모르는(↔ contented 만족하고 있는) ☐ voracious a. 게걸스럽게 먹는, 과식하는; 탐욕스러운 ☐ avid a. 탐욕스러운; 열심인 ☐ ravenous a. 게걸스러운; 몹시 굶주린, 탐욕스러운 ☐ rapacious a. 약탈하는; 탐욕스러운, 만족할 줄 모르는

그의 삶이 얼마나 외로웠는지가 갑자기 분명해졌다. 학문을 끝없이 갈구하는 사람인 그는 이곳에서 성년 생활의 대부분을 지적인 고립상태에서 살 수밖에 없었다.

**47** 2016 이화여대      ①

☐ unequivocal a. 모호하지 않은, 분명한(↔ ambiguous 애매한, 모호한) ☐ obnoxious a. 밉살스러운, 불쾌한, 싫은 ☐ palpable a. 손으로 만질 수 있는; 매우 뚜렷한, 명백한 ☐ predictable a. 예언할 수 있는, 예상할 수 있는 ☐ encouraging a. 장려하는, 고무시키는

결과는 분명했다. 욕을 듣는 것에 대해 젊은이들이 어떻게 반응하는지에 있어서 명확한 차이가 있었다.

**48** 2015 이화여대      ①

☐ caregiving n. 간병, 돌봄 ☐ corroborate v. 제공하다, 확증[입증]하다(↔ controvert 반박[반증]하다) ☐ tremendous a. 엄청난, 굉장한 ☐ burden n. 부담 ☐ strain n. 부담, 중압감 ☐ concede v. 인정하다, 수긍하다 ☐ conflate v. 융합하다, 혼합하다 ☐ complicate v. 복잡하게 하다, 뒤얽히게 만들다 ☐ counterfeit v. 위조[모조]하다

간병에 관한 연구 결과는 알츠하이머 환자를 돌보는 가족이 엄청난 부담과 중압감을 겪고 있다는 것을 계속 입증해 주고 있다.

**49** 2015 이화여대      ④

☐ persevere v. 참다, 인내하다; ~에 굴하지 않고 꾸준히 하다(↔ give up 포기하다) ☐ counterpart n. 상대, 대응 관계에 있는 사람[것] ☐ take away 제거하다, 치우다 ☐ send out ~을 보내다 ☐ put into ~에 들어가다; ~을 착수하다 ☐ bring forward 제시하다

과학과 관련된 직업에 정진하는 사람들은 다른 분야의 사람들보다 더 많은 취업 기회와 고용 안정성을 찾게 될지도 모른다.

**50** 2015 이화여대      ④

☐ dubious a. 의심하는, 수상쩍은(↔ convincing 설득력 있는, 확실한) ☐ momentum n. 탄력, 가속도 ☐ integration n. 통합 ☐ shabby a. 다 낡은[해진], 허름한; 부당한 ☐ thoughtless a. 무심한, 배려심 없는 ☐ perplexing a. 당황하게 하는, 난처하게 하는 ☐ stringent a. 엄중한; 긴박한

이 보고서는 국가의 경제가 세계 경제에 보다 급진적으로 통합됨으로써 탄력을 받을 수 있다는 의심스러운 개념을 조장하기 위해 만들어진 것이다.

**51** 2015 이화여대      ④

☐ deter v. 그만두게 하다, 저지하다 ☐ whistle-blowing n. 고발, 밀고, 비밀누설 ☐ discreet a. 신중한, 조심스러운(↔ inconsiderate 사려 깊지 못한) ☐ informer n. (특히 범죄의) 밀고자, 정보 제공자 ☐ high-profile a. 세간의 이목을 끄는, 눈에 띄는 ☐ intelligent a. 총명한, 똑똑한 ☐ modest a. 보통의; 겸손한 ☐ secretive a. 비밀스러운 ☐ suspicious a. 의심스러운, 수상쩍은

내부고발을 막지 않기 위해서, 우리는 세간의 이목을 끄는 부패 사건에 연관된 제보자들의 신원에 대해 신중을 기할 필요성에 대한 논의를 장려해야 한다.

**52** 2015 이화여대      ④

☐ engender v. (어떤 감정·상황을) 낳다, 불러일으키다(↔ remove 치우다, 제거하다) ☐ incongruity n. 부조화, 모순, 부적합 ☐ provoke v. 유발하다 ☐ mystify v. 혼란스럽게[얼떨떨하게] 만들다 ☐ clarify v. 명확하게 하다 ☐ stimulate v. 자극[격려]하다

공상과학 소설은 논리적인 부조화를 발생시키는 경향이 있는 것 같다.

**53** 2015 이화여대      ④

☐ merger n. (조직체·사업체의) 합병 ☐ consolidation n. 합동, 합병; 통합(↔ fragmentation 분열) ☐ provocation n. 도발, 자극 ☐ restriction n. 제한, 규제 ☐ opposition n. 반대 ☐ instigation n. 선동, 부추김

합병에 거듭 성공을 거둔 은행들은 합병이 완료되는 순간 곧바로 활용할 수 있는 합병을 위한 청사진을 가지고 있다.

**54** 2014 이화여대      ②

☐ virtue n. 미덕, 선행 ☐ measure v. 측정하다; 판단하다 ☐ approximation n. 접근, 근사 ☐ proper a. 적당한, 타당한, 상응하는; 고유의 ☐ manifest v. 명시하다, 드러내다 ☐ implicit a. 은연중의, 함축적인, 암시적인(↔ overt 명시적인) ☐ noble a. 고귀한; 고상한, 숭고한 ☐ absurd a. 불합리한; 부조리한 ☐ tacit a. 무언의; 침묵의 ☐ inherent a. 본래부터 가지고 있는; 선천적인

미덕은 계급이 가진 고유한 모습에 얼마나 가까운지 여부로 측정된다. 심지어 『보물섬(Treasure Island)』과 같은 간단한 모험 소설조차도 이런 암묵적인 계급적 시각을 분명하게 드러내고 있다.

**55** 2014 이화여대      ④

☐ ethereal a. 가뿐한; 공기 같은; 하늘의; 무형의(↔ tangible 분명히 실재하는) ☐ aspect n. 양상, 모습; 국면 ☐ define v. 규정하다; 정의를 내리다 ☐ formlessness n. 모양이 없음, 무정형 ☐ medium n. 매개, 매개물, 매체 ☐ haunt v. (유령 등이) 출몰하다; (생각 따위가) 늘 붙어

따라다니다 ☐ sublime a. 장엄한, 숭고한; 탁월한 ☐ divine a. 신의; 신성(神性)의; 신성한 ☐ incorporeal a. 실체가 없는; 영적인 ☐ spectral a. 유령의, 괴기한

소리의 무형적 측면에 대한 그의 최근 연구에서, 데이비드 톱(David Toop)은 소리를 모양이 없는 것으로서, 여러 장소와 사람들을 따라다니는 매개물로 정의하고 있다.

## 56　2014 이화여대　①

☐ trip up 넘어뜨리다, 거꾸러뜨리다; 딴죽을 걸다 ☐ evasion n. (책임·의무 등의) 회피(↔ confrontation 대면, 직면) ☐ deceit n. 속임수; 책략 ☐ gag n. 재갈; 발언금지, 입막음 ☐ a kick in the pants 비참한 패배; 노골적인 비난 ☐ trick n. 책략, 계교, 속임수 ☐ fact n. 사실, 실제 ☐ quibble n. 핑계, 구차한 변명 ☐ blame n. 비난

그 장(章)의 요지는 의식이 행동하거나 말하고자 하는 것을 무의식이 종종 반대하며, 온갖 종류의 회피, 속임수, 억압, 그리고 노골적인 비난을 통해 자주 그것을 좌절시킨다는 것이다.

## 57　2014 이화여대　⑤

☐ voluntarily ad. 자발적으로 ☐ delay v. 지연시키다; 연기하다 ☐ gratification n. 만족(↔ dissatisfaction 불만) ☐ tolerate v. 참다, 견디다; 관대히 다루다 ☐ self-imposed a. 자진해서 하는, 스스로 맡아서 하는 ☐ willpower n. 의지력, 정신력 ☐ resilience n. 탄성, 탄력; 회복력 ☐ acceptance n. 받아들임; 수락 ☐ pleasantness n. 즐거움, 유쾌함; 상냥함 ☐ gratitude n. 감사, 보은의 마음 ☐ indulgence n. 멋대로 하게 둠, 관대; 탐닉, 방종

즉각적인 만족을 자발적으로 지연시키는 능력, 즉 보상을 자진해서 미루는 것을 견뎌내는 능력은 의지력, 자아 강도, 그리고 자아 회복력에 대한 대부분의 개념에서 핵심적이다.

## 58　2014 이화여대　①

☐ alternative a. 양자택일의; 선택적인; 대안적인 ☐ mechanism n. 기계, 기구; 구조, 기제 ☐ normative a. 표준의, 규범적인(↔ atypical 이례적인) ☐ morphogenesis n. 형태 형성[발생] ☐ accumulation n. 축적, 누적 ☐ innovation n. (기술) 혁신, 쇄신 ☐ conformist a. 순응적인 ☐ customary a. 습관적인, 관례에 의한 ☐ preceptive a. 교훈의, 교훈적인; 명령적인 ☐ abortive a. 유산의; 실패의

규범적 형태생성의 대안적 기제는 혁신을 축적하는 것이다.

## 59　2014 이화여대　⑤

☐ ingredient n. 성분, 원료, 재료 ☐ resilience n. 탄성, 탄력; (원기의) 회복력(↔ stagnation 침체, 정체) ☐ optimistic a. 낙관적인, 낙천적인 ☐ positive a. 확신하는; 긍정적인; 적극적인 ☐ convalescence n. 차도가 있음, 건강회복 ☐ recovery n. 회복, 복구 ☐ recuperation n. 회복, 만회 ☐ retrieval n. 만회, 복구, 회복

회복력의 구성요소 가운데 하나는 낙관적인 태도, 그리고 자신과 인간 본성에 존재하는 긍정적인 면에 주의를 집중하는 것이다.